ISBN: 9781313301855

Published by:
HardPress Publishing
8345 NW 66TH ST #2561
MIAMI FL 33166-2626

Email: info@hardpress.net
Web: http://www.hardpress.net

Wycliffe College
TORONTO

SHERATON
MEMORIAL LIBRARY
EASTER, 1906

BX9175 M23
74+M

Shelf No.

Register No. 10,148

THE
WORKS OF THOMAS MANTON, D.D.

VOL. XVII.

COUNCIL OF PUBLICATION.

W. LINDSAY ALEXANDER, D.D., Professor of Theology, Congregational Union, Edinburgh.

JAMES BEGG, D.D., Minister of Newington Free Church, Edinburgh.

THOMAS J. CRAWFORD, D.D., S.T.P., Professor of Divinity, University, Edinburgh.

D. T. K. DRUMMOND, M.A., Minister of St Thomas's Episcopal Church, Edinburgh.

WILLIAM H. GOOLD, D.D., Professor of Biblical Literature and Church History, Reformed Presbyterian Church, Edinburgh.

ANDREW THOMSON, D.D., Minister of Broughton Place United Presbyterian Church, Edinburgh.

General Editor.
REV. THOMAS SMITH, D.D., EDINBURGH

THE COMPLETE WORKS

OF

THOMAS MANTON, D.D.

VOLUME XVII.

CONTAINING

SERMONS ON SEVERAL TEXTS OF SCRIPTURE.

LONDON:
JAMES NISBET & CO., 21 BERNERS STREET.
1874.

PRINTED BY BALLANTYNE AND COMPANY
EDINBURGH AND LONDON

CONTENTS.

                                                              PAGE

SERMONS ON SEVERAL TEXTS OF SCRIPTURE, PART I.—*Continued.*

SERMONS UPON MARK x. 17–27—*Continued.*

    Sermon VIII. "And take up the cross," &c., . . . 3
    IX. "And he was sad at that saying," &c., . 13
    X. "And Jesus looked round about," &c., . 24
    XI. "And the disciples were astonished at his words," &c., ... 36
    XII. "It is easier for a camel to go through the eye of a needle," &c., ... 48
    XIII. "And they were astonished out of measure," &c., ... 59
    XIV. "And Jesus, looking upon them, saith," &c., . 72
    XV. "With God all things are possible," . . 82

SERMONS UPON 2 THESSALONIANS i. 3—

    Sermon I. "We are bound to thank God always," &c., . 95
    II. "We are bound to thank God always," &c., . 105
    III. "Your faith groweth exceedingly," &c., . 117
    IV. "Your faith groweth exceedingly," &c., . 126
    V. "Your faith groweth exceedingly," &c., . 135

SERMON UPON MATTHEW viii. 5–10, ... 146

SERMON UPON MATTHEW xv. 21–28, ... 155

SERMON UPON JOHN viii. 56, ... 167

SERMON UPON ROMANS iv. 18–21, ... 179

CONTENTS.

SERMONS UPON MARK iii. 5—

    Sermon I. "And Jesus looked round about on them with anger, being grieved for the hardness of their hearts," 191

    II. "And Jesus looked round about on them with anger," &c., ... 199

    III. "And Jesus looked round about on them with anger," &c., ... 209

SERMONS UPON EXODUS iv. 21—

    Sermon I. "I will harden his heart, that he shall not let my people go," &c., . . . 221

    II. "I will harden his heart," &c., . . . 231

SERMON UPON GENESIS iii. 15, ... 241

SERMONS UPON GENESIS xxiv. 63—

    Sermon I. "And Isaac went out to meditate in the field at the eventide," 263

    II. "And Isaac went out to meditate," &c., . 274

    III. "And Isaac went out to meditate," &c., . 281

    IV. "And Isaac went out to meditate," &c., . 288

    V. "And Isaac went out to meditate," &c., . 298

    VI. "And Isaac went out to meditate," &c., . 306

    VII. "And Isaac went out to meditate," &c., . 314

    VIII. "And Isaac went out to meditate," &c., . 323

    IX. "And Isaac went out to meditate," &c., . 331

    X. "And Isaac went out to meditate," &c., . 339

SERMONS ON SEVERAL TEXTS OF SCRIPTURE, PART II.—

    Epistle Dedicatory, ... 351

SERMONS UPON LUKE xvi. 30, 31—

    Sermon I. "And he said, Nay, father Abraham: but if one went unto them from the dead," &c., . 353

    II. "And he said, Nay, father Abraham," &c., . 363

SERMON UPON HEBREWS xiii. 20, 21, . . . 373

SERMON PREACHED ON A DAY OF PUBLIC THANKSGIVING, . 383

CONTENTS.

	PAGE
SERMON UPON LUKE xxii. 31, 32,	395
SERMON UPON HEBREWS i. 9,	407
SERMONS UPON ACTS xxiv. 14–16—	
Sermon I "Believing all things which are written in the law and the prophets," &c.,	419
II. "Believing all things which are written," &c.,	428
SERMON UPON ZECHARIAH xiv. 20, 21,	441
SERMON UPON JOHN iii. 14, 15,	453
SERMONS UPON 1 THESSALONIANS v. 16—	
Sermon I. "Rejoice evermore,"	469
II. "Rejoice evermore,"	479
SERMON UPON 1 THESSALONIANS v. 17,	491

SERMONS

ON

SEVERAL TEXTS OF SCRIPTURE.

SERMONS UPON MARK X. 17-27.

SERMON VIII.

And take up the cross.—MARK x. 21.

DOCT. 3. All those that follow Christ should prepare their shoulders for the cross.

Here I shall show—(1.) What it is to take up the cross; (2.) The reasons why they must so do.

I. What it is to take up the cross.

1. Negatively.

[1.] Not to devise a voluntary affliction to ourselves; as Baal's priests gashed themselves: 1 Kings xviii. 28, 'They cried aloud, and cut themselves after their manner with knives and lances, till their blood gushed out upon them;' and the pharisees had their self-disciplines. Christ is a lover of human nature, and he hath put no such severe penance upon us. This is to make the cross, not to take it up. Origen, that was too allegorical in plain texts, was too literal when he castrated himself upon that text, Mat. xix. 12, 'There be eunuchs which have made themselves eunuchs for the kingdom of heaven's sake.' Christ only intended power over our natural affections.

[2.] Not to draw sufferings upon ourselves by our own rashness and folly: James i. 2, 'My brethren, count it all joy when ye fall into divers temptations.' He saith, when ye 'fall into them,' not when ye draw them upon yourself. It was Tertullian's error to say that afflictions are to be sought and desired. Man is never satisfied with his present condition; sometimes we question God's love when we have no afflictions, and anon when we have nothing but afflictions. In all these things we must refer ourselves to God's pleasure, not desire troubles, but bear them and improve them when he layeth them on us. Christ hath taught us to pray, 'Lead us not into temptation;' it is but a fond presumption to cast ourselves upon it. Philastrius and Theodoret speak of some that would compel men to kill them out of an affectation of martyrdom; this was a mad ambition, not a true zeal. And no less fond are they that seek out crosses and troubles rather than wait for them, or by their own violence and miscarriage draw a just hatred upon themselves. Christ would not that for his sake we should run headlong into dangers, and without necessity; there is a medium between faintness and rashness. Christ himself did not take up the cross till it was laid upon him. If a man set fire to his own house, he is liable to the law; if it be fired by accident he is pitied and relieved. Therefore we are not to seek the cross, or make it, but bear it, and take it up; not to fill the cup ourselves, but to drink it off when God puts it into our hands to take it up; when we cannot avoid it without sin, or a breach upon our consciences, we are not to shift then, or avoid it by unlawful means.

2. Positively. To bear it patiently and willingly when we cannot avoid it without sin. When we are brought into a necessity of either suffering or sinning, in such cases there must be a cheerful, free, voluntary submission of ourselves to suffer the whole will of God. To take up the cross implieth—(1.) Faithfulness and integrity without shifting; (2.) Patience and submission without murmuring; (3.) Joy and cheerfulness without fainting.

[1.] Faithfulness and integrity without shifting. Many distinguish themselves out of their duty, and when God calleth them to suffering put a fallacy upon their souls: Gal. vi. 12, 'As many as desire to make a fair show in the flesh, they constrain you to be circumcised, only lest they should suffer persecution for the cross of Christ.' They cannot live without honour, and ease, and plenty, and therefore turn and wind themselves to shift the cross. Our Lord Jesus offered himself: Ps. xl. 7, 8, 'Then said I, Lo, I come; in the volume of the book it is written of me, I delight to do thy will, O my God, yea, thy law is within my heart.' So should we resign ourselves when the will of God is so, and give up the comforts of our lives when we can hold them no longer, and be glad we have something of value to esteem as nothing for Christ. The apostle speaks of some 'who are enemies of the cross of Christ, whose god is their belly, whose glory is in their shame, who mind earthly things,' Phil. iii. 18, 19. *Multum interest inter theologum gloriæ et theologum crucis.* Men that have no love to God, but only serve their fleshly appetites, and look no higher than riches, and honours, and pleasures, and applause, will never be faithful to Christ. There are a sort of men that study to save themselves, not from sin, but from danger, and accordingly accommodate themselves to every interest. As the men of Keilah dealt with David, they entertained him for a while, but when Saul pursued him, they resolved to betray him, they would come into no danger and trouble for him; so they deal with religion.

[2.] Patience and submission without murmuring. We show our obedience to God in suffering his will, as well as doing his will. He is sovereign in his acts of providence as well as in his laws. And this we must do without murmuring or repining against God, as if he did us wrong, or did deal hardly with us: Isa. xxx. 15, 'In quietness and confidence shall be your strength;' that is, in faith and patience, humbly submitting to God's will, and depending on his favour and gracious protection. There must be a submissive attendance upon God: Ps. lxii. 1, 'Truly my soul waiteth upon God; from him cometh my salvation;' Ps. xxxix. 9, 'I was dumb, I opened not my mouth, because thou didst it;' not uttering impatient words; God's will silenceth all.

[3.] Cheerful behaviour under the cross: Rom. v. 3, 'And not only so, but we glory in tribulation also;' James i. 2, 'My brethren, count it all joy when ye fall into divers temptations.' Afflictions to God's people do not only minister occasion of patience, but great joy: 2 Cor. vii. 4, 'I am exceeding joyful in all our tribulation,' ὑπερπερισσευομαι τῇ χαρᾷ; I overflow with joy. A dejected spirit doth not behave itself answerably to its principles, privileges, and hopes. Are you at peace with God, and have you communion with him at every turn? And have you hopes of glory, and are you so troubled when you are a little cut short in your temporal comforts? A christian should be at an indifferency, to rejoice as if he rejoiced not, and mourn as if he mourned not. Dejection of spirit argueth too great addictedness to worldly comforts, and love of ease and flesh-pleasing, and ingratitude for all the spiritual good we have received. Shall God lay in such great comforts, and after such great receivings do you take it ill to be put to a little expense? Job xv. 11, 'Are the consolations of God small with thee?' If you had a due sense of the world to come, you would be glad to keep your conscience, though you lose your coat: Heb. x. 34, 'Ye took joyfully the spoiling of your goods, knowing in yourselves that ye have in heaven a better and an enduring substance,' Rom. viii. 18, 'For I reckon that the sufferings of this present time are not worthy to be compared with the glory which shall be revealed in us.' Do you look for a glory to be revealed in you? Then look upon all the sufferings of this life as a feather put into the scales against a talent. We are to have a sense of our condition, yet in regard of the honour done to us to bear a part of Christ's cross, and in regard of the comfort and happiness provided for us we should be cheerful, that it may not be known to be an unwilling patience, and extorted by force. There is one expression more: Luke ix. 23, 'Let him take up his cross daily.' How daily? There are fair days as well as foul days, and the face of heaven doth not always look sad and lowering. How then are we to take up the cross daily? I answer—

(1.) It notes a daily expectation of it; the first day that we begin to be christians, we must reckon on the cross: Mat. xvi. 24, 'If any man will come after me, let him deny himself, and take up his cross, and follow me.' These words are the christian's indenture, and every one must seal to this before he can call Christ master. As porters stand in a street waiting for a burden for them to carry, so must a christian be ready and prepared to meet with any hardship which God may lay out for him in his christian course; or as the Israelites ate the first passover 'with their loins girded, their shoes on their feet, and their staff in their hand,' Exod. xii. 11, as ready for a journey, so should a christian be ready to go forth at God's call: Acts xxi. 13, ἑτοίμως, ἔχω, 'I am ready not to be bound only, but also to die at Jerusalem for the name of the Lord Jesus.' Evils familiarised are less burdensome; by renewing our daily resolution the evil is the less when it cometh.

(2.) The frequency of our conflicts, as if every day there were some exercise for our faith and patience. We are not to prescribe to God how long or how much affliction he shall exercise us with. No; though it were all the days of our lives, we must be content; it is but a moment to eternity. We must take up our cross as often as it lieth in our way, and we cannot baulk it without sin: Gen. xlvii. 9, 'Few and evil have the days of the years of my life been.' Man is born to trouble. The world is a valley of tears, not the mount of the Lord, where is fulness of joy, If there were no cross, we should not be in tune and consort with the rest of the world, for here all the creatures are a-groaning.

(3.) The word 'daily' showeth that private and personal calamities are a part of the cross, as well as the afflictions of the gospel, and for the profession of the name of Christ. Afflictions are either for God or from God. Sickness and death of friends and loss of estate by an immediate providence are a part of our cross. There is an enduring persecution for the name of Christ, and an enduring affliction at the will of Christ. Ordinary crosses do not exclude the comforts of christianity; these occasion experience of God and trial of grace, and are a part of God's discipline for the mortifying of sin, and are happy opportunities to discover more of God and of grace to us. Yea, there is more reason for submission in these, because God taketh us into his own hands. A man that stormeth when a bucket of water is cast upon him, is patient when he is wet with the rain that cometh from heaven.

II. The reasons why those that follow Christ should prepare their shoulders for the cross.

1. That we may be conformed to our head. He had a bitter cup tempered for him by his Father's hand: John xviii. 11, 'The cup that my Father hath given me, shall I not drink it?' and we must pledge him. Jesus Christ was 'a man of sorrows, and acquainted with grief,' Isa. liii. 3, and there would be a strange disproportion between head and members if we should altogether live in delicacy, ease, and pleasures. The bitter cup goeth by course and round, first to Christ, then to his apostles, and it goeth from hand to hand ever since. The apostle speaks of ὑστερήματα τῶν θλίχεων χειστοῦ, Col. i. 24, 'that which is behind of the afflictions of Christ.' There is Christ personal and Christ mystical. Christ personal, as he is complete in himself, so his sufferings are complete; but the sufferings of Christ mystical are not perfect until every member have their own alloted share and portion. Indeed our sufferings are but the drops upon the brim of the cup; he drank up the dregs. The great wave of affliction did first beat upon him, and being thereby broken, some small sprinklings of it do light upon us; we bear the hinder part of the cross of Christ. It is but reason that those that will partake with Christ in his kingdom should be partakers with him in his sorrows, and that the soldiers should follow 'the captain of their salvation,' Heb. ii. 10, and fare as he fared: John xv. 20, 'Remember the word that I said unto you, The servant is not greater than the Lord; if they have persecuted me, they will also persecute you.' We cannot in reason expect better entertainment than he found in the world. If you had an high esteem of Christ, and a low esteem of yourselves, you would easily consent to submit to the will of God herein. It is an unseemly daintiness to be nice and tender of carrying the cross after Jesus Christ, as if we were better than he. Many christians will seem to express much devotion to a crucifix, or those chips of wood which importers cry up for pieces

of the cross of Christ; but here is true respect to the cross of Christ, to be willing for Christ's sake to bear afflictions with patience and humble submission. The apostle counted all things but dross and dung: Phil. iii. 10, 'That I may know him, and the power of his resurrection, and the fellowship of his sufferings, being made conformable to his death.' There is a great deal of sweetness and spiritual comfort in suffering after, for, and with Christ; we should count all things dung and dross to gain this experience. This should be comfort enough to a gracious heart, that thereby he is made more like his Lord and master.

2. Because of the world's hatred: John xv. 19, 'If ye were of the world, the world would love its own; but because ye are not of the world, but I have chosen you out of the world, therefore the world hateth you.' A thorough christian will be sure to meet with opposition. We are told, 2 Tim. iii. 12, 'Yea, and all that will live godly in Christ Jesus shall suffer persecution.' If a man will be lukewarm, not caring how things go, he may find friendship with the world; but he that hath any zeal and conscience, and would be faithful, the world will hate him as an object reviving guilt: 1 John iii. 12, 'Not as Cain, who was of that wicked one, and slew his brother; and wherefore slew he him? because his own works were evil, and his brother's righteous.' The spiritual and carnal seed cannot agree; Gal. iv. 29, 'For as then he that was born after the flesh persecuted him that was born after the spirit, so it is now.'

3. It is needful, in order to our following Christ, that our pride and carnal affections should be broken by the cross: 1 Peter i. 6, 'Now for a season (if need be) ye are in heaviness through manifold temptations.' There is a need of the cross to reclaim us from our wanderings, to cut off the provisions and fuel of our lusts, to make us mindful of heavenly things, and that we may retreat to our great privileges, and to humble us for sin, to stir us up to prayer, and to wean us from the world. *Tribulatio tam nobis necessaria est quam ipsa vita, immo magis necessaria, et multo utilior quam totius mundi opes et dignitates*— Affliction is as necessary to us as life itself, yea, more necessary and profitable than all the wealth and honours of the world; and therefore, being so necessary and profitable for us, we should be willing to take up the cross.

Use 1. Is of information. It informeth us—

1. With what thoughts we should take up the stricter profession of christianity, namely, with expectations of the cross. We cannot but expect great inconveniences and troubles in Christ's service, therefore let us not flatter ourselves. Many think they may be good christians, and yet live a life of ease and peace, free from troubles and afflictions; this is all one as if a soldier, going to the wars, should promise himself peace and continual truce with the enemy, or as if a mariner, committing himself to the sea for a long voyage, should promise himself nothing but fair weather and a calm season, without waves and storms; so irrational it is for a christian to promise himself a life of ease and rest here upon earth.

2. That a christian had need be a mortified and resolute man.

[1.] A mortified weaned man: 'That which is lame is soon turned out of the way,' Heb. xii. 13. If we have any weak part in our souls, there the assault will be most strong and fierce. A garrison that looketh to be besieged takes care to fortify the weak places, and where there is any suspicion of entrance; so should a christian mortify every corrupt inclination lest it betray him, be it love of honour, pleasure, or profit.

[2.] He had need be a resolved man: 'His feet shod with the preparation of the gospel of peace,' Eph. vi. 15; or else in hard ways he will soon founder and halt. That ἑτοιμασία, that preparation is a resolved mind to go through thick and thin, and to follow Christ in all conditions. Well, then, it is no easy matter to be a christian indeed. Nature in the general is against bearing the cross. Christ himself, his human nature recoiled and shunned it without sin; and to us it is more grievous to suffer: Heb. xii. 11, 'No affliction for the present seemeth to be joyous, but grievous.' And besides, lusts, if they be not purged out, will tempt us to stumble, and we need to be armed with great resolution, or else after we have launched out into the deep with Christ, we shall be ready to run ashore again. Now most christians are not mortified, and so they trip up their own heels. Most christians are not resolute, and do but take up religion as a walk for recreation, not as a journey, so as to be prepared for all weathers.

[3.] What fools they are that take up religion upon a carnal design of ease and plenty in the world: they quite mistake it. There are inconveniences that attend religion in peaceable times, but the profession will afterwards engage us in the greater troubles; and therefore men do but make way for the shame of a change, and other inconveniences to themselves, that hope for temporal commodity by the profession of the gospel. The great drift of the gospel is to draw us off from the comfort of this world to the concernments of a better, and to bring us to follow a naked Christ upon unseen encouragements; therefore they that have temporal things in their eye quite change the nature of the gospel, and make Christ another Christ.

[4.] That the course which Christ taketh to draw in proselytes is quite different from that of Satan and the world. Satan showeth us the bait and hideth the hook, but Christ telleth us the worst at first. The world useth to invite followers with promises of honours and riches, and Christ telleth us not of the crown, but the cross. Why so? Partly to discourage hypocrites, who will come and cheapen and taste, but will not buy. Christ will not deceive them, but have them count the charges. Partly to forearm his people, that they account afflictions will come, and prepare accordingly. We entered upon the ways of godliness on these terms, to be willing to suffer afflictions when the Lord seeth fit, and therefore we should arm ourselves with a mind to endure them, whether they come or no. God never intended Isaac should be sacrificed, yet he will have Abraham lay the knife to his throat. Partly because sorrows foreseen leave not so sad an impression upon the spirit, the evil is more familiarised before it cometh: Job iii. 25, 'For the thing which I greatly feared is come upon me, and that which I was afraid of is come unto me.' When we suffer our fears to prophesy, and do expect evils, they smart less; *præcogitati mali mollis ictus;* but when they come unlooked-for, it is the more burdensome.

He saith his lesson best that often conned it over. Partly because it allayeth the offence when we see nothing befalleth us but what we were warned of beforehand: John xvi. 1, 'These things have I spoken to you, that you should not be offended;' and ver. 4, 'But these things have I told you, that when the time shall come, ye may remember that I told you of them.' The scripture speaketh nothing at random; we pretend to believe them when they are read, and yet we complain when they are fulfilled. For all these reasons it is necessary that those that will be Christ's disciples must be forewarned in peaceable times of approaching troubles, and the rather because we are so apt still to promise great things to ourselves.

Use 2. Is of reproof of several sorts.

1. Of those that suffer per force, by compulsion and constraint, not willingly. It is not enough to bear the cross, but we must take it. It is said of the three children, that 'they yielded their bodies that they might not serve nor worship any god except their own God,' Dan. iii. 28; that is, they cheerfully suffered themselves to be cast into the furnace, rather than worship any but the true God. Many suffer, but it is unwillingly and against stomach, with repining and impatience under the hand of God, like refractory oxen, that draw back, and are loath to submit their necks to the yoke, especially such as have not been acquainted with sufferings. Patience per force is no true patience, little better than the patience of the devils and damned in hell, who suffer misery and torment against their wills, being forced to it. Rebellion and want of subjection is the very curse of crosses; it maketh the burden heavier than otherwise it would be, and causeth God to redouble his strokes, as a stubborn child under the rod hath the more blows.

2. Those that murmur not against the cross in general, but such a cross; if it were any other they could bear it. Christ saith, 'Take up the cross,' indefinitely, whatever God is pleased to lay on us; we must not be our own carvers, but stand to God's allowance. The patient is not to choose his own physic; God knows what is best for us. Men under their troubles wish that God would afflict them in another kind, lay any trouble upon them rather than that which is laid, and think they could bear it better. The poor man wishes any other cross but poverty, the sick man he could bear poverty better than the pain of sickness. He that hath a long and lingering sickness wisheth for a sharp fit so it might be short; and, on the contrary, another feeling a sharp and violent sickness, could wish for a longer, so it were less painful. Thus we are apt to dislike our cross, which God layeth on us for the present. But this is disobedience to God and folly too, for if God should leave us to ourselves to choose our own crosses, we should choose worse for ourselves than the Lord doth, that affliction which is hurtful and dangerous for us. The Lord knows what is best for us and in what vein to strike us.

3. Those that desert their duty and their station, as being discouraged by the cross; these are more culpable than the former: Ps. cxxv. 5, 'As for such as turn aside unto their crooked ways, the Lord shall lead them forth with the workers of iniquity.' He had been speaking of 'the rod of the wicked resting on the lot of the righteous,' ver. 3; and therefore by them 'that turn aside' he meaneth such as dare not trust

God, nor adhere to the comfort of the promises; these are in the same rank with open enemies: Rev. xxi. 8, 'The fearful and unbelieving' are joined together.

4. Those that seek to make their worldly advantage and the profession of the gospel agree further than they ever will; and when they cannot frame the world and their conveniences to the gospel, they will fashion a gospel to the world and their carnal courses in it. It is a pity such had not been of the Lord's counsel, when he first contrived and preached the gospel, that they might have helped him to some discreet and mild course, that would have served the turn for heaven and earth; but do what ye can, 'the way is narrow that leadeth to life,' Mat. vii. 14; 'Take my yoke upon you, &c., and ye shall find rest unto your souls,' Mat. xi. 29.

5. Those that suffer, but it is for their evil-doing; these take not up the cross of Christ, but the cross of the thieves. Or if a man put himself upon needless danger, he taketh not up Christ's cross, but his own, and so hath his amends in his own hands. Afflictions so coming may be sanctified by repentance, good in their use, though not in their cause. When we suffer for our faults, we ought to bear it patiently, but we cannot suffer so cheerfully: 1 Peter iv. 15, 'But let none of you suffer as a murderer, or as a thief, or as an evil-doer, or as a busy-body in other men's matters.'

Use 3. To press us to take up the cross, and to take heed of grudging and heartless discouragement. Now, that you may so take up the cross, see the hand and counsel of God in it. So it was as to Christ's cross: Acts ii. 23, 'Him being delivered by the determinate counsel and foreknowledge of God, ye have taken, and by wicked hands have crucified and slain;' John xviii. 11, 'The cup which my Father hath given me,' &c.; and so as to the christian's cross: 1 Thes. iii. 3, 'That no man should be moved by these afflictions, for yourselves know that we are appointed thereunto.' All things must obey God's appointment, and every one must yield up himself to the disposal of God. And we have Christ's example, who took up his cross for us, and doth not call us but to walk in such ways as he hath trodden before us: 1 Peter ii. 21, 'For even hereunto were ye called, because Christ also suffered for us, leaving us an example, that ye should follow his steps.' He hath paved the way with the blessing of his example, whatever the cross be. Are we banished our country? Our Lord Jesus was a stranger upon earth, and when he was in the cradle he was carried into Egypt. Are you poor? You cannot be poorer than Christ, who had not where to rest his head. Are you constrained to hard fare? He thought a draught of water a courtesy: John iv. 7, 'Jesus saith unto her, Give me to drink;' and on the cross they gave him vinegar to drink when he was athirst. Christ preached in a boat in the midst of the waves. Do but read the history of Christ's life, and the hardship he endured, and will you be scandalised at a little suffering? Are you reproached? Christ himself was called a devil, accused of blasphemy and sedition, and you must not think to be better used than he was. *Quum Christus ipse crucem et supplicia passus sit tantum illis pretii accessit, ut nemo istis dignus sit*, saith Luther—Since Christ hath endured the cross, there hath such a value and honour accrued to it thereby, that no man is worthy to have this honour put upon him. We bear it together with Christ: Rom. viii. 26, 'The Spirit also helpeth our infirmities,' συναντιλαμβάνεται; 1 Cor. x. 13, 'He will with the temptation also make a way to escape, that ye may be able to bear it.' Such a master may well expect cheerful servants. He will give us peace and comfort in all our sufferings: John xvi. 33, 'These things I have spoken unto you, that in me ye might have peace: in the world ye shall have tribulation; but be of good cheer, I have overcome the world;' 2 Cor. i. 5, 'For as the sufferings of Christ abound in us, so our consolation also aboundeth by Christ.' Jacob, when he slept, and had a heap of stones for his pillow, had then the visions of God; and usually when we are taken off from the comforts of the world, then we have the clearest manifestations of the love of God: Rom. v. 5, 'The love of God is shed abroad in our hearts by the Holy Ghost, which is given unto us.' It is an honour for us to suffer with Christ and for Christ: Phil. i. 29, 'For unto you it is given in behalf of Christ, not only to believe on him, but also to suffer for his sake.' And all this, how bitter soever it be for the present, will end well: Acts xiv. 22, 'We must through many tribulations enter into the kingdom of God.' After this howling wilderness there will be a Canaan. We have had our times of good, and is it nothing to pass over so much of our time in peace and comfort? Job ii. 10, 'Shall we receive good at the hands of God, and shall we not receive evil?'

Use 4. If all that enter themselves disciples of Christ must prepare for the cross, then are we indeed prepared for it? You will think all this needeth not in times of peace, when religion is under the covert and protection of the laws, and we are not called to the afflictions of the gospel, yet certainly such questions as these are not to be entertained coldly and carelessly. Have you prepared your shoulders for the cross of Christ? It is necessary to put it to you—

1. Because of private crosses, which are incident to all, such as loss of goods and relations, pains of body, sickness, reproach, contempt, and the like. There is none get out of the world without some exercises: 1 Peter v. 9, 'Knowing that the same afflictions are accomplished in your brethren that are in the world;' Heb. vi. 12, 'That ye be not slothful, but followers of them who through faith and patience inherit the promises.' All the heirs of salvation have their conflicts before they come to enjoy their hopes. The earth is a middle place between heaven and hell, and partaker of both; it is only evil that is in hell and only good that is in heaven; but here our state is mixed, our afflictions are tempered with some comforts, and our comforts seasoned with some afflictions. Earth must be earth, and heaven must be heaven; here we must expect our trials: Job ii. 10, 'Shall we receive good at the hand of the Lord, and shall we not receive evil?' therefore we need to be provided; there is good that need to be tried, and bad that need to be purged out.

2. Because we should be always ready to encounter the greatest difficulties. Though we do not always lie under tribulations and persecutions, yet we should be always prepared, *præparatione animi*, as Joseph prepared for the years of scarcity in the years of plenty. The wise virgins had not only oil in their lamps, but oil in their vessels;

we should not only have grace for present use, but against future temptations. Now have you indeed this preparation of heart? And because a man may crack and vaunt it before the temptation cometh, let us consider who hath this preparation of heart, so as cheerfully, willingly, and patiently to bear the cross, and who hath it not.

[1.] He that is not strict and holy in a time of peace will not be cheerful in a time of trouble: Acts ix. 31, 'Then had the churches rest, &c.; and walking in the fear of the Lord, and in the comfort of the Holy Ghost, were multiplied.' When we are not called to passive obedience and suffering, our active obedience should be more cheerfully performed. Now where is it so? Our fathers suffered more willingly for Christ than we speak for him; they were not ashamed to die for a crucified Jesus, they endured the fire better than we can a frown or scoff.

[2.] He that is not mortified to the world, but loveth a flesh-pleasing life, is but ripening himself for apostasy: James v. 5, 'Ye adulterers and adulteresses, know ye not that the friendship of the world is enmity with God? whosoever therefore will be a friend of the world is the enemy of God.' A fond and delicate person, that hath a value for worldly contentments, will be grieved when he cometh to part with them; he that is corrupted with prosperity, will be dejected with adversity; but no man is prepared but he that is crucified to the world by the cross of Christ, that liveth in a holy weanedness in the midst of his present enjoyments: Gal. vi. 14, 'But God forbid that I should glory, save in the cross of our Lord Jesus Christ, by whom the world is crucified to me, and I unto the world.'

[3.] He that is not abounding in charity, and willing to part with temporal things in a way of free distribution, will be loath to part with them by constraint, and by way of sacrifice and voluntary surrender to God, when he calls for them. I offer this, because the churches that were free from persecution are still charged with the duty of charity; and it is a general precept, Gal. vi. 10, 'As we have therefore opportunity, let us do good unto all men, especially unto them who are of the household of faith;' because he that will not part with his superfluities willingly to God, will never part with his substance and the main of his estate with rejoicing, when it is made a prey to the violence of men. It is irrational to think that he that grudgeth at a command that requires him to part only with a little of his temporal conveniences, will not storm at the violence when all is taken away: James v. 1, 'Go to now, ye rich men, weep and howl for your miseries that shall come upon you.' There are their howling times, when that wealth which they sat abroad upon is taken away in an instant.

[4.] He that cannot digest lighter afflictions, how will he bear greater? Jer. xii. 5, 'If thou hast run with the footmen, and they have wearied thee, then how canst thou contend with horses? and if in the land of peace, wherein thou trustedst, they wearied thee, then how wilt thou do in the swelling of Jordan?' The prophet was all in a pet because the men of his town and neighbourhood had conspired against him, and were very troublesome to him. God tells him, If thou canst not bear this, how wilt thou do when thou art exposed to greater trials? There are private persecutions, therefore father and mother are put into the catalogue of things to be renounced by us when we take to Christ : Luke xiv. 26, 'If any man come to me, and hate not his father and mother, and wife and children, and brethren and sisters, yea, and his own life also, he cannot be my disciple.' If a frown and disgrace, and loss of preferment, be so much, how will you endure rapine, and torture, and all manner of violence and evil?

[5.] He that begrudgeth a little pains for God, and counts it so tedious to converse with him a little while in duties of holiness, and reckons all labour too much, and is loath to 'strive to enter in at the strait gate,' Luke xiii. 24, how will he endure torments, and expose the body to all kind of sufferings? *Necesse est, ut ei honestum vile sit, cui corpus carum est*—He that is so tender of his ease, so delicate that he cannot endure the labours of the gospel, how will he bear the afflictions of the gospel? If it be irksome to put the body to a little trouble in prayer or meditating, or other holy duties, how will he rejoice in the midst of all tribulations that shall befall him for Christ's sake? Thus you see how few are prepared for the cross.

SERMON IX.

And he was sad at that saying, and went away grieved, for he had great possessions.—MARK x. 22.

WE have hitherto seen the young man at his best; now we shall find him discovered and laid open in his own colours. It was well that he came to Christ with such reverence and seriousness about such a weighty question as 'What shall I do that I may inherit eternal life?' It was well if he could say truly, 'All these have I kept from my youth.' But now, here is the event and issue of this interlocutory discourse between him and Christ; when Christ bid him 'Sell all, and take up his cross, and follow him,' then 'he went away sad,' &c.

Here observe—

1. How he was affected with Christ's advice, 'He was sad at the saying, and went away grieved.'

2. The reason of his sorrow, or why he was thus affected, 'For he had great possessions.'

In the first part we may observe—

[1.] The kind of the affection; he was not angry, but sorry; he doth not fret and fume, but goes away sorrowful.

[2.] Observe the degree of it; it is expressed here by two things—a sad heart, and a heavy countenance. The sadness of his countenance I gather from the word στυγνάσας ἐπὶ τῷ λόγῳ, 'He was sad at that saying.' The word properly signifies he lowered at that saying; the lowering of the heavens is expressed by that word, 'So the sky was red and lowering,' Mat. xvi. 3, πυρράζει γὰρ στυγνάζων ὁ οὐρανός. Then the sadness of his heart, ἀπῆλθη λυπούμενος, 'He went away grieved.' In Luke xviii. 23, it is περίλυπος ἐγένετο, 'He was very sorrowful.' Note, that he went away, and we hear no more of him; like those, John vi. 66, 'At that time many of his disciples went back, and walked no more with him.'

Secondly, here is the reason of this, 'For he had great possessions.' In Luke it is said ἦν γὰρ πλούσιος σφόδρα, 'He was very rich;' he had both κτήματα possessions, and χρήματα, riches too, as appears by the next verse. And observe, that the bare having is rendered as the reason, 'He had great possessions,' and therefore he went away sad. It is hard to have them without lustful affections to them. It may be, if he had so little as the poor fishermen, or the other disciples whom Christ called, he would sooner have left all and followed Christ; but having so much to lose, it was the more difficult for him to forsake all: 'He went away, for he had great possessions.'

To give you a few brief points—

1. That a man may go very far, and be zealous and forward at first, yet afterwards cool and fall away.

2. That trials bring men forth to the light, and make them manifest what they are.

3. A man wedded to the world will renounce Christ and his commands rather than the world whenever it comes to a proof.

4. A carnal worldly man may be very sorrowful when he cannot have heaven in his own way.

5. The disease of worldlings is very incident to great men, and it is a very hard matter to keep the heart of such open and free for Christ.

Doct. 1. That a man may go far, and be zealous and forward at first, and yet cool and fall away at last.

Witness this young man, who comes to Christ to learn of him the way of life, and that in such an humble and reverent manner, and makes profession that he hath kept the commandments from his youth; and yet when Christ tells him what he must do more, he was troubled, and falls off. So Judas walked with Christ for a while, but afterwards proveth a traitor to him: John vi. 70, 'Have not I chosen you twelve, and one of you is a devil?' When others were turning away from Christ, and were offended at his doctrine, he continues in Christ's company, and yet a devil for all that. Judas was not carried away with the stream of the defection; he kept the bag, and his temptation was not yet come, yet his heart was not sound. So 'Herod heard John gladly, and did many things,' yet afterwards put him to death: Mark vi. 20, 'Simon Magus, he believed, and when he was baptized, he continued with Philip and wondered, beholding the miracles and signs which were done,' Acts viii. 13. Here was faith and solemn profession and fellowship with Philip, and this not feignedly, but out of a sense and conviction of a power that accompanied his doctrine, and yet afterwards he discovered that he was but 'in the gall of bitterness and bond of iniquity,' ver. 23. The reasons of this are—

1. They take up religion upon foreign and extrinsic reasons, and when those reasons fail, their religion faileth also. As puppets moved by the wires to which they are fastened, so they are moved by credit and esteem and countenance in the world; they court religion while it hath a portion for them. Thus we read of some that followed Christ for the loaves: John vi. 26, 'Ye seek me, not because ye saw the miracles,

but because ye ate of the loaves, and were filled;' and 'ye rejoiced in his light for a season,' John v. 35. Curiosity and novelty made them rejoice in his light for a while. *Vix queritur Jesus, propter Jesum.* Religion is scarce received in the world for religion's sake. Now foreign things, as they are accidental to religion, *possunt abesse et adesse*, so must the respect built upon them be casual and accidental, and very uncertain, even as those reasons vary. Men upon these foreign reasons may be very zealous for a time, as interest will urge men more than conscience; and when it is their interest to follow or promote such a way, they are vehement sticklers for it. Therefore the difference between false and sincere professors is not altogether taken from their zeal and outward diligence; they may be exceeding zealous and forward upon the impulsion of false principles who have a base heart lurking under it, because the motions of lusts disguised with religion are rapid and earnest, and byends have a powerful influence. Though lust be served, yet because it is in the way of religion, men's affections are much aloft, and they may seem to have great fits and zealous pangs in the service of God, and yet all this comes to nothing.

2. Because they many times rest in externals without internal grace. This young man for outward conformity went very far. There is nothing for external duties that a child of God doth but a hypocrite may do also; he may pray, preach, confer, hear the word, though not in a holy and gracious manner. A painter may paint the external colour of fire, but not the internal virtue and heat of it, or the limbs, shape, figure, and colour of a man, but the life cannot be painted, there is no counterfeiting that; so many men deceive themselves and others by a show of religion, and their diligence in external duties, when they are void of the truth and power of it; the power of religion cannot be counterfeited. Now externals will in time be cast off, where there is not the root to feed them.

3. Because that internal affection which they seem to have to the ways of God is not rooted and fixed, only a slight tincture, that may easily be worn off: Luke viii. 13, 'They on the rock are they which, when they hear, receive the word with joy, and these have no root which for a while believe, and in time of temptation fall away.' At first men have some taste, and seem to feel some sweetness in the word, and that begets a little affection to it, and that affection begets profession, and that profession begets external reformation; so far it is good; but in time they lose their relish and taste, and then their affection is gone and dried up, and then their leaf falls, and afterwards run from their profession into profaneness and a plain distaste of the ways of God.

4. Their corrupt lusts were only restrained, not mortified and weakened, and so it is but like a sore that is skinned over, and festers inwardly, and will at length break out again. This is the case of many: Luke viii. 14, 'That which fell among thorns are they which, when they have heard, go forth, and are choked with cares and riches and pleasures of this life, and bring no fruit to perfection.' Many an unsound professor seems to cast the world and their old fashions behind their back, yet their hearts are not wholly weaned from them, nor are they wholly cast out; some prevalent lust remains that will make them turn back to their old vomit again; so dangerous it is to have Satan

only gone out for a while, and not cast out, Luke xi. 24, to have anything wherein to delight besides Christ when we close with him, or to have those things which we formerly seemed to slight to seem great and lovely again, and bear bulk in our eyes. This point is but reductive to this place, therefore I shall not handle it at large.

Use. It doth press us unto two things—to search for a sound work, and to watch against declinings.

1. To search for a true sound work. We have need to shift and ransack all the corners of our souls, to see that there be no one reserved lust as a seed of our revolt and apostasy from Christ. One leak let alone will ruin the ship, so will one lust the soul: Ps. cxix. 133, 'Order my steps in thy word, and let not any iniquity have dominion over me.' Whilst any one sin remains unbroken, all that we do in conformity to God will be lost; and therefore let us search and see, that our love to the ways of God be founded in a complete resignation to his use and service, and a renouncing of every fleshly interest, if we would constantly persevere with Christ. Profession will fail unless there be a good and an honest heart to bear it out; and what is that but a resolution to make this our great business and interest, to get the love of God in Christ whatever it cost us? It is not enough to have good offers and inclinations; one idol left in the heart will estrange us from God: Ezek. xiv. 4–6, 'Every man of the house of Israel that setteth up his idols in his heart, and putteth the stumbling-block of his iniquity before his face, and cometh to the prophet, I the Lord will answer him that cometh according to the multitude of his idols; that I may take the house of Israel in their own heart, because they are all estranged from me through their idols. Therefore say unto the house of Israel, Thus saith the Lord God, Repent and turn yourselves from your idols, and turn away your face from all your abominations.' And what is prized besides Christ will be soon prized above Christ; therefore, unless the sweetness of his grace makes all the baits of the flesh unsavoury to us, we cannot be sound.

2. To watch against declinings, for we lose ground every day, as a thing running down the hill falls lower and lower, if we do not keep up a constant relish and savour of good things. When you lose your first love, you will leave your first works: Rev. ii. 4, 5, 'Nevertheless I have somewhat against thee, because thou hast left thy first love. Remember therefore from whence thou art fallen, and repent, and do thy first works.' We see it is very ordinary for new converts to be carried on with a great measure of affection and zeal, because of the newness of the thing, and the edge upon their affections is not yet blunted by change of condition, or multiplicity of business, and the Lord restrains furious temptations, till they be a little confirmed and engaged in his way, and he has a deeper sense of comfort. Now take heed to keep up this, for when this edge is blunted and taken off, a man loses ground. Therefore the apostle saith, Heb. iii. 6, 'Whose house are we, if we hold fast the confidence and the rejoicing of the hope firm unto the end.' Upon our first acquaintance with Christ there is a mighty joy of heart, and comfort in the hopes of a pardon and of eternal life. Oh! you must keep up this to the end. If you quite lose your savour, you run into total apostasy; and if you lose it

in part, you grow remiss and lazy. If you have not such delight in God, you can read and hear the offers of grace and eternal life without any considerable joy and thankfulness, you have not that lively sense you were wont to have; take heed, you are upon decay.

Doct. 2. That trials bring men forth to the light, and make them manifest what they are.

Here upon the trial the young man is discovered. Who would but have thought this young man good till now? But when he heard Christ's terms, 'he was sad at that saying, and went away grieved.' As lime seems cold, and to have no heat and warmth in it, till you pour water upon it, then it burns and smokes, so our corrupt affections lie hid till there be an occasion to try them. Trials are either extraordinary or ordinary. Extraordinary, as that of Abraham: Gen. xxii. 1, 'And it came to pass after these things that God did tempt Abraham;' that is, try him for his discovery, by the command for sacrificing of his son, his only son, the son whom he loved, the son of the promise. So this young man, Christ tries him, 'sell all.' But then God's ordinary trial is in the course of his providence or by his word. By his providence, either by affliction: Dan. xi. 35, 'And some of them of understanding shall fall, to try them;' 1 Peter i. 7, 'That the trial of your faith, being much more precious than of gold that perisheth, though it be tried with fire, might be found unto praise;' or some other occasion offered to discover either grace or sin, as Joseph was tried by the temptation of his mistress. Or by his word, which doth search and try our hearts, when it pursueth them within, and followeth them home to their consciences: John vi. 60, 'When they heard this, they said, It is a hard saying, who can hear it?' They are offended when it toucheth upon a bosom sin, pride, sensuality, or covetousness, or unlawful pleasure, they are tried by it.

Again, trial is either for the discovery of grace or corruption, to discover the corruption of their hearts or the weakness of their graces. So God trieth his people, as he tried Hezekiah: 2 Chron. xxxii. 31, 'Howbeit in the business of the ambassadors of the princes of Babylon, who sent unto him to inquire of the wonder that was done in the land, God left him to try him, that he might know all that was in his heart.' So Christ tried his apostles: John vi. 6, 'And this he said to prove them, for he himself knew what he would do.'

Reasons.

1. It is for good that men should be discovered, the graces of his people to their comfort, and their weakness that it may be repaired; as when a man tries a leaky vessel with an intent to make it more stanch, and a man that is diseased, by walking and stirring the disease appears; it is better it should be discovered that it might be remedied, than to lie hid in the body till it kill us. The hypocrite is tried that he may be discovered: Prov. xxvi. 26, 'His wickedness shall be showed before the whole congregation.' It is a great part of God's providence to uncase hypocrites. It is for the church's good, lest men get a name to do religion a mischief; and—

2. It is for the glory of God, that men may appear what they are, and for the reclaiming of offenders. Many were likely to have grace, if they were discovered to themselves and knew they had no grace.

Trials are ordered by God for this end and purpose. God is wise, and knows in what vein to strike. God tries not to inform himself, but to discover us to ourselves: Ps. cxxxix. 2, 'Thou understandest my thoughts afar off.' God knows not only conclusions and events, but the first contrivances, though afar off. As a man in the air may see a river in the rise, fountain, and course all at once, so God doth see things altogether, but he tries us, that we may be discovered to ourselves, and suits the means accordingly.

Use. Well, then, expect trials, and see to it how you behave yourselves under them.

1. Expect trials. Mat. vii., we read of two builders, the one built upon the sand, the other on the rock; when they had built, the tightness of the building was to be tried; the winds blew, the rain fell, the waves did swell and arise; that that was built on the rock stood, that that was built on the sand fell. Whosoever buildeth a confidence for heaven must look to have his building tried. Count it not strange we are loath to forecaste and to think of trials. You shall see even the people of God many times are subject to security when trials are nearest. When the shepherd was to be smitten and the sheep scattered, then the disciples were asleep, Mat. xxvi. 40; and they were dreaming of ease and of dividing kingdoms when the cross was at their heels: Acts i. 6, 'Lord, wilt thou at this time restore again the kingdom to Israel?' We promise ourselves perpetual exemption, if we have but a little breathing time: Ps. xxx. 6, 'In my prosperity I said I shall never be moved.' We take a carnal pillow, and lie down upon it, and count it strange when it comes.

2. Be careful how you acquit yourselves in trials. When the hour of temptation is come upon the earth, then we should be cautious: Rev. iii, 10, 'Because thou hast kept the word of my patience, I also will keep thee from the hour of temptation, which shall come upon all the world, to try them that dwell upon the earth.' Whatever a man doth, he will behave himself well when he is upon his trial.

Doct. 3. That a man wedded to the world will renounce Christ and his commands rather than the world when it comes to a proof.

When two persons walk together, you cannot tell to whom the servant that follows them belongs, but when they part company then it is seen; so when Christ and the world part, then the servant of the world and the servant of Christ is seen; for he that is addicted to the world will break all the commands of Christ for the world's sake. It must needs be so, for the world diverts the heart from Christ, and sets the heart against Christ.

1. The love of the world diverts the heart from Christ, that there is no room for holy things. The heart will be where the treasure is, Mat. vi. 21, and so the delight that we should have in heavenly things will be intercepted, the stream will be carried another way, the heart will be withdrawn from God, whom we should love with all our soul and might. Look, as in a pair of balances, what you take out of one scale, you make the other so much the more weighty; just so our souls hang like a pair of balances between God and the world; what you give to the world you take from God, and what you give to heavenly things you take from the world: Col. iii. 7, 'Set your affections on

things above, not on things of the world.' Our desires cannot be carried out after heavenly things with any intention unless they be remitted to the world.

2. The love of the world sets the heart against Christ, and carries it to contrary things. I shall prove it by three considerations—it disposeth and inclineth the soul to all evil; it incapacitateth us for the doing of any good; and it hinders us from the receiving any good.

[1.] It disposeth and inclineth the soul to all evil. It makes a man break every command of the law of God: 'The love of money is the root of all evil,' 1 Tim. vi. 10. Let it once reign in the heart, and then a man sticks at no sin, and he becomes a ready prey for Satan when his heart is intoxicated with the love of present things: Micah ii. 2, 'Covet fields, and take them by violence, and houses, and take them away; so they oppress a man and his house, even a man and his heritage.' First they covet, and then they will stop at nothing, but break out into all that is unseemly. Let Judas but enchant his thoughts with the pleasure of a supposed gain that he can make of his master, and he will soon come with a *Quid dabitis?*—What will you give me? Gehazai, let him but affect a reward, and he will dishonour God and lay a stumbling-block in the way of a new and noble convert. Let Achan's heart be tickled and pleased a little with the sight of it, and he will be purloining the wedge of gold and Babylonish garment. Let Balaam hear of gold and silver, and he will curse Israel against his conscience, and venture though there be an angel in the way to stop them. Ahab will consent to Naboth's blood when his vineyard is in the chase. Ananias and Sapphira will keep back part of what was dedicated to God, if they look upon what they part withal. Simon Magus will deny religion, and return to his old sorceries, that he may be some great one among the people. So that there is no sin so foul but the love of the world will make it plausible, and reconcile it to the thoughts of men.

[2.] It incapacitateth us, and makes us incapable of doing service to God in our general and particular calling.

(1.) In our general calling.

(1*st.*) It destroys the principle of obedience, which is the love of God: 1 John ii. 15, 'If any man love the world, the love of the Father is not in him.' The great principle which sways and inclines the heart to do the will of God is love; now the love of the world and the love of God are contrary and inconsistent. Love anything besides Christ, and you will soon love it above Christ. Why? Because the love of God is a stranger and foreigner, the love of the world is a native.

(2*d.*) It is contrary to the matter of our obedience. The commands of God and the commands of mammon are contrary: Mat. vi. 24, 'No man can serve two masters, for either he will hate the one and love the other, or he will hold to the one and despise the other. Ye cannot serve God and mammon.' God saith, Pity the afflicted, relieve the miserable, venture all for a good conscience, seek heaven in the first place with your most ardent affection, with your most earnest diligence. But now mammon saith, Be sparing of your substance, follow the world as hard as you can, stick at nothing, lie, steal, comply with the lusts of men, and then you shall be rich. Well, now, he that is ruled by mammon, whose eyes the god of this world hath blinded, that is, enchanted with the love of worldly goods, he can never serve God; he loves wealth above all, he trusts it above all, he serves it more than God himself; though his tongue dare not say earth is better than heaven, and that the things of this life are better than everlasting blessedness, and therefore they shall have more of his heart and care, yet his life says it; he can part with God for the matters of this world. In short, it unfits us not only for one duty, but for all duties required of us. God's laws are for our respects to God, neighbour, and self; this inordinate love of the world denies what is due to God, what is necessary for our neighbour, and what is comfortable for ourselves. A man that loves the world is unthankful to God, unmerciful to his neighbour, and cruel to himself.

(3d.) It slights the encouragements of obedience, which are the rewards of God, as it weakeneth all our future hopes, and depresseth our heart from looking after spiritual and heavenly things. They despise their birthright, Heb. xii. 16, and when they are invited to the wedding, Mat. xxii., they prefer their farm, oxen, and merchandise, before the rich feast of grace which God invites us to.

(2.) He that loves the world will break with God in the duties of his particular calling for the world's sake. What manner of men ought magistrates to be? Exod. xviii. 21, 'Such as fear God, men of truth, hating covetousness;' not only not covetous, but hating covetousness; for let this once possess his heart, it will make him base, and act unworthily; nay, for a piece of bread will that man transgress. Then for a minister, what a poor meal-mouthed creature will it make him! One qualification of a minister is, 1 Tim. iii. 3, 'Not to be greedy of filthy lucre.' If his heart be set upon that, it makes him sordid, low-spirited, flattering and daubing to curry favour with men, more intent upon his gain and profit than the saving of souls. See the work of a minister: 1 Peter v. 2, 'Feed the flock of God that is among you, taking the oversight thereof, not for filthy lucre, but of a ready mind.' What a low flat ministry will that be that is inspired with no other aim but outward profit! If that be their inducement to undertake, and their prime encouragement to discharge the work of their calling, how soon will they strain themselves to please men, especially great ones, and writhe themselves into all postures to soothe the humours and lusts of others; as Balaam: 2 Peter ii. 15, 'Who loved the wages of unrighteousness,' and therefore would fain curse the people whom God blessed. This base, powerful, imperious lust will draw men to very base and unworthy actions. Saith God, Ezek. xiii. 19, 'Will ye pollute me among my people for handfuls of barley and pieces of bread, to slay the souls that should not die, and to save the souls of people alive that should not live by your lying to my people that hear your lies.' That is to say, What! will you declaim against the good, and harden the evil in their evil, and comply with the fashions of the world thus to humour men? So if a man be a master of a family: Prov. xv. 27, 'He that is greedy of gain troubleth his own house.' What a burden and trouble will he be to his servants and all about him! In short, it is love of the world that makes one an oppressing landlord, another a false tradesman and an ill neighbour, that makes him study iniquity of traffic: Ezek. xxviii. 5, 'By thy great wisdom, and by thy traffic hast thou increased thy riches.' So that it is the pest and bane of human societies.

[3.] It hinders the receiving of good, and those means of reformation that should make us better. A man that is under the power of worldly lusts is prejudiced against whatever shall be spoken for God, and for the concernments of another world: Luke xvi. 14, 'The pharisees also, who were covetous, heard all these things, and derided him.' If the word stir us a little, and men begin to have some anxious thoughts about eternal life, these thorns, which are the cares of this world, will choke the good seed, and stifle our convictions, so as they come to nothing: Mat. xiii. 22, 'He also that receiveth seed among the thorns is he that heareth the word, and the cares of this world and the deceitfulness of riches choke the word, and he becometh unfruitful.' They will distract the head with cares, and put out all thoughts of our eternal condition. If a man begins to do some outward thing, it will make us soon weary of religion and attendance on holy duties, as if all time laid out upon God were lost; and they cry out, 'When will the sabbath be over that we may set forth wheat,' Amos viii. 5. The heathens counted the Jews a foolish people, as Seneca saith, because they lost a full seventh part of their lives; he speaks it with respect to the sabbath; so other men are of his mind; they think all lost that is laid out upon God. And it distracts us in duty, and carries away our heart: Ezek. xxxiii. 31, 'They come unto me as the people cometh, and they sit before thee as my people, and they hear thy word, but they will not do them; for with their mouth they show much love, but their heart goeth after their covetousness.' It interlines our prayers and holy services with worldly projects and thoughts; nay, it turns religion into a trade and market. Men live by it; it makes religion to serve their worldly ends; they make a market of their devotion, as the Shechemites, for then, say they, 'their substance and their cattle will be ours.'

Use. To inform us of the evil of worldliness. We need to be set right in that, for most men stroke it with a gentle censure. They will say, He is a good man, but a little worldly, as if it were no great matter to be so; nay, men are apt to applaud those that are guilty of this sin: Ps. x. 3, 'They bless the covetous, whom the Lord abhorreth.' He that by hook and crook gets honour and riches is the only prudent man in their account. If our children are loose, and drunkards, and riotous, we are offended, but if we see them worldly, we are not troubled. Oh! it is a foul sin, but the men of the world will not believe it. Surely we have too mild thoughts of it, and therefore we do not watch and strive against the love of the world: Luke xii. 15, 'Take heed and beware of covetousness.' The words are doubled for the more vehemency; he doth not say, 'Take heed' only, but 'Take heed and beware of covetousness.' Sins that are more gross and sensual are easier discovered, and such a sinner is sooner reclaimed, but this is a secret sin that turns away the heart from God. And to make you more careful to avoid it, in scripture a covetous man is called 'an idolater,' Eph. v. 3, and covetousness is called idolatry, Col. iii. 5; and is that a small crime? What! to set up another god? Who are you that dare to harbour such an evil in your bosoms, and make no great matter of it? Will you dethrone that God which made you, and set up the world in his stead? It is called 'adultery,' James iv. 4; it is a breach of your conjugal vow. You did promise in your baptism to renounce the world, and give up yourselves unto Christ's service, and will you cherish such whorish and disloyal affections as will carry you to the creature instead of God? Oh! we cannot think bad enough of such a sin.

Doct. 4. A carnal worldly man may be sorrowful when he cannot win heaven in his own way.

When he cannot get heaven, and his own will in the world also, as this young man was, when he could not be a christian at a cheaper rate. He departed from Christ sad, as loath to miss this felicity, and yet loath to pay so dear for it. There is a sorrow 'that worketh repentance to salvation never to be repented of,' 2 Cor. vii. 10; but this is of another nature; it makes a wound in the conscience, and doth no more. It troubled him much that he had moved this question when he did not find Christ's answer according to his desire and expectation; and this is just the disposition of a man that hath a sense of eternity, and yet is wedded to his lusts. Fain he would be happy hereafter, but will not leave his lusts now; so they are troubled; they cannot have Christ and the world too, Christ for their consciences, and the world for their affections. They love this world, and yet would fain be saved in the world to come, and therefore are grieved when they cannot have both. On the one side they are troubled with a sense of religion, and on the other side with a fear of losing their worldly interests. See a like trouble in Herod: Mat. xiv. 9, 'The king was sorry; nevertheless for his oath's sake, and for them that sat with him at meat, he commanded it to be given her.' He was loath to put John to death, and yet loath to deny her. So Balaam would have the reward, and yet loath to go against the express command of God, Num. xxi., xxii. So Pilate was loath to condemn Christ against his own conscience. Thus shall we be affected till we seek God with our whole hearts.

This sorrow of the young man will give us some light as to the difference between those conflicts that are in a gracious and renewed man, and those conflicts that are in the unregenerate. There are conflicts in both, yet they differ much. In the unregenerate graceless soul the conflict is between conviction and corruption; conscience wrestles with their lusts, and lusts wrestle with conscience, and so men are sorrowful upon carnal, not godly reasons; whereas the conflict in the regenerate is in the same faculty, carnal reason against spiritual reason, and carnal will against spiritual will, carnal affections against spiritual affections; the battle is fought in every faculty. In the conflict betwixt the flesh and spirit in the regenerate, the spiritual part prevails. Herod, and Pilate, and Balaam had a conflict, natural conscience did restrain them for a while, but at last they yielded; and here the young man yielded, and went away sorrowful. This conflict and sorrow may leave a wound in the conscience, but it doth not prevail to cause them to look after heaven on Christ's own terms.

The last point is taken from the reason of his heavy and sorrowful departure. 'For he had great possessions.' He had them: is that a fault? Here is no note of crime put upon him as to his getting of them. He is not taxed with an insatiable desire of riches, nor with unconscionable means to get them; only it is said that he was marvellously rich and had great possessions, and therefore he went away sorrowful; so that the point will be this—

Doct. 5. That the disease of worldliness is very incident to great persons and men of quality.

If we have not a mortified heart, the very having an estate may prove a snare to us. I observe this, because many please themselves in this, that they have not got what they have by extortion or cosenage, or by any fraudulent or unlawful means, that their heritage comes to them lawfully, in the fair way of providence; but if they have it, and they look not to their hearts, it will enchant them. It is not the means of gathering wealth, but the deceitfulness of it, however gathered, that chokes the word. The very possession and presence, though it be not greedily sought for nor unlawfully purchased, may enchant our minds, and render us unapt to obey Christ's commandments. Take three propositions—

1. That it is possible, yea, very likely, that our hearts may be inordinately set upon wealth lawfully gotten; and therefore God gives us that caution: Ps. lxii. 10, 'If riches increase, set not your heart upon them.' Though they should increase by God's providence, yet consider, a man may drink too freely, and be intoxicated with his own wine. The mind may be enchanted with a secret delight and desire to retain and increase riches lawfully gotten. A man may be a slave to his wealth, and loath to part with it upon religious reasons. It is very likely it will be so when men have anything in the world. Saith Austin, *Nescio quomodo cum superflua et terrena diliguntur, arctius adepta quam concupita comprimunt; nam unde juvenis, iste tristis discessit, nisi quia magnas habebat divitias? Aliud est enim nova incorporare, quia desunt; aliud jam incorporata divellere; illa enim velut cibi repudiantur, ista vero velut membra præciduntur*—I do not know how it comes to pass, but so it is, there is more danger in possessing wealth than in getting it; this young man went away sad, for he had great riches; and it is one thing, saith he, to refuse that we have not, another thing to part with what we have: we may refuse that we have not, as we do some meats; but that we have, we are loath to part with it, as we are with the members of our bodies. Covetousness is not to be determined by a greedy thirst only, but also by complacency, delight, and acquiescence of soul in worldly enjoyments. Though we would not desire more, yet if our hearts be glued to that we have already, we are unapt for the kingdom of God; these are torn from us as members. In short, it is the corruption of our hearts that we are very prone to affect worldly goods too much, and so much the more by how much the more plenty and abundance of them is enjoyed. The moon is never in an eclipse but when she is at the full; so when we are at the full these things prevail over us. They that have much flax and gunpowder in their houses had need be careful to keep fire from it; so a christian, that enjoys a great store of wealth, had need look to his heart, that corruption do not meet with it; that aversion from God, and conversion to the creature is so natural to us, that when we have great store of the world's goods, we are ready to set our hearts too much on them.

2. That the gathering of a spiritual disease is very secret and insensible. Bad humours breed in the body, and are not discovered till a strain ; much more distempers breed in the soul ere we are aware, and therefore the more caution is necessary : Prov. xxx. 9, 'Give me not riches, lest I be full, and deny thee, and say, Who is the Lord ?' Every man is afraid of want and poverty, but who is afraid of riches ? Yet Agur is as much afraid of that as of poverty. Our greatest learning is to learn how to abound. The worldly-minded judge riches and abundance a happy condition : Oh ! blessed is the man, they will say, that is in such a case. It is the sum of every man's wish ; but to be shy of the world, to suspect danger in plenty, it can never enter into their hearts. But alas ! as a rank soil is apt to breed weeds, so many snares are incident to this condition and this sort of life. Alas ! they that have great and plentiful estates, how apt are they to pamper the flesh, to grow forgetful of God, slight in holy things, to be wedded to worldly greatness. A corrupt heart will take mischief in every course of life, as a drunken man will stumble in the plainest way, but especially in a plentiful condition. As soon as men have anything in the world, their heads are lifted up above their brethren, and they grow proud, scornful of God's word, slighting of holy things, and we are wholly enchanted with pleasures of such an estate, but consider not the snares that secretly are laid for their souls.

3. There is no means to prevent the danger but by the continual exercise of good works, and a prudent carefulness to improve our substance for God's glory and helpfulness to others. Look, as we clip the wings of birds that they may not fly away from us, or as we cut off the superfluous boughs of trees that they may not hinder their growth and height, so this should be your care, not to join house to house, and field to field, for then our desires will swell into so vast an excess and proportion, as will not become grace and hopes of heaven. No ; but your business should be how you should honour God : Prov. iii. 9, 'Honour the Lord with thy substance, and with the first-fruits of all thy increase ; "Give alms, and all shall be clean unto you,' Luke xi. 41. A man's care should rather be for contracting and cutting short his desires, and how to make use of it in order to eternal life. Unless there be this constant solicitude upon the heart, it is impossible 'for a rich man to enter into the kingdom of heaven.'

SERMON X.

And Jesus looked round about, and saith unto his disciples, How hardly shall they that have riches enter into the kngidom of God !— MARK x. 23.

You have heard this young man was loath to sell all, and yet loath to quit his hopes of eternal life. He did not go away murmuring and frowning against Christ, but, because he could not bring both ends together, 'He went away sad, for he had great possessions.' The instance of this young man had raised them all into wonder, and therefore when they were full of thoughts about it, our Lord would make use of this for the instruction of his disciples. You find our Lord edifying his disciples upon all occasions, and improving every occurrence for their good. As a wise man passing by the field of the sluggard learns wisdom, and hath a sensible discovery of the loss and ill effects of idleness and careless indilgence; so by this young rich man's refusal of Christ's terms, the disciples might know the snares of the wealthy, and what a pull-back from Christ the love of the world is. Surely they that were sent forth to gain the world need such an instruction partly that they might be more diligent in warning rich men of their danger and duty: 1 Tim. vi. 17, 'Charge them that are rich in this world, that they be not high-minded, nor trust in uncertain riches, but in the living God, who giveth us richly all things to enjoy;' and partly that they might not be offended if their doctrine should be despised by men of that rank and order. The rich and full-fed worldlings were likely to despise the doctrine of a crucified Saviour and oppose his worshippers: James ii. 6, 7, 'But ye have despised the poor. Do not rich men oppress you, and draw you before the judgment seats? Do they not blaspheme that worthy name by the which ye are called?' Now they are forearmed against this contempt by seeing Christ himself refused by a rich man. And partly for themselves, that, laying aside all thoughts of worldly greatness, they might the better bear their own poverty, riches being such a hindrance and impediment to the kingdom of God; for they were leavened with the conceit of a carnal Messiah, that they should be mighty men in the world, and until the Spirit was poured out they had this conceit; for these and such like reasons, 'Jesus looked round about him, and saith to his disciples, How hardly shall they that have riches enter into the kingdom of God!' In this verse we have—

1. Christ's gesture, 'And Jesus looked round about him,' $\pi\epsilon\rho\iota\beta\lambda\epsilon\psi\acute{a}\mu\epsilon\nu o\varsigma$, the gesture of one that is to speak or do some notable thing: Luke vi. 10, 'And looking round about upon them all, he said unto the man, Stretch forth thy hand.' So here he looked round about to every one of them, to see how they entertained this passage and occurrence of providence, and to stir up their attention, and to cause them to be affected with it as a matter of some great weight and moment, that, when this moral, sweet-natured, forward young man came with such respect, kneeling to him, and asking him such a question, and went away sad, Jesus looked round about, as if he had said, How do you entertain this?

2. Here is Christ's speech, 'He saith to his disciples, How hardly shall they that have riches enter into the kingdom of God.' I will take notice of the matter and the form.

[1.] The matter, where the persons spoken of, 'They that have riches.' The privilege denied, entering into the kingdom of God.

[2.] The form. It is by way of question, 'How hardly?' he would appeal to them. See now what the love of the world did. They were leavened with it, and thought of great offices in the kingdom of the Messiah; but how hard is it for a rich man to enter into the kingdom of heaven. 'How hard?' It is—(1.) *Questio admirantis.* It is propounded in the form of an admiring question. (2.) It is *questio dolentis*, of one that bewails the corruption of human nature, that men should turn God's good gifts and blessings into a snare. Alas! 'How hard!' &c.

For the matter, there is not an utter impossibility, but a very great difficulty. It is spoken of such men as have riches only; and Christ explains himself in the next verse, 'Children, how hard is it for them that trust in riches to enter into the kingdom of God!' It doth not lessen the wonder, but increase it, for then 'they were astonished out of measure among themselves, saying, Who can be saved?'

By the kingdom of God is meant the kingdom of grace, or the kingdom of glory. How hardly do they submit to the doctrine of Christ, or enter into the kingdom of grace here! Or how hardly are they made partakers of his glory in the kingdom of heaven hereafter!

Doct. It is a very hard matter for such as abound in worldly wealth to enter into the kingdom of heaven.

1. I shall explain the point by the circumstances of the text.
2. Show whence the difficulty doth arise.
3. Make application.

I. To explain the point by the circumstances of the text. And here—

1. The persons spoken of, 'They that have riches.' The very having layeth us open to a snare. It is true Christ explains himself in the next verse, 'Children, how hard is it for them that trust in riches to enter into the kingdom of God!' The plain sense of the words is this, It is hard to have them and not trust in them. The disciples were astonished at his words when he said, 'How hardly shall they that have riches,' &c.; but when he said, 'How hard is it for them that trust in riches,' &c., they were astonished out of measure. And we see Agur, when he prays to God, not only deprecates the sin, but the estate, 'Give me not riches, lest I be full and deny thee, and say, Who is the Lord?' Prov. xxx. 8, 9. James ii. 6, 'Do not rich men oppress you, and draw you before the judgment-seats?' He doth not say, Do not wicked rich men oppress you? but simply 'rich men.' As a fat and fertile ground produceth weeds, if it be not carefully tilled and planted with better seed, so do riches usually prove a temptation to us.

But you will say, Why doth he speak so hardly against one order and sort of men whom God hath set up in the world? Are not riches in themselves God's blessings? Prov. x. 22, 'The blessing of the Lord maketh rich;' and are they not promised to his people? Ps. cxii. 3, 'Wealth and riches shall be in his house;' and accordingly are bestowed upon them. For we read of Abraham, Gen. xxiv. 25, 'The Lord hath blessed my master greatly, and he is become exceeding great;' saith Eliezer. So was Job, chap. i. 3, 'The greatest of all the men of the East.' So David, Solomon, and Lazarus of Bethany, Joseph of Arimathea, and others; and therefore is it not to calumniate our Master's bounty to say, that the very having of riches is an impediment to us in our heavenly pursuits, and a snare to us? I answer—No.

[1.] The fault is not in riches, but in our abuse of them: 2 Peter i. 4, 'The corruption that is in the world through lust.' It is your unmortified corruption that spoils all, not wealth in itself. The poison is not in the flower, but in the spider. The carnal disposition which remains in us maketh us ready to drown our mind, our time and affections, our life and love in the world, and the cares and pleasures thereof, and so they are ensnared thereby, and hindered from looking after heavenly happiness. Riches are an advantage of doing liberal, magnificent things, if they be used well; and to blame riches simply, were to blame him that made them, and distributeth them according to his will, as if he did bait his hook with seeming blessings, and did set golden snares to entangle the souls of men. The goods of this world are profitable to them that can make a good use of them, as giving them the means of being more God-like, and more useful in their places; for certainly 'it is more blessed to give than to receive,' Acts x. 35. They do not make us corrupt, or put corruption into us, but only discover the corruption that is there already; as when we fill a leaky vessel, the unsoundness of it is seen, as soon as it is filled it begins to run out. Our corruptions are drawn out by these things, and plainly discovered to the world, when the fault is not in the riches, but in the lust.

[2.] When wealth is spoken of as an estate full of spiritual danger, it is rather to check our desires of it than to lessen God's bounty, as if there were no obligation upon us by those temporal blessings. If we covet and seek great things for ourselves, we do but run into the mouth of temptation: 1 Tim. vi. 9, 'They that will be rich fall into temptation and a snare, and into many foolish and hurtful lusts, which drown men in destruction and perdition.' We are to bless God for his bounty, but we are to guard our own hearts, and contract our desires before the will of God is declared. When we ask riches, we know not what we ask. Do not aim at great things for yourselves in the world.

[3.] Wealth, considered not as sought by us, but as given by God, needeth peculiar and special grace to improve it, because we must not only look to the manner of acquisition, but to the manner of fruition. It is true we have honestly acquired it, it comes to us fairly, but then we must see how we enjoy it. Some are rich because they are wicked, having gotten their wealth by unjust and indirect means; but others are wicked because they are rich, being corrupted by the enjoyment of them. There are some gifts of God that are *absolute bona*, so absolutely good that they can never be evil, such things do certainly make the owner, or him that possesseth them, good too; as the graces of the Spirit, faith in Christ, the love of God, fear of his name; but one may be rich, but yet never the better. Nay, consider man *in statu lapso*, fallen from God to the creature: he is easily made worse, and usually is too, and that by the good things he doth enjoy, if the Lord doth not vouchsafe to him his grace.

[4.] I answer again—When temporal blessings follow eternal, then it is well, as wisdom with an inheritance is good; and Solomon asked wisdom, and with it God gave him riches and honour in great abundance; but where they are given singly and apart, so they are given to God's enemies. Elijah was poor, and Ahab rich; Paul, that holy man, was in prison, and bound with a chain, and Nero at the same time emperor of the world. God hath gifts for all his creatures: some in one way, some in another, shall find him a good God. Jesus Christ, that gave his Holy Spirit to the best of the apostles, gave the bag to Judas. Nay, Jesus Christ himself, that had the Spirit without measure, chose a poor estate. He that made a fish to pay him tribute could as well have made men to do so; he that multiplied a few loaves could have increased his stock; he that made the world could have built himself a stately palace; but 'when he was rich, yet for our sakes he became poor,' 2 Cor. viii. 9, that he might sanctify holy poverty in his own person, and honour it by his own example; and usually he cuts his children short, while wicked men live in plenty. Therefore they that merely have riches, that is, that have it apart from grace, are in a worse condition than those that are kept low and bare. As a child may be dieted for its health, while a servant is left to a free allowance, so God knows our weakness; and they understand nothing in divinity that do not know this, that God works congruously, and will not only give strength, but will also abate the temptation itself, and not suffer us to have overmuch in the world, lest it should become a snare to us. So much for the persons spoken of, 'They that have riches.'

2. The privilege in debate, that which is denied or hardly vouchsafed to them is, 'Entering into the kingdom of God.' By which is meant—

[1.] The kingdom of grace; and so the meaning is, they are incapable of the doctrine of Christ, as the thorny ground was of the good seed. Now what are they that answer to the thorny ground? 'They that are choked with the cares, and riches, and pleasures of this life,' Luke viii. 14; that is, the heart wherein christianity cannot enter with any good effect and success: these choke and destroy many hopeful seeds of grace, which would otherwise spring forth in a lively diligence, and earnest pursuit of that one thing necessary. And this may be the meaning of 'How hardly do they enter!' viz., the great difficulty of rich men's becoming the disciples of Christ; and the truth is, at the first setting forth of the gospel, it was verified by plain experience, for it is said, Mat. xi. 5, among other miracles which Christ wrought, he tells us 'the poor have the gospel preached unto them;' it is $\pi\tau\omega\chi o\grave{\iota}$ $\epsilon\grave{v}\alpha\gamma\gamma\epsilon\lambda\acute{\iota}\zeta o\nu\tau\alpha\iota$, they are all to be gospelled; and $o\grave{v}$ $\pi o\lambda\lambda o\grave{\iota}$, 'Not many wise men after the flesh, nor many mighty, nor many noble are called,' 1 Cor. i. 26; not many of that order and rank.

[2.] Entering into the kingdom of God may be expounded of being made partakers of his glory in the kingdom of heaven; this follows necessarily upon the former, for if they are incapable of grace, they are incapable of glory. And this is true too: James ii. 5, 'Hath not God chosen the poor of this world, rich in faith, and heirs of the kingdom?' And this was such a truth that even the scoffers and opposers of the christian religion took notice of it. Julian the apostate, in his epistle to Ecebolius, speaking scoffingly of those passages, saith, I have taken away from these Galileans some of their wealth, that they might not be deprived of the heavenly kingdom which their master promised them.

3. The thing spoken of these persons with respect to that privilege; there the form, $\pi\hat{\omega}s$, 'How:' it is $\theta\alpha\upsilon\mu\acute{\alpha}\sigma\tau\iota\kappa o\nu$ $\epsilon\pi\iota\rho\rho\eta\mu\alpha$, saith Hesichius, a form of admiration; and the matter, 'How hardly!' It is not an utter impossibility, but a very great difficulty. All men are

saved with difficulty: 'If the righteous scarcely are saved,' 1 Peter. iv. 18. It is no easy matter, but it is more difficult for them than others. It is passionately expressed, 'Oh, how hardly!' it is the greatest difficulty imaginable, such as made the disciples wonder: 'They were astonished at his words,' ver. 24. Afterwards it is set forth by the proverb of 'a camel passing through the eye of a needle,' ver. 25. Many foolish conceits men have about this, whereas in truth it is nothing but a Jewish proverb, to show it is a very unusual thing, of extraordinary difficulty, not to be removed, but by the almighty power of God, 'but with God all things are possible,' ver. 27. Not that riches are evil in themselves, but that it is hard for such creatures as we to possess them without sinful and inordinate affections.

4. Consider who it is that speaks it. Alas! if it had been the saying of any private divine or particular minister, we might tax it as rash and rigorous; but the mouth of truth itself hath spoken it, even Jesus Christ, whom we own as our Lord and Master. He knew the way of salvation, and knew the state and danger of souls, and he hath interposed his authority, and represents the difficulty. It is Jesus Christ, that had so much wisdom to judge aright of matters, Jesus Christ, that had so much regard to the comfort and happiness of men, that he would not fright them with a needless danger; and therefore certainly you should take such an admonition to heart from the mouth of him whom you call your Lord and master, and from whom at last you expect your doom and judgment; he hath said it. If any wise man had said it from the experience of almost all ages and persons, you ought to have regarded it; but when our Lord hath said it, he who is the 'Amen, the faithful and true witness,' why should we not believe him? I pray what do you think of Christ? Was not he able to judge of the case? It was the saying of Plato, ἀγαθὸν εἶναι διαφερόντως, καὶ πγούσιον εἶναι διαφερόντως ἀδύνατον—It is impossible to be excellently good and eminently rich; therefore Celsus, a heathen who sought all occasions to disgrace the gospel, saith that Christ borrowed this saying of Plato, but he is confuted by Origen in his book against him. This proud heathen was sensible there was wisdom in the speech, therefore he would deprive Christ of the honour of it. But now since we believe the doctrine of Christ, and own it as the speech of Christ, who is our Lord and master, therefore it should more sink into our hearts. Thus for the explanation of the point, from the circumstances of the text.

II. Let us see whence this difficulty doth arise? I answer—Because of the sins to which a wealthy estate doth expose us.

1. Riches are apt to breed atheism and contempt of God. They that are wholly drowned in pleasures of sense do not look into the invisible world, and see God which is the Father of spirits: Prov. xxx. 9, 'Lest I be full, and deny thee, and say, Who is the Lord?' There is a practical atheism when men forget or despise God, and a speculative atheism when they deny God. Now the rich are apt to do both. A man that tumbles in wealth, ease, and plenty is apt to forget and despise God: 'But Jesurun waxed fat, and kicked; thou art waxen fat, thou art grown thick, thou art covered with fatness, then he forsook God which made him, and lightly esteemed the rock of his salva-

tion,' Deut. xxxii. 15. Nay, in some sort they deny God; they live as if there were no God at all, none to call them to account. Men that have seen no changes, and were never humbled under God's mighty hand, never think of an invisible power. I remember the psalmist saith, Ps. lv. 19, 'Because they have no changes, therefore they fear not God;' they have not an awe or reverence, or due sense of a divine power upon their hearts, because they never have been acquainted with changes; the condition they have lived in hath been a constant tenure of worldly happiness. So Zeph. i. 12, 'They are settled upon their lees;' that is, are not tossed from vessel to vessel, as wine that is racked. They live in an even course of worldly prosperity, and in abundance of worldly comforts, without a change, and this chokes and gluts the heart, that they have no sense of the Lord's goodness. Changes do more awaken us, and make us look to God, as the fountain of good and evil. *Istæ vices magis in nobis excitant sensum divinæ bonitatis, quam continuus tenor fœlicitatis, qui nos inebriat.* In short, the pleasures and thoughts of the world do so take up their hearts, that there is no place for any serious thought and solemn remembrance of God, such as should beget an awe in us. It is said, Isa. v. 12, 'The harp and the viol, and tabret and pipe, and wine are in their feasts; but they regard not the work of the Lord, neither consider the operation of his hands.' Thoughts of God are suppressed as soon as they do arise, and they take no notice of the work of God's hands, nor what he doth in their days to revive the sense of his eternal power and Godhead; nor do they take their comforts out of God's hands, but look altogether to natural and to second causes, as being sufficient to themselves, to live of themselves. Indeed, they may seem in opinion to own a God, as others do; they take up the current opinions, and perform customary worship, but they do not glorify him as God, or repair to him with that life and fervency as those that stand in need of him, nor consecrate their best time, and strength, and affections to his service. It is usually the broken-hearted godly poor, and those that have had frequent experiences of the changes of providence, that exercise themselves to godliness, and seek after God in good earnest. The great landlord of the world hath more rent from many poor cottages than from divers great palaces, for they wallow in plenty, and never think of God.

2. Riches keep men from being broken-hearted and seeing their need of Christ. It is the poor needy soul, sensible of its own sin and misery, that is likely to thrive in religion, and prosper in any heavenly design and pursuit. Now those that are rich have so many entertainments of sense to inveigle their minds and divert their thoughts, and are so besotted and enchanted with present delights and pleasures, that they have no feeling of their condition, or sense of the necessity of God's grace; therefore it is our Lord begins his description of blessedness: Mat. v. 3, 'Blessed are the poor in spirit, for theirs is the kingdom of heaven.' How few of them that are rich in estate are poor in spirit! The sense of their present ease and welfare makes them forget all thoughts of their spiritual condition, and reconciling themselves to God by Christ. The prodigal never thought of going to his father till he began to be in want, Luke xv. 17, 18. While men have any-

thing in the world, they are senseless and secure in the midst of all their sin and misery; and if they can live without God and apart from God, they will not come at him: Jer. ii. 31, 'Wherefore say my people, We are lords, we will come no more unto thee?' As if this merry world would always last, and there were no judgment to come, and God would never bring them into his presence, but they live a life of estrangement from God; they can live upon themselves, and their own supplies, and things that fall to them by the bounty of God's providence.

3. Suppose these worldly rich men should take to the serious profession of religion, as some of them do, and so mask and varnish over a heart wholly wedded to the world and worldly things with some kind of form and garb of religion, and it may be the strictest too, yet they can never walk worthy of it, nor hold and maintain it with any power and vigour: 'They are enemies to the cross of Christ;' and why? 'They mind earthly things,' Phil. iii. 18, 19. Christ speaks of selling and forsaking all, and they are for getting and taking all into their own hands. Now it is more difficult for them that have anything in the world to comply with Christ's commands. Surely they that live in a lower condition have less temptations. The young man here went away sad, 'For he had great possessions.' I shall mention a story of a soldier of Antigonus, which is well known, because it helps to set forth what we have now in hand. This person had a very loathsome disease upon him, which made his soul desire to be divorced from his body, and then none so ready and forward to venture himself in all battles as he, and when the general, admiring his valour, got him to be cured, then he, that had been so prodigal of his life before, was as shy, tender, and wary of it as others; when he had a life worth the keeping, he was loath to venture and expose it to danger. I apply it to this purpose. It may be when the world disappoints thee thou art ready to venture thy little all for christianity, but if anything may make the world sweet to thee, none so sparing, so afraid and ashamed to own Christ as they. Certainly it conduceth much to the safety of grace to have the temptation removed, as well as to have the lust abated: *Rebus in angustis facile est contemnere vitam*—He that hath little can soon part with it, whereas riches expose to apostasy: 2 Tim. iv. 10, 'Demas hath forsaken us, having loved this present world.'

4. It maketh men apt to take up their rest here, and to sit down satisfied with the world as their chiefest good, without any earnest longing for or looking after a better estate: Ps. xvii. 14, 'From men of the world, which have their portion in this life;' small hope or desire of the pleasures of another world; they will have their heaven here, and therefore 'How hardly shall they enter into the kingdom of heaven.' The Lord will not remove us *a deliciis ad delicias*, from Delilah's lap to Abraham's bosom, from carnal to spiritual delights; and the truth is they have no mind to be removed: James v. 5, 'Ye have lived in pleasure on the earth and been wanton.' Here we are in a place of exile, banishment, separation from God, where God doth not exhibit himself in that latitude which he doth in the other world, and yet here they seek their felicity: Luke vi. 24, 'Woe unto you that are rich, for you have received your consolation.' God requires of us

contentation, and allows us a temperate use, and holy delight in the blessings of his providence, but we are not to take our whole comfort here (for that is meant by our consolation), and sit down drunk with temporal happiness, that will make us mindless of those other things offered to us in the gospel, and kept for us in the world to come.

5. They are apt to wax proud and scornful, and impatient of reproof, and so grow licentious, and lose the benefit of the remedies that might reclaim them from their errors: 1 Tim. vi. 17, 'Charge them that are rich in this world, that they be not high-minded.' I interpret it of this sort of pride, when men grow scornful of admonition, licentious in sin, and hate reproof. All pride is incident to riches, but especially this pride; for as soon as a man hath anything about him, he begins to speak higher, and look higher, and fare higher, and to display the ensigns of his vanity in his apparel; but chiefly his heart is higher, and so grows impatient of check, and so cannot bear the means God hath appointed to warn him of his danger and duty. They think we are too bold thus to deal with them and speak to them. It is observed of beasts, that they never grow fierce but when they are in good plight; so usually men when they are full, grow scornful and fierce, and cannot endure to hear the mind of God powerfully and plainly set forth. Great men have great spirits, and they will not stoop to such base and mean persons as the messengers of Christ: Jer. v. 5, 'I will get me to the great men, and will speak unto them, &c., but they have altogether broken the yoke and burst the bonds;' Jer. xiii. 15, 'Hear ye, and give ear, be not proud, for the Lord hath spoken.' Men are high and scornful, and if they have anything to bear them out in contempt of the Lord's message, they set themselves to oppose Christ and his interest, and dash against the corner-stone, though they are broken in pieces. They are the great and yokeless men of the world that will come under no rule, and no awe of christianity.

6. They are wanton and sensual, and so must needs be careless of heaven and heavenly things: partly as sensuality brings a brawn and deadness upon the heart, and takes off all sense and feeling and savouriness of spirit: Hosea iv. 11, 'Whoredom and wine and new wine take away the heart;' that is, infatuate men, and make them of such a base brutish spirit, that they are incapable of sound reasoning, or of entertaining the doctrine of godliness: 1 Tim v. 6, 'She that liveth in pleasure is dead while she liveth.' A life of pleasure brings on a strange deadness and infatuation upon the soul, partly as sensuality engrosseth the time, and causeth us to waste those precious hours in which we should make provision for eternity; to eat, drink, and be merry, and knit one carnal pleasure to another, and so leaves no room for any serious sober thoughts of God, Christ, and the world to come, and necessity of regeneration and taking the way of holiness: Luke xii. 19, 'I will say to my soul, Soul, thou hast much goods laid up for many years; take thine ease, eat, drink, and be merry.' And partly as sensuality doth strengthen our enemy. The greatest enemy we have is the flesh, and the more we please it, the more we set back our salvation. Now when men nourish their heart, and strengthen their corruptions, how can they be overcome by the power of the Lord's grace? James v. 5, 'Ye have nourished your hearts as in a day of

slaughter.' They add fuel to their lusts, and make corrupt nature more active and stirring than otherwise it would be. Now rich men are very sensual and apt to please the flesh; yea, they can hardly avoid it in the plenty of accommodations they enjoy, as scripture and experience witnesseth. Sodom was a pleasant and fruitful place, and was as the garden of God. What were the sins of that place? 'Pride, fulness of bread, and abundance of idleness,' Ezek. xvi. 49; and that fulness did *dispumare in libidinem,* as Tertullian saith, issue out into monstrous lusts. Alas! where there is such a glut of worldly things, what hope is there to prevail, and bring men under the power of strict religion and that holiness Christ calls for. Men grow excessive in their pleasure, and they refresh not their labours with some kind of pleasure (for that God hath allowed), but they refresh one pleasure with another, and so set up the flesh in God's stead: 'Their god is their belly,' Phil. iii. 19, and they are 'Lovers of pleasure more than lovers of God,' 1 Tim. iii. 4. Men think sensuality no sin in those that are rich. Indeed greedy getting or griping to raise an estate the world will condemn. Oh! but when a man lives plentifully, and is at heart's ease, without considering whether he nourish a temptation or no, the world takes no notice of that: Ps. xlix. 18, 'While he lived, he blessed his soul; and men will praise thee when thou doest well to thyself;' that is, when thou spendest freely upon carnal satisfactions, that is accounted more honourable. Nay, and they themselves do applaud themselves in this course, and think because their estates will bear it, therefore they may indulge their carnal desires. Oh! do not think so. You are to consider things with respect to eternity and the world to come. Plenty will be no excuse. You would be angry with your cook if he should make your meat too salt because he had store of salt by him; so may God be angry with you, if you have plenty, such as would refresh the hungry, and supply the needy, and you altogether lay it out upon pomp and pleasure, above what your estates and what your bodies will bear, but chiefly what your souls will bear; for you should keep up the welfare of your souls, and be ready and free towards God. Do you think you were made only for idleness and pleasure, and others must glorify God only by labour and service? The rich glutton was cast into hell; here was no oppression, but 'he fared deliciously every day,' and sucked out the sweetness of his wealth, and the indictment that is brought against him is this: Luke xvi. 25, 'Son, remember that thou in thy lifetime receivedst thy good things.' A slavery to pleasures will make the hardship and duties of religion intolerable. You are brought into bondage and under the power of these things, and then you cannot leave them that you may attend upon the good of your souls and upon the things that relate to eternity: 1 Cor. vi. 12, 'All things are lawful for me, but I will not be brought under the power of any.'

7. The more rich, the more wedded we are to the world; for *crescentem sequitur cura pecuniam;* usually the more we have, our desires are increased to get more: Eccles. v. 10, 'He that loveth silver shall not be satisfied with silver, nor he that loveth abundance with increase.' Men when they are low are modest; food and raiment is enough, and they receive it with great thankfulness; but if they had a little more

in the world, then they should serve God without distraction, and if they had such a proportion they would care for no more; but if those desires be granted, they find themselves entangled, and their hearts deceived, and still they must have more and more, until they settle into a worldly course. As a river, the greater it grows by receiving of little brooks, the wider and deeper still it wears the channel, so outward things, the more they increase, the more they enlarge desires. Men would be a little higher in the world, a little better accommodated; and when they have that, they would have a little more, and still a little more, and so keep 'joining house to house, and field to field, till there be no place that they may be placed alone in the midst of the earth,' Isa. v. 8. They would seize upon all things within their grasp and reach. As fire increaseth with new fuel, so this burning desire doth increase on their hands; whereas we should still take thankfully what God vouchsafeth to us, without those vast cravings and desires, and look after no more than will serve us in our passage to heaven. Mariners freighted for a near haven will not victual for a long voyage. *Magno viatico breve iter non instruitur*—'Time is short,' 1 Cor. vii. 29. Thus there is very great difficulty with respect to the sins that are incident to a plentiful estate, and grow upon us insensibly.

Use 1. This doctrine showeth us how contented we should be with a mean condition, if God reduce us thereunto. We can hardly be poorer than Christ and his apostles, and shall we murmur? Many have more than they had, take them altogether, and yet think their condition hard and strait: 1 Tim. vi. 8, 'And having food and raiment, let us be therewith content.' God hath freed thee from those snares and occasions of sin which others are subject unto, and so thy way to heaven is made more easy. Certainly they that do indeed intend the kingdom of heaven would not desire a more difficult passage; therefore be content with a mean estate, though you have no more than necessaries. Contract your desires, and your trouble will be lessened. The Israelites said to the king of Edom, 'Let us go through your land in peace;' but the cravings of carnal men are endless, 'They enlarge their desire as hell,' Hab. ii. 5. Not to be content with our lot and portion, especially when it is competent, is a great sin. When you hunt after more, what do you but increase your temptations, and multiply your snares? 'You load yourselves with clay,' Hab. ii. 6; base riches which pollute you, thorns which make your condition more uneasy. And when will there be an end of these desires? Lust will grow with the possession; the more wood you put on, the more the fire increaseth. Therefore, rather bring your minds to your estates than your estates to your minds; if you be not content with what you have now, you will never be contented hereafter; a greater estate will not do it, if grace do not do it; as in some diseases, *non opus habent impletione, sed purgatione*, there is more need of purging than filling; a man is still hungry though he hath eaten enough, and still thirsty though he hath drunk enough. The way is, not to increase our substance, but to moderate our desires.

Use 2. It teacheth us patience and comfort under loss of goods. We should possess the things of this world as if we possessed them not, and therefore when God taketh away our plenty, we should mourn as if we mourned not. You may find gain in this loss, and profit in this trial. The Lord seeth fit many times to take away the fuel of our pride and other lusts, to draw us to seek better treasure in heaven, the purchase whereof is certain, the possession firm, and the price incomprehensible. The Lord will keep you aloof from temptations; he knows that if you were rich, you would grow sensual, insolent, and negligent of spiritual things. God knoweth what condition is best for you; you should have a greater account to make; he expecteth from others charity, from you patience. Besides, says Job, chap i. 21, 'The Lord gave, and the Lord hath taken away; blessed be the name of the Lord.' Some think it is the greatest misery to have been sometimes happy, but that is through corruption, when former enjoyments make men more nice, delicate, and tender, and so less able to bear the present cross. But if we consider rightly, the less we have been afflicted, the less are our afflictions on that behalf. Is it nothing that God hath given us to pass over some of our days with peace and comfort? should we be so unthankful as to account that no benefit because it is past? Job ii. 10, 'What! shall we receive good at the hand of God, and shall we not receive evil?' is not what you have received a pledge of what he can do for the future?

Use 3. To the rich, to show them what need they have of special grace to manage that condition aright. It would seem a hard censure upon this sort and order of men, yet it is a truth, and spoken by him who is truth itself. It concerneth you to look after special grace more than others; your danger is great, and your difficulties in order to eternal life not a few. You need peculiar grace—

1. To prevent the evils and to heal those diseases that are incident to riches; as contempt of God. We are apt to neglect and despise him when our necessities do not drive us to him, such is the pravity of our natures: Hosea v. 15, 'In their affliction they will seek me early.' Make God your refuge and he will be your habitation: Ps. xci. 9, 'Because thou hast made the Lord thy refuge, even the Most High thy habitation.' Neglect of Christ and salvation by him; they that have an happiness in their hands already see no want in their condition: 'The whole need not a physician.' Take heed of being heart-whole, then you will have no relish for the gospel. It disposeth to apostasy; you have something of value which you must esteem as nothing for Christ. It maketh us neglect heaven: Ps. iv. 6, 7, 'There be many that say, Who will show us any good? Lord, lift thou up the light of thy countenance upon us: thou hast put gladness in my heart, more than in the time that their corn and their wine increased.' An estate without God is not good. Lord, let me not have my all here, for these things must be left. It maketh you proud and scornful; remember there are the true riches, without which a person is but vile. He is most honourable before God that hath most grace. The value of men is otherwise in the world to come than in the present world. Your humility is your crown. It makes you to be more sensual. Wealth is the pander of pleasure, the purveyor for the flesh, but it should not be thus. There is more cause of fear than rejoicing: Gal. vi. 8, 'He that soweth to the flesh shall of the flesh reap corruption.' It makes us worldly, as chains to detain us under the power of Satan,

and enslave us to the world. It doth but betray you into mischief. Do you desire your way to heaven should be made more hard, that is hard enough already?

2. That you might devote your riches to the Lord, and be holy and heavenly in the midst of so great temptations; that you may not by momentary and temporal things forfeit eternal, but rather further them: Luke xii. 21, 'So is he that layeth up treasures for himself, and is not rich towards God;' 1 Tim. vi. 18, 19, 'That they be rich in good works, ready to distribute, willing to communicate, laying up in store for themselves a good foundation against the time to come, that they may lay hold of eternal life.' Wealth rightly employed makes us capable of a greater reward hereafter, as it makes us more useful here.

SERMON XI.

And the disciples were astonished at his words. But Jesus answered again, and said unto them, Children, how hard is it for them that trust in riches to enter into the kingdom of God!—MARK x. 24.

IN these words you have two things—

1. The entertainment which the disciples gave to his former speech, 'They were astonished at his words.'

2. Christ's further explication of himself, 'But Jesus answered again, and said unto them, Children, how hard is it for them that trust in riches to enter into the kingdom of God!' Wherein observe—

[1.] The manner of our Saviour's speaking, in that kind compellation, 'Children.'

[2.] The matter of the explication, 'How hard is it for them that trust in riches to enter into the kingdom of God!'

1. For the entertainment which the disciples gave to his former speech, 'They were astonished at his words.' This astonishment was caused either by the legal dispensation under which obedience was rewarded with visible and temporal blessings, and therefore they marvelled that rich men should find such difficulty of entering into heaven; or else it was occasioned by the Jewish expectation of a pompous Messiah; wherewith the disciples themselves were leavened, expecting to share of the honours and riches of that kingdom which Christ would set up. Now Christ's answer was quite blank contrary to these carnal hopes, therefore they marvelled. Or it may be upon the common reason that the gates of heaven should be shut to them to whom the gates of the world do always lie open. Thus hardly are good men brought to disesteem worldly things, and rightly to ponder and weigh the doctrine of the cross, which Christ had so frequently taught them.

2. For Christ's explication; and there—

[1.] The compellation, τέκνα, 'Children;' so he bespeaks them who were sincere for the main, though a little leavened with carnal conceits, and to sweeten the doctrine which seemed so contrary to their humour: 1 Thes. ii. 11, 'As you know how we exhorted, and comforted, and charged every one of you, as a father doth his children.' Novices and weak ones are to be used with all indulgence, for they had not received the Spirit in that plentiful measure as afterward.

[2.] The matter of his explication, 'How hard is it for them that trust in riches,' &c. He had said before, 'How hardly do they that have riches;' now he explains himself, they 'that trust in riches.' He instanceth in this—

(1.) As one common disease of rich men, as soon as they have anything in the world, they are apt to trust in it. Some abuse riches one way, some another; some to increase their worldly cares and desire of having, others to feed their pride and sensuality; this way, or that way, according to their different temper and constitution of body and soul, but they all agree in this, both the muckworm and the epicure, that they trust in riches.

(2.) He instanceth in this trust rather than love of riches, not how hard is it for them that love riches, but how hard is it for them that trust in riches, because this is more, and doth more express the disposition of worldly men. We love many things in which we do not put our trust, but we put our trust in nothing but what we love. A glutton loves his belly-cheer, but he doth not trust in it, as thinking to be protected by it, as the covetous doth by his estate; and therefore though he make his belly his god, or his chief good, and last end, yet he doth not make it the first cause and fountain of his happiness. But now this gives all the titles and privileges of God to wealth. Trust makes wealth to be the first cause, the chief good, and the last end. Well, then, for these two reasons doth Christ instance in this one sin, as being a common disease and cause of all the rest, or implying them at least. This young man, who went away sorrowful from Christ, thought he should be despised, and grow necessitous if he should forsake all upon the command of Christ; he made his riches to be the fountain of his hope and confidence; and therefore doth Christ say, 'How hard is it for them that trust in riches to enter into the kingdom of God!'

Doct. That rich men are very prone and apt to put their confidence in riches, and so thereby render themselves incapable of the kingdom of God.

In the handling this point I shall—(1.) Show there is such a sin as trusting in riches; (2.) The heinousness and evil of it; (3.) The signs and discoveries of it; (4.) The remedies.

I. That there is such a sin, and that a very common sin. The scripture shows it plentifully. Job, when he protested his innocency, among other sins he reckoned up, he disclaims this, chap. xxxi. 24, 25, 'If I have made gold my hope, or said to the fine gold, Thou art my confidence; if I rejoiced because my wealth was great, and because my hand had gotten much.' Job to vindicate himself from hypocrisy reckons up the usual sins of hypocrites, and among the rest this for one, making riches our hope and confidence. He had immediately before waved the crime of extortion and oppression, but he thinks not that sufficient to clear himself, and therefore he further denieth also the crime of carnal confidence. It is not enough that our wealth be not gotten by fraud, cosenage and extortion, but we must not trust to it. Symmachus renders it ἀφοβίαν, my safety and security, the cause why I am not afraid. The world looketh upon wealth as that which will help us to all we want, defend us from all we fear, and procure to us all we do desire; as if by that we were out of the reach of all danger, and in a capacity to live longer and happier under the patronage and provisions which our money shall procure to us. Another place is Prov. xviii. 10, 11, 'The name of the Lord is a strong tower, the righteous runneth into it and is safe: the rich man's wealth is his strong city, and an high wall in his own conceit.' Mark, what the name of the Lord is to the believer, that is wealth to the carnal rich man in his own conceit. A godly man never thinks himself safe till he can get into the name of the Lord, and be within the compass and verge of the covenant; but a carnal rich man, if he be walled and entrenched within his wealth, thinks himself secure against all changes and chances, and so God is laid aside and little cared for. That there is such a sin you see, but I shall prove that it is a common sin, very incident to all men, and that it is a very secret sin, but yet of a pestilential influence.

1. It is very natural to all men, yea, impossible almost to be free from it. Consider man as degenerate, and in that corrupted estate in which he is, as fallen from God as his chief good and last end, and so he is an idolater, and makes the creature his god, or sticketh too much to it, more especially to wealth. Wealth is the great instrument of commerce; it cannot be denied to have a power and influence upon human affairs: Eccles. x. 19, 'Money answereth all things.' It can do much in this lower world, and saveth us out of many dangers: Prov. xiii. 8, 'The ransom of a man's life are his riches.' It hath its use in this world as a means in God's hands to sustain and preserve life. But what more common than for a man to look to the subordinate means, and neglect altogether the first cause. As children will thank the tailor, and think they owe their new clothes to his provision rather than to their parents' bounty, so we look to the next hand, and set up that instead of God. Rich and poor cannot be exempted from this sin.

(1.) The poor, and those that have not wealth; they idolise it in fancy and conceit, that if they had estates this would make them happy and glorious; and because they have not, they trust in those which have, which is idolatry upon idolatry. See Ps. lxii. 9, 'Surely men of low degree are vanity, and men of high degree are a lie.' To appearance men of low degree are nothing and can do nothing towards our relief, and so are vanity; but men of high degree, they are a lie, because they disappoint those that trust in them, to the wrong of God. Alas! they have neither power to help nor hurt, if the Lord will not: 2 Kings vi. 27, 'If the Lord do not help thee, whence shall I help thee?' And therefore we need not fear the hazard of their frowns nor of their displeasure; we need not with such restlessness court their favour and trust in them that have wealth. (2.) But chiefly this is incident to worldly great men, to trust in what they have; their minds are secretly enchanted by their estates when they are increased to them. Still the distemper grows with the increase of worldly accommodations: Ps. lxii. 10, 'Trust not in oppression, and become not vain in robbery: if riches increase, set not your heart upon them.' As soon as we begin to have anything about us, from thence forward we date our happiness and security. Many that in want despise wealth, and live in an actual dependence upon God's providence, as soon as they have somewhat in the creature, they begin to value themselves at a higher rate, as if they could live alone without God, and their hearts are altogether for increasing their store, or keeping and retaining what they have already gotten.

2. It is a very secret sin, and found in those that are least sensible of it. We seldom or never mistrust ourselves of this confidence, which is so natural and so common; and why? Because we have too gross a notion of this sin of trusting in riches. A man doth not think he makes money his idol if he do not pray to it, or offer sacrifice to it, or adore it with outward ceremonies, as the heathens did their idols of gold and silver; whereas this sin is to be determined *non exhibitione ceremoniarum, sed oblatione concupiscentiarum*, not by the formal rights of worship, but by the secret workings of the heart towards it. Though we do not actually say to the fine gold, Thou art my confidence, or use such gross language to riches as, Ye shall deliver me, or I will put my trust in you, yet secretly we idolise it, and set it up in the place of God. It would have been a sorry vindication of Job's innocency to deny that; few hypocrites say so in open language, but our hearts say so though we perceive it not. There is nothing so close and secret in the bosom of man as his trust. But the heart hath a tongue as well as the mouth, and thoughts are called the sayings of the heart. Yea, divines usually observe that there are two sorts of thoughts, *implicit* as well as *explicit*. The scripture calls them inward thoughts: Ps. xlix. 11, 'Their inward thought is that their house shall continue for ever.' * This is the interpretation of our actions when we do not make God our portion, but trust in the abundance of our riches; this is our inward thought, the saying of our heart, Ye are my God; we do in effect say, Thou art my confidence, my hope, and my joy, and will stand by me when all things cease and fail, and wilt not suffer me to want or to be wronged as long as thou lastest; these are the secret speeches of our hearts. Christians, many may, orator-like, declaim against the vanity of the creature, and speak as basely of money as others do, and say, We know it is but a little refined earth, but their hearts close with it, they are loath to part with it for God's sake or upon God's declared will. As he that speaketh good words of God is not said to trust in God, so speaking bad words of worldly riches doth not exempt us from trusting in them. There is a difference between declaiming as an orator, and acting like a christian; well, then, it is a common but secret sin.

II. My next work is to show the evil of this sin, and how great it is, both in regard of its heinous nature and in regard of its mischievous effects.

1. In regard of its heinous nature. It is a renouncing of God, and setting up another in his stead.

[1.] It is a renouncing of God, and taking away his honour. The heart of man is so conscious to itself of its own weakness, that it will not be long without a prop, it must have something to rest upon.

Now, naturally, we have no respect to invisible things, so as to choose them and to rest upon them, but easily take up with what comes next to hand. By a vile ingratitude we pervert God's bounty to a defection from him. As harlots love the gifts rather than the man, so we take the gifts of God, and rest upon them, and set them up in God's stead. No man can trust God and riches too, therefore if we trust in riches, the heart is diverted and carried away from God: Jonah ii. 8, 'They that observe lying vanities forsake their own mercy.' They turn their back upon God, and take up with these vain comforts here in the world. The same temple will not serve God and Dagon; the Philistines could not bring it to pass, do what they could; nor the same heart God and the world: 1 Tim. 6, 17, 'Charge them that are rich in this world, that they trust not in uncertain riches, but in the living God.' If we trust in the one we disclaim the other. Now consider what a dishonour is this to leave God for the creature! the fountain of living waters for broken cisterns: Jer. ii. 13, 'My people have committed two evils, they have forsaken the fountain of living waters, and hewed out cisterns, broken cisterns, that can hold no water.' They leave the husband for a slave, treasure for coals, things precious for dung.

[2.] As there is a leaving of God, so there is the setting up another god in his stead; therefore covetousness is called 'idolatry,' Col. iii. 5, and a covetous man an 'idolater,' Eph. v. 5. Mammon is the idol, and the worldling the priest. Our trust is not only diverted, but placed elsewhere, while we expect that from wealth which is to be expected from God alone. Trust in God is a confidence that no evil shall befall us, and nothing truly good shall be wanting to us while we keep in with him; such a kind of confidence we place in riches, therefore this must needs be a heinous sin. So that besides apostasy and forsaking the true God, there is idolatry: we set up another god. Trust is a prime affection, which keeps up all commerce between us and God. Our allegiance and respect to the crown of heaven is mainly preserved by dependence, and the heart is never kept in a right frame but when we look for all from God. Let a man but think himself sufficient to his own happiness, and God will soon be laid aside. As soon as we can live without God, we presently omit all kind of worship and respect to him. Our first parents greedily catched at the bait: 'Ye shall be as gods,' Gen. iii. 5. How as gods? Not in a blessed conformity, but in a cursed self-sufficiency. Thus we all affect to be sufficient to ourselves, to be able to live without God. The prodigal son, when he had his portion in his own hands, soon left his father. If we can live without God, we will never care for him. You dethrone God, and put money in his place, and set up something as God.

2. The mischievous effects and fruits of carnal confidence. You may consider these effects *meritorie* and *effective*.

[1.] Consider it *meritorie*, the merit of it; it maketh us incapable of eternal life. God is disparaged from being our paymaster and giving us our reward when we trust in money. Look, as God sent the Israelites to their idols, to see whether they could deliver them: Judges x. 14, 'Go and cry unto the gods which ye have chosen; let them deliver you in the time of your tribulation;' so he will send us to the things we trust to. A man seeks his heaven and happiness here, while he is content to enjoy wealth without God, and so dischargeth God from providing a reward for him: Luke vi. 24, 'Woe unto you that are rich, for ye have received your consolation;' you have the happiness you pitch upon. God once said, Woe to you that are rich, but never said, Woe to you that are poor. They that have their heaven, their happiness here without God, can expect no more from him. Therefore meritoriously this is the fruit of it, it will make us incapable of eternal life.

[2.] Consider carnal confidence *effective*, in the influence of it; the effects of it are very mischievous.

(1.) It is the ground of all miscarriage in practice. When men think they cannot be happy without wealth, or so much coming in by the year, then they will soon come to this, they dare not obey God for fear they shall lose their worldly comforts, wherein their happiness lies. It is notable, when the Holy Ghost speaks of keeping the commandment, and that the commandments of God are not grievous to his people, presently he speaks of victory over the world: 1 John v. 3, 4, 'For this is the love of God, that we keep his commandments, and his commandments are not grievous; for whatsoever is born of God overcometh the world, and this is the victory that overcometh the world, even our faith.' Why? What is the reason of this connection? The world is a great hindrance and let in keeping the commandment. Unless a man overcome his worldly appetites and worldly desires, he cannot keep the law of God to any purpose; and therefore David saith, Ps. cxix. 36, 'Incline my heart unto thy testimonies, and not to covetousness;' implying that while our hearts are carried out so strongly after worldly things we can never be thorough and upright with God in the way of his testimonies.

(2.) It hinders us from looking after heavenly things. It is impossible a man should in good earnest seek things above whilst he trusts in the world, and promiseth himself a long and happy life here. Trust is *acquiescentia cordis*, the rest and complacency of the soul; it seeks no further when it hath something to rest in; therefore when we rest here, all other happiness is neglected; there is no want in their condition: Luke xii. 19, 'Soul, thou hast much goods laid up for many years; take thine ease.' They cannot endure to think of a change, of leaving this, and going to a world to come, of shooting the gulf, and launching out into another world, and therefore make no provision for eternity. Well, then, trusting in riches is bad, as it takes off the heart from depending upon God's providence for the present, for so far a creature exempts itself from the jurisdiction and dominion of God; but much more bad as it takes us off from depending on God's promises for the future, as it flatters us with hopes of long and happy days, and causeth us to put off all thoughts, and all care about eternity and blessedness to come. He that trusts in riches judgeth all his happiness to be in this life; let him enjoy the world to the full, and he hath enough; here is his happiness, and his heaven too: he saith as that cardinal, He would not give his portion in Paris for his portion in paradise. Tell a worldly man of laying up treasures in heaven, and of the riches of the heavenly inheritance, he smiles at it, and will not give a foot of land here for an acre in heaven. Tell them of growing rich towards God, and it is but a fancy : Luke xii. 21, 'So is he that layeth up treasure for himself, and is not rich towards God.' So they may enjoy present satisfactions, they will give God a discharge for other things. As the Reubenites and Gadites would stay on this side Jordan, and consented to abate their portion in the land of Canaan, because they were already in a rich country, so they can be content to abate heavenly happiness, for if it be well with them here, they are satisfied, for other things they need not trouble themselves : 1 Cor. xv. 32, 'Let us eat and drink, for to-morrow we shall die;' and there is an end of the world with us,

(3.) It is the ground of all the disquiet and discontent of mind that we meet with. If a man would live a happy life, let him but seek a sure object for his trust, and he shall be safe: Ps. cxii. 7, 'He shall not be afraid of evil tidings; his heart is fixed, trusting in the Lord.' A man that puts his confidence in God, if he hears bad news of mischief coming towards him, as suppose a bad debt, a loss at sea, accidents by fire, tempests, or earthquakes, as Job had his messengers of evil tidings, which came thick and threefold upon him, yet he is not afraid, for his heart is fixed on God, he hath laid up his confidence in God, therefore his heart is kept in an equal poise; he can say, as Job, 'The Lord hath given, and the Lord hath taken away; blessed be the name of the Lord,' Job i. 21. His comforts did not ebb and flow with the creature, but his heart was fixed trusting in the Lord. But now when a man puts his joy and his contentment under the creature's power, he is always liable to great dejections and anxious disquiets: Jer. xlix. 23, 'They have heard evil tidings, they are faint-hearted.' His life and happiness consists in the presence of creatures, and in the affluence of the world which, being mutable, so must his comfort needs be; so that he that trusts in riches, to be sure doth but make way for sore and sad troubles of spirit. Good David, when he had abused his prosperity to a carnal trust and security, he felt the more trouble afterwards, and so gives us the instance of himself in this kind : Ps. xxx. 6, 7, 'I said in my prosperity, I shall never be moved. Lord, by thy favour thou hast made thy mountain to stand strong, thou hidest thy face, and I was troubled.' He shall never want troubles that placeth his trust in anything on this side God, but is up and down as his worldly comforts ebb and flow; whereas a christian, who makes God his trust, and the favour of God his greatest interest, is like the nave or centre of the wheel, which still remains in its own place and posture in all the circumgyrations and turnings about of the wheel. So in all the turnings of providence, when the spokes are sometimes up and sometimes down, sometimes in the dirt and sometimes out of the dirt, the nave and centre is still where it was. Well, then, if you would be acquainted with true peace, let not your hearts be set upon great estates, which are liable to so many changes, but trust in the Lord, and your heart shall be established.

III. I come to give some signs and discoveries of this secret evil, confidence and trust in riches.

1. When men oppress, and do that which is evil, and think to bear it out with their wealth, power, and greatness, as if there were no God above to call them to an account, or as if there had not been, or could not be such a turn of human affairs as God can lay them low enough,

and their honour be laid in the dust, and the poor and afflicted shall be exalted. God hurls the world up and down, that misery may not want a comfort, nor power a bridle. Sometimes God puts up this, sometimes the other sort of men, that still by all these changes he may keep the world in order, that think they may do anything because it is in the power of their hands: Micah ii. 1, 'Woe unto them that devise iniquity, and work evil upon their beds; when the morning is light they practise it, because it is in the power of their hand.' Usually the world is governed by interest rather than conscience; they count everything right which they are able to effect, and justice is measured by present safety, not by principles of conscience; it is in the power of their hands, and therefore they will do it. The Lord gives caution against this: Ps. lxii. 10, 'Trust not in oppression, become not vain in robbery; if riches increase, set not your heart upon them.' When a man thinks he is able to carry it against others, and to do his adversary two wrongs for one, then he makes no conscience, but does all that he can, not all that he ought. Alas! this poor creature rests upon his vain support, and that which seems to be his present advantage will in time prove his loss and ruin, when the course of providence is altered. How soon can God turn poor worms into dust! bring them down from their altitudes, and make them become the scorn and shame of those afflicted poor that wait upon the Lord! Ps. lii. 6, 7, 'The righteous shall see and fear, and shall laugh at him. Lo, this is the man that made not God his strength, but trusted in the abundance of his riches, and strengthened himself in his wickedness.' This is that brave, that gallant man in the world, that never thought of securing his greatness by God's protection, nor applied himself to piety and justice, nor imagined that such things would be useful to his present security, but resolved by wealth and wicked enterprises to establish and perpetuate his greatness; but how hath God confuted all his vain and false hopes, and brought utter destruction upon him! Thus it hath been, and thus it will be again, till the world learn to grow wiser by all the changes that God hath wrought before their eyes. And therefore, this is a sign of trusting in wealth, when men grow proud, insolent, and overbearing, and speak roughly: Prov. xviii. 23, 'The rich answereth roughly,' and are high-minded: 1 Tim. vi. 17, 'Charge them that are rich in this world, that they be not high minded, nor trust in uncertain riches, but in the living God.'

2. An inordinate care and solicitousness to get wealth. Multiplying of worldly practices cometh from unbelief in God and confidence in the means: Prov. xxiii. 4, 'Labour not to be rich; cease from thine own wisdom.' This toiling and labour to get the world into our hands argues we esteem of it beyond what it deserves. Indeed there is a lawful labour; wealth may be sought for the necessities of life and exercise of good works; but when men make it their main care, they place their happiness in it. Now, because it is hard to distinguish honest labour from worldly care, the best way will be for you to consider the disproportion of your endeavours to earthly and spiritual and heavenly things; for our Saviour, when he describes the carnal fool, that trusted in the abundance of his riches, he tells us, Luke xii. 21, 'So is he that layeth up treasure for himself and is not rich towards God.'

When men seek the world in good earnest, and make slender provision for heaven and the happiness of their precious and immortal souls, when they never look after the assuring of their interest in things to come, when the lean kine devour the fat, when that which should be sought first, either is sought last or not at all, then men trust in these outward things. Surely you fancy a greater happiness in the enjoyment of worldly things than you should. The scripture notes as a sign of this inordinate respects a making haste to be rich: Prov. xx. 21, 'An inheritance may be gotten hastily at the beginning, but the end thereof shall not be blessed;' and chap. xxviii. 20, 'He that maketh haste to be rich shall not be innocent;' and ver. 22, 'He that hasteth to be rich hath an evil eye, and considereth not that poverty shall come upon him.' When men are so earnest to commence into an estate, taking all opportunities, seeking to get it by indirect means, and think thereby to make them and theirs happy, this inordinacy will prove their bane and ruin. In bestowing it as God directs, none so slow; in getting it, none so earnest: certainly he that believeth will not make haste.

3. When men think themselves better provided by a wealthy apostasy than by a close adhering to God all-sufficient. Sometimes the keeping of wealth and religion come in competition. Now, when a man debates with conscience, Here is your duty, and there is your loss, can you trust in wealth rather than in the promises of God? If the Lord for our duty should reduce us to never so great straits, he is able to make it all up to us again, this should suffice us: 'The Lord is able to give thee much more than this,' 2 Chron. xxv. 9. But if in the debates of conscience gain bears sway, it is a sign we trust in wealth rather than in the promises of God.

4. When men slacken or omit prayer, because they are well at ease and have worldly abundance. This is a certain truth, that trust in God, or prayer, or an acknowledgment of God, always go together: Ps. lxii. 8, 'Trust in him at all times, ye people; pour out your hearts before him.' If the heart be taken off from the creature, it will be much with God; but when men are full, and think they need him not, and therefore grow cold and careless in their addresses to him, it may be in their affliction God shall hear from them, but at other times the throne of grace lies neglected, they have other trusts, and depend on something on this side God, or God would be oftener acknowledged.

5. When men think wealth shall sufficiently secure them against all changes, and that when they have it they shall see nothing but happy days, and therefore give up themselves securely to enjoy the pleasures of this life: Luke xii. 19, 'Soul, thou hast goods laid up for many years; take thine ease, eat, drink, and be merry.' Sensuality, security, and pride are the fruits of carnal confidence: 'They trust in their wealth, and boast themselves in the multitude of their riches,' Ps. xlix. 6. As if their felicity and chiefest stay lay in them, not only against the chances of this life, but against God's threats and vengeance and judgment; thence men fetch their support and comfort, and hope for them and theirs: Prov. x. 15, 'The rich man's wealth is his strong city.' A penny in their purse is better than the God of heaven. Here is their great assurance, the sure pledge of their happiness, as if God could not bring them down wonderfully.

6. When men are so loath to forego riches when God calls them thereunto, it is a sign they trust in them, not in God. The soul of man should be justly poised, and at a point of indifferency to worldly things, to get or keep, to want or have, as God will. Until our resolutions be as easily cast the one way as the other, we shall never be said to be wholly free from this sin of trusting in riches; but certainly we are deeply tainted with it when we are so over dejected with worldly losses: 1 Cor. vii. 31, 'They that mourn as if they mourned not;' and 2 Peter i. 5, 'Add to temperance, patience.' If there were a moderation in the use of worldly things, it would make way for patience. Gregory saith, Job lost his estate without grief, because he possessed it without love; but it is a sign we love them too much when we murmur against God, and the heart is so depressed when they are taken away by God's providence, as if all our happiness were gone. Certainly riches are too highly prized, and the world too impatiently desired, when they are so deeply lamented; if when they take wings, and are gone, they bewail it as if their god were gone: Judges xviii. 24, 'Ye have taken away my gods which I made, and the priest, and are gone away, and what have I more? and what is this that ye say unto me, What aileth thee?' Thence ariseth their trouble, grief, and sorrow of heart.

IV. For the remedies against this secret and great mischief of putting our confidence in earthly things.

1. By way of consideration.

[1.] Consider the uncertainty of riches should check our trust in them: 1 Tim. vi. 17, 'That they trust not in uncertain riches.' What depends upon more uncertainty than our outward estates; and will you trust in them? Who would trust another that is sure to fail him at his greatest need? Prov. xxiii. 5, 'Wilt thou set thine eyes upon that which is not? for riches certainly make themselves wings, and fly away, as an eagle towards heaven.' A man is not better and more sufficiently provided for his dinner because there is a flock of wildfowl now pitched upon his fields; they may soon fly away. Riches are like winged creatures, compared to eagles which fly away towards heaven. How are they gone! how many ways may the Lord take them away from us! There is the fire, the thief, fraudulent bargains, vexatious lawsuits, public judgments, the displeasure of the times. Many are the wings that riches have, and therefore unless a man hath a mind to be deceived, why should he trust in them? This should be deeply thought of in our greatest prosperity, especially when we have many instances before our eyes. Alas! how many are there that have laid out all their wit, and labour, nay, and venture conscience, to get an estate, and all is gone in an instant, and they have heirs that they never thought of! And yet the world is as greedy upon these things as ever.

[2.] Consider, none ever trusted to the world but they have cause to complain in the issue. We think wealth can do great things for us, and stand us in stead beyond any other thing to make us happy, but we shall find it otherwise. God is jealous of our trust, and the creature that is of itself vain is made more vain by our dependence upon it. God will set himself to disappoint a carnal trust: Prov. xi. 28, 'He that trusteth in his riches shall fall.'

[3.] Consider, the more wealth, many times the more danger, therefore shall we trust in this? In a net, when great fishes are taken, the lesser make their escape. A great tree by the largeness and thickness of its boughs provoketh others to lop it, or it falleth by its own weight. Nebuchadnezzar led the princes and nobles captive when the poor were left in the land. As many times thieves and robbers cut off the finger for the ring's sake when they cannot otherwise pluck it off, so is a man destroyed and made a prey for his wealth's sake.

[4.] Consider the unprofitableness of wealth without God; it cannot make you contented, and safe, and happy, and comfortable: Luke xii. 15, 'A man's life consisteth not in the abundance of the things which he possesseth.' A man doth not live upon his wealth: 'Not by bread alone,' Mat. iv. 4, but by the providence of God. I do not only say they cannot make you happy and wise; certainly they cannot do that; but they cannot make you more healthful, cheerful, and comfortable; so that whether you will or no, at length you are brought to depend upon God. But especially is their unprofitableness seen in the day of death and in the day of wrath. In the day of death, when a man must shoot the gulf of eternity, and launch out into the deep ocean of the other world: Job xxvii. 8, 'What is the hope of the hypocrite, though he hath gained, when God taketh away his soul?' When you must die, and nothing shall remain with you but the bitter remembrance of an estate, either ill-got or ill-spent (for it is all one), oh! how bitter and grievous will this be to you to call to mind the iniquity of traffic, to remember the cries of the oppressed widow or orphans, or neglected poor, or your pride and luxury, and sowing to the flesh, when God comes to take away the soul! Or else in the day of wrath: Prov. xi. 4, 'Riches profit not in the day of wrath.' Of internal wrath, when a spark of God's anger lights upon the conscience, and our thoughts are awakened against us, and fall as a heavy burden upon us, oh! what will all riches do! To allude to that Prov. vi. 35, 'He will not regard any ransom, neither will he rest content, though thou givest many gifts.' Justice will not be bribed, neither will all the money you have buy you a pardon. And in the day of external wrath: Zeph. i. 18, 'Neither their silver nor their gold shall be able to deliver them in the day of the Lord's wrath.' As Absalom's mule left him hanging by the hair of the head, so will riches leave and forsake you in all your misery.

[5.] Think seriously of this, that God is the author of all wealth, and the sovereign disposer of it; and therefore, whether we have it or have it not, we must trust in God. If wealth fails, that we have it not, then it is manifest it is not to be trusted in. If it should increase, yet it should occasion us to trust in God, who gives us what we have; by what means soever it comes to our hands, it is his gift: 'It is the blessing of the Lord that maketh rich,' Prov. x. 22. If riches come to you by inheritance from your ancestors, it was by the providence of God that you were born of rich and noble friends, and not of beggars. If it come by gift, it is God that made them that gave it you able and willing. If it comes by industry and skill, it is God that gives the faculty, the use, and the success; so that still God is to be trusted in, not the creature, for he hath a mighty hand in the disposal of things in the world.

2. By way of practice.

[1.] Pray more to be kept from this sin than from poverty, namely, to have riches, and not to trust in them. It is an extraordinary gift of God, and to be sought with greater care, diligence, and frequency of prayers and fastings, than either health, preferment, life, or any other thing: ver. 27, 'With men it is impossible, but not with God, for with God all things are possible.' God only can do it thoroughly. This should be the constant request of rich men, Lord, let me not trust in what I have; this is a greater blessing than the greatest abundance in the world.

[2.] Be more ready to watch opportunities of charity, to distribute and dispense your estate than to increase it; for there is nothing will free us from this sin so much as the continual exercise of charity, or the giving of alms. Therefore your great care and delight should be to hearken after charitable occasions for the relief of the poor and for the church of God, and be glad when occasions of doing good are offered. They that hunt after opportunities of gain trust in riches, but they that seek opportunities of doing good show they are clear from this sin: Luke xii. 33, 'Sell that you have, and give alms; provide yourselves bags which wax not old, a treasure in the heavens, that faileth not;' then you trust in the promises. Your office is not that of a treasurer, but of a steward, to have them in your hands, not in your hearts; otherwise not you but your chest is rich.

[3.] Labour by faith to make God your trust and confidence: 1 Tim. vi. 17, 'That they trust not in uncertain riches, but in the living God.' To rely upon his power, mercy, and goodness for all that you have and stand in need of: 'Give us this day our daily bread;' for protection and provision. When God giveth you riches, suspect what your heart may do with them. It is good to fear always, especially when we have what we wish for or desire. Therefore, still be looking to God, taking your maintenance out of his hands, and praying to him, and blessing him daily for your supply, and this will make your estate sweet and comfortable to you, and free from those snares wherewith otherwise it will be encumbered.

[4.] Be sure you get grace together with an estate, for otherwise singly it will be a snare to you: Prov. xiv. 24, 'The crown of the wise is their riches, but the foolishness of fools is folly.' Riches are as they are used; if they fall to the share of a man that is godly and wise, they are a crown and ornament, otherwise a snare; for the one employeth them to the honour of God, and the good of the church and state, and is more publicly useful, but the other groweth more haughty and fierce, and scornful of holy things, and sensual and vain, and eateth and drinketh, and swaggereth away the good gifts of God, which might have a more noble use. So Eccles. vii. 11, 'Wisdom is good with an inheritance;' it is good without it, but more conspicuously good with it. It is not said an inheritance is good without wisdom or grace. No; it is reserved to the owners for their hurt. So Prov. xvii. 16, 'Wherefore is there a price in the hand of a fool to get wisdom, seeing he hath no heart to it.' Many a man hath a price, but he hath not a heart; an estate is but as a sword in the hand of a madman, when a man wants grace to improve it.

[5.] Be sure your esteem of riches come below your esteem of religion and good conscience. As Nazianzen said of his eloquence, he had something of value to esteem as nothing for Christ. By all my wealth and glory, this alone I have gained, that I have something to which I might prefer my Saviour. This is like 'the woman clothed with the sun, and the moon under her feet,' Rev. xii. 1, contemning all worldly and sublunary things for Christ.

[6.] Think of changes in the midst of your fulness: 'Surely every man at his best estate is altogether vanity,' Ps. xxxix. 5; not only at his worst estate, when God rebuketh him for sin. We should make suppositions, and see how we can bear the loss of all things, when they are represented but in conceit and imagination: Hab. iii. 17, 18, 'Although the fig-tree shall not blossom, neither shall fruit be in the vine, &c., yet I will rejoice in the Lord, and joy in the God of my salvation.' The fool durst not suppose the accidents of that night: Luke xii. 20, 'Thou fool! this night thy soul shall be required of thee.' Security is a coward; acquaint the soul with a supposition of loss and danger.

SERMON XII.

It is easier for a camel to go through the eye of a needle, than for a rich man to enter into the kingdom of God.—MARK x. 25.

I HAVE now read you a sentence, that at first view may seem to cut off the greatest and most splendid part of the world from all hopes of salvation. Had it been my saying only, you might take liberty to tax it as rash and rigorous, but the mouth of truth itself hath spoken it, even Jesus Christ, whom we own as our Lord and master. He sufficiently knew the worth and way of salvation, and the state and danger of souls. Now he interposeth his authority: Mat. xix. 24, 'I say unto you, It is easier for a camel to go through the eye of a needle, than for a rich man to enter into the kingdom of God.' If we believe him, then let rich men look to themselves. He had already told them, that it is hard for them that have riches; then he shows wherein the difficulty lay, because of their trusting in riches. Now, he represents the difficulty by a similitude; it is as hard for them to enter into the kingdom of God, as for a thing of the greatest bulk to pass through the straitest place; for what more strait than a needle's eye, and a camel is a creature of a great bulk. A camel cannot pass through a needle's eye without a miracle, nor a rich man enter into the kingdom of God without the singular power of God's grace. For the expression: Some say there was a gate at Jerusalem, called the eye of a needle, a strait gate, by which a camel could not enter. *Nisi deposito onero, et flexis genibus*, without laying aside his burden, and bending his knee. But no approved history mentions this, and the conceit lesseneth the force of our Saviour's speech. Others say that the word κάμελος signifies a cable, by which mariners do fasten the anchor, but that also is a mistake; for that word is otherwise spelt, κάμιλος and doth also rarely occur in that sense, and therefore rather the beast is intended than the cord or cable.

It was an ordinary proverb among the Jews, and is so even to this day, that an elephant cannot pass through the eye of a needle. Our Saviour indeed a little changeth the proverb, instead of the elephant, a beast which few had seen, putting a camel, a creature very ordinary in Syria; 'It is easier for a camel to go through the eye of a needle.' I will not say that this similitude was chosen because they were wont to lade their rich wares upon camels, and so the camel doth most decipher the rich man, who is the packhorse of his wealth, and hath the burden, but not the use of it. However, two things I may gather from it, as Origen hath done before us—

1. That there is something in turning christian, or entering into the kingdom of God, that answers the needle's eye, and that is the strait gate and the narrow way which leads to life, Mat. vii. 14, the strait gate of repentance, and the narrow way of constant mortification.

2. That there is something on the rich man's part which answers the camel, namely, that they grow so great and bulky, in regard of their pride, worldly lusts, joys, and confidences, that they cannot reduce themselves to those straits that are necessary for entering into the kingdom of God, as the camel's bulk and bunchback hinders his entrance into a strait place. This without straining I might observe; though I must tell you, I think the main intent of this proverbial speech is nothing else but this, to express an extraordinary difficulty on the rich man's part, not to be removed but by the almighty power of grace. Such similitudes are frequent in scripture: Jer. xiii. 23, 'Can the Ethiopian change his skin, or the leopard his spots?' so Mat. xxiii. 24, 'Ye blind guides, which strain at a gnat and swallow a camel.'

Well, then, you see it noteth the difficulty, if not utter impossibility, for men of that rank, without peculiar grace to avoid the snares of Satan, or to render themselves capable of eternal blessedness. And since Christ doth again and again press this—we have had it three times, and now doth amplify it by a comparison—I shall observe—

Doct. That the danger of riches, and the difficulty of rich men's salvation, is a point ought much to be pressed and seriously thought of.

There are two propositions included in this observation—(1.) That the salvation of rich men is very difficult; (2.) That this must be much pressed and seriously thought of.

I. The difficulty of their salvation. I have formerly proved this by reason of the sins incident to this state and condition of life, therefore now I shall quit that, and prove there is a great deal of difficulty for rich men to enter into the kingdom of God, because of the duties required of them.

1. There are common duties that concern them and all christians.

2. There is something peculiar and singular expected from the rich, which makes their entrance into heaven more difficult.

1. There are common duties that concern them and all christians, that are more difficult for them than for others to perform, and these

are set down Mat. xvi. 24, 'If any man will come after me, let him deny himself, and take up his cross, and follow me.' Christ saith, 'If any man,' without exception; small and great, rich and poor, they must all submit to those terms. The duties are three, and they make way one for another—(1.) He must deny himself, and he must comply with this; (2.) That he may take up his cross, and bear it kindly and willingly; and that fits for the (3.) Duty, following Christ, or cleaving close to him. These are the three duties that are required of all that will come after Christ, and would follow him as their great Lord and master, and captain of their salvation: He must 'deny himself,' his own wit, his own will, his own affections and interests, and be wholly at the disposal of God, pleasing him in all things. Till we come to this, nothing else in christianity will down. Well, when this is done, then he must 'take up the cross;' first deny ourselves, that bows the back of a sinner; then take up, and bear the cross kindly; that is to say, rather suffer the loss of all than wilfully sin against God, and hazard his favour. And after this he must follow Christ, not forsake him because of the cross, but stick the closer to him, walking according to his doctrine and example. Let us treat of these duties apart, and withal show how hard it is for the rich man to comply with them.

[1.] He must deny himself, whatever his corrupt heart desires, how dear and pleasing soever it be; though his parting with the contentments of the flesh should be like 'cutting off the right hand, and plucking out the right eye,' Mat. v. 29, 30, yet this must be done, and he must fully resign up himself to please God in all things. Now this is very hard and difficult for all men, which we may soon be sensible of if we do but consider how earnestly man affects a dominion and sovereignty over himself, to be *sui juris*, at his own dispose, as those rebels against God said, Ps. xii. 4, 'Our lips are our own, who is lord over us?' A libertine yokeless spirit possesseth them. We conceit that our hearts are our own to think what we please, our tongues our own to speak what we please, our hands our own to do what we please. Man affects to be a god to himself, and to be solely under the government of his own will, and to have all his comforts in his own hand and at his own dispose, denying himself nothing which his heart affects; as Solomon saith he did, Eccles. ii. 10, 'Whatsoever mine eyes desired, I kept not from them, I withheld not my heart from any joy.' Natural pride and self-love is such that we cannot endure the yoke of any restraints, but we let loose the reins to a full fruition of whatever our hearts affect. Now, as self-denial is difficult to all, because of this yokeless and libertine spirit, much more to the rich and to the great, and to those that flow in ease and plenty, and have no bands and restraints of providence upon them; they are more licentious, impatient of contradiction, or of having their wills thwarted, and therefore by a lawless liberty they wholly seek to please themselves, and to feed their own lusts, without any care and respect to God: Jer. v. 5, 'I will get me to the great men, and will speak unto them, but they have altogether broken the yoke, and burst the bonds;' that is, they cast off all the bonds of loyalty and obedience to God. And why? Because they think they can subsist alone and apart from him: Jer. ii. 31, 'Wherefore do my people say, We are lords, we will come no more unto thee?'

Men think themselves to be lords of their own fortune, and therefore slight God, break through the restraint of his laws, cannot deny themselves anything that their corrupt hearts affect. Those that are in a low condition, kept bare, and in a daily need of providence, are more humble and submissive to God; but when they grow great, they turn the back upon him, and cannot endure his strict government. So Jer. xxii. 21, 'I spake to thee in thy prosperity, but thou saidst, I will not hear.' Those that are rich and well at ease are loath to be controlled in their will, even by God himself: Exod. v. 2, 'Who is the Lord, that I should obey his voice to let Israel go? I know not the Lord, neither will I let Israel go.' Who so self-willed, proud, and scornful of God as they? who so apt to please themselves, and to use their riches to feed their lusts, and to provide accommodations for their flesh and corrupt nature? Self-denial and a flesh-pleasing course are inconsistent; and therefore, because of the lawless liberty which they take to please themselves and to make provision for the flesh, they cannot comply with this precept of Christ, 'Let him deny himself.'

[2.] To take up the cross, that is another of Christ's precepts, and to be willing to suffer affliction, either from the hands of God or from the hands of men for God's sake. This is one thing that we must reckon upon: if we would be christians and Christ's disciples, first or last we shall be called to this exercise. Ignatius, when he was led bound before the tribunal, Now, saith he, I begin to be a disciple of Christ. Many think it is factious to talk of the cross in days of peace and liberty, but Christ puts it into our indentures. If we should never suffer for Christ, yet we must be sure that we have a heart that would suffer if God calls us to it. It is possible a man may go to heaven without suffering, but he cannot go to heaven without a resolution to suffer when God will. Now the cross makes it hard to all: Heb. xii. 11, 'Now no chastening for the present seemeth to be joyous but grievous.' It is not pleasing to the flesh to endure blows, suffer smart, and to account all that we have as 'dung and dross in comparison of Christ;' to be joyful in tribulation, and so wholly swallowed up with the hopes and interests and concernments of the world to come, and to be dead to present things. Oh! how irksome is the remembrance of this to those that are high in place and office, and sail with a full tide and current of worldly felicity! To be averse to suffering is natural to man, and is in itself no sin, for nature is to seek its own welfare and preservation, but when it goes to excess, it argues a tenderness of the flesh, and that we have consulted with Satan: Mat. xvi. 22, said Peter, 'Be it far from thee, Lord; this shall not be unto thee;' but Christ said, ver. 23, 'Get thee behind me, Satan.' Now the more men have to lose, the more tender they are of losing it; a little is sooner quitted. This young man went away sad, for he had great possessions. Great men, when once they come to be noted for the profession of the truth, they shrink and fall off presently; they have not learned to leave all for Christ's sake. Judas, that had the bag, turns apostate and traitor to Christ, John xii. 6; when he saw nothing but opposition increasing, the supposed kingdom not to go forward, and heard Christ speaking of nothing but the cross and suffering, he thinks of betraying his master; heaven is no pennyworth for him if it cost so dear.

[3.] Let 'him follow me.' He that will be Christ's disciple must follow him, his doctrine, and his example.

(1.) His doctrine; that is, the directions he hath given us in his word. Now what is the drift of Christ's doctrine? The doctrine Christ brought out of the bosom of God is to draw us off from the world to heaven, from the pleasures of the flesh and the baits of this life, to seek things to come and things eternal. This is one great excellency of the christian faith, that it reveals the doctrine of eternal life and a blessed estate to come, which all other professions in the world could only guess at. Christ hath made it manifest, and brought it to light, that there is such a thing: 2 Tim. i. 10, 'He hath brought life and immortality to light through the gospel.' And the gospel reveals the way that leads to it; it makes a free offer of it upon the condition of faith in Christ: John iii. 16, 17, 'God so loved the world, that he gave his only-begotten Son, that whosoever believeth in him should not perish, but have everlasting life: for God sent not his Son into the world to condemn the world, but that the world through him might be saved.' And walking in all holiness of life: Heb. xii. 14, 'Follow peace with all men, and holiness, without which no man shall see the Lord.' And the gospel lays before us the highest motives to quicken us to walk therein, and take off our affections from the world: Col. iii. 1, 2, 'If ye then be risen with Christ, seek those things which are above, where Christ sitteth at the right hand of God: set your affections on things above, not on things of the earth.' This must be our great scope and business, that we may get home to God with a neglect of present advantages. The gospel tells us that we should not be troubled though our outward man decay, whilst 'this light affliction, that is but for a moment, worketh for us a far more exceeding and eternal weight of glory,' 2 Cor. iv. 17. Well, then, seeing this is the great design of the doctrine of Christ, that here we should ply our work, that hereafter we may receive our wages; that here we should study holiness, that hereafter we may be blessed with him. Now what doctrine can be more contrary than this to those 'that have their portion here,' Ps. xvii. 14, 'That have received their consolation here,' Luke xvi. 32, 'That have received their good things in their lifetime,' Luke xvi. 25? To tell them of a dislodging and removal, and of foregoing the things they love and see for a God they never saw, oh! how tedious is this to a carnal heart! They are already happy and blessed, and cannot endure to think of a change, and therefore are incapable of following this doctrine, that drives us off from carnal vanities to look after the interests and concernments of the world to come.

(2.) His example. I shall only instance in two things—we are to follow him in humility of heart and purity of life.

(1*st.*) In humility: Mat. xi. 29, 'Learn of me, for I am meek and lowly of heart.' This is the great thing the Son of God would recommend to us, in which we should take after him, even to be of an humble and lowly spirit: 'Let the same mind be in you that was in Christ Jesus,' Phil. ii. 5. Christ was the Son of God. He did not affect to be a God by robbery, as the angels had rebellious thoughts against the empire and majesty of God, and they were thrust down from heaven for their aspiring; but the Son of God was equal with God the Father:

'He thought it no robbery to be equal with God,' ver. 6 ; and yet 'he made himself of no reputation, took upon him the form of a servant and was made in the likeness of man, and being found in fashion as a man, he humbled himself,' ver. 7, 8. Certainly, if any had cause to stand upon his terms, Jesus Christ had much more. That preface is notable and very magnificent, John xiii. 3, 'Jesus knowing that the Father had given all things into his hands, and that he was come from God, and went to God.' And what follows? 'He washed his disciples' feet,' ver. 4, 5. Thus the boughs that are most laden hang their heads, and the sun at the highest casts the least shadow. Jesus Christ indeed was high, excellent, and glorious, yet he would condescend to set his disciples such a pattern of humility. But now who more proud and disdainful than the rich? When men have anything in the world, they grow high and lofty. Oh! when we consider the pride of man to man, we may more stand wondering at the condescensions of God to man. As soon as a man hath any estate in the world, he is altered presently: 1 Tim. vi. 17, 'Charge them that are rich in this world, that they be not high-minded.' Many that in their low estate were humble and meek, in prosperity grow proud and disdainful ; many that were forward and zealous, grow cold and slothful in spiritual things ; many that, while they were kept dependent upon God, were diligent in hearing, profitable in conference, thought it no disgrace to instruct their families, were patient of reproof, but when the world comes in upon them, no such matter. As the moon is never eclipsed but in the full, so all the grace that they seemed to have it is under an eclipse when they are in the full of prosperity.

(2d.) In purity and holiness: 'He that saith he abideth in him, ought himself so to walk even as he walked,' 1 John ii. 6, and 1 John iii. 3, 'Every man that hath this hope in him purifieth himself even as he is pure;' and 1 John iv. 17, 'As he is, so are we in the world.' Now prosperity and true holiness seldom go together ; they are afflictions that promote holiness: 'They verily for a few days chastened us after their own pleasure, but he for our profit, that we might be partakers of his holiness: now no chastening for the present seemeth to be joyous but grievous, nevertheless it yieldeth the peaceable fruit of righteousness unto them that are exercised thereby,' Heb. xii. 10, 11. Then are men most serious when they feel the rod and are pinched with some necessity ; but when they are full, they wax wanton, kick with the heel, and throw off all respects to God and godliness.

2. As the difficulty ariseth from the general duties that are common to them with others, so it ariseth also from this: more is required of them that are rich and great in this world than of others They should be eminent and exemplary for holiness. They have larger accounts to make to God than others, for our account must be according to our receipts: Luke xii. 48, 'Unto whomsoever much is given, of him shall be much required ; and to whom men have committed much, of him they will ask the more.' Among men this is a constant rule, and so it is with God ; the account is according to the thing with which ye are trusted ; they that have more must account for more. Now certainly more is required of great and rich men than of others upon four accounts—they have greater obligations, more opportunities for spirit-

ual improvement, they have larger abilities and advantages of honouring God, and because of the influence of their example.

[1.] They have greater obligations. Certainly they to whom God hath been more bountiful, are bound to be more dutiful than others. It is not enough to render to God, but we must render according to what we have received. It was Hezekiah's fault, 2 Chron. xxxii. 25, 'Hezekiah rendered not again according to the benefit done unto him.' The rent must be paid according to the value of the farm. God will not accept that at the hands of a rich man which he would accept from a poor man, which hath not such great obligations. A man that hath tasted of the bounty of God's providence, and hath had fulness and plenty of all things, it is required he should serve God more cheerfully than others, Deut. xxviii. 47. Their duties are greater, and their sins are greater; as you know the prophet aggravates David's sin by the mercies he had received, in 2 Sam. xii. 7–9, 'I anointed thee king over Israel, and I delivered thee out of the hand of Saul; and I gave thee thy master's house, and thy master's wives into thy bosom, and gave thee the house of Israel and of Judah; and if that had been too little, I would moreover have given unto thee such and such things: wherefore hast thou despised the commandment of the Lord, to do evil in his sight?' They have tasted more of the bounty and goodness of his providence, and have had more than others to revive the sense of God, and keep up the memorial of God in their hearts.

[2.] They have more opportunities of being free to good duties, as being not so straitly bound to bodily labour for present maintenance, nor burdened with so many cares and distractions of this life, and so have more time and leisure for studying the mind of God in his word and improving themselves in the knowledge of the truth, and meditating the statutes of God, as David professeth he did all the day long. And look, as the apostle speaks of married and single persons, 1 Cor. vii. 32, 33, 'He that is unmarried careth for the things that belong to the Lord, how he may please the Lord; but he that is married careth for the things that are of the world, how he may please his wife;' they that are in a single estate have more leisure to attend the service of God, greater opportunities of holy privacy and meditation upon the promises of God, are less distracted and divided with the cares of the world, and have nothing else to do but to serve God and study to please him; so it is true of poor and rich; those that live in a plentiful condition, oh! what a great deal of time and leisure have they for religious duties, better education, more helps, more advantages, therefore they are more bound to addict and give up themselves to the study of divine things. A little knowledge of God he will accept of in a poor tradesman that is divided and distracted with the cares of the world, and have not such leisure to attend the service of God, and the opportunities of holy privacy and meditation, which he will not accept of in the rich, that have so many opportunities to furnish themselves with knowledge, and have little else to do but to serve God and labour to please him, and to study the promises of God, that they may grow in grace; and yet, when they abandon themselves to sensuality, and live from one week's end to another, and can scarce tell what to do with their time, and yet cannot afford it to God, how culpable are they!

[3.] They have greater advantages of furthering the duties of piety and mercy, and of honouring God with their substance, Prov. iii. 9, and of relieving others, of 'making themselves friends of the mammon of unrighteousness,' Luke xvi. 9. I say they have greater opportunities of being 'rich in good works,' 1 Tim. vi. 18. Others that have hearts have not estates, and cannot be so publicly useful. God expects from every man according to his ability, and therefore they should abound in all acts of mercy and piety, for the promoting the honour and service of God, and relief and comfort of others. But alas! usually it is here as in nature, those mountains in the bowels of which there are most mines of gold and silver are most barren; so rich men, for the most part, live most unprofitably as to the fruits of grace, piety, and charity. They that have great estates have least heart to do anything for God, and men of a middle condition do exceedingly outstrip those that are vastly and excessively rich, in being liberal and open-handed for honouring of God and the relief of others.

[4.] More is required of them because of the influence of their example. They are as the first-sheets, others are printed off by them. The more any are exalted and lifted up above others, the more conspicuous are their actions. The example of an eminent person is never single, for when such a one doth evil, he carries others with him as the stream doth that which floats upon it. If they do good, their countenance and example doth exceedingly provoke many to follow after that which is good; therefore they should specially take care to fear God, and be diligent in the exercise of godliness, and serious in the business of eternal life. But alas! who authorise sin and propagate it in the poor more than they that have a plentiful fortune and estate to bear them out in it? Who are more dissolute and lascivious, and profaners of God's holy name and day, and deriders of God's word, and holy services and servants? and so wherever they go, they leave their dregs behind them, and leaven others, and draw them into sin, which makes the difficulty of their salvation so much the greater.

II. The other proposition that is contained in this observation is, that this ought to be much pressed, seriously thought of, for Christ inculcates it again and again.

1. To keep up a remembrance of God and heavenly things in the hearts of rich men. Security and forgetfulness of God is the cause of all the mischief rich men are liable to. Men that have so much in the world never think of God and salvation. The heart is so full of the world, that it leaves no place for the thoughts and remembrance of God. When God would offer to come in upon them, it doth fare with him as it did with Christ; when he was born at Bethlehem, 'there was no room for him in the inn,' Luke ii. 7. When God would lodge in the understanding, the upper chamber of the soul, that is full of worldly or sensual projects. If he would enter into the memory, that is the world's warehouse, and it is pestered with cares about present things. If he would enter into their hearts and affections, they are prepossessed already, that is the world's storehouse, there their treasure lies; and so, what with this and that, it comes to pass, that 'God is not in all their thoughts,' Ps. x. 4. The awful remembrance of God is a strange uncouth thing to those that are full, and live plentifully

in the world. This appears by the whole current of scripture; God forewarns his people of it: Deut. xi. 12, 'When thou shalt have eaten and be full, beware lest thou forget the Lord thy God.' When men are full, and abound with so much accommodation, God is banished out of their thoughts. He complains of this as the cause of his people's forgetting him: Hosea xiii. 6, 'According to their pasture, so were they filled; they were filled, and their heart was exalted, therefore have they forgotten me.' God is forgotten in prosperity, when we have not such a sensible need of him and of his help. Men can live alone and apart from God, and therefore cast off all thoughts of him: 1 Tim. vi. 17, 'Charge them that are rich in this world that they be not high-minded, nor trust in uncertain riches, but in the living God, who giveth us richly all things to enjoy.' Plenty easily breeds forgetfulness of God, therefore it needs often to be inculcated and enforced upon, and thought of by them.

2. This ought to be much pressed and seriously thought of, to awaken suspicion; there may be a snare in our estate. To suspect danger is a good means to prevent it, and therefore, that we may draw men to self-suspicion, being compassed about by the snares of the devil, we must again and again tell you how hard it is for rich men to be saved. Agur was afraid of riches and the evil influence of them, and therefore prays for a competency: Prov. xxx. 8, 9, 'Give me neither poverty nor riches; feed me with food convenient for me, lest I be full and deny thee, and say, Who is the Lord?' Whereas men that never think of danger are surprised with it before they are aware; therefore it is good to be suspicious of a prosperous estate, to be afraid of the world more when it smiles than when it frowns. Most men are afraid of poverty, but few are afraid of wealth, and yet there the snares and temptations lie; and the reason is, because they prize their temporal interest more than their eternal salvation. Poverty is against their temporal interests, but wealth, fulness, and plenty is a hindrance to their eternal salvation, and men will venture their souls rather than their bodies. It is fat and rank soil that feedeth weeds; therefore think of it often; here lies the difficulty to have the world at will and not to be ensnared by it; to learn to abound is the harder lesson. Paul had learned both, so must we: Phil. iv. 12, 'I know both how to be abased, and I know how to abound; everywhere and in all things I am instructed both to be full and to be hungry, both to abound and to suffer need.' We say of a proud man or woman, Such a one would do well to be a lord or lady; but it is harder than you imagine. How few are there that have any lively thoughts of eternity, or make any serious preparation for death and judgment, when they have health and wealth, and all the accommodations which the carnal nature desires? And therefore be suspicious when you find delight, and what is pleasing to the flesh, it is not likely to be safe for your soul. Oh! possess your estates with fear. The fear of a snare may help to avoid it. How easily may such a carnal heart as yours be enticed from God, and grow cold and remiss about the great things of your salvation!

3. This ought oft to be pressed and seriously thought of, to stir up observation how it is with us. There is no man that observes his heart but will find this effect, that riches make the business of salvation more

difficult. Good David observed that his heart was corrupted by his condition: Ps. x. 6, 'He hath said in his heart, I shall never be moved; for I shall never be in adversity.' And elsewhere we find he was sensible that worldliness was creeping upon him: Ps. cxix. 36, 'Incline my heart unto thy testimonies, and not to covetousness.' A child of God hath not the bent of his heart so perfectly fixed towards God but it is ever and anon returning to its old bent and bias again. The best may find that they cannot keep their affections as loose from the world when they have houses, and lands, and all things at their will, as they could when they are kept low and bare. The best may find that their love to heavenly things is on the wane as worldly things are on the increase. It is reported of Pius Quintus that he should say of himself, that when he first entered into orders, he had some hopes of his salvation; when he came to be a cardinal, he doubted of it; but since he came to be pope, he did even almost despair. Many may find a very great change in themselves, much decay of zeal for God's glory, and love to and relish of God's word, and mindfulness of heavenly things, as it fares better with them in the world. Now it is good to observe this before the mischief increaseth. Look, as jealousy and caution is necessary to prevent the entrance and beginning of this mischief, so observation is necessary to prevent the increase of it. When the world doth get too deep an interest in our hearts, when it begins to insinuate and entice us from God, and weaken our delight in the ways of God and zeal for his glory, then we need often to tell you how hard it is for a rich man to enter into the kingdom of heaven.

4. To stir up supplication for special and peculiar grace, that it may not be so with us, that the Lord would keep us from the snares of our condition; for 'with God all things are possible;' that we may go to God, and say, Lord, let not my estate be my bane and poison. On the one side, it is a great judgment that God brings upon wicked men when 'their table becomes their snare,' Ps. lxix. 22, when their comforts are cursed to them, and when their hearts are drawn from God by their plentiful condition in the world. On the other side, it is a peculiar grace and favour from God when we be heavenly-minded in the midst of plenty, and keep up lively spiritual exercises of godliness notwithstanding our opulency and plentiful condition in the world. Jehoshaphat is an instance to encourage you to pray for this: 2 Chron. xvii. 5, 6, it is said of him, 'He had riches and honour in abundance, and his heart was lift up in the ways of the Lord.' Christians, it is hard to carry a full cup without spilling, to have riches and honour, and all this with great abundance, and yet to have a lively zeal towards God and a great delight in his ways. Now this is possible with God, and this God hath bestowed, and therefore it should be asked. There is nothing that quickens to prayer so much as a constant sense and apprehension of the danger and difficulty which attends such an estate; therefore this must ever be laid before you, that your thoughts may be steeped in this consideration.

Use 1. It serveth to check the desire of greatness and increase of wealth. If you had more your duty would be more, and your account greater, and your snares and temptations and stumbling-blocks in the way to heaven would be much more multiplied; and therefore you should be contented with what you have. If we cannot thrive in the valleys, and keep up a lively and warm respect to the world to come in a low condition, how should we expect to grow on the tops of the mountains, where we are more exposed to tempests, and the soil is more barren? therefore you should strive rather to give a good account of a little than to make it more. The Lord knoweth that if you were a step higher, you would be apt to be proud, licentious, secure, mindless of eternal life, further off from God, and then better you had lived in beggary all your days. The time will soon come about when you will judge so, and therefore do not enlarge your desires, as if you could never have enough.

Use 2. It teacheth us patience, not only in the want, but in the loss of outward riches. It is more irksome to lose than to want, as it was an unnatural thing for the sun to go back ten degrees in Ahaz's dial. Yet this is to be borne, for when God taketh away your wealth from you, he maketh your way to heaven more easy; if God taketh away riches, he doth but take a bush of thorns out of the way that would prick and gore your souls. The world is apt to turn away your heart from true happiness, and to hinder you in the way that leadeth to it. Now God's grace is seen not only in fortifying the heart, but in abating the temptation; he seeth you are apt to sleep upon a carnal pillow, and therefore taketh it from under your heads to awaken you. If you believe the word of God, that riches and honours do easily prove a snare, why should you be grieved when the snare is broken? Do you love to have your salvation hindered or hazarded? and therefore why are you so impatient when God cuts you short in these outward things?

Use 3. Let rich men think of this, and make application of this sentence to their own hearts, that they may possess their estates with fear. To this end, consider—

1. The person speaking is Christ, who had so much wisdom and love to the comfort and happiness of men, that he would not fright them with a needless danger. (See before on ver. 23.)

2. Whom it is spoken of; rich men, those that can live of themselves in the world without the supply of others. The disciples, that had little, cried out, 'Who then can be saved?' We fancy it is spoken only to the overgrown rich; but they that have but one talent must improve it, and it is hard to do so. We must give an account of one talent as well as ten. The sensualist will turn this upon the covetous, and the covetous upon the sensualist, the voluptuous gallant upon the cormorants of the city, and they upon the epicures; but Christ saith indefinitely, 'the rich.'

3. What is spoken of, entering into the kingdom of God. It is salvation and eternal life; not a trifle. Christ doth not say, He shall do no worthy exploits in the world, or arrive at no great degree of grace, but, He shall not enter into the kingdom of God.

4. How it is spoken. It is represented by a similitude that implieth impossibility, or at least an extraordinary difficulty without a miracle of peculiar grace.

Then look about you, sirs. Such speeches of Christ were doubly entertained—with wonder, as by the disciples in the next verse, 'They were astonished out of measure, saying among themselves, Who then can be saved ?' or with scorn: Luke xvi. 14, 'The pharisees also, who were covetous, heard all these things, and derided him.' For the reverence you bear to Christ, I hope you will not entertain it with scorn, but rather with wonder, holy fear, and solicitude.

I expect now you will say, What shall we do to prevent this mischief?

[1.] Remember your condition in the world. You are not a freeholder, but a tenant-at-will: Luke xii. 20, 'Thou fool! this night thy soul shall be required of thee, then whose shall all those things be which thou hast provided?' You are not owners, but stewards; not lords and masters of what you have, but only must improve it for God; and you must give an account: Luke xvi. 2, 'Give an account of thy stewardship, for thou mayest be no longer steward.' You are not citizens but strangers: 1 Peter ii. 11, 'Dearly beloved, I beseech you, as strangers and pilgrims, abstain from fleshly lusts, which war against the soul.' . The world is our inn, where we abide but for a night; our dwelling is there where we live longest.

[2.] Judge of your estates to be good or bad to you, not as they do accommodate the flesh, but as they help or hinder you in your way to heaven. Make heaven your end, and consider all things else as means and helps. Ordinances are the next means, riches and estates are remote helps to heaven. All things are measured by the great and last end, therefore you are to judge of all things as they help you on in heaven's way. Better to be preserved in brine and pickle than to rot in honey.

[3.] Devote your wealth to the Lord: Luke xii. 21, 'So is he that layeth up treasure for himself, and is not rich towards God.' Riches are snares, and will certainly prove means of our damnation if we do not so.' That is the best condition for us in which we may do most service to God, and not to the flesh: Gal. vi. 8, 'For he that soweth to the flesh shall of the flesh reap corruption, but he that soweth to the Spirit shall of the Spirit reap life everlasting.'

SERMON XIII.

And they were astonished out of measure, saying among themselves, Who then can be saved?—MARK x. 26.

IN this verse you have the entertainment of Christ's doctrine concerning the difficulty of rich men's being saved. The effects of it are two —(1.) A great wonder or deep sense of this difficulty, 'They were astonished out of measure;' (2.) An anxious question, 'And they said among themselves, Who then can be saved?'

For the first branch, their great wonder, περισσῶς ἐξεπλήσσοντο, they were struck at heart, 'astonished out of measure.' We meet with it before at the first proposal of this difficulty, 'They were astonished at his words;' but now, when Christ had rendered the reason, and reassumed the former difficulty, 'It is easier for a camel,' &c., this doth increase the astonishment, and it is not barely said, 'they were astonished,' but 'out of measure.' Let us a little inquire into the reason of this wonder. Why should the disciples be so troubled at this speech? They were poor, or, however, had left all and followed Christ, as it is in the next words.

1. Some say it was for others, to see so great a part of the world cut off from all hopes of salvation. Though all have not wealth, yet there are few but do desire it, and that desire may hinder as well as the enjoyment; therefore, they being solicitous for the salvation of others, they were astonished, and said, 'Who then can be saved?' Certainly it is good not only to work out our own salvation, but to effect the salvation of others. We have a saying, *Omne bonum est sui diffusivum*—All good seeks to propagate itself; as fire turns all things about it into fire. This is the disposition of God's people; when they have found any comfort and benefit by Christ themselves, they desire others should share with them, and be partakers of the same grace and heirs of the same promises. David, after many roarings and disquiets, when he had found that penitent confession of sin was such a notable way for the easing of his own conscience, and had seen the fruit of humble dealing with God, he pens the 32d psalm, which is 'Maschil, a psalm of instruction,' and so is willing to teach others the way. So Andrew calls Peter when he had found Christ, John i. 41, and Philip calls Nathanael, ver. 45. Carnal things are possessed with envy. They that are rich and great in the world would shine alone, and when they are gotten to the top themselves, they are loath to teach others the way to climb up after them. But it is not so with spiritual things, grace is charitable and communicative. Indeed, where any take up religion out of faction and carnal aims, they would enclose the common salvation, and envy the profession and hope of it to others, that they may be the better esteemed and respected themselves. It is observed of mules and other creatures that are of mixed and bastard production, that they never procreate and beget after their kind. Mongrel christians are envious rather than communicative; but those that have really tasted of the sweetness of Christ themselves are glad of company, and it is a great satisfaction to them to hear that others are in a towardly or hopeful way of salvation: 1 John i. 3, 'That which we have seen and heard declare we unto you, that ye also may have fellowship with us, and truly our fellowship is with the Father, and with his Son Jesus Christ.' The apostle had fellowship with Christ, and therefore was so zealous to bring others to the enjoyment of that privilege; therefore, this might be one reason why the disciples, that were safe as to their own particular, and had left all and followed Christ, were troubled to hear that it was so hard for rich men to be saved. Surely this charitable disposition becomes us well, and answers the great patterns we have in the world. We read of some that were so zealous for the salvation of others that in some sense they preferred it before their own: 'Blot me out of thy book that thou hast written,' saith Moses, Exod. xxxii. 32; and Paul, 'I could wish that myself were accursed from Christ for my brethren, my kinsmen according to the flesh,' Rom. ix. 3. So much of personal happiness as resulted to him

from communion with God, he could even lay it down at God's feet for their sake. These are rare instances I confess, but some portion of this spirit all should have: 'Charity seeketh not her own,' 1 Cor. xiii. 5. Chrysostom saith, I cannot believe it is possible for that man to be saved who doth not labour to procure and further the salvation of his neighbour; for whoever would go to heaven would not go to heaven alone, but laboureth to draw others along with him. *Vide* Chrysostom de Sacerdot., lib. vi. It was out of zeal for the salvation of others.

2. The former reason was good, and argued a gracious disposition in them, but this that I shall now give is of a worse alloy, and argues weakness. And yet I cannot but think that this had an influence upon them, viz., the hopes of an earthly kingdom, and the great emoluments and preferments they expected thence. Christ's own disciples were deeply leavened with a conceit of an earthly kingdom which the Messiah should set up. And though they had left all and followed him in his poor estate, yet they expected greatness and honour, and the confluence of all worldly blessings, when the kingdom of the Messiah should begin; and therefore, when they heard Christ again and again expressing himself concerning the difficulty of rich men's entering into the kingdom of God, 'They were astonished out of measure,' as finding all their carnal hopes dashed at once. I cannot but think this was one cause of their astonishment, because in all their converses with Christ they bewrayed a spice of this humour. Two instances I shall give as a pregnant proof of it. One when they were at the sacrament, a little before the death of Christ: 'There was a strife amongst them which of them should be accounted the greatest,' Luke xxii. 24. They understood that the kingdom was consigned to them in that ordinance, and they were framing of principalities, and striving who should have the highest preferment and office in this kingdom. Nay, you shall see after Christ had suffered such ignominious things at Jerusalem, this conceit abode with them; and therefore after his resurrection they come to him with this question, 'Lord, wilt thou at this time restore again the kingdom to Israel?' Acts i. 6. They thought the Messiah would set up a temporal kingdom over all nations, and that they should at least be princes and lords under him, in the exercise of his dominion and sovereignty. Justin Martyr tells us that the heathens imagined some insurrection that the christians would be guilty of against magistracy, because they spoke so much of the kingdom of heaven; and well might they be excused of their jealousy and of this surmise, since Christ's own disciples were so far mistaken in it, whom he had so often warned of the cross, and to whom he had expressly said, that 'his kingdom was not of this world.' But we see hence that the best are too carnal, and too apt to mind earthly things, and to please themselves with the dreams of a happy estate in the world. The appetite of temporal dominion, and wealth, and honour, and peace is natural to us, and we think God doth us wrong if he doth not make us flourish here. All God's children find something of this disposition in themselves, even whilst they are under the cross; they do too little comfort themselves with the meditation of the glory of the world to come, but are always feeding themselves with desires and hopes of an

earthly happiness, and of turning the tide and current of affairs that seem to be against them, that the world may more smile upon them, and befriend them more; and when they are frustrated and disappointed of this hope, their soul faints, and they are astonished out of measure. Oh! this is a sign that our conversation is not in heaven, and that we do not seek the things that are above, and are not perfectly subdued to the will of God, who many times sees the cross to be necessary and profitable for us; and therefore, to please ourselves still with carnal hopes and dreams of a commodious and comfortable condition in the world, is not for a christian.

3. The sense of this difficulty might revive the thoughts of other difficulties. Other things besides riches might obstruct them, and hinder their passage to heaven; and therefore, even those that had left all and followed Christ were astonished out of measure, when they understood the way to heaven to be much harder than they formerly conceited. Certainly it is good to think of the general case when one instance is given. Is it hard to the rich and not to the poor? have they no temptations? When we hear strict doctrine pressed, we should not put it off to others, but fear for ourselves. The poor disciples were astonished out of measure when Christ spake to the rich, How hard it was for them 'to enter into the kingdom of heaven.'

4. Possibly this astonishment might arise from fear of the success of the gospel, wherein they were to be employed as instruments, when they heard that rich men were not likely to prove friends, but rather enemies to the kingdom of God. Alas! what should they do that had parted with all, and were like to be left destitute to the mercy of an unkind world! If the great and mighty men of the world, who should be their props and supports, should so hardly be gained, alas! then how should they go abroad and preach with any efficacy for the saving of souls! Now, whether this or that or all caused the wonder, I will not now determine; all these have an influence upon it, and for these reasons they were astonished out of measure. This is the first effect, their wonder.

The second effect is a doubt moved among themselves privately, 'Who then can be saved?' This question may be looked upon either—

1. As a question of anxious solicitude. Alas! how is it that any can be saved! Or—

2. Of murmuring and secret dislike. Why, if it be so, who is able to receive this severe doctrine, or to enter upon this strict course? Now which of these shall we take it to be? Either for a question of anxious solicitude, or a question of murmuring and secret repining? I answer—

[1.] I suppose this question expresseth their anxious solicitude, and so for the main it is a good question. When we hear strict doctrine, it is good to be moved with it, and fall a-questioning. Many hear it over and over again, yet are slight, no wonder, no astonishment in their hearts; therefore it is good when it is weighed and laid to heart. This question of the apostles brings to mind a saying of one, when he heard Christ's sermon on the mount read to him, he cried out, *Aut hoc non est evangelium, aut nos non sumus christiani*—Either this is not true gospel, or we are not true christians.

[2.] There might be something of weakness, mixtures of infirmity. I cannot say there was nothing of murmuring and dislike; the muttering or saying this among themselves seems to infer it; they durst not make Christ conscious to the question, for it is in the text, 'They said among themselves;' that is, they muttered privately, and so it argues there was something of dislike.

[3.] This weakness was not to a prevalent degree, so as to make them take offence, and depart from Christ, as we find others did upon the like occasion, when Christ had preached something strict and contrary to their humour: John vi. 60, 61, 'Many of the disciples when they heard this, said, This is a hard saying, who can hear it? When Jesus knew in himself that his disciples murmured at it, he said unto them, Doth this offend you? What and if you shall see the Son of man ascend up where he was before, &c. And from that time many of his disciples went back, and walked no more with him,' ver. 66. Now these, though they were astonished at the strangeness of the doctrine of Christ, yet they did not reject or refuse the belief of it. There was more of anxious solicitude, but somewhat of muttering, 'Who then can be saved.'

Doct. When the difficulties of salvation are sufficiently understood and laid forth, we shall wonder that any are or can be saved?

I shall prove—(1.) That it is a difficult thing to be saved; (2.) Wherein the difficulty of salvation doth lie; (3.) Show how this ought to be seriously minded and regarded by us, that it is such a difficult thing to go to heaven.

I. That it is a difficult thing to be saved. Christ showeth that, Mat. vii. 14, 'Strait is the gate, and narrow is the way that leadeth unto life, and few there be that find it.' The way to heaven is somewhat like that which is described, 1 Sam. xiv. 4, 'And between the passages by which Jonathan sought to go over unto the Philistines' garrison, there was a sharp rock on the one side and a sharp rock on the other side.' So is our way to heaven a strait way, between rock and rock; here is the rock of vain presumption, and there the rock of despairing fears. Indeed, the text tells us of two things, the gate strait, the way narrow. The gate is strait, the entrance into religion hard; there must be repentance and bewailing our former sins, the working up the heart to a fixed resolution against sin, and a serious dedicating ourselves to God. Oh! how hard is it to pass through this gate! And then there is a narrow way, full of difficulties to corrupt nature; our lusts are impatient of any restraint, and we are loath entirely to give up ourselves to do and suffer God's will. So Mat. xi. 12, 'The kingdom of heaven suffereth violence, and the violent take it by force.' It is no wonder that earthly kingdoms are surprised by violence, but it is strange that the kingdom of heaven should suffer violence; how shall we understand this? Violence doth not signify unlawful attempts, but earnest diligence. It is not an injurious violence, such as snatches at earthly crowns, but the industrious violence, a resolution to break through all impediments, and take no nay; no discouragements can much abate our edge, and take us off from our pursuit of the heavenly kingdom. So 1 Peter iv. 18, a righteous man is 'scarcely saved,' μόλις σωθήσεται; with much ado he gets to shore, he makes a hard shift to get to heaven. This is enough to intimate the general truth, that there is difficulty to get to heaven.

II. Wherein lies the difficulty of salvation? The reason of doubting is this, because God's terms upon which heaven is offered are gentle and sweet: Mat. xi. 30, 'My yoke is easy, and my burden is light.' The law which God hath given us is holy, just, and good, becoming a God to give and a creature to receive: Rom. vii. 17, 'The law is holy, and the commandment is holy, and just, and good;' a law such as a man would choose if he were at liberty, and at his own option and choice. Therefore how is it so difficult, especially since there is so much strength given. Habitual strength: Eph. ii. 10, 'We are his workmanship, created in Christ Jesus unto good works.' We are fitted by his grace; and there is so much actual strength: 'I can do all things through Christ, which strengtheneth me,' Phil. iv. 13. God is no Pharaoh, to require brick where he gives no straw. And therefore, since the way is so good, his yoke so easy, and there is so much strength given, and since the encouragements are so many, both from the work and from the wages. From the work itself: 'Her ways are ways of pleasantness, and all her paths are peace,' Prov. iii. 7. There is a great deal of peace, comfort, and sweetness in walking with God, as those that travelled to Sion, 'Passing through the valley of Baca, make it a well, the rain also filleth the pools,' Ps. lxxxiv. 6; so they meet with many comfortable refreshings in a course of godliness. And then for the wages, 'God is a rewarder of them that diligently seek him,' Heb. xi. 6. Well, then, to sum up all, these things concur, since the way is plain, the helps many, the promises full and sure, why is it so difficult to go to heaven? I answer—The fault is not in God, but in our own selves, in our own hearts, in our addictedness to temporal satisfactions; and therefore when God calls us off from the interests and concernments of the present world, wholly to look after the interests and concernments of the world to come, the disposition of our flesh or carnal nature and the course of God's institutions will not suit. And this must needs be a very great difficulty, not easily removed, because—(1.) It is natural to us; (2.) It is increased by custom; (3.) It hath a powerful efficacy upon us to hinder us from walking in the ways of God, that are so sweet and pleasant.

1. This is natural to us, to be led by sense, or to be addicted to present things. There are three sorts of beings in the world—angels, that are pure spirits without flesh, these were made for heaven, and not earth; there are brute creatures, that are flesh without immortal souls, these were made for earth, and not heaven; and there is man, a middle nature between both these, that hath a fleshly substance and an immortal soul, made partly for heaven and partly for earth, as partaking of both; he hath a body that was made out of the dust, and so fitted to live in this world, and he hath a soul that came down from the superior world, and must return thither again. Now these two things must be regarded according to the dignity of the parts of which man consisteth, his earthly part and his heavenly part. The soul being the better part, the perfection and happiness of it should chiefly be looked after. The good of the soul is the enjoyment of the ever-blessed God, this should be our main work and business; and the good of the

body should be looked after in an inferior and subordinate manner. The good of the body is meat, drink, wealth, honour; these things are to be looked after in our passage to heaven. The good of the soul is the chief good, and so should be looked after as our great end and scope, and the good of the body minded only as a means. Man was made for earth in his passage and way to heaven, but his home and happiness is in heaven, where he is to enjoy the blessed God among his holy angels, and those blessed creatures that dwell above in the region of spirits. This was the end for which man was created, and while man continued innocent he had a heart inclined and disposed towards God as his chiefest good; he sought the good of his soul, and was to love him, and fear him, and serve him, and depend upon him as the fountain of his happiness. But by the fall man was drawn off from God to the creature to seek his happiness there: 'They have forsaken the fountain of living waters, and hewed them out cisterns, broken cisterns, that can hold no water,' Jer. ii. 13. Not only Adam in his own person, but all his posterity are turned from God to the creature. Now man in his pure naturals is inclined to the creature, which conduceth to the satisfaction of the earthly part, and not to God, wherein the happiness of his soul lies. This will be evident to you if you consider that though the soul be created by God, yet it is created destitute of grace or original righteousness; and being destitute of the image of God or original righteousness, it doth only accommodate itself to the interests of the body, and seek the happiness of the body; for where there is not a principle to carry us higher, it can only close with things present and known, such as are the pleasures of the body and the interests of the bodily life, and so forgets God and what concerns the enjoyment of him. And so it is said, Rom. viii. 5, 'They that are after the flesh do mind (or savour) the things of the flesh, and they that are after the Spirit, the things of the Spirit.' Therefore take man in in his pure naturals, as destitute of grace, his soul forgets its divine original, and so conforms itself to the body, and only seeks its welfare and happiness; and thence proceeds all our mindlessness of God and averseness to him, our unruly and inordinate appetites of temporal things, and the confusion, weakness, and disorder that is seen in the life of man and all his operations and faculties. Hence comes that dulness and slowness that is in his understanding to conceive of spiritual things, his acuteness in back and belly concernments: 'He that lacketh these things is blind, and cannot see afar off,' 2 Peter i. 9. He is sharpsighted in all things that concern the present world, but cannot see things to come; and until the Lord make a gracious change upon him, he sees nothing of the worth of salvation, or of a need of Christ, and making any serious preparation for eternity. Hence comes that averseness of will to what is truly good, that he cannot endure to hear of it: Rom. viii. 7, 'The carnal mind is enmity against God, for it is not subject to the law of God, neither indeed can be.' And while the soul is so, it hath such a bent and proneness to that which is evil, or what concerns our interest in the world. Hence it is that our memories are so frail and slippery as to that which is good, and so tenacious of that which is evil. Good things easily slip from us, as clear water through a grate; but evil things, as slime and mud, stick with us. Hence comes his affections to be like tinder, to take fire at the spark of every temptation; the affections are awakened and stirred presently; but in holy things they are like fire in wet wood, that needs much blowing and much excitation. Hence it is that in the course of our lives we take up with the interests of the present world, and make no provision for a better life; we are 'lovers of pleasure more than lovers of God,' 2 Tim. iii. 4, and forsake God for the present world: 1 Tim. iv. 10, 'Demas hath forsaken us, having loved the present world.' Well, then, by a natural constitution we are utterly at a loss, the soul being destitute of a principle that should carry it to look after spiritual things as its great scope and interest; it wholly purveys and caters for bodily pleasures, and the honours and profits of the present life. Here lieth the great difficulty in the way of salvation.

2. This addictedness to present things is increased by our converse in the world; so that besides natural inclination there is inveterate custom, whereby this inclination to carnal satisfactions, such as riches, pleasures, ease, safety, and sensual delights, is strengthened and deeply engraved in us. The first years of a man's life are merely governed by sense, and the pleasures of the flesh are born and bred up with us, by which means we come to be stiff, and settled in a carnal frame. Custom is another nature, and therefore the more we are accustomed to delight in any course of life, we are weaned from it with the greater difficulty: Jer. xiii. 23, 'Can the Ethiopian change his skin, or the leopard his spots? then may ye also do good, who are accustomed to do evil.' Every act disposeth the soul to the habit, and after the habit or custom is produced, every new deliberate act adds a stiffness of bent, or sway unto the faculty, wherein the custom is seated; so that by degrees we grow into an obstinacy and strength of will in a carnal course, which is called 'hardness of heart,' or 'a heart of stone,' in scripture. A man is ensnared by his customs, whatever they be; for an addictedness in the general to carnal satisfactions brings a slavery upon us. So if men be addicted to this or that carnal satisfaction, it brings slavery upon them; as a man that is given to wine: Titus ii. 3, 'Not given to much wine.' The word in the original is δεδουλωμένος, ensnared by wine; or a man that is given to women: 2 Peter ii. 14, 'Having eyes full of adultery, and that cannot cease from sin.' Men by the tyranny of custom become so impotent to resist their lusts, that the satisfaction thereof becomes their very element, out of which they cannot live; it is their Eden and their heaven, their very paradise, though at length indeed they find it to be their hell. And of all evil customs, covetousness or worldliness is most dangerous, because it is of more credit and of less infamy in the world; and besides, it doth multiply its acts most, and works incessantly; and therefore we read of 'hearts exercised with covetous practices,' 2 Peter ii. 14. Their hearts are always running on the unworthy things of this present world. Now, while worldly men's hearts are so deeply dyed with such desires as carrieth them out to such things, they are hardly saved. Well, then, here is another reason of the difficulty that our lusts are born and bred with us from our infancy, and can plead prescription, and religion cometh afterwards, and findeth us biassed and prepossessed with other inclinations, which by reason of long use cannot easily be broken and shaken off.

3. Let us now consider the great efficacy and power which this inclination to temporal things hath upon us, and then you will see it is very difficult for us to enter into heaven.

[1.] This inclination and addictedness to present things weakens our sense of the world to come, and then our reward hath no influence upon us to move us and encourage us to serve God. Whilst the world bears bulk in our eye, heavenly things are of small or of no value with us. Satan blinds us as 'the god of this world,' 2 Cor. iv. 4; that is, by the love of the world. Christ cured the blind man by anointing his eyes with clay, but the devil puts out the eyes of our souls with this thick clay, for gold is so called: Hab. ii. 6, 'That ladeth himself with thick clay.' He blinds us so as we cannot have a true sight and persuasion of the truth and worth of things to come. We cannot look afar off into the other world: 2 Peter i. 9, 'He that lacketh these things is blind, and cannot see afar off.' Mountains seem molehills only at so great a distance; heaven is as a matter of nothing in comparison of present things; as in a prospective glass, look at one end of it, it greatens the object, at the other end it lessens the object. Thus when we look upon things to come through the glass of our own passions and carnal affections, they are nothing, they have no force nor power to move us. Saith Austin, Men do not look after heavenly things; *Quia in terrena prori dorsum eorum semper incurvum est,* their backs and necks are bowed down, that they cannot look upward and have any true sight of heavenly things; the world and the profits of it are real and substantial, but heavenly things are shadows, dreams, matters of conceit and mere imagination. And therefore, since this addictedness to temporal things hath such force upon us, to hinder the sight of the world to come, it must needs be difficult to us to be saved.

[2.] This addictedness to present delights and pleasures makes us impatient of the restraints of religion. Our natural desires carry us to those things which religion forbids. We cannot endure to be bridled, and kept from forbidden fruit, but we have all an appetite after it: Ps. ii. 3, 'Let us break their bonds asunder, and cast away their cords from us;' and Jer. v. 5, 'They have altogether broken the yoke and burst the bonds;' and Rom. viii. 7, 'The carnal mind is enmity against God, for it is not subject to the law of God, neither indeed can be.' *Nitimur in vetitum,* the prohibition doth but irritate corruption, as a stream if checked grows more furious. A man wholly given up to present satisfactions cannot endure the yokes and fetters religion would lay upon him; he would be a free creature, and live as he list. Indeed it is to be a captive creature, but this he accounts his liberty and freedom.

[3.] It maketh those duties seem irksome and unnecessary which are necessary as the way to salvation. Look into the book of God, and you will find we are called upon to strive to enter into heaven, and required 'to work out our salvation with fear and trembling,' Phil. ii. 12, with all holy solicitude, with all lively diligence, to be still employed in this work; 'To strive to enter in at the strait gate,' Luke xiii. 24; 'To walk worthy of God, who hath called us to his kingdom and glory,' 1 Thes. ii. 12. Now they that are addicted to ease, pleasure, and sensual delights cannot endure to be held to this work; they do either openly refuse this work, or delay it, which is the more modest denial, or else are cold in it. Some profane persons cast off all care of duty, as if religion were but a point of policy, heaven but a dream, and hell but a false fire, the gospel but a fable to busy men's heads with, and so resolve to please the flesh, and never trouble themselves about uncertain futurities. Many thus live in defiance of God and christianity, or else they delay to a more convenient season, they have no mind to the work: Acts xxiv. 25, 'Go thy way for this time; when I have a more convenient season, I will send for thee.' Lust must have present satisfaction, but Christ comes always out of season. When Christ makes an offer of heaven to their souls, hereafter they will be glad to hear of him, but now he comes before the time. As he said in Seneca, *A quinquagessima in otium discedam*—When I am fifty years old, then I will retire and study philosophy; so when their youthful vanities are spent, then they will look after these things. When the heart cannot keep out light and conviction of our duty, it seeks to keep off care, and so by making fair promises for the future we elude the importunity of present conviction. Or else a heart addicted to present satisfaction is very cold in religion, for the heart that is diverted by other pursuits cannot make religion its work, but only minds it by the by. The world, that is their business, but religion, that is put in the place of a recreation, and 'they mind earthly things,' Phil. iii. 19. Their heads and hearts are full of the world, so that they have no room for God. Their time, thoughts, discourses are wholly swallowed up of present things and complying with their present lusts.

[4.] This addictedness to present satisfactions will make us shrink at the trials God exerciseth us with before we go to heaven: Acts xiv. 22, 'Through much tribulation we must enter into the kingdom of God.' All good things are hard to come by, and God will show that heaven is worth something. When men have cheap thoughts of it, God will enhance the price of heaven. There must be striving and suffering before we get thither. The howling wilderness was the ready way to Canaan. The captain of our salvation was made perfect through suffering. We should else neither esteem the cross of Christ nor long for heaven; but present ease, present safety, present wealth doth wonderfully enchant us, to have good days here, and a quiet life without any trouble. If we could compound with God for this world and heaven too, then we should like it; but now, while we are so wholly inclined and addicted to present things, it must needs be a difficult thing to hear of trials and crosses that we must endure.

III. This difficulty must be sufficiently understood and seriously thought of by us. And here—

1. *Negatively.* We should so reflect upon the difficulty—(1.) Not to murmur against God because heaven is not to be had upon cheaper terms, and his ways lie so cross to our desires. Take heed of this; as if he were envious, and had not a good respect for the happiness of his creature. It is but reasonable that we should labour for heaven, as we do for all other things that are good and excellent; that which costs nothing is worth nothing. Besides, there are so many corruptions to be mortified, duties to be performed, and trials to be endured, that the faith of the elect 'may be found to the more praise and honour,' 1 Peter i. 7, and therefore all the pains, and shame, and loss, and trouble, is but

necessary. This is an ill use and end to murmur against God and repine against his sovereignty and dominion over the creature; and yet this is the use that many make of it: John vi. 60, 'Many of his disciples when they heard this, said, This is a hard saying, who can hear it?' What! nothing but mortifying our desires? nothing but thwarting our pleasing inclinations? nothing but performing such works which we cannot abide. Why hath God planted such desires in us if he would not have them satisfied? (2.) Not that we should despair or wholly despond, as those, Jer. xviii. 12, 'There is no hope, but we will walk after our own devices, and we will every one do the imagination of his evil heart;' and Jer. ii. 25, 'There is no hope; no, for I have loved strangers, and after them will I go.' Well, I see my condition is helpless and hopeless, therefore I resolve to make the best of it. When men hear how hard it is to go to heaven, they throw off all in a despondency, they shall never bring their hearts to this work. But we should not despair; and think it altogether impossible προαίρησις οὐκ ἐστὶν ἀδυνάτων; there cannot be a pursuit of that which is impossible. Past cure, they say, past care. Many, their affections are so strongly set upon carnal things, and they are so inveigled with the comforts of the world and the pleasures of the flesh, that they are discouraged, and so think it impossible to do otherwise than they do. Oh, no! that is not the use of it. Do not say, There is no hope of the world to come, therefore let us make the best of this life. God would have the fallen creature to despair of himself indeed: 'With man it is impossible, but with God all things are possible,' as in the next verse.

2. Positive. Why should these difficulties be thought of and laid to heart? to what end?

[1.] To prevent slightness of spirit. There is not a greater bane to religion, nor a greater judgment lights upon a creature, than a vain, frothy, slight heart; and therefore, to prevent this, and that we may in good earnest mind the things of our eternal peace, it is good to understand sufficiently the difficulty of it. A slight heart thinks it no such great matter to get to heaven, there is no such danger of missing it as men talk of; though they be not so religious as preachers would have them, nor so strict in conscience as to abstain from every smaller matter, yet through the grace of God they shall do well enough. Hell is made for the devil and devilish men and outrageous sinners; if they live fairly, and do as their neighbours do, they shall do well enough, though they do not pine and whine over their sins, or busy their brains about clearing up their interest in God; though they be not so nice and scrupulous, and take God's word too strictly, they shall do well enough for all that. Christians, these conceits, with which most men are leavened, are the bane, and eat out the heart of all religion. It is no such easy matter to go to heaven as the world imagines. A cold faint wish will never bring us thither, nor a desire to enjoy it when we can live here no longer. No; there must be watching, and labouring, and striving; this must be your great business and employment: Ps. xxvii. 4, 'One thing have I desired of the Lord, that will I seek after, that I may dwell in the house of the Lord all the days of my life, to behold the beauty of the Lord, and to inquire in his temple.' Oh! whatever is neglected, this business must be looked after day after day, namely, in what posture we are for the enjoyment of the blessed God: Phil. iii 12, διώκω, 'I follow after it, if that I may apprehend that for which also I am apprehended of Christ ;' Acts xxvi. 7, 'Unto which hope the twelve tribes served God instantly,' some render it; but it is ἐν ἐκτενείᾳ, with all their strength, 'day and night, hope to come.' Now it is necessary men should be sensible of the difficulty of being saved, to quicken their endeavours, and to bring them out of this slight frame of heart which is so natural to us; they think there needs not so much ado that we make the way straiter than God hath made it; they will not believe it is half so hard as it is. We see how great is our sloth and negligence. Now, if after he hath told us it is as hard as to go through the eye of a needle, what would we do if all were easy? Think of the difficulty to prevent this slight heart.

[2.] To keep us in a due dependence upon and an admiration of grace, God would have us sensible of the difficulty. What carnal hearts have we! how hard a matter is it to guide and govern them in the fear of God that we may keep up an admiration of the power of God that is perfected in our weakness! 2 Cor. xii. 10, 'When I am weak, then am I strong.' Alas! when we look to ourselves, we may cry out, when we think of these things, 'Who can be saved?' This awakeneth our prayers for special grace from day to day, and maketh us to look up to God for new supplies, because we find it is not in ourselves: 'The way of man is not in himself, it is not in man that walketh to direct his steps,' Jer. x. 23; 'We are not sufficient of ourselves to think anything as of ourselves, but our sufficiency is of God,' 2 Cor. iii. 5.

[3.] That we may be forearmed with resolutions. They that take a walk for recreation do not prepare for all weathers, as they that resolve upon a journey; or they that go to sea for pleasure, if they see a storm coming, easily go to shore again, but they that go for business resolve upon all hazards to finish their voyage. Now, that we may resolve to make a thorough work of christianity, and to hold on our way in Christ's strength notwithstanding all difficulty, our Lord would have us to sit down and count the charges, Luke xiv. 28, to consider what it will cost us to go to heaven; not to discourage us, but to provoke us to put on the more resolution, lest we tire when we find more difficulty than we did expect, and that we may resolve to hold on with God, whatever it cost us.

Use 1. This shows us the reason of that presumption which is so common. We use to say that despair kills thousands, but presumption its ten thousands. What is the reason that many presume? Oh! the difficulties of salvation are not well weighed. True hope is a middle thing between presumption and despair; the object of hope is *bonum, futurum, arduum, sed possibile*. Hope considers its object as hard, for that which is easy to come by is as if it were already enjoyed; a man cannot be said to hope for that which he may have with the turn of his hand. Well, then, it considers the good to come as difficult, to awaken diligence and serious endeavours; but then it considers it as possible, for otherwise we are really discouraged from looking after it; for why should we look after that which is impossible? Paul's mariners gave over working when all hope that they should be saved was taken away, Acts xxvii. 20. But now presumption leaves out the difficulty, and reflects only upon the possibility. Some may be saved; surely God will not damn all his creatures; therefore I shall be saved. But suppose the contrary, few are saved; then what shall become of me? On the other side, despair reflects only upon the difficulty, and leaves out the possibility. Oh! it is hard, it is impossible with men, therefore they give it over. I shall make no work of it, saith despair. Now the scripture, that would breed and nourish in us a true hope, doth all along lay forth the difficulty, to prevent slightness of spirit, and yet represents the possibility to prevent despair; the difficulties to quicken our endeavours, and the possibility to encourage men to hope for the grace of God.

2. It presseth us to mortify our addictedness to present things. O christians! if you could overcome the world, you pluck out the root of all temptations, and then the commandments of God would not be grievous: 1 John v. 3, 4, 'For this is the victory whereby we overcome the world, even our faith;' the world is the great let which hinders us from keeping the command, from being so exact, punctual, and sincere with God. Overcome the world, and the work will be easy. Take heed of pleasing the flesh, or letting the world have too great an interest in your hearts; let it not seem a great thing in your eye. Until your hearts are drawn off from present things, and you are wholly baptized into that spirit that suits with the world to come, to make that your main care and desire, you will never prosper in heaven's way, until your thoughts be loosened from the world, and you are carried out more to heaven and heavenly things. Consider, why should you be addicted to present things? You that are strangers and not inhabitants, your happiness lies not here: 'If our hopes were only in this life, we were of all men most miserable,' 1 Cor. xv. 19. We are but probationers for heaven: 'Our conversation should be in heaven,' Phil. iii. 20.

3. To fortify us against the difficulties in the way of salvation. You must be at some pains and labour: John vi. 27, 'Labour not for the meat that perisheth, but for that meat that endureth unto everlasting life.' Do not slacken your endeavours. To quicken you, consider—

[1.] If you love your salvation, you will be at some cost about it. It it is a sign you make no reckoning of heaven, and have no great sense of things to come, when you grudge your pains; it is a sign you slight it when you are so slow in the pursuit of it: Phil. iii. 14, 'I press towards the mark for the prize of the high calling of God in Christ Jesus.' Oh! did you value heaven, or had you any esteem of heavenly things, you would not think much of a little pains, of striving with God in prayer, of wrestling, and denying your lusts, to bring your hearts to a readiness and cheerfulness in the service of the ever-living God. No trade in the world you can drive on by idleness. Who ever prospered in any course of living if he followed it with a slack hand? We cannot think to have those great invisible things of the Lord's kingdom and his glory if you will do nothing for it.

[2.] There is difficulty both in the way to heaven and hell. Lusts are ravenous things, and cannot be fed or kept without much self-denial. You must deny yourselves either for God or the devil. You must deny your comforts, and your estate. Men will venture much for their lusts and for their sensuality; there must be a great deal of charge to feed this humour, to satisfy the pleasures of the flesh; it is costly to be an epicure. Worldliness wastes the spirits, racks the brain. For ambition, how many hazards do men run for their greatness in the world? how many men sacrifice their lives upon the point of honour, for revenge, and for a little vainglory! Now, if a man will take pains to go to hell, shall he not take pains to go to heaven? When men will be at such costs for lusts as to deny conscience and slight many of the comforts of the present world for lust's sake, shall we take no pains and exercise no self-denial for heaven?

[3.] If we be at a little labour it will not be in vain in the Lord: 1 Cor. xv. 58, 'Be steadfast and unmovable, always abounding in the work of the Lord, forasmuch as you know that your labour is not in vain in the Lord.' Whether you consider your vales or wages, your labour is not in vain. Your vales: Christ's servants have a great deal of comfort and sweetness: Prov. iii. 17, 'Her ways are ways of pleasantness, and all her paths are peace.' And for the world to come there is a full and sure reward; therefore do not stick at a little pains; though it be difficult, yet remember it is for salvation.

4. Let us look to our own selves; how is it with us? are we in the way to hell or heaven? Let us look to our own standing; do we leave the boat to the stream? do we give up ourselves to the sway of our corrupt and carnal affections? or else do we row against the stream and current of flesh and blood? It is no easy matter to be saved. I do not ask now what will become of those that never minded salvation, that never busied their thoughts about it, but even in effect say, Let them take heaven that list; but I ask, what will become of those slothful perfunctory christians that count a little slight and formal religion enough, which is without any life, alacrity, and power? Will this do the deed? Such will fall short of heaven.

SERMON XIV.

And Jesus, looking upon them, saith, With men it is impossible, but not with God; for with God all things are possible.—MARK x. 27.

WE have seen the disciples' wonder returning. Christ, that is never wanting to his in their trouble and astonishment, graciously looketh upon them, and in words full of comfort giveth a solution of that which was such a riddle to them, 'And Jesus, looking upon them, saith,' &c. Here we have—

1. Christ's gesture, 'Jesus looked upon them.'
2. Christ's answer, by a distinction how it is impossible and how not. In the first part of the distinction there is a concession, 'That with men it is impossible.' In the second branch there is a correction, 'But not with God.' This latter branch is confirmed by a general reason, 'For with God all things are possible.' In this text three

things are asserted—(1.) The impotency of nature; (2.) The sovereign efficacy of grace; (3.) The general truth upon which it is grounded, and that is the omnipotency of God. Accordingly the points are three—

1. That it is impossible for mere man by his own natural strength to get to heaven.

2. Men that are discouraged with the sense of their own impotency should consider the power of God.

3. That this power of God is all-sufficient, and can do all things.

Doct. 1. That it is impossible for mere man by his own natural strength to get to heaven.

Two things will evidence that—

1. There is *legalis exclusio;* we are all excluded by the sentence of God's law, and therefore it is impossible for any mere man to get to heaven. The law knows no way of justifying a sinner, but only of saving a creature holy and innocent; and if we be not holy and innocent, there is a sentence in force against us. That scripture expresses the tenor of the law: Gal. iii. 10, 'For as many as are of the works of the law are under the curse; for it is written, Cursed is every one that continueth not in all things which are written in the book of the law to do them.' An innocent nature is presupposed, for the person must *continue*, it doth not say *now begin.* The law doth not treat with man as lapsed or fallen, or as having already broken with God, but as in a good and sound estate; and therefore, since by the fall we are sinners, we are also under the curse by nature: Eph. ii. 3, 'And were by nature the children of wrath, even as others;' liable to the stroke of God's vindictive wrath. Well, now, 'with man it is impossible.' God hath placed a cherub with a flaming sword that keeps the passage into paradise. Heaven's gates are shut against us now. No mere man can appease an angry God, or redeem his soul from the curse that keeps him out of heaven. We are weak and without strength: Rom. v. 6, 'For when we were yet without strength, in due time Christ died for the ungodly.' Weakness or without strength there beareth the same sense with unworthiness. We are unable to perform the work or duty through the curse of the first covenant, and when we were altogether sinful and unworthy, then Christ died for us, and therefore it is impossible in regard of his legal exclusion; for suppose we could obey perfectly for the future, yet the paying of new debts doth not quit old scores. We are without strength, because we cannot expiate former transgressions, and so the law is become impossible through the weakness of our flesh: Rom. viii. 3, 'For what the law could not do in that it was weak through the flesh, God sending his own Son in the likeness of sinful flesh, and for sin condemned sin in the flesh.'

2. There is *evangelica difficultas;* there are difficulties by the gospel which mere man cannot overcome. Though the gospel giveth hopes of entrance into heaven, or reversing the strict conditions of the law, yet upon such terms as we must be beholden to grace for them. Christ, that requires the conditions of the gospel, must also give them to us: Acts v. 31, 'Him hath God exalted with his right hand to be a prince and a saviour, for to give repentance to Israel, and forgiveness of sins.' He is not only a prince and lawgiver, but also a saviour, or the author and fountain of grace. He doth not only give the privilege, remission;

but he gives the condition, repentance. If you conceive of Christ that he doth give the privilege, and require the conditions, and no more, you legalise Christ, as the Samaritans had a temple without an ark and a mercy-seat; so to speak of a law without grace, or if you separate the law of the gospel from the grace of the gospel, it is impossible.

Why is it thus impossible with man upon gospel terms? The legal impossibility all will acknowledge, but whence is this evangelical difficulty? It ariseth from three things—there is *vitiosa contrarietas*, a corrupt nature; there are *externa impedimenta*, many outward snares; and there is *inimica oppositio*, a great deal of enmity and opposition; therefore with man it is impossible.

[1.] There is *vitiosa contrarietas*, a corrupt nature, inclined to evil and averse to good: Gen. vi. 5, 'God saw that the wickedness of man was great in the earth, and that every imagination of the thoughts of his heart was only evil continually.' Man hath such a heart that, if left to itself, will always be minting evil thoughts and evil desires and carnal and inordinate motions. And as the heart of man is prone to evil, so it is averse to what is good, and so averse that it cannot do any of the great duties that God hath required of him. Look upon this averseness and impotency with respect to duties; he cannot know, believe, nor obey. He cannot know: 1 Cor. ii. 14, 'The natural man receiveth not the things of the Spirit of God; for they are foolishness unto him, neither can he know them, because they are spiritually discerned.' And he cannot believe: John vi. 44, 'No man can come to me, except the Father which hath sent me draw him;' it is not said, he *doth not*, but he *cannot*. And he cannot obey: Rom. viii. 7, 'The carnal mind is enmity against God, for it is not subject to the law of God, neither indeed can be.' And consider this impotency with respect to our thoughts, words, and deeds. He cannot think a good thought: 2 Cor. iii. 5, 'Not that we are sufficient of ourselves to think anything as of ourselves.' He cannot speak a good word: Mat. xii. 34, 'How can ye, being evil, speak good things?' He cannot do any good thing: John xv. 5, 'Without me ye can do nothing.' He doth not say, *nihil magnum*, you can do no great thing, you cannot acquit yourselves in some eminent temptation with honour, or in some notable duty; but *nihil*, you can do nothing without me. Well, then, when we cannot know, nor believe, nor obey, nor think, nor speak, not do anything without grace, surely it is impossible man of himself should perform the conditions of the gospel; he is wholly impotent, and unable to help himself.

[2.] There are *externa impedimenta*, outward impediments. Man is impotent and corrupt naturally, and his corruption is fed and strengthened by worldly things, and so his outward condition proves a snare to him: 1 John ii. 16, 'All that is in the world, the lusts of the flesh, the lust of the eyes, and the pride of life, is not of the Father, but is of the world.' Lust or distempered appetite finds an answerable diet. There are sensible objects which to our souls as thus constituted prove shrewd and dangerous temptations and snares. If we will find the lust, the world will afford us the object. For 'the lusts of the flesh,' there are pleasures and carnal delights to beset our souls, to inveigle and entice us from the strictness and severity of the christian profession. For 'the lusts of the eye' there are riches and all kinds of profits. For 'pride of life' there are dignities, and superiorities, and popular acclamations, and all sorts of preferments, or anything men are naturally proud of; so that a poor creature living in the midst of so many snares and temptations, may sadly cry out, as Bernard doth, Oh, woe is me! here are snares and temptations, and there is a sensual nature in us that is strongly drawn forth by all that is about us. It is true, riches, pleasures, and honours were not snares in their original institution or God's intention, but they prove so through our corrupt affection. God ordained them as *miserimæ necessitatis solatia*, as Jerome tells us, to be helps and comforts in our mortal condition; but through the strong affection we bear to them they prove snares: 2 Peter i. 4, 'The corruptions that are in the world through lust.' It is from unmortified corruption and lustings after them. Here, then, is that which increaseth the difficulty; these sensible objects to which we have a great inclination by nature, and which are continually present with us, do enchant and divert the heart from God and heavenly things, so that we either sin in them or for them. In the use of them, or for the getting and keeping of them, we offend God many times, and cross the rule that is given unto us; so that besides the natural impotency that is in us to all things spiritual, the soul is further depraved and corrupted by evil habits, or particular inclinations to any of these sensible objects. This is a superadded impediment to our condition by nature, as a crooked stick by growing becomes more difficult to be made straight. It is impossible for any mere man to receive the things of the Spirit, but much more for one that is wedded to any of these sensible things; for here Christ puts the impossibility upon a carnal rich man, because he hath so much of the world to divert his heart from God and true happiness. There are degrees of impossibilities; as some have fewer lets and impediments, and some have more, so it is more or less impossible, as they need more or less of God's special and extraordinary grace. For let us consider any dispositions to these sensible objects. Let us consider any of the dispositions to these sensible things, be it riches, 'the lusts of the eye,' so he calls covetousness, or an inclination to riches, for by the eye the heart is wounded, and so the difficulty of salvation is increased. When once men set up this as their scope, and make it their business to be rich and great in the world, 'They that will be rich fall into temptation and a snare,' 1 Tim. vi. 9. Or be it an inclination to honour, either to popularity or esteem of the people; or to ambition, or an inordinate desire of preferment by the magistrates and potentates of the world, John v. 44, 'How can ye believe that receive honour one of another?' it makes the impotency the greater. Or if it be an inclination to pleasures, 'Lovers of pleasures more than lovers of God,' 2 Tim. iii. 4. But mostly doth our Lord here put the difficulty upon riches. Why? Because that is a complicate temptation, and that is the fuel of pleasure, and the means by which we get to honours and greatness in the world; therefore here is the greater difficulty for a rich man in his corrupt estate to enter into the kingdom of God.

[3.] There is *inimica oppositio* if we would go to heaven, there are enemies to oppose. The devil: 1 Peter v. 8, 'Your adversary the devil as a roaring lion walketh about, seeking whom he may devour.' And wicked men: John xv. 19, 'If ye were of the world, the world would love its own, but because ye are not of the world, but I have chosen you out of the world, therefore the world hates you;' and 'Whosoever will live godly in Christ Jesus shall suffer persecution,' 2 Tim. iii. 12. But because the great opposition is from Satan, therefore I shall insist upon Eph. vi. 12, 'We wrestle not against flesh and blood, but against principalities, against the rulers of the darkness of this world, against spiritual wickedness in high places.' There is a more terrible and dangerous party against us than bodily and human power. Indeed we have bodily enemies, and they are great lets and great discouragements in the way of salvation, when the Lord lets loose their hands against us. These are but Satan's auxiliary forces whom he stirs up and employs; but the principal part of our conflict and wrestling is against devils and damned angels, enemies of great power and strength and influence upon the rulers of the darkness of this world; they have a mighty power upon the ignorant, carnal, and blind part of the world, and it is with these we contend and wrestle about the things which concern the honour of God, and the eternal welfare of our souls. Now this terrible opposition, how soon will it bear down a poor creature that stands merely by his own strength! Alas! set creature against creature, and Satan is too hard for us; he exceeds us in the rank of beings, and so we are no match for the devil. Our adversary is of a spiritual, immaterial substance, and so invisible both in his nature and approaches, and doth often reach us a deadly blow before we know it is he, and in the very simplicity of our hearts we run into the snare. And again, he is so restless in his assaults, so unwearied in his motions: 1 Peter v. 8, 'Your adversary the devil as a roaring lion walketh about, seeking whom he may devour.' The best christian will be surprised if there be not a greater than he to stand by him and for him. He is either weakening our comforts, or enticing us to sin, or making us weary of the ways of God. If he cannot pervert us, and draw us by some gross sin to dishonour God, he ceaseth not to vex us, and make our heavenly course uncomfortable to us. The devil never ceases to pursue his designs, but observes all our motions, all the postures of our spirits; when we are merry and when we are angry, when we are laughing and when we are mourning. He sees how the tree leans, and then joins his force to run us down. And he is of great power, one that can make terrible opposition, of great authority and influence over the carnal world, of great cunning and dexterity in setting our sins a-work. Certainly unless we 'be strong in the Lord, and in the power of his might,' there is no standing, Eph. vi. 10–12, compared.

But why hath God left it impossible to man, when he hath offered hopes by the new covenant?

(1.) That all the glory of the good that is in us may redound unto his grace: Eph. i. 6, 'To the praise of the glory of his grace, wherein he hath made us accepted in the beloved.' That is God's end in the new covenant, that we might ever admire and highly esteem his glorious grace. And therefore it is not only grace that opens the door, that removes the flaming sword that is against us, that takes away the curse of God, but in the whole business of salvation all is to be ascribed to grace: 'It is not of him that willeth, nor of him that runneth, but of God that showeth mercy,' Rom. ix. 16. The words *willeth* and *runneth* are considerable. The Lord, that brings us into this state, keeps us in this state.

(2.) To keep the creature in a constant dependence upon him, and that he might often hear from us. As long as a man is sufficient to himself, he never comes to God: Jer. ii. 31, 'We are lords, and will no more come unto thee.' If a man had the dominion over his own spirit, and were sufficient to himself, God would never hear from him. The prodigal went away from his father when he had his portion in his own hands and he never thought of returning till he had spent all and began to be in want, Luke xv. 14. Thus should we do with God. Prayer and all trading with heaven would cease if we were sufficient of ourselves as to do anything; and therefore with man it is impossible.

Use 1. Take heed that you do not make a wrong use of this impossibility, namely, so as to be discouraged and throw off all, as if there were no hope. God hath left it so as that we may despair of our own strength, but not of his help. We should not be discouraged, since he worketh in us what he requireth of us.

1. God can overcome all this difficulty. He that made the heart is above it, and can frame it to himself. Evangelical difficulty lies in three things — the corruption of our nature, outward impediments, and Satan's opposition. Now the scripture represents God as able to do all for us. He can change our hearts, sanctify our condition, and help us to vanquish our temptations.

[1.] He can change our hearts by regeneration. Alas! we cannot change our natures or turn ourselves to God, and therefore we are apt to be cast down when we look upon God's holy ways and the strength of our own lusts. But God is able to change those hearts of ours, and take away their reluctancy; not by making a violent impression, as we force a stone upward, but by imprinting in our hearts the habits of grace, whereby we are carried out willingly in the ways of God, and so our business becomes easy: Titus iii. 4, 'According to his mercy he saved us, by the washing of regeneration, and renewing of the Holy Ghost;' 'No man can come unto me except the Father which hath sent me draw him,' John vi. 44; 'Draw me, and we will run after thee,' Cant. i. 4. He puts forth his mighty power upon the heart, and changeth the bent of our souls, and so we come in.

[2.] God can sanctify our condition, that it shall not be a snare. Christians, whatever you think of it, it is not easy to keep yourselves unspotted from the world, to live in the midst of so many temptations and to carry on an equal, holy, heavenly frame of heart, such as the apostle mentions, 1 Cor. vii. 29–31, 'It remains that they that have wives be as though they had none, and they that weep, as though they wept not; and they that rejoice, as though they rejoiced not; and they that buy, as though they possessed not; and they that use this world, as not abusing it.' This is our duty; but how shall we do to get such a weaned heart? With man it is impossible but not with God. He can give a rich man such grace as to contemn the world, to lay up treasures in heaven, and upon religious reasons to leave all for Christ's sake. God taught Paul this holy weanedness: Phil. iv. 12, 'I know both how to be abased, and I know how to abound; everywhere and in all things I am instructed both to be full and to be hungry, both to abound and to suffer need.' And he can teach it you if you will wait upon him. Our own natural spirits indeed carrieth us quite another way: James iv. 5, 6, 'The spirit that dwelleth in us lusteth to envy, but he giveth more grace.' Our natural spirit is all for temporal things; it envies the greatness of others, it designs for ourselves; but when lusts rage, he can bridle them; the Lord is able to give us a holy weanedness and moderation of our desires in the midst of all those baits and snares that we are compassed about withal.

[3.] To conquer temptations. It is God that rescues the prey, and plucked us at first by a strong hand out of Satan's power: Luke xi. 21, 22, 'When the strong man armed keepeth his palace, his goods are in peace; but when a stronger than he shall come upon him, and overcome him, he taketh from him all his armour, wherein he trusted, and divideth his spoils.' God can bind Satan, and dispossess him, and 'recover you out of the snares of the devil, wherein you are taken captive by him at his will,' 2 Tim. ii. 26. And when we are once in a state of grace, he can preserve you in despite of men and devils. The world assaults the children of God with great force and power, and the devil is in the design; but, saith the apostle, 'Greater is he that is in you than he that is in the world,' John iv. 4. God is greater in counsel, greater in strength, greater in his providence and watchfulness for the good of his people. Till this divine power interpose it can never be.

[4.] We have no reason to doubt of his will, for he hath promised to take away the heart of stone: Ezek. xxxvi. 26, 'A new heart will I give you, and a new spirit will I put within you, and I will take away the stony heart out of your flesh, and I will give you an heart of flesh.' There is nothing within the compass of our christian calling of which we have not a promise in the covenant. The precept and the promise go hand-in-hand; therefore the promise will be made good, and so we have no reason to despair, but humbly wait upon God in the use of means till these promises be accomplished.

2. What use shall we make of it then? Go to God for this power, and give God all the glory of any saving grace wrought in us by this power.

[1.] Go to God for this power when you are sensible of your impotency. In vain do we talk of power to men that are not sensible of weakness, and will not so much as essay whether they have power or no: 2 Cor. xii. 10, 'When I am weak, then am I strong.' When creatures are helpless and shiftless, God takes pity upon them; therefore when you have been tugging and wrestling in the business of salvation, and it doth not come on kindly, but you find your weakness, then you may come to God for his power. Bewail your impotency, and say, as Jehoshaphat, 2 Chron. xx. 12, 'Lord, we have no might, neither know we what to do, but our eyes are unto thee;' or rather as Ephraim, Jer. xxxi. 18, 'Thou hast chastised me, and I was chastised, as a bullock unaccustomed to the yoke; turn thou me, and I shall be turned.' God's chastisement revived the sense of his duty, and thinking of his duty made him feel his impotency, and feeling his impotency that made him groan to God, and wait for his power. Oh! it is well when practical experience convinceth us of our weakness and necessities, and our weakness and necessities lead us to the promises, and the promises to Christ, in whom they are 'Yea and amen;' and Christ to God as the fountain of grace, and then we rest upon the power of God. And therefore, since it is impossible with man, go to God, and say, Lord, I confess the debt, I acknowledge my impotency, but thou hast forbidden me to despair, therefore I come to thee; give what thou commandest, and command what thou wilt.

[2.] If it be impossible with men, let God have all the glory of any saving grace wrought in thee. Mark this, because there is a deceit. God must not only have some glory, but all the glory, for in the new covenant there is no glorying but in the Lord. All will acknowledge and count it a piece of religious manners to speak of some help of grace, but they do not give it its due praise. The pharisee could say, 'God, I thank thee I am not as other men,' Luke xviii. 11. As, for instance, if a man should say, It is all from God indeed, but only in a Pelagian sense, as he is *author naturæ*, the author of nature, as he created us at first with a rational soul, and gave us an understanding and will, whereby he enableth us freely to choose that which is good; here is God's power acknowledged, but at too remote a distance. The very heathens would acknowledge grace, as sacrilegious as they were in robbing God of his due. *Quod vivamus*, that we live, and that we had reasonable natures, that was the gift of the gods; but *quod bene vivamus*, that we live well, that is of ourselves. This confounds nature and grace; we sacrifice the wax to God, and keep the honey to ourselves. Again, we should acknowledge God not only in the grace of external revelation, revealing the object, that God hath given us an excellent religion, there is his grace, but in working upon the faculty. Here God is acknowledged, but at too low a rate, for we need not only the sunlight, but eyes: Eph. i. 18, 'The eyes of your understanding being opened, that ye may know what is the hope of his calling, and what the riches of the glory of his inheritance in the saints.' Or if we will go further, and acknowledge internal grace is necessary, but not absolutely necessary, but only for facilitation, to do it the more easily, for the work is very difficult if mere man were left to himself; here God's power is acknowledged, but not enough; grace is absolutely necessary, not as a horse to a journey, but as legs and feet. Again, if we should acknowledge it as absolutely necessary for God to excite and move us, but give the main stroke to our own will, this is not praise high enough; it is God inclines the heart, it is God that gives us the will, the beginning and ending of all is from him; with man it is impossible, therefore God must have all the glory.

Doct. 2. Those that have a deep sense of their sinful impotency and carnal distempers should seriously consider and encourage themselves by the sovereign power of God's grace.

Of the power of God as generally considered I shall speak by and by. Now I shall speak of it as it worketh in a way of grace, to bring us into a state of grace, and to preserve us therein.

1. The scripture speaks of this power that bringeth us into a state

of grace: Eph. i. 19, 'And what is the exceeding greatness of his power to us-ward who believe, according to the working of his mighty power.' Mark, there is a mighty glorious power that is seen in converting a sinner, and turning him from sin to holiness, even greater than the power by which God made the world. When God made the world, as there was nothing to help, so there was nothing to hinder; but such is the perverseness of man's nature within, such is the opposition from without, and so great an enemy is Satan, that nothing less than God's powerful grace can begin such a saving work in them: 2 Peter i. 3, 'According as his divine power hath given unto us all things that pertain unto life and godliness.' There is a divine power that gives us life, or a gracious spirit within, and a divine power that helps us to walk in a course of godliness without. So Rom. xi. 23, 'God is able to graff them in again.' The Jews are of all people most obstinate and averse from God; they have no natural goodness of disposition in them; they 'please not God, and are contrary to all men;' and shall the Jews be converted? Yes; 'for God is able to graff them in again,' and bring them into a state of grace.

2. This power of grace is seen in preserving us in a state of grace, and carrying on this work in despite of men and devils, till grace be crowned in glory. Alas! if God did never so much for us at first, yet if he did not keep us, we should be made a prey, and be shipwrecked in the haven's mouth; therefore from first to last the power of God is seen—

[1.] In defending the habit of grace that is begun in the soul. When the apostle had told us that God 'of his abundant mercy had begotten us again unto a lively hope,' 1 Peter i. 3, presently he saith, ver. 5, 'Who are kept by the power of God through faith unto salvation.' First we are begotten, then kept, heaven is kept for us, and we are kept for it; first the power of grace is a quickening power, and then a preserving power, defending the work God hath begun in us.

[2.] God actuates and quickens our graces in us: 'It is God which worketh in you to will and to do of his good pleasure,' Phil. ii. 13, inspiring and breathing holy motions into us: 'Awake, O north wind; come, O south wind; blow upon my garden, that the spices thereof may flow forth,' Cant. iv. 16. And then strengthening those graces, and defending them in all assaults and temptations, and causing us to grow: Col. i. 11, 'According to his glorious power, unto all patience and long-suffering, with joyfulness;' and Eph. iii. 16, 'That he would grant you, according to the riches of his glory, to be strengthened with might by his Spirit in the inner man.' And thus he continueth to do till they be perfected and completely glorified. Thus the Lord puts forth his power in defending, quickening, and increasing the grace that he hath wrought in us. We have seen there is a power put forth in a way of grace.

Now this should be considered by them that have a deep sense of their impotency and carnal distempers, for these reasons—

(1.) Because it is a great relief and prop to the soul. Oh! what cannot the working of this mighty power do for us! It exceedeth all the contrary power, whether in sin, the world, or the devil, and so answers our doubts and fears. But you will say, How is the power of

God such a relief to the soul? We can easily grant that God is able, but how shall we know that he will put forth this mighty power for us? I answer—(1.) In agonies of conscience; it is not the fear of hell only that troubles us, but our rooted distempers. Indeed, fears of hell awaken us, but when we come to see our inveterate and rooted carnal distempers, this troubles us. A poor soul that is anything far gone in this preparative work cries out, It is impossible this blind heart of mine should ever be enlightened, this vain mind be made serious, this hard heart be softened, these bewitching lusts renounced. It is the difficulty of parting with sin troubleth the conscience; therefore it is a relief to represent God as able. So in the midst of assaults and temptations, when we are dangerously beset, and fear we shall never be able to hold out, think of the power of God: 2 Tim. i. 12, 'I know whom I have believed, and I am persuaded that he is able to keep that which I have committed unto him against that day;' Jude 24, 'Unto him that is able to keep you from falling.' Our great trouble is for want of power. (2.) Again, it must needs be a relief to the soul, because if we be persuaded of his power it gives us some hope of his will also; so that we may go to God, and say as the leper, Mat. viii. 2, 'Lord, if thou wilt, thou canst make me clean.' Look, as beggars, if they see an ordinary man pass by, they do not use much clamour and importunity with him, but if they see a man well habited and well attended, they will follow after him, and plead hard for relief, and say, Sir, it is in the power of your hands to help us; so it doth encourage us to consider God is thus able, and can easily help, and do this for us. Nay (3.) God's power is engaged by promise, and therefore in many cases we may reason he is able to keep us, and therefore he will: Rom. xiv. 4, 'He shall be holden up, for God is able to make him stand;' and Rom. xi. 23, 'They shall be grafted in, for God is able to graft them in again.' The two pillars of the temple were called Jachin and Boaz, strength and stability; he hath strength, and therefore he will establish, for he hath power enough to make good his word.

(2.) Difficulties are left for this very end, to drive us to the throne of grace, that we may set the power of God a-work, that where man leaves off, there God may begin, and when the creature hath spent its allowance, the Creator may show forth his strength. Look, as in the outward case, God promiseth to deliver his people, 'when he seeth that their power is gone,' Deut xxxii. 26, so in the inward case, 'He giveth power to the faint, and to them that have no might he increaseth strength,' Isa. xl. 29.

Use 1. Let this support us in all the difficulties that we meet with in our way to heaven. When we are at a loss, God is not at a loss: Zech. viii. 6, 'If it be marvellous in the eyes of the remnant of this people in these days, should it also be marvellous in my eyes, saith the Lord.' God's power is not to be measured by our thoughts and by our scantling. Things may seem strange to us, but God can easily effect them. He that bringeth forth in the spring such beautiful flowers out of the earth, which looked with such a horrid and dismal face in the winter, what cannot he work in our souls? This is a great support to a fainting soul; it is easy with God to do what we count impossible. A stranger cannot charm a mastiff dog, when the master of the house can with a word. The shepherd can call off the dog from the flock; so the Lord can easily rebuke Satan, when he finds him most violent, and he can subdue and quell the strongest lust.

2. When we are sensible of our weakness, let us observe the laws God hath set to the creatures. God will be attended upon, and waited for in the use of means. We must come to the throne of grace, and therefore our Lord, when he teacheth us to pray, he saith, 'Thine is the kingdom, the power, and the glory.' We must come to God, if we would have his power exerted; and God will be believed in, and have his power rested upon and applied: Mark xv. 28, 'O woman! great is thy faith; be it unto thee even as thou wilt;' John xi. 40, 'If thou wilt believe, thou shouldest see the glory of God;' that is, his power. If in desperate exigences we would have the power of God put forth, God must be sought to, and rested upon; and you must abstain from all sin. Sampson received strength no longer from God than he kept the law of his profession. When we entangle ourselves, and wilfully run into sin, and turn away from God, we discharge God from looking after us.

3. Observe what experience you have of the power of his grace; have you found it working in you? Mere reading and hearing will not evidence this truth so much as experience, that there is power put forth in a gracious way. Alas! otherwise we shall but speak of it as strangers to it, with cold notions; therefore can you say, 'I can do all things through Christ strengthening me?' Phil. iv. 13. And are you 'strong in the Lord, and in the power of his might?' Eph. vi. 10. Have you learned this holy art of conquering your distempers and temptations by the power of God?

SERMON XV.

With God all things are possible.—MARK x. 27.

DOCT. 3. I come to the general truth upon which this is grounded, that God is omnipotent, and can do all things. This I shall prove, explain, apply.

First, I shall prove by scripture and by reason.

1. By scripture, because it is an article of faith, and the scriptures that concern this point may be ranked thus: You will find the question propounded, Gen. xviii. 14, 'Is anything too hard for the Lord?' and this answered, Jer. xxxii. 17, 'There is nothing too hard for God.' The affirmative is in the text; and Mat. xix. 26, 'With God all things are possible;' and the negative, which binds it the more strongly, is in Luke i. 37, 'With God nothing shall be impossible.' The general is in the text, 'All things are possible with God;' and the particular is in Job xlii. 2, 'I know that thou canst do everything.' So that the power of God is not only propounded in the lump, but particularly parcelled out. Certainly God is almighty.

2. I shall prove it by reason.

[1.] The creation of the world shows it. The apostle tells us, Rom.

i. 20, 'That the invisible things of him from the creation of the world are clearly seen, being understood by the things that are made, even his eternal power and godhead.' If you will know what God is, look upon his creatures. Every creature that hath passed his hand hath some prints and some stamp upon it, that may discover God, his godhead, and his power; that is the most visible thing seen in the creation. His wisdom and goodness is seen in the creation, but his power lies upward; and the most natural notion that we have of God is God Almighty. God made all the things that are seen, and more than are seen. He that made all things is omnipotent, and can do whatever is possible to be done. Creatures only can do what is possible to be done in their own kind. A man is one kind of creature, an angel is another; both have their essence limited. Man can do things belonging to a man, an angel can do all things belonging to an angel; but God made all things, and therefore he can do all things. In short, 'He that stretcheth out the heavens as a curtain,' Isa. xl. 22, he that handles the great ocean as a child newly come out of the womb, he that 'appointed the clouds a garment thereof, and thick darkness a swaddling band for it,' Job xxxviii. 8, 9, 'He that hangs the earth upon nothing,' Job xxvi. 7, What cannot he do? The earth, that vast and ponderous body, has nothing to support it but the fluid air, that will not so much as support a pin or feather. It hangs like a ball in the midst of the heavens; where are the pillars and props that sustain this mighty mass? It is upheld by nothing but the power of God. And for the manner of making, how did he make all things? By his word. This great builder needed no instruments and tools: Heb. xi. 10, 'Whose builder and maker is God;' he commanded, and they were created,' Ps. xlviii. 5. What more easy than a word? One asks what is become of the tools and engines wherewith God made the world? Tully brings in a philosopher disputing against the creation of the world: With what spade did God dig the sea? where was the trowel wherewith he arched the heavens? and the line and plummet by which he laid forth the foundations of the earth? There was nothing but his word that brought all things out of the womb of nothing. This is the omnipotent, the glorious God, that can do all things. And then, *ex parte termini*, he brought all things out of nothing, which philosophers could not so much as conceive how it should be done. What a large stride and gap is there between being and not being! He that out of mere nothing brought forth all this world, certainly nothing can be too hard for him. A man cannot work without materials and preparations to his work, but God works when he hath nothing to work upon. As long as the creatures endure, as long as heaven and earth stands, which is a monument of God's power, we need not doubt of his all-sufficiency; and therefore in difficult and hazardous cases the scripture refers us to God as a creator: 1 Peter iv. 19, 'Wherefore let them that suffer according to the will of God commit the keeping of their souls to him in well-doing, as unto a faithful creator.' Why as unto a creator? At that time they carried their lives in their hands; they had nothing to subsist upon, no visible interests to defend them. Well, go on cheerfully in well-doing, and commit yourselves to him that can work all things out of nothing;

your souls, that is your lives; put your lives into the Creator's hands. There may be something of love in the expression, He that created you will take care of you, and there is also something of power implied; they had but only from day to day, and then he bids them trust in God as a creator. So Ps. cxxiv. 8, 'Our help is in the name of the Lord, who made heaven and earth.' Whilst you see heaven and earth, doubt not of God. He hath not lost nor spent his power. He that made heaven and earth is as ready and as able to work as he did at first. Though a potter (it is Basil's similitude) make a thousand vessels, his art is not lessened by the making, but increased rather; so whatever God doth, he doth not spend by giving; his power is the same, and his word is as mighty as ever: 'He spoke, and it was done, he commanded, and it stood fast;' Ps. xxxiii. 9, and that when there was nothing to work on. The will and the word of God, what mighty things can they do! He can do the greatest things without any visible means; things are done in the world, and nobody can tell how or by what. So the apostle tells us that he still acts according to his mighty power, which he wrought in the creation: 1 Cor. i. 28, 'God hath chosen τὰ μὴ ὄντα, things that are not, to bring to nought things that are.' God will ever triumph over human improbabilities, and will have no flesh to despair because of the smallness of the means, or to glory in his sight because of the greatness of them; for he doth all things, and that by his mighty power: Rom. iv. 17, his creating power is there again alluded to, 'He calleth those things that are not as though they were.' As when God created the world, he spoke light out of darkness; and so still when he finds nothing to work upon he 'calls things that are not as though they were;' speaking of fulfilling his promises to Abraham. So he works grace in the hearts of his people according to his creating power: 2 Cor. iv. 6, 'For God, who commanded the light to shine out of darkness, hath shined in our hearts to give us the knowledge of the glory of God in the face of Jesus Christ.' So that nature well considered is a great help to grace; when we consider the creation, and busy our thoughts therein, it helps us more to enlarge the power of God in our apprehensions.

[2.] As creation, so providence shows it. Take it either for God's external or internal providence.

(1.) His external providence, preserving all things in their proper place, and for their proper use: Heb. i. 3, 'He upholdeth all things by the word of his power.' All things that are in the world are held up by God's hand; they do not subsist by their own nature so much as by divine manutenency: 'He upholds all things.' It is an allusion to a weighty body that is held up by the hand of man, which if loosened, it falls to the ground; so the creature would fall to nothing if not kept up by God. Now what an almighty grasp hath he that holds up all things! He that feedeth so many mouths with the opening the hand of his bounty: Ps. cxlv. 15, 16, 'The eyes of all wait upon thee, and thou givest them their meat in due season: thou openest thy hands, and satisfiest the desire of every living thing;' he that sustains and guides so many creatures, that preserves the confederacies of nature, that sets bounds to the sea, and makes decrees for the waves to obey, beyond which they shall not pass: Jer. v. 22, 'Which have placed the sand for the bounds of the sea, by a perpetual decree, that it cannot pass it; and though the waves thereof toss themselves, yet can they not prevail; though they roar, yet can they not pass over it;' he that holds the winds in his fist, is not he mighty and strong? And therefore, if God should but loosen his hand, the world would soon fall into confusion and nothing. Thus his sustaining and preserving all things speaks him an all-powerful God.

(2.) His internal providence. The providence of God is chiefly seen in his power over the spirits of men that are voluntary agents. He hath such a power over them that they are not masters of their own affections and dispositions, but act contrary many times to their intended purposes: Prov. xxi. 1, 'The king's heart is in the hand of the Lord as the rivers of waters; he turneth it whither soever he will.' Look; as a man by cutting a channel draws the water this way or that way, hither and thither, so doth God move the hearts of all men in the world, nay, even of kings and princes: Prov. xvi. 7, 'When a man's ways please the Lord, he maketh even his enemies to be at peace with him.' Strange thing that God can put a bridle upon the spirits of men, and they shall be at peace with him whom they hated; their hearts are turned many times to what formerly they resolved against. Esau is an instance; he had vowed Jacob's death, and meets him with purpose to destroy him, but when God brings them together, Esau falls embracing of Jacob: Gen. xxxiii. 4, 'And Esau ran to meet him, and embraced him, and fell on his neck, and kissed him.' Egypt dismissed Israel with jewels. Balaam comes to curse, and he falls a blessing Israel. This bridling, turning, changing the hearts of men, it is a notable discovery of God's omnipotency. Look, as there is more power seen in governing a skittish horse than in rolling a stone, so in ruling those beings which have a principle of resistance doth the Lord show forth his power. Angels, men, and devils can do nothing but as God will, and as God gives them leave. The devils are fain to ask Christ's leave to enter into the herd of swine, Mat. viii. 31; and therefore how may the flock of Christ's sheep rest secure under the power of his providence, when those damned spirits are held in by the irresistible providence of God that they can do nothing but what God will! As Tertullian said, If the bristles of swine be numbered, much more are the hairs of the saints. God hath such a mighty power, that not a creature can be troubled without his leave, even by those spirits that are most opposite to him; so that his power over the affections and hearts of men shows he is a great and mighty God.

[3.] That God is almighty appears by the strength that is in creatures, which is an effect and shadow of the power of God. All the power that is in creatures is from God, and he wastes not by giving as we do. That expression suits to this case; God took from the spirit of Moses, and put it upon the elders, and yet Moses had not the less because of their participation. We cannot communicate to others but we lessen ourselves, but God remaineth in an infinite fulness; and therefore, if he hath given power to creatures, he hath more power himself. Now there is great power in creatures: Job xli. 8, Job tells us of great whales that have bones as brass, and strong as pieces of iron; and David tells us of 'angels that excel in strength,' Ps.

cxxxiii. 20, so that one of them slew a hundred fourscore and five thousand in one night in Sennacherib's host. And if there be such strength in creatures, what is there in God from whom they have it? for nothing is in the effect but what was first in the cause.

Secondly, Let me come to explain this power of God by three distinctions—

1. God's power is twofold—either absolute or actual. (1.) His absolute power is that by which he can do that which he never will do. This is spoken of Mat. xxvi. 53, 'Thinkest thou not that I cannot now pray to my Father, and he shall presently give me more than twelve legions of angels?' Mat. iii. 9, 'God is able of these stones to raise up children to Abraham;' he can do more than ever he did or will do. He can do not only what men and angels conceive can be done, but what he himself conceiveth can be done. (2.) His actual power is that by which he doth whatever he will: Ps. cxv. 3, 'Our God is in the heavens; he hath done whatsoever he pleaseth;' and Ps. cxxxv. 6, 'Whatsoever the Lord pleased, that did he in heaven and in earth, in the seas, and all deep places.' Never shall anything be done but what God wills, and what God wills shall surely come to pass; which is a notable support in all accidents.

2. God's power is ordinary and extraordinary. (1.) Ordinary is that which is according to the course of second causes and law of nature, when he preserves the creatures, and works by them according to the order which he himself hath established: Ps. cxix. 91, 'They continue this day according to thine ordinance, for all are thy servants.' All the creatures, sun, moon, and stars, do keep the track and path which God hath set unto them, and God preserves the beings of all things, and keeps the 'covenant of night and day,' as it is called in the prophet. (2.) There is God's extraordinary power, by which he can suspend the whole course of nature, as he hath done sometimes upon eminent occasions; as when the sun stood still in the valley of Ajalom, Josh. x. 12, 13, or when the sun went back ten degrees on the dial of Ahaz, 2 Kings xx. 11; his interdicting the Red Sea that it should not flow, Exod. xiv. 21, 22; his causing iron, which is a heavy body, to swim upon the top of the water at the prayer of Elisha, 2 Kings vi. 6; his suspending the burning of the fire when the three children were in the furnace, Dan. iii. 27; his shutting the mouths of the hungry lions when Daniel was in the den with them, Dan. vi. 22; his making the ravens, which are by nature birds of prey, to be caterers to Elijah, 1 Kings xvii. 6.

3. *Distinction.* There are *impossibilia naturæ*, and *impossibilia natura*, things impossible to nature, and things impossible by nature. Things impossible to nature God can do, but not things impossible by nature; he will do things above nature, and besides it, but nothing against it. Things impossible by nature are such as either respect the agent or the object. (1.) With respect to the agent, that which is repugnant to his own essential perfection. Thus God cannot lie: Titus i. 2, 'Which God, that cannot lie, hath promised;' Heb. vi. 18, 'That by two immutable things, in which it is impossible for God to lie, we may have strong consolation.' God cannot deny himself: 2 Tim. ii. 13, 'If we believe not, yet he abideth faithful; he cannot

'deny himself;' for these things imply weakness, and not power. God cannot die, God cannot sleep. It is no discredit to a wise man that he cannot play the fool, or to a valiant man that he cannot be a coward. God can do all things, so as that he is still God; those things that are repugnant to the perfection of his nature he cannot do. (2.) With respect to the object, such things as imply a contradiction; as that a thing should be, and not be, to make a creature finite and infinite, dependent and independent at the same time and in the same respect; limited to a place and yet in every place; to make the sun shine and not to shine at the same time; these are against the nature of the things themselves. These distinctions have their use in many controversies that are about religion.

Use. For exhortation. To press you to believe that God is almighty, and to improve it.

1. Believe it. Need we press men to that? It is a piece of natural divinity, a truth held forth to us, not only in the book of scripture, but of nature. That light which finds out a deity will discover him to be almighty; and therefore need we any great ado to persuade men to believe it? Yes, certainly; for this is the great thing that we question in cases of difficulty; we doubt more of the power of God than of his will. Our seeming doubts of his will are but pretences to cover our shameful and atheistical doubts of his power; that which works subtly and underground in us, and weakens our confidence in God, and hinders the rejoicing of our faith, is a doubt of his power. Surely God knows us better than we do ourselves; and the scripture shows all along that our doubts are about God's power. When there was a promise brought from God that Sarah should conceive with child, she did not believe the promise: Gen. xviii. 13, 14, 'And the Lord said unto Abraham, Wherefore did Sarah laugh, saying, Shall I of a surety bear a child, which am old? Is anything too hard for the Lord?' There was her doubt and difficulty. So Moses, the man of God, the Lord had told him face to face that he would feed his people, and give them flesh to eat, and he doubted of God's power: Num. xi. 21, 23, 'The people among whom I am are six hundred thousand footmen, and thou hast said, I will give them flesh, that they may eat a whole month. Shall the flocks and herds be slain for them to suffice them? or shall all the fish of the sea be gathered together for them to suffice them? And the Lord said unto Moses, Is the Lord's hand waxed short?' So when the prophet foretold there should be such plenty in Samaria, where there was great scarcity, saith the nobleman, 2 Kings vii. 2, 'Behold, if the Lord should make windows in heaven, might this thing be?' There was his doubt. So the Virgin Mary, when the angel comes with the message of the great mystery of the incarnation of the Son of God, that he should be born of her, Luke i. 34, 'Then said Mary unto the angel, How can this be, seeing I know not a man?' At this rate still doth unbelief speak in the wilderness; as the children of Israel: Ps. lxxviii. 19, 20, 'Can God furnish a table in the wilderness? Behold he smote the rock, that the waters gushed out, and the streams overflowed; can he give bread also? can he provide flesh for his people?' Certainly the scripture knows what is the special language of our hearts better than we ourselves. Now unbelief is still

represented as doubting of God's power. Besides, doubts haunt us only in times of difficulty, and when mercies expected are hard to come by. If we did doubt of God's will because of our unworthiness, why do we not doubt at other times, when things are easy? But these doubts surprise us only when the things we expect from God according to his promises are difficult and hard to come by. And the reason why we are so apt to doubt of God's power is the imperfection of our thoughts about God's being. We are inured to principles of sense, and converse with limited beings, and therefore confine God to a circle of our own making: Ps. lxxviii. 41, 'They turned back and tempted God, and limited the Holy One of Israel.' We confine God to the course of second causes, with which we wholly converse, and when there is difficulty, there our hearts fail; therefore there is need to press you to believe God's power.

2. Improve it to strengthen our faith and encourage our obedience.

[1.] To strengthen our faith, either in prayer or in waiting. In prayer: Oh! when you come to God, remember 'he is able to do abundantly above all that we ask or think,' Eph. iii. 20. How hard and difficult soever the thing be that we ask of God, he is able to do it. When our Lord taught us to pray, what are the encouragements he gives us? see the conclusion of the Lord's prayer, Mat. vi. 13, 'Thine is the kingdom, the power, and the glory.' As God hath a kingdom and authority to dispose of all things for his glory and our good, so he hath a power to back it; it is not an empty title. Pray for help with such cheerfulness and confidence as if it were the easiest thing in the world to be done. All those things that are so difficult to be obtained, either the sanctification of our souls, or the promotion of Christ's kingdom, or any of those things, 'Thine is the power;' there is that which holds up our hands in prayer, and gives us confidence towards God. So to strengthen our faith in waiting, touching the performance of all God's promises for ourselves and others. Abraham believed above hope and against hope. Why? 'Being fully persuaded that what he had promised he was able also to perform,' Rom. iv. 21. This is the great security of the soul, that confirms us in waiting upon God, when the accomplishment of his promises is unlikely to reason, 'God is able.' If you expect of God preservation in the midst of difficulties, such a fickle and such a changeable creature as man is, how can that be? 1 Peter i. 5, 'Who are kept by the power of God through faith unto salvation.' The power of God is engaged for our defence. So for temporal difficulties, when we see no means, no likelihood to escape, yet we are not thoughtful of this matter, for 'our God whom we serve is able to deliver us from the burning fiery furnace, and he will deliver us out of thy hand, O king,' Dan. iii. 17. In death, when we go to the grave, to moulder into dust and rottenness, then to look upon the morsels of worms as parcels of the resurrection, what shall uphold and support our hearts in waiting upon God for this? Phil. iii. 21, 'Who shall change our vile body, that it may be fashioned like unto his glorious body, according to the working whereby he is able to subdue all things unto himself.' The scripture still refers us to the mighty power of God, whereby he can subdue and cause all to fall under him. The destruction of antichrist and enemies of the church, who are supported by great and strongly combined interests, how can that ever be hoped for? Rev. xviii. 8, 'Her plagues shall come in one day, death and mourning, and famine, and she shall be utterly burnt with fire, for strong is the Lord God who judgeth her;' and that is the greatest cordial of the soul. The life of faith lies in the belief of God's power and all-sufficiency. He can raise up the church from her low condition, and all without any means; when all is dry bones, then God can put life into his people.

[2.] To encourage us in obedience; it is good to believe and improve the power of God.

(1.) That we may carry it more humbly and more dutifully: 1 Peter v. 6, 'Humble yourselves under the mighty hand of God.' This is that which begets a deep awe and reverence of his majesty. Shall we not submit to that God that is able to crush us? Oh! therefore let us study to please him in all things. When you sin, you bid defiance to the Almighty, and enter into the lists with God, and provoke him to jealousy: 1 Cor. x. 22, 'Do we provoke the Lord to jealousy? are we stronger than he?' Do you know what it is to dash against God and contest with God? He that is almighty is the most desirable friend or the most dreadful adversary, and therefore humble yourselves, and carry it dutifully towards him. Every one would be in with the Almighty. Be sure to keep in with the Lord: Deut. x. 17, 'For the Lord our God is a God of gods and Lord of lords, a great God, a mighty and a terrible, which regardeth not persons, nor taketh reward.' Will you provoke him and dare him to his face?

(2.) To keep us upright in obedience, without warping and using any carnal shifts: Gen. xvii. 1, 'I am the Almighty God; walk before me, and be thou perfect.' God alone is enough to you. The reason why we so often step out of the way is, because we do not believe God to be almighty, that he is more able to defend than man to hurt. Even God's own children may warp for want of a sound belief of this. Abraham saved himself by a lie, because he would not trust God with his preservation, Gen. xx. 11. Moses was backward to do the Lord's message, Exod. iv. 13, as if God could not bear him out before Pharaoh, and before the Egyptians. There was a promise Jacob should have the blessing, but Rebecca puts him upon using indirect means to obtain it, because she could not trust God's all-sufficiency to bring it about. He that will not trust God and rest upon his power cannot be long faithful to him; because they think there is not enough in God, they will seek elsewhere. All sincerity ariseth from these two things (and until you get your hearts into this frame you never will be sincere), submitting all things to God's will, and resting upon God's power. How desperate soever the case be, this will relieve you, and keep you sincere and comfortable, the Lord is a powerful God, and knows how to provide for his glory, and for your sustentation.

Now to quicken you thus to believe and improve the power of God, I will offer these considerations—

(1.) Consider the amplitude of God's power, which is not to be measured by our scantling and model. We can do something, but God can do all things; we must have matter prepared, but God works out of nothing; we do things difficultly, and must have time, but God can do all things in a moment; he needs no instruments or tools, no pattern or copy, but worketh all things according to the counsel of his will. We rust with age, and our strength is dried up, but 'the Lord's hand is not shortened that it cannot save,' Isa. lix. 1. His strength is never wasted or dried up. When anything is to be done or expected from God, is it greater than making the world? and God is where he was at first. Our knowledge of things is by effects, but God never had an effect adequate to his power; he hath done great things, but he hath power to do greater: Mal. ii. 15, 'And did not he make one? yet had he the residue of the Spirit.' When he created the world, he had the residue of the Spirit, he could have made more worlds. All created effects are finite, and therefore not fully answerable to the force of the cause. Let us be still enlarging in our thoughts of God's power. This is a power that needeth not the concurrence of visible means, but can work without them; yea, opposite power is no hindrance to God. Rubs are plain ground to him: Isa. xxvii. 4, 'Who would set the briers and thorns against me in battle? I would go through them, I would burn them together.' What can briers and thorns do against a devouring flame? they are fit fuel to increase the fire, but cannot hinder the burning. God works through all opposition: Isa. xliii. 13, 'I will work, and who shall let it.'

(2.) Consider this power is ready to be employed for our use, so far as it shall make for God's glory and our good. God is ours if we be in covenant with him; and if so, all that is in God is ours also, *quantus, quantus est*. As great as he is, God makes over himself in covenant. I am yours, therefore almightiness is yours, to be set a-work for you. And, as Aristotle said, τῶν φίλων παντα κόινα, all things are common between friends and confederates: 1 Kings xxii. 4, 'Jehoshaphat said unto the king of Israel, I am as thou art, my people as thy people, my horses as thy horses.' Surely, being in covenant with God, it is a relation of friendship, and whatever is God's is ours; and that is the reason of this expression, Eph. vi. 10, 'Be strong in the Lord, and in the power of his might.' In all our faintings and fears we should look upon God's almighty power as a guardian for our good. All that God hath is forthcoming for our use; as all other things, so his almighty power and strength.

(3.) Whatever his will is, or whatever God hath determined to do concerning us, yet he would have us magnify his power, and with comfort cast ourselves upon it: Isa. viii. 12, 13, 'Fear not their fear, nor be afraid; sanctify the Lord of hosts himself, and let him be your fear, and let him be your dread.' You should set power against power, that you may not be dismayed, Isa. l. 10. It is not meant spiritually only, but also in temporal cases: 'Let him trust in the name of the Lord, and stay upon his God.' You should comfort yourselves in the power and all-sufficiency of God.

(4.) Consider how angry God hath been with his children for not resting upon his power. Nothing hath hindered the discovery of God's power and the manifestation of his love to them so much as distrust of his power: Mark vi. 5, 'He could there do no mighty work.' It is not said, he would not, but he could not do any mighty works there, because of their unbelief. Unbelief doth put a bar and rub in the way of God's omnipotency; and John xi. 40, 'If thou wouldst believe, thou shouldst see the glory of God.' God doth not put forth himself because we do no more rest upon him and his all-sufficiency to help us. See how angry God hath been on this account with his own children and people; with Moses and Aaron: Mat. xx. 12, 'Because ye believed me not, to sanctify me in the eyes of the children of Israel, therefore ye shall not bring this congregation into the land which I have given them.' The believing of God's power is not determining the success, but when we encourage ourselves to pray and wait, and to be sincere and faithful upon the account of God's power, that God is able. Many troubles and perplexities have befallen God's children for not believing his power. Zacharias, John's father, was struck dumb for not believing: Luke i. 20, 'Behold, thou shalt be dumb, and not able to speak until the day that these things shall be performed, because thou believest not my words, which shall be fulfilled in their season.' And God let the nobleman live to see himself confuted, and then he was crushed to death: 2 Kings vii. 2, 'Then a lord on whose hand the king leaned answered the man of God, and said, Behold, if the Lord should make windows in heaven, might this thing be? And he said, Behold, thou shalt see it with thine eyes, but thou shalt not eat thereof.'

(5.) Consider it is a notable argument in prayer to conjure the Lord by his power. As the leper comes to Christ, Mat. viii. 2, 'Lord, if thou wilt, thou canst make me clean;' do what thou wilt, but this I know, that thou canst, thou hast power enough. See how Moses insinuates: Num. xiv. 15, 16, 'Now if thou shalt kill all this people as one man, then the nations which have heard the fame of thee will speak, saying, Because the Lord was not able to bring this people into the land which he sware unto them, therefore he hath slain them in the wilderness;' as if he should say, Lord, thou wouldst have the glory of thy power seen in the eyes of the nations, that they may know thee as a mighty powerful God; now they will say, The Lord was not able to bring them into Canaan.

(6.) All our courage, and all the strength of our comfort and obedience, and all the blessings of obedience, depends upon the belief and the improvement of God's power. Look into the book of God, and you shall see all the generous acts that worthy men have performed came from hence. Abraham, the father of the faithful, offered up his son, his only son, the son of the promise, and that freely; and why? 'Accounting that God was able to raise him up, even from the dead, from whence also he received him in a figure,' Heb. xi. 19. In such a trial, what would support and bear us out? So when the fiery furnace was heated seven times hotter than ordinary, burning and flaming exceedingly, the three children ventured into it upon this principle, 'Our God whom we serve is able to deliver us from the burning fiery furnace, and he will deliver us out of thy hand, O king,' Dan. iii. 17. What is the reason we are so cowardly and dastardly? We look to things sensible and visible, and cannot set the power of God against it or above them, and consider how he can bring good out of evil, and so carnal fears and hopes draw us aside. Why are we discouraged, and turn from God in difficult cases rather than in easy cases, but that we do not believe that he can do all things?

Paul believed, therefore in the face of opposition he goes on in his work unweariedly: 1 Tim. iv. 10, 'Therefore we both labour and suffer reproach, because we trust in the living God, who is the Saviour of all men, especially of them that believe.' This made him in the midst of reproaches and all manner of difficulties to go on with courage.

(7.) When we run to carnal shifts because we cannot trust this power of God, then we engage his strength, that should be for us, against us, and it is just with God to blast us. Jonah runs from his work, and God sends a storm after him. Jonah was afraid of the Ninevites, but mischief will sooner or latter overtake them that run from their duty, and they have worse inconveniences by their own shifts. Jacob would get the blessing by a wile, but that cost him dear; he was banished from his father's house upon it, lest Esau should kill him. Indirect courses will certainly prove a loss; though you may obtain your purpose, yet you plunge yourselves into greater difficulties afterward, and obtain your desires with more trouble than if you had waited upon God.

(8.) If the thing be not done for us which we need and desire when we trust upon the power of God, it is because it is not best for us. He that trusts upon the power of God cannot miscarry. A cross is best, and a low estate is best, and troubles are best. It is not for want of power and love that we are afflicted of God; he will deliver us and support us, and turn it to the best: Ps. lxxxiv. 11, 'For the Lord God is a sun and a shield, he will give grace and glory, and no good thing will he withhold from them that walk uprightly,' Ps. xxxiv. 9, 'The young lions do lack and suffer hunger, but they that seek the Lord shall not want any good thing.' If we want anything we would have, certainly it is not good for us.

(9.) The less power we have in ourselves, the more experience we have of God's power: Isa. xl. 29, 'He giveth power to the faint, and to them that have no might he increaseth strength.' So Deut. xxxii. 36, 'The Lord shall judge his people, and repent himself for his servants, when he seeth that their power is gone, and there is none shut up or left.' When human help begins to fail and is spent, then God's power is seen. The lean cheeks, and the faint voice, and the pale colour of a hunger-starved beggar moves more than all the canting entreaties of a sturdy one. When we are sufficiently humbled in the sense of our own unworthiness, and can entirely cast ourselves upon God, out of a confidence of his power, help will not be far off, for he really pities those that are indeed miserable, and have a sense of it, and sets his power on work for their relief.

(10.) We can never expect to be free from biting cares and perplexities about the various occurrences of this life until we can entirely cast ourselves upon God's all-sufficiency and power. Oh! but when you are once got upon the rock, then you will not be tossed with the uncertain waves: Isa. xxvi. 3, 4, 'Thou wilt keep him in perfect peace whose mind is stayed on thee, because he trusteth in thee: trust ye in the Lord for ever, for in the Lord Jehovah is everlasting strength.' In the ebbings and flowings of the creature a man is safe and fixed, for he hath that which answers all things. A man that hath no lands, yet if he hath money, the wise man tells us, that answereth all things.

and he may do well enough; so if a man hath nothing in the creature, yet if he hath the power of God, that answereth all things; he can rejoice in God when creatures fail, Heb. iii. 17, 18: 'As having nothing, yet possessing all things,' 2 Cor. vi. 10. The Almighty God carrieth the purse; we have all things in God, and he will supply us as he seeth it to be best with respect to his own glory and their eternal condition; and therefore, if you would be freed from all these floating uncertainties, and those tempestuous agitations of spirit by which you are tossed to and fro, you will never come to this till you encourage yourselves in the sense of God's power and all-sufficiency.

SERMONS UPON 2 THESSALONIANS I. 3.

SERMON I.

We are bound to thank God always for you, brethren, as it is meet, because that your faith groweth exceedingly, and the charity of every one of you all towards each other aboundeth.—2 Thes. i. 3.

The first part of this epistle is gratulatory, for the Thessalonians' perseverance and increase in grace; in which—(1.) The apostle giveth thanks to God; (2.) He telleth of the fame thereof in the churches, ver. 4, that he might the better encourage and exhort them to continue. By both he intimateth his love and spiritual affection to them.

In his thanksgiving to God we may take notice of—
1. The affectionate manner.
2. The matter of this thanksgiving, the increase of their faith and charity.

For the manner, it is done emphatically, 'We are bound to thank God always for you, as it is meet.' There are three emphatical words: 'Always;' this work of God among them was much upon his heart, and still give him new matter of praising God in their behalf. Then there is the obligation from justice and equity, signified in those words; ὀφείλομεν, 'We are bound,' and καθὼς ἄξιον ἐστιν, 'As it is meet;' there the expression is stronger. He doth not only tell them that he did it, but that he ought to do it, 'We are bound, and it is meet.' The first expression respects the mercy of God, so there was a debt of duty lying upon him; there was justice in the case. The second respects their estate, 'It was meet;' becoming the condition into which grace had brought them, and so there was equity in the case. Some refer this last clause to the performance of the duty, that he gave thanks as was meet; that is, in that manner which so great a benefit deserveth, not slightly and perfunctorily, but with great rejoicing. But rather it refers to the apostle's judgment of their estate: 'As it is meet,' hearing what I do, for me to judge of you; for a parallel expression doth thus explain it, Phil. i. 7, 'Even as it is meet for me to think thus of you all.' He conceived himself bound to judge of them all to be such as had owned the Lord with a sincere faith, and his people with a sincere love, and were likely to continue therein. Not his affection, but his judgment inclined him to think so; the church of the Thessalonians and every member thereof had given such real and evident signs of the grace of God in them, that he was bound to give God special thanks for this grace. The gospel hath and may be blessed in some places, so far that all the members of particular churches have given positive evidences of true grace in them, and that to the most discerning christians, and those who were best able to judge. It is yet possible, and therefore why should we not endeavour after it? It is meet for me to judge so; I hope you are so; therefore I count myself bound to give thanks to God.

From this preface four points are observable—

1. That it is a debt we owe to God to give thanks for his benefits.
2. That in thanksgiving to God we should specially own his spiritual benefits.
3. That not only the spiritual benefits vouchsafed to ourselves, but to others also, must be acknowledged with thankfulness.
4. That in thanksgiving for spiritual benefits, whether to ourselves or others, the increase of grace must be acknowledged, as well as the beginnings of it.

In the former epistle he gave thanks to God for their faith and love, here for the increase and growth of both, 'Your faith groweth exceedingly, and your love aboundeth.'

Doct. 1. That it is a debt we owe to God to give thanks for his benefits.

Paul saith here not only, 'We do,' but, 'We are bound.'

1. Justice requireth it, for the benefits were given upon this condition, that we should praise God for them: Ps. l. 15, 'Call upon me in the day of trouble; I will deliver thee, and thou shalt glorify me.' This is God's pact and agreement with us, that we shall have the benefit, and he will have the glory. As the king of Sodom said to Abraham, Give me the persons, and take the goods to thyself again, Gen. xiv. 21; so in effect God saith to us, You shall have the comfort, but let me have the honour. We ourselves consent to this covenant; we seldom make prayers in our distress but we promise thankfulness: Hosea xiv. 2, '.Take away all iniquity and receive us graciously, so will we render the calves of our lips.' We engage to offer praise when our requests are heard. Now, when God heareth and granteth our requests, there is an obligation upon us to glorify God for the mercies received. But now, though God be sought to in our necessities, there is no more mention of him when our turns are served. We are forward in supplications, but backward in gratulations. All the lepers could beg health, yet 'But one returned to give God the glory,' Luke xvii. 18. Surely we should be as much affected, or rather more, in receiving the mercies than we were in asking them; for before we only knew them by guess and imagination, but then by actual feeling or experience of the comfort of them. But chiefly the argument is, that justice requireth it. It is a kind of theft, and unjust detention of what is another's, if in our necessities we crave help, and afterward there is no more mention of God than as if we had these blessings from ourselves.

2. God by his precept commanding it and we in our distress promising it, he expecteth that there should be thankful returns of the

mercies afforded to us. That is the second argument, God's expectation; which must be interpreted θεοπρεπῶς, becoming the excellency of his being. One may be said to expect a thing *de jure*, rightfully, or *de facto*, really and actually. God knoweth that he hath to do with unthankful creatures, and that the stupid world will not take notice of his kindness; therefore *de facto*, actually, he expecteth no more than is given him, having a full and clear prospect of all future events; but *de jure*, of right, he might expect. So these expressions are to be interpreted: Luke xiii. 7, 'These three years I come seeking fruit on this fig-tree, and find none.' So Isa. v. 4, 'When I looked it should bring forth grapes, brought it forth wild grapes.' So we may fail his expectation, but still to our loss: 2 Chron. xxxii. 25, 'Hezekiah rendered not again according to the benefit done to him, for his heart was lifted up; therefore there was wrath upon him, and upon Judah and Jerusalem.' All our receipts call for a return, and a return suitable, which if we perform not, God's wrath is kindled against us, and therefore a good man should make conscience of his returns: Ps. cxvi. 12, 'What shall I render unto the Lord for all his benefits towards me?'

3. It keepeth up the intercourse between us and God, which would be interrupted and broken off if we should discontinue our addresses to him as soon as we have what we would have, and when our wants are supplied God should hear no more from us. By the laws of Ezekiel's temple, the worshippers were so required to go in at one door and out at another, that none of them might at any time turn their backs upon the mercy-seat, Ezek. xlvi. 9, but which way soever they entered they were to go away right against it. God cannot endure men should turn their backs upon him when their turn is served. Prayer and praise still keep up communion and familiarity with God, that still there may be a commerce between us and him, by asking all things, and taking all things out of his hands. Prayer and praise are our continual work: Heb. xiii. 15, 'By him therefore let us offer the sacrifice of praise continually, that is, the fruit of our lips, giving thanks unto his name.' The supreme benefactor and fountain of all goodness must still be owned; there must be a constant course in it. Some mercies are so general and beneficial that they should be remembered before God every day; and God is still blessing his people, and by new mercies giving new matter of praise and thanksgiving.

4. It continueth a succession of mercies, for the more thankful we are for them the more they are increased upon us, as an husbandman trusts more of his precious seed in fruitful soils. The ascent of vapours maketh way for the descent of showers. The sea poureth out of her fulness into the rivers, and they all return again into the sea: Ps. lxvii. 5, 6, 'Let the people praise thee, O God, let all the people praise thee, then shall the earth yield her increase, and God, even our God, shall bless us.' Or when the springs lie low, we pour in a little water into the pump, not to enrich the fountain, but to bring up more for ourselves. I do the rather observe it, because it is not only true of outward increase, but spiritual also: Col. ii. 7, 'Rooted and built up in him, and established in the faith, as ye have been taught, abounding therein with thanksgiving.' If we give thanks for so much grace as we have already received, it is the way to increase our store. The

reason why we do no more thrive in grace or advance in the spiritual life is because we do no more give thanks.

5. In thanksgiving all spiritual graces are acted and promoted. (1.) Faith is acted in thanksgiving when we see and own the invisible hand that reacheth out our supplies to us: 'All things come of thee, and of thine own have we given thee,' 1 Chron. xxix. 14. Stupid and carnal creatures look to the next hand, as if he that bringeth the present were more to be thanked than he that sendeth it: Hosea ii. 8, 'She did not know that I gave her corn, and wine, and oil.' We are unthankful to God and man, but more to God, because blessings that come from an invisible hand we look upon as things of course, and do not praise the giver. Beasts own the next hand: Isa. i. 3, 'The ox knoweth his owner, and the ass his master's crib, but Israel doth not know, my people doth not consider.' (2.) Love: It is love that doth open our mouths, that we may praise God with joyful lips: Ps. cxvi. 1, 'I will love the Lord, because he hath heard the voice of my supplications;' and then, ver. 2, 'I will praise him as long as I live.' The proper intent of mercies is to draw us to God. When the heart is full of the sense of the goodness of the Lord, the tongue cannot hold its peace. Self-love doth more put us on prayers, but the love of God on praises, therefore to seek and not to praise, it is to be lovers of ourselves rather than of God. (3.) Hope is acted. While we give thanks for the very grant, for the promise, for the preparations, with greater assurance we expect what is behind; as Abraham built an altar in the land of Canaan, and offered thanksgivings to God, when he had not a foot in the country, Gen. xiii. 18. (4.) Our humility: The humble soul is most delighted in the praise of God, but the proud soul in its own praises: 'They sacrifice to their net, and burn incense to their drag,' Hab. i. 16. Whilst others sacrifice to God, they deprive God of his honour, and exalt anything rather than the author of felicity; they ascribe all to themselves, whilst the others profess their unworthiness of the least mercies from God: Gen. xxxii. 10, 'I am not worthy of the least of all thy mercies, and of all the truth which thou hast showed unto thy servant;' and 2 Sam. vii. 18, 'Who am I, O Lord God, and what is my house, that thou hast brought me hitherto?' God is never exalted till the creature be abased.

6. It preventeth many sins; as—(1.) Hardness of heart, and security in enjoying the blessings of God's common providence. These common mercies point to the author, and discover their end to the thankful soul, but to the unthankful they prove occasions to the flesh; so 'their table is made a snare to them, and their welfare a trap,' Ps. lxix. 22. But when we sip and look upward, and acknowledge God on all occasions, the creature is sanctified to us: 1 Tim. iv. 4, 'Every creature of God is good, and nothing to be refused, if it be received with thanksgiving.' Where there is a due acknowledgment of the donor, we have it with a blessing. So (2.) It suppresseth murmuring, or that quarrelling, fretting, impatient humour which venteth itself against God, even in our prayers and complaints, and soureth all our comforts. Murmuring is an anti-providence, the scum of discontent, by which we entertain crosses with anger, and blessings with disdain. Man is a touchy creature, always querulous, especially when God

retrencheth him in some worldly conveniences which he fancieth.
Now a thankful spirit counterbalanceth crosses with comforts: Job
ii. 10, 'What! shall we receive good at the hand of the Lord, and
shall we not receive evil?' It taketh notice how gracious God hath
been notwithstanding his seeming severity, therefore it can bless God
in every condition: Job i. 21, 'The Lord gave, and the Lord hath
taken away, blessed be the name of the Lord.' This fretting humour
is cured; as long as we see occasion of giving thanks, it causeth us to
submit to his disposing will. (3.) It prevents distrust and carking
cares. This remedy is prescribed by the apostle: Phil. iv. 6, 'Be
careful for nothing, but in everything by prayer and supplication,
with thanksgiving, let your requests be made known unto God.' When
we acknowledge what God hath done for us, it prevents distrust:
Ps. lxxvii. 10, 11, 'I said, This is my infirmity, but I will remember
the years of the right hand of the Most High: I will remember the
works of the Lord; surely I will remember thy wonders of old.' There
are great convulsions in an earthquake, but when it findeth a vent all
is quiet. When we can bless God for favours already received, we
will not doubt of his goodness for the future, but quietly compose ourselves to wait for the good end of the Lord. (4.) It cureth spiritual
pride to consider who must be praised and owned for all the good
which is in us: 1 Cor. iv. 7, 'Who maketh thee to differ from another?
and what hast thou that thou didst not receive? Now if thou didst receive it, why dost thou glory as if thou hadst not received it?' The
more we have, we are more indebted to grace. We have all from God
and for God, not for ourselves, our own glory and ostentation. God
will be angry if we rob him of it, as Herod was smitten 'because he
gave not God the glory,' Acts xii. 23. The receiver is as bad as the
stealer; we consent to this robbery and usurpation.

Use. Oh! then, let us be more abundant in thanksgiving and praise.
It is God's will concerning us in Christ: 1 Thes. v. 18, 'In everything give thanks, for this is the will of God in Christ Jesus concerning you.' But there are other reasons to persuade us; as—(1.) Our
profit both spiritual and temporal. It argueth a good spirit, great
faith and love, when we look to God in everything, and a submissive
spirit when we take anything kindly at his hands, the nations had
never fallen to idolatry if they had kept up thankfulness, and considered God in all their mercies: Acts xiv. 16, 17, 'Who in times past
suffered all nations to walk in their own ways; nevertheless he left
not himself without witness, in that he did good, and gave us rain from
heaven and fruitful seasons, filling our hearts with food and gladness.'
Setting up the idol chance was the great cause of perverting mankind.
Besides, this is noble and delightful work, the work of angels, our work
in heaven. Well, then, observe what matter of praise God vouchsafeth
to you continually. If you did want many of the comforts you now
enjoy, how miserable would your lives be! A thing too near the ball
of the eye is not seen well; our comforts must be set at a distance to
make us value them. (2.) Our continual dependence. It is with us
as it was with the raven and the dove which Noah sent forth out of
the ark, Gen. viii. 7, 8: the raven, feeding on the floating carrion,
returned no more; but the dove, finding not whereon to rest the sole

of her foot, returned with an olive branch. Carnal men, if they can get anything from God to support them, and they have their stock in their own hands, they care no more for him, but live apart from God: Jer. ii. 31, 'Wherefore say my people, We are lords, we will come no more unto thee?' (3.) Consider how thankful others are for less than what we enjoy. There are many that would be glad of our leavings, but usually those that enjoy the greatest possessions pay the least rent, and God receiveth more praise from a poor cottage than from a rich palace. But I proceed to the second point.

Doct. 2. That in thanksgiving to God we should especially own his spiritual benefits.

These are usually overlooked, but yet these deserve the chiefest acknowledgments.

1. Because these are discriminating, and come from God's special love, which floweth forth to his own people. Corn, and wine, and oil are bestowed upon the world, but faith and love upon his saints. David prayeth, Ps. cvi. 4, 'Remember me, O Lord, with the favour which thou bearest unto thy people.' To have the favourite's mercy is more than to have a common mercy. Protection is the benefit of every common subject, but intimate love and near admission are the privileges of special favourites. Now by the common effects of his providence, love or hatred cannot be known: Eccles. ix. 1, 2, 'No man knoweth either love or hatred by all that is before them; all things come alike to all,' &c. The things without us, and the things before us, and the things promiscuously dispersed, will not discover his special love to us. Christ gave his purse to Judas, the worst of the disciples, but his Spirit to the rest as the choicest gift.

2. Because these concern the better part, the inward man: 2 Cor. iv. 16, 'For which cause we faint not, but though our outward man perish, yet the inward man is renewed day by day.' He doth us more favour that healeth a wound in the body than he that seweth up a rent in the garment. Is not the body more than raiment? So is not the soul more than the body? Yea, further, and the soul furnished with grace, than the soul furnished only with natural gifts and endowments? 1 Cor. xiii. 1–3, 'Though I speak with the tongues of men and of angels, and have not charity, I am become as sounding brass, or a tinkling cymbal: and though I have the gift of prophecy, and understand all mysteries and all knowledge; and though I have all faith, so that I could remove mountains, and have no charity, I am nothing: And though I bestow all my goods to feed the poor, and though I give my body to be burned, and have not charity, it profiteth me nothing.' I am nothing without saving grace; therefore these are the mercies for which God will be praised.

3. These are brought about with more ado than temporal favours. God as a creator and upholder of all his creatures doth bestow temporal blessings upon the ungodly world, even upon the heathens that know him not, that never heard of Christ; yet saving grace he bestoweth only as the God and Father of our Lord Jesus Christ, who was to purchase these blessings by his death and bloody sufferings before we could obtain them: Eph. i. 3, 'Blessed be the God and Father of our Lord Jesus Christ, who hath blessed us with all spiritual

blessings in heavenly places in Christ.' Other blessings run in the channel of common providence, these in the channel of Christ's mediation.

4. Because these are pledges of eternal blessings, and the beginnings of our eternal well-being. The life that is begun in us by the Spirit is perfected in heaven: John v. 24, 'He that heareth my words, and believeth on him that hath sent me, hath everlasting life, and shall not come into condemnation, but is passed from death to life.' It is a spark that shall not be quenched, and the food that feedeth it is the meat that 'perisheth not, but endureth to everlasting life,' John vi. 27. Those graces and eternal blessedness are to be linked together, that they cannot be separated: Rom. viii. 30, 'Whom he did predestinate, them he also called, and whom he called, them he also justified, and whom he justified, them he also glorified.' Sanctification is included in the last word; here in the beginnings by sanctification, and hereafter in the full possession of eternal glory. So 2 Cor. iii. 18, 'We all with open face, beholding as in a glass the glory of the Lord, are changed into the same image, from glory to glory, even as by the Spirit of the Lord.' It loseth itself in the ocean of eternal glory and happiness.

5. These incline and fit the heart for praise and thankfulness to God. There is an occasion to praise God, and a disposition and a heart to praise God. Outward benefits give us the occasion to praise God, but these not only the occasion, but the disposition; other benefits are the motives, but these the preparations, as they do fit and incline the heart. The work of faith and love do set the lips wide open to magnify and praise the Lord. Grace is the matter of God's praises, and gives also a ready will to praise him, yea, the very deed of praising him: Ps. lxiii. 5, 'My soul shall be satisfied as with marrow and fatness, and my mouth shall praise thee with joyful lips.' When they feel the love of God shed abroad in their hearts, they are inclined to praise God.

6. Temporal favours may be given in anger, but the graces of the Spirit are never given in anger. God may give us worldly honour and riches in judgment, and indulge large pastures to beasts fatted for destruction; but he giveth not faith and love in anger, or a renewed heart in anger, but as a token of his special love: 'To you it is given to know the mysteries of the kingdom of heaven,' Mat. xiii. 11; 'To you it is given to believe,' Phil. i. 19. So that for these principally we should praise the Lord. We have a quick sense in bodily mercies, but in soul concernments we are not alike affected. We think God dealeth well with them to whom he giveth greatness and honour; but doth he not deal well with you to whom he hath given his Spirit?

7. These render us acceptable unto God. A man is not accepted with God for his worldly blessings; he is indeed the more accountable unto God, but not of greater account with him: Luke xii. 48, 'For unto whomsoever much is given, of him shall the more be required.' The more helps and the more encouragements, the more work and service God expecteth, but they are not more precious in his sight for temporal things' sake. Under the law the rich and poor paid the same ransom; the rich is not accepted for his riches, nor the poor man despised for his poverty; but now the saving graces of his Spirit are acceptable with God. It is said, 1 Peter iii. 4, 'A meek and quiet

spirit is in the sight of God of great price.' God esteemeth this more, and therefore it should heighten the esteem of grace in our hearts, and quicken us more to get and increase it.

8. These benefits should be acknowledged, that God may have the sole glory of them, for he is 'the Father of lights, from whom cometh every good and perfect gift,' James i. 17. It was the opinion of the stoics, *Quod vivamus deorum munus est, quod bene vivamus nostrum*—Our natural being we ascribe to God, but our moral perfections we are apt to usurp the glory of them to ourselves. *Judicium hoc est omnium mortalium*, saith Tully. All men think that prosperity and success is to be asked of the gods, but prudence and good management belongeth to us. But these opinions are sacrilegious, and rob God of his chiefest honour; therefore, to prevent spiritual pride, we must be sure to bless God for spiritual blessings; our crowns must be 'cast at the feet of the Lamb,' Rev. iv. 10, 11, for he only is worthy to receive honour, and blessing, and glory, and power. Whatever we do, it is from him who worketh all our works in us: Isa. xxvi. 12, 'Thou wilt ordain peace for us, for thou also hast wrought all our works in us;' and 1 Chron. xxix. 14, 'All things come of thee, and of thy own have we given thee.' By his grace we are what we are: 1 Cor. xv. 10, 'By the grace of God I am what I am;' and Luke xix. 16, 'Thy pound hath gained ten pounds.'

Use. Is to exhort us to two things—(1.) To be in a capacity to bless God for spiritual blessings; (2.) To be most affected with these mercies.

1. See that you be in a capacity to bless God for spiritual blessings. First see that you have these mercies, and then bless God for them. It would trouble a man even to trembling to hear slight and vain persons take up a form of thanksgiving which no way is proper to them, as to bless God for their election before time, their sanctification in time, and their hopes of glory after all time. As if a leper should give thanks for perfect health, or a madman that he is made wiser than his neighbours, or a man that is ready to die to thank God that he is pretty well and recovering, so they give thanks for grace which they never knew nor felt. This is to mock God while we pretend to adore him. It is true there are spiritual mercies for which all are bound to give thanks, such as the mystery of redemption, the new covenant, the offers and invitations of grace, means, and time to repent; these you should value more, and bless God for them. But for men that know not their own great necessities and benefits, but slight their chiefest mercies, and account them burdens, they can more feelingly thank God for a gluttonous meal, or unjust gain, or some vain pleasure, but for the means of grace they bless him not. But now, the flower of thanksgiving is when we can bless God for Christ, for his Spirit, for heaven, for faith and love; and therefore we should labour to get these things, and to make our sincerity more unquestionable; for these are the chiefest matters for which God expecteth praise from us. The apostolical forms insist upon these things: 1 Peter i. 3, 'Blessed be the God and Father of our Lord Jesus Christ, which according to his abundant mercy hath begotten us again unto a lively hope, by the resurrection of Jesus Christ from the dead.'

2. To be most affected with these mercies. Other mercies may be

overvalued, especially if we look upon them under the notion of provision for the flesh; so our very thankfulness may be a snare. Lust engrosseth our hearts, but religion tippeth our tongues. Men will thank God for their preferment more than for the offer of Christ, and pardon and life by him. Our esteem is known by this, what it is that moveth us to thankfulness; if it be for the world, as used for the pleasure of the flesh rather than for the service of God, it is but lust disguised in a religious form. Therefore, what are you most affectionately thankful for, worldly or spiritual good things? God is to be thanked for all, for temporal encrease, but chiefly for spiritual mercies. Now what endeareth God to your hearts, that he is so good in Christ, or that he blesseth your outward estate? You should not lessen that favour, but look for a better and more distinguishing expression of his love.

Doct. 3. That not only the spiritual blessings vouchsafed to ourselves, but to others also, must be acknowledged with thankfulness.

1. It suiteth with our relation of members in the same mystical body of Christ, and so is a part of the communion of saints: 1 Cor. xii. 26, 'And whether one member suffer, all the members suffer with it; or one member be honoured, all the members rejoice with it.' The members care for one another, and are affected with each other's woe or weal. If the toe be trod upon, the tongue will cry out, You have hurt me; therefore, they that have lost sympathy and feeling seem to have cast themselves out of the body, as if they were no way concerned in their fellow-members in Christ. If we be in the body, we must be affected with others' concernments as with our own: Phil. i. 7, 'I have you in my heart.' Where sincere love is among christians, there will be a communion of prayers and praises, therefore they bless God for others' mercies as their own. See Rom. xii. 15, 'Rejoice with them that do rejoice, and weep with them that weep.' Spiritual love is but acted and personated if we only drop some words of prayer and praise, and do not look upon ourselves as under a debt, and that it is meet so to do, and do it upon inclination, and not merely upon the invitation of others. We should give thanks for all their mercies, especially for such spiritual mercies as constitute the union, such as faith and love. By faith we are united to the head, by love to the fellow-members: Col. i. 3, 4, 'We give thanks to God, and the Father of our Lord Jesus Christ, praying always for you, since we heard of your faith in Christ Jesus, and of the love which you have to all the saints.' These graces qualify for this spiritual communion.

2. The glory of God is concerned in it. Wheresoever his goodness shineth forth, especially with any eminency, it must be acknowledged: Rom. i. 8, 'I thank my God through Jesus Christ for you all, that your faith is spoken of throughout the whole world.' When Christ's kingdom doth thrive extensively or intensively, by the addition of more peace or the increase of grace; if we love our Master, we must be glad when he getteth more servants, and our joy must be expressed in praises. When Paul was converted, he saith, Gal. i. 24, the saints 'glorified God in me;' that is, praised God in his behalf, and gave him the honour of that great work, that so useful an instrument was gained to the faith.

3. The spiritual blessings vouchsafed to others conduce to a common good, therefore our profit and interest inviteth us to this duty. The good of some is the gain of the whole; we have benefit by their

example, and are confirmed by having companions in the faith and patience of the gospel, and the common profession groweth by their accession to the faith: 1 Thes. i. 7, 8, 'Ye were examples to all that believe in Macedonia, and Achaia; for from you sounded out the word of the Lord, not only in Macedonia and Achaia, but also in every place your faith to God-ward is spread abroad.' Eminent christians promote the interest of the gospel, and their gifts make them serviceable: 1 Cor. i. 4, 5, 'I thank my God always on your behalf, for the grace that is given you by Jesus Christ, that in everything ye are enriched by him, in all utterance, and in all knowledge;' and Rom. i. 12, 'That I may be comforted together with you, by the mutual faith both of you and me.' It is a comfort to meet with our Father's children everywhere, and that we have hopes of having more companions in heaven.

4. If we have no profit by them, yet the thing itself is a benefit to us, for if we have anything of the bowels of Christ or love to souls, surely we are gratified when any are converted to God. If the salvation of our brethren be dear to us, whatever is given in order thereto we must reckon among our benefits, and we should rejoice in one another's gifts and graces as our own. True goodness is communicative, and diffusive of itself, as fire turneth all about it into fire. Hypocritical profession is accompanied with an envy; they would shine alone; and mules and creatures of a bastard production do not propagate.

5. We increase their faith and comfort when we give thanks to God for them. To that end doth the apostle mention his thanksgiving, that they might be encouraged to go on: Phil. i. 3-6, 'I thank my God upon every remembrance of you, being confident of this very thing, that he which hath begun a good work in you will perform it until the day of Jesus Christ.'

Use 1. They are monsters of men that repine at the riches poured down by their own or other men's ministry upon others; yet such a base spirit reigneth in many; they cannot endure any should be godly and serious.

Use 2. Let us bless God for others. The angels rejoice at the conversion of a sinner, Luke xv. 10. Now this should never be omitted —(1.) When there is some eminent work accomplished, either for the multitude of objects or degree of grace. As when Cornelius was gained to the faith as the first-fruits of the Gentiles, Acts xi. 18, 'When they heard these things, they held their peace, and glorified God, saying, Then hath God also unto the Gentiles granted repentance unto life;' and ver. 21, 'The hand of the Lord was with them, and a great number believed, and turned unto the Lord;' and ver. 23, 'Barnabas was glad when he had seen the grace of God, and exhorted them all, that, with purpose of heart, they would cleave unto the Lord.' (2.) When there are special circumstances, as if we have been instrumental to do them good, and God hath blessed our word, or converse, or example: 1 Thes. ii. 19, 20, 'For what is our hope, or joy, or crown of rejoicing? are not even ye in the presence of our Lord Jesus Christ at his coming? for ye are our glory and joy.' Or if we have prayed for anything for others, whatever we have prayed for must be thankfully acknowledged when brought to pass: 2 Cor. i. 11, 'You also helping together by prayer for us, that for the gifts bestowed upon us by the means of many persons, thanks may be given by many on our behalf;' and 3 John 4, 'I have no greater joy than to hear that my children walk in the truth.'

Doct. 4. That in thanksgiving for spiritual benefits, whether to ourselves or others, the increase of grace must be acknowledged as well as the beginnings of it.

The degree is from God. He that beginneth perfecteth: Phil. i. 6, 'He that hath begun a good work will perfect it to the day of Christ.' The whole progress of the work, from the first step to the last, is all from God, not from the power of our own free-will, or the strength of our resolutions, or the stability of our gracious habits. For the first, that it is not from the power of our own free-will, is plain from John vi. 44, 'No man can come to me except the Father which hath sent me draw him.' And then for the second, that it is not from the strength of our resolutions: Ps. lxxiii. 2, 'As for me, my feet were almost gone, my steps had well-nigh slipped.' And for the third, that it is not from the stability of gracious habits, see Rev. iii. 2, 'Be watchful, and strengthen the things which remain, and are ready to die, for I have not found thy works perfect before God;' and 1 Peter v. 10, 'The God of all grace, who hath called us unto his eternal glory by Jesus Christ, after that you have suffered a while, make you perfect, establish, strengthen, settle you.' He that beginneth the work of grace in us doth still carry it on to perfection; he doth establish what is attained, and increase our spiritual strength for all difficulties and duties; so Luke xvii. 5, 'The apostles said unto the Lord, Increase our faith.'

Use. Take notice of God's favour in the addition of every new degree of grace, because the change is more remarkable. We may ascribe our first conversion to God, but we must also our after-growth. We are still under the love and care of Christ; though we are passed from death to life, yet not from earth to heaven. You are in continual need of Christ for direction, intercession, pardon, further sanctification, support, comfort, and peace; therefore take notice of every degree. If there be greater fervour, if more delightful exercise, if more ability and strength to overcome opposition, let God have the glory of all. He many times chastiseth our pride and unthankfulness with lapses or decays if we do not acknowledge him; as Peter and David, what grievous lapses had they!

SERMON II.

We are bound to thank God always for you, brethren, as it is meet, because that your faith groweth exceedingly, and the charity of every one of you all towards each other aboundeth—2 Thes. i. 3.

In these words we have observed—(1.) An affectionate form of thanksgiving; (2.) The matter of it.

For the first, it is a blessed thing when complaints are turned into thanksgivings, both for ourselves and others. For ourselves we should not be always craving and always complaining. Gratulation should find a place in our addresses to God, as well as acknowledgments of sin and supplications for grace: Col. iv. 2, 'Continue in prayer, and watch in the same with thanksgiving.' So for others, we should rather take notice of their excellences than of their blemishes. We give occasion to others to suspect us to have a rough imperious spirit, to be always finding fault, never acknowledging the grace they have received or the good they have done. This was far from Paul's temper, who was ever ready to acknowledge anything of Christ wherever he found it, especially where grace was discovered with eminency, as in these Thessalonians; therefore he saith, 'We are bound to thank God always for you, brethren, as it is meet;' whence we observed four doctrines.

I am now to speak of the matter of this thanksgiving, 'Because that your faith groweth exceedingly, and the charity of every one of you all towards each other aboundeth;' where observe these six things—

1. That it is a comfort that our inward man is in a good state, however it be with us as to our outward condition before the world. These Thessalonians were poor and afflicted. We read in the first epistle, 'They received the gospel in much affliction,' 1 Thes. i. 6; and in the verse next the text he speaketh of their 'patience and faith in all their persecutions and tribulations;' and the following words tend wholly to comfort them under their sore troubles. Yet their condition before God was thriving and prosperous, and matter of thanksgiving rather than lamentation. So 2 Cor. iv. 16, 'For this cause we faint not,' saith the apostle, 'but though our outward man perish, yet the inward man is renewed day by day.' We should count this world's goods well exchanged if the want or loss of them be recompensed to us by the increase of spiritual graces, and be glad if it go well with our souls, though our bodily interests be infringed. If God by an aching head will give us a better heart, by a sickly body an healthy soul, as he did to Gaius, 3 John 2, by lessening us in the world, or reducing us to straits, make us 'rich in faith,' James ii. 5; by troubles and oppositions excite us to a more lively exercise of grace. We should not barely submit to such a dispensation, but give thanks. The children of God are always set forth to be of this temper: Ps. cxix. 71, 'It is good for me that I have been afflicted, that I might learn thy statutes;' 2 Cor. xii. 9, 10, 'I will rather glory in my infirmities, that the power of Christ may rest upon me; therefore I take pleasure in infirmities, in reproaches, in necessities, in persecution, in distresses for Christ's sake; for when I am weak, then am I strong;' if the afflictions and troubles of the world may do us good, and our knowledge and holiness be increased as our estates are diminished. So Heb. xii. 11, 'No chastening for the present seemeth to be joyous, but grievous, nevertheless afterward it yieldeth the peaceable fruit of righteousness unto them which are exercised thereby.' All the honours and riches of the world are not worth the least degree or drachm of grace.

2. Their condition was not only good, but growing better every day. It is not enough barely to be good, but we must grow from good to better, and be best at last. God's children wait on the Lord, and he is not wont to be sparing and straitened to those that attend upon him: Isa. xl. 31, 'They that wait on the Lord shall renew their strength.'

They are planted in his courts, and that is a fertile soil : Ps. xcii. 13, 14, 'Those that are planted in the house of the Lord shall flourish in the courts of our God ; they shall still bring forth fruit in old age, they shall be fat and flourishing.' There are ordinances by which they receive a supply of the Spirit; their hearts are upon the ways that lead home to God: Ps. lxxxiv. 7, 'They shall go on from strength to strength.' When our hearts are set upon a thing, we will neither go off nor go back, but still gain ground. They find new encouragement in God's ways: Prov. x. 29, 'The way of the Lord is strength to the upright;' the more they walk in it, the more encouragement they find to do so, all which doth condemn our laziness, that we make no more progress. Surely our reward should encourage us: Phil. iii. 14, 'I press towards the mark for the prize of the high calling of God in Jesus Christ.' In a race where there is so great a prize, we should not stand at a stay, but still be running, and getting nearer the goal; the way is so pleasant that we have no occasion to tire in it : 2 Peter iii. 18, 'But grow in grace, and in the knowledge of our Lord and Saviour Jesus Christ.' We have so many benefits by Christ, that surely we are encouraged to seek for more. Besides, consider God's expectation. God expecteth more from some than others, according to their years and standing: Heb. v. 12, 'For when for the time ye ought to be teachers' (having had so much means and advantages), 'ye have need that one teach you again which be the first principles of the oracles of God.' So Luke xii. 48, 'Unto whomsoever much is given, of him shall be much required; and to whom men have committed much, of him they will ask the more.' We expect he should come sooner that rideth on horseback than he that goeth afoot. Now, that we may grow, carnal affections must be weakened: John xv. 2, 'Every branch that beareth fruit, he purgeth it that it may bring forth more fruit.' This purging is by mortification ; faith, the mother grace, must be increased: Rom. i. 17, 'Therein is the righteousness of God revealed from faith to faith; as it is written, The just shall live by faith.' We must still continue to live by faith. The means of grace must still be attended upon : 1 Peter ii. 2, 'As new-born babes, desire the sincere milk of the word, that ye may grow thereby.'

3. Their growth was considerable ; they arrived to a great degree of eminency, ὑπεραυξάνει ἡ πίστις ὑμῶν, καὶ πλεονάζει ἡ ἀγάπη. Here is high faith and great love. Certainly they did not overgrow their duty, but it was a wonderful growth, considering the difference between them and themselves, what they were before the gospel came to them, and what now; considering also the difference between them and others, how they had outgrown their equals, yea, those who had received the gospel before them. Surely we should not only grow in grace, but seek to excel in grace ; God will have more glory, and we more comfort. Now those that would excel—(1.) Should be more humble ; for, James iv. 6, 'God resisteth the proud, but giveth grace to the humble.' The Lord increaseth his grace where all is ascribed to God and nothing to ourselves, but he is an enemy to those that lift up themselves, and puff up themselves and set the crown upon their own heads. (2.) They should be diligent in the use of their gifts, for 'to him that hath shall be given,' Luke viii. 18; that is, that useth what he hath, that carrieth himself

according to the helps vouchsafed, and employeth and improveth what he hath, he shall have more. They shall have more faith, more love from the same Spirit who gave them the first grace. If in the effect you show what you have, and declare what you have, you shall have more; the original stock shall be increased. (3.) There should be thankfulness. They own God in all: Col. ii. 7, 'Rooted and built up in him, and stablished in the faith, as ye have been taught, abounding therein with thanksgiving.' The creature then robbeth not God of the glory of his gifts, and therefore shall have more. (4.) There must be obedience to the word of God as our rule, the sanctifying motions of the Spirit as our principle, and the author of that grace which we have. Now the more ready we show ourselves to comply with the directions of his word and the motions of his Spirit, the more is grace strengthened in us; for disobedience to the word is a provocation to God, which hindereth the due impression of it on our souls: Jer. viii. 9, 'They have rejected the word of the Lord, and what wisdom is in them?' And disobedience to the Spirit is a grief to him: Eph. iv. 30, 'Grieve not the Holy Spirit of God, whereby ye are sealed unto the day of redemption.' So that sin hindereth our growth, and letteth out our strength. But what shall we say of them that beat down the price of christianity as low as they can, and content themselves with what is barely necessary to salvation, as if the safest way were to go as near the brink of destruction as possible? These men care not though they dishonour God, so they may be saved, but they will in time see that the greatest grace is no more than needeth.

4. They grow in both graces, both in faith and love. These two graces are inseparable companions: Col. i. 4, 'Since we heard of your faith in Christ Jesus, and of the love which ye have to all the saints.' So 1 Tim. i. 13, 'Hold fast the form of sound words which thou hast heard of me, in faith and love, which is in Jesus Christ.' The one concerneth our personal benefit and safety, the other the good of the body, that we may have a tender care of the unity, honour, and prosperity of Christ's church. We are to build up ourselves in our most holy faith, and we are also to edify others, which is done by love principally. Besides, this connection is necessary, because all religion is exercised by these two graces. The mysteries of religion are received and improved by faith, and the precepts and duties of it are acted by love: 1 Cor. xvi. 13, 14, 'Watch ye, stand fast in the faith, quit yourselves like men, be strong; let all things be done with charity.' And therefore that qualification which entitleth us to the privileges of the new covenant is made to be 'faith working by love,' Gal. v. 6. The one grace without the other is not saving and sincere. Faith without love is dead, James ii. 17, and love without faith is but a little good-nature, or facile inclination to others, not derived from the Spirit of God, nor built on our belief of his grace in Christ; they depend upon one another, as the effect upon the cause. Faith produceth love, as it showeth the true grounds of union, and from a sense and apprehension of God's love to us causeth us to love others. In short, both graces are recommended by the same authority: 1 John iii. 23, 'And this is his commandment, that we should believe on the name of his Son Jesus Christ, and love one another, as he gave us commandment.' He that

maketh conscience of the one will make conscience of the other also. Again, the one referreth to God, the other to men; faith for God, charity for our brethren. The one keepeth us from defection from God, the other preventeth a schism and a breach with our fellow christians. Well, then, here was the commendation of those Thessalonians, their adherence to the faith was very constant, and they lived in unity and amity with one another. There is no surer argument of sincerity and proficiency in christianity than this growth of faith and love. They are the fountain of all other duties; and if you would be accounted thorough and growing christians, you must excel in both these graces, for true solid godliness is rooted in faith, and acted by love towards God and men, which is the all of christianity.

5. This growth and proficiency was found in all; not only some among them were eminent for faith and love, but all. If the apostle had only said, The charity of you all aboundeth, it might seem to refer to the church, that there was no schism there; but he saith, 'Of every one of you all towards each other.' In other epistles, the believers, to whom the apostle wrote, have all the style of 'churches,' or 'men sanctified,' &c.; but afterwards notorious and particular miscarriages are reproved, which showeth that the denomination was *a potiori parte*, from the better part; but here he mentions all and every one; they were a choice sort of christians. Where shall we find their fellows? It is our duty to be such, and it should be our care; for here we see what the grace of God can do if we be serious, and what an advantage it is to be in good company, and to have good examples about us, and how much living coals do enkindle one another when they lie together.

6. He saith, faith groweth, but love aboundeth. Love must not only increase, but abound to each other. A thing may be increased *intensive* or *extensive*; intensively, when it is more rooted, when there is a greater fervour and vigour of faith and love; extensively, either as to effects or objects; as to effects, in doing more good, as when we abound in works of mercy; or as to objects, by doing good to more persons, not confining our love to one only, or a few, but extending it to all. This was the case of those Thessalonians; their love was not a lank or lean love, but an abounding love, full of all good fruits; and this not to some, but to all, even the meanest christians among them. If we would give others occasion to bless God for us, let us imitate their example. Occasions are many, objects are many, to whom we may be beneficial, therefore our charity must not be straitened, but abounding.

[1.] The internal affection must increase: Phil. i. 9, 'This I pray, that your love may abound yet more and more;' that is, both their love to God and their neighbours, especially to those who are God's. There are so many things to extinguish it, or make it grow cold, that we should always seek to increase this grace, that it may be more fervent and strong, and not grow cold and dead.

[2.] The external expressions should abound both as to acts and objects.

(1.) As to acts. In duties of charity we should not be weary. Now we may be weary upon a double occasion, either because we meet not presently with our reward; to that the apostle speaketh, Gal. vi. 9, 'Be not weary of well-doing, for in due time we shall reap, if we faint not;' duties of charity have their promises annexed, which are not presently accomplished, but in their season; they will be either in this life, or in the next; or because of continual occasions, when there is no end: Heb. vi. 10, 11, 'For God is not unrighteous to forget your work and labour of love, which you have showed towards his name, in that ye have ministered to the saints and do minister; and we desire that every one of you do show the same diligence, to the full assurance of hope unto the end.' Meaning that formerly they had a courage to own Christ and his despised ways, and to be charitable to poor christians; now he desireth them to be so still; as long as the occasion continueth, so long should the charity continue, that at length they might reap the reward, 'Ye have ministered, and do minister.' This is tedious to nature and to a niggardly and base heart, but love will be working and labouring still, and ever bringing forth more fruit. Where this heavenly fire is kindled in the soul, it will warm all those that are about them. But love is cold in most; it will neither take pains, nor be at charge to do anything for the brethren; but christian love is an immortal fire, it will still burn and never die; therefore we should continue the same diligence, zeal, and affection that formerly we had.

(2.) As to objects. Christ telleth us, 'The poor ye have always with you,' Mat. xxvi. 11. As long as God findeth objects, we should find charity; and the apostle saith, Gal. vi. 10, 'As we have opportunity, let us do good to all men.' Expensive duties are distasteful to a carnal heart. It may be they would part with something which the flesh can spare, and will snatch at anything to excuse their neglect; they have done it to these and these; but as long as God bringeth objects to our view and notice, and our ability and affection doth continue, we must give still. If our ability continueth not, providence puts a bar, and excuseth; but if our affection doth not continue, the fault is our own.

Now I come more particularly to speak of the growth of faith, 'Your faith groweth exceedingly.'

Doct. That it is well with christians when their faith groweth and doth considerably increase.

The scripture speaketh of a weak faith and a strong faith, therefore it concerneth us to consider whether our faith be weak or strong, in the wane or in the increase. Now we shall best judge of the growth of faith—(1.) By the nature of it; (2.) The properties of it; (3.) The examples of scripture.

First, Let us see the nature of it, and thereby we shall best judge of the growth of it. Faith is a grace whereby we believe God's word in general, and especially the doctrine of salvation by Christ, and do receive him and rest upon him for grace here and glory hereafter.

First, The general object of faith is the whole word of God: Acts xxiv. 14, 'Believing all things which are written in the law and the prophets.' Certainly the general faith goeth before the particular, for there is no building without a foundation; so that the general faith is a firm and hearty assent to such things as are revealed by God, because revealed by him. In which description we may consider—(1.) The object of this grace, things revealed by God, as revealed by him; (2.) The act, it is an assent; (3.) The adjuncts or qualifications of this act, it is a firm, cordial, or hearty assent.

1. The objects of faith, considered materially, are such things as are contained in the divine revelation. Formally these things by faith are apprehended under that consideration as revealed by God, by virtue of the truth and authority of his testimony. The objects of faith materially considered are all such things as are contained in the word of God or revealed by him, which are of a different nature, precepts, promises, threatenings, histories of facts done, mysteries of godliness; all these are apprehended, and improved by faith, to the use of holy living or entertaining communion with God through Christ; only among these objects some are more noble and excellent, others of lesser weight and moment. The chief objects of faith are those things which are absolutely necessary to salvation, and without which we can neither be holy here nor happy hereafter. Such are those things which we specially call articles of faith, as briefly comprehending all the mysteries of salvation, the decalogue, &c. But many other things are contained in the word of God, and conduce to the confirmation and fuller understanding of these things, though not of like weight and importance with them; as, for instance, divers histories and miracles which are spoken of in scripture, as also some lesser doctrines, which only belong to the greater fulness and perfection of knowledge. The first sort of things must be explicitly and distinctly known and believed; an implicit faith may suffice for the rest. Now an implicit faith we call that faith by which we believe things not distinctly and apart, but as they are contained in their common principle; as, for instance, he that believeth the book of Judges to be a book divinely inspired, and yet hath never read it or heard it read by others, he doth indeed believe the histories contained therein to be true, but not by an explicit faith, for he knoweth them not but by an implicit and general faith, as he is persuaded the book was indited by the Spirit of God; but he who hath read the book, and knoweth particularly what is said of Sampson, Gideon, Barak, and others of the Lord's worthies, and believeth it, he hath a distinct and explicit faith of these things. The believers of the Old Testament knew the Messiah and Redeemer of the world implicitly, and not with that particularity which is required of believers in the New. And so do many weak christians assent to all things contained in the word of God by an implicit faith, though they do only expressly and explicitly believe things necessary to salvation; which is not said to justify laziness in any, or an overly carelessness in any matters of religion, as if we should acquiesce in the knowledge of a few necessary things, and seek no further. No; 'The word of God must dwell in us richly, in all wisdom,' Col. iii. 16; for though things absolutely necessary are but few, yet other points have their use, and conduce both to the confirmation and improvement of the rest. But hitherto we have only spoken of the object of faith materially considered; we must speak also of the formal consideration. Things revealed by God, as revealed by him; for every assent, even that which is given to things contained in the word of God, cannot be called faith. For instance, if a man should certainly hold and maintain any point of religion, as the creation of the world out of nothing, but not upon the account of God's revealing any such truth, but for some other reason which seemeth necessary and cogent to him, he cannot be said to believe this article, or to understand it by faith; as it is said, Heb. xi. 3, 'Through faith we understand

that the worlds were framed by the word of God;' for faith is an assent to a divine testimony; but when we know things by other ways and means of assurance, it is not faith, whatever it be. So if a man should believe the passages of God's providence towards the Israelites, upon the relation of Josephus the historian, and not upon the authority of the sacred writers who have delivered it to us, he cannot be said to have faith; which also may be said of them who adhere to the true religion only out of custom, and the happy chance of their birth and education, or because they received it by tradition from their ancestors, or the bare warrant of their present teachers, or evidence of reason.

2. The next thing which the description offereth to us is the act of faith about this object, which is an assent. The formal object of faith is some divine truth, as we have seen. Now the understanding hath a double act about truth—apprehension and dijudication, or exercising a judgment about it. So in these divine truths first we apprehend the nature or tenor of them, or consider what is propounded to us in the word of God, which is knowledge or apprehension; but then secondly we judge or determine concerning the truth of these things, which is acknowledgment or assent, and this is the act proper to faith.

3. The adjuncts or qualifications of this assent come now to be considered. They are two—(1.) It is a firm assent; (2.) It is a cordial and hearty assent

[1.] As it is a firm assent, so faith is distinguished from many things that look like it, or pass for it in the world; as (1.) Non-contradiction, or not questioning the truths of religion, which is all the faith that most have, and cometh from their inadvertency and carelessness about divine matters. They do not object against the truth of what the gospel propoundeth, because they do not regard it and weigh it in their serious thoughts. This differeth little from children's learning questions of catechism, or saying things by rote; they can say over the articles of their belief, and never doubted of them; you may teach them to think and say anything, what you please, for they say it, and never consider of it. So most men in the christian world talk at the same rate that others do, but consider not what they say, nor whereof they affirm, only ignorantly and inconsiderately swallow down the current opinions, without 'knowing the certainty of those things wherein they have been instructed,' Luke i. 4. And so though they never doubted of the truth of their religion, it is because they are never assaulted with temptations to the contrary, and all the strength of their faith lieth in their inconsideration or non-attention. If they have any ground and bottom, it is only men's saying so, and therefore their belief (if they have any) should rather be called human credulity than christian faith. In short, they that believe everything believe nothing, which soon appeareth when a temptation cometh. (2.) It distinguisheth it from conjecture, which is a lighter inclination of mind to a thing, as possibly or probably true, whereby men get no higher than, It may be so, and yet there are shrewd suspicions to the contrary. A guess is not an assent, much less a firm and strong assent, as faith is. (3.) It distinguisheth it from opinion, which is a trembling, fearful, uncertain assent. Opinion is beyond conjecture, but short of faith. Conjecture only supposes it may be so, but opinion asserts that it is so, though not without some fear of the contrary; but above all, this faith is an undoubted persuasion of the truth of things revealed by God. By opinion one may be so convinced of the truth of divine things as not to be able reasonably to contradict them; but by faith a man is so convinced of the truth of the gospel that he seeth all the reason in the world to embrace and follow it: Col. ii. 2, 'That their hearts might be comforted, being knit together in love, and unto all riches of the full assurance of understanding, to the acknowledgment of the mystery of God, and of the Father, and of Christ:' and 1 Thes. i. 5, 'For our gospel came not unto you in word only, but also in power, and in the Holy Ghost, and in much assurance, as ye know what manner of men we were among you for your sake;' and Heb. x. 22, 'Let us draw near with a true heart in full assurance of faith, having our hearts sprinkled from an evil conscience, and our bodies washed with pure water.'

[2.] The next qualification of this assent is that it is a cordial or hearty assent: I mean, such as doth engage the will and affections to pursue the happiness which God hath revealed, in the way and by the means which God hath prescribed. We read in scripture of 'believing with the heart,' Rom. x. 9, 10, 'and with all the heart,' Acts viii. 37. The object of faith is not only true, but good, and therefore produceth a cordial adherence to the truths of which it is persuaded. There is not only a conviction of the mind, but a bent and inclination of the will, which followeth the persuasion of faith if it be firm and strong; for it considereth not only the evidence of the things propounded, but the worth, weight, and greatness of them: 1 Tim. i. 15, 'This is a faithful saying, and worthy of all acceptation;' otherwise it will not serve the end and purpose of the gospel, which requireth us to crucify our lusts, and sacrifice our interests, and perform duties displeasing to corrupt nature, and all this upon the hopes only which it offereth to us, and to wait upon God for his salvation in the midst of all pressures and afflictions. Therefore certainly believing is an heart-business, not a simple, naked, and speculative assent. This latter qualification doth exclude two things from true, lively, and saving faith—(1.) That which divines call historical; (2.) That which they call temporary faith.

(1.) Historical faith, which is a simple and naked assent to such things as are propounded in the word of God, and maketh men more knowing but not better, not more holy and heavenly; they are not excited thereby to pursue that happiness which the gospel offereth in the way of holy living or patient continuance in well-doing. So Simon Magus believed the preaching of Philip, Acts viii. 13, yet his heart was not right with God, but he still remained in the gall of bitterness and bond of iniquity. And so many believed in the name of Christ, to whom Christ 'committed not himself, because he knew all men,' John ii. 23, 24; and this faith even the devils may have: James ii. 19, 'Thou believest that there is a God, thou doest well; the devils also believe, and tremble;' and that not only in truths evident by natural light, such as that is there mentioned, that there is a God, but in gospel truths, as that Jesus is the Son of God: Mark i. 24, 'The devil cried out, saying, Let us alone; what have we to do with thee, thou

Jesus of Nazareth? I know thee who thou art, the Holy One of God.' Now this kind of faith is called historical faith, not from the object of it, as if it did only believe the histories of scripture. No; they that have it may believe the promises, the doctrines, the precepts as well as the histories; but from the manner in which it is conversant about its object, namely, thus: as we read histories in which we are no way concerned; we nakedly read them for knowledge' sake, not to make a party in their broils and interests, but only to know what was done; so they that have only this kind of faith, read the scriptures as persons unconcerned, and rest in idle speculation, without referring those notable truths to choice and practice. I cannot say that this cannot be called faith, because they that have it do believe those things which are true, and do truly believe them; but yet lively saving faith it is not, for he who hath that, findeth his heart engaged to Christ, and doth so believe the promises of the gospel concerning pardon of sins and life eternal that he seeketh after them as his happiness, and doth so believe the mysteries of our redemption by Christ as that all his hope and peace and confidence is drawn from thence, and doth so believe the commandments of God and Christ as that he determineth to frame his heart and life to the observance of them, and doth so believe the threatenings, whether of temporal plagues or eternal damnation, as that, in comparison of them, all the frightful things of the world are as nothing: Luke xii. 24, 'Be not afraid of them that can kill the body, and after that have no more that they can do.' Destruction from God is a terror to them, beyond all the evil that man can threaten; as he said to the emperor, Thou threatenest a prison, but Christ threateneth hell.

(2.) It is distinguished from temporary faith, which is an assent to scriptural or gospel truth, accompanied with a slight and insufficient touch upon the heart, called 'a taste of the heavenly gift, and of the good word of God, and the powers of the world to come,' Heb. vi. 4-6. By this kind of faith, the mind is not only enlightened, but the heart affected with some joy, and the life in some measure reformed, at least from grosser sins, called, 'escaping the pollutions of the world,' 2 Peter ii. 20; but the impression is not deep enough, nor is the joy and delight rooted enough to encounter all temptations to the contrary. Therefore this sense of religion may be choked, or worn off, either by the cares of this world, or voluptuous living, or great and bitter persecutions and troubles for righteousness' sake. It is a common deceit; many are persuaded that Jesus is the Christ, the only Son of God, and so are moved to embrace his person, and in some measure to obey his precepts, and to depend upon his promises, and fear his threatenings, and so by consequence to have their hearts loosened from the world in part, and seem to prefer Christ and their duty to him above worldly things, as long as no temptations do assault their resolutions, or sensual objects stand not up in any considerable strength to entice them; but at length, when they find his laws so strict and spiritual, and contrary either to the bent of their affections or worldly interests, they fall off, and lose all their taste and relish of the hopes of the gospel, and so declare plainly that they were not rooted and grounded in the faith and hope thereof. This is true faith generally considered, which foundation being laid, it will be easy to show the nature of special faith, which now followeth to be discussed.

Secondly, The special objects of faith are God's transactions about man's salvation by Christ; therefore, besides the general faith, there is a special faith, whereby we receive Christ, and rest upon him. Saving faith is called a receiving of Christ: John i. 12, 'To as many as received him, to them gave he power to become the sons of God, even to them that believe in his name;' and Col. ii. 6, 'As ye have received Christ Jesus the Lord, so walk ye in him.' We take him as God offereth him, and to the ends for which God offereth him; to do that for us and to be that to us which God hath appointed him to do for and to be unto poor sinners. The general work of Christ as mediator is to bring us to God: 1 Peter iii. 18, 'For Christ also hath once suffered for sins, the just for the unjust, that he might bring us to God.' And the great use that we make of him, is to come to God by him. There is implied in faith an intention of God as our chiefest good, for otherwise Christ is of no use to us; and a consent to Christ's undertaking, that he may bring us to God, or a thankful acceptance of him for those ends. All they are rejected that will have none of him: Ps. lxxxi. 11, 12, 'But my people would not hearken to my voice, and Israel would none of me; so I gave them up unto their own hearts' lust, and they walked in their own counsels;' that 'will not come to him that they may have life,' John vi. 40; that 'will not have him to reign over them,' Luke xix. 27. But they who consent to receive him as their lord and saviour are accepted with him; only let us see how this consent is qualified.

1. It is not a rash consent, but such as is deliberate, and serious, and well-advised. When God in the gospel biddeth us to take Christ, men are ready to say, With all their hearts; but they do not consider what it is to receive Christ, and therefore retract their consent as soon as it is made. No; you must sit down and count the charges, Luke xiv. When you have considered his strict laws, and made a full allowance for incident difficulties and temptations, and can resolve, forsaking all others, to cleave to him alone for salvation, it is an advised consent.

2. It must not be a forced and involuntary consent, such as a person maketh when he is frightened into a little righteousness for the present; such as a person would not yield to if he were in a state of liberty. It may be in a distress or pang of conscience; by all means they must have Christ when sick, when afraid to die, when under some great judgment. No; the will must be effectually inclined to him, and to God the Father by him, as our utmost felicity and end. Christ's people are a willing people: Ps. cx. 3, ' Thy people shall be willing in the day of thy power.'

3. It must be a resolved consent, a fixed, not an ambulatory will, which we take up for a purpose, or at some certain times, for a solemn duty, or so. No; you must cleave to him: Acts xi. 23, 'He exhorted them all, that with purpose of heart they would cleave unto the Lord.' You must trample upon everything that will separate you from him: Phil. iii. 8, 9, 'Yea, doubtless, and I count all things but loss for the excellency of the knowledge of Christ Jesus my Lord, for whom I have suffered the loss of all things, and do count them but dung, that

I may win Christ,' &c.; and Rom. viii. 38, 39, 'I am persuaded that neither death, nor life, nor angels, nor principalities, nor powers, nor things present nor things to come, nor height, nor depth, nor any other creature, shall be able to separate us from the love of God, which is in Christ Jesus our Lord.'

4. It must be not a partial consent, but total; not only to take Christ as offered with his benefits, but a consent of subjection to him as our Lord. We are to take him and his yoke: Mat. xi. 29, 'Take my yoke upon you, and learn of me.' We are to take him, and his cross: Mat. xvi. 24, 'If any man will come after me, let him deny himself, and take up his cross, and follow me.' It is accompanied with a resolution to obey his laws and keep his commandments, that we may abide in his love.

Thirdly, Besides this consent, there must be a recumbency, dependence, resting, or a fiduciary reliance upon him for all things we stand in need of from him. Recumbency is a special act of faith: Isa. xxvi. 3, 'Thou wilt keep him in perfect peace whose mind is stayed on thee, because he trusteth in thee.' Now what do we rest upon him for? For somewhat here and somewhat hereafter—(1.) Here; for the inward man, for all kind of grace, justification, sanctification, privileges, duties, for the beginning and continuance: Phil. i. 6, 'Being confident of this very thing, that he which hath begun a good work in you will perform it until the day of Jesus Christ;' and Acts v. 31, 'Him hath God exalted to be a prince and a saviour, for to give repentance to Israel, and forgiveness of sins.' He is the author and fountain of grace, as well as a Lord and lawgiver, and the ground of our hope and confidence, as giving us that righteousness whereby we may stand before God, and have comfortable access to him. And then for the outward man, God hath not only undertaken to give us heaven and happiness in the next world, but to carry us thither with comfort, supplying us in a way most conducible to his glory and our welfare: Ps. lxxxiv. 11, 'The Lord is a sun and shield; the Lord will give grace and glory; no good thing will he withhold from them that walk uprightly.' All things are yours, ordinances, providences: 1 Cor. iii. 21, 'For all things are yours, whether Paul, or Apollos, or Cephas, or the world, or life, or death, or things present, or things to come, all are yours, and ye are Christ's, and Christ is God's.' (2.) Hereafter; that Christ will give us eternal glory and happiness in the other world: 1 Tim. i. 16, 'For this cause I obtained mercy, that in me first Jesus Christ might show forth all long-suffering, for a pattern to them which should hereafter believe in him to life everlasting;' and John xx. 31, 'These are written, that ye might believe that Jesus is the Christ, the Son of God, and that believing, ye might have life through his name.' This is the main blessing which faith aimeth at: 1 Peter i. 9, 'Receiving the end of your faith, even the salvation of your souls.' By this all temptations of sense are defeated.

Now, if you would know whether your faith groweth or no, you must discover it by the firmness of your assent, or the resolvedness of your consent, or the peace and confidence of your reliance.

1. For assent. If you believe the word of God, especially the gospel part, with an assent so strong that you can resolve to venture your

whole happiness in this bottom, and let go all that you may obtain the hopes which the gospel offereth to you, certainly he hath a strong faith who taketh God's promises for his whole felicity, and God's word for his only security; he needeth no more, nor no better thing, nor surer conveyance to engage him to hazard all that he hath, when the enjoyment of it is inconsistent with his fidelity to Christ.

2. Your consent. A full, entire, hearty consent to resign yourselves to Christ; not a feeble consent, such as is contradicted by every foolish and hurtful lust, but a prevalent consent, such as can maintain itself notwithstanding difficulties, temptations, and oppositions of the flesh, and control all other desires and delights whatsoever.

3. For reliance. When you can trust him for deliverance from the guilt, power, and punishment of sin, and to quicken, strengthen, and preserve grace in you to everlasting life. You trust him in all his offices; as a priest, when you believe his merits and sacrifice, and comfort yourselves with his gracious promises and covenant, and come to God with more boldness and hope of mercy upon the account of his intercession, especially in all extremities and necessities: Heb. iv. 14-16, 'Seeing then that we have a great high priest that is passed into the heavens, Jesus the Son of God, let us hold fast our profession; for we have not an high priest which cannot be touched with the feeling of our infirmities, but was in all points tempted like as we are, yet without sin: let us therefore come boldly unto the throne of grace, that we may obtain mercy, and find grace to help in time of need.' You trust him as a prophet when you give up yourselves as his disciples to the conduct of his word and Spirit, being persuaded that he will infallibly teach you the way to true happiness: John vi. 68, 'Lord, to whom shall we go?. thou hast the words of eternal life.' You trust him as a king when you become his subjects, and are persuaded that he will govern you in truth and righteousness in order to your salvation, and defend you by his mighty power from all your enemies: 2 Tim i. 12, 'I know whom I have believed, and I am persuaded, that he is able to keep that which I have committed unto him against that day;' and 2 Tim. iv. 18, 'And the Lord shall deliver me from every evil work, and will preserve me unto his heavenly kingdom; to whom be glory for ever and ever. Amen.'

SERMON III.

Your faith groweth exceedingly, and the charity of every one of you all towards each other aboundeth.—2 Thes. i. 3.

The growth and increase of faith may be judged of—(1.) By the nature of faith; (2.) The properties of it; (3.) The examples and instances of great faith in scripture.

We are now upon the second thing, the properties.

1. A dependence upon God for something that lieth out of sight.

That this is an essential property of faith appeareth by the description of it: Heb. xi. 1, 'The evidence of things not seen;' that is, not seen by sense and reason. Some things are invisible by reason of their nature, as God, for 'no man hath seen God at any time,' John i. 18; and therefore he is called 'the invisible God,' Col. i. 15. And some things by reason of their distance, because they are absent and future, as the glory of the world to come, and therefore it is an object of faith and hope: Rom. viii. 24, 'For hope that is seen is not hope; for what a man seeth, why doth he yet hope for it?' Vision and possession exclude hope, and leave no room and place for it. Now without faith a man can have no sight of these things: 2 Peter i. 9, 'He that lacketh these things is blind, and cannot see afar off.' There is a mist upon eternity, and we cannot look beyond the clouds of this lower world unless we have the eagle-eye of faith; but by faith we can see them, so as to frame our lives accordingly: 2 Cor. v. 7, 'For we walk by faith, and not by sight.' By sense we see what is pleasing or displeasing to the flesh, but by faith what conduceth to the saving or losing of the soul. Faith being very much like sight, and serving us for the government of the soul, as sight doth for the body, it may much be explained by it. Now to bodily sight there must be an object, a medium to make the object conspicuous, and a faculty or organ. (1.) The great object of faith is eternal life, as procured by Christ and promised in the gospel. There is no use of sight where nothing is to be seen; therefore the object is set before us in the view of faith, in the promises of the gospel, Heb. vi. 18, and xii. 2. God's truth is as certain as sight itself can be in it; we see all things promised as sure and near. (2.) The medium; as we see colours in the light of the air, so these spiritual and heavenly things in the light of the Spirit: 1 Cor. ii. 11, 12, 'For what man knoweth the things of a man, save the spirit of a man which is in him? even so the things of God knoweth no man, but the Spirit of God. Now we have received not the spirit of the world, but the Spirit which is of God, that we might know the things that are freely given us of God.' (3.) The eye, or visive power. A blind man cannot see at noonday, nor the sharpest sight at midnight. Now this eye is faith, which is the evidence of things not seen; we are as sure of them as if we saw them with our eyes, or as we are of those things which we now see with our eyes.

The sight of faith may be considered either—(1.) As to its certainty and clearness; (2.) As to its power and efficacy.

[1.] As to its certainty and clearness. We do so see God, heaven, Christ, that we are affected in some measure as if we saw them with our bodily eyes. God, whilst we walk before him: Acts ii. 25, 'I foresaw the Lord always before my face.' Christ: Gal. iii. 1, 'Before whose eyes Jesus Christ had been evidently set forth, crucified among you.' Christ was set forth before their eyes, as if they had seen him hanging and dying upon the cross. Heaven; they have it in their eye, and are affected in some measure, as if they were in the midst of the glory of the world to come. I say, only in some measure; for compare the light of faith and the light of glory, and there is a difference in the degree. The light of glory nullifieth sin, the light of faith only mortifieth it; but yet really it maketh us do those things which we would do if we saw the glory of heaven, shun those things which are to be avoided as if we saw the flames of hell. There is a certainty and firm belief which hath a great influence upon us, so compare it with the light of sense. Those things which we are to see and feel move the more passionately, for while the soul dwelleth in flesh, and looketh out by the senses, the objects of sense are more apt to move the passions, but yet faith doth effectually move us, though not so passionately.

[2.] As to efficacy and prevalency, this sight prevails over those things which we see and feel. A christian hath senses as well as others, and knoweth that he dwelleth in a world full of sensible objects, which are pleasing to that flesh which he still carrieth about with him; but God hath opened the eyes of his mind, by which he seeth better and more glorious things, which take up his heart and mind, life and love, care and time, and so is weaned from sense-pleasing vanities, and can deny them, and trample upon them, for the enjoyment of these better things; and neither life, nor anything comfortable to life, is counted so dear as that, for their sake, he should hazard the favour of God, his Redeemer's blessing, and the happiness of the world to come. If sight and sense invite and entice him to sin, and forsake his God and Christ, the objects of faith prevail against the amusements of sense, and sway his choice, and incline his heart, and govern his resolutions in the whole course of his life. He looketh not to things as they seem for the present, or relish to the flesh, or as they appear to short-sighted men who are governed by sense, but as they will appear at last, and will prove to all eternity, and so can leave things which he seeth and feeleth for things which he never saw, but expecteth shortly to enjoy.

Well, then, this is the essential property of faith, to look to things not seen by sense, but revealed by God in his word; and this property showeth itself in all the acts of faith, elicit and imperate. Elicit acts are those which are proper to this grace; imperate are such as belong to other graces, but faith hath an influence upon them by virtue of which they are produced. We may more plainly call them acts and effects.

(1.) As the acts of faith, which are assent, consent, trust, or dependence.

(1*st.*) For assent to such truths as God hath revealed in his word. When we have sufficient evidence of this revelation, the less sensible helps we need to underprop our assent, the stronger is our faith. Let me instance in the great article of the christian faith, Christ's person and office. I shall produce that place of the apostle, 1 Peter i. 8, 'Whom having not seen ye love, in whom though now ye see him not, yet believing, ye rejoice with joy unspeakable, and full of glory.' Though they had never seen Christ in the flesh, and he was now absent from them in regard of his bodily presence, being withdrawn into the heavenly sacrary, yet this did not hinder their faith; they loved him and rejoiced in him as if they had seen him and conversed with him bodily. It was an advantage certainly to have seen Christ in the flesh, and to converse with him personally here upon earth, to see his miracles and hear his gracious words; but faith can embrace him as offered in the promise though it never saw him in the flesh; and the fewer sensible helps faith hath besides the word, it is the more highly esteemed by Jesus

Christ. The same appeareth by Christ's words to Thomas: John xx. 29, 'Thomas, because thou hast seen, thou hast believed; but blessed are they that have not seen, yet have believed.' Thomas must have the object of faith under the view of his senses, which argued a great weakness and imbecility: 'Unless I see in his hand the print of the nails, and put my finger into the print of the nails, I will not believe.' What if Christ would not give him that satisfaction, but other sufficient evidence? This was his infirmity, therefore Christ telleth us they have the stronger and more acceptable faith that do not give laws to heaven, or prescribe to God upon what terms they will believe, but accept of the assurance God offereth, without satisfaction to sense.

(2d.) For consent, when we come to enter into covenant with God, God is invisible who maketh the promise, and heaven, which is the great promise that he hath promised us, is future and yet to come, and lieth in another world, and before we get thither we must encounter many difficulties, yea, shoot the gulf of death; but the believer can as really and heartily transact with the great God, and give the hand to the Lord to become his, as he can with a man that is present, and offereth a good bargain upon easy terms and conditions; he hath so firm a belief of the life to come, that he taketh it for his portion and happiness: 2 Cor. iv. 18, 'While we look not at the things which are seen, but at the things which are not seen;' he looketh to things unseen, which he taketh for his treasure and happiness, and is resolved to be anything and do anything which God will have him be and do, that he may obtain it.

(3d.) Another elicit act of faith is trust and dependence, which maintaineth us in a course of patient and cheerful obedience to God, though our happiness be yet to come; yea, though for the present we are harassed with great troubles and afflictions, and it may be, see not the signs, *i.e.*, any sensible tokens of God's favour and respect to us, yet the sight of an invisible God, and confidence of a future reward, keepeth up joy in the soul, and no violence of temptation is able to break it, and remove us from the truth: Rom. viii. 24, 25, 'We are saved by hope, but hope that is seen is not hope, for what a man seeth, why doth he yet hope for? But if we hope for that we see not, then do we with patience wait for it.' They are confident that in God's time they shall have salvation and final deliverance, though it be not to be seen anywhere but in God's promise by Jesus Christ. Well, then, the fewer external comforts we need, the stronger is our faith; the more, the weaker. Weak christians must be carried in arms, dandled on the knees, fed with sensible pledges and ocular demonstrations, or else they are ready to faint.

(2.) The imperate acts or effects of faith, they are produced by virtue of this property, faith's prevailing oversight and sense. I shall name four—

(1st.) To promote holiness, and reduce us and reclaim us from the false happiness. Surely none will accomplish the work of faith with power, and so glorify God and Christ in the world, that is, live in all holy conversation and godliness, but those that have that faith which is the evidence of things not seen. Those that live always as in the sight of an invisible God, are the thorough christians. What greater check can there be to temptations to sin than to live always in the sight of an invisible God? Gen. xxxix. 9; or to temptations to the world, than an invisible glory; or to the troubles and molestations of the world? Rom. viii. 18, 'For I reckon that the sufferings of this present time are not worthy to be compared with the glory which shall be revealed in us;' and 2 Cor. iv. 17, 'Our light affliction, which is but for a moment, worketh for us a far more exceeding and eternal weight of glory.' If godliness expose us to difficulties, molestations, and troubles, faith seeth the final rest, glory, and happiness. If we are inclined to the honours and pleasures of the world, faith seeth the most shining glory will soon burn out, and end in a snuff: Ps. cxix. 96, 'I have seen an end of all perfection, but thy commandment is exceeding broad;' and 1 John ii. 17, 'The world passeth away, and the lust thereof, but he that doth the will of God abideth for ever.' If sense present the bait of present profit, pleasure, or honour, faith seeth the final shame, ignominy, and loss; and so we are guarded on all sides against right-hand and left-hand temptations. This is a general; I shall speak of more particular effects.

(2d.) To keep the heart tender and in awe of God's word. Surely it is a blessed frame of spirit, and very useful to us, to tremble at the word of God: Isa. lxvi. 2, 'To this man will I look, even to him that is poor and of a contrite spirit, and trembleth at my word;' and to stand in awe of his word: Ps. cxix. 161, 'My heart standeth in awe of thy word.' Now this can never be unless we have that faith which is the evidence of things not seen; for many times the word threateneth evils which are not likely to come to pass, if we look to the visible face of things, and all that part of God's discipline is lost unless we can believe unseen things. See Heb. xi. 7, 'By faith Noah, being warned of God of things not seen as yet, moved with fear, prepared an ark to the saving of his house, by which he condemned the world, and became heir of the righteousness which is by faith.' The world was then in a jolly condition, and little dreamt of a flood. The earth flourished as much as ever, and there was building, and marrying, and planting; but God had told him of a universal destruction of all things by a deluge, therefore he admonisheth the careless world, and provideth for his own and family's safety. So we read of Josiah, when he heard of the words of the 'book of the law, he rent his clothes,' 2 Kings xxii. 11. We do not read of any actual trouble that was then in the land, or any danger nigh. When an age is very corrupt and ripe for judgment, God giveth warning. But alas! few take it or lay it to heart, for the world is led by sense, and not by faith: they are not affected with things till they feel them. Few can see a storm when the clouds are ingathering, but securely build on the present ease and peace, though God be angry. But in the eye of faith a sinful estate is always dangerous; therefore they fall a praying and humbling themselves, and cry to God mightily, and use all means of safety, while a judgment is but yet in its causes.

(3d.) To support us against the greatest dangers and terrors: Heb. xi. 27, 'By faith Moses forsook Egypt, not fearing the wrath of the king, for he endured as seeing him that is invisible.' To depend upon God's aid and succour in a time of great extremity and danger needeth a strong faith. As to appearance, he was ready to be swallowed up, being pursued by a wrathful and puissant king; the sea was before him, the Egyptians behind him, and the craggy and inaccessible mountains on each side; but the terrors of sense may be easily vanquished by those invisible succours which faith relieth upon; an invisible God can bear us out against visible dangers.

(4.) To teach us how to carry an equal mind in prosperity and adversity. In prosperity, when we are borne up by the chin, we have but too much confidence, and when we are lessened and cut short in the world, we are full of diffidence and distrustful fears: Ps. xxx. 6, 'In my prosperity I said, I shall never be moved.' When a child of God hath gotten a carnal pillow under his head, he lieth down, and sleepeth sweetly, dreaming many a pleasant dream of uninterrupted felicity in the world, but if God taketh away his pillow from under his head, then he is as diffident as formerly confident, then 'God will be favourable no more.' God is the same, his promises the same, the covenant the same, the Mediator the same, but our condition is changed, because we look to things seen, live upon things seen, and still imagine of things according to what we see and feel. So for supplies of maintenance and provision; if we have them not in view and sight, how little can we depend upon God! If sense be against the promises, the promises do us but little good. How few can comfort themselves in God when all faileth, Hab. iii. 18, or make his all-sufficiency their storehouse! Gen. xvii. 1. No; they must have a full heap in their own keeping. How few can take his promises for their heritage! Ps. cxix. 11. No; they must have lands and fixed revenues, or else they know not where to have food and raiment for themselves and children. How few can be contented to trust the purse in God's hands, and be contented to take their daily allowance from him! which yet is a necessary point of faith, of continual practice. How few can see all things in God when they have nothing in the creature! 2 Cor. vi. 10. Many talk of living by faith, but it is when they have enough in the world to live upon; they eat their own bread; wear their own apparel, only call it by God's name. The life of sense is more evident than the life of faith. Well, now, this being the nature of faith, thereby we may know the measure of it; for the excellency and degree of everything is known by the essential properties.

2. The second property of faith is self-denial, or a venturing of all in Christ's hands, or a foregoing all for Christ. That this is included in the nature of faith, yea, essential to it, I must prove to you—

[1.] By the description of faith in scripture: Heb. x. 39, 'We are not of the number of them that draw back to perdition, but of them that believe to the saving of the soul;' ἐκ πίστεως εἰς περιποίησιν ψυχῆς, the purchasing of the soul; not purchasing in the way of merit, but means. A true and sound faith will cause us to save the soul, though with the loss of other things. The flesh is for sparing or saving the body, but faith is for saving the soul whatever it costs us. The flesh saith, Favour thyself; faith saith, Hazard all for Christ.

[2.] By reason. I will prove that it not only necessarily results from the nature of faith, but is included in it; for faith builds upon the promise of salvation by Christ. Now this promise is not only true but good, 1 Tim. i. 1. It is certainly true, and requireth the firmest belief; it is eminently good, and worthy to be regarded above all other things; the happiness is most desirable, and the assurance of enjoying it as strong as can be given us. Now we do not close with this promise rightly unless we assent and embrace, take the thing promised for our whole happiness, and the promise itself for our whole security. The thing promised we do not take for our whole happiness unless we forsake all other hopes and happiness, and can let go all pleasures, profits, worldly reputation, and honour; yea, life itself, when it is inconsistent with our fidelity to Christ, or the way we should take to enjoy the blessedness that he offereth. Not only wilful sin, and all carnal pleasures, but anything, though never so near and dear to us. No; we will not take up with any other portion and felicity for all the temptations in the world. And also there must be a confidence of God's promise in Jesus Christ, that we may venture our all upon this security, and, if God call us to it, actually forsake all; so that without self-denial we can neither trust God nor be true to him.

[3.] This suiteth with the nature of the conditional and baptismal covenant. There is an absolute covenant whereby God promiseth to give faith to the elect, and a conditional covenant sealed in baptism, wherein it is said that 'He that believeth and is baptized shall be saved,' Mark xvi. 16. Now by this covenant none can be believers or disciples of Christ, but those that forsake all for Christ's sake: Mat. xiii. 45, 46, 'The kingdom of heaven is like to a merchant-man seeking goodly pearls, who when he had found one pearl of great price, he went and sold all that he had and bought it.' Christ knew the nature of faith better than we do. Many cheapen the pearl of price, but do not go through with the bargain, because they do not sell all to purchase it, all that is inconsistent with this choice and trust. So Luke xiv. 26, 'If any man come unto me, and hate not father, and mother, and brother, and sister, yea, and his own life, he cannot be my disciple.' Shall we think to go to heaven at a cheaper rate, after such express declarations of the will of Christ? All christians are not called to this, but all must be ready for this: Eph. vi. 15, 'Your feet shod with the preparation of the gospel of peace;' Acts xxi. 13, 'I am ready not to be bound only, but also to die at Jerusalem for the name of the Lord Jesus;' 1 Peter iii. 15, 'Be ready always to give an answer to every man that asketh you a reason of the hope that is in you, with meekness and fear.' This every disciple must be, prepared to undergo martyrdom if God calls him to it.

[4.] I prove it by the instances of believers, ordinary and extraordinary. Faith was ever a venturing all and a forsaking all upon God's veracity and truth of his promises.

(1.) Extraordinary. Noah had but God's bare word for the flood, Heb. xi. 7, yet notwithstanding the mocks of the incredulous world, with vast expense and care he prepareth an ark, which was the prescribed means to save himself and household. Abraham leaveth his father's house, though he knew not whither God would call him, Heb. xi. 8. Here was venturing all on God's fidelity; and afterwards we read that he was ready to offer Isaac, leaving the way to God how to fulfil his promises, ver. 17, 18. So the Israelites passing through the Red Sea, ver. 29, there they put their all into God's hands, when upon his word themselves and little ones and all their substance ventured into the great deep. So Christ's trial of the young man: Mark x. 21, 'Go thy way, sell whatsoever thou hast, and give to the poor, and thou shalt have treasure in heaven,' &c.; but the promise of eternal life and great treasure in heaven could not part the young man and his great estate.

(2.) Ordinary. Moses: Heb. xi. 24–26, 'By faith Moses, when he was come to years, refused to be called the son of Pharaoh's daughter, choosing rather to suffer affliction with the people of God than to endure the pleasures of sin for a season, esteeming the reproach of Christ greater riches than the treasures in Egypt, for he had respect unto the recompense of reward.' So those that the apostle speaketh of, Heb. x. 34, 'Ye took joyfully the spoiling of your goods, knowing in yourselves that ye have in heaven a better and an enduring substance.' They had such a faith in Christ, that though they had lost their goods, yet because they lost not Christ and the hopes of heaven by him, they thought themselves happy enough. So Paul's quitting all honour and respect with his countrymen: Phil. iii. 8, 'I count all things but dung and dross for the excellency of the knowledge of Christ Jesus my Lord.' It is endless to instance in all, but this is enough to show you that the true believers are still known by their self-denial. But you will say, if this be necessary to the very truth and being of faith (as certainly it is), how shall we know our growth, for we can but forsake all? I answer—By your readiness and willingness to part with all for Christ. The weakest believer can part with no more but all, but the stronger this faith is, he doth it with the more readiness of mind, and with least defaults in his duty and blots in his fidelity to Christ. Would you know then whether your faith be strong or weak? know it by this—The more you can adhere to Christ, whatever temptations you have to the contrary, if you can venture not only some, but all things, upon the account of the promise of eternal life—

(1st.) Deny the sinful pleasures of the flesh; they were never worth the keeping. If I cannot deny a little vain pleasure, what can I deny for Christ? Surely momentary delight is bought too dear if it must be bought with the loss of eternal joys. Esau is represented as a profane person, that sold his birthright for one morsel of meat, Heb. xii. 15. If the vain delights of the world prevail so with men that all the promises of the gospel cannot reclaim them, these comply with the motions of the flesh, which is importunate to be pleased, but have no sense of the offers of Christ, who calleth upon us to save our souls. The true christian is a stranger and pilgrim on the earth, whose mind and heart is set upon better things, which are to come, 1 Peter ii. 11. Upon the security of God's word, he is taking his journey into another world.

(2d.) We must be willing to sacrifice all our interests: Mat. xvi. 24, 'If any man will come after me, and be my disciple, let him deny himself, and take up his cross and follow me.' If God be trusted as our felicity, worldly felicity must be no impediment to our duty; therefore, if we cannot incur blame and shame with men, yea, damage and loss, that we may be faithful with God, our faith is worth nothing.

(3d.) If God call you not to sufferings, yet there are some expenseful and self-denying duties which ever are incumbent upon you, Mat. xxv. 35. Visiting the sick, clothing the naked, feeding the hungry: Luke xii. 33, 'Sell that ye have, and give alms; provide yourselves bags which wax not old, a treasure in the heaven that faileth not.' Can you trust Christ upon such promises, and be at some loss for the gospel? for a religion that costs nothing is worth nothing. Most men love a cheap gospel, and the flesh engrosseth all; faith gets little from them to be laid out for God. These men run a fearful hazard of being rejected for ever; they sow to the flesh: Gal. vi. 8, 'He that soweth to the flesh shall of the flesh reap corruption, but he that soweth to the Spirit shall of the Spirit reap life everlasting.'

(4*th*.) If your faith maketh you to submit to providence. When we first entered into covenant with God, we entirely and absolutely gave up ourselves to God, to be governed by his commanding will, and to be ordered by his disposing will. You cannot shift yourselves out of his hands, but your voluntary submission to anything, if you may have Christ and heaven at last, is the trial of your faith: Job i. 21, 'The Lord gave, and the Lord hath taken away; blessed be the name of the Lord;' Phil. i. 20, 'So Christ be magnified in my body, whether it be by life or death.' He was come to a point; nothing should be reserved. So Christ may be glorified, and you may have his saving grace, let him give or take; the more willingly you do this, the stronger is your faith. Certainly to deny all is an essential property of faith.

3. The third evidence of a growing faith is when our light is turned into love; for faith is not a bare knowledge, but a sound, a savoury and effective knowledge, a knowing things as we ought to know them 1 Cor. viii. 1, 2. A knowledge with a taste; for such a difference as there is between the sight of meat and the tasting of it, such a difference there is between speculative knowledge and the apprehension of faith, 1 Peter i. 3. You may dispute him out of his belief that seeth, but you can never dispute him out of his belief that tastes, for you cannot make him go against his own sense. The steadfastness of unlearned christians cometh mainly from their taste and love; they adhere more closely to Christ than those that have only a dead opinion, because they received the truth not only in the light but love of it, 2 Thes. ii. 10. Now the more taste we have of the things we know and believe, the stronger is our faith. Now, besides the manner of apprehension, the truths apprehended tend mainly to raise our love to God, that we may love him that loved us first, 1 John iv. 19. We know God that we may love him, and faith is nothing else but a beholding the love of God in the face of Jesus Christ, that our hearts may be warmed, attracted, and drawn to God. Faith is the bellows to enkindle the fire of love in our souls; and therefore faith, the more sound and sincere it is, the more it worketh by love, Gal. v. 6. Faith is required *sub ratione medii;* love, *sub ratione finis.* The end of the gospel institution is love, 1 Tim. i. 5. Well, then, when you make it your great business to love God, and count it your great happiness to be beloved by him, then may you best judge of the growth of your faith. The gospel representeth the goodness and amiableness of God, that he may be more lovely to us, and be beloved by us; for this was the end of reconciling and saving man by Christ; his incarnation, life, sufferings,

death, resurrection, ascension, and intercession is all to reveal the love of God in Christ, and to work our hearts to love God again. To this end also tend his merciful covenant and promises, and all the benefits given to the church, all the privileges of the saints, his Spirit, pardon, peace, glory, all these to warm our hearts, and fill them with a sense of the love of God. Now if we slightly reflect upon these things, with cold and narrow thoughts, we have not the true faith, certainly not a grown faith.

SERMON IV.

Your faith groweth exceedingly.—2 Thes. i. 3.

The fourth essential property of faith is its respect to the word of God. That I may explain this with more full satisfaction, I shall open four things—(1.) The relation of the word to faith; (2.) The acts of faith about the word; (3.) The effects of faith thus exercised; (4.) The notes whereby we may discern a strong or grown faith.

First, The relation of the word to faith.

1. It is a means to beget and breed faith: Rom. x. 14, 15, 'How shall they call on him on whom they have not believed? and how shall they believe on him of whom they have not heard? and how shall they hear without a preacher? and how shall they preach except they be sent?' Every part of the gradation hath its weight. First, what I am bound to adore and invocate; I must believe in him as a divine power. For the second, how shall men believe in Christ as a God unless they have heard of him? Faith is a believing such things as God hath revealed because he hath revealed them; therefore the divine revelation must be conveyed to them by some means or other. The third, there is no hearing without a preacher; some messenger or interpreter that may bring tidings of pardon and life by Christ. Then for the fourth branch, 'How shall they preach except they be sent?' that is, come with authority, evidence, and power, whereby it may be known that he is a messenger authorised and sent by God, that the things propounded may be received as a certain truth of God's own revelation, that we may depend upon the credit of his word, and that with such a lively and effectual belief as may prevail with us to assent unto it, and embrace it notwithstanding all difficulties and objections to the contrary. Now such is the doctrine of salvation by Christ, which inviteth us to call upon his name or name ourselves by the name of Christ, because we may believe in him, and run all hazards for him, 2 Tim. i. 12. Why? Because we have heard of him; the fame of his doctrine, so suitable to the glory of God and the necessities of mankind; and the fame of his miracles, especially his death and resurrection, and that by authentic preachers, or faithful men authorised by God, and sufficiently owned by him, as those that are commissioned to instruct the world, and to teach them the way of salvation; so that the word is the great means to work faith.

2. It is the warrant of faith, which stateth the laws of commerce between us and God, which showeth how far God hath obliged himself, and we may depend upon him, as appeareth by the words of Christ: John xvii. 20, 'Neither pray I for these alone, but for them also that shall believe in me through their word.' The principal object of faith is Christ; we believe in him; and the warrant of faith is the word, that is, the doctrine which by the apostles is consigned to the use of the church. For these and no other Christ prayeth, and according to this way or law of grace God offereth himself to be reconciled to his creatures. So that here you may hold him to his covenant; the word is gone out of his lips, and without this you make promises to yourselves which God will not stand unto.

3. It is the object of faith, or the thing which we do believe: Acts xxiv. 14, 'I believe all things which are written in the law and the prophets;' and add to that, in the writings of the apostles. To make the object of the christian faith complete, take in also what is written in the apostles, for 'We are built upon the foundation of the apostles and prophets, Jesus Christ himself being the chief corner-stone,' Eph. ii. 20; that is, the doctrine of the apostles and prophets, Jesus Christ being the chief sum and scope of it, who is to be accepted of as he is revealed and offered in the scriptures of the Old and New Testament, betwixt which there is a sweet harmony and agreement. But because this is too bulky and large for us to manage at one time, let us consider the sum of the scriptures in the method wherein God hath put it, and that is, the covenant of grace ratified by the blood of Christ, which is the most glorious discovery whereby God hath made known himself to his creatures: Ps. cxxxviii. 2, 'I will praise thy name for thy loving-kindness and thy truth, for thou hast magnified thy word above all thy name.' There we see that God's word is the chiefest discovery that he hath made of himself to the creature, for it is magnified above all his name; that is, it doth set forth God above all that is named, famed, spoken, or believed, or known, or understood of God. And what is the matter of his word? His loving-kindness and his truth; that is, in the word there are contained admirable promises, which God will certainly perform to the utmost importance of them. There we see his mercy and loving-kindness in making such great promises. The promises of the new covenant are beyond all expression great and precious, 2 Peter i. 4; they contain as much as the heart of man can desire, all spiritual and eternal riches, pardon of sin, taking away the stony heart, eternal life; these are offered to men to believe. And then his truth and fidelity in performing these promises most punctually to all those that do believe, and will accept the pardon, grace, and blessedness offered, and behave themselves accordingly. Well, then, God's mercies in Christ to them that repent, believe, and obey God are the matter and object of our faith.

4. The word is the security and strength of our faith—(1.) As it puts God's grace into the way of a promise; (2.) As this promise is the promise of God.

[1.] We have much advantage in believing by the formality of a promise. A promise is more than a purpose, more than a doctrinal declaration, more than a prediction of prophecy.

(1.) More than a purpose. A purpose is only the thought of the heart, a thing secret and hidden, but a promise is open and manifest. A purpose is the intention of a person, a promise is his intention revealed, whereby we have a knowledge of the good intended to us. If God had only purposed to give us eternal life, we might at last have enjoyed it, but we could not have known it beforehand; it would have been as an hidden treasure. Promises are the eruptions and overflows of God's love to us; his heart is so big with kindness and designs of goodness that it cannot stay till the accomplishment of things: Isa. xlii. 9, 'Before they spring forth I tell you of them.' God's purposes are a sealed fountain, but his promises are a fountain broken open, bubbling forth. He might have done us good, and given us no notice, but love concealed would not be so much for our comfort. Besides, they are obligations which God taketh upon himself *promittendo se fecit debitorem.* So far as God hath promised, so far he hath made himself a debtor. God's purposes are unchangeable, but his promises are a security put into our hands, so that we have a greater holdfast upon God now the word is gone out of his lips, Ps. lxxxix. 34. We may put the bond in suit, throw him in his handwriting: Ps. cxix. 49, 'Remember thy word unto thy servant, upon which thou hast caused me to hope.' We have the pawn of the thing promised, which we must hold fast till performance cometh. His truth and holiness lie at stake, and are as it were impawned with the creature.

(2.) It is more than a doctrinal declaration. It is one thing to reveal a thing, another to promise it. A doctrine maketh a thing known, but a promise maketh a thing sure. A doctrine giveth us notice, but a promise giveth us right and interest if we be qualified. Christ hath brought life and immortality to light through the doctrine of the gospel, 2 Tim. i. 10; but he hath not only manifested, but granted, assured it to believers by the promises of the gospel, 1 John ii. 25. It is so conveyed to us as that we may be sure of obtaining it.

(3.) It is more than a prophecy or simple prediction. Scripture prophecies will be fulfilled because of God's veracity, but scripture promises will be fulfilled, not only because of God's veracity, but also because of his fidelity and justice. As by our promise another man cometh to have a right to the thing promised, therefore it is just it should be given unto him, so it is in God; it was his mercy and goodness to make the promise, but his holiness and justice bindeth him to make it good: 1 John i. 9, 'He is faithful and just to forgive us our sins.' And as for pardon, so for life: 2 Tim. iv. 8, 'Henceforth there is laid up for me a crown of righteousness, which the righteous judge shall give me on that day.' It becometh a debt of grace. This may be illustrated by what divines say of an assertory lie and a promissory lie. An assertory lie is when we speak of a thing past or present otherwise than it is, and a promissory lie is when we speak of a thing for the time to come which we never intend to perform; and this is the worst sort of lies, because it doth not only prevent the end of speech, which is truth, but also defeateth another of that right which we seem to give him by our promise in the thing promised, which is a further degree of injustice. Now we should apprehend God to be very far from this: Titus i. 2, 'In hope of eternal life, which God, that cannot lie, promised before the world began;' and Heb. vi. 18, 'That by two immutable things, in which it was impossible for God to lie, we might have a strong consolation.'

[2.] It is the promise of God. In every promise, that it be certain and firm, three things are required—(1.) That it be made seriously and heartily, with a purpose to perform it; (2.) That he that promiseth continue in his purpose without change of mind; (3.) That it be in the power of him that promiseth to perform what he hath so promised. Now in the promise of God there can be no doubt of any of these things. Certainly God meaneth as he speaketh, when he promiseth eternal life to the faithful servants and disciples of Jesus Christ; for what need had he to court his creatures into a false and imaginary happiness which he never meant to bestow upon them? to send his Son with a commission from heaven, to assure them of it, who also wrought miracles to confirm the message that he brought from God, died upon this truth, and rose again, and entered into the happiness that he spoke of, to give us assurance, and a visible demonstration of the truth of it? sent abroad his apostles to invite the world to embrace it, his Holy Spirit accompanying them, and sealing their message also with divers signs and wonders? And surely he doth continue in the same mind, for there is no repeal of this law of grace. And he is able to perform it; for what difficulty is there which omnipotency cannot subdue and overcome? Surely what God hath promised he is fully able to perform.

Secondly, The acts of faith about the word.

1. We are to believe and credit it upon solid and sufficient evidence. It is said, Heb. xi. 11, 'They saw these things afar off, and were persuaded of them;' and Acts xiii. 48, 'When the gentiles heard this, they glorified the word of God, and believed;' that is, blessed God for his glorious mercy revealed in the gospel. The sound belief and firm assent leadeth on other things, for the most powerful truths work not till they are believed: 1 Thes. ii. 13, 'Ye received the word not as the word of man, but (as it is in truth) the word of God, which effectually worketh also in you that believe.' Here beginneth the efficacy. Now usually we receive the truth at first upon low and insufficient evidence, but afterwards our assent is upon better grounds, and more valid and strong; as the Samaritans: John iv. 42, 'Now we believe, not because of thy saying, for we have heard him ourselves, and know that this is indeed the Christ, the Saviour of the world.' Her saying was much, for the woman had testified that she had met with an holy person that had told her of all that ever she did. So Nathaniel was drawn to Christ by Philip's persuasion, but when he perceived that he knew the heart and secret things, John i. 48, 49, 'He saith unto him, Whence knowest thou me? Jesus answered and said unto him, Before that Philip called thee, when thou wast under the fig-tree, I saw thee. Nathaniel answered, and saith unto him, Rabbi, thou art the son of God, thou art the king of Israel. Christ then promiseth him further assurance and greater evidence, which should beget a more confirmed and strong faith: ver. 50, 'Jesus answered and said unto him, Because I said unto thee, I saw thee under the fig-tree, believest thou? thou shalt see greater things than these.' The church is in possession of a religion which

God hath blessed throughout successions of ages, and we received the doctrine of the gospel and new covenant upon report and hearsay; hereafter we see farther and better grounds, and the scriptures are owned with more certainty of evidence. Well, then, here is the first thing, assent, or a receiving all truths about supernatural things upon the credit of God's word.

2. The work of faith is to apply these things; for the closer such blessed truths are laid to our own souls, the more we feel the virtue of them: Job v. 27, 'Lo, this it is; know thou it for thy good;' Rom. viii. 31, 'What shall we then say to these things?' The promise includeth you as well as others, and promiseth and offereth you pardon and life if you will believe in Christ; therefore the application I press you to is not a claim of privileges (stay a while there), but an exciting yourselves to perform the duties of the gospel, that you may turn away from all other ways of felicity, and choose this alone. Faith must be applicative, and the closer the application the better; but there is a difference between the application which is an excitement of your duty, and that application which is an assurance of your interest: Acts xiii. 20, 'To you is this word of salvation sent.' It is my duty to make general grace particular, but not presently, and at first dash to enter my plea and claim, but to oblige me to take God's way. God calleth upon me to repent and believe in Christ, that I may have pardon and life.

3. We are heartily to consent to this blessed covenant which is contained in the word of God, taking the promises offered for our happiness, resolving upon the duties required as our work: Acts ii. 41, 'They received the word gladly, and were baptized.' There was a precept and a promise, ver. 38; they accepted the counsel, and waited for the promise. Our respect to the word is made up of a mixture of obedience and dependence; there must be a consent to both, and we must resolve for the holy and heavenly life. Faith is an act of the will as well as of the understanding: Heb. xi. 13, 'These all died in faith, not having received the promises, but having seen them afar off, and were persuaded of them, and embraced them.' Besides being persuaded, there is embracing: 'The promises of God in him are Yea, and in him Amen, unto the glory of God by us,' 2 Cor. i. 20; and they are 'exceeding great and precious promises,' 2 Peter i. 4. In one place you have both: 1 Tim. i. 15, 'This is a faithful saying, and worthy of all acceptation, that Christ Jesus came into the world to save sinners.' Therefore embrace them you must with all your hearts, and submit to this way of covenanting with God.

4. Your judgments must highly esteem these promises, and your hearts find full contentment and satisfaction in them. We read often of receiving the word with joy, and the confidence and rejoicing of hope, Heb. iii. 6. Usually the word of God hath too cold and slight entertainment in our affections, and we do not value those precious promises as we ought to do. They should be dearer to us than our lives, and give us more satisfaction than all the enjoyments of the world: Ps. cxix. 111, 'I have taken thy testimonies as an heritage for ever; they are the rejoicing of my soul.' They do you good to your very heart, and the more you are acquainted with them, the

more you will see the worth of them : Luke vi. 23, 'Rejoice and leap for joy, for great is your reward in heaven.' And of the eunuch, when he had sealed covenant with God, Acts viii. 39, it is said, 'he went his way rejoicing.' Faith cannot do its office, that is, out of an holy gratitude to God, to draw us off from the allurements of sense, and fortify us against adversities and troubles, and engage us to the duties of christianity, which are distrustful to flesh and blood, unless it did fill our hearts with an higher and better joy than the world yieldeth. Surely it is comfortable to be pardoned and reconciled to God, to be in the way, and under the hopes of eternal life.

Thirdly, The effects which these acts produce. These may be stated by the several uses for which the word of God serveth. (1.) It is the seed of a new life; (2.) The constant rule of all our actions; (3.) The sure charter of our hopes; (4.) Our strength and preservation against all temptations from the devil, the world, and the flesh; (5.) Our comfort and cordial in all afflictions.

1. It is the seed of a new life : 1 Peter i. 23, 'Being born again, not of corruptible seed, but of incorruptible, by the word of God, which liveth and abideth for ever;' and James i. 18, 'Of his own will begat he us, with the word of truth, that we should be a kind of first-fruits of his creatures;' and also, 2 Peter i. 4, 'Whereby are given unto us exceeding great and precious promises, that by these you might be partakers of the divine nature.' When we so believe the pardon, and grace, and blessedness offered, that our hearts are changed into the life and likeness of God; for the truth is not rightly owned and believed till this change be wrought both in heart and life, then we are cast into the mould of this doctrine : Rom. vi. 17, 'Ye have obeyed from the heart that form of doctrine that was delivered to you.' Gospel truths serve not for speculation or mere talk and discourse, but for sanctification; and therefore if this seed be sown and engrafted in your hearts, and you begin to live to God an holy and heavenly life, you have the surest evidence of your faith; for causes are made sensible to us by their effects. It is usually brought as a proof of the word, the sanctifying virtue of it; so it is of the sincerity of your faith, for the word profiteth not unless it be mingled with faith; and since both faith and the word concur to this effect, it may be ascribed to either. Surely therefore if we believe the word of God, and value it as we ought, it doth leave the impression of God's image upon us, for it is the fairest draught and representation of God that ever was in the law and life of Christ, 2 Cor. iii. 18. If our souls and lives be a transcript of the word, this image is thence deduced to us by the Spirit, and of necessity it must be so, for Christ's comforting promises of mercy and glory are made to these new creatures who live the holy and heavenly life. They have God's mark and signature upon them, and therefore are said to be 'sealed to the day of redemption,' Eph. ii. 30, and Eph. i. 3. This renovation of the soul is the seal of God, the pledge of his love, and the earnest of the heavenly inheritance.

2. The constant rule of all our actions. There is a fixed determined rule from whence we cannot swerve and vary without sin, and if we would have communion with God here or enjoy him hereafter. We must keep close to this rule : Gal. vi. 16, 'As many as walk according

to this rule, peace be on them, and mercy, and upon the Israel of God.' This rule, that is the word of God, which directeth us as to our general path and way, and all our steps or particular actions: Ps. cxix. 105, 'Thy word is a lamp unto my feet and a light unto my paths.' We must hide the word in our hearts: Ps. cxix. 110, 'Thy word have I hid in my heart, that I might not sin against thee.' We must consult with it upon all occasions, as willing to understand our duty: Ps. cxix. 24, 'Thy testimonies also are my delight, and my counsellors.' And because we may mistake through error of mind, or be tempted aside through aversion of heart and manifold temptations, therefore we must earnestly beg it of God: Ps. cxix. 133, 'Order my steps in thy word, and let not any iniquity have dominion over me.' And we must use all study ourselves, Rom. xii. 2, and constant watchfulness: Eph. v. 15, 'See then that ye walk circumspectly, not as fools, but as wise.' Now that which I say is this: When the word ruleth the main course of our lives, and teacheth us how to live in the world, soberly, righteously, and godly, the tenderness of the word, and high respect to it, that we dare not transgress it whatever temptations we have so to do, showeth that faith hath obtained its effect in us; for trembling at the word, fearing of a commandment, and whatever of that kind is spoken of in the scripture, they are all fruits of faith.

3. It is the charter of our hopes: John xx. 31, 'These things are written that ye might have life through his name;' 1 John v. 11, 'This is the record that God hath given unto us eternal life, and this life is in his Son.' Now the work of faith is to 'lay hold upon eternal life,' 1 Tim. vi. 12; that is, seize upon it as ours, as assured to us by the word of God, or to take it as our happiness, and accordingly pursue after it: Eph. i. 13, 'In whom ye trusted after ye heard the word of truth, the gospel of your salvation.' Now, when we choose this felicity for our portion, set our hearts upon it, make it the chief care and business of our lives to seek it, and do all as means thereunto, carry ourselves as strangers and pilgrims in the world, and look for no great matters here, but wholly depend upon God's faithful word for this happiness to come, then is faith wrought in us.

4. It is our strength and preservative against all temptations from the devil, the world, and the flesh. The word of God is the 'sword of the Spirit,' Eph. vi. 17, a weapon of excellent use in the spiritual warfare; and it is said, 1 John ii. 14, 'Ye are strong, and the word of God abideth in you, and ye have overcome the wicked one.' This helpeth us to ward off the blow of any temptation. When the heart is well stocked and furnished with this word of God, you have something to oppose still to darken the splendour of the world, to check the desires of the flesh, and so do the better carry on a continual warfare and watchfulness. And so the fleshly inclination is overruled, and the profits, honours, and pleasures of the world have less force upon us. When the devil showeth the bait, and the flesh is ready to swallow it, faith showeth the hook. A belief of the word of God being of a lively and vigorous nature, produceth noble effects in us. It casteth down all that rebelleth against God, and casteth out all that would be preferred before him: Ps. xxxvii. 31, 'The law of his God is in his heart, none of his steps shall slide.' A lively active sense of his duty is kept fresh upon his heart.

5. To be our comfort and cordial in our afflictions: Ps. cxix. 59, 'This is my comfort in my affliction, thy word hath quickened me;' ver. 92, 'Unless thy law had been my delight, I should then have perished in my affliction,' Heb. xii. 5; 'Ye have forgotten the exhortation which speaketh unto you as unto children, My son, despise not thou the chastening of the Lord, nor faint when thou art rebuked of him.' So Ps. xciv. 19, 'In the multitude of my thoughts within me thy comforts delight my soul.' God's comforts are such as God alloweth, or God worketh. The matter of both is in the scriptures, though the Spirit be the author of them, and the instrument he worketh by is faith. In wants and straits how sweet is it to a believer to consider how amply we are provided for in the covenant. When God's hand is heavy upon us, and providence represents him as an angry judge, yet the covenant represents him as a father. In a time of trial, one promise of God will give you more true comfort and support than all the arguings of men.

Fourthly, The notes whereby we discern a strong and grown faith as to this property of it, its respect to the word.

1. When the consolations laid down in the word of God are more prized than any extraordinary dispensations. Certainly it is a weakness when men undervalue the comforts of the word, as slender, empty, unsatisfactory, and would have the manifestations of God's love exhibited to them in some singular and extraordinary way. Eliphaz chargeth it on Job wrongfully, Job xv. 11, 'Are the consolations of God small with thee? is there any secret thing with thee?' God's ordinary way is the sure way, the other layeth us open to a snare. Surely our consciences are best settled in the ordinary way of God's word, in a way of faith, repentance, and close walking with God; but as Naaman despised the waters of Jordan, so many despise the ordinary comforts, and would have signs and wonders to assure them. These may long sit in darkness, because if God comforts them not in their way, they will not be comforted at all. Now, though God sometimes, in condescension to his people, may grant their desires, as Christ did to Thomas, yet it is with an upbraiding of their weakness and unbelief, John xx. 28. You should acquiesce in the common allowance of God's people, lest you seem to reflect on the wisdom and goodness of God, and lay open yourselves to some false consolation and dream of comfort, while we affect new rules without the compass of the word; especially when we find not our expectations there speedily answered, like hasty patients ready to tamper with every medicine they hear of, rather than submit to a regular course of physic. Gregory telleth us of a lady of the emperor's court that never ceased importuning him to seek from God a revelation from heaven that she should be saved. *Rem difficilem petivit et inutilem.* It was a thing difficult, and unprofitable; difficult for him to obtain, and unprofitable for her to ask, having a surer way by the scriptures: 2 Peter i. 19, βεβαιότερον λόγον, 'We have a more sure word of prophecy' than oracles. The adhering of the soul to the promises is the unquestionable way to obtain peace. Luther, as he confesseth, was often tempted to ask for signs or some special revelation. He tells also how strongly he withstood these temptations, *Pactum feci cum Domino meo, ne mihi mittat visiones, vel etiam angelos; contentus enim sum hoc dono, quod habeo scripturam sanctam quæ abunde*

docet et suppeditat omnia quæ necessaria sunt, tam ad hanc vitam, tam ad futuram—I indented with the Lord my God that he would never send me dreams and visions; I am well contented with the gift of the scriptures.

2. When the word is matter of joy and firm confidence to us before there is any appearance of performance. This in two cases—

[1.] In case of delay, when it is long ere God appeareth, and faith doth not require the existence and pre-essence of the thing believed, only the promise of it. Therefore though the promise be delayed, it eyeth the blessing at a distance: Heb. xi. 13, 'These all died in faith, not having received the promises, but having seen them afar off, were persuaded of them, and embraced them.' Abraham was one of them: John viii. 56, 'Your father Abraham rejoiced to see my day, and he saw it, and was glad.' And we, if we would be strong believers, must do likewise: Heb. vi. 12, 'Be not slothful, but followers of them who through faith and patience inherit the promises.' A christian is not to be valued by his enjoyments, but his hopes; heaven is all performance. Here he dealeth with us by promises, but you will find his payment sure, and that God in effect is better than all his promises; for they cannot signify and convey the full sense of all that God meaneth to bestow. Therefore we must wait, whether the promise be to be fulfilled in this life or the life to come; let us dig the pit, and tarry till God fill it with rain from heaven.

[2.] In case of difficulties, wants, distresses, the naked promise must be ground of hope and comfort to you; though it seem to be contradicted in the course of God's providence, when it is neither performed nor likely to be performed, you are to go by his word whatever his dispensation be: Rom. iv. 18, 'Abraham against hope believed in hope;' and David saith, Ps. lvi. 4, 'In God will I praise his word, in God I have put my trust; I will not fear what man can do unto me.' So ver. 10, 'In God will I praise his word, in the Lord will I praise his word.' The best holdfast faith can have on God is to take him by his word; though he withholdeth comfort and deliverance from us, yet we may praise him as long as we have his word. His dispensation giveth no satisfaction, yet the soul can find rest and contentment in his word. Well, then, if the word be an impregnable bulwark against all fears and dangers, and comfort against all wants and distresses, your faith is grown; for the more simply our dependence is upon the word of God, without sensible encouragements, the stronger is our faith.

3. When all the trust we have in God concerning the comforts we expect by the way is still referred to the great blessing of eternal life. We are to trust God by the way for our protection and defence, as well as for the reward at the end of the journey; by swimming in the shallow brooks we learn to venture in the great ocean, but still in subordination to the main blessing. This is the great comfort: Luke xii. 32, 'Fear not, little flock; it is your Father's good pleasure to give you the kingdom.' And our faith in the word tendeth to this: Rom. xv. 4, 'Whatsoever things were written aforetime were written for our learning, that we through patience and comfort of the scriptures might have hope.' Therefore strength of faith is hereby determined.

4. Because the word is not only our charter, but our rule. The strength of faith is known by this. If we value the word of God as it maketh us wise unto salvation, therefore we delight in the plain word without the ornaments of wit, as painting in glass windows hindereth the light. Everything communicateth to its own nature; heat causeth heat, cold causeth cold. Ministers speak as the oracles of God, and so the people receive.

SERMON V.

Your faith groweth exceedingly, and the charity of every one of you all towards each other aboundeth.—2 THES. i. 3.

WE come to the fifth property of faith, which is an high value and esteem of Jesus Christ. I mention this—

1. Because faith in the new covenant mainly and distinctly respects Christ: Acts xx. 21, 'Testifying both to the Jews, and also to the gentiles, repentance towards God, and faith towards our Lord Jesus Christ.' Why repentance respects God I showed you lately, because from God we fell, and to God we return. We fell from him as we withdrew our allegiance and sought our happiness elsewhere; we return to him as to our rightful Lord and proper happiness. But faith respects the Mediator, who is the only remedy of our misery, and the means of eternal blessedness. He opened the way to God by his merit and satisfaction, and actually bringeth us into this way by his renewing and reconciling grace, that we may be in a capacity to please and enjoy God, and that is the reason why faith in Christ is so much insisted on, as it begets a title to the blessings of the new covenant. It hath a special aptitude and fitness for this work of our recovery from sin to, God, partly because a guilty conscience is not easily settled, and brought to look for all kind of happiness from one whom we have so much wronged. Adam, when once a sinner, was shy of God, Gen. iii. 10. Guilt is suspicious, and maketh us hang off from God, Ps. xxxii. 13; and if we have not one to lead us by the hand, and bring us to God, we cannot abide his presence.

2. Partly because the comfort of the promises is so rich and glorious, and the persons upon whom it is bestowed so unworthy, that it cannot easily enter into the heart of a man that God will be so good and gracious to us, unless we have a sound belief of his merit who hath procured these mercies and hopes for us: 1 Cor. ii. 9, 'Eye hath not seen, nor ear heard, neither hath it entered into the heart of man, the things which God hath prepared for them that love him.' Therefore since sense and reason could look for no such thing, a strong faith is necessary.

3. The way God hath taken for our deliverance is so supernatural and strange that nothing but faith can receive it: John iii. 16, 'God so loved the world, that he gave his only-begotten Son, that whosoever believeth on him should not perish, but have everlasting life;

and Rom. viii. 32, 'He spared not his own Son, but gave him to die for us.'

[4.] The chief of our blessings lie in another world, and nature cannot see so far off: 2 Peter i. 9, 'He that lacketh these things is blind, and cannot see afar off.' Unless we believe Christ, and his message to us, we shall never entertain these things.

[5.] For the present Christ's people are assaulted, and afflicted with so many difficulties, and so seemingly forsaken, and temptations to unbelief in this lower world are so manifold and pressing, that we can take no comfort in the new covenant unless we have faith in Christ, who is able to maintain and defend us till he hath brought us home to God: 2 Tim i. 12, 'I know whom I have believed, and I am persuaded that he is able to keep that which I have committed unto him against that day.'

[6.] Faith in Christ is most fitted for the acceptance of his free gift. Faith and grace go always together, and are put as opposites to law and works: Rom. iv. 16, 'Therefore it is of faith, that it might be of grace;' and Eph. ii. 8, 'By grace ye are saved, through faith, and that not of ourselves, it is the gift of God.' Faith establisheth the free grace and favour of God, or his condescension to us in the new covenant, wherein pardon and life are offered to penitent believers. What we receive by the grace of God in Christ cannot be of right, or such as we may challenge by virtue of obedience to the law upon that account. He might condemn us, but he doth accept us upon these new terms which Christ propounded of his mere grace: and therefore faith solveth the interest of grace in our pardon and salvation.

[7.] Because the duties of the new covenant are opposite to the bent of the carnal heart, which is set upon liberty and uncleanness: Rom. viii. 7, 'The carnal mind is enmity against God, for it is not subject to the law of God, neither indeed can be.' And nothing will bind us but faith in Christ, to whom we must give an account in the solemn judgment: Acts xvii. 30, 31, 'He commandeth all men everywhere to repent, because he hath appointed a day wherein he will judge the world in righteousness, by that man whom he hath ordained; whereof he hath given assurance unto all men, in that he hath raised him from the dead.' In which words I observe four things—(1.) That God requireth of all that will submit to the gospel repentance and new obedience; (2.) That the binding consideration is, that the judgment of every man's estate is put into Christ's hands, who in the day appointed will declare and determine every man's right and qualification; (3.) That the efficacy of this consideration dependeth on the strength of our faith or belief in Christ; (4.) That the strength of our faith dependeth on that assurance given, $\pi\acute{\iota}\sigma\tau\iota\nu\ \pi\alpha\rho\alpha\chi\grave{\omega}\nu\ \pi\hat{\alpha}\sigma\iota\nu$. Woe be to those that now refuse Christ, or do not believe him so as to obey him: 2 Thes. i. 8, 'In flaming fire, taking vengeance on them that know not God, and that obey not the gospel of our Lord Jesus Christ.'

[8.] Till we believe in Christ all his offices are useless to us, and therefore without faith he will do us no good. Who would learn of him that doth not believe him to be the great Prophet sent of God to teach the world the way to true happiness? Who would obey him that doth not believe that he is our Lord, that he hath power over all flesh, at whose judgment we must stand or fall? Who would depend upon the merit of his obedience and sacrifice, and be comforted with his gracious promise and covenant, and come to God with boldness and hope of mercy in his name, and be confident that he will justify and save, who doth not believe that he is a priest who once made an atonement, and doth continually make intercession for us? In the days of his flesh, all that would have benefit by Christ he did put them to this question, whether they did believe he was able to do it? To the father of the possessed child, 'Believest thou that I am able to do this?' Mark ix. 23; to Martha, John xi. 26, 'Whosoever liveth and believeth in me shall never die: believest thou this?' So still it holdeth good; this is the most necessary grace, that maketh way for all other respect to Christ.

That this respect is an high value and esteem of Christ above all other things. That faith implieth an esteem of Christ is plain by that of the apostle, 1 Peter ii. 7, 'Unto you therefore which believe he is precious.' And that it is a transcendental respect and esteem, so as that all other things are lessened in our opinion of them, and estimation of them, and respect unto them in comparison of Christ, appeareth by other scriptures; as Phil. iii. 8, 'I count all things but loss for the excellency of the knowledge of Christ Jesus my Lord, for whom I have suffered the loss of all things, and do count them but dung, that I may win Christ.' He had counted, and did count, as not repenting of his choice; he could deny his own honour, ease, profit, and estate, his own everything but his own God and his own Christ. So Mat. xiii. 45, 46, 'The kingdom of heaven is like unto a merchant-man seeking goodly pearls, who when he had found one pearl of great price, he went and sold all that he had and bought it.' The pearl was accounted of great price, if he would sell all things for it. Christ is so dear and precious, that the most excellent things are not dear and precious when they are to be ventured for his sake: Acts xx. 24, 'But none of these things move me, neither count I my life dear unto myself, so that I might finish my course with joy, and the ministry which I have received of the Lord Jesus, to testify the gospel of the grace of God.' No faith but this will allure and draw our hearts to Christ, and no faith but this will keep our hearts to him, there being so many other things either to keep us, or to draw us off from him. Nothing but this transcendental respect begets the close adherence to Christ.

Now I will show three things—(1.) That Christ hath deserved this esteem; (2.) That faith only will give it him; (3.) The notes, or how this esteem of Christ will show itself.

1. That he deserveth it; and that—

[1.] By what he is in himself, the Son of God and the Saviour of the world. This is the chief ground of our respect to the mediator: Acts viii. 37, 38, 'If thou believest with all thy heart, thou mayest; and he answered and said, I believe that Jesus Christ is the Son of God.' So Martha maketh her confession of faith: John xi. 27, 'Yea, Lord, I believe that thou art the Christ, the Son of God that should come into the world.' So Peter in his own name and the name of his fellow-disciples: John vi. 69, 'We believe and are sure that thou art the Christ, the Son of the living God.' This is the ground of adherence to him and dependence upon him, that he whom the christian world hath hitherto called their Saviour is the very Son of God, appointed by God to execute the office of king, priest, and prophet to the church. This giveth us ground to adhere to him, and vanquish all temptations: 1 John v. 5, 'Who is he that overcometh the world, but he that believeth that Jesus is the Son of God.' The most part of the christian world leap into this opinion, and the name of Christ is prized, but his office is neglected; there is a fond esteem of his memory, but no real improvement of his grace. *Quandoquidem panis Christi jam pinguis factus est, tractatur in conciliis, disceptatur in judiciis, disputatur in scholis, laudatur in eclisiis, questiosa res est nomen Christi.* But this is the true ground of a christian's esteem, when soundly persuaded that he is the Christ.

[2.] What he hath done for us. Christ requireth not so much at our hands as he himself hath voluntarily performed for our sakes. He 'pleased not himself,' that he might promote the glory of God and our salvation, Rom. xv. 3; 'He became poor that we might be rich,' 2 Cor. viii. 9; He 'was obedient to the death, even the death of the cross,' that we might have life, Phil. ii. 7; 'He was made sin for us, that we might be the righteousness of God in him,' 2 Cor. v. 21; 'He was made a curse for us,' that we might have the blessing; Gal. iii. 13. Doth he require so much of us? It is grievous to the flesh to be crossed, but he hath suffered greater sorrows and agonies, that we might have eternal life.

[3.] What he still doth for us. He is 'our life,' Gal. ii. 20. You live upon and by his life: John xiv. 19, 'Because I live, ye shall live also.' We use him not as an instrument which is laid by when our turn is served, but as an head and root. He is your righteousness, 1 Cor. i. 30, and 2 Cor. v. 21, 'He hath made him to be sin for us who knew no sin, that we might be made the righteousness of God in him.' You have the effect of his merit and obedience to plead to God; he is your blessedness for the present: Col. i. 27, 'Christ in you the hope of glory.' All the fatherly goodness of God cometh to you by him; all your helps, mercies, and hopes are founded in him alone. It is he presents your requests to God, and you take all your mercies out of his hands: 1 Cor. viii. 6, 'To us there is but one God, the Father, of whom are all things, and we in him; and one Lord Jesus Christ, by whom are all things, and we by him.' Your petitions are presented by the hands of him who is the beloved of God.

2. That faith doth give him this esteem, as it is an assent, consent, and affiance.

[1.] As an assent, we believing what he is, hath done, and doth still do for us, therefore we prize him. Faith knoweth him partly by what the word revealeth: John iv. 10, 'If thou knewest the gift of God, and who it is that saith to thee, Give me to drink, thou wouldest have asked of him, and he would have given thee living water;' and John vi. 40, 'This is the will of him that sent me, that every one which seeth the Son and believeth on him may have everlasting life.' They see such an excellency, fulness, and all-sufficiency in him as draweth off their hearts from all other things, and they cleave to him alone. Partly by experimental feeling, that he is such an one to us. As they see him to be such, they find him to be such: 1 Peter iii. 3, 'If so be that ye have tasted that the Lord is gracious.' The word revealeth, and experience findeth him to be so.

[2.] As it is a consent. We see Christ is so necessary for us, so beneficial to us, that we accept him for our Lord and Saviour, and count all the choicest concernments in the world but base things in comparison of his grace; therefore, forsaking all others, we devote ourselves to him, and are married to the Lord, that we may bring forth fruit to God, Rom. vii. 4. Nothing is allowed to rival Christ in the soul, or to be a competitor with him: Hosea iii. 3, this is the form of the conjugal covenant, 'Thou shalt not be for another, but thou shalt be for me.'

[3.] As it is a trust and affiance in him, that we may be reconciled to God, and saved by him from sin and punishment, and so be brought safe into a state of perfect happiness. Every one of these benefits doth endear him to the soul. Surely dependence will beget observance, and we will love him and please him in whose hands we venture our all, even our eternal interests and concernments.

3. The notes, or how this esteem will show itself.

[1.] In labouring to get Christ above all. This is the prime care, and must be carried on, whatever is left undone: Mat. xvi. 33, 'Seek ye first the kingdom of God and his righteousness, and all these things shall be added unto you;' Ps. xxvii. 4, 'One thing have I desired of the Lord, that will I seek after; that I may dwell in the house of the Lord all the days of my life, to behold the beauty of the Lord, and to inquire in his temple;' Prov. iv. 7, 'Wisdom is the principle thing, therefore get wisdom, and with all thy getting get understanding.' The accessary things must give way to the principal, the arbitrary things to the necessary. Food and raiment is not so necessary as Christ; temporal want is not so great an evil as eternal misery. Well then, communion with God in Christ must be minded, whatever is neglected. Most men's time and labour is laid out upon unsatisfying vanities; their life, and love, and time, and strength, and care is spent on worldly things, and they have seldom and cold thoughts of salvation by Christ, cannot deny themselves a little worldly pleasure or carnal ease, that they may attend upon this work, to get an interest in Christ's renewing and reconciling grace. Of those that were invited to the marriage-feast it is said, Mat. xxii. 5, 'They made light of it.'

[2.] A care in keeping Christ above all. Nothing should be so near and dear to you as Christ; he is your life and your strength. Your great care is, that he may lie as a bundle of myrrh in your bosoms: Cant. i. 13, 'A bundle of myrrh is my well-beloved unto me; he shall lie all night betwixt my breasts;' or 'dwell in your hearts by faith,' Eph. iii. 17. Christ is all in all to you. You are loath to put the comforts of his presence to hazard for a little carnal satisfaction, are chary and tender of your respects to your Redeemer, that he be not displeased or provoked to withdraw by any unkind dealing of yours. Whatever temptations would withdraw you from your duty you reject with loathing and indignation. Christ hath pitched upon this as the true and proper evidence of our love to him and esteem of him: John xiv. 21, 'He that hath my commandments, and keepeth them, he it is that loveth me; and he that loveth me shall be loved of my Father, and I will love him and will manifest myself to him.' We are apt to flatter ourselves with an airy religion, that we value Christ and prize Christ; if so, we will be careful he be not offended and displeased.

[3.] By a willingness to lose all rather than lose Christ: Luke xiv. 33, 'Whosoever he be of you that forsaketh not all that he hath, he cannot be my disciple.' Counting the most dishonourable things in the world as honourable for his sake: Heb. xi. 26, 'Esteeming the reproach of Christ greater riches than the treasures in Egypt, for he had respect unto the recompense of reward;' Acts v. 41, 'And they departed from the presence of the council, rejoicing that they were counted worthy to suffer shame for his name.' They see a beauty in his despised ways. You can worship Christ as the wise men did, though in a stable, and are contented to be made vile for his sake: 2 Sam. vi. 22, 'I will yet be more vile than thus, and will be base in my own sight.' And we read of Marsacus, when he was led forth to suffer, and because of his quality they bound him not as they did others, he cried out, *Cur non et me quoque torque donas, &c.*—Why do you not give me also my chain, and make me a knight of this noble order? Some will pretend to prize Christ, but can hardly suffer a disgraceful word for him, or endure to be browbeaten with a frown.

[4.] By delighting in him and the testimonies of his love above all things else. Faith must breed such a confidence in Christ as keepeth up our delight in him, and such a delight and well-pleasedness of mind as we find not elsewhere: Ps. iv. 7, 'Thou hast put gladness in my heart, more than in the time that their corn and their wine increased;' and Cant. i. 4, 'We will be glad and rejoice in thee; we will remember thy loves more than wine.' The choicest contentments of the flesh are nothing so satisfying as the joy of his salvation. This joy is called 'unspeakable and glorious,' as being better felt than uttered, 1 Peter i. 8. The strength of it is seen when other comforts fail: 'How precious are thy thoughts unto me, O God! how great is the sum of them!' Ps. cxxxix. 17.

Sixthly, The sixth property of faith is victory over the world: 1 John. v. 4, 5, 'For whatsoever is born of God overcometh the world, and this is the victory that overcometh the world, even our faith: who is he that overcometh the world, but he that believeth that Jesus is the Son of God?' I shall despatch this briefly, and shall show you—

1. What is the world that is to be overcome? All worldly things whatsoever, so far as they lessen our esteem of Christ and heavenly things, or as they hinder us in our duty to God. In short, the delights and terrors of this world; for we must be armed on both sides with the armour of righteousness, both on the right hand and the left, 2 Cor. vi. 7. The fears of this world are apt to stagger us, so do snares prevent and inveigle us. Moses had temptations of all kinds, right-hand temptations from riches, honours, pleasures: Heb. xi. 24–26, 'By faith Moses, when he was come to years, refused to be called the Son of Pharaoh's daughter, choosing rather to suffer affliction with the people of God than to enjoy the pleasures of sin for a season, esteeming the reproach of Christ greater riches than the treasures in Egypt;' left-hand temptations: ver. 27, 'By faith he forsook Egypt, not fear-

ing the wrath of the king, for he endured as seeing him who is invisible.' The armour of the right hand is called temperance; of the left hand, patience: 2 Peter i. 6, 'To knowledge temperance, and to temperance patience.' In the parable of the sower sowing his seed we read that which fell on the stony ground withered in persecution: Luke viii. 13, 'They on the rock are they which, when they hear, receive the word with joy; and these have no root, which for a while believe, and in time of temptation fall away. That which was sown in the thorny ground was choked with the cares, riches, and pleasures of the world: ver. 14, 'And they which fell among thorns are they which, when they have heard, go forth, and are choked with cares and riches and pleasures of this life, and bring no fruit to perfection.' If the terrors of sense assault our constancy, we must set loss against loss, pain against pain, fear against fear: Mat. x. 28, 'Fear not him that can kill the body, and do no more, but fear him that can cast both body and soul into hell.' If they threaten a prison, remember God threatens hell; if they threaten fire, God threatens everlasting fire; if they threaten loss of estate, loss of heaven is much worse. If the delights of sense are likely to corrupt us, to pervert or divert our minds from better things, we must look to it, and remember what better things are reserved for us. Persecution is opposite to profession without, but this obstructs the very vigour, life, and power of godliness within: 1 John ii. 15, 'If any man love the world, the love of the Father is not in him.' And then for pleasures: 2 Tim. iii. 4, 'Lovers of pleasures more than lovers of God;' Heb. xii. 16, 'Or profane person as Esau, who for one morsel of meat sold his birthright.' Honours are baneful to our faith: John v. 44, 'How can ye believe which receive honour one of another, and seek not the honour that cometh from God only?' They eat out the heart of it. These are our daily temptations.

2. The necessity of overcoming the world.

[1.] It is by the world that our spiritual enemies have advantage against us. The devil seeketh to tempt or fright the fleshly nature in us either by the terrors or allurements of sense. Therefore conquer the world, and the tempter is disarmed; he blindeth us as the god of this world: 2 Cor. iv. 4, 'In whom the god of this world hath blinded the minds of them which believe not, lest the light of the glorious gospel of Christ, who is the image of God, should shine unto them.' He vexeth as the prince of this world, and having a strong party in the world, he findeth it no great matter to entice a sensual worldly mind to almost anything that is evil. The baits and provisions of the flesh are in the world: 1 John ii. 16, 'For all that is in the world, the lust of the flesh, the lust of the eyes, and the pride of life, is not of the Father, but is of the world.' The world fits us with a bait agreeable to every appetite, or a diet that suiteth with every distemper of our souls. A proud mind must be honoured and humoured, and will go nothing lower than high place and pomp of living. A sensual mind must have its pleasures, and the covetous the increase of wealth, and religion is either cast off or neglected and made an underling.

[2.] The world is the great let and impediment to our obedience.

In the first epistle of John, chap. v., in the context to the words that I am now explaining, ver. 2, 3, it is said, 'By this we know that we love the children of God, when we love God, and keep his commandments; for this is the love of God, that we keep his commandments, and his commandments are not grievous.' Then it followeth, ver. 4, 'For whatsoever is born of God overcometh the world,' &c. So Titus ii. 11, 12, 'For the grace of God that bringeth salvation hath appeared to all men, teaching us, that denying ungodliness and worldly lusts, we should live soberly, righteously, and godly in this present world.' The one must be done that the other may be done. We shall soon be tempted to make a breach upon righteousness, sobriety, or godliness if we do not labour to overcome the world. So Ps. cxix. 36, 'Incline my heart unto thy testimonies, and not to covetousness.'

[3.] This victory over the world distinguisheth the spiritual from the animal life. The world of mankind is distinguished into two sorts—some that live the animal life, and some that live the spiritual life. They that live the animal life are such as only behave themselves merely as living creatures, or as a wiser sort of beasts, and the comfort of their life is only kept up by the good things of this world, land, heritages, honours, pleasures, riches; and so reason is subjected to sense, all their contrivance is for the flesh. But the spiritual and divine life is supported by the comforts of the Spirit and the foresight of eternal joys in the world to come, and so reason is raised and sublimated by faith. These two lives are distinguished: John iii. 6, 'That which is born of the flesh is flesh, and that which is born of the Spirit is Spirit;' 1 Cor. ii. 14, 15, 'But the natural man receiveth not the things of the Spirit of God, for they are foolishness unto him; neither can he know them, because they are spiritually discerned: but he that is spiritual judgeth all things, yet he himself is judged of no man;' and Jude 19, 'These be they who separate themselves, sensual, having not the Spirit.' Now the more we live this spiritual life, the more thorough christians we are. Another kind of spirit cometh upon a man, he liveth as a man of another world; he can bear up when the outward and animal life is exposed to the greatest difficulties, 2 Cor. iv. 16; he fetcheth his solace and comfort from those great and glorious things which are kept for him in heaven. It is a mighty thing to have this spirit of faith.

[4.] We cannot hold out with Christ whilst any temporal and sensitive thing lieth too near the heart: 1 Tim. vi. 10, 'For the love of money is the root of all evil, which while some coveted after, they have erred from the faith, and pierced themselves through with many sorrows,' and 2 Tim. iv. 10, 'Demas hath forsaken us, having loved this present world.' The devil hath them in a string, and we are easily taken again, though we seem to make some escape from him.

3. Faith is the grace that is employed in overcoming the world. It is not only said to be a means of overcoming, but the victory itself; for it is the nature of faith. There are terms in it as in other graces; it is a recess from the world, and an access to God, a drawing off the heart from things visible and temporal to those which are invisible and eternal. How doth faith overcome the world?

[1.] As it is an assent to God's word, and chiefly to the promises of the gospel. Now this strong and firm assent doth prepossess the mind with the glory of the world to come: Heb. xi. 26, 'Moses had an eye to the recompense of reward;' and 2 Cor. iv. 18, 'We look not to the things which are seen, but at the things which are not seen;' and Heb. xi. 1, 'Faith is the substance of things hoped for, the evidence of things not seen.' By this sight and view of heavenly things our esteem of the world is abated, so by consequence the force of the temptation. Alas! whatever this world offereth must be left on this side the grave, pomp, pleasure, estate: 1 Tim. vi. 7, 'For we brought nothing into this world, and it is certain we can carry nothing out.' Here we lust for greatness, but death soon endeth the quarrel. In the grave no difference is to be discerned between rich and poor, both are alike obnoxious to rottenness and corruption; but faith persuadeth us of better things: Heb. xi. 13, 'These all died in faith, not having received the promises, but having seen them afar off, and were persuaded of them, and embraced them, and confessed that they were strangers and pilgrims on the earth.'

[2.] As it is a consent. It causeth us to surrender ourselves to Christ's discipline, or that religion which wholly draweth us off from this world to the world to come. Its purpose and drift is that we may deny ourselves, bear the cross, and follow him. This we promise in baptism: 1 Peter iii. 21, 'Baptism saveth us (not the putting away the filthiness of the flesh, but the answer of a good conscience towards God), by the resurrection of Jesus Christ.' The spirit of our religion is not the spirit of the world: 1 Cor. ii. 12, 'Now we have received not the spirit of the world, but the Spirit which is of God, that we might know the things that are freely given to us of God.'

[3.] As it is a dependence and trust in Christ's power and sufficiency to maintain you, and defend you safe, till you are brought home to God. He died for this end: Gal. i. 4, 'Who gave himself for our sins, that he might deliver us from this present evil world, according to the will of God and our Father.' He intercedeth for us to the Father for this end: John xvii. 15, 'I pray not that thou shouldest take them out of the world, but that thou shouldest keep them from the evil.' He overcame the world in his own person for this end, not only to encourage us, but to enable us by his example: John xvi. 33, 'These things I have spoken unto you, that in me ye might have peace; in the world ye shall have tribulation, but be of good cheer, I have overcome the world.' He sendeth his Spirit into our hearts to preserve us against the assaults of the devil, the world, and the flesh: 1 John iv. 4, 'Ye are of God, little children, and have overcome them; because greater is he that is in you than he that is in the world.' And because every state of life is thick-set with temptations, he reneweth his influence upon us: Phil. iv. 13, 'I can do all things through Christ which strengthens me.' He had before spoken of carrying an equal mind in all conditions; Christ enabled him as well as taught him this contentment.

Well, then, reckon the growth of your faith by the exercise of your mortification and weanedness from the world, rather than by strong confidence of your good estate or highflown joys and comforts. The comforts of the Spirit will not be tasted by an unmortified worldly heart. Most men's confidence cometh from their security and mindlessness of these things. The comforts are more suspicious when the mortification is a sure note.

Seventhly, The seventh property of faith is quieting the heart against fears and doubts, and waiting on God. I join these two things together because the scripture doth : Lam iii. 26, 'It is good that a man should both hope, and quietly wait for the salvation of God.' But we must handle them asunder.

1. Waiting. Sense is all for present satisfaction, but faith can tarry God's leisure till these good things which we do expect do come in hand : Isa. xxviii. 16, 'He that believeth shall not make haste.' Men that cannot tarry for relief will yield up a town upon the basest terms. The children of God were always forced to eat their words when they spoke in haste : Ps. xxxi. 22, 'For I said in my haste, I am cut off from before thine eyes; nevertheless thou heardest the voice of my supplication when I cried unto thee;' and Ps. cxvi. 11, 'I said in my haste, All men are liars.' But where faith and hope is there is patience: Rom. viii. 25, 'If we hope for what we see not, then do we with patience wait for it;' James v. 7, 8, 'Be patient therefore, brethren, unto the coming of the Lord. Behold the husbandman waiteth for the precious fruit of the earth, and hath long patience for it, until he receive the early and latter rain. Be ye also patient; stablish your hearts, for the coming of the Lord draweth nigh.' Unbelief leapeth overboard on the first danger. Impatience and precipitation is the cause of all mischief. What moved the Israelites to make the golden calf, but impatience in not waiting for Moses till he came down from the Mount, where he was with God? What made Saul to offer sacrifice, but want of patience till Samuel came? 1 Sam. xiii. 8–10, 'He tarried seven days, according to the set time that Samuel had appointed. But Samuel came not to Gilgal, and the people were scattered from him. And Saul said, Bring hither a burnt-offering to me, and peace-offerings; and he offered the burnt-offering, and it came to pass that as soon as he had made an end of offering the burnt-offering, behold Samuel came,' &c. What made the bad servant to smite his fellow-servant, and to eat and drink with the drunken, Mat. xxiv. 40, but this, 'My Lord delayeth his coming?' Hasty men are loath to be kept long in doubtful suspense. The voluptuous cannot wait their time, when they shall have pleasures at God's right hand for evermore, therefore take up with present delights, like those that cannot tarry till the grapes be ripe, but eat them sour and green. Solid everlasting pleasures they cannot wait for, therefore choose the pleasures of sin that are for a season. A covetous man will wax rich in a day, cannot tarry the leisure of God's providence : Prov. xx. 21, 'An inheritance may be gotten hastily at the beginning, but the end thereof shall not be blessed.' The ambitious man will not stay till God gives crowns and honours in his kingdom. All revolts and apostacies from God proceed hence; they cannot wait for God's help, and tarry the fulfilling of his promises, but finding themselves pressed and destitute, the flesh, which is tender and delicate, groweth impatient. It is tedious to suffer for a while, but they do not consider it is more tedious to suffer for evermore. Thence come murmurings and unlawful attempts, stepping out of God's way. An impetuous river is always troubled and thick, so is a precipitated impatient spirit, out of order, and ready for a snare.

2. Quieting the heart against doubts, fears, and cares. By a grown faith thoughts are established: Prov. xvi. 3, 'Commit thy works unto the Lord, and thy thoughts shall be established.' Fire well kindled casteth the least smoke. We have firm ground to stand upon, therefore we must not reel to and fro in a doubtful agitation of mind: James i. 6–8, 'Let him ask in faith, nothing wavering; for he that wavereth is like a wave of the sea, driven with the wind and tossed; for let not that man think that he shall receive anything of the Lord. A double-minded man is unstable in all his ways.' Faith fixeth the heart against fears: Ps. cxii. 7, 'He shall not be afraid of evil tidings; his heart is fixed, trusting in the Lord;' Isa. xxvi. 3, 'Thou wilt keep him in perfect peace whose mind is stayed on thee, because he trusteth in thee;' Rom. v. 1, 'Therefore, being justified by faith, we have peace with God through our Lord Jesus Christ;' Phil. iv. 7, 'And the peace of God which passeth all understanding shall keep your hearts and minds through Christ Jesus;' Rom. iv. 20, 'Abraham staggered not at the promise of God through unbelief, but was strong in faith, giving glory to God;' and Mat. vi. 30, 'Wherefore if God so clothe the grass of the field, which to-day is, and to-morrow is cast into the oven, shall he not much more clothe you, O ye of little faith!' so Mat. viii. 26, 'He saith unto them, Why are ye fearful, O ye of little faith!' The weak are mated with every difficulty: Mat. xiv. 31, 'O thou of little faith, wherefore didst thou doubt?' Ps. xlii. 5, 'Why art thou cast down, O my soul? and why art thou disquieted within me? Hope thou in God, for I shall yet praise him for the help of his countenance.' Well, then, here is a sure note of a grown faith, the more we can quiet ourselves in the promises of God, and wait his leisure for their accomplishment.

SERMON UPON MATTHEW VIII. 5–10.

And when Jesus was entered into Capernaum, there came unto him a centurion, beseeching him, and saying, Lord, my servant lieth at home sick of the palsy, grievously afflicted. And Jesus saith unto him, I will come and heal him. The centurion answered and said, Lord, I am not worthy that thou shouldest come under my roof; but speak the word only, and my servant shall be healed. For I am a man under authority, having soldiers under me : and I say to this man, Go, and he goeth; and to another, Come, and he cometh; and to my servant, Do this, and he doeth it. When Jesus heard it, he marvelled, and said to them that followed, Verily I say unto you, I have not found so great faith, no, not in Israel.—MAT. viii. 5–10.

I COME now to the instances of a grown faith, and begin with the faith of the centurion; and that deservedly, for—

1. Christ owneth it as great faith: ver. 10, 'I have not found so great faith, no, not in Israel;' that is, a faith so ripe and mature, and that in a military man and an heathen.

2. Because he marvelled at it. In ordinary cases wonder is a fruit of ignorance. When we are ignorant of a thing, or a thing exceedeth our capacity or apprehension, we wonder at it. But this cannot be imagined in Christ, for he knoweth what is in man, and could not be surprised, being the author of this faith. Therefore some interpret it of some external gesture of wondering, which he used to commend the centurion's faith. Why not the passion of wonder itself? for we wonder at things strange and unusual though we be not ignorant of them; and Christ would discover all our sinless infirmities; therefore this showeth it was a remarkable thing. We read that twice Christ wondered; once here, and another time, Mark vi. 6, 'And he marvelled because of their unbelief.'

3. Because he was the first-fruits of the gentiles: ver. 11, 12, 'And I say unto you, that many shall come from the east and west, and shall sit down with Abraham, Isaac, and Jacob, in the kingdom of heaven. But the children of the kingdom shall be cast out into utter darkness; there shall be weeping and gnashing of teeth.' This was the first occasion which Christ took to speak of the rejection of the Jews and

the calling of the gentiles. This man was a Roman and an heathen, but it seemeth had gotten some knowledge of the true God and the true religion; and though he were not a proselyte, yet the Jews gave him this testimony, Luke vii. 5, 'He loveth our nation, and hath built us a synagogue;' and indeed we read nothing but well of him. The very errand that brought him to Christ was care of his servant, and looking out for cure for him. Many have no more care of their servants than they have of their horses and oxen; but this man was of another temper, good to the Jews, good in all his relations. Now, that we may profit by this example, let us consider these three things—(1.) What was his faith, and wherein the greatness of it lay; (2.) How this faith was bred and begotten in him; (3.) The effects and fruits of it, or how it discovered itself.

I. The nature of his faith. It was a firm persuasion that all power and authority was eminently in Christ, and that he could do what he pleased. The great end of Christ in all his miracles was to discover himself to be the Son of God, and one in whom the divine nature and power resided, and so by consequence that true Messiah and Saviour of the world. This was Peter's confession of faith: Mat. xvi. 16, 'Thou art Christ, the Son of the living God;' the promised Messiah, the anointed Saviour of the world. And with Peter all the rest of the disciples join: John vi. 69, 'We believe, and are sure, that thou art that Christ, the Son of the living God.' This the Samaritans, being convinced and converted, confessed also: John iv. 42, 'We know that this is indeed the Christ, the Saviour of the world.' This Martha acknowledges: John xi. 27, 'She saith unto him, Yea, Lord, I believe that thou art the Christ, the Son of God, that should come into the world.' This was it which the apostles preached: Acts xiii. 23, 'Of this man's seed hath God, according to his promise, raised unto Israel a saviour, Jesus.' This they required of all whom they converted to the christian faith: Acts viii. 37, 'I believe that Jesus Christ is the Son of God.' Now this the centurion cometh off roundly with, being firmly persuaded of a divine power and authority in Christ; for he ascribeth an omnipotency to his word, and reasoneth it out notably: 'Speak but the word, and my servant shall be healed;' ver. 8, 9, 'For I am a man under authority, having soldiers under me; and I say to this man, Go, and he goeth; and to another, Come, and he cometh; and to my servant, Do this, and he doeth it.' Here then was the greatness of his faith.

Object. You will say then, All have great faith, for all the christian world professeth this truth that Jesus is the Son of God, papists and protestants, carnal and renewed; the rabble of nominal christians as well as the seriously godly are of this opinion that Jesus is the Son of God and the Saviour of the world.

Ans. 1. *Distingue tempora*—You must distinguish of the times In that age there was no human reason to believe this truth. Antiquity was against it, and therefore, when Paul preached Jesus, they said, 'He seemeth to be a setter forth of strange gods,' Acts. xvii. 18. Authority was against it: 1 Cor. ii. 8, 'Which none of the princes of this world knew, for had they known it they would not have crucified the Lord of glory.' Authority, not only civil, but ecclesiastical, was against it: 'Acts iv. 11, 'This is the stone which was set at nought of you builders.' The universal consent of the habitable world was against it; only a small handful of contemptible people owned him: Luke xii. 32, 'Fear not, little flock,' μικρὸν ποίμνιον. At that time it was the critical point, the hated truth, that the carpenter's son should be owned as the son of God. Those bleak winds that blow in our backs, and thrust us onward to believe, blew in their faces, and drove them from it; those very reasons which move us to own Christ moved them to reject him. For many ages the name of Christ hath been in request and honour, but then it was a despised way. For men to lay aside their old religion, and temples, and altars, and ceremonies, and rights of worship, for the new way of Jesus of Nazareth, never heard of before, born of a Jewish woman, living in a mean way, crucified like a malefactor, and dead and buried; that he should be owned as the Son of God and the Saviour of the world, what could be to appearance more unreasonable? Alas! what should we have done, if we had been put to encounter with these difficulties and prejudices? And no sooner did any man own this truth, but he was presently exposed to all manner of troubles and persecutions, brought before magistrates, tortured, murdered by all the cruel deaths that could be devised; and all this to be endured upon the hopes of an unseen world. Therefore then it was an undoubted truth: 1 John v. 1, 'Whosoever believeth that Jesus is the Son of God is born of God;' and 1 John iv. 2, 'Every spirit that confesseth that Jesus Christ is come in the flesh is of God.' Nay, somewhat less than faith and great faith. At his first appearance a certain persuasion, impressed upon the soul by the Spirit of God, of the divine power and all-sufficiency of Christ, so as to repair to him for help, was faith and great faith; when the veil of his human nature and infirmities did not keep the eye of faith from seeing him to have a divine power, though they could not unriddle all the mysteries about his person and office, this was accepted for saving faith.

2. The speculative belief of this truth was not sufficient then, no more than it is now, but the practical improvement. Grant that truth, that Jesus is the Son of God, and other things will follow, as that we must obey his laws, and depend upon his promises, and make use of his power, and trust ourselves in his hands; otherwise the bare acknowledgment was not sufficient. If a man had at that time with some kind of belief owned Christ as the Son of God, and yet could not overcome the shame and fear of the world, he would not have been accepted; for it is said, 1 John v. 5, 'Who is he that overcometh the world, but he that believeth that Jesus is the Son of God.' Unless that effect followed, the belief was vain. Therefore it is said, John ii. 23–25, 'Many believed in his name when they saw the miracles which he did. But Jesus did not commit himself unto them, because he knew all men, and needed not that any should testify of man, for he knew what was in man.' Christ knew the inside of men, and therefore knew this faith was unlikely to bear any stress, or hold out against temptations. Men might be convinced of some excellency and divine power in Christ, and yet remain unconverted. So Acts viii., Simon Magus believed in Christ, yet remained in the 'gall of bitterness and bond of iniquity.' So we

read again, John viii. 30, 31, 'As he spake these words, many believed on him. Then said Jesus to those Jews which believed on him, If ye continue in my word, then are ye my disciples indeed.' Some are his disciples in show, not truly and really, being not settled and rooted in the faith. So it is noted, John xii. 42, 43, 'Nevertheless among the chief rulers also many believed on him; but because of the pharisees they did not confess him, lest they should be put out of the synagogue; for they loved the praise of men more than the praise of God.' They had faith, but it was too weak to encounter temptations; they were too tender of their reputation, lest they should be despised, and turned out of their places for deserting the old way wherein they were bred. But none of this can be imputed to our centurion, whose faith Christ approved and rewarded; for in contemplation of this faith the cure was wrought: ver. 13, 'And Jesus said unto the centurion, Go thy way; and as thou hast believed, so be it unto thee.' And he ventureth the credit he had with his nation; and though the particular address concerned not him, but his servant, yet he maketh an open acknowledgment of Christ.

II. How was this faith wrought and bred in him?

I answer—The groundwork was laid in his knowledge of the omnipotency and power of God, and his acquaintance with the scriptures of the Old Testament, though he were not a professed Jew. This prepared for his faith in Christ; the report or hearing was the ground of faith: Isa. liii. 1, 'Who hath believed our report?' He had heard by fame of his excellent doctrine: Mat. vii. 29, 'That he taught as one having authority, and not as the scribes.' And he had heard the rumour of his miracles, more particularly the late instance of curing the leper, which was notorious and public; for Christ biddeth him 'show himself to the priests,' Mat. viii. 4; and also the miracle in recovering the ruler's son, an instance near, which was done in time before this: John iv. 46, 47, 'And there was a certain nobleman, whose son was sick at Capernaum; and he heard that Jesus was come out of Judea into Galilee, and he went unto him, and besought him that he would come down and heal his son, for he was at the point of death.' By all which he was moved to ascribe the omnipotency of God, which he knew before, to Jesus Christ. The Spirit of God can bless slender motives to a willing heart; and there is a readiness in holy souls to believe sooner and easier than others: Acts xvii. 11, 'These were more noble than those of Thessalonica, in that they received the word with all readiness of mind, and searched the scriptures whether these things were so or no.' They were not light of belief, for they searched the scriptures; yet they were more ready to believe than perverse and prejudiced persons, πρόθυμοι. When there is sufficient evidence, they can hold out no longer. Thus the Spirit of God blessed the knowledge of this centurion, and the rumours that were brought to him of Christ's doctrine and miracles.

III. The effects or fruits of it, or how it discovered itself.

1. In that he applieth himself to Christ. They that believe in Christ will come to him, and put him upon work, whilst others prize his name but neglect his office. A gracious heart will find occasions and opportunities of acquaintance with Christ, if not for themselves yet for others; for when they have heard of him, they cannot keep from him. Faith

never wants an errand to the throne of grace; either necessity brings us thither, or delight. Christ inviteth us to come for what he hath to give: Mat. xi. 28, 'Come unto me, all ye that labour and are heavy laden, and I will give you rest.' He is angry that we will not come: John v. 40, 'And ye will not come to me that ye may have life.' If we be backward, he sendeth afflictions upon ourselves and families: Hosea v. 15, 'In their affliction they will seek me early.' Surely it is a delight to him to do his office in helping distressed creatures, or else he would never have taken it upon him. The elect shall be brought to him upon one occasion or another, and he will kindly receive them: John vi. 37, 'All that the Father giveth me shall come to me, and he that cometh to me I will in no wise cast out.' An apoplexy fallen on a beloved servant bringeth this centurion to Christ. Well, then, since Christ is 'able to save to the uttermost all that come to God by him,' Heb. vii. 25, let us not neglect the occasions of coming to him, but get nearer to God by repentance and faith in our Lord Jesus Christ. Would Christ stoop so low as to take our nature and purchase us with his blood, and be strange to us when we come for the fruits of his purchase and his mercy, to help us and ours?

2. That he accounteth misery an object proper enough for mercy to work upon. The centurion came to him, saying, 'Lord, my servant lieth at home sick of the palsy, grievously tormented,' ver. 6; that is, grievously affected with the disease. Alas! what can we bring to Christ but sins and sicknesses? Justice seeketh a meet object, for it giveth to every one what is due, but mercy only seeketh a fit occasion. It doth not consider what is deserved, but what is desired and wanted. *Etiam si sim indignus, sum tamen indigens*, saith Romeranius—I am not worthy, but I am needy. The more affected we are with our misery, the fitter for Christ's mercy: Ps. ix. 18, 'The needy shall not always be forgotten.' The more hope we have, the more we are sensible of our need: Ps. xl. 17, 'But I am poor and needy, yet the Lord thinketh upon me.' Faith giveth us this ground of hope, that misery is a motive to God's pity. Though we have nothing within us or without us to commend us to Christ, yet he will not despise the miserable and the needy, and they shall not perish who in the sense of that need repair to him. God bringeth all-sufficiency to the covenant, we bring nothing but all-necessity; as the widow was only to provide empty vessels; the oil failed not till the vessels failed. Christ's bowels yearn towards the distressed.

3. When Christ offereth to come and heal him, ver. 7, 'I will come and heal him' (which was the great condescension of the Son of God to a poor servant), see how the centurion taketh it, ver. 8, 'He answered and said, Lord, I am not worthy that thou shouldest come under my roof.' Humility is a fruit of faith. A sound believer hath an high esteem of Christ and a low esteem of himself, and the one breedeth the other; they see Christ so excellent and themselves so vile, in regard of past sin and present infirmities. What! the Son of God come to the house of an ethnic, and one that hath lived in idolatry and the worship of false gods! The godly are ever acknowledging their vileness and baseness, and indignity and unworthiness, when they have to do with God and Christ: Gen. xviii. 27, 'And Abraham answered, and said,

Behold, now I have taken upon me to speak unto the Lord, which am but dust and ashes;' 2 Sam. vii. 18, 'Then went David in, and sat before the Lord, and he said, Who am I, O Lord God, and what is my house, that thou hast brought me hitherto?' Gen. xxxii. 10, 'I am not worthy of the least of all thy mercies, and of all the truth which thou hast showed unto thy servant.' So Mat. iii. 11, 'Whose shoes I am not worthy to bear.' So when Christ had let out a beam of his divinity in that great draught of fishes, Peter said, 'Lord, depart from me, for I am a sinful man,' Luke v. 8. The prodigal: Luke xv. 19, 'I am not worthy to be called thy son.' So 1 Cor. xv. 9, 'I am the least of the apostles, and am not meet to be called an apostle.' So though the Jews had said of our centurion, Lord, go to him, for 'he is worthy,' Luke vii. 4: yet he saith of himself, 'Lord, I am not worthy that thou shouldest come under my roof.'

Quest. Why are true and sound believers so ready to profess their unworthiness?

Ans. They have a deeper sense of God's majesty and greatness than others have, and also a more broken-hearted sense of their own vileness by reason of sin. They have a more affective light and sight of things; God is another thing to them than before, so is sin and self. The more unworthy they are in their own apprehension, the more is God and Christ exalted. Faith is an emptying grace, and the best men have lowest thoughts of themselves. A proud man thinketh all things due to him, but an humble man nothing.

4. He is content with Christ's word without his bodily presence: 'Speak but the word, and my servant shall be healed.' God's word is enough to a believer; he doth not limit him to a certain way of working as if there were no way of working but that way only; that is a sign of weakness of faith: Ps. lxxviii. 41, 'They limited the Holy One of Israel.' We are to depend upon him and submit to him, and not prescribe how and when he should help us, nor straiten and confine his power to such or such means. Compare John iv. 47, 48, with this centurion: 'A certain nobleman, whose son was sick at Capernaum' (the town where this centurion was in garrison), he again and again 'besought Jesus that he would come down and heal his son, for he was at the point of death. And Jesus said, Except ye see signs and wonders ye will not believe.' The cure must be done in their way: ver. 49, 'The nobleman saith unto him, Sir, come down ere my child die.' Christ refuseth to go to the ruler's house, being twice entreated, but here he offereth to come to visit this poor servant; but the centurion saith, 'Speak but the word;' he was loath to give him this trouble to come to his house; one word will as easily cure him as if he come personally; he doth not tie his virtue to his bodily presence, but ascribeth all to his word. God made the world by a word, sustaineth the world by a word, therefore the centurion only desireth a word. There is a threefold word of God—

[1.] *Verbum scriptum*, his written word, his promise, and that is the food of faith; and a believer can make a feast to himself in the promises when he is seemingly starved in the creature.

[2.] There is *verbum benedictionis*, his word of blessing. So Mat. iv. 4, 'Man liveth not by bread only, but by every word that proceedeth out of the mouth of God.' It is quoted out of Deut. viii. 3. In the wilderness, where they had neither bread nor water, they were not famished with want, nor compelled to use unlawful means for their relief, God blessed manna. He that provided forty years for such an huge multitude in the desert will not be wanting to his own Son who had fasted but forty days. It is not bread, but the blessing of God that sustaineth us. If they reserved aught of the manna till morning, it putrified and stank; yet the same manna, kept by the commandment of God, was sweet and good in the Ark. God gave his blessing to the one, and not to the other.

[3.] There is *verbum potentiæ* the word of his power: 'He spake, and it was done,' Ps. xxxiii. 9. So here the centurion desireth a word. The word made the world, and the word upholdeth it: Heb. i. 3, 'Upholding all things by the word of his power.' The powerful word of God doth all in the world: 'He sendeth forth his commandment upon earth; his word runneth very swiftly,' Ps. cxlvii. 15. So Ps. cvii. 20, 'He sent his word, and healed them;' it is *dictum factum* with God. So 'the word of the Lord tried them.' Ps. cv. 19; that is, his power; there is a powerful commanding word, which is enough.

5. Here is Christ's power and dominion over all events, and events that concern us and ours, fully acknowledged, and that is a great point gained: 'He is Lord both of the dead and living,' Rom. xiv. 9. Health and sickness are at his command. So Isa. xlv. 7, 'I form the light, and create darkness; I make peace, and create evil; I the Lord do all these things.' So Job xxxiv. 29, 'When he giveth quietness, who then can make trouble? and when he hideth his face, who then can behold him? whether it be done against a nation, or against a man only?' Here is a clear confession of Christ's omnipotency and sovereign dominion. This sovereign dominion is backed with omnipotency, and extendeth to all things. To devils: Mark ix. 25, 'I charge thee come out of him, thou dumb and deaf spirit.' To sickness: Luke iv. 39, 'He rebuked the fever, and it left her.' Christ can speak to the leprosy: 'I will; be thou clean,' Mat. viii. 3. To the winds and seas: 'Then he arose, and rebuked the winds and the seas, and there was a great calm,' Mat. viii. 26, 27. To death: 'Lazarus, come forth,' John xi. 43. To nothing, as if it had ears and reason: Rom. iv. 17, 'And calleth those things which are not as though they were.' To the fishes in the sea: Jonah ii. 10, 'The Lord spake to the fish, and it vomited up Jonah upon the dry land.' Thus all creatures have an obediential ear, to hearken to what God saith, and God can make use of them according to his own pleasure; yea, he can speak to sinners, who are the most stubborn and obstinate pieces of the creation: Ezek. xvi. 6, 'I said unto thee, when thou wast in thy blood, Live;' Eph. v. 14, 'Wherefore he saith, Awake thou that sleepest, and arise from the dead, and Christ shall give thee light.' Every creature is a servant of omnipotency, and doth suspend or exercise its natural operations as God biddeth it. Christ hath this power as God and heir of all things.

[1.] Let us see what is this all-sufficient power and dominion of Christ. It lieth in three things—(1.) A right of making and framing anything as he will, in any manner as it pleaseth him: Jer. xviii. 6, 'Behold, as the clay is in the potter's hand, so are ye in mine hand, O house of Israel.' (2.) A right and power of possessing things so made.

all is his; they are rebels that said, Ps. xii. 4, 'Our tongues are our own; who is lord over us?' (3.) A right of using, governing, and disposing of all things so possessed: Mat. xx. 15, 'Is it not lawful for me to do what I will with my own?' whether men or any other creature in the world.

[2.] This dominion and all-sufficient power is a great stay to the souls of true believers, to cause them with comfort to trust themselves and all their affairs in the hands of Christ. We have no reason to doubt of his care, protection, and merciful disposal of us; and if poor, sick, and desolate, you may go to him; it is in the power of his hands to help you. (1.) There is no want, but he can easily supply it: Ps. xxiii. 1, 'The Lord is my shepherd; I shall not want.' (2.) There is no pain or suffering, but he can easily mitigate or remove it: Mat. viii. 2, 'Lord, if thou wilt, thou canst make me clean.'

[3.] There is no danger so great from which he is not able to deliver thee: Dan. iii. 17, 18, 'If it be so, our God whom we serve is able to deliver us, and he will deliver us out of thine hand, O king: but if not, be it known unto thee, O king, that we will not serve thy gods, nor worship the golden image which thou hast set up;' 2 Cor. i. 10, 'Who delivered us from so great a death, and doth deliver; in whom we trust that he will yet deliver us.' Where can we be so safe as in the love and covenant of such an almighty saviour? Get but this imprinted upon your hearts, and it will beget a strong and steadfast confidence in him.

6. He reasoneth from the strict discipline observed in the Roman armies, where there was no disputing of commands or questioning why and wherefore: 'I am a man under authority, having soldiers under me; and I say to this man, Go, and he goeth; and to another, Come, and he cometh; and to my servant, Do this, and he doeth it,' ver. 9. Where he compareth person with person: I am a man, thou a God; condition with condition, a subordinate officer with Christ the supreme Lord; he knew what it was to obey and to have power over others; power with power, his power over soldiers and servants with Christ's command over all events, health and sickness, life and death. Reasoning for God and his promises is a great advantage. We are naturally acute in reasoning against faith, but when the understanding is quick and ready to invent arguments to encourage faith, it is a good sign.

Use. Go you and do likewise. From the example of the centurion let me encourage you—

1. To readiness of believing: James iii. 17, 'The wisdom that is from above is first pure, then peaceable, gentle, and easy to be entreated.' This is opposite to that slowness of heart to believe which we read of, Luke xxiv. 25, 'O fools, and slow of heart to believe all that the prophets have spoken.' These are more receptive and easy to entertain a doctrine than others: John. vii. 17, 'If any man do his will, he shall know of the doctrine whether it be of God.' The sincere and renewed need less ado to convince them. There is a light credulity: Prov. xiv. 15, 'The simple believeth every word;' and there is the readiness of a sincere mind to embrace the truth. We are to captivate our understandings to the obedience of faith, but not every fancy, lest we be like children, 'tossed to and fro, and carried about with every wind

of doctrine,' Eph. iv. 14. No; a christian must not be like a reed shaken with the wind, nor believe every spirit; but yet, where the truth is sufficiently evidenced, we must embrace it. Most of our hesitancy in religion comes not so much from the conflict between our light and the doubts of our mind, as from the conflict between our light and lusts, which maketh us irresolute; but a sincere heart soon overcometh the difficulty.

2. To represent our necessity to Christ, and refer the event to him, to commit and submit all to him. There is an all-sufficiency of power, and infinite pity and goodness, that we need not trouble ourselves about the event. Submission before the event is faith, as after it is patience. This is true faith, in such cases as the centurion came about, to refer all to Christ.

3. To be humble. In all our commerce with Christ, faith must produce a real humility. Faith is most high when the heart is most low: Luke xviii. 11-14, 'The pharisee stood and prayed, saying, God, I thank thee I am not as other men are, &c. I fast twice a week, I give tithes of all that I possess. And the publican, standing afar off, would not so much as lift up his eyes to heaven, but smote upon his breast, saying, God be merciful to me a sinner! I tell you, this man went down to his house justified rather than the other; for every one that exalteth himself shall be abased, and he that humbleth himself shall be exalted.' The one challenged a debt, the other begged a favour. Humble supplications to God become us better than proud expostulations.

4. To meditate often on the sovereign dominion of Christ, and his power over all things that fall out in the world. To keep us from warping and running to unlawful shifts, God propoundeth his all-sufficiency to our faith when we enter into covenant with him: Gen. xvii. 1, 'I am the Almighty God; walk before me, and be thou perfect.' He hath power enough to help, defend, and reward us; we need not seek elsewhere for a protector or paymaster; the word of his providence is enough. He can heal our diseases, supply our necessities, or bless a little, as he did the pulse to the captive children: Dan. i 15, 'Their countenances appeared fairer and fatter in flesh than all the children which did eat the portion of the king's meat.'

SERMON UPON MATTHEW XV. 21-28.

Then Jesus went thence, and departed into the coasts of Tyre and Sidon. And behold, a woman of Canaan came out of the same coasts, and cried unto him, saying, Have mercy on me, O Lord, thou Son of David; my daughter is grievously vexed with a devil. But he answered her not a word. And his disciples came and besought him, saying, Send her away; for she crieth after us. But he answered and said, I am not sent but unto the lost sheep of the house of Israel. Then came she and worshipped him, saying, Lord, help me. But he answered and said, It is not meet to take the children's bread and cast it to dogs. And she saith, Truth, Lord: yet the dogs eat of the crumbs which fall from their master's table. And Jesus answered and said unto her, O woman, great is thy faith: be it unto thee even as thou wilt. And her daughter was made whole from that very hour.—MAT. xv. 21-28.

WE come now to the second instance of a great and grown faith; this ought to be considered by us. In the centurion we had an instance of a reasoning faith, now of a wrestling faith—faith wrestling with grievous temptations, but at length obtaining help from God. We ought to consider this for these reasons—

1. Because Christ pronounceth it to be great faith, and so proper for our imitation, 'O woman, great is thy faith.' It is the faith of a woman; a woman not proselyted or embodied with the visible people of God at that time; a woman whose faith is approved and commended by Christ. And surely this should provoke every christian heart to be furnished with a like faith.

2. To instruct us that the life and exercise of faith is not easy, but will meet with great discouragements. We must reckon of trials, and prepare for them. They that leap into profession, and do not count the charges, will soon find their rash confidence disappointed. They may meet with rebukes from men. David's enemies said, 'There is no help for him in God,' Ps. iii. 2. Or from mistaking friends, as those that would not have Christ hindered in his passage: Mark x. 48, 'Many charged him that he should hold his peace; but he cried the more a great deal, Thou son of David, have mercy on me!' But this woman seemeth to be checked and disappointed by Christ himself, who at first answereth her not a word, and then seemingly defeateth her

confidence. To wrestle, not only with temporal discouragements, but disappointments of our hope in God, is the sorest trial. The blind man wrestled with the rebukes of men, but she with the rebukes of Christ himself. Yea, here is trial upon trial; she is put back after a first and second address. Christ, as God, knew the strength of her faith at first, but yet he would exercise her faith to the uttermost; as in another miracle it is said, 'He himself knew what he would do, but this he said to prove him; 'John vi. 6, 'Whence shall we buy bread, that so great a company may eat.' Christ loveth to try them with whom he hath to do, sometimes the weakness, sometimes the strength of their faith.

3. Because of the success: ver. 28, 'Be it unto thee even as thou wilt; and her daughter was made whole from that very hour.' When faith is sufficiently tried, Christ can hold out no longer. As Joseph's bowels yearned, and he could not refrain himself: Gen. xlv. 3, 'I am Joseph;' so when the strength of faith is sufficiently discovered, Christ cannot continue the conflict any longer; the believer shall have what he doth desire: Hosea xi. 8, 'Mine heart is turned within me, my repentings are kindled together;' and Jer. xxxi. 20, 'Is Ephraim my dear son? Is he a pleasant child? For since I spake against him, I do earnestly remember him still; therefore my bowels are troubled for him. I will surely have mercy upon him, saith the Lord.' So Isa. xl. 1, 2, 'Comfort ye, comfort ye my people, saith your God; speak ye comfortably to Jerusalem, and say unto her that her warfare is accomplished, that her iniquities are pardoned; for she hath received of the Lord's hand double for all her sins.' Now it is enough; let them have their mercies and their comforts.

In opening this instance, let us consider—

1. The quality of the woman. She is called in Mat. xv. 22, 'a woman of Canaan;' in Mark vii. 26, 'a Greek,' a Syrophœnician by nation. Phœnicia was that country which was inhabited by the relics of the ancient Canaanites: she was by nation a Phœnician, and by religion a Greek; for the term of Jew and Greek distinguished the then world: Rom. i. 16, 'It is the power of God unto salvation, to the Jew first, and also to the Greek;' and it is as much as Jew and gentile. She was a devout woman among the gentiles, that, bordering upon the people of God, was acquainted with the true religion, though she professed it not.

2. That she was a believer appeareth by her coming to Christ to cure her daughter, who was bodily vexed with the devil. How she was acquainted with Christ, it is said, Mark vii. 25, 'She heard of him;' that is, by the rumour of his miracles. And if God blessed rumours, or the fame of Christ's miracles, we may be ashamed that we do no more improve a clear word. And not by her coming only, but also by the title she gave to Christ; her calling him, 'The Son of David,' ver. 22. This was the solemn name of the true promised Messiah. So the blind men, Mat. xx. 30, 'Have mercy on us, O Lord, thou Son of David.' So Bartimeus (if it be a distinct story), Mark x. 47, 'Jesus, thou Son of David, have mercy on me.' 'Son of David' was the common title by which our Saviour was called and known among the Jews: Mat. ix. 27, 'Thou Son of David, have mercy on us;' because Christ was

to be born of the seed and posterity of David: Jer. xxiii. 5, 'Behold, the days come, saith the Lord, that I will raise up unto David a righteous branch;' Rom. i. 3, 'Concerning his Son Jesus Christ our Lord, who was made of the seed of David according to the flesh.' The Messiah was to come as a king, to rule and feed his church, and therefore he is called sometimes 'David' in the prophets; and in the days of his flesh, in the addresses that were made to him, 'Son of David.' So that in this she showeth her faith. There is in faith knowledge, assent, and affiance, and all three are in this woman's faith. That the Messiah was to be the Son of David, there is her knowledge. There was her assent, that Jesus was the Christ or true Messiah, for she applieth the title to him upon the rumours of his miracles. Then there was her affiance and dependence in this address to him, as one that was able and willing to help all distressed creatures; and that she renewed her suit after so many repulses showed a notable confidence in his mercy and power.

3. *The greatness and strength of her faith.* To set forth that we must consider—(1.) Her trials and temptations; (2.) Her victory over them, by her importunity, humility, and resolved confidence.

First, Her temptations; they are four—

1. Christ's silence, 'He answered her not a word,' ver. 23.
2. The coldness of the disciples' dealing in her behalf, in the same verse, 'His disciples besought him, Send her away, for she crieth after us.'
3. Christ's answer to his disciples, seeming to exclude her out of his commission, ver. 24, 'He answered and said, I am not sent but to the lost sheep of the house of Israel.'
4. Her renewed importunity draweth another answer from Christ, which implieth a contempt of her, or at least a strong reason against her, ver. 26, 'It is not meet to take the children's bread and cast it unto dogs.' So that you see here are sore trials, multiplied trials; but yet she keepeth begging and arguing with Christ till he giveth her satisfaction.

First, Christ's silence: ver. 23, 'And he answered her not a word.' It is a great trial to our faith, but such as the people of God usually meet withal. It is sad to go to a dumb oracle, and get not a word from God; so here. What! not a word from a merciful and gracious Saviour, who was so ready to hear and help upon all occasions, and to cure all those that came to him! But she gets not a word, though her daughter was grievously tormented by the devil; a notable temptation to a poor woman, who had heard so much of Christ's power and compassion towards all those that came to him for relief. He heard well enough what she asked, but not a word of answer gets she from him. I will show you, that though Christ love our persons, and dislikes not our petitions, but meaneth to grant them, yet for a time he will seem to take no notice of them.

1. That this is a sore temptation.
2. That it should not yet weaken our faith.

1. That it is a sore temptation appeareth by the complaints of the saints and servants of God: Lam. iii. 8, 'When I cry and shout, he shutteth out my prayer;' as if God had locked up himself, that their

prayers should not come at him, or find access to him. So ver. 44, 'Thou coverest thyself with a cloud, that our prayer should not pass through;' as if God had wrapped up himself in a thick cloud of displeasure against our sins, that our prayers could find no entrance. So the spouse: Cant. v. 6, 'I sought him, but I could not find him; I called him, but he gave me no answer.' That God should refuse and reject our prayers is a grievous trial to the faithful, who value communion with God. Nay, this delay may be so long till the cause seem hopeless: Ps. lxix. 3, 'I am weary of my crying; my throat is dried, mine eyes fail, while I wait for my God.' So Ps. xxii. 2, 'O my God, I cry in the daytime, but thou hearest not; and in the night season, and am not silent.' And all this while God seemeth to forsake them, nor to regard the suit, as if he had no respect to their hard condition. To lose our labour in prayer is one of the saddest disappointments that we can meet with, when our loud and importunate cries bring no relief to us. But—

2. It should not weaken our faith; for God's delay is for his own glory and our good.

[1.] For his own glory and the beauty of his providence. We read, John xi. 5, 6, 'Jesus loved Martha, and her sister and Lazarus; and when he heard he was sick' (even to death), 'he abode still two days in the same place where he was.' There is little love in that, you will think, to a sick friend who was ready to die. Martha expostulateth with him about it, ver. 21, 'Lord, if thou hadst been here, my brother had not died.' But Christ giveth the true account of it, ver. 40, 'Said I not unto thee, that if thou wouldest believe thou shouldest see the glory of God.' It was more for the glory of God to raise a dead man than to cure a sick man. So when the disciples were in a storm, Christ made a show of passing by: Mark vi. 48, 'He cometh unto them, walking on the sea-side, and would have passed by them.' So Christ delayeth the woman as to appearance, and denieth her, that the glory and greatness of her faith might be more seen. "$\mathit{Iνα\ στεφανώσῃ\ τὴν\ γυναῖκα}$, saith Chrysostom, that he might crown the woman as a notable believer.

[2.] For our good, and to exercise our faith, patience, love, and desire.

(1.) Our faith, to wait and depend upon God for things we see not; for faith is a dependence upon God for something that lieth out of sight. This woman was delayed, but had at last that which she desired; but first her great faith was discovered.

(2.) Our patience in tarrying God's leisure. His dearest children are not admitted at the first knock. David saith in three verses, 'I cried, I cried, I cried,' Ps. cxix. 145-147. Our Lord Jesus prayed thrice before he got any comfort in his agony: Mat. xxvi. 44, 'And he left them, and went away again, and prayed the third time; and then an angel appeared to him from heaven, and strengthened him,' Luke xxii. 43. Elijah prayed thrice for the dead child ere he got him to life: 1 Kings xvii. 21, 'And he stretched himself upon the child three times, and cried unto the Lord, and said, O Lord my God, I pray thee let this child's soul return unto him again.' Paul prayed thrice: 2 Cor. xii. 8, 'For this thing I besought the Lord thrice, that it might depart from me.' The Lord useth the like dispensation to us that are their followers: Heb. vi. 12, 'Be followers of them who through faith and patience inherit the promises.' We are told, Lam. iii. 26, 'It is good that a man should both hope and quietly wait for the salvation of the Lord.' It is *bonum bonestum et utile.* It is our duty, and it is our profit. Our times are always present with us. Hungry stomachs must have the meat ere it be sodden or roasted. We would have our mercies too soon, like the foolish husbandman who would reap his corn and get it into the barn before it be ripened.

(3.) Our love; though we be not feasted with felt comforts and present delights, or bribed with a sensible dispensation, or indulged with a ready condescension to our requests. God will try the deportment of his children, whether we love him or his benefits most; whether sensible consolations, especially external, be more to us than a God in covenant: Isa. xxvi. 8, 'Yea, in the way of thy judgments, O Lord, have we waited for thee.' A child of God will love him for his judgments and fear him for his mercies. God will try whether we can rejoice in himself in our greatest wants and destitutions: Hab. iii. 17, 18, 'Although the fig-tree shall not blossom, neither shall fruit be in the vines; the labour of the olive shall fail, and the fields shall yield no meat; the flocks shall be cut off from the fold, and there be no herd in the stalls; yet I will rejoice in the Lord, I will joy in the God of my salvation.' A resolute dependence on an unseen God is the power and glory of faith, and a resolute adherence to a withdrawn God is the vigour of love. Lime, the more water you sprinkle upon it, the more it burneth. 'Many waters cannot quench love, neither can the floods drown it,' Cant. viii. 7.

(4.) To enlarge our desires, and put greater fervency into them. A sack that is stretched out holds the more. Delay increaseth importunity: Mat. vii. 7, 'Ask, seek, knock;' the door is kept bolted that we may knock the harder. The choicest mercies come to us after great wrestlings. She prayeth, but Christ keepeth silence. Silence is an answer, and speaketh thus much, Pray on, and continue your praying still. Though Christ loved the supplicant, and meaneth to grant the petition, yet at first he answereth her not a word.

Secondly, Her next temptation was from the small assistance she had from the disciples: ver. 23, 'Send her away, for she crieth after us.' Interpreters dispute whether this was spoken out of commiseration or impatience. I incline to the former, and the sense is, 'Send her away by granting her request; do that for her which she desireth, that she may be quiet.' But though it were commiseration, yet they spake too coldly as to her distress, and seem to have a greater respect to their own trouble than the woman's affliction, that they might not be troubled with her cries, but they desire for quietness' sake that she might be despatched one way or another. Many a poor benighted soul pray themselves, and set others on praying, till they are weary, and God heareth not, which is a great discouragement to a poor afflicted creature; but yet it is but a temptation; for though man's drop be soon spent, yet God's ocean of compassions faileth not. When they are troubled, yet importunity is welcome to Christ.

Thirdly, Her next temptation is sorer. Christ seemeth to exclude her out of his commission: ver. 24, 'But he answered and said, I am not sent but to the lost sheep of the house of Israel.' This was a truth, for Christ in the days of his flesh' was a minister of the circumcision, Rom. xv. 8. His personal and particular ministry was principally designed for the people of the Jews; they were to have the morning market of the gospel, and the first handsel of the Redeemer's grace; which, by the way, was a rebuke to the Jews that they did no more prize his ministry and dispensation when this stranger was so importunate to receive the benefit of it. But, however, it was a great trial to the woman, as if she were not one of these lost sheep whom Christ came to seek. When salvation itself refuseth to save us, when Christ shall in effect say, I am a Saviour, but not unto thee; thou art not one of my redeemed ones: this is an amazing thing. Poor believers, when they are in this conflict, seem to be driven from Christ, not only by their own misgiving hearts, but the denunciation of his word: they question their election and the intention of God's grace, whether ever it were meant to them or no. But this is but a temptation; we must not betray our duties by our scruples; though it be midnight now, we cannot say it will never be day. Our rule, which we must stick to in such cases, is, God may do what he pleaseth, I must do what he commandeth. Our necessities are great, and so are Christ's compassions; therefore a believing soul must not be put off by groundless fears, nor must the threatenings of the word drive us from, but to the promise; for God opposeth for a while that he may at length give faith the victory.

Fourthly, when the woman reneweth her suit: ver. 25, 'Then she came, and worshipped him, saying, Lord, help me.' Yet ver. 26, 'He answered and said, It is not meet to take the children's bread and cast it to dogs.' By implication Christ reckoneth her among the dogs; a grievous word to drop from the mouth of a gracious Saviour. But when Christ trieth us, he will try us to the quick, and humble us to the very dust. Our Lord speaketh this according to the common rate of language among the Jews, who accounted all the heathens as dogs, and without the covenant. Such as were within the covenant and pale of grace were holy and consecrated to God; others who were without the covenant, because of their false religion, were accounted profane and unclean. Dogs and sheep were opposed one to another. The people of Israel are deciphered by the appellation of 'lost sheep;' others are called 'dogs;' Rev. xxii. 15, 'Without are dogs,' a term applied to this day by all oriental people to those whom they count to be misbelievers. Surely one would think now here were an end of her faith and address to Christ. No; the humble soul maketh an advantage of this: ver. 27, 'Truth, Lord; yet the dogs eat of the crumbs which fall from their master's table.' Faith is quick to observe all advantages whereby it may strengthen itself. A dog is allowed to creep under the children's table, and to feed on what falls down there. Thus she maketh a seeming rebuke to be a kind of claim and title. And then Christ can hold out no longer, for he will at length yield, and will not always hide himself from the seeking soul. They that wrestle will at length overcome: Mark vii. 29, 'And he said unto her, For this saying, Go thy way; the devil is gone out of thy daughter.'

Secondly, Her victory over these temptations. (1.) By her importunity: (2.) Her humility; (3.) Her resolved confidence; all which are the fruits of great faith.

1. Her importunity. She will not be beaten off by Christ's silence; but she maketh some advantage of it; for it is not said, he 'heard her not a word,' but 'answered her not a word.' Christ may hear his people when he doth not presently answer them. She seemed to be excluded out of Christ's commission, but neither this nor reproach of her own condition doth hinder the exercise of her faith, but still she reneweth her suit, 'Lord, have mercy on me; Son of David, help me.' The woman will not be put off praying when Christ seemeth to forbid or not to regard her praying. Her daughter was sore vexed, and she must have help from Christ or none. The more God seemeth to refuse us, the more instant should we be in prayer, and pursue our suit constantly. Let God answer how he pleaseth; if he be silent, we must resolve to follow the suit till we get audience; if he seem to deny, we must get ground by denials; if he rebuke us, we must still make supplications. Be it a suspension, a seeming denial, a contrary providence, faith will not give over. To sink under the burden argueth weakness, but it is strength of faith to wrestle through it. We read of Pherecides, a Grecian, in a naval fight between his nation and Xerxes, that he held a boat in which the Persians were fighting, first with his right arm, when that was cut off with his left, when that was cut off with his teeth, and would not let go his holdfast but with his life. This doth somewhat represent an importunate soul. This woman, when Christ doth seem to turn away from her and refuse her prayer, yet she prayeth, 'Lord, help me.' When he reasoneth from his charge, yet still she will come and worship him. When he putteth her off with the common reproach which the Jews did cast upon all that were not of their religion, his doctrines and miracles were children's bread, she turneth a discouragement into an argument, and maketh her claim, 'The dogs eat of the crumbs that fall from their master's table.' Thus all true believers are in good earnest; come what will of it, they are resolved to pray still. Thus blind Bartimeus, the more they rebuked him, the more he cried, Mark x. 48. Faith is like fire, the more it is pent up, the more it striveth to break out, and worketh effectually in us. We read of Jacob's wrestling with God: Gen. xxii. 24, 'There wrestled a man with him until the breaking of the day.' And it is explained, Hosea xii. 3, 4, 'He had power with God; yea, he had power over the angel, and prevailed; he wept, and made supplications to him.' Wrestling souls that are good at holding and drawing with the Almighty will not let him go till he bless them. The woman doth not turn her back upon Christ, but draws the nearer to him the more he seemeth to drive her away from him, and keepeth arguing with him, and beseeching of him, till he giveth her satisfaction.

But how shall we do to keep up prayer in the midst of so many discouragements? *Ans.* (1.) Our necessity should quicken us; and (2.) God's goodness and power should support us. Faith pressed with need is earnest in prayer, when it is dealing with a God gracious and powerful; why should we give over the suit?

2. Her humility. We read of no murmuring and impatience or discontent at Christ's carriage. No; if we will wrestle with God, we must

wrestle with prayers and tears, with humble and broken hearts; there must be no complaining of God, but to God. The woman doth not tax Christ as harsh and severe, but only maketh supplication, 'Lord, have mercy upon me; Son of David, help me.' It is said, Mat. xv. 25, 'She worshipped him.' But in Mark. vii. 25, it is said, 'She fell at his feet.' She fell prostrate before him, and owneth the term of 'dog,' that justly she might be accounted so, and maketh it her plea and claim. Humility is contented to be humbled as deeply as the Lord pleaseth, but cannot bear this, to be excluded from Christ and the benefit of his grace. In all faith there is always a deep humility. When Christ rebuketh her as a dog, she doth not make a murmuring retort, but an humble plea, that some of the mercy provided for Israel might be spared to a poor Canaanite, a crumb at least.

3. A resolved faith under our greatest pressures: Job. xv. 14, 'Though he slay me, yet I will trust in him.' As Antisthenes told his master that taught him philosophy, that he should not find a club big enough to beat him from him. Faith will not quit its adherence to God for any difficulty whatsoever; when God seemeth to quit the believer, the believer will not quit God, but take him as a friend when he seemeth to deal as an enemy, and still put a good construction upon his providence. This resolute adherence is seen in three things—

[1.] An adherence to his way, how little soever he seemeth to own it: Ps. xliv. 17, 18, 'All this is come upon us, yet have we not forgotten thee, neither have we dealt falsely in thy covenant: our heart is not turned back, neither have our steps declined from thy way.' Sharp afflictions do not discharge us from our duty in professing the truth; as our steps must not decline, so not our hearts: Dan. iii. 17, 18, 'Our God whom we serve is able to deliver us from the burning fiery furnace, and he will deliver us out of thy hand, O king; but if not, be it known unto thee, O king, that we will not serve thy gods, nor worship the golden image which thou hast set up.' However God disposes of us, we must keep to our duty.

[2.] In perseverance in the use of means: Rom. xii. 12, 'Continuing instant in prayer.' We are to use the duty still, though we have no satisfaction as to the event, and as long as there is life in the duty, it will come to something at the last: Luke v. 15, 'We have toiled all night, and have taken nothing; nevertheless, at thy word we will let down the net.' It is enough that these means are appointed by God, and we must use them, though hitherto we have gained little comfort and success by them.

[3.] In a dependence upon his promises and powerful providence. The woman sticketh to Christ as only able to help her, though there was little appearance of any help from him. She runneth not away to another helper, but worshippeth him, cleaveth to him. Better lie dead at Christ's feet than die in a state of alienation from him. We must resolve to be his, though we cannot know that he is ours. No trouble, how great soever, is a warrant to quit our trust; and whatever disappointment saith to us, it doth not say, put your confidence elsewhere, or trust no longer in God. This resolute confidence is justifiable upon these grounds.

(1.) His providence will never give his word the lie. Let God do what he will, they are approved who are approved by his word, and they are condemned who are condemned by his word: Ps. lxxiii. 17, 'When I went into the sanctuary of God, then understood I their end;' Job. iii. 3, 'I have seen the foolish taking root; but suddenly I cursed his habitation.' And, on the contrary, Ps. iv. 3, 'But know that the Lord hath set apart him that is godly for himself; the Lord will hear when I call unto him;' Isa. iii. 10, 'Say ye to the righteous that it shall be well with him; for they shall eat of the fruit of their doings.'

(2.) There is more good-will in his heart than is visible in his dealings. The merciful nature of God should be a support to us, though we see nothing of the effects of it in his providence: Job. x. 13, 'These things hast thou hid in thine heart; I know that it is with thee.' He speaketh of his favourable inclination to show pity to distressed creatures. We are not able always to reconcile his present dispensations with his gracious nature yet faith must not quit its holdfast. We must see what is hid in God's heart, and comfort ourselves with that favour and mercy which we know to be essential to him. Though the mercy and pity be not visible and obvious to sense, the disposition and inclination abideth in God unchangeable and sure. God is a merciful God still, and Christ a compassionate Saviour, though the effects be suspended to try and sharpen our faith.

(3.) Because God loveth to bring light out of darkness, to give the valley of Achor for a door of hope to 'bring meat out of the eater, and sweetness out of the strong,' to bring about his people's mercies by means very improbable and contrary, that he may train us up to hope against hope. When deliverance is a-coming, it is not always in sight. Christ at a wedding calls for water when he intended to give wine: John ii. 7, and here he rebuketh the woman as a dog when he meant to treat her as a daughter of Abraham.

(4.) When he seemeth to resist and be opposite to his people, he giveth them secret strength to prevail over him. When Jacob wrestled with God, it was by God's own strength; God in Jacob seemed to overcome God without him, or against him. Was not the spirit of Christ at work in the heart of this woman all the while he seemed to be struggling with her? He never striveth with his servants but he giveth them suitable strength to the task he imposeth on them: 1 Cor. x. 13, 'God is faithful, who will not suffer you to be tempted above that you are able: but will with the temptation also make a way to escape, that ye may be able to bear it;' Ps. cxxxviii. 3, 'In the day when I cried, thou answeredst me, and strengthenedst me with strength in my soul.' He heareth not as to deliverance, but yet he heareth as to support.

(5.) Because the saints are wont to train up themselves for these difficulties, by proposing hard cases to themselves; as Ps. iii. 6, 'I will not be afraid of ten thousands of people that have set themselves against me round about;' Ps. xxvii. 3, 'Though an host should encamp against me, my heart shall not fear; though war should rise against me, in this I will be confident;' Ps. xlvi. 1, 2, 'God is our refuge and strength, a very present help in trouble.' Therefore will we not fear though the earth be removed, and though the mountains be carried into the midst of the sea.' Presumption is a coward, and a runaway from all thoughts of danger; but faith meeteth its enemy in open field; it supposeth the worst, that the heart may be fortified aforehand against whatever may fall out. They much inure their thoughts to God, and dwell in and with the Almighty, and reckon upon the changes of a reeling world, and so are prepared to be martyrs, and suffer the worst for God.

Use. You have heard this faith opened to you; labour to get such a wrestling faith in expecting the benefits of the Messiah. You may have your difficulties—

1. About your spiritual estate and acceptance with God in Christ. You would have the devil cast out of your souls: you beg it of God, but he seemeth not to hear you; you are to wait, not to give over the matter as hopeless, and in despondency to throw up all at first: 'The Lord is righteous, for I have rebelled against his commandment,' Lam. i. 18. He hath called, and you would not hear, and therefore now God may delay. It may be you have doubts whether ever God will hear you, and you question your election; then consider God's mercy and your necessity. Christ hath taught us how to pray for the spirit: Luke xi. 8, 'Though he will not rise and give him because he is his friend; yet because of his importunity he will rise and give him.' You continue praying, and it is with you as before; it may be worse: Rom. vii. 9, 'But when the commandment came, sin revived, and I died.' A bullock is most unruly at first yoking; fire at first kindling casteth forth much smoke. What then? Should you give over seeking to Christ? That is to shut the door upon yourselves. God seemeth to shut you out, and you are discouraged with a deep sense of your own unworthiness. Will he look upon such a dead dog as I am? In such cases you should creep in at the back door of the promise, as Paul doth: 1 Tim. i. 15, 'This is a faithful saying, and worthy of all acceptation, that Jesus Christ came into the world to save sinners, of whom I am chief.' If Christ came to save sinners, I am sinner enough for Christ to save; or, as the woman here, 'dogs lick up the crumbs.'

2. In some prevailing carnal distempers, that you have long wrestled with to get rid of, and you desire the physician of souls should cure you. Follow the means, lay open before him the plague and sore of your own heart. You do not presently find success; will you therefore give over the business as hopeless, and go still with a wound or thorn in your conscience? No; consider—(1.) It must be cured; (2.) If ever it be cured, it must be by Christ; (3.) Use all his healing methods; (4.) And beg a blessing upon all by prayer, 'Lord, if thou wilt, thou canst make me clean,' Mat. viii. 2; (5.) Believe his grace to be sufficient for thee. Be earnest and importunate; we scratch the face of sin, but we do not seek to root it out. If you are resolved, you will take no nay. In a little time, and after some serious wrestling with God, you will be eminent in the contrary grace.

3. In great straits and pressures you seek to God; plead his covenant, and yet no answer cometh. Will you turn atheist, and say, It is in vain to pray to God? No; 'He that believeth will not make haste,' Isa. xxviii. 16. Or will you faint and give over the suit? Where then is the exercise of your faith and patience? It may be

God showeth himself strange to you in your troubles; as Jonah ii. 4, 'I said, I am cast out of thy sight, yet I will look again toward thy holy temple.' Let faith look to heaven and the covenant made with Christ. Will you give way to the temptation till you are bribed by sense? No; look again and again. Let faith triumph over difficulties, and the issue will be comfortable.

4. For the church, as God's children prefer Zion above their chief joy. You pray for the welfare of it, and God giveth no comfortable answer; what then? Will you neglect your duty or abate of your love? It may be the clouds are thickened, dangers greater. What! will you swell against providence? Hab. ii. 4, 'Behold his soul, which is lifted up, is not upright in him; but the just shall live by his faith.' No; it is importunity, humility, resolved confidence will do you good at the last; follow the suit still, and say, 'For Zion's sake I will not hold my peace, and for Jerusalem's sake I will not rest, until the righteousness thereof go forth as brightness, and the salvation thereof as a lamp that burneth,' Isa. lxii. 1. There should be an unwearied solicitation of God for the church's restitution. Christ is the church's advocate, we are her solicitors. This is an example, not to gaze upon, but to imitate.

SERMON UPON JOHN VIII. 56.

Your Father Abraham rejoiced to see my day; and he saw it, and was glad.—JOHN viii. 56.

THE next instance and pattern of a strong faith we find in Abraham. We must consider his faith in two things—

1. His clear sight of things to come, before the exhibition of Christ or his coming in the flesh.

2. His overlooking the difficulties which seemed to obstruct the accomplishment of the promise. A believer hath two great works to do—to open the eye of faith, and shut that of sense. In both Abraham was eminent. His opening the eye of faith is spoken of here, 'He saw my day.' His shutting the eye of sense in Rom. iv. 13, 'And being not weak in faith, he considered not his own body now dead, when he was about an hundred years old, neither yet the deadness of Sarah's womb.' The former falleth under our consideration now, Your Father Abraham rejoiced to see my day; and he saw it, and was glad.' The Jews were always cracking and boasting that they were children of Abraham. Christ disproveth their claim because they did not his works: John viii. 39, 'If ye were Abraham's children, ye would do the works of Abraham;' and in particular, because they imitated not his faith with respect to Christ; they despised what Abraham made great account of. Abraham rejoiced to see what you see, but they rejoiced not in him, and the privileges of the gospel offered by him. He desired to see me, though future and absent, and you despise me now present. He valued what you scorn, and therefore they were degenerate children of Abraham.

In the words observe three things—

1. The earnest desire Abraham had to see Christ's day, 'Abraham rejoiced to see my day.'

2. His obtaining his desire in some sort, and in that way which pleased God, 'And he saw it.'

3. The effect of that sight: it bred joy and contentment in his mind, 'And he was glad.'

Some explicatory questions shall be handled—

[1.] What was Christ's day?
[2.] In what sense he earnestly desired to see it?
[3.] How he saw it?

[4.] The gladness which was the fruit of it.

[1.] What was Christ's day? I answer—His coming in the flesh, and setting up the gospel dispensation. *Day* in scripture is put for all that space of time wherein any one hath lived, together with the state of things during that time. So Christ's day was the time when Christ came to fulfil his office of a redeemer, and the state of the gospel kingdom there begun.

[2.] How he earnestly desired to see it. His earnestness is employed in that word ἠγαλλιάσατο, 'He rejoiced to see my day.' With great pleasure of mind he thought of Christ's coming into the world to save sinners, and desired it might fall out in his time. He had no greater desire than to see Christ's kingdom set up and flourish in the world. He rejoiced, he vehemently and with ardent affection desired this might come to pass.

[3.] How he saw it? Not with bodily eyes; that negative is proved: Luke x. 24, 'Many prophets and kings have desired to see those things which ye see, and have not seen them; and to hear those things which ye hear, and have not heard them.' Abraham was one of these. But affirmatively he saw it with the eye of faith: Heb. xi. 13, 'All these died in faith, not having received the promises, but having seen them afar off, and were persuaded of them, and embraced them.' There it is explained. The object to be seen was revealed and set before them in the promise, and their eye and visive power was faith. Thus God granted him his desire in a better way. God may suspend the satisfying the desires of his people in their own way all their days, and yet in effect grant them in a way that is as good, and better for them. Moses would fain enter into the land of Canaan, but God would only give him a Pisgah-sight. The exhibition of Christ in the flesh was denied to Abraham and the patriarchs during their lives, but yet he gave that which was better than a simple bodily sight, a spiritual sight of him in the word of promise. We desire the restoration of the church speedily, but it may be it doth not suit with the harmony of God's providence; therefore we must submit our will to the wisdom of his counsels.

[4.] He was glad, and heartily rejoiced at it: Gen. xvii. 17, 'Then Abraham fell on his face and laughed.' Not as Sarah laughed, as doubting of the event, Gen. xviii. 12, but wondering, rejoicing at it, being strong in faith that God could and would make good his promise. There is the laughing of exultation, and the laughing of derision, when one telleth an improbable thing. Sarah's was the laughter of derision and unbelief; Abraham's was the laughing of exultation. The exhibition of the Messiah, and the setting up his kingdom in the world, was matter of great joy and consolation to him.

Doct. That a strong faith giveth such a clear sight of Christ as produceth an holy delight and rejoicing in him.

In handling this point—
1. I shall speak of the ground of Abraham's faith.
2. Of the strength of it, set forth by a double effect—(1.) His clear vision and sight of Christ; (2.) His deep affection, or rejoicing in it.

1. The ground of his faith; for except the thing to be believed be represented to us in a divine revelation, it is not faith but fancy. This

sure ground was the promise of God. And if you ask, What promise had his faith to work upon? I answer—That which you have: Gen. xii. 3, 'In thee shall all the families of the earth be blessed.' 'In thee,' that is, in thy seed, as it is explained, Gen. xxii. 18, 'In thy seed shall all the nations of the earth be blessed.' Now, to open this promise we must inquire—(1.) What this seed was; (2.) What this blessedness was.

1. What was this seed? We must distinguish of a twofold seed of Abraham—his seed to whom the blessing was promised, which was to be blessed, and his seed in whom both Abraham himself and also his seed and all nations were to be blessed. The promise of blessing to his seed is spoken of, Gen. xvii. 7, 'I will establish my covenant between me and thee, and thy seed after thee in their generations, for an everlasting covenant, to be a God unto thee, and to thy seed after thee.' Now this promise to his seed was either to his carnal seed which descended from his loins (God was there God, in visible covenant with them), or his spiritual seed: Gal. iii. 7, 'Know ye therefore that they which are of faith, the same are the children of Abraham;' because they walked in the steps of Abraham, and did receive and obey the doctrine of faith or covenant of grace which he himself believed and received. But then there was another seed, in whom he himself and all the families of the earth were to be blessed, that is, in the Messiah who was to come, who is the Lord Jesus Christ. The promise of multiplication and blessing of his seed was but an appendage of this promise, and the means to effectuate it, and so subservient to it.

2. What was this blessedness? All that good which resulteth to us from God's covenant; chiefly reconciliation with God and life eternal.

[1.] Our reconciliation with God, which consists of two parts—remission of sins, and regeneration; without these two no man can be capable of blessedness, and both these are included in the covenant made with Abraham.

(1.) Remission of sins. Certainly they are blessed whose sins are forgiven: Ps. xxxii. 1, 2, 'Blessed is he whose transgression is forgiven, whose sin is covered; blessed is the man unto whom the Lord imputeth not iniquity.' And this is included in the blessing of Abraham; for it is said, Gal. iii. 8, 'And the scripture, foreseeing that God would justify the heathen through faith, preached before the gospel unto Abraham, saying, In thee shall all nations be blessed.' So that justification by faith, a principal part of which is remission of sins, is that gospel blessing which was purchased by Christ for Abraham's seed.

(2.) Regeneration was included also, as a considerable part of the Mediator's blessing: Acts iii. 25, 26, 'Ye are the children of the prophets, and of the covenant which God made with your fathers, saying unto Abraham, And in thee shall all the kindreds of the earth be blessed. Unto you first, God having raised up his Son Jesus, sent him to bless you, in turning away every one of you from his iniquities.' There the blessing is interpreted.

[2.] That eternal life is included in it also is evident from the nature of the thing; for this being the chief blessedness, it cannot be excluded; and may be further proved from the double reasoning of the apostle from this covenant.

(1.) Because the patriarchs sought it by virtue of this promise: Heb. xi. 13–15, 'All these died in faith, not having received the promises, but having seen them afar off, and were persuaded of them, and embraced them, and confessed that they were strangers and pilgrims on the earth. For they that say such things declare plainly that they seek a country; and truly if they had been mindful of that country from whence they came out, they might have had opportunity to have returned. But now they desire a better country, that is, an heavenly.' The argument is, they did not think themselves to be at home in Canaan, but sojourned there as in a strange country. The apostle is speaking of Abraham, Isaac, and Jacob, who were heirs of the same promise, namely, of blessedness in the seed of Abraham; they still sought another place.

(2.) Because else God could not act suitably to the greatness of his covenant love and relation, and did not make good his title: ver. 16, 'Wherefore God is not ashamed to be called their God, for he hath prepared for them a city.' God, having made so rich a preparation for them, may be fitly called their God. Note our Saviour's reasoning: Mat. xxii. 31, 32, 'But as touching the resurrection of the dead, have ye not read that which was spoken to you by God, saying, I am the God of Abraham, and the God of Isaac, and the God of Jacob? God is not the God of the dead, but of the living.'

II. Come we now to the strength of his faith; that is seen in two things—(1.) His clear vision; (2.) His deep affection.

1. His clear vision and sight of Christ: 'He saw my day.' The eagle eye of faith will see afar off and through many impediments, and draw comfort not only from what is present, visible, and sensible, but from what is distant and future, and but obscurely revealed. The sight of faith may be illustrated by bodily sight.

Three things argue the strength of bodily sight—

[1.] When the things are afar off that we see; for a weak eye cannot see afar off.

[2.] When there are clouds between, though the things be clear; to pierce through these clouds argueth the sight is strong.

[3.] When there is but a little light to see by. To see a thing at a distance, either in the morning or evening twilight, argueth a strong sight. All these concur here.

[1.] The things to be seen were at a great distance, not to be accomplished in their time, nor a long time after. Thousands of years and many successions of ages intervened ere the Messiah was exhibited to the world, and came in the flesh to erect his gospel kingdom; yet they went to the grave in assurance of this promise, that in due time the redemption of sinful man should be accomplished. Well, then, we see the nature of faith, that it can look upon things absent and future as sure and near; and without it man looketh no farther than present probabilities: 2 Peter i. 9, 'But he that lacketh these things is blind, and cannot see afar off,' τυφλός καὶ μυωπάζων. A purblind man cannot see things at a distance from him; but faith surmounts all successions of ages, and can fly over many thousands of years in a moment to the object expected; as the apostle John: Rev. xx. 12, 'I saw the dead, small and great, stand before God.' He saw it in the light of prophecy; but the light of faith and prophecy differ little. They agree in the general ground, viz., divine revelation; they differ only as the general revelation is the ground of faith; a particular revelation is the ground of prophecy. They agree in the manner of perception, by divine illumination; the Spirit enlighteneth believers, and the Spirit enlightened the prophets, for they were moved by the Holy Ghost. But only believers by that general way of illumination, which is common to all the saints; the special illumination is peculiar to prophets. They agree in the object, things absent and future and at great distance; here there is no difference. They agree in the certainty of apprehension; only by prophecy they may define particular events; by the other, the accomplishment of general promises. They agree as to the affections of the heart, but they differ in the degree; the one hath more esctatic motions, the other is a more temperate confidence. So that you see by this comparison a strong faith can see things at a distance, and we are affected with them in some manner as if they were present.

[2.] When clouds come between faith and the object to be seen. When the promise was given to Abraham, he was childless, and so remained a long time. In the course of nature his own body and Sarah's womb were dead; and after he had a son, God commands him to slay him and offer him in sacrifice; a command not only against his natural affection, but hope. And then afterwards his seed was few in number for a long time, and when they did multiply they were oppressed, which was revealed to Abraham. Now, to strive against all these difficulties was 'to believe in hope against hope,' Rom. iv. 18. But this I must reserve to the next time. However it is said of Abraham, 'He saw my day;' he rested in the truth and power of God, and by it resolved all difficulties. To see through such natural impossibilities argueth a strong sight of faith.

[3.] For their light to go by, it was but a little; the revelation was but obscure; the patriarchs had only that promise, Gen. iii. 15, 'And I will put enmity between thee and the woman, and between thy seed and her seed; it shall bruise thy head, and thou shalt bruise his heel.' Abraham's was a little clearer; all that he had was but this, 'In thy seed all nations shall be blessed.' Yet this was but a small glimmering light in comparison of what we enjoy, far short in clearness and plainness of the many precious gospel promises which are made to us. The daylight is not only broken out, but it draweth nigh to high noon. Though they saw not Christ so nearly and clearly revealed as we do, yet they could do more mighty things with their faith than we can do with ours, and did more excel both in comfort and holiness.

You will say, What is this clear vision of Christ to us? How shall we judge of the strength or weakness of our faith by this?

Ans. 1. As to Christ, there is a sight of Christ past, present, and to come, which still belongeth to faith.

(1.) Past: To see him whom we have not seen, that is, so to be affected with his miracles and acts of mediation as if we had seen him in the flesh, is still the work and exercise of our faith. So the apostle telleth the Galatians, chap. iii. 1, 'Before whose eyes Christ Jesus hath been evidently set forth crucified among you;' that is, before you he hath been convincingly declared, as if he were set before your eyes nailed to the cross. We should receive Christ as it were crucified in the midst of us; and the more lively and impressive thoughts we have of this in the word and sacraments, the stronger is one's faith. We do so believe it, and our hearts are so warmed by it, as if it were all done before our eyes. Such evidence and conviction should we have as to warm our hearts.

(2.) Present: To see him so as to make him the object of our love and trust: John vi. 40, 'And this is the will of him that sent me, that he that seeth the Son, and believeth on him, may have everlasting life.' There is a clear sight of Christ still necessary to believing; we must see him and know him spiritually. Though he be removed from us within the curtain of the heavens, yet we must see him, and such worth and excellency in him as may draw off our hearts from other things; see him so as to believe that he is at the right hand of God, negotiating for us, that we may trust ourselves and our all in his hands. Stephen said, Acts vii. 56, 'Behold, I see the heavens opened, and the Son of man standing at the right hand of God.' He saw the Lord Jesus as in a posture of readiness to assist and help him; that was by extraordinary vision, for it is said, 'The heavens opened.' But faith doth the like in its degree and proportion. Especially must we see him at the right hand of God ready to receive us when we die.

(3.) Future: We must see him; that is, be assured of his second coming, and thoroughly persuaded that we shall see him; as Job, chap. xix. 25–27, 'For I know that my Redeemer liveth, and that he shall stand in the latter days upon the earth; and though after my skin, worms destroy this body, yet in my flesh I shall see God; whom I shall see for myself, and mine eyes shall behold him.' At the resurrection we shall get this sight and blessed vision of God. Now faith must overlook all impediments to assure ourselves of this.

Ans. 2. There are other objects about which the vision of faith is exercised, as the glory and blessedness of the world to come. Faith is the perspective of the soul, by which it can see things at a distance as present. It can look beyond and above the world, and draw unspeakable joy from the hope of eternal life. Moses, Heb. xi. 26, 'Esteemed the reproach of Christ greater riches than the treasures of Egypt; for he had respect to the recompense of reward,' ἐπέβλεπεν; he looked to it. The glory of the world to come is represented and set before us in the promise; we see it clearly there: Heb. vi. 18, 'That by two immutable things, in which it was impossible for God to lie, we might have strong consolation, who have fled for refuge to lay hold upon the hope set before us;' Heb. xii. 2, 'Looking unto Jesus, the author and finisher of our faith, who, for the joy that was set before him, endured the cross, despised the shame, and is set down at the right hand of the throne of God.' To this we should look, and see it as if it were before our eyes, that we may not be allured or terrified by the things that are before our eyes. But of this I have already spoken in the nature of faith. (See Sermons on Heb. xi. 1.) Only let me advise you now to keep the eye of faith clear, that Christ and heaven may be always in view. The devil seeks to shut it: 2 Cor. iv. 4, 'In whom the god of this world hath blinded the eyes of them which believe not, lest the light of the glorious gospel of Christ, who is the image of God, should shine unto them.' He doth it by the world, deluding and bribing the flesh, and enchanting the mind with worldly felicity, so that God and heaven are forgotten, and that necessary care which we should use in preparation for it is neglected and omitted. But it is opened by the Spirit: Eph. i. 17, 18, 'That the God of our Lord Jesus Christ, the Father of glory, may give unto you the Spirit of wisdom and revelation in the knowledge of him; the eyes of your understanding being enlightened, that ye may know what is the hope of his calling, and what the riches of the glory of his inheritance in the saints.' And therefore we should always pray for this spiritual eyesalve, that we may have a due sense of the world to come fresh and strong upon our hearts.

2. The next effect is deep affection or rejoicing in Christ, and all the work of redemption done in his day. Certainly a sight of Christ by faith doth bring true joy and peace into the soul.

Here I shall show—

[1.] That no other affection will become Christ, and the salvation offered by him and received by faith, but great joy. This is evident by the whole drift and current of the scriptures. The angels told the shepherds at Christ's birth, Luke ii. 10, 'And the angel said unto them, Fear not, for behold I bring you good tidings of great joy, which shall be to all people.' Surely tidings of Christ, the Redeemer of the world, are tidings of great joy, because then there was a way found out for our reconciliation with God, and the taking up that dreadful controversy between us and him, that heaven and earth may kiss each other, and meet again in a covenant of love and peace and grace, purchased by Christ, whereby we might overcome the devil, the world, and the flesh. The great enemies of our salvation are defeated, and a proportionable happiness found out for man, without which he would have been as Leviathan in a little pool. So when this grace was offered to any, as to Zaccheus, by Christ's coming into his house and bringing salvation with him: Luke xix. 6, 'He made haste, and came down, and received him joyfully;' or published in the word: Acts xiii. 48, 'When the gentiles heard these things, they were glad, and glorified the word of the Lord, and as many as were ordained to eternal life believed.' Now we are concerned as well as they. The gospel should never be as stale news to sinners, or as a jest often told. Our necessities are the same with theirs, and the benefits are offered to us as well as them. The Virgin Mary was thus affected: Luke i. 47, 'My spirit hath rejoiced in God my Saviour;' that Christ was to be born of her, and was formed in her. The eunuch, when Philip had preached to him Jesus, and he was baptized into this faith, Acts viii. 39, 'He went on his way rejoicing;' as men do that have met with a good bargain, and have sealed it and made it sure. So the jailer: Acts xvi. 34, 'He rejoiced, believing in God with all his house;' he was but newly converted, and recovered out of the suburbs of hell, ready to kill himself just before, so that a man would have thought you might as easily fetch water out of a flint or a spark of fire out of the bottom of the sea, yet he rejoiced when he was acquainted with Christ. So that you see none reflect seriously on the gospel but they find cause of joy. We cannot consider and believe the great things which Christ hath done and purchased for us, with some hope of the enjoyment of them, without joy.

[2.] The reasons of this joy. These must be considered with respect to the object, the subject, the causes.

(1.) The excellency of the object, which is Jesus Christ, and the incomparable treasure of his grace.

(1st.) He is excellent in himself, as being the eternal Son of God. Now, when he will come down, not only to visit, but redeem a sinful world, this should be matter of joy to us. He came down, was not thrust down; he came as the pledge and instance of the Father's love: John iii. 16, 'God so loved the world, that he gave his only-begotten Son.' To make divine nature more amiable, that we might not fly from him as a condemning God, but return to him as a pardoning God, and willing to be reconciled to sinful man: 2 Cor. v. 19, 'God was in Christ reconciling the world to himself, not imputing their trespasses to them.' And in our nature died for us: Rev. i. 5, 'Who hath loved us, and washed us from our sins in his own blood.' Christ would show us a love that passeth knowledge, and would surprise men and angels with a heap of wonders in the whole business of our deliverance from sin and misery. And surely we bring down the price of these wonders of love if we entertain them with cold thoughts, and without some considerable acts of joy and thankfulness.

(2d.) He is also necessary for us: Rom. iii. 19, 'And all the world may become guilty before God,' ὑπόικος Θεῷ; subject to the judgment of God, or obnoxious to his wrath and vengeance. What could we have done without his passion and intercession? If he had not died for sinners, what had we to answer to the terrors of the law or accusations of conscience, or to appease the fears of hell and approaching damnation? How could you look God in the face, or think a comfortable thought of him, or call upon his name, or pray to him in your necessities? In good sadness what could you do? Would you bewail sins past; but what recompense or ransom for your souls was there? If you had wept your eyes out, it would not have been accepted without a redeemer or some satisfaction to divine justice: Micah vi. 6, 7, 'Wherewith shall I come before the Lord, and bow myself before the high God? Shall I come before him with calves of a year old? will the Lord be pleased with thousands of rams, or with ten thousand of rivers of oil? shall I give my first-born for my transgression? the fruit of my body for the sin of my soul?' Would you commit sin no more, or serve God for the future exactly? If that had been possible with a sinning nature, yet payment of new debts doth not quit old scores; or paying what we owe doth not make amends for what is stolen; you might have lain in your blood. We could not find out a ransom which God would accept: Ps. xlix. 7, 8, 'None of them can by any means redeem his brother, nor give to God a ransom for him; for the redemption of their soul is precious, and it ceaseth for ever.' No; it is the Lord's mercy to find out a ransom for us: Job xxxiii. 24, 'Then he is gracious unto him, and saith, Deliver him from going down to the pit; I have found a ransom.'

(3d.) He is so beneficial to us. We have cause to rejoice if we consider the many benefits we have by him: 1 Cor. i. 30, 31, 'But of him are ye in Christ Jesus, who of God is made unto us wisdom, and righteousness, and sanctification, and redemption: that according as it is written, He that glorieth, let him glory in the Lord.' Ignorance alienates from God; depraved nature brings doubts and fears, which always haunt us about eternity and the way thither. Now, when God hath provided such a suitable and all-sufficient remedy, should we not rejoice, and esteem him, and delight in him, and count all things but dung and dross in comparison of him, that we may gain him and his grace?

(2.) The subject.

(1st.) They are affected with their misery; for according as our sense of our misery is, so is our entertainment of the remedy. Those that heal their wounds slightly little care for the physician. A doctrinal sight of sin maketh way for a dead opinion about Christ. It is they that are often in tears and groans, through the feeling of sin and fears of the wrath of God, who do most esteem Christ and rejoice in him: Mat. ix. 13, 'I am not come to call the righteous, but sinners to repentance;' Acts ii. 37, 'And when they heard this, they were pricked in their hearts, and said unto Peter and the rest of the apostles, Men and brethren, what shall we do?' A saviour is welcome to them, for he is to them a comfortable and suitable remedy.

(2d.) They mind their end, which is to return to God as their proper happiness. When the soul seeth nothing better than God, then nothing is sweeter than Christ. Intention of the end maketh the means acceptable: John xiv. 6, 'Jesus saith unto him, I am the way, the truth, and the life; no man cometh to the Father but by me;' Heb. vii. 25, 'Wherefore he is able to save to the uttermost all those that come unto God by him, seeing he ever liveth to make intercession for them.' Christ is of no use but where God is our chiefest good; for if we be indifferent as to the favour of God, why should we prize Christ?

(3d.) Their heart is suited to spiritual things. To excite delight and complacency there are two things necessary—the attractiveness of the object, and the inclination of the faculty. Delight and pleasure is *applicatio convenientis convenienti.* If the object be never so lovely, yet, if the faculty be not suited, there is no delight. We use to say, One man's food is another man's poison: Rom. viii. 5, 'For they that are after the flesh do mind the things of the flesh; but they that are after the Spirit, the things of the Spirit.' Every man's taste is according to his constitution; some are so lost and sunk in the dregs of pleasures, honours, and profits, that they have no relish for better things. Though Christ be so excellent and so suitable, and so all-sufficient to soul-necessities, yet carnal men cannot savour him: this excellency is only valued by a spiritual mind. Scarlet maketh no more show in the dark than a better colour. The mystery of redemption to the carnal is but a cold story, and the rose of Sharon but as withered flowers, and the promises of the gospel are as dry chips.

(3.) The causes of it; they are the Holy Ghost, and faith as his instrument. This joy is stirred up by the Holy Ghost, therefore often called joy in the Holy Ghost: Rom. xiv. 17, 'For the kingdom of God is not meat and drink, but righteousness and peace, and joy in the Holy Ghost;' 1 Thes. i. 5, 'For our gospel came not unto you in word only, but also in power and in the Holy Ghost.' And the comforts of the Spirit: Acts ix. 31, ' Walking in the fear of the Lord, and in the comfort of the Holy Ghost.' But then faith is the means: Rom. xv. 13, ' Now the God of hope fill you with all joy and peace in believing;' 1 Peter i. 8, ' Whom having not seen, ye love; in whom, though now ye see him not, yet believing, ye rejoice with joy unspeakable and full of glory.' So that it is a fruit of faith as well as a work of the Holy Ghost. Faith joined with love will bring much love into the heart of a believer, and will cause it to be deeply affected with Christ's grace.

[3.] The nature of this joy and gladness. Here we must distinguish—

(1.) There is a superstitious joy which ariseth from knowing Christ after the flesh: 2 Cor. v. 16, ' Wherefore henceforth know we no man after the flesh; yea, though we have known Christ after the flesh, yet now henceforth know we him no more;' which is seen in this, it prizeth Christ's name but neglects his office, pretends a fond esteem of his memory but despises his benefits. As the Jews would fly in the face of any that would not count them Abraham's children, yet would not do the works of Abraham, so is the nominal christian's joy. This joy venteth itself in a carnal way, by outward theatrical pomp and ceremonial observances, but not in real affection to Christ; yea, they are rather enemies to his spiritual kingdom and cause and servants, and express their rejoicing rather as votaries of Bacchus than as disciples of Christ, in a gross and carnal way. This joy is a rejoicing in Christ for a day, but we are to make it our daily work, a holy festival that lasteth our whole lives: Phil. iv. 4, ' Rejoice in the Lord always, and again I say, Rejoice.' This is a different thing from Abraham's rejoicing. He had a prospect of Christ's day, and was exceeding glad; but this is a carnal owning of the god of the country, and no more.

(2.) There is a holy rejoicing which may be considered—(1.) As to the lively acts; (2.) Or solid effects.

(1*st.*) As to the lively acts, in solemn duties, as the word, and meditation, and Lord's supper, it doth your hearts good to think of Christ: Cant. i. 4, ' We will be glad and rejoice in thee; we will remember thy love more than wine;' Ps. xxii. 26, ' The meek shall eat, and be satisfied; they shall praise the Lord that seek him: your heart shall live for ever;' Heb. xi. 13, ' All these died in faith, not having received the promises, but having seen them afar off, and were persuaded of them, and embraced them;' that is, when they thought of it; the time of the gospel was a sweet time to them, and so it is to all other believers. A man cannot think of his pelf or any petty interest in the world without comfort; and can a believer think of the promises and not be affected with them? In solemn meditation and other duties is faith and joy acted.

(2*d.*) As to its solid effects,

(1st.) It is such a joy as doth enlarge our hearts in duty, and strengthen us in the way of God: Neh. viii. 10, ' For the joy of the Lord is your strength;' Ps. cxix. 14, ' I have rejoiced in the way of thy testimonies as much as in all riches.' The hardest services are pleasant to one that delighteth in Christ. This joy is the very life of obedience; a christian cannot be without it.

(2d.) It sweeteneth our calamities and crosses. (1.) Common afflictions. It can never be so sad with us in the world but we have cause of rejoicing in Christ: Hab. iii. 17, 18, 'Though the fig-tree do not blossom, &c., yet I will rejoice in the Lord, and joy in the God of my salvation;' for we have better things in him than any natural comfort which can be taken from us. This should not diminish the solid satisfaction of our souls. (2.) The afflictions of the gospel: Luke vi. 23, 'Rejoice ye in that day, and leap for joy: for your reward is great in heaven; for in like manner did their fathers unto the prophets;' Heb. x. 34, 'And took joyfully the spoiling of your goods, knowing in yourselves that in heaven ye have a better and enduring substance.' They are fit occasions to show how much we value Christ above all our own interests, how near and dear soever they be to us.

(3d.) It draweth us off from the vain delights of the flesh. Every man must have some oblectation; for love and delight cannot lie idle in the soul; either it is taken up with the joys of sense or with the joys of faith. And it is good for every man to observe what it is that puts gladness into his heart, where his solid contentment and pleasure is. A brutish heart fetcheth all its solaces from the world, but a gracious heart from Christ; the one loves pleasures more than God, but to the other Christ and his benefits are matter of joy and comfort; this is that they are cheered with, as they get more of Christ into their hearts: Ps. iv. 7, 'Thou hast put gladness in my heart, more than in the time that their corn and their wine increased;' as David calleth God his 'exceeding joy,' Ps. xliii. 4. They need not the carnal mirth, without which others cannot live: Ps. iv. 6, 'Who will show us any good?'

Use. Well, then, you see faith is not only a sight, but a taste, or a feeding on the promises with delight: Ps. cxix. 111, 'Thy testimonies I have taken for an heritage for ever; for they are the rejoicing of my heart.' And such a delight as draweth off our hearts from other things, as the man that hath found the true treasure, Mat. xiii. 44, 'For joy thereof goeth and selleth all that he hath, and buyeth that field.'

I observe a double joy in Abraham—

1. In desiring, 'He rejoiced to see my day.' The spiritual desires of God's people after Christ are full of joy. There is a joy that accompanieth seeking before we attain what we seek after: Ps. cv. 3, 'Let the hearts of them rejoice that seek the Lord.' Before complacential joy there is a seeking joy. Better be a seeker than a wanderer, and delight in Christ keepeth up this seeking.

2. There is a joy after faith hath given some satisfaction. First, ἠγαλλιάσατο, 'he rejoiced;' and then, ἐχάρη, 'he was glad.' A man sick of a mortal disease, when he heareth of a famous physician, he desires to see him; it is some contentment to a sick man to see him; but when his cure is wrought, he much more rejoiceth. So when we feel the benefit in our own souls, it causes joy: Rom. v. 11, 'And not only so, but we also joy in God through our Lord Jesus Christ, by whom we have now received the atonement.'

SERMON UPON ROMANS IV. 18-21.

Who against hope believed in hope, that he might become the father of many nations, according to that which was spoken, So shall thy seed be. And being not weak in faith, he considered not his own body now dead, when he was about an hundred years old, neither yet the deadness of Sarah's womb: he staggered not at the promise of God through unbelief; but was strong in faith, giving glory to God; and being fully persuaded that what he had promised he was able also to perform.—Rom. iv. 18-21.

We are now come to handle the other branch of Abraham's faith. A believer hath but two works to do—to open the eye of faith, and to shut that of sense. I shall speak of this latter now. This instance deserveth to be considered by us—(1.) Because he is called once and again, 'The father of the faithful,' ver. 11, 16, meaning thereby that his faith is the pattern according to which our faith is to be cut out, or the copy to be transcribed by us; or, as the apostle's expression is, ver. 12, 'That we should walk in the steps of the faith of our father Abraham.' (2.) Because this was great and grown faith. It is negatively expressed, ver. 19, 'He was not weak in faith;' and affirmatively, ver. 20, 'That he was strong in faith, giving glory to God.'

Now in Abraham's faith we shall consider three things—

First, The ground of it.

Secondly, The excellency and strength of it, set forth by four expressions—

1. That 'he believed in hope against hope,' ver. 18.
2. That he considered not the difficulties, ver. 19, 'He considered not his own body now dead, neither yet the deadness of Sarah's womb.'
3. That 'he staggered not at the promise through unbelief,' ver. 20.
4. That he had a full persuasion of God's power, 'Being fully persuaded that what God had promised he was able to perform,' ver. 21.

Thirdly, The fruit and effect of it, an exact, ready, and self-denying obedience to God, not spoken of in the text, but to be supplied from other scriptures, especially in those two eminent acts of self-denial, his leaving his country, and offering his son. Thus was Abraham's faith tried, by promises of things strange and incredible, and by commands of the hardest duties.

First, The ground of his faith was the promise of God, as is often implied in the text; for it is said, ver. 18, 'That he might become the father of many nations, according to that which was spoken, So shall thy seed be;' and ver. 20, 'He staggered not at the promise of God;' and ver. 21, 'Being fully persuaded that what he had promised,' &c. There were many promises made to Abraham, but those to which the apostle alludeth are contained in Gen. xv., as appeareth by his dispute all along, and the comparing the two chapters. Now the promise was either general or particular.

1. The general promise: Gen. xv. 1, 'I am thy shield, and thy exceeding great reward.' That God would take him into his protection, and abundantly reward his obedience. The like promise is made to all the faithful: Ps. lxxxiv. 11, 'The Lord God is a sun and a shield; the Lord will give grace and glory, and no good thing will he withhold from them that walk uprightly.' The only one and true God, Father, Son, and Holy Ghost, will exercise all his wisdom, power, and goodness to protect us, and deliver us from all evil, and to give us all those blessings which are necessarily required to make us fully and eternally happy. He will be a shield to save us and protect us, either by way of prevention or removal of all evil, both temporal and spiritual, and he will be a reward to give us all good things, yea, 'a great reward,' yea, again 'an exceeding great reward,' which cannot come short of heaven's glory and eternal happiness, which is the aggregation of all blessings. It is implied also in the metaphor of being a sun to us. Here he is as a sun at its first rising, shining upon us with his morning beams of favour and compassion, which are very cherishing and comfortable; but then our sun shall be in its meridian, when he shall directly, fully, and for ever shine upon the saints.

2. The other promise was particular, and thus occasioned: When God had told Abraham that he would be his shield and exceeding great reward, he replied, 'Lord what wilt thou give me, seeing I go childless, and the steward of my house is this Eliezer of Damascus?' and again, 'Behold thou hast given to me no seed; and lo, one born in my house is mine heir,' Gen. xv. 2, 3. These words of Abraham imply some diffidence, or conflict with unbelief, or a weakness of faith at least; though they also may be conceived to represent his condition to God, and revive the remembrance of an old promise made to him some time before: Gen. xii. 3, 'In thee shall all the families of the earth be blessed.' And they in effect speak to this sense: Lord, how can I take comfort in the promised reward, since I do not see the fulfilling of thy promise touching my seed? But now mark the Lord's reply: ver. 4, 'This shall not be thine heir, but he that shall come forth out of thine own bowels shall be thine heir;' that is, thou shalt have posterity, the promised seed shall at length come of thy loins. And then God led him forth: ver. 5, 'And he brought him forth abroad, and said, Look now toward heaven, and tell the stars, if thou be able to number them.' Ocular demonstration leaveth a stronger impression upon the mind: 'And he said unto him, So shall thy seed be;' upon this 'Abraham believed in the Lord, and he counted it to him for righteousness,' ver. 6; that is, upon this he began to grow stronger in the faith, more and more overcoming the doubts of the flesh, and embracing the great promises which God had made him. He was a believer before, but now he commenceth a strong believer; this is

that which is said, ver. 18, 'He believed in hope against hope, that he might become the father of many nations, according to that which was spoken, So shall thy seed be.'

Secondly, The excellency of his faith, in four expressions—

I. 'He believed in hope against hope.' Abraham was still childless, and so remained for some years after this assurance from God, and in the course of nature he had little reason to expect a child; but he hoped in the word of God, when according to the order of nature all hope of issue was cut off. We learn, then, that spiritual hope can take place when natural hope faileth; as Abraham had a strong hope in God when all appearances seemed to forbid hope. Most men's faith is borne up by outward likelihoods and probabilities, and when they fail, their faith faileth; they can trust God no further than they can see him; but true faith dependeth upon him when his way is in the dark, and there is little appearance of the things we wait for; as Paul could assure them not a man should be lost, when all hope that any should be saved was taken away, Acts xxvii. 20–22. I prove this—

1. From the genius and nature of faith. There must be some difficulty in the thing to be believed, or else it is not an object of faith: Rom. viii. 24, 'But hope that is seen is not hope; for what a man seeth, why doth he yet hope for?' The nature of faith and hope is so that it is not of things presently enjoyed; for vision and possession exclude hope, and what is easy and next at hand, it is as if it were already enjoyed; therefore it is no trial of your faith to wait for probable things, and such as are within the view of sense or reason; but to hope against hope, when God disappointeth our confidence, and seemeth to beat us off from believing, yet to adhere to him, this is the disposition of faith.

2. From the warrant of faith, which is the word of God. Now we must believe God upon his bare word, though we know not what time or way he will take, or by what means the things promised may be accomplished. In things future and invisible, we believe against sense. To say with Thomas, 'Except I see, I will not believe,' John xx. 25, this maketh way for atheism. In things incredible we believe against reason: Heb. xi. 1, 'Faith is $\accentset{}{\ἔλεγχος\ τῶν\ μὴ\ βλεπομένων}$, the evidence of things not seen;' provided they be revealed by God. We must not be false prophets to ourselves, and make promises which God never made; that is to interest his glory in our vain conceits: Jer. iv. 10, 'Ah, Lord God, surely thou hast greatly deceived this people and Jerusalem, saying, Ye shall have peace;' meaning the false prophets using his name. And it is a snare to ourselves; we dream of deliverance when God intendeth a further trial: 1 Thes. v. 3, 'For when they shall say, Peace and safety, then sudden destruction cometh upon them, as travail upon a woman with child, and they shall not escape.' But when the promise is clear, then we must believe in hope against hope. Sense, nature, and human reason must not be heard against faith: Ps. xxvii. 3, 'Though war should rise against me, in this I will be confident;' whatever the danger was, for he had a particular promise of coming to the throne. It must not be, saith sense: It cannot be, saith natural reason: It both can and will be, saith faith. Though what God had promised to do, do far exceed the power of nature, his word is enough to faith.

But if we have no express promise, may we not believe in hope against hope?

Ans. If believing be meant only of a confidence in God's power, not determining the certainty of the event. Many times we are cast upon God's providence, all human refuge and help faileth, there is no possibility of escape; yet God forbiddeth despair, and thus driveth us to himself: 2 Cor. i. 9, 'But we had the sentence of death in ourselves, that we should not trust in ourselves, but in God, which raiseth the dead.' He means, when the furious multitude at Ephesus was let loose upon him for his adherence to his way: Ps. xliv. 19, 20, 'Though thou hast sore broken us in the place of dragons, and covered us with the shadow of death, we have not forgotten the name of our God.' We have sometimes that which is equivalent to a promise, even the usual practice of God: Deut. xxxii. 36, 'For the Lord will judge his people, and repent himself for his servants, when he seeth their power is gone, and there is none shut up or left;' Gen. xxii. 14, 'In the mount of the Lord it shall be seen.'

3. The object of faith, God all-sufficient. We must neither measure his goodness nor power by our scantling and module. Not his goodness: Isa. lv. 8, 9, 'For my thoughts, are not your thoughts, neither are your ways my ways, saith the Lord; but as the heavens are higher than the earth, so are my ways higher than your ways, and my thoughts than your thoughts;' Hosea xi. 9, 'I will not execute the fierceness of mine anger, I will not return to destory Ephraim; for I am God and not man.' We sin as men, but he pardoneth like a God. Nor his power: Zech. viii. 6, 'If it be marvellous in the eyes of the remnant of this people in these days, should it also be marvellous in mine eyes? saith the Lord of hosts.' The promises then made seemed impossible or improbable to be performed; for the Jews were a despicable remnant, and the times full of dangers and fears. Reason and probability is not our support, but faith, which looketh to God, to whom nothing is impossible. Nothing can be laid in opposition to his power, or can overbalance his promises. We are at a loss many times, but God is never at a loss. You would think that man ridiculous that should say an horse cannot carry him upon his back because a fly cannot. It is more ridiculous to confine God to human likelihoods and probabilities. We cannot do this, therefore God cannot: Ps. lxxviii. 41, 'They limited the Holy One of Israel;' that is, straitened his power, as if their wants were so great God was not able to supply them; or their miseries so grievous, that he were not able to remove them; or their enemies so strong, that he were not able to vanquish them. If there be any difficulty in the case, it is the fitter for an almighty power. Certainly we have no strong faith, if any faith, when we cannot see the truth of God's promises, unless we see the possiblity of their accomplishment by natural means. If it pass the power of the creature, we say, How can these things be? Alas! you do not know God's infinite power. Can you say, Thus far God can go and no further; this much God can do, and no more?

II. He considered not the difficulties: ver. 19, 'And being not weak in faith, he considered not his own body now dead, when he was about an hundred years old, neither yet the deadness of Sarah's womb.' Here we learn that we must not oppose natural impediments to the power and truth of God. Unbelief will stir up many objections, great reasonings within ourselves against the promise. To hearken to these is to tempt ourselves, and choke our own faith. As in other sins, to pore upon the temptation is to parley with the devil, and suffer the evil to fasten itself upon our spirits; so, in point of believing, Abraham considered not how dead and unmeet he and his wife were as to prolification.

First, I shall examine how we are, or are not to consider difficulties.

1. In some sense it is our duty to consider them, that we may not go about the most serious work hand-over-head. Christ bids us sit down and count the charges: Luke xiv. 28, 'For which of you, intending to build a tower, sitteth not down first, and counteth the cost, whether he have sufficient to finish it?' The saints are wont to put hard cases to themselves: Ps. iii. 6, 'I will not be afraid of ten thousand of people that have set themselves against me round about;' and Ps. xxiii. 4, 'Yea, though I walk through the valley of the shadow of death, I will fear no evil.'

2. Therefore the ends must be observed. We must consider them to prevent slightness, and to weaken our security, but not to weaken our confidence in the promise. When they are urged against the promise, they impeach the truth of God; but when we consider them to prevent slightness, it is good. The difficulties of salvation must be sufficiently understood, otherwise we think to do the work of an age in a breath: Luke xiii. 24, 'Strive to enter in at the strait gate; for many I say unto you will seek to enter in, and shall not be able;' Josh. xxiv. 19, 'And Joshua said unto the people, Ye cannot serve the Lord; for he is a holy God.' It is not so easy a matter as you take it to be.

3. Difficulties must be thought on to quicken faith, not to weaken it. If they be pleaded against the promise, they weaken faith; if they be pleaded to drive us to the promise, they quicken faith. What greater arguments are there to press us to dependence than to consider our impotency, the looseness of our hearts, and the strength of temptations? 2 Chron. xx. 12, 'For we have no might against this great company that cometh against us, neither know we what to do, but our eyes are unto thee.' But to plead against the promise is to consult with the wisdom of the flesh, and it hath ever fared ill with the saints: Luke i. 18, 'And Zacharias said unto the angel, Whereby shall I know this? for I am an old man, and my wife well stricken in years.' Therefore for a while he was struck dumb. So Moses: Num. xx. 12, 'Hear now, ye rebels; must we fetch you water out of the rock?' God had bidden him smite the rock, and assured him the water should flow; but he pleadeth the natural impossibility, therefore he was shut out of Canaan. So that nobleman, 2 Kings vii. 2, 'Then a lord on whose hand the king leaned answered the man of God, and said, Behold, if the Lord would make windows in heaven, might this thing be? And he said, Behold thou shalt see it with thine eyes, but shalt not eat thereof.' But he that will not believe the truth of a promise, shall not partake of the benefit of it. Well, then, as Abraham regarded not the great difficulties that might be pleaded to his faith from his own and his wife's age, so must not we.

Secondly, I shall show you the inconveniences of this sinful considering the difficulties in all the parts of faith, assent, consent, and affiance.

1. As to assent. There are many difficulties which may be objected against the truths propounded in the word; but it is enough to a believer that God hath revealed them in his word, and propounded them to his faith. Reason is apt to reply, as Nicodemus, when Christ spake to him of regeneration: John iii. 9, 'How can these things be?' Carnal reason keepeth men from simple believing, or resting on what is revealed, till they see a reason for everything. Now we see a reason why we do believe, and that is the word of God or divine revelation, though we do not see a reason of everything which we do believe, for many things are mysteries. In such cases we must receive truths as we do pills, not chew, but swallow them, take them upon the credit of the revealer. To chew produceth a loathsome ejection; to swallow a wholesome remedy. Believing in the common notion of it is a receiving of truths upon trust from another, so it differeth from knowing; and divine faith is a receiving such things as God hath revealed, because he hath revealed them. Therefore our first inquiry is, whether these things be so or no? Not, how they can be so? There we begin at the wrong end. In many cases, *constat de re ;* the thing is evident in scripture whereby it is revealed, but how it can be is beyond our reach; the *modus* is not certain. Now, when we should believe, we dispute, and so cavil rather than inquire. If it be not plainly revealed by God, you may reject it without sin and danger; but if it be, you must not contradict all that you cannot comprehend, otherwise dangerous mischiefs will ensue. The true God will be no God to you, because you cannot comprehend the trinity of persons in the unity of the divine essence. Christ will be no Christ, because you cannot comprehend how a virgin should conceive, or how a God should become man. It is sufficient that it is revealed in scripture, which carrieth its own evidence in its forehead, shining by its own light, hath the seal and stamp of God upon it; and moreover is confirmed by miracles, and handed and brought down to us by the universal tradition of the church through the successions of all ages, in whose experience God hath blessed it to the converting, comforting, and sanctifying of many souls. In short, to see a thing in its evidence is not to believe, but to receive it on the credit of the testifier. If you will not credit it unless the thing be evident in itself without his word, you do not believe Christ, but your own reason; and instead of being thankful for the revelation, you quarrel with his truth, because it is in some things above your capacity. You should be satisfied with the bare word of God, and captivate your understandings to the obedience of it.

2. As to consent and acceptance. There are many things may be objected against entering into covenant with Christ, as our unworthiness, the fickleness and looseness of our hearts; how unable we are to keep covenant with him; but these things must not be alleged against our duty and the free offers of the Lord's grace.

[1.] Our great unworthiness. This is one reason why the instance of Abraham is produced by Paul as a pattern of faith to the gentiles. As Abraham considered not his natural incapacity to have children, so they not their unworthiness to be adopted into God's covenant. The gentiles were not a people unto God, but were overlooked in the dispensations of his grace; but, Hosea ii. 23, 'I will have mercy upon her that had not obtained mercy; and I will say unto them that were not my people, Thou art my people, and they shall say, Thou art my God.' Our condition is not so desperate that the mercy of the new covenant cannot reach us and recover us. So for particular christians, they exclude and repel comfort, because they are so vile and unworthy and such sinners. If you be such a sinner, the more need of a saviour. You would laugh at him that would argue thus: I am too cold to go to the fire, too sick to send for the physician, too poor to take alms, too filthy to go to the water to be washed. You must not consider what you have been, but what you would be. Christ doth not invite us because we are holy, but that we may be holy. The objection were of weight if we did only advise you to be eased of your smart, but not to be rid of your burden; if this consent were only a claim of privileges, and not an obligation to duties, or a submission to Christ's healing methods. Celsus objected against christianity, that it was a sanctuary for naughty persons and men of a licentious life. Origen answereth him that it was not a sanctuary to shelter them only, but an hospital to cure them. It is not the worthy are invited, but the thirsty and the needy; you are unworthy to the very last, but are you hungry? You are unworthy to receive Christ, but God is worthy to be obeyed. It is not a matter of privilege only, but duty.

[2.] Your hearts are so loose and changeable, you are afraid to bind yourselves to God. The truth is, this consent implieth a delivery over of yourselves to Christ, to seek happiness in the way that he hath appointed; it is the first egress of the soul towards the execution of the duty of a christian, our entry into the practice of the holy life, and an entry withal into a resolved war with the devil, the world, and the flesh, who will resist us herein; and you must consider difficulties so as to fortify your resolution: Mat. xvi. 24, 'If any man will come after me, let him deny himself, and take up his cross, and follow me.' He will surprise no man: Mat. xx. 22, 'Are ye able to drink of the cup that I drink of? and to be baptized with the baptism that I am baptized with?' And not to consider is to discourage your consent.

Object. You will say you cannot do it by your own strength, and you are uncertain of God's assistance.

Ans. Do not foretell the event, but charge yourselves with your duty. It is your duty to engage your hearts to God, though you cannot lay wagers upon your own strength. You must resolve, but continually depend upon Christ for the performing of your resolutions. He will maintain you in your way to heaven: 2 Tim. i. 12, 'For I know in whom I have believed, and I am persuaded that he is able to keep that which I have committed unto him against that day.' In a sense of your own insufficiency and deceitfulness of heart, you must still rely upon his grace and spirit, who hath made many promises to support and to keep you by his power, through faith unto salvation.

3. For affiance in the great promise of the gospel, or offer of pardon and life by Christ. There seemeth to be an impossibility to sense and reason from first to last. If the difficulties of salvation were suffi-

ciently understood, we should see, from the beginning to the end, from the first step to its last period in everlasting glory, it is the mere grace and power of God that carrieth it on, in despite of men and devils; and therefore it is said, Eph. i. 19, 'And what is the exceeding greatness of his power to us-ward who believe, according to the working of his mighty power?' As for instance, the reconciling of a guilty soul to God: Eph. ii. 3, 'Among whom also we had our conversation in time past, in the lust of our flesh, fulfilling the desires of the flesh and of the mind, and were by nature children of wrath even as others.' The changing of a naughty and obstinate heart: Jer. xvii. 9, 'The heart is deceitful above all things, and desperately wicked: who can know it?' And the giving us an holy nature and life: Job xiv. 4, 'Who can bring a clean thing out of an unclean? not one.' Or to quicken us that were dead in trespasses and sins: Eph. ii. 1, 'You also hath he quickened, who were dead in trespasses and sins.' To strengthen a feeble and weak creature: 2 Cor. iii. 5, 'Not that we are sufficient of ourselves, to think anything as of ourselves, but our sufficiency is of God.' That things meet with so much opposition by the way: Eph. vi. 12, 'For we wrestle not against flesh and blood, but against principalities, against powers, against the rulers of the darkness of this world, against spiritual wickedness in high places.' What can maintain us in the midst of so many temptations? We at length die and rot in the grave as others do; now the raising of our bodies after it is eaten by worms and turned to dust is a thing incredible, and to flesh and blood wholly impossible; it is wholly within the reach of God's power. Now since we have ground to hope for all this from the word of God, even to pardon our many sins: Isa. lv. 7, 'Let the wicked forsake his way, and the unrighteous man his thoughts, and let him return unto the Lord, and he will have mercy upon him, and to our God, for he will abundantly pardon;' to change this sinful nature, that we may become an holy people to God: Titus iii. 5, 'Not by works of righteousness which we have done, but according to his mercy he saveth us, by the washing of regeneration, and renewing of the Holy Ghost;' to overcome our obstinacy, perverseness in evil, fickleness in good; to maintain grace in the midst of temptations: Jude 24, 'To him that is able to keep you from falling;' and finally to raise us up out of the grave, we must not consider and plead the difficulties to damp faith, but to quicken it, going on with our duty, and wait for his salvation.

III. 'He staggered not at the promise through unbelief.' Strong faith is so satisfied with God's promise, that it leaveth no place for considerable doubtings; as Abraham here admitted no doubts or questionings touching the promise of God, but, without disputing or arguing to the contrary, depended fully upon the Lord, being persuaded he could do what he had promised. There are two reasons hereof—the immutability of his nature: Heb. vi. 18, 'That by two immutable things, in which it was impossible for God to lie, we might have strong consolation;' and his tenderness of his word: Ps. cxxxviii. 2, 'For thou hast magnified thy word above all thy name.' Both these breed this assured persuasion of God's faithfulness and steadfastness, and make his promise the great prop and support of faith. Now this staggering or not staggering at the promise, and so the weakness and strength of our faith, may refer to three acts or parts of faith—

1. A strong assent or clear sight of the evidence of the truth. If we have the word and promise of God, we should believe anything as surely as if we had the greatest evidence in the world. Thus some of the disciples doubted of the truth of Christ's resurrection: Mat. xxviii. 27, 'And when they saw him, they worshipped him, but some doubted;' Luke xxiv. 21, 'But we trusted that it had been he which should have redeemed Israel.' This argueth a weak faith, not vigorous and active; but faith is strong as it overcomes our speculative doubts, and so doth settle and establish our souls in the truth: Acts ii. 36, 'Let all the house of Israel know assuredly that God hath made that same Jesus, whom ye have crucified, both Lord and Christ.'

2. There is a doubting or staggering, as faith is a consent; when the consent is weak and wavering, faith is weak: Heb. x. 23, 'Let us hold fast the profession of our faith without wavering, for he is faithful that promised.' But such a confirmed resolution as leaveth no room for wavering and looking back argueth a strong faith: Acts xxi. 13, 'Then Paul answered, What! mean ye to weep and to break my heart? for I am ready not to be bound only, but to die at Jerusalem for the name of the Lord Jesus.'

3. As faith implieth a dependence and trust: James i. 6-8, 'But let him ask in faith, nothing wavering; for he that wavereth is like a wave of the sea, driven with the wind and tossed; for let not that man think that he shall receive anything of the Lord: a double-minded man is unstable in all his ways.' Divided between God and other confidences: 1 Tim. ii. 8, 'I will therefore that men pray everywhere, lifting up holy hands, without wrath and doubting;' Mat. xiv. 31, 'O thou of little faith! why didst thou doubt?' Well, then, it is a strong faith that causeth such a fortitude, that we pass through all difficulties and trials without distrust or anxiety of mind. It is opposite to fainting: Ps. xxvii. 13, 'I had fainted unless I had believed to see the goodness of the Lord in the land of the living.' To fears and troubles: Mat. viii. 26, 'Why are ye fearful? O ye of little faith!' Strength of assent doth exclude speculative doubts and errors; strength of resolution doth fortify us against worldly temptations, which beget uncertainty; temptations of profit, pleasure, or vainglory, if the heart be secretly biassed with these, it is opposite to faith: John v. 44, 'How can ye believe, which receive honour one of another?' And strength of confidence doth exclude those doubts which arise from fears of danger and terrors of sense; in such cases we dispute away the comfort of the promises.

IV. 'He was fully persuaded that what God had promised he was able also to perform.' A strong, steady, and full persuasion of the power of God argueth a great faith.

1. There is no doubt of his will when we have his promise; but the ability of the promiser is that which is usually questioned. Unbelief stumbleth at his *can:* 'Can God furnish a table in the wilderness?' Ps. lxxviii. 19; and, 'How can these things be?' Luke i. 34. So 2 Kings vii. 2, 'If the Lord should make windows in heaven, might this thing be?' Nay; and the children of God themselves. Sarah was rebuked when she laughed: Gen. xviii. 12-14, 'Therefore Sarah laughed within herself, saying, After I am waxed old shall I have pleasure, my lord being old also? And the Lord said unto Abraham,

Wherefore did Sarah laugh, saying, Shall I of a surety bear a child, which am old? Is anything too hard for the Lord?' Her laughter was not the laughter of exultation, but dubitation. Moses: Num. xi. 13, 'Whence should I have flesh to give unto all this people? for they weep unto me, saying, Give us flesh that we may eat.' The case is clear; we doubt not but in case of danger, then we are full of fears and suspicions; if of his will, it is because we are so vile and unworthy; but we are vile and unworthy out of danger as well as in danger, therefore it is of his power.

2. God's power and all-sufficiency is to the saints the great support of faith in their greatest extremities. They are relieved by fixing their eye on God's almightiness; as Abraham here. So Heb. xi. 19, λογισάμενος, 'Accounting that God was able to raise him up even from the dead.' So for perseverance: Jude 24, 'Now unto him that is able to keep you from falling.' And for the resurrection: Phil. iii. 21, 'Who shall change our vile body, that it may be fashioned like unto his glorious body, according to the working whereby he is able to subdue all things to himself.' His power reacheth to the grave and beyond the grave. So for the calling the Jews: Rom. xi. 23, 'And they also, if they abide not still in unbelief, shall be grafted in; for God is able to graft them in again.' In short, to question his power is to put him out of the throne, to deny him to be God, as if he were not able to help his friends, and to be a terror to his enemies. Well, then, in matters absolutely promised we have nothing to do but to exalt his power; therefore you may reason thus: He will do it, for he is able to do it: Rom. ii. 23, 'They shall be grafted in, for God is able to graft them in again.' In matters conditionally promised we must magnify his power, and refer the event to his will: Mat. viii. 2, 'Lord, if thou wilt, thou canst make me clean.'

3. There are two things enlarge our thoughts and apprehensions about the power of God; they are mentioned ver. 17, 'Whom he believed, even God who quickeneth the dead, and calleth those things that be not as though they were.' We have to do with a God that can say to the dead, Live. God's power can bring life out of death, something out of nothing; resurrection and creation are easy to him. He that can quicken the dead can quicken those that are dead in trespasses and sins. By the word of his power he maketh all things to be that are not; 'Let there be light,' and there was light; 'Lazarus, come forth,' and he came forth. He causeth things to appear and exist that had no being before.

Thirdly, The fruit and effect of his faith; an exact and constant obedience: Isa. xli. 2, 'Who raised up the righteous man from the east, and called him to his foot.' The righteous man is supposed to be Abraham, often designed by that character; and he was called to his foot, to go to and fro at God's command; as the centurion said, Mat. viii. 9, 'I am a man under authority, having soldiers under me, and I say to this man, Go, and he goeth; and to another, Come, and he cometh; and to my servant, Do this, and he doeth it.' There are two great instances of Abraham's obedience—

1. His self-denial in leaving his country: Heb. xi. 8, 'By faith Abraham, when he was called to go out into a place which he should

after receive for an inheritance, obeyed, and he went out not knowing whither he went.' It was a sore trial to forsake kindred, friends, lands, father's house and inheritance, and to seek an abode he knew not where. Such a total resignation there must be of ourselves to the will of God. This was done by him, and must be done by all that will be saved. We know where the land of promise is, and the way to it, but it lieth in an unknown world.

2. Another trial was, Heb. xi. 17, 18, 'By faith Abraham, when he was tried, offered up Isaac, and he that had received the promise offered up his only-begotten son, of whom it was said, that in Isaac shall thy seed be called.' Because God would make Abraham an example of faith to all future generations, therefore he puts him to this trial, to see whether he loved his Isaac more than God. Now Abraham gave him up wholly to God's disposal, even Isaac, on whom the promise was settled; being assured of God power, he made all things ready for the sacrifice.

Use. Let us get such a faith, even such a sincere, hearty, giving up ourselves to Christ, firmly to rely upon the promises, and faithfully to obey all his commands delivered in the gospel. The gospel is a summary of what we are to believe and do: Ps. cxix. 166, 'I have hoped for thy salvation, and done thy commandments.' Stick to this whatever trial is made of you, and you have the faith of Abraham.

SERMONS UPON MARK III. 5.

SERMON I.

And Jesus looked round about on them with anger, being grieved for the hardness of their hearts.—MARK iii. 5.

In the first verse of this chapter we read that 'there was a man which had a withered hand,' who came to Jesus for relief on the sabbath-day. Here was a fair occasion offered to the pharisees to display their malice. The sabbath was of high esteem and veneration among the Jews, and therefore now they thought by this means to blast the repute of Christ among the people. In case he should heal on the sabbath-day, their noise and clamour against him might seem to be justified; therefore it is said, 'They watched him whether he would heal on the sabbath-day,' ver. 2. But Christ is not daunted; he goeth on with his work for all their prejudices; nay, to make the miracle more manifest, he biddeth him 'stand forth,' ver. 3. However, to satisfy the people, he disputeth with them; they themselves would do more to a beast than he was requested to do to the man with a withered hand: ver. 4, 'He saith unto them, Is it lawful to do good on the sabbath-day, or to do evil? to save life, or to kill?' In Mat. xii. 10, it is said they propounded the question to him; and in the 11th verse, by way of answer, he maketh use of an argument from a beast fallen into a pit: 'He said unto them, What man shall there be among you that shall have one sheep, and if it fall into a pit on the sabbath-day, will he not lay hold on it and lift it out? But they held their peace.' They could reply nothing by way of answer and sufficient confutation, and they would reply nothing by way of approbation and consent. At their malicious silence Christ is both angered and grieved. There is an excellent temper and mixture in his affections. In Christ's anger there is more of compassion than of passion; he knew how to distinguish between the man and the sin, and to manifest his displeasure and grief at the same time. The cause of both is assigned in the text, 'for the hardness of their hearts,' ἐπὶ τῇ πωρώσει τῆς καρδίας αὐτῶν. He was softened for their hardness.

The point which I mean to handle is the grievousness of the sin of hardness of heart. Christ was grieved with it in the pharisees, and there is not a greater cause of offence to his Spirit.

Doct. That hardness of heart is a grievous sin, very offensive and provoking to Jesus Christ.

I shall—(1.) Open the terms; (2.) Show you the nature of this evil frame of heart; (3.) The kinds of it; (4.) The causes of it; (5.) The heinousness of it; (6.) Some observations concerning this spiritual malady.

I. For the terms by which it is expressed, they are two, 'Heart,' and 'Hardness.'

1. 'Heart.' This hardness is sometimes ascribed to the neck; as Prov. xxix. 1, 'He that, being often reproved, hardeneth his neck, shall suddenly be destroyed, and that without remedy.' And then it is a metaphor taken from refractory oxen, that will not endure the yoke; and so it noteth disobedience. Sometimes to the face; as Jer. iii. 5, 'They have made their faces harder than a rock;' and so it noteth impudence; they can no more blush than a rock or stone. But most usually it is ascribed to the heart, as in the text. So Ezek. iii. 7, 'The house of Israel will not hearken to thee, for they will not hearken to me; for all the house of Israel are impudent and hard-hearted;' and so it noteth obstinacy. All go together, an hard heart, an hard neck, and an hard face. Men are first disobedient, then obstinate, then impudent. But it is the heart that we are to consider, which naturally, and in its first sense, signifieth a piece of flesh in the body, which is the chief seat and shop of life; but morally and metaphorically it signifieth the soul: 1 Sam. xii. 20, 'Serve the Lord with all your heart;' that is, with all your soul. Now in the soul there are many faculties—the mind, the conscience, the memory, the will and affections; and they are all expressed by this term 'Heart.' The mind is called heart: Rom. i. 21, 'Their foolish heart was darkened;' that is, their mind. The conscience: 1 Sam. xxiv. 5, 'David's heart smote him;' that is, his conscience. The memory: Phil. i. 7, 'I have you in my heart;' that is, I am mindful of you. But usually it signifieth the will and affections; as Mat. xxii. 37, 'Thou shalt love the Lord thy God with all thy heart.' And this is the faculty in which this disease is seated. Blindness is incident to the mind, searedness and benumbedness to the conscience, slipperiness to the memory, deadness to the affections; but hardness is incident to the will, that part of the soul by which we choose and refuse good or evil.

2. 'Hardness.' It is expressed by different terms in scripture; sometimes by $\pi\omega\rho\omega\sigma\iota\varsigma$ $\tau\hat{\eta}\varsigma$ $\kappa\alpha\rho\delta\iota\alpha\varsigma$, as in the text, and Eph. iv. 18, which noteth a callous, brawny, insensible hardness, such as is in the labourer's hand or the traveller's heel; sometimes by $\sigma\kappa\lambda\eta\rho\omicron\kappa\alpha\rho\delta\iota\alpha$, or $\sigma\kappa\lambda\eta\rho\omega\tau\eta\varsigma$ $\tau\hat{\eta}\varsigma$ $\kappa\alpha\rho\delta\iota\alpha\varsigma$, so it is a metaphor taken from dry bodies, when the parts are more condensed, and so more impenetrable. *Durities est qualitas, densas et bene compactas habens partes, difficulter cedens tactui.* It doth not easily yield to any impressions from without. So it is set forth by the hardness of the adamant: Zech. vii. 12, 'They made their hearts as an adamant stone.' They can no more be wrought upon to receive any impression of grace and reformation than the diamond or flint or hardest rock can be engraved or fashioned to any form by the tool of the artificer.

II. I must open the nature of it. The hardness of heart discovereth itself by two properties : it is κῆρ ἀναισθήτον καὶ ἀκίνητον, an insensible heart, and an inflexible heart.

1. An insensible heart, as a brawny substance or callous piece of flesh, like the labourer's hand and traveller's heel. This the apostle intimateth, Eph. iv. 18, 19, 'Having the understanding darkened, being alienated from the life of God, through the ignorance that is in them, because of the blindness of their heart: who being past feeling,' &c. In one verse he chargeth them with hardness of heart, and in the first words of the next verse with loss of feeling. Feeling, of all senses, though it be not the most noble, yet it is the most necessary; there is no life without it ; it is diffused throughout the whole body; and in what member soever it is lost, there is no more intercourse of vital and animal spirits ; and where it is totally lost, there is no more life. There may be life when other senses are wanting ; a man may be deaf and yet live, blind and yet live ; but if he utterly lose his feeling, he cannot live. Such a dead senseless heart is the hard heart, as appeareth in the wicked by that great security, ease, and quiet which they naturally have, though lying under the guilt of many and grievous sins; and though they be obnoxious to the wrath of God, yet they are never troubled nor affected with any sense of their condition; they can sin freely in thought, foully in act, without any remorse and shame. *Ab assuetis non fit passio.* Men are not moved by such things as they are much used to. As they that live by the fall of great waters sleep quietly because they are accustomed to the noise, so men that are accustomed to sin can swear, and be drunk, and commit filthiness, or go on in some other trade of wickedness, and are never troubled. Mithridates through the custom of drinking poison made it so familiar to him that he drank it without danger. *Elementa non gravitant in suis locis*—Elements weigh not in their proper place. A fish in the water feeleth no weight; sin is not burdensome to wicked men, it is in its own place. This insensibleness is the greater where men will not be awakened out of their lethargic fit by all the means which God useth to them, by the threatenings of his word, or the judgments of his providence. There is a method in God's dispensations ; he threateneth that he may not punish, and punisheth now that he may not punish for ever. Now the children of God are startled at the threatenings, and tremble when they see a storm in the clouds before it falleth ; as Josiah had a tender heart, and melted at the threatening, 2 Chron. xxxiv. 27. And they are said to 'tremble at the word,' Isa. lxvi. 2, and Ezra ix. 4. But wicked men think this is a vain scarecrow ; and though they are most obnoxious to the judgment and wrath of God, yet they have no sense and tender feeling of it; therefore God goeth on to his second dispensation; he punisheth now that he may not punish for ever. As Absalom set Joab's barley-field on fire that he might draw him to come and speak with him, so God seeketh to make men serious, to bring them to the throne of grace, and sue out their pardon, by many temporal judgments. But still wicked men start aside, and will not turn to him that smiteth them: Jer. v. 3, ' Thou hast stricken them, but they have not grieved ; thou hast consumed them, but they have refused to receive correction.' As the anvil is smoothed into hardness by many blows and strokes, so are men more

insensible of their condition, and will not regard the meaning of God's providences. Well, then, a hard heart is insensible of what they have done against God, or what God hath or may do to them. And so far as we lose our sense and tenderness, so far is the heart hardened.

2. It is an inflexible heart; it is not easily bent to God's purpose; say he what he will, men are as light, as vain, as mindless of heavenly things, as basely wedded to the delights of the flesh as ever, and obstinately, and against all means to the contrary, refuse the counsel of God for their good. Though God hath the highest reasons on his side, and great variety of powerful and alluring motives to gain souls to his obedience, and these represented not only to the ear by his messengers, but to the heart by his Spirit, yet men are so addicted to their own wills and lusts, that they will not suffer themselves to be persuaded by him to accept of his offers and rich mercies in Christ; they will not obey the sweet directions of his word, nor regard the motions and strivings of his Spirit, to let their beloved lusts go, and comply with the will of God.

[1.] They are inflexible to the counsels of his word, where God interposeth in the way of the highest authority, straitly charging and commanding us under pain of his displeasure, and reasoneth with us in the most potent and strong way of argumentation, from the excellency of his commands, and their suitableness to us as we are reasonable creatures; from his great love in Christ, whom he hath given to die for us; from the danger if we refuse him, which is no less than everlasting torment; from the benefit and happiness of complying with his motions, which is no less than eternal and complete blessedness both for our bodies and souls; and all is bound upon us by a strict impartial day of accounts, when we are to answer for our neglects, or else to receive the reward of our diligence. But alas! the hard heart defeateth the end of this whole contrivance. Neither the awe of God's authority, nor the reasonableness of his commands, nor the wonderful love of Christ, nor the joys of heaven, nor the horrors of everlasting darkness, nor the strictness of the last day's account, will work man to a sense of his duty, or gain him to make serious preparation for his own happiness and everlasting salvation. Out of what rock was the heart of man hewn? What will work upon you if this doctrine, upon which God hath laid out all the riches of his wisdom and grace, will not work upon you? Hath God another Son to die for you? a better heaven to bestow upon you? or an hotter hell to scare you withal? Would you have the day of judgment more exact and severe? or greater obligations to all holiness and godliness of conversation than those already propounded? or more charms and persuasiveness added to the gospel? Oh, no! that cannot be. Infinite wisdom hath already stated these things. Or would you have God save you against your wills? or thrust these things upon you without your consent? Surely it is obstinacy, plain obstinacy and hardness of heart, that maketh you stand out against God: Ps. lviii. 4, 5, 'They are like the deaf adder that stoppeth her ear, which will not hearken to the voice of charmers, charming never so wisely.' So Mat. xi. 17, 'We have piped unto you and ye have not danced; we have mourned unto you, and ye have not lamented.' The sweetest strains of grace move not the obstinate sinner.

If an angel come from heaven, he cannot bring you better arguments, for the gospel is 'the wisdom of God,' 1 Cor. i. 24. If one came from the dead, he cannot present you with more powerful motives: Luke xvi. 31, 'If they hear not Moses and the prophets, neither will they be persuaded though one rose from the dead.' Oh! why will you not be persuaded? You do in effect say, Let God do or say what he will, he shall not have my heart. Well, then, this unteachableness and unpersuadableness is another property of hardness of heart; and slowness of heart and backwardness to God's work is a degree to it.

[2.] It is inflexible to the motions of God's Spirit. God doth not only invite sinners by the word, but knocketh at their hearts by the pressing motions and impulsions of his grace, and yet they do not open to him to give him entrance. How often have we eluded the importunity of many warm convictions, and baffled many pangs and checks of conscience! Acts vii. 51, 'Ye stiff-necked, and uncircumcised in heart and ears, ye do always resist the Holy Ghost.' Their ears are said to be uncircumcised, as they do resist the counsels of the word; and their hearts, as they do resist the motions of the Spirit, who enforceth truths with a clearer light and conviction upon their hearts. There are many importunate motions and convictions which they slight and oppose. An hard heart goeth to hell with violence; the word standeth in the way, and the Spirit standeth in the way; but still they break through, and so their condemnation is more just; as the prophet said, Isa. vii. 13, 'Is it a small thing for you to weary men, but ye will weary my God also?' Wicked men do not only grieve God's ministers and messengers, but his Spirit, in refusing to accept his gracious offers. The crime would be less if the counsel of the messengers were not enforced by the motions and inspirations of the Holy Ghost. God is not behindhand with a sinner. If the words of men offer occasion of suspicion and prejudice, yet these inward checks and excitements in their own bosoms to be more serious and diligent carry their own evidence with them; and upon such a close application we should be ashamed to give God the denial. But they resist all inward and outward means of reformation; they resist the Spirit as well as despise the minister. But can the Spirit be resisted? Certainly no, when he worketh according to an eternal purpose of grace; for God never made a creature too hard for himself. Yea, it is said even of wicked men, Acts vi. 10, 'They were not able to resist the wisdom and Spirit by which he spake.' The meaning is, they could not hinder his workings, though they thwarted his motions; the light was so clear that they could not hinder the shining of it, nor contradict it, but out of obstinate malice. But how are they said to resist the Holy Ghost? We had need to vindicate the place, because it is usually urged against the efficacy of divine grace. The operation of the Spirit is not irresistible, say they, for the Jews did always resist it. We may grant the whole. Wicked men of an hard heart may resist the common operations of the Spirit, his light and his motions, but the opposition of the elect is overpowered by the efficacy of grace. There is a spirit of resistance in us, but the stronger operation of the Holy Ghost maketh it to give place; we may kick against the pricks till the soul be awakened, and then God hath us at his own beck. Though the grace of conversion be not common to elect and reprobate, yet the grace that tendeth to conversion is common,—and this may be resisted. God may knock at the heart that is never opened to him; they may have excitements, but alas! they are as the rock or adamant to the tool. There is no impression left upon them. *Object.* But if God will use a fainter operation, why are they to blame? I answer—God is not bound, but they are bound to prepare their hearts to receive his motions; let them prove God a debtor, and they may excuse themselves for their disobedience.

III. The kinds of hardness. These will be known by these distinctions—

1. The first distinction is, that hardness of heart is either—(1.) Natural; or (2.) Voluntary and acquired; or (3.) Penal and judicial.

[1.] Natural hardness of heart is a part of inbred corruption, which remaineth with us till God take it away by grace: Ezek. xi. 19, 'I will take away the stony heart out of their flesh, and I will give them an heart of flesh.' The stone in the heart is a disease that all Adam's posterity are subject unto; it runs in the blood. It is not incident to Nabals only, or such as he was, men of a churlish and crabbed temper. No; all men are sick, and most men die of this disease. We brought with us into the world a strong bent to carnal things, and by consequence an averseness from God; and it is a mighty work of grace if we do not carry it with us out of the world. When Nabal died, his heart was as a stone, and so might yours.

[2.] Acquired and voluntary, when men do wittingly and willingly reject the counsel of God, and strengthen themselves in their natural disobedience and obstinacy; or being invited to faith and repentance by God, out of love to sin resist God's call, and put away the word from them, and refuse to obey: Ps. xcv. 8, 'Harden not your hearts.' It is our own act. And 2 Kings xvii. 14, 'They would not hear, but hardened their necks, like to the neck of their fathers.' This increaseth our natural hardness, and maketh it grow more and more, till it be stiffened and settled in an aversion to God; as a crooked stick or twig by growing becometh more difficult to be made straight. By every act of sin we lessen our awe of God; and having ventured once, grow more bold to sin a second time. Men when they first put forth to sea are very fearful, but afterwards laugh at storms; so when a man cometh off safe from sin, he will venture again. By every act of disobedience our incapacity to receive grace is increased, and our inclination to carnal vanities is strengthened; by frequent acts we are confirmed in the habit. But nothing increaseth this voluntary hardness so much as refusing grace; as no water is so apt to freeze as that that hath been once heated. God is provoked when we refuse his grace upon a closer application, and the heart is encouraged to continue in sin. So that by their carelessness and delay men are hardening by degrees. Every call defeated addeth one degree of hardness more; and so God is more apt to desert us and forsake us.

[3.] Penal and judicial hardness. This adds to voluntary hardness, as voluntary hardness implies something above natural. Man, as naturally hardened, doth not turn to God; as judicially hardened, he cannot. There is a great impossibility he should. This is God's act; he hardeneth as a just judge, not by infusing evil, but withdrawing grace. In scripture God is said to harden two ways—(1.) By leaving some in their natural hardness: Rom. ix. 18, 'Therefore hath he mercy on whom he will have mercy; and whom he will, he hardeneth.' So it is an act of dominion; he passeth them by. He may do it justly; he is Lord of his own grace, and is not bound to save sinners. This is not an act of justice, but dominion. God doth not act as a judge, but as a Lord; it is matter of favour to soften, not right. (2.) By giving up others to a reprobate sense, which is a penal and judiciary act: Acts xxviii. 26, 27, 'Hearing ye shall hear, and shall not understand; and seeing ye shall see, and shall not perceive: for the heart of this people is waxed gross, and their ears are dull of hearing, and their eyes have they closed,' &c. There is consideration had of man's sin and foregoing provocations. God punisheth them by their own sin. Men first harden themselves; they go before *peccando*, by sinning; then God cometh after *judicando*, by inflicting this judgment of hardness of heart on them. They harden themselves, and God leaveth them under their hardness. As Jeroboam stretcheth out his arm against the prophet and then God layeth a judgment upon him, that he could not pull it in again to him, 1 Kings xiii. 4, so men hardening themselves, God layeth this judgment upon them, that they shall not return to any softness.

2. The next distinction is, that hardness of heart is either total or partial. Some are in the state of hardness, others complain of it as their present frame. There is a difference between hardness of heart and an hard heart. Some hardness of heart is in God's children: Mark vi. 52, 'They considered not the miracle of the loaves, for their heart was hardened;' and Mark xvi. 14, 'He upbraided them for their unbelief and hardness of heart.' Original hardness of heart is not altogether taken away by grace. Much of the heart of stone, or old averseness from God and holy things, remaineth with God's children; but yet they are not wholly insensible, and wholly inflexible to God's purpose; their hearts are bent to his testimonies, though ever and anon they are apt to fall back to the old bias. Therefore David prayeth, Ps. cxix. 36, 'Incline my heart unto thy testimonies, and not to covetousness.' The children of God do often complain of deadness and unaptness for holy things; yet there is not in them that obstinacy, impenitency, and hardness of heart, that is in the wicked: Rom. ii. 5, 'But after thy hardness and impenitent heart, treasurest up unto thyself wrath against the day of wrath.' In the one it is bemoaned, in the other not; in the one it ariseth from negligence and drowsiness, in the other from flat disobedience and enmity to God. When God's children give too free a contentment and license to the flesh, they have not that sense, that liveliness in prayer, that readiness to obey, that delight in the word, as at other times; but the other are contemptuous and scornful, and do not set their hearts this way, to please God or enjoy his favour. In the wicked there is a careless security, no sense of their eternal condition; they banish it out of their thoughts: Amos vi. 3, 'Ye put far away the evil day.' If it intrude upon them, they look upon it as a melancholy interruption; they seek to put off what they do not put away; yea, there is a plain reluctancy and opposition to good things, and a contempt of God's messages. But in the other

there may be some hanging off from God, for original sin is not quite done away, especially under a distemper occasioned by carnal liberty: Luke xxi. 34, 'Take heed to yourselves, lest at any time your hearts be overcharged with surfeiting, and drunkenness, and cares of this life; and so that day come upon you unawares.' A christian is a compound creature; he hath hardness as well as softness. When their hardness prevaileth, for the present they mourn less for sin, and do not tremble at the word, and are not affected with providences, slight the warnings and motions of the Holy Spirit, are more dead in duty, find not alike savour in the promises, and duties seem more irksome to them. An hard heart maketh their work seem hard and tedious.

3. The next distinction is, that hardness of heart is either felt or unfelt.

[1.] Felt, as by men under a preparative work, and in God's children for hardness there may be in them; yea, it is their condition as long as they are in the world. Grief for hardness is a good sign that there are some tender parts left. An heart judicially hardened can never feel that hardness, nor grieve for it; but the children of God fear it as the greatest evil, and complain of it as the greatest burden, and so accordingly strive against it. Thus Ephraim bemoaned himself, and his obstinacy and inflexibleness: Jer. xxxi. 18, 'I have surely heard Ephraim bemoaning himself thus: Thou hast chastised me, and I was chastised as a bullock unaccustomed to the yoke: turn thou me, and I shall be turned; for thou art the Lord my God.' There is hope of cure when they are sensible of the disease: they fear it in themselves and others as the greatest evil: Heb. iii. 12, 13, 'Take heed, brethren lest there be in any of you an evil heart of unbelief, in departing from the living God: but exhort one another daily, while it is called to-day, lest any of you be hardened through the deceitfulness of sin.' Of all judgments, the judgment of the hard heart is worst. They complain of it as the greatest burden: Isa. lxiii. 17, 'O Lord why hast thou made us to err from thy ways, and hardened our heart from thy fear?' They find much deadness and dulness of spirit; they are not affected with God's presence in duties, nor with his providences in the world. This is their complaint and burden, Lord I have a stiff neck, that will not easily be brought under the strict duties of religion, to meditate and to pray in private; I have a proud stubborn heart, too hard for me to take down. Thus do they complain of these things, and strive against it. As a man that hath a stone in the bladder, he useth good means to soften it, and is careful of his diet, so are God's children sensible, and therefore fearful and careful, often bemoaning themselves.

[2.] Unfelt; so it is in wicked men, who never consider the frame of their hearts, or bemoan themselves because of spiritual evils. The heart of stone is not sensible of itself; and so God's children for a while may be under great desertions and the guilt of heinous sins, and be insensible; after gross falls they may lie in hardness for a while, till God rouse them up again. Great falls are like a blow upon the head, that stuns us and amazes us for a while, and it is some good while ere we recover again. David's conscience was not presently awakened. Spiritual lethargies are long fits. David lay ten months from the conception to the birth of his child, and yet all this while did formally use God's ordinances and public service. Nathan comes to him after the child was born: 2 Sam. xii. 14, 'The child that is born unto thee shall surely die.' And he never relented till Nathan came to him, as appeareth by the title of the 51st psalm, 'A Psalm of David, when Nathan the prophet came to him after he had gone into Bathsheba.' All this while grace was not dead, but in a deep sleep. The least sin maketh way for hardness of heart, much more sins against conscience; there is a more long sequestration then. God will not let you enjoy the comforts and effectual presence of his spirit. These blows and wounds will leave you for dead for a long while.

SERMON II.

And Jesus looked round about on them with anger, being grieved for the hardness of their hearts.—MARK iii. 5.

IV. THE causes of hardness of heart.

1. Ignorance. The blind mind and the hard heart always go together: John xii. 40, 'He hath blinded their minds, and hardened their hearts, that they should not see with their eyes, nor understand with their hearts.' Men are first unteachable, then unpliable. Obstinacy beginneth at sottishness of conceit. He that knoweth not what he ought to do careth not much what he doth. The children of God never feel hardness in their hearts but when the light in their minds is unactive or obscured; there is a kind of darkness for that time. We see that the most carnal wretches, when they come to die, are sensible; when the mind is cleared from the fogs of lust, and conscience is awakened, then they feel a great weight of sin upon them. Light always begets tenderness, as in a clear vessel the dregs do soon appear. Well, then, either they are ignorant, or have but a naked theory, not the lively light of the Spirit; and hence it is that their hearts are hardened.

2. Unbelief; for it is faith that maketh all truths active and lively. The great motives and arguments of religion are mainly fetched from things to come. Now it is not enough to know the things of the world to come, but there must be an hearty assent to them, as if we did see them before our eyes. Things that are at a distance are as nothing to us, as the stars appear as so many spangles, they lose much of their greatness. Men sin, and no evil cometh of it, therefore they grow bold and senseless in sin: Eccles. viii. 11, 'Because sentence against an evil work is not executed speedily, therefore the heart of the sons of men is fully set in them to do evil.' They grow remiss and slack in their duty. The reward is not by and by: Mal. iii. 14, 'Ye have said, It is in vain to serve God, and what profit is it that we have kept his ordinances, and that we have walked mournfully before the Lord of hosts?' We are for a present good. Now, 'Faith is the substance of things hoped for, and the evidence of things not seen,' Heb. xi. 1. It maketh

things present as if we did see them with our eyes, as if the judgment-seat were set and the books were opened. Those that hardened their hearts did not believe what God said was true, Heb. iii. 7–18. If men did believe there were an heaven, and hell, and judgment to come, they would not lie in their sins, they could not be unpliable to God's motions. All disrespect of promises and threatenings cometh from unbelief. Christ did chide his disciples for their unbelief and hardness of heart, Mark xvi. 14. What is the reason that though we preach the law and the judgment of God so much to you, and beseech you to come in and receive Christ, and you shall be saved, and this time after time, and day after day, and yet the word hath no effect upon you, you are as ignorant and careless as ever? The reason is you do not believe. Certainly the word would work otherwise than it doth if you did believe it. If one should tell a man that such an earthly potentate, if he would but come to him and visit him, would raise him to great honour, it would be the first thing he would do. Truly so, if you did believe that coming to Christ were the only way to happiness, you would mind it more seriously than you do. Again, if you did believe that the word of God is true, that God is a just God; if the drunkard did believe that drunkards should be damned; or the adulterer did believe that no adulterer shall inherit the kingdom of God; or if the vain person or the gamester did believe that they must give an account of their misspent time, and idle words, and vain communication, they would not sport themselves in their sins as they do. If men did believe that God calleth when and whom he listeth, they would not defer their repentance and put off the motions of the Spirit, but would strike while the iron is hot, and let out the sails when the wind bloweth. But men do not believe, and therefore go on in their sins as they do. Tell men of earthly things, of a commodity which, if they would but buy, it would yield an hundred for one, surely they would not neglect the market. We press men to renounce but a little ease and carnal pleasures, and to use diligence to get Christ into their hearts, and they shall have a hundred for one; but men want faith, therefore Christ lieth by as a refuse commodity. There is nothing breedeth hardness of heart so much as unbelief of what God can and will do.

3. Custom in sinning. As an highway is trodden hard by long travelling in it, so the heart by long custom groweth more obstinate every day. In sin there is not only a fault, guilt, but a blot, a stronger inclination to the practice of the same sin again; as a brand that has been once in the fire is more apt to burn again. Every new oath is as oil to the tongue, to make it more glib and fleet in the repetition of that oath or vain speech. There is a natural tenderness in men whilst young, at least, a lesser degree of hardness, which will get strength by use and age if not in time cured: Jer. xiii. 23, 'How can ye do good that are accustomed to do evil?' Water when it first freezeth will not bear the weight of a pin, but afterwards by continual freezing it cometh to bear a cart-load.

4. Hypocrisy. Take it for dissembling, whereby we deceive others; or formality, whereby we deceive ourselves. For dissembling: the pharisees were a dissembling generation, and they are the famous instances of hardness of heart in the first gospel days. Hypocrisy is a

constant lie, and every lie is a sin against light. When men take a religion out of design, their pretences condemn them. Men sin, and are secured against the stroke of the word and checks of conscience by their fame and plausible appearance. Then for formal performing of good duties: Prov. vii. 14, 'I have peace-offerings with me; this day have I paid my vows.' I do this and that, I read so many chapters a day, and keep to my church. Men think they have done enough though they have done never so little. Hardness of heart is often occasioned by the ordinances. Now how do ordinances harden? They may harden partly as they irritate corruption, but chiefly as they are trusted in. Duties soundly done humble men, as new wine rendeth and breaketh old bottles all to pieces. But when formal duties are used as a sleepy sop to stop the mouth of conscience, the heart is insensibly hardened. Every man must have a religion to lean to. Conscience, like the stomach when it hath no solid food, draweth wind.

5. Pride and stubborness against God. Men scorn to be controlled: Exod. v. 2, 'And Pharaoh said, Who is the Lord, that I should obey his voice to let Israel go? I know not the Lord, neither will I let Israel go;' Neh. ix. 29, 'They dealt proudly, and hearkened not unto thy commandments, but sinned against thy judgments, and withdrew the shoulder, and hardened their neck, and would not hear;' Jer. xiii. 15, 'Hear ye, and give ear; be not proud, for the Lord hath spoken.' Men scorn to submit to ordinances, to be checked by God's messengers, and say, What have we to do with them? In this light of christianity the contempt is cast upon the messenger, though indeed the heart riseth against the authority of God himself. One great cure of hardness of heart is seriously to meditate on God's power: Deut. x. 16, 17, 'Circumcise therefore the foreskin of your heart, and be no more stiffnecked; for the Lord your God is God of gods and Lord of lords, a great God, a mighty, and a terrible, which regardeth not persons, nor taketh reward.' Do you know what God is? Will you contend with him? You will fail in the enterprise; you cannot be hard-hearted if you would, in the issue of the combat. Pride is the root of all sin. What is the reason men dare sin? They think they shall carry it out well enough for all God, and so suffer their lusts to perk above the commandment.

6. The deceitfulness of sin: Heb. iii. 15. 'Lest any of you be hardened through the deceitfulness of sin.' Now, how doth sin deceive us, and so harden the heart?

[1.] By general invectives. We all cry out of sin, and complain of sin, and yet all this while regard it in our hearts. We make sin a notion, and so defy it in the general, when in particulars we love it all the while; as many ignorant people defy the devil but hold the crown upon his head, for he is the ruler of the darkness of this world. The devil careth not for ill words so he can keep possession of the heart. We make sin the common packhorse to bear all our burdens. Men content themselves with empty declamations or forms of satire and invective, yet the heart liketh it well enough, and so is insensibly hardened; they are not serious and particular. Men look upon matters of religion as abstracted ideas and matters of fancy. Oh! take heed of this.

[2.] By delaying: Acts xxiv. 25, 'Go thy way for this time; when I have a convenient season I will call for thee.' Christian, it is but a deceit; take heed thy heart be not hardened by it. What reason hast thou to presume of that which God can only give? If Cæsar had read the letters overnight to prevent the conspiracy, he had been safe. What security have you, either of time or grace, but your own presumptions? and he that is security to himself is a fool. It is true all may be redressed by repentance, but this is not in thy power, and thy hardness by delaying increaseth every day.

[3.] It cometh lapped up in carnal baits of profit and pleasure, to gratify our lusts and interests. Sin pretends great advantage; but be not deceived, it will harden thy heart, and destroy thee; it cannot profit thee.

[4.] It hath many colours wherewith to beguile a man. It presents itself in another dress than its own; and therefore we have need to have our eyes about us: Prov. xxviii. 14, 'Happy is the man that feareth always: but he that hardeneth his heart shall fall into mischief.' Many sins lie secret, unrepented of, and so the heart is hardened.

[5.] It will increase upon thee; it groweth to a custom by degrees; it is of a bewitching nature, and soaketh into a man insensibly, from thought to consent, then to action, then to reiteration, then to custom. First men excuse sin, then justify it, then glory in it, and in time they grow senseless and confirmed in a habit of sin, and are loath to quit it. At first temptations seemed horrible; the first committing of sin much perplexed the soul; but in time it is not so burdensome, yea, it is become pleasing and delightful. Be not deceived and hardened by saying, It is a little one, and my soul shall live; unless we take it betimes, as Peter went out immediately and wept bitterly, it cannot easily be subdued. Sampson knew that Delilah had purposed to betray him into the Philistines' hands, and yet he could not leave her. Though sin cost men temporal and eternal life, yet they cannot give it over.

[6.] That God will be merciful; this is another thing whereby we are deceived, a presumption of impunity: Ps. l. 21, 'These things hast thou done, and I kept silence; thou thoughtest that I was altogether such an one as thyself; but I will reprove thee, and set them in order before thine eyes.' So Deut. xxix. 19, 20, 'And it came to pass, when he heareth the words of this curse, that he bless himself in his heart, saying, I shall have peace, though I walk in the imagination of mine heart, to add drunkenness to thirst.' Be not deceived; mark what follows: 'The Lord will not spare him, but then the anger of the Lord and his jealousy shall smoke against that man, and all the curses that are written in this book shall lie upon him, and the Lord shall blot out his name from under heaven.' Take heed of the deceitfulness of sin. These are the causes of hardness of heart.

V. The heinousness of it.

1. It is a contending with God, $\theta\epsilon o\mu a\chi ia$, a fighting with God. The hard heart is the greatest enemy God hath on this side hell. That there is a contest between God and a hard heart who shall have the better, the instance of Pharaoh showeth, God sendeth a message to him, and meeteth with a repulse. His message to Pharaoh was, Exod. v. 1. 'Thus saith the Lord God of Israel, Let my people go.' And

this proud creature hath the boldness to deny him: ver. 2, 'And Pharaoh said, Who is the Lord, that I should obey his voice to let Israel go? I know not the Lord, neither will I let Israel go.' And he standeth it out after many warnings and foregoing judgments. And he doth not stand alone, but hath more fellows in the world: Neh. ix. 29, 'They dealt proudly, and hearkened not to thy commandments, but sinned against thy judgments, and withdrew the shoulder, and hardened their neck, and would not hear.' Every command of God, every offer of grace, is a message from God: 'To you is the word of this salvation sent,' Acts xiii. 26; and it should be respected with as much reverence as if an angel himself were the messenger. Only here is the difference; God saith to Pharaoh, 'Let my people go;' to us he saith, 'Let sin go.' It is pity he should have the repulse. Sin will be as bad an inmate to the soul as the Israelites were a snare to Egypt; they were fain to thrust them out at length, and were glad they could be so rid of them. I say, this is the contest between God and his creatures, whether sin shall go or tarry, whether Christ shall be accepted or no? He sent Moses and Aaron to Pharaoh; and he hath sent prophets, apostles, pastors, and teachers to us. Let idols, images, and false worship go; swearing, sabbath-breaking, adultery, murder, disobedience to parents, lying, covetousness, let it all go; there should not be a hoof left. This is God's message. Now, if you will try it out, you shall see 'whose word shall stand, God's or yours?' Jer. xliv. 28; his threatenings, or your vain and delusive imaginations? If you put it to the trial, you have more boldness than an angel: Jude 9, 'Yet Michael the archangel, when contending with the devil (he disputed about the body of Moses), durst not bring against him a railing accusation.' An angel durst not use one passionate word, and will you dare to set up other gods, to profane the sabbath, to swear, lie, or be drunk, and to say, We will not let these things go, let God say or do what he will to the contrary? The contest on God's part is managed for a long time in a mild condescending way. He beseecheth his own creatures: Jer. xiii. 15, 16, 'Hear ye, and give ear; be not proud, for the Lord hath spoken: give glory to the Lord your God, before he cause darkness, and before your feet stumble upon the dark mountains; and while ye look for light, he turn it into the shadow of death, and make it gross darkness.' Be not obstinate; it is better that you should take down the stoutness of your hearts than that I should pull it down. Let me have the glory of this conquest voluntarily; I shall carry it at length. You dream of happiness and pleasure; alas! you cannot enjoy these vain delights long. Come, leave them, and I will make you as happy as heart can wish, but if not, take that that followeth; you will stumble into the dungeon of hell, and then be as miserable as almightiness can make you: Job ix. 4, 'He is wise in heart, and mighty in strength; whoever hardened himself against God and prospered?' You will never get the day of God; if you contend with him, there is nothing to be expected but blows. You may indeed overcome him, but it is not by resisting, but stooping; a tender heart overcometh him: Jer. xxxi. 20, 'Is Ephraim my dear son? is he a pleasant child? for since I spake against him, I do earnestly remember him still; therefore my bowels are troubled for him, I will surely have mercy upon him, saith the Lord;' and Isa. lvii. 18, 'I have seen his ways, and will heal him; I will lead him also, and restore comforts to him, and to his mourners.' But an hard heart is no match for God; it is ever foiled in the enterprise: if they yield not to his mercy, they are consumed by his wrath. Pharaoh would contend with God, but found his maker too hard for him at last; so Julian the apostate. Ezek. xxii. 14, 'Can thy heart endure, or can thy hands be strong in the days that I shall deal with thee? I the Lord have spoken it, and will do it;' and 1 Cor. x. 22, 'Do we provoke the Lord to jealousy? are we stronger than he?' It is a foolish contest; it ever endeth with our destruction.

2. It is in itself the sorest of all judgments. When other means are urged in vain, God giveth them up to hardness of heart; it is one of the chains of darkness, in which captive souls are held unto eternal judgment. A stormy conscience, that lieth under the power of perplexing despairing fears, is not so bad as an hard heart. They are both chains of darkness, despair, and obstinacy, as in the devils; but in men, despair may make way for repentance. God hath them in the briers; many are brought to heaven by the gates of hell. God hath begun with them, but left these. Again, it will end in despair. The heart that is not sensible now will then be sensible enough. We read of 'the worm that never dieth, and the fire that shall never be quenched,' Mark ix. 44. In hell men will remember how every sabbath God did stretch out the arms of his mercy to embrace them, and they would not; how Christ offered a plaster of his own heart's blood to cure them, but they refused it, and made light of it; how the Holy Ghost put many good motions into their hearts, but they rejected these thoughts, and would not be interrupted in their ease and false peace. Oh! the deep wounds and stings these thoughts will occasion when it is too late!

3. It never goeth alone, but bringeth other judgments along with it. Pharaoh had plague upon plague: Zech. vii. 12, 'They made their hearts as an adamant stone, lest they should hear the law, and the words which the Lord of hosts hath sent in his Spirit, by the former prophets; therefore came a great wrath from the Lord of hosts;' more than ordinary displeasure. So Prov. xxix. 1, 'He that, being often reproved, hardeneth his neck, shall suddenly be destroyed, and that without remedy.' They shall be destroyed, not afflicted only, and that without remedy; there shall be none to help. And Rom. ii. 5, 'After thy hardness and impenitent heart, treasurest up unto thyself wrath against the day of wrath, and revelation of the righteous judgment of God.' God will harden his heart against you, shut up his bowels against you in your greatest straits; when his patience is quite spent, God will retaliate: Zech. vii. 12, 13, 'They made their hearts as an adamant stone, lest they should hear the law, &c. Therefore it is come to pass, that, as he cried and they would not hear, so they cried and I would not hear, saith the Lord of hosts.' There is a time when the stoutest-hearted sinner, who careth least for God, shall stand in need of his help, and would give the whole world for one favourable look from God. But, oh, no! not a glimpse, not the least answer. God's children meet with sad suspensions sometimes: Cant. v. 6, 'I sought him, but I could not find him; I called him, but he gave me no answer.' He seemeth

not to hear their prayers when they are dead to his counsels; he will make them sensible of their unkind, ungracious treating of him.

4. It is the great hindrance in the spiritual life; it depriveth you of grace. The Spirit of God will not animate a stony heart; a body of flesh is only fit to be animated with a living soul; so the heart of flesh, or tender heart, by the Spirit of God: Ezek. xi. 19, 20, 'I will give them one heart, and I will put a new Spirit within you, and I will take the stony heart out of their flesh, and will give them an heart of flesh, that they may walk in my statutes, and keep my ordinances, and do them; and they shall be my people, and I will be their God.' So Isa. lvii. 15, 'Thus saith the high and lofty One that inhabiteth eternity, whose name is Holy; I dwell in the high and holy place, with him also that is of a contrite and humble spirit, to revive the spirit of the humble, and to revive the heart of the contrite ones.' There is God present with his graces. God hath two places of special residence—the highest heaven, and the humblest heart. In the one is the presence of his glory, in the other of his grace. When the spirit is humbled and softened, it is a fit pillow for God to rest on; the hard heart hindereth us in duty, it is an hard heart that maketh our work hard. If once the will were gained, all things would be easy in religion: Rom. viii. 7, 'The carnal mind is enmity against God, for it is not subject to the law of God, neither indeed can be.' It is not subject to God, but averse from him.

VI. The observations concerning this spiritual malady.

1. With spiritual hardness of heart there may be a natural and sinful tenderness. Some men have a natural softness and sweetness of spirit as to commerce with men, yea, rather a faulty easiness, yet they are very hard-hearted as to God; as Zedekiah: Jer. xxxviii. 5, 'The king is not he that can do anything against you.' He was easily drawn by company and evil counsel. Usually it is so; an hard heart is like wax to the devil, but as a stone to God, hardened against goodness, but exorable and easy to be entreated by sin and Satan. If the devil do but whist, they find an irresistible power in his temptations. If carnal men do but hold up the finger, it is a strong cord to draw them to excess. The looks and speeches of the harlot are enough to cause them to follow, though it be like an ox to the slaughter: Prov. vii. 21, 22, 'With much fair speech she caused him to yield; with the flattering of her lips she forced him: he goeth after her straightway as an ox to the slaughter, or as a fool to the correction of the stocks.' God may plead and tell us of grace and glory, but we mind it not. A diamond is not wrought upon but by its own dust. On the contrary, men may have a stout heart in dangers that are very yielding and trembling in point of sins: Prov. xxviii. 14, 'Happy is the man that feareth always; but he that hardeneth his heart shall fall into mischief.' David could encounter lions, bears, and giants, yet in what a weeping humble posture is he when he hath to do with God! It is good to be a coward in sin, puling and weak-hearted as to any contest with God.

2. Small sins harden as well as great sins; it is hard to say which most. It is confessed for the present little sins do not deaden and harden the heart so much as great; as a prick of a pin maketh a man start, but an heavy blow stunneth him, and leaveth him dead for a while. David, when he cut off the lap of Saul's garment, and had some revengeful

intention against his soveriegn, he quickly perceived his error: 'His heart smote him,' 1 Sam. xxiv. 5. But when he committed the foul sin of adultery, he lay insensible for a long space of time. But on the other side, little sins do by degrees harden. Great sins are apparent and liable to the judgment of conscience, but we neglect small sins, and so a custom groweth upon us, and we are insensibly hardened by our carelessness and constant neglect of our souls. A surfeit or violent distemper maketh us run to the physician, but when a disease groweth upon us by degrees, it proveth mortal ere we regard it; therefore we should make conscience of daily failings: Heb. iii. 13, 'Exhort one another daily, while it is called to-day, lest any of you be hardened through the deceitfulness of sin.' Great falls, as they astonish us for the present, so they awaken conscience afterwards, and so we regard that and other sins; as when a great sound hath awakened us out of a deep sleep, we easily hear lesser sounds; but men slide into a carnal frame of heart unawares. *Qui nunquam delirat, semper erit fatuus.* We would never grow wise but for some notable acts of folly. Chrysostom saith that we should be more watchful of small sins than of great. Nature abhorreth these, but the other slide into us. A little leak unespied drowneth the ship as well as a great breach. If we would look more to small things, so many great mischiefs would not ensue.

3. Sins of omission harden as well as sins of commission, yea, sometimes more; a neglect of duties as well as the practice of gross sins; because they use not the means whereby the heart may be kept soft and in a due remembrance of God and their duty to him. An instrument never so well in tune, if it lie by, it soon groweth out of kilter. In every sin of commission there is a sin of omission, but not the contrary. A man may be civilly harmless, inoffensive, and yet have a very hard heart, if he hold no communion with God, and neglect the means whereby the heart may be kept tender. The neglect of good duties is a more general means of destruction than the commission of evil. Men are estranged from God by the neglect of the word and prayer: Ps. xiv. 4, 'They call not upon the Lord;' attend not upon the means of grace with that life and seriousness they ought to do.

4. None are so confident of the goodness of their hearts as those that have an hard heart; for the more any spiritual disease increaseth upon us, the less it is felt. There is hope, whilst there is some complaining of sin, that there is some tenderness left. The hardest heart must needs be the most confident, because they use no recollection and reflection upon themselves: Jer. viii. 6, 'No man repented him of his wickedness, saying, What have I done?' What am I, what have I done? Yea, they slight their danger, take up every vain pretence and allegation to maintain their carnal peace and quiet: Deut. xxix. 19, 'And it come to pass, when he heareth the words of this curse, that he bless himself in his heart, saying, I shall have peace, though I walk in the imagination of my heart, to add drunkenness to thirst: the Lord will not spare him,' &c. Broken-hearted christians are sensible of the holiness of God, and what an hard matter it is to hold communion with him, and observe their own weakness and unworthiness; and therefore they complain of the badness of their hearts, that there is no greater bent towards God, and are always suspicious of their spiritual condition.

5. Hardness of heart is most apt to creep upon us in times of ease and prosperity. Solomon saith, Prov. i. 32, 'The prosperity of fools shall destroy them;' and Rom. ii. 4, 5, 'Despisest thou the riches of his goodness, and forbearance, and long-suffering; not knowing that the goodness of God leadeth thee to repentance? but after thy hardness and impenitent heart, treasurest up unto thyself wrath against the day of wrath.' Usually in the times of God's goodness and patience, men are besotted with the pleasures of the flesh, and then lose their feeling. Nothing bringeth a brawn upon the heart so much as sensuality and an inordinate use of the creatures; it taketh away the heart; and usually in a prosperous condition men grow sensual and careless. Pharaoh himself, when under the rod, could speak as good words as another; but when he was well at ease, then his hardness returned upon him; as metal in the furnace is very yielding and melting, capable of any impression, but out of the furnace it returneth to its wonted firmness and consistency. The greatest plague was upon his heart when he wanted other plagues. Men do well in their wickedness, enjoy themselves with comfort, and then fear nothing. We see in the brute creatures, when they are in good plight, they grow more fierce; so doth man that aboundeth in ease and pleasure; his worldly happiness maketh the heart gross and senseless. We had need to take heed of an hard heart at all times, but especially when we are like to be corrupted with ease and pleasure. A sensual heart will be senseless.

6. Hardness of heart is a grievous sin at all times, but then most sinful when most unseasonable; for time is an aggravating circumstance in all things, so in this. Now when is it unseasonable? In times of judgment and times of gospel grace.

[1.] In times of judgment: 2 Chron. xxviii. 22, 'In the time of his distress did he trespass yet more against the Lord: this is that king Ahaz.' There is a brand set on him. Certainly the times we live in are extraordinary times. We have seen many changes and great effects of God's anger for sin; we have now many spiritual judgments upon us, error and blasphemy, great divisions and breaches among God's people, and scandals of them that profess the gospel. An hard heart now is most unsuitable; it is like a garland of rosebuds in a day of mourning. Clearly upon some the strokes of God's providence have lighted very sore; if they shall add hardness of heart to their other plagues, who will pity them? When all the corrections of an angry God cannot draw any sensible and serious thoughts from them, how sad is this! I tell you, christians, it looketh like hell to continue sinning under suffering, and to be obstinate against God and the counsels of his grace for your salvation; it speaketh much of a spiritual plague added to temporal judgments. If we did persuade you to a party only, it were more excusable; but when we press you to come to Christ, and you still remain obstinate and hard-hearted, this is sad. If the ministry were only used as a state engine to engage you in such a faction and design, you might have something to plead for yourselves. Pardon me for dealing thus freely with you; we are debtors to all, Rom. i. 14. Would you be troubled if the base should rise against the honourable? It were a judgment certainly; but what are you to

God? Poor base worms! will you contend with your maker? You would complain of it as an heavy burden, and strange inversion of all states and conditions, if men of mean and low fortunes should be at the top, and have power and domination over the ancient gentry and nobility of the land. Be it so; but I would have you to consider in the mean time what an horrible presumption it is, and how God may take it, that you stout it out against the fear of God. Alas! there is a greater distance between you and him than between you and your fellow-creatures. For you to contest it with God, to swagger it and outbrave his ordinances, to contend with his Spirit! how may God complain of this, if it be so grievous to you to be outbraved by your fellow-creatures!

[2.] Times of light and great gospel grace. An hard heart in gospel days is the very reproach of ordinances. Many think the ministry and ordinances useless things. Why? Because there is so little success. You make them useless, and then there will not want those that decry them apace: 2 Cor. vi. 1, 2, 'We then, as workers together with him, beseech you also that ye receive not the grace of God in vain; for he saith, I have heard thee in a time accepted, and in the day of salvation have I succoured thee: behold now is the accepted time, behold now is the day of salvation.' An hard heart should be a thing now quite out of fashion. In a time of ignorance, or a time of restraint of preaching, when visions are not open, or under a dead sleepy ministry, God might dispense with what he will not under a clear discovery of his will. But now, when the doctrine of the gospel is so clearly opened, and Christ so freely tendered, now to be estranged from the fear of God is as unsuitable as if we should revert to the fashions of barbarism, or those kind of clothes or dresses which our ancestors wore before they were reduced to this pitch of civility whereunto we are now arrived. You would laugh at garments of an antique fashion, and if the gallants of the age should put on the dress of Adam, or be clothed with skins newly taken from the beasts offered in sacrifice; a blind mind and a sottish obstinate heart is more uncomely in the eye of God. Will you be strangers in Israel, and lose the blessings of the times by refusing the stricter ways of God?

7. Hardness of heart groweth and increaseth on us more and more, if we let it alone: Zech. vii. 11, 12, 'But they refused to hearken, and pulled away the shoulder, and stopped their ears, that they should not hear; yea, they made their hearts as an adamant stone, lest they should hear the law, and the words which the Lord of hosts hath sent in his Spirit by the former prophets.' There are so many degrees mentioned; first they grow slight and careless, and do not care to hear what you say; then they refuse to obey what they have heard; then they grow sermon-proof; they can hear, and have no benefit by it. As long as the word doth any way affect a sinner, there is some hope; but within a while conscience smiteth not, and men have gotten the victory over their fears and scruples; and thus they go on from natural to voluntary, and from voluntary to judicial hardness of heart, and so are a ready prey for the devil.

8. Dilatory excuses are the last refuge of an hard heart. When they can no longer withstand a conviction, they adjourn and put off

the compliance with God's will, and so elude the importunity of the present conviction. Felix his heart boggled: Acts xxiv. 25, and as he reasoned of righteousness, temperance, and judgment to come, Felix trembled, and said, Go thy way for this time; when I have a convenient season I will call for thee.' Mind the present season, when God is affording opportunities of getting grace: Heb. iii. 7, 8, 'To-day, if ye will hear his voice, harden not your hearts;' Ps. cxix. 60, 'I made haste, and delayed not to keep thy commandments.' Zaccheus, Luke xix. 6, 'He made haste, and came down, and received him joyfully.' Peter and Andrew, Mark iv. 20, 'They straightway left their nets and followed him: Paul, Gal. i. 16, 'Immediately I conferred not with flesh and blood.' If God hath given you any will and inclination for the present, it is an advantage. Sin, the longer it continueth, the stronger it groweth. He that doth not go over at the fountain-head will not be able to go over when the stream groweth broader; and the farther he goes downward, the broader still he findeth it. Every day's impenitency bringeth on a new degree of hardness. Would a man that is to drink that which to his knowledge is poisoned put the more into his cup, and then take it off, out of a presumption that at length he shall find an antidote? Alas! thou mayest be poisoned and dead before the antidote comes.

SERMON III.

And Jesus looked round about on them with anger, being grieved for the hardness of their hearts.—MARK iii. 5.

USE 1. Of trial. Is this our state? Take the two properties to judge by—insensibleness and inflexibleness.

First, A hard heart is insensible; insensible of providences, of the word, and of the state of the soul.

1. Insensible of providences.

[1.] Of mercies: either of the author of mercies; they never look up to the God of their mercies: Hosea ii. 8, 'She did not know that I gave her corn, and wine, and oil, and multiplied her silver and gold;' as swine, that feed upon the acorns, but never look up to the tree from whence they fall: Cant. iv. 1, 'Behold thou art fair, my love; behold thou art fair; thou hast doves' eyes.' As doves peck, and look upwards. It is a sign of a tender heart to see God in every mercy. A drowsy and inattentive soul never heedeth it, is wholly swallowed up in present enjoyments, and looketh no further. It is our privilege above the beasts to know the first cause; other creatures live upon God, but they are not capable of knowing God; they glorify God in their kind, but we may know him. Idolatry and sottishness had never crept into the world if men had owned the first cause; or of the end of mercies, which is to draw in our hearts to God: therefore they are called cords of a man: Hosea xi. 4, 'I drew them with cords of a man, with bands of love;' Esther vi. 3, 'What honour and dignity hath been done to Mordecai for this?' 2 Sam. vii. 2, 'Then the king said unto Nathan the prophet, See now I dwell in an house of cedar, but the ark of God dwelleth within curtains.' When the heart is urging to duty upon this score, God hath been good to me, he hath given me food and raiment; what have I done for God? Now the heart is hard when we are not sensible of his daily providence and gracious supplies in this kind: 2 Sam. xii. 7-9, 'Thus saith the Lord God of Israel, I anointed thee king over Israel, and delivered thee out of the hand of Saul; and I gave thee thy master's house, and thy master's wives into thy bosom, and gave thee the house of Israel and of Judah; and if that had been too little, I would moreover have given unto thee such and such things. Wherefore hast thou despised the commandment of the Lord, to do evil in his sight?' David had lost his awe of God, because he had not a thankful sense of the mercies of God.

[2.] Of corrective providences. The body is a tender part with wicked men; when they are straitened for bodily conveniences, they will complain; yet the hard heart is still insensible of judgments. They are insensible of the author or deserving cause; they do not look upward nor inward; and though doctrinally right in these things, yet they do not seriously consider it, and recall it to mind. Opinion is one thing, and consideration is another. Wicked men may take up good opinions, but they do not consider the force and consequence of them.

(1.) They do not see the hand of God in them: Isa. xxvi. 11, 'Lord, when thy hand is lifted up, they will not see.' They look on these things but as a chance: 1 Sam. vi. 9, 'And see, if it goeth up by the way of his own coasts to Bethshemesh, then he hath done us this great evil; but if not, then we shall know that it was not his hand that smote us, it was a chance that happened to us.' If men own God's hand, they should take up the matter with him; but they own it doctrinally, though not practically. A godly man hath explicit thoughts of God. Job doth not say, The Sabeans and the Chaldeans, but, 'The Lord gave, and the Lord hath taken away,' Job i. 21. They do not complain, when they are crossed, of chance, but the Lord is angry; and when they are stricken, they consult with him, and humble themselves before him. Wicked men are sensible of the smart of the rod, but not of the hand that holds it.

(2.) They do not see the deserving cause of them, which is sin: Lam. iii. 39, 40, 'Wherefore doth a living man complain, a man for the punishment of his sins? Let us search and try our ways, and turn again to the Lord.' If sickness cometh, if a relation be taken away, if an estate be blasted, a waking conscience looks to the cause; they would see the mind of God in the rod. When Israel fell before the men of Ai, Joshua looketh out for the troubler; so do God's children.

2. Insensible of the power of the word; they have no taste, no feeling of the powers of the world to come: Jer. xxiii. 29, 'Is not my word like a fire, saith the Lord, and like a hammer that breaketh the rock in pieces?' There is a breaking and a melting power in the word.

[1.] What law-work hath been wrought on you? what shakings of heart, and feeling of the powers of the world to come? Have you been roused and startled out of your natural condition? Many will assent to this truth, that all are miserable by nature; but wast thou ever sensible that this was thy case, and accordingly affected? Wert thou ever feelingly convinced of thy misery? Otherwise we do but learn these things as a parrot learneth them, by rote. What feeling have you of your cursed estate by nature? Have you had any experience of the terrors of the Lord? You know the misery of man by nature, but have you ever felt it?

[2.] What gospel-work hath been wrought on you? what taste have you had of the good word of God? what experience of the efficacy of the Spirit? 1 Peter ii. 3, 'If so be ye have tasted that the Lord is gracious.'

3. Insensible of the state of the soul; they never look after it. If the body feel but the scratch of a pin, or want but a night's sleep, we complain presently; but the poor soul, though oppressed with lusts and unfit for duties, is never minded nor regarded, and they have no heart to pray for a release out of that spiritual judgment. To own the plague of our own hearts argueth tenderness: 1 Kings viii. 38, 'Which shall know every man the plague of his own heart.' When we complain of lusts more than fevers, and indisposition of soul more than weakness of body, the languishing of grace more than outward consumption, the stone in the heart more than the stone in the bladder and kidneys. We find Ephraim bemoaning himself, being ill at ease for an untoward heart: Jer. xxxi. 18, 'I have surely heard Ephraim bemoaning himself thus: Thou hast chastised me, and I was chastised, as a bullock unaccustomed to the yoke.' Did you ever complain of the hardness of your heart, and lay it before God? Do you not bemoan your spiritual distempers when lazy and backward? Where is your relish for the word? your delight in spiritual things? Isa. lxiii. 17, 'O Lord, why hast thou made us to err from thy ways, and hardened our heart from thy fear?'

Secondly, A hard heart is inflexible. That will be known where it is more gross.

1. By a refusal of the word, when men will not give God the hearing: Zech. vii. 11, 12, 'But they refused to hearken, and pulled away the shoulder, and stopped their ears, that they should not hear; yea, they made their hearts as an adamant stone, lest they should hear the law, and the words which the Lord of hosts hath sent in his Spirit by the former prophets.' They refused to hear, either to vouchsafe their presence or attention: Acts xiii. 46, 'Ye put it from you, and judge yourselves unworthy of eternal life.' The case is clear in these, whereas to others it is doubtful; what needeth more dispute in the matter?

2. By an unteachableness, so as not to apprehend ought that is spiritual. To be ignorant is one thing, to be unteachable is another: Ezek. xii. 2, 'Son of man, thou dwellest in the midst of a rebellious house, which have eyes to see, and see not; they have ears to hear, and hear not: for they are a rebellious house;' Acts xxviii. 26, 'Go unto this people, and say, Hearing ye shall hear, and shall not understand; and seeing ye shall see, and shall not perceive.' They do not see what they do see; they have no spiritual discerning, though a grammatical knowledge: Job v. 14, 'They meet with darkness in the daytime, and grope

in the noonday as in the night.' They are simple in the midst of rational advantages; as the disciples: Luke xxiv. 16, 'Their eyes were holden, that they should not know him. They see the general truth, but make no application. When a man is shown a thing, and he minds it not, but his mind is on another object, that man may be said to see and not to see, because he doth not regard it. Or a man that hath a matter come before him, he heareth it, but his mind being otherwise employed, he regardeth it not; in which sense he may be said to hear and not to hear. Not to apply is not to regard; in seeing rationally and literally, he doth not see spiritually, with any life and power. There is a literal knowledge, and there is a spiritual knowledge; the literal knowledge is that which the hard heart may have. It is said, 2 Cor. iii. 3, 'Ye are manifestly declared to be the epistle of Christ, ministered by us; written not with ink, but with the Spirit of the living God; not in tables of stone, but in the fleshly tables of the heart.' It is an allusion to the law of Moses. Consider it in the letter, as separated from the Spirit, and only as a law written in stone, wherein there is a naked direction of life, but no power; so a stony heart may see, but in seeing they see not. But the Spirit of Christ writeth it on the mind and heart, and maketh the heart docile and tractable: Rom. vii. 6, 'That we should serve in newness of spirit, and not in the oldness of the letter.' The letter of the law only manifested duty, but gave no power to perform it; it discovered corruption, but gave no strength to subdue it; it was written in tables of stone, to show the hardness of man's heart. But now the law, when it cometh in upon us with a spiritual light, softeneth and strengtheneth the heart, and maketh it docile and pliable to God's counsel.

3. By an unwillingness to be admonished in public or private; if in public, the greater the evil. Private admonition is a kind of charge, a closer application. To storm against private admonition argueth an ill spirit, when men are loath to be disturbed in the ways of sin. But much more against public admonition, where the application ariseth not so much from a personal charge as from their own consciences. When men cannot endure sound doctrine, it is a dangerous crisis, that which the prophet Jeremiah speaketh of, chap. vi. 10, 'To whom shall I speak and give warning, that they may hear? Behold, their ear is uncircumcised, and they cannot hearken; behold, the word of the Lord is unto them a reproach, they have no delight in it.' Surely men delight in Satan's arms when they are loath to be plucked from thence. Satan hath made his nest there, and is loath to be disturbed: 2 Sam. xxiii. 6, 7, 'But the sons of Belial shall be all of them as thorns thrust away, because they cannot be taken with hands; but the man that shall touch them must be fenced with iron and the staff of a spear.' The sons of Belial are compared to thorns that cannot be touched with hands, but rend and tear those that meddle with them. Men are angry that they cannot quietly enjoy their lusts. Plausible strains are very suitable to a carnal heart, or tame lectures of contemplative divinity; but sound doctrine, that rendeth and teareth the conscience, is not endured.

4. By scoffing at the word. The chair of the scorner is a preferment in sin: Ps. i. 1, 'Blessed is the man that walketh not in the counsel of the ungodly, nor standeth in the way of sinners, nor sitteth

in the seat of the scornful;' Jer. xxiii. 34–36, 'And as for the prophet, and the priest, and the people that shall say, The burden of the Lord, I will even punish that man and his house. Thus shall ye say every one to his neighbour, and every one to his brother, What hath the Lord answered? and what hath the Lord spoken? And the burden of the Lord shall ye mention no more; for every man's word shall be his burden; for ye have perverted the words of the living God, of the Lord of hosts our God,' &c. The prophets used to begin their prophecies with 'The burden of the Lord;' and they would in mockery demand, What burden they had from the Lord for them? Now shall we hear again of the burden of the Lord. Saith God, 'Every man's word shall be his burden;' that is, you shall dearly pay for this scoffing language; your words shall be your burden. But these marks may not be close enough, let me propound other things.

[1.] Did you ever lay down the buckler before God, and say, I have done foolishly; I will do so no more? Were you ever feelingly convinced, and your lusts powerfully subdued? Did you ever say, as Paul, Acts ix. 6, 'Lord, what wilt thou have me to do?' Every man carrieth on his opposition against God till he be brought to yield by a mighty Spirit breaking in upon him. When were the wings broken that you could fly no longer? the will subdued, that you said, Lord I have too long stouted it out against thee, so that you were willing to be at peace with God? Isa. xxvii. 5, 'Let him take hold of my strength that he may make peace with me, and he shall make peace with me.' Were you ever forced to cry quarter? Didst thou ever apprehend God ready to smite and give fire upon thee, and then in a submissive posture did entreat him to stay his hand?

[2.] What effect hath the word upon you? Isa. lxvi. 2, 'To this man will I look, even to him that is poor and of a contrite spirit, and trembleth at my word.' It is a great part of sensibleness to tremble at the word. What meltings and yieldings of heart do you express? Doth it put you upon recourse to God? 2 Chron. xxxiv. 27, 'Because thine heart was tender, and thou didst humble thyself before God when thou heardest his words against this place, and against the inhabitants thereof, and humbledst thyself before me, and didst rend thy clothes and weep before me, I have even heard thee, saith the Lord.' Didst thou ever humble thyself before the Lord, to clear up matters between God and thy soul, and to get thy doubts resolved, and thy lusts mortified?

[3.] What pliableness has there been in thee to the Holy Ghost's motions? A man that hath a tender heart yieldeth to the motions of the Holy Spirit: Ps. xxvii. 8, 'When thou saidst, Seek ye my face; my heart said unto thee, Thy face, Lord, will I seek.' There is a quick echo to God's voice: Isa. vi. 8, 'I heard the voice of the Lord saying, Whom shall I send? and who will go for us? Then said I, Here I am; send me.' There is not only a readiness to obey, but he offers himself to the work. When we grow lazy and backward in holy things, and hang off, it is a high degree of hardness of heart.

Use 2. Exhortation.

1. To press us to beware of hardness of heart; it is a grievous sin, I shall use three arguments—

[1.] It depriveth you of grace. (See before, p. 205.)

[2.] It unfitteth you for duty while we are under the power of it. An hard heart is forced and superstitious. With what coldness and formality did David pray during the suspension of God's grace! We come into God's presence with great backwardness and reluctancy while we are under the power of a hard heart.

[3.] It fitteth for judgment. The heart groweth harder and harder, and the mind blinder and blinder, till it be cast into an utter indisposition and impossibility of repentance. Hardness of heart turns a man into a beast, nay, into a devil; and according to our sin so is God's wrath: Rom. iii. 5, 'After thy hardness and impenitent heart, thou treasurest up unto thyself wrath against the day of wrath, and revelation of the righteous judgment of God.'

2. To press us to come out of this evil frame of spirit. Arguments—

[1.] As long as the heart is hard you are very remote from the comforts of the gospel. Christ came 'to heal the broken-hearted,' Luke. iv. 18. So Mat. ix. 12, 13, 'They that be whole need not the physician, but they that are sick: I came not to call the righteous, but sinners to repentance.' You are full of sin, but not sick; as a toad is full of poison, but the toad is not sick, because it is natural to him. Will a physician go about to cure a toad? Men lie under a great weight of sin, yet they sleep, and eat, and drink, and trade, and look as well as ever, feel no pain, nor anything to trouble them. These men have no need and will to be cured, and, of all men, are most properly said to be dead in trespasses and sins; they neither break an hour's sleep, nor abate one drachm of their carnal delights, but are heart-whole. The physician hath no desire to meddle with them that will not take what he prescribeth, as carnal men will not submit themselves to God's directions.

[2.] You are very remote from the work of the gospel. As God maketh a way for his anger, so he maketh a way for his mercy and grace. The heart is fitted and prepared for the Spirit's residence. It is softened before it is quickened: Ezek. xxxvi. 26, 27, 'I will take away the stony heart out of your flesh, and I will give you an heart of flesh; and I will put my Spirit within you, and cause you to walk in my statutes, and ye shall keep my judgments and do them.' The vital spirit is not infused till the body be organised and formed. God made Adam out of the dust of the ground, and then breathed into him the breath of life. The Spirit of grace coming into the tender heart maketh way for itself.

Now for the cure of it, I will recommend unto you two means, two graces, and two ordinances.

First, Two means, light and love.

1. Light: Jer. xxxi. 19, 'Surely after that I turned I repented; and after that I was instructed I smote upon my thigh; I was ashamed, yea, even confounded, because I did bear the reproach of my youth.' Men that know not the nature and danger of sin are little troubled about it. Where there is no knowledge there is little conscience. When the troops of Syria were smitten with blindness, they were easily led into the midst of their enemies, 2 Kings vi. 18, 19; and when they thought themselves at Dothan they were in Samaria. Ignorance,

because it is not always accompanied with gross acts, is little thought of; but it is a bloody sin. If men did know God and themselves more, they could not be satisfied with their condition. Ignorance is the greatest cause of hardening.

2. Love. I do not consider it as a grace, but as an argument to melt the soul. It is a forcible argument and a kindly argument.

[1.] It is a forcible argument. Saul relented when David had an advantage against him, and spared him in the cave: 1 Sam. xxiv. 16, 17, 'Saul lift up his voice and wept; and he said to David, Thou art more righteous than I; for thou hast rewarded me good, whereas I have rewarded thee evil.' To make the heart relent, it is good to study God's kindness, not only how he hath spared us, but how he hath blessed us.

(1.) For temporal mercies, creation and providence. For the mercies of creation: We all condemn the rebellion of Absalom for rising against his father. God made us out of nothing; none so much a father as God, and yet we rebel against him. If we had lost a limb, an eye, a tooth, or an arm, would we injure him that could restore us these things? God gave them to us at first; how should the thoughts of this soften our hearts! Then for the mercies of providence: Nathan mentions God's mercies to David to humble him: 2 Sam. xii. 7–9, 'I anointed thee king over Israel, and I delivered thee out of the hand of Saul; and I gave thee thy master's house, and thy master's wives into thy bosom, and gave thee the house of Israel and of Judah; and if that had been too little, I would moreover have given unto thee such and such things. Wherefore hast thou despised the commandment of the Lord, to do evil in his sight?' It is God that feedeth and maintaineth you, and preserveth you. Men stand upon their honour in the world, to be true to their interest, not to be unthankful to their preservers. Now God giveth us life and breath and all things. You value these things when they are given you by men, much more should you when they are given you by God. Is water the worse because it cometh from the fountain and not from the cistern? Water is purer in the fountain. We have more reason to value mercies when they come from God, that so great a majesty should look after you: Ps. cxiii. 6, 'Who humbleth himself to behold the things that are in heaven and in the earth;' that God that standeth not in need of you, as man doth of the meanest; that God whom you have offended, whose favour you are so much concerned about. In a small gift from a king, the favour is valued: we are continually fed and maintained at the expense and care of his providence.

(2.) For spiritual mercies; they melt the heart. What great love Christ showed in the business of our salvation, what he left, what he suffered, what he purchased!

(1*st.*) What he left. That love that is accompanied with self-denial is accounted the highest. How many degrees did the sun of righteousness go back! ἐκένωσιν ἑαυτὸν; Phil. ii. 8, 'He humbled, or emptied himself.' There was a veil upon his godhead: when 'he was rich, for our sakes he became poor,' 2 Cor. viii. 9. In the fulness of the Godhead he abstained from the use of it. Did Christ leave heaven, and wilt not thou leave thy lusts? Was he made the Son of man, and wilt not thou be made the son of God? It was his abasement, but it is our advancement.

(2*d*.) What he suffered. We are more affected with what men suffer for us than with what they do for us. *Cubitum sine manu.* To show the stump of the arm where the hand was lost was an effectual plea: Zech. xii. 10, 'They shall look upon me whom they have pierced; and they shall mourn for him, as one mourneth for his only son, and be in bitterness for him, as one that is in bitterness for his first-born.' Sin doth most affect the heart when we consider the wrong done to Christ by it. *Amor doloris causa*—The more a man loveth another, or apprehends that he is loved of him, the more he is grieved that he hath any way injured him. Your sins strike at Christ, and have pierced him; shall not your hearts be pierced when his head was pierced with thorns, his hands and feet with nails, his heart with sorrows? Can you look upon Golgotha with dry eyes and a careless stupid heart? Think that you heard Christ say, Behold, is any sorrow like to my sorrow? Will you still go on in your rebellion against me? Is all nothing, all that I have done and suffered for you?

(3*d*.) What hath he purchased for us? He gave himself a ransom and price, a ransom to free us from death and hell. We would love a man that should get a pardon for our lives when we are condemned to die: 1 Thes. i. 10, 'Even Jesus, who delivered us from the wrath to come.' There was never any such wrath past or present; it is a thing to come, when we shall stir up all his wrath. And a price to purchase for us the favour of God, and our eternal abode with him in heaven. Heaven is called 'the purchased possession,' Eph. i. 14. If we were to be annihilated, or to spend our time in some obscure place, it were mercy; but to be for ever with the Lord, and to be filled up with God, who can express the greatness of this mercy? And all this is freely offered to you in the gospel. Things that concern us affect us; and therefore surely this should melt the heart: Rom. xii. 1, 'I beseech you therefore, brethren by the mercies of God.' What! shall not mercy prevail? Joel ii. 13, 'And rend your heart, and not your garments, and turn unto the Lord your God; for he is gracious and merciful, slow to anger, and of great kindness, and repenteth him of the evil.' Surely God's graciousness and readiness to receive returning sinners should work upon us. An hammer will easily break an hard stone against a soft bed; but if it be laid on an hard solid body, that will not give way underneath, strike as hard as you will, it is kept from breaking; so smite thy soul on the gospel, hell and damnation may be the hammer; but then lay thy soul upon the gospel and gospel considerations, then it breaketh all to shatters. Strike thy soul with the blows of God's wrath against the law, and it resists still; all doth but make us desperate; but now remember the mercies of the Lord, how freely he inviteth returning sinners, and this breaks the heart to pieces.

[2.] It is a kindly argument; the heart is not till then kindly humbled for sin as sin. An apprehension of wrath is one thing, godly sorrow is another thing; the former is necessary, but not enough: 2 Kings xxii. 19, 'Because thine heart was tender, and thou hast humbled thyself before the Lord, when thou heardest what I spake against this place, and against the inhabitants thereof, that they should become a desolation and a curse, and hast rent thy clothes, and wept before me, I also have heard thee, saith the Lord.' Threatenings may terrify, but this melts the heart, and begets a serious remorse for sin, as offensive, displeasing, and grievous unto God: 2 Cor. vii. 10, 'For godly sorrow worketh repentance to salvation, not to be repented of; but the sorrow of the world worketh death;' Ezek. vi. 9, 'And they that escape of you shall remember me among the nations whither they shall be carried captives; because I am broken with their whorish heart, which hath departed from me, and with their eyes, which go a whoring after their idols; and they shall loath themselves for the evils which they have committed in all their abominations.' Not only for the evils which they have suffered, but which they have committed; for the evil that is in sin, not for the evil that is after sin: 2 Chron. xxxii. 26, Hezekiah, 'humbled himself for the pride of his heart.' Not only for the inconvenience and mischief done thereby, but because God was offended. That christian Niobe wept much 'because she loved much,' Luke vii. 47.

Secondly, There are two graces—faith and fear.

1. Faith. As reason maketh a difference between a man and a beast, so doth faith between a man and a man. It is faith bringeth us under the power of a truth, and maketh light active. Three times Christ reproached his disciples for hardness of heart, and still the cause given is unbelief: Mark vi. 52, 'They considered not the miracle of the loaves for their hearts were hardened;' Mark viii. 17, 'Why reason ye because ye have no bread? Perceive ye not yet, neither understand? have ye your heart yet hardened?' Mark xvi. 14, 'Afterwards he appeared unto the eleven as they sat at meat, and upbraided them because of their unbelief and hardness of heart, because they believed not them which had seen him after he was risen.' A man is dull, stupid, and senseless till faith maketh light break in upon the heart with power; till then he will not make use of his eyes, ears, or memory. All affections follow persuasion. Faith persuadeth of death, and hell, and judgment to come. We would not trifle away the day of grace if we did believe the goodness of God offering favour and life eternal in Christ. *Hæc audiunt quasi somniantes*—Men entertain these things as a dream, and are only a little troubled for the present, till they thoroughly believe them.

2. Fear. It is always made a preservative against hardness of heart: Isa. lxiii. 17, 'O Lord, why hast thou made us to err from thy ways, and hardened our heart from thy fear?' Fear argueth a constant sense of God's presence, and a deep respect to him, so as that we are loath to offend him; it makes the soul to walk as in God's company, and therefore it is kept humble: Prov. xxviii. 14, 'Happy is the man that feareth alway; but he that hardeneth his heart shall fall into mischief.' It will make us tender of offending God, and yielding to our own corruptions, though never so secret. Who is the man that is opposed to him that hardeneth his heart? 'He that feareth alway.' Carelessness breedeth senselessness; but now, when we are continually watchful, and say, Shall I thus and thus offend God? the heart is kept in a good frame.

Thirdly, There are two ordinances—the word and prayer; for water, if never so scalding, will return to its natural coldness.

1. The word: 2 Chron. xxxiv. 19, 'It came to pass, when the king had heard the words of the law, that he rent his clothes;' and ver. 27, 'Because thine heart was tender, and thou didst humble thyself before God, when thou heardest his words against this place, and against the inhabitants thereof, and didst rend thy clothes, and weep before me, I have even heard thee also, saith the Lord;' Heb. iii. 7, 8, 'To-day, if ye will hear his voice, harden not your hearts.' A conscionable hearing the word will prevent hardness of heart: Jer. xxiii. 29, 'Is not my word like a fire, saith the Lord, and like a hammer that breaketh the rock in pieces?' There is the double work of the word—legal and evangelical; the breaking and the melting power of it. There is a great deal of difference between breaking the ice with a staff, and thawing or melting it: break it in one place, and it freezeth in another; melting is more universal. There are legal breakings and gospel meltings; there sin is discovered, here it is subdued. But then you must use the word as an ordinance, receive it in faith and obedience; use it in obedience, when you are discouraged in point of faith: Luke v. 5, 'Master, we have toiled all the night, and have taken nothing; nevertheless at thy word I will let down the net.' But use it not only in obedience, but in faith; you must hear the word, not only as a moral lecture or legal discourse, or as a means of literal instruction, but evangelically, waiting for the power and presence of God.

2. Prayer. God will be specially owned in this work. No creature in the world can soften and turn the heart, but only God. He that made the heart can only change it: Ezek. xi. 19, 'And I will give them one heart, and I will put a new spirit within you; and I will take the stony heart out of their flesh, and will give them an heart of flesh.' It is God only that gives a teachable mind, a pliable will, and ready affections. Go, then, and practise this duty; beg of God to give you a heart more pliable to the work of grace, more capable to be renewed, more soft and ready to receive the impressions of grace, and be earnest with him for this.

I shall now give you some further advice.

1. In the first place, begin with conversion to God; look for a change of state. Repentance in particular cases is neither right nor acceptable, as long as men do not mind conversion to God, and a change of state by regeneration. When the tree is good, then the fruits are answerable. Get the heart of stone taken away, and then labour to preserve a tender frame. It is a fruitless course to look after a good frame, till we are brought into a good estate. Natural hardness is the cause of habitual hardness; till that be taken away by regeneration all cometh to nothing.

2. Be tender how you use your light. Men wax bold by sinning against light, and seem to get a victory over their consciences. When the candle is put out, lust will be stirring. Light and reason is God's bridle on man to keep him in awe. Well, then, use your light tenderly. If it be but an half light, search further; if it be a full light, walk by it. If you are children of the light, you will have no fellowship with the unfruitful works of darkness.

3. After you have sinned, take up betimes; as Peter went out, and wept bitterly; for sin will fret, and soak in more and more.

4. Use frequent recollection and communing with your hearts. Man hath reason, and can talk with himself. God, that cannot err, surveyed every day's work, and found it good. Cast up your account at the foot of every page. He that runneth in debt, and never casteth up his accounts, will sink at last. A man is insensibly hardened for want of searching and ransacking his conscience; there is no serious repentance without it: Lam. iii. 40, 'Let us search and try our ways, and turn again to the Lord.' God will search you if you leave the work to him.

5. Improve afflictions. It is a means God hath appointed to shake us out of our security. We are apt to be lulled asleep with the delights and pleasures of sin till we feel the sharp rod of afflictions: 2 Chron. xxviii. 22, 'And in the time of his distress did he trespass yet more against the Lord: this is that King Ahaz.' They are monsters of nature and hopeless wretches that are not reclaimed by afflictions. God sets a brand on Ahaz, like a dogged servant that will not stir, beat him never so much. Unprofitableness under the rod is an ill presage. In hell sinners are always suffering and always sinning.

6. Beware of those things which are both steps unto, and causes of, hardness of heart; for one degree is the cause of another; as when sin is committed without remorse, and swallowed without grief.

7. Beware of extenuating sin, of having less thoughts of it, and being less troubled about it. At first it seemed a horrible thing, a burden too heavy for us; but afterwards it grows less light, and the heart more insensible, and sin more delightful. The burden of sin increaseth in the children of God as light and acquaintance with God increaseth. That which they made nothing of at first groweth very heavy.

8. Keep grace in a constant exercise. Let the fire be kept always in that came down from heaven, 2 Tim. i. 6, 'Wherefore I put thee in remembrance, that thou stir up the gift of God that is in thee.'

9. Frequent the society of God's people. Want of care of our company is a great fault; for company hardeneth in sin or humbleth. The very example of God's people will be a great help to you; how tender they are, how watchful, what meltings of heart they have in prayer, how they make conscience of the least sin, how they complain of themselves, Oh! what a hard heart have I! Coals lying together keep fire. This is a means to keep us tender: Heb. iii. 13, 'But exhort one another daily while it is called to-day, lest any of you be hardened through the deceitfulness of sin.'

SERMONS UPON EXODUS IV. 21.

SERMON I.

I will harden his heart, that he shall not let my people go.—
Exod. iv. 21.

I HAVE spoken of hardness of heart as it is proper to man. I shall now speak of that judicial hardness which is inflicted by God; a notable instance whereof we have in Pharaoh, that was raised up that God might in him make his power known; that is, he was born into the world, and advanced to royal dignity, that the world may know what God can do against an obstinate contradicting creature. And accordingly it is applied by the apostle: Rom. ix. 17, 'For the scripture saith unto Pharoah, Even for this same purpose have I raised thee up, that I might show my power in thee, and that my name might be declared throughout all the earth.' Therefore it is an instance worth the viewing.

In this place God acquainteth Moses of it aforehand, to fortify him against all discouragements. He was to deal with an obstinate creature, but it was that which God had foreseen and foredecreed: 'I will harden his heart, that he shall not let my people go.'

The point or head of doctrine is, God's hardening of sinners. You may take it in the form of a proposition, for the help of the weakest.

Doct. God himself hath a hand in the hardening of obstinate sinners.

About fourteen times is the hardness of Pharaoh's heart spoken of; and thrice it is said, 'He hardened his own heart:' Exod. viii. 15, 'When Pharaoh saw that there was respite, he hardened his heart, and hearkened not unto them, as the Lord had said.' So ver. 32, 'And Pharaoh hardened his heart at that time also, neither would he let the people go;' and again, chap. ix. 34, 'And when Pharaoh saw that the rain, and the hail, and the thunders were ceased, he sinned yet more, and hardened his heart, he and all his servants.' In all the other places it is ascribed to God himself. Man hardeneth, and then God hardeneth. When God blindeth a man, he first closeth his own eyes; and when God hardeneth a man, he first contracteth a brawn and stiffness upon his own heart. Pharaoh in hardening himself is charged with two things— slighting of the judgment: chap. vii. 23, 'And Pharaoh turned and went into his house, neither did he set his heart to this also.' And contempt of the threatening: chap. viii. 15, 'He hardened his heart, and hearkened not unto them, as the Lord had said.' And the very same thing also is said to be of God: chap. vii. 13, 'He hardened Pharaoh's heart, that he hearkened not unto them, as the Lord had said.'

For the clearing of this, I shall—(1.) Give you some observations from the story; (2.) Show you how God hardeneth; (3.) The causes of it.

I. I shall give you some general observations from the story; for in the story of Pharaoh we have the exact platform of an hard heart.

1. Between the hard heart and God there is an actual contest who shall have the better. The parties contesting are God and Pharaoh. (See the first Sermon on Mark iii. 5.)

2. The sin that hardened Pharaoh, and put him upon this contest, was covetousness and interest of state. Jacob's seventy souls that he brought down to Egypt were grown to six hundred thousand fighting men, besides children; and to let such a company of men go, whom they used as slaves, besides the prey of their herds and flocks, seemed hard to Pharaoh. Which is not only an item to magistrates, to retain nothing which God hateth out of interest and reason of state, but also to private christians. Whatever of gain and advantage we may fancy in sin, it will at length prove a certain loss. If God send a message for our right eye, we must pluck it out; or for our right hand, we must cut it of. It is dangerous to deny God anything. If he demand Israel, and all the flocks and herds, let them go; the sweetest interests, the dearest pleasures, the most gainful employments, if they are unlawful, let them go. There is an usual contest between interest and duty, between pleasure and obedience, between profit and the command; but it is better our own faith should give the command, the victory, than God's power: 1 John v. 4, 'This is the victory that overcomes the world, even our faith.' He had before spoken of keeping the commandments, ver. 3, and presently he speaketh of 'victory over the world.' The world is the great enemy of the commandments; and till it be overcome, a christian can have no comfort, but still be contesting with God, as Pharaoh was, and slighting every message.

3. This contest on Pharaoh's part is managed with slightings and contempt of God; on God's part, with mercy and condescension. On Pharaoh's part with slightings and contempt of God: Exod. v. 2, 'And Pharaoh said, Who is the Lord, that I should obey his voice to let Israel do? I know not the Lord, neither will I let Israel go.' Words of profane contempt. 'Who is the Lord?' as if he should say, Am not I king of Egypt? who is my peer, much less my superior and my lord? 'I know not the Lord.' Ere God hath done with Pharaoh he shall know him to the purpose. Mark the words, 'I know not;' and then, 'I will not.' Hardness is the usual effect of blindness. Errors of mind go on to errors of heart. I will not know, I will not hear of it; I care not for such a duty, nor will I weigh or consider what is God's will concerning me. The eye affecteth the heart. Pharaoh did not consider what it was to deal with God, and then doubleth the burdens of the Israelites. But now, on God's part

it is managed with sweetness and kindness. God from the beginning foreknew the hardness of Pharaoh's heart, and therefore might have swept him away of a sudden, but he giveth him frequent warnings and convictions. He would have men convinced ere they are punished. Foregoing mercy showeth the righteousness of ensuing wrath. In all the progress of the story the first miracles were before him, the next upon him. And every judgment is threatened before it be executed; God telleth what he would do to warn Pharaoh. In one plague it is notable that God doth not only threaten the judgment, but sendeth a gracious warning to bid him take his cattle out of the fields: Exod. ix. 19, 'Send therefore now, and gather thy cattle, and all that thou hast in the field; for upon every man and beast which shall be found in the field, and shall not be brought home, the hail shall come down upon them, and they shall die.' To show that God delighteth not in the ruin and destruction of the creature, and to make Pharaoh the more liable to condemnation, and to spare such among the Egyptians as had some fear of God remaining in them, but chiefly to harden Pharaoh the more: Exod. x. 1, 'And the Lord said unto Moses, Go in unto Pharaoh, for I have hardened his heart, and the heart of his servants, that I might show these my signs before him.' Moses might say, Lord, therefore let me never go to Pharaoh; but saith God, 'Go in unto him, for I have hardened his heart.' God continueth the means, though he denieth grace; and the wicked must be admonished, though they will not be reformed. In the hardening of sinners, God usually observeth this course: by mercies and the means of grace they are convinced and hardened at the same time; there is still new matter of glorifying God, and hardening the creature.

4. The first plague on Pharaoh's heart is delusion. Moses worketh miracles, turneth Aaron's rod into a serpent, rivers into blood, bringeth frogs, and the magicians still do the same; God permitteth these magical impostures, to leave Pharaoh in his wilful error. It is probable that what the magicians did was not real, but a mere delusion of the senses; but the Lord doth not discover the cheat, because his present aim was not to shame Satan, but to harden Pharaoh; therefore he suffered the devil to imitate the true miracles without discovery. It is sad when men choose false teachers to themselves, and God suffereth them to be blinded: Hosea iv. 17, 'Ephraim is joined to idols; let him alone.' They may have some parts, plausible elocution, gifts of prayer; there may be common effects wrought by them; these things blind men, and their hearts are set upon familism and antinomianism; let them alone: Exod. vii. 22, 'The magicians of Egypt did so with their enchantments, and Pharaoh's heart was hardened.' This was one means of hardening his heart, the magicians wrought the same miracles that Moses and Aaron did. God suffereth men to be hardened by their own choice.

5. God was not wanting to give Pharaoh sufficient means of conviction. The magicians turned their rods into serpents, but 'Aaron's rod swallowed up their rods,' Exod. vii. 12; which showeth God's supereminent power. They could not deliver him from the frogs, though they could bring frogs. God may suffer the devil to add to the judgment, but to relieve them is an act of mercy: the magicians could add

to the plagues, but they could not deliver him from them; the devil can sooner bring a plague than remove it. This was warning enough; there was difficulty enough to harden them, and light enough to convince them. Again, the magicians were nonplussed in their art: Exod. viii. 18, 'And the magicians did so with their enchantments to bring forth lice, but they could not.' They sought to bring forth lice, and could not, being hindered by God's will. They that could bring forth frogs could not bring forth lice; the greater the possibility, the more are the magicians abashed; this was an easy miracle. All colour of excuse is taken away from Pharaoh; they confess, 'This is the finger of God,' Exod. viii. 19; and yet Pharaoh's heart was hardened; as many will not be won to the truth by the confession of those that led them into the mistake. Nay, afterwards the magicians themselves were smitten with boils: Exod. ix. 11, 12, 'And the magicians could not stand before Moses because of the boils; for the boil was upon the magicians, and upon all the Egyptians. And the Lord hardened the heart of Pharaoh, and he hearkened not unto them.' If the hard heart go to hell, it is not for want of light, but grace. We may wonder as much at the success as at the plagues. To what a height of obstinacy will man come if he be let alone to plagues! for all this while Pharaoh's heart was hardened.

6. Observe, in one of the plagues Israel might have stolen away, whether Pharaoh would or no: Exod. x. 22, 23, 'And Moses stretched forth his hand towards heaven, and there was a thick darkness in all the land of Egypt three days; they saw not one another, neither rose any from his place for three days; but all the children of Israel had light in their dwellings.' They were not only deprived of the light of heaven, but of candles and torches; the air was condensed with thick clouds, and the mists and vapours so thick, that they would easily have damped them, and put them out again. Now whilst they were under the power of three days' darkness, the Israelites might have stolen away, and have gone three days' journey in the wilderness before they could have made any pursuit; but God had more miracles to be done. When he hath to do with a hard heart, he will not steal out of the field, but go away with honour and triumph. This was to be a public instance, and for intimation to the world: 1 Sam. vi. 6, 'Wherefore then do ye harden your hearts, as the Egyptians and Pharaoh hardened their hearts? when he had wrought wonderfully among them, did they not let the people go, and they departed?' The Philistines took warning by it, and it will be our condemnation if we do not.

7. In all these plagues I observe that Pharaoh now and then had his devout pangs. In an hard heart there may be some relentings, but no true repentance. We have him confessing, Exod. ix. 27, 'I have sinned this time: the Lord is righteous; and I and my people are wicked;' and chap. x. 16, 17, 'I have sinned against the Lord your God, and against you: now therefore forgive, I pray thee, my sin only this once, and entreat the Lord your God, that he may take away from me this death only.' So chap. xii. 32, 'Be gone, and bless me also.' Hardened sinners may have their gripes and sensible touches, and so some faint purposes of reformation. But that which was defective, and showeth it was not true repentance, was—

[1.] Because it was only extorted by present horror: Job xxvii. 10, 'Will he always call upon God?' A still will send forth water as well a fountain, but it is by drops, and by force: Prov. v. 11–13, 'And thou mourn at last, when thy flesh and thy body are consumed; and say, How have I hated instruction, and my heart despised reproof? and have not obeyed the voice of my teachers, nor inclined mine ear to them that instructed me?' The lecher hath his penitent moods. A malefactor on the rack will confess freely. Vows of men are very frequent. Oh! that men would be such when they are well as they promised to be when they were sick!

[2.] Because the aim of all was ease and safety. Pharaoh's cry is not, Take away iniquity, but, Take away this plague. Offers of nature after ease are found in hypocrites. Esau sought the privileges of the birthright with tears, *quia perdiderat, non quia vendiderat*; not because he sold it, but because he had lost it. Nature may be sensible of present evil.

[3.] Because it was vanishing. The good motions of an hard heart are of no long continuance; they pass through, and are gone like a flash of lightning. Pharaoh's remorse for the frogs and grasshoppers was as a cloud soon blown over. Till there be sound repentance, remorse must needs be short, for it is an unpleasing penance. Water heated is the colder afterwards, because it is rarefied; after it hath thawed a little, it will freeze the harder. Pharaoh after every respite was hardened anew; it is the temper of those that are doomed to destruction.

[4.] Because his purposes came so short and lame of what God expected. An hard heart, when it cannot prevail against God, would fain compound with him. First he gave leave: Exod. viii. 25, 'Go ye, sacrifice to God in the land;' then ver. 28, 'I will let ye go, that ye may sacrifice to the Lord your God in the wilderness, only ye shall not go very far away;' then chap. x. 11, 'Go now, ye that are men, and serve the Lord.' Their children were to remain for hostages. Then, ver. 24, 'Go ye, serve the Lord, only let your flocks and your herds be stayed; let your little ones also go with you.' Their cattle were to remain for a pawn, and their flocks and their herds for a forfeiture if they returned not, and a recompense for the damage of Egypt. But God would not abate him a hoof. An hard heart yieldeth to God by halves. Pharaoh hucketh with him; first they might sacrifice in the land; then go a little way, three days' journey; then he would keep their children, then their flocks and herds. An hard heart never yieldeth to God his whole demand; the devil is loath to let go his hold. How do men huck with God in duties contrary to their affections or prejudicial to their interests? 2 Kings v. 18, 'In this thing the Lord pardon thy servant, that when my master goeth into the house of Rimmon to worship there, and he leaneth on my hand, and I bow myself in the house of Rimmon; when I bow myself in the house of Rimmon, the Lord pardon thy servant in this thing.' They have their reservations, and in this and that thing they will be excused. These are but deceitful pangs. Pharaoh doth often eat his words, and retract every grant.

8. In process of time his hardness is improved into rage and downright

malice: Exod. x. 28, 'Get thee from me, take heed to thyself, see my face no more; for in the day thou seest my face thou shalt die.' Vessels, when they come to the lees, they grow sour and tart; so Pharaoh began to run dregs. Or as beasts by long baiting grow mad and furious, so it was with Pharaoh. Men first slight the truth, and then are hardened against it, and then come to persecute it. A river, when it hath been long kept up, swelleth and beareth down the bank and rampire; so do wicked men rage when their consciences cannot withstand the light, and their hearts will not yield to it.

9. At length Pharaoh is willing to let them go. After much ado God may get something from a hard heart; but it is no sooner given, but retracted; like fire struck out of a flint, it is hardly got, and quickly gone: Hosea vi. 4, 'Your goodness is as a morning cloud, and as the early dew it goeth away.' Many may have some show of goodness, at least at some times, who yet are little the better, and their condition nothing the better; it proveth a great snare and neck-break to them; its unsoundness is presently seen in its inconstancy.

10. The last news that we hear of hardening Pharaoh's heart was a little before his destruction: Exod. xiv. 8, 'And the Lord hardened the heart of Pharaoh king of Egypt, and he pursued after the children of Israel.' Pharaoh begrudgeth his own grant, as if he had yielded too far. Hardness of heart will not leave us till it hath wrought our full and final destruction. God always besotteth when he meaneth to destroy. Never any were hardened but to their own ruin. As God, that loveth his own, loveth them to the end, so God, that hateth those that are hardened, hateth them to the end. Pharaoh is first plagued and then destroyed. This is the upshot of all: Job ix. 4, 'Who hath hardened himself against him, and prospered?' The beginning is imposture and delusion, the middle obstinacy, and the end ruin.

11. How God hardeneth. It is a point that needeth explication. God is not and cannot be the author of sin; if God should cause it, man should sin of necessity, and then his punishment would not be just, he being under force. God hath not brought upon any necessity of sinning; and God, that is good, cannot be the cause of evil. If God were the immediate author, it would be no sin, for whatever God doth is good.

How then doth he harden the heart? I answer—(1.) Negatively; (2.) Affirmatively.

1. Negatively. In the explication of this matter we must avoid both extremes; some say too much of it, others too little.

[1.] We must not say too much, lest we leave a stain and blemish upon the divine glory.

(1.) God infuseth no hardness and sin as he infuseth grace. All influences from heaven are sweet and good, not sour. Evil cannot come from the Father of lights. God enforceth no man to do evil.

(2.) God doth not excite the inward propension to sin; that is Satan's work. He persuadeth it not; it hath neither command, nor approbation, nor influence, nor impulse from heaven. In all these ways we must look upon man's sin. All sin is a child begotten by that incubus of hell on the corrupt soul of man; it is poured out as milk into the womb of their hearts, and there it is curdled as cheese.

[2.] We must not give it too little. God doth not harden by bare prescience, because God foreseeth other sins, and yet they are not ascribed to God; he is not said to kill, or to steal, or to do wrong, as he is to harden. There is a difference between God's concurrence to this sin and others. It is not only by way of manifestation, that is, by his plagues and judgments he declareth how hard it is. God hardened Pharaoh, say some, that is, by frequency of judgments showed how hard his heart was. The prayer by which we deprecate this evil showeth the meaning of it. We would not say, Lord, show not how hard I am by thy many judgments upon me; but, Lord harden not my heart, lead me not into temptation, incline not my heart to any evil thing. And it doth not hold good in other instances: Deut. ii. 30, 'Sihon king of Heshbon would not let us pass by him, for the Lord thy God hardened his spirit, and made his heart obstinate.' There was no such long process to make it evident they had hard hearts. So Josh. xi. 20, 'For it was of the Lord to harden their hearts, that they should not come against Israel in battle.' So that there is somewhat besides an evident manifestation to the world by continued judgments that it is hard. Nor is it by a mere idle permission (for there is besides that his decree, and a judicial action of providence), as if God were like the heathen's Jupiter, who was feasting in Ethiopia while things were out of order in Greece. Or at least such think God hath no more to do than a man that standeth on the shore and seeth a ship ready to be drowned when he might have helped it; there is somewhat more than so. Nor is it merely by desertion and suspension of grace. It is true this is a part, but not all; as a captain leaving his soldiers in the midst of a battle, may be said to leave them in the enemies' hands. God concurreth not only by way of permission and patience, but by way of action and power; not making hardness, but doing and willing the things whereby the sinner is hardened. Besides his decrees, there is his judicial sentence, and an active providence in order thereunto. Many things concur to the hardening of the heart, all which God willeth and intendeth, but justly. The wicked take these occasions of their own accord; Satan tempteth out of his own malice; but all this cannot be done without the will of God; there is at least a permissive intention. If there were not God's overruling it, then he were not God omnipotent; there is a supreme power overruling and ordering everything that is done in the world. It was God's will that Pharaoh should be hardened, that he might dispose of it to the ends of his providence: Exod. ix. 16, 'And in very deed for this cause have I raised thee up, for to show in thee my power, and that my name may be declared throughout all the earth.' If there were only a naked idle permission, then it may be said that he suffereth the heart to be hardened rather than hardeneth it, which is the phrase used.

2. Affirmatively, how God doth harden. The inward way is wonderful; as God's drawing sinners is secret, so is his hardening. But if you ask me by what means it is accomplished? I answer—

[1.] By desertion, by taking away the restraints of grace, whereby he letteth them loose to their own hearts: Ps. lxxxi. 12, 'So I gave them up unto their own hearts' lusts, and they walked in their own counsels.' Man in regard of his inclinations to sin is like a greyhound held by a slip or collar; when the hare is in sight, take away the slip, and the greyhound runneth violently after the hare, according to his inbred disposition. Men are held in by the restraints of grace, which, when removed, they are left to their own swing, and run into all excess of riot. Thus God took away his good Spirit from Saul: 1 Sam. xvi. 14, 'But the Spirit of the Lord departed from him, and an evil spirit from the Lord troubled him.' Take away the pillar that sustaineth the house, and then the house falleth of itself. God taketh away his grace, and then all runneth to ruin; as darkness ensueth upon the withdrawing of light. Now herein God is not to be blamed.

(1.) Because he is debtor to none. He may give his grace to whom he pleaseth, and withhold it as he will; he is not bound to give or continue, but is free to bestow or withhold. Man sinneth when he doth not hinder sin, because he is bound to hinder it all that he can: Neh. xiii. 17, 'Then I contended with the nobles of Judah, and said unto them, What evil thing is this that ye do, and profane the sabbath-day?' When the people profaned the sabbath, and they did not restrain them.

(2.) He knoweth how to make the best of any evil, to turn the greatest evil into the greatest good, which man cannot do, and ought not, being under a rule. We must not do evil that good may come of it: Rom. iii. 8, 'And not rather, as we be slanderously reported, and as some affirm that we say, Let us do evil, that good may come; whose damnation is just.'

(3.) There is an actual forfeiture. God is so far from being bound to continue grace, that he is bound in justice to withdraw what is given. When men stop their ears, God may shut them. But—

[2.] By tradition. He delivereth them up to the power of Satan, who worketh upon the corrupt nature of man, and hardeneth it; he stirreth him up as the executioner of God's curse; as the evil spirit had leave to seduce Ahab: 1 Kings xxii. 21, 22, 'And there came forth a spirit, and stood before the Lord, and said, I will persuade him. And the Lord said unto him, Wherewith? And he said, I will go forth, and I will be a lying spirit in the mouth of all his prophets. And he said, Thou shalt persuade him, and prevail also; go forth and do so.' There is a permissive intention, not an effective; Satan is the efficient and instrument, God is the judge; he permitteth Satan to excite and stir up their evil natures: they grieve his Spirit, and then God withdraweth, and leaveth them to an evil spirit; as in Saul: 1 Sam. xvi. 14, 'But the Spirit of the Lord departed from Saul, and an evil spirit from the Lord troubled him.' The light of the Spirit of the Lord is gone, and then Satan filled him with rage and fury and cruelty. It is said, 'An evil spirit from the Lord,' because he was sent from God to punish him for his sins.

[3.] There is an active providence, which disposeth and propoundeth such objects as, meeting with a wicked heart, maketh it more hard. God maketh the best things the wicked enjoy to turn to the fall and destruction of those that have them. Sometimes natural comforts: Jer. vi. 21, 'Therefore thus saith the Lord, Behold, I will lay stumbling-blocks before this people; and the father and the sons together shall fall upon them, the neighbour and his friend shall perish.' Their table is made a snare, and an occasion and preparation and means to ruin them. They harden themselves by despising the goodness and patience of God : Rom. ii. 4, 'Or despisest thou the riches of his goodness, and forbearance, and long-suffering, not knowing that the goodness of God leadeth thee to repentance?' Sometimes corrections and chastisements; these produce nothing but a greater contumacy; as a resty horse, the more he is spurred forward, the more he goeth backward; or as a fierce bull or bear groweth mad with baiting. In what a sad case are wicked men left by God! Mercies corrupt them, and corrections enrage them; as unsavoury herbs, the more they are pounded, the more they stink. Sometimes by spiritual ordinances and advantages; the most spiritual means do them no good: Isa. vi. 10, 'Make the heart of this people fat, and make their ears heavy, and shut their eyes, lest they see with their eyes, and hear with their ears, and convert and be healed.' He that bringeth in the light blindeth the owl. Water poured on lime maketh it burn the more; so do the means of grace hurt wicked men, irritating their corruptions, or they resting in them. Sometimes by withdrawing the word and means of grace and prayers of his people: Acts xix. 9, 'When divers were hardened, and believed not, but spake evil of that way before the multitude, he departed from them;' Jer. vii. 16, 'Pray not thou for this people, neither lift up cry nor prayer for them, neither make intercession to me, for I will not hear thee.' Do not any longer strive between me and them. Sometimes by disposing and ordering the deceits of false teachers: 2 Thes. ii. 10, 11, 'They received not the love of the truth, that they might be saved: and for this cause God gave them up to strong delusions, that they should believe a lie;' Job xii. 16, 'The deceived and the deceiver are his.' This doth not fall out without a providence. The water runneth its own course, but the miller maketh use of it to drive his engine. As all things work together for good to them that love God, so all things work for the worst to the wicked and impenitent. Providences and ordinances; we read of them that wrest the scriptures to their own destruction, 2 Peter iii. 16. Some are condemned to worldly happiness; by ease and abundance of prosperity they are entangled: Prov. i. 32, 'The prosperity of fools shall destroy them;' as brute creatures, when in good plight, grow fierce and man-keen. If we will find the sin, God will find the occasion. I shall instance in Judas; Christ had reproved him for begrudging Mary's bounty, and ye read, Mark xxvi. 16, 'From that time he sought opportunity to betray him.' He was offended with Christ's reproof. Judas was hurried on with wrath and avarice; and when men are resolved, God in his providence suffereth them to have a fit opportunity. The priests, alarmed with the miracle of raising Lazarus from the dead, by which many were drawn to believe in him, were thinking how to seize on him, and Judas comes in the nick, and asketh them, What will ye give me, and I will betray him to you?

Use. Let us take warning by Pharaoh's example, that this great judgment light not upon us. The Philistines, that were otherwise a blind and stupid people, yet were affected with it. Dagon was broken in pieces, and they were smitten with emrods once and again, and they begin to consult what to do. Their diviners told them, 1 Sam.

vi. 6, 'Wherefore do ye harden your hearts, as the Egyptians and Pharaoh hardened their hearts? when he had wrought wonderfully among them, did they not let the people go, and they departed?' God delighteth not in judgment, and therefore he hath made a precedent once for all; here is Pharaoh set up, that all succeeding ages may stand in fear. God would not have us learn to our bitter cost, but take example by others. *Qui alieno malo non sapit, gravius punitur*—He that will not take warning by others shall be more grievously punished. In judgments it is better to take example than to become examples. If thy life should be nothing else but Pharaoh's story acted over again (for certainly there is an exact parallel between this case and the course of every obstinate sinner), how great will thy doom be! God was angry with Belshazzar because he was not warned by Nebuchadnezzar's example: Dan. v. 22, 'And thou his son, O Belshazzar, hast not humbled thine heart, though thou knewest all this.' You have known and heard of the way of God with Pharaoh; God hath a quarrel with some of you for your lusts and vanities; do you think to bear it up against warnings with peace and quiet? Your lusts may not bring you to present ruin, that you may be the more hardened in them; but be sure that God will have the best at last; and then I leave you to judge what will be your condition when you fall under the weight of his displeasure. Have you not some qualms of conscience sometimes about your eternal condition? doth not conscience say, Surely I am not so careful to make my peace with God as I should be? Upon every such stirring you are the more estranged from God if you do not improve it. Conscience will repeat over these warnings to you when you lie upon your death-beds; and then you will sadly howl over your neglects, and wish your magicians and old companions far from you; then you will send for Moses and Aaron, and it may be too late. When God is showing mercy, the last mercies are the best, and the farther he goeth the sweeter he is; and when God is punishing, the last punishments are the sorest, and the farther he goeth the more bitter.

I will propound two considerations—

1. From the evil of an hard heart.

[1.] It is a contest with God, not only with his greatness and power, but also with his goodness and mercy, and therefore it must needs succeed ill with us. Before God breaketh out with fury he treateth with us in a mild condescending way; he beseecheth his own creature: Jer. xiii. 15, 16, 'Hear ye, and give ear; be not proud, for the Lord hath spoken: give glory to God before he cause darkness, and before your feet stumble upon the dark mountains; and while ye look for light, he turn it into the shadow of death, and make it gross darkness.'

[2.] An hard heart makes us rebels to God and slaves to everything else; for we are wedded to some inferior thing; we are our own Pharaohs, and will not let ourselves go: 2 Tim. iii. 4, 'Lovers of pleasures more than lovers of God.'

[3.] It is in itself the sorest of all judgments.

[4.] It never goes alone, but brings other judgments along with it.

[5.] It is the great hindrance of the spiritual life. (See Sermon on Mark iii. 5.)

2. From the parties whom it may befall, not only the open wicked, but in some measure God's own children; for God may harden two ways—as a judge, and as a father; by way of punishment, and by way of correction. By way of punishment again two ways—totally and finally. Some are totally hardened, and have nothing of a soft heart in them, and yet not finally; the dreadful sentence of obduration is not yet passed upon them, as it may be upon others, and that during life, when God leaveth them to their own hearts' counsels, without any check or restraint of providence, or purpose to reclaim them. These three kinds I must then speak of—God's hardening the wicked in general, his final hardening, and his hardening in part his own children.

SERMON II.

I will harden his heart, that he shall not let my people go.—
Exod. iv. 21.

First, Of God's hardening wicked men in general as a judge. The causes of it are—

1. Ignorance; for light and love make the heart tender. Light is that which we are now to take notice of. Light begets tenderness, as it discerneth sin, and maketh us sensible of it, especially the lively light of the Spirit: Rom. vii. 9, 'I was alive without the law once; but when the commandment came, sin revived, and I died.' Sense of guilt and punishment soon flashed in his face; as in a dungeon the worms crawl as soon as light is brought in: Jer. xxxi. 19, 'After I was instructed, I smote upon my thigh; I was ashamed, yea, even confounded, because I did bear the reproach of my youth.' Instruction breedeth remorse, and awakeneth men out of their stupid security; but while men continue in their ignorance they are stupid and senseless. Now thus men may be for a long time, and yet afterwards God may make the scales fall off from their eyes, and 'open their eyes, and turn them from darkness to light, and from the power of Satan unto God,' Acts xxvi. 18. However, affected and vinceable ignorance, when men are willingly ignorant and err in their hearts, that is, when men have powerful and enlightening motives and yet remain ignorant, this is very dangerous. And for the present, that ignorance is one cause of their hardening is evident, because the worst usually when they come to die are sensible; their mind is then cleared from the fogs and steams of lust, and conscience being awakened, they then feel their load, and a great weight of sin lying upon them, and most wish they had lived in a more strict and ready obedience to God's will.

2. Unbelief. There is an hardness of the heart against the light and offers of the gospel, when Christ is tendered, but not received, and the cause of that is ignorance, affected ignorance; and there is an hardening of the heart against the truth once received, out of love of

their temporal peace, liberty, and safety of life and estate; this cometh from unbelief, and want of a sufficient sense and sight of the world to come; which hardness is caused by the veiglement and importunities of the flesh, craving its satisfactions in the present world, and denying or disbelieving the blessedness to come. If men did believe heaven and hell, they would be more pliable to God's motions, and more deaf to the importunities of the flesh; but that this is a cause of hardening appeareth by Christ's chiding his disciples for their unbelief and hardness of heart: Mark xvi. 14, 'Afterward he appeared unto the eleven as they sat at meat, and upbraided them with their unbelief and hardness of heart, because they believed not them which had seen him after he was risen.'

3. Sinning against light, either by way of omission or commission. This provoketh God to give us over to more hardness of heart. By way of commision is easily granted, but it is also by way of omission: James iv. 17, 'To him that knoweth to do good, and doeth it not, to him it is sin.' They will find it to be sin in the sad effects of it. (See Sermon on Mark iii. 5.)

4. Custom in sinning. (See Sermon on Mark iii. 5.)

5. Small sins may occasion this judgment, and harden the heart as well as great sins. It is not easy to say which doth most; indeed great sins get into the throne presently, but small sins insensibly and by degrees: Ps. xix. 13, 'Keep back thy servant also from presumptuous sins; let them not have dominion over me,' A small sin may get the upperhand of a sinner, and bring him under in time; and after that, it is habituated by constant custom, so that he cannot easily shake off the yoke, and redeem himself from the tyranny thereof, as if a man be addicted to any vanity and foolish delight. These do not exercise dominion over the enslaved soul till they have gotten strength by many and multiplied acts. But presumptuous sins by one single act weaken the Spirit, and give a mighty advantage to the flesh, even almost to a complete conquest. So that for the present little sins do not harden the heart so much as greater. (See Sermon on Mark iii. 5.)

Now all these causes concur to the hardening of the heart, and making it as a stone, but yet out of these stones God can raise up children to Abraham.

Secondly, Of God's final hardening, when God leaveth men to perish, and will no more treat with them. Now here I shall show—(1.) That there is such a dispensation; (2.) The causes of it.

1. That there is such a dispensation.

[1.] It is an usual dispensation for God to leave men to perish in their sins, and that irreversibly, even before death, and will be entreated no more for them. It appears by many places of scripture: Rev. xxii. 11, 'He that is unjust, let him be unjust still; and he which is filthy, let him be filthy still.' Those which remain obstinate after many warnings and calls, it is usual with God to give them over to their lusts, that they may be ripe for hell: Ezek. iii. 27, 'He that heareth, let him hear; and he that forbeareth, let him forbear; for they are a rebellious house.' As if God should say, Let them now do what they will, I am at a point. Now sometimes their condition is irreversible, which is clear, because when God hath given them over, how shall they repent, and break off their sin? God's oath is passed: Ps. cxv. 11, 'Unto whom I sware in my wrath, that they should not enter into my rest.' God standeth sworn to condemn and destroy them. If they should have any anguish of conscience and remorse stirred up in them, God will have no regard to it: Prov. i. 26, 27, 'I also will laugh at your calamity, I will mock when your fear cometh; when your fear cometh as desolation, and your destruction cometh as a whirlwind, when distress and anguish cometh upon you;' Hosea v. 6, 'They shall go with their flocks and with their herds to seek the Lord, but they shall not find him, he hath withdrawn himself from them.' When men have neglected God's seasons, and begin to be surprised with death, then they would fain have comfort and pardon; but instead thereof the Lord puts them off. No; you would have none of me: Ps. lxxxi. 11, 12, 'But my people would not hearken to my voice, and Israel would none of me: so I gave them up unto their own hearts' lust, and they walked in their own counsels.' Instead of compassion they are mocked, and turned over to their evil courses and carnal company: John viii. 21, 'I go my way, and ye shall seek me, and shall die in your sins.' That this may be before death appeareth because grace is confined to a season: Isa. lv. 6, 'Seek ye the Lord while he may be found, call ye upon him while he is near.' And that season is not always as long as life: Luke xix. 42, 'If thou hadst known, even thou, at least in this thy day, the things which belong to thy peace! but now they are hid from thine eyes.' The day of grace is bright but short. We may mourn over many thus; when the measure of their iniquities is filled up, God giveth over calling and expecting and waiting for their repentance. It is true the time is not to be known by any man of himself, nor by others concerning him; we cannot state the number of calls, because circumstances are diverse, and light breaketh in with warnings in a different degree. There is a great deal of variety in the Lord's dispensations, therefore all must use the means, and warn we must to the last. We can only say in the general, that after God hath done with them, and expects no good from them, he may let them live for the glory of his justice; as after God had hardened Pharaoh's heart, yet he continued his life, that he might show his power in him: Exod. ix. 16, 'And in very deed for this cause have I raised thee up, for to show in thee my power, and that my name may be declared throughout all the earth.' You may survive your final hardness, as a monument of God's justice in the world.

[2.] It is a just dispensation. It is just with God to take the refusal and be gone, and to cease to deal with your hearts any more, when, after all the melting entreaties of his grace, you cast him off; he commands, and you will not obey; he is willing, and you are not willing; he entreats, and you will not hearken; he wishes: Deut. v. 29, 'O that there were such an heart in them, that they would fear me, and keep all my commandments always, that it might be well with them, and with their children for ever!' he laments: Ps. lxxxi. 13, 'O that my people had hearkened unto me, and Israel had walked in my ways!' and you will not join with him. He is grieved that his offer of grace is not received, and you will not lament. It is but just that a man should be left to his own choice, that a man should miss of that salvation which he cared not for; that if, after warnings, convictions, and entreaties, he will be filthy, he should be filthy still. In hell conscience will acquit God; ἐγὼ ἐμοῖ τούτων αἰτία, I have been the cause of all this to myself.

[3.] It is a merciful dispensation to the rest of the world. We are told of these things beforehand, not that we may despair, that is an ill consequence; but that, as we love our souls, we should take heed of resisting grace, and turning our backs upon our own mercies. It is a merciful and fatherly warning to strike in betimes, and own the God of our mercies. Delay is that that undoeth all the world. Now this is the best cure of delay.

2. The causes of it.

[1.] Sinning away the light of nature. By nature men have some knowledge of good and evil. There are κοῖναι ἔννοιαι, some common principles, as that God is, and must be worshipped, that we must do wrong to none, nor pollute ourselves with promiscuous lusts. The heart of a pagan would rise against it: Rom. ii. 14, 15, 'For when the gentiles, which have not the law, do by nature the things contained in the law, these, having not the law, are a law unto themselves, which show the work of the law written in their hearts.' Now, when men hold the light of nature 'in unrighteousness,' Rom. i. 18, when they hold poor truth fettered and bound that it cannot break out into an holy conversation, this provoketh God to give them up to hardness. There are many sins which nature discovereth, and may be avoided upon such reasons and considerations as nature suggesteth. Now, when men put the finger into nature's eye, or will not suffer reason to exercise any dominion, but let loose the reins to lust, God leaveth them to a carnal and sottish heart. Though by the light of nature men cannot convert to God, yet by the light of nature men may practise many duties and avoid many sins. The gentiles were left to an unsound injudicious mind. When men fall into foul sins against the light of nature, conscience loseth its feeling and tenderness: Eph. iv. 19, 'Who being past feeling, have given themselves over unto lasciviousness, to work all uncleanness with greediness.' Hearts prejudiced against the things of God may grow to very stones.

[2.] Refusing God's many calls: Prov. xxix. 1, 'He that, being often reproved, hardeneth his neck, shall suddenly be destroyed, and that without remedy.' God may bear with us a while after one or two or more reproofs, but when we are often reproved and often convinced, and yet will not be reclaimed, God may give us over. The exact date of Christ's patience, or the number of his calls ere the fatal period of final induration cometh, we know not; but when it is often, you are in danger. Take heed of forfeiting your own mercies by refusing the most earnest motions of the word and Spirit. When God importuneth to be heard and obeyed, his Spirit being thus resisted and refused, God will be at length wearied, and will not give as much grace as before: Isa. lxiii. 10, 'But they rebelled, and vexed his Holy Spirit; therefore he was turned to be their enemy, and he fought against them.' *Sævit infelix amor.* Gen. vi. 3, 'My Spirit shall not always strive with man, for that he also is flesh.' The heathens did acknowlege that the τόπικοι θεοὶ, the gods of cities and nations, did for the provocation of the inhabitants forsake their altars and temples. The more calls and convictions we resist in this kind, the more difficult and improbable is the reducing a sinner to God; every day he groweth more wicked and profane. To resist the clamours of conscience is sad, but to weary and grieve the Spirit is dreadful: Ezek. xxiv. 13, 'In thy wickedness is lewdness; because I have purged thee, and thou wast not purged, thou shalt not be purged from thy filthiness any more, till I have caused my fury to rest upon thee.' God sets them over the fire till their hearts begin to be warmed, and then lets the sun remain on them.

[3.] Gross hypocrisy. This is a constant lie, a contempt of God, an habitual and customary stifling and smothering of checks of conscience; for their form and profession showeth what they should be, and if they were what they seem to be, all would be well. Men have light enough to take on the form of religion, and sin enough to resist the power of it. And therefore their judgment is the greater; for their whole life being a constant rebelling against the light, they are left to perish by their own deceivings: 2 Thes. ii. 10, 11, 'Because they received not the love of the truth, that they might be saved, for this cause God shall send them strong delusions, that they should believe a lie.' The carnal christian being not brought to true faith and sincere repentance, God giveth them up that they may be deceived by every vain pretence.

[4.] Apostasy from grace received. Men are not only warmed, but begin to have a taste. They that take up with some profession of the things of God, but afterwards fall away again to looseness and vanity and worldliness, they are more left by God than others: Heb. vi. 4–6, 'For it is impossible for them who were once enlightened, and have tasted of the heavenly gift, and were made partakers of the Holy Ghost, and have tasted the good word of God, and the powers of the world to come, if they shall fall away, to renew them again to repentance.' For they dishonour him more, and bring an evil report upon God. The devil hath more power over them; as a prisoner that hath made his escape, if he be taken afterwards, hath more chains put upon him: 2 Peter ii. 21, 22, 'For it had been better for them not to have known the way of righteousness, than after they have known it to turn from the holy commandment delivered unto them: for it is happened unto them according to the true proverb, The dog is turned to his own vomit again, and the sow that was washed to her wallowing in the mire.' They themselves are made more incapable of ever owning the ways of God again; it is impossible they should renew themselves, it groweth up into wilful malice: Heb. x. 26, 'For if we sin wilfully after we have received the knowledge of the truth, there remaineth no more sacrifice for sins.' Grace will not pardon them, the Mediator will not intercede for them. *Apostatæ sunt maximi osores sui ordinis*—Apostates hate the ways they have professed: Hosea v. 2, 'The revolters are profound to make slaughter.' None so cross and malicious and perverse in their cause.

[5.] Sottish despair (there is a raging despair, and a sottish despair; the one is when conscience is terrified, the other when it is stupefied), when to custom in sinning there is added a passionate will: Jer. ii. 25, 'Thou sayest, There is no hope; no, for I have loved strangers, and after them will I go;' Jer. xviii. 11, 'And they said, There is no hope, but we will walk after our own devices, and we will every one do the imagination of his evil heart.' Προαίρησις οὐκ ἐστὶν ἀδυνάτων, men do not use to consult about things that are impossible. It is said of the Israelites, Exod. vi. 9, 'They hearkened not unto Moses for anguish of spirit and for cruel bondage.' Lust is so deeply rooted that they cannot help it; the case is desperate, they are at a point; as we use to say, Past cure, past care; they grow out of heart, and so lie down under the power of their lusts; they resolve to persist in their sins, to live as they list, and it is to no purpose to speak to them.

Thirdly, Of God's hardening as a father, in a way of the highest fatherly anger and displeasure. This may be so: Isa. lxiii. 17, 'O Lord, why hast thou made us to err from thy ways, and hardened our heart from thy fear?' This is a partial hardness. There may be desertion in point of grace, though some tenderness left in the understanding, that discerneth good and evil; in the conscience, that is dissatisfied in its present state; in the will, that owneth the ways of God; so that there is a general purpose to please him in all things. Yet the heart groweth dead and stupid; there is an inaptness for holy things; they are less sensible of the evil of sin; they have not such delight in the word, nor rejoicing in hope, nor freedom for prayer, nor patience under afflictions, nor complacency in communion with God. And it is sad when it is so, when to sense there is little difference between them and the wicked; there is hardness in a stone, and hardness in a piece of wax. I will show the causes of this, and the means to cure it.

1. The causes of this are—

[1.] Sinning against conscience. There are sins of daily incursion and sudden surreption; and there are sins of presumption, into which God's children may in some rare cases fall, but then they make great waste and havoc in their souls; as David's great sin, by which he lost that free spirit, and was forced to beg a new creation, as if all were to begin again: Ps. li. 10–12, 'Create in me a clean heart, O God, and renew a right spirit within me; cast me not away from thy presence, and take not thy Holy Spirit from me; restore unto me the joy of thy salvation, and uphold me by thy free Spirit.' Many are the mischiefs which come by such sins. Partly God's love is obstructed, that he is not so ready to do them good: Isa. lix. 2, 'Your iniquities have separated between you and your God, and your sins have hid his face from you, that he will not hear;' that is, the good-will and favour of God is, as it were, bound up, and hindered from showing itself in all those gracious effects which otherwise it would put forth for our comfort and peace. He doth not actually pardon their sins, nor make them partakers of spiritual benefit sin so ample and full a measure as otherwise he would; but holds his hand, and cuts you short in spiritual blessings, which otherwise he would plentifully dispense unto his people. Partly they exceedingly weaken the work of grace which is wrought upon their hearts. Their faith is more dead, their love is more cold than it was, hope is languid, the spiritual life is interrupted, and at a stand; though the seed of God remains, yet it cannot put forth itself with such vigour and efficacy. Yea, they may never recover such a portion of the Spirit as they had before: 2 Chron. xvii. 3, 'Jehoshaphat walked in the first ways of his father David,' as having some note of blemish n his latter ways. These sins, in short, as a wound in the body, let ut our blood and strength. As a prodigal, that hath once broken after he hath been set up, is not trusted with a like stock again, so God's children may not recover that largeness of spirit and fulness of inward strength and comfort which they had before; as many after a great disease do not regain that pitch of health which formerly they had, but may carry the fruits of their disease with them to their graves. Partly because acts are intermitted. When the soul is distempered, it is unfit for action. Either duties are omitted, or else done in such an overly manner as doth increase our distemper, and harden us the more. In what a sorry fashion did David worship till God awakened his conscience by Nathan! Prayer is interrupted: 1 Peter iii. 7, 'As heirs together of the grace of life, that your prayers be not hindered.'

[2.] Grieving the Spirit: Eph. iv. 30, 'And grieve not the Holy Spirit of God, whereby ye are sealed unto the day of redemption. All sin is a grief to the Spirit, especially filthiness and bitterness. Compare this with ver. 29, 31, 'Let no corrupt communication proceed out of your mouth, but that which is good to the use of edifying, that it may minister grace unto the hearers. Let all bitterness, and wrath, and anger, and clamour, and evil-speaking be put away from you, with all malice.' Now the grieving of the Spirit makes a great breach in our grace and comfort, as the Spirit is our sanctifier and comforter. To speak only of the last: When the Spirit is grieved, we have not such a sense of God's love: 'For the love of God is shed abroad in our hearts by the Holy Ghost, which is given unto us,' Rom. v. 5. We have not that liberty and confidence in prayer we once had: 1 John iii. 21, 'Beloved, if our heart condemn us not, then have we confidence towards God.' Nor those lively hopes of glory and final redemption, in that text, Eph. iv. 30, 'Grieve not the Holy Spirit of God, whereby ye are sealed unto the day of redemption.' Nor that comfort in reproaches, nor courage in afflictions, nor strength to resist sin, nor that readiness and cheerfulness in obedience that once they had. So that a christian is like Sampson when his locks are gone; all delightful communion with God is suspended, and a christian doth not act like a servant that is in his master's favour.

[3.] Carnal liberty. When a man giveth too much contentment to the flesh, the spirit or better part is in bonds: Ps. cxix. 37, 'Turn away mine eyes from beholding vanity, and quicken thou me in thy way.' A man that lets loose the reins to worldly vanity will soon find hardness coming on his heart, and see a need to ask quickening grace: Luke xxi. 34, 'Take heed to yourselves, lest at any time your hearts be overcharged with surfeiting, and drunkenness, and cares of this life.' Worldly comforts over-affected or immoderately used clog and enslave the heart, and so we are more unpersuadable and disobedient to the motions of his Spirit, and the counsels of his grace. Therefore, if we will take heed that our hearts be not hardened, let them not out too freely to worldly things, lest they be withdrawn from God; but rejoice here as if you rejoiced not, that you may keep up your liberty to God.

[4.] Pride and self-sufficiency: 2 Chron. xxxii. 31, 'Howbeit in the business of the ambassadors of the princes of Babylon, who sent unto him to inquire of the wonder that was done in the land, God left him to try him, that he might know all that was in his heart.' Paul was permitted to be buffeted, that he might be kept humble: 2 Cor. xii. 7, 'And lest I should be exalted above measure through the abundance of the revelations, there was given to me a thorn in the flesh, the messenger of Satan to buffet me, lest I should be exalted above measure.' When you trust to yourselves, God leaveth you to yourselves; and then we are as a glass without a bottom, broken as soon as out of hand: James iv. 6, 'God resisteth the proud, but giveth grace to the humble.' It is not so much understood of a moral humility, or a lowly carriage towards men, as of an evangelical humility, which consists in brokenness of heart, or a sense of our unworthiness and weakness; these are influenced by grace, but others are left to fall and miscarry by their own presumptuous confidence. And therefore, if we would not incur any degree of this judgment, we must take heed of pride and spiritual security. Those that feel the daily and hourly necessity of grace have more of the supplies of the Spirit, they are oftener waiting upon God: Ps. xxv. 5, 'On thee do I wait all the day.' Christ hath taught us to beg daily bread, daily pardon, and daily strength against temptations, that he might engage us to be often with God, and keep in a constant dependence on him, that the heart might be kept more awful, tender, and serious.

[5.] Carelessness and spiritual sloth. When we carelessly entertain the motions of his Spirit, and lie upon the bed of ease, he is gone: Cant. v. 2, 3, 'I sleep, but my heart waketh: it is the voice of my beloved that knocketh, saying, Open to me, my sister, my love, my dove, my undefiled: for my head is filled with dew, and my locks with the drops of the night. I have put off my coat, how shall I put it on? I have washed my feet, how shall I defile them?' and ver. 6, 'I rose up to open to my beloved, but my beloved had withdrawn himself, and was gone.' God's children may stifle many a pressing conviction and motion in their souls, hang off from the throne of grace and other good duties, and upon every frivolous pretence keep away from God. This unkind and ungracious dealing will cost them dear. Neglect of the means of grace quencheth the Spirit: 1 Thes. v. 19, 20, 'Quench not the Spirit; despise not prophesyings.' Therefore we should be more diligent in the use of means: Mark iv. 24, 'Unto you that hear shall more be given.' We must more carefully obey the sanctifying motions of the Spirit if we mean to avoid hardness of heart.

2. The means to cure it.

[1.] Bewail the evil, and complain of it before God, who alone can help us. We complain of hard times, of the hard dealings of men, of hard duties. *Durus est hic sermo*, this is a hard saying, and who can hear it? But we seldom complain of that which we should most complain of, hardness of heart. The Lord is pleased with these complaints: Jer. xxxi. 18, 'I have surely heard Ephraim bemoaning himself thus; Thou hast chastised me, and I was chastised as a bullock unaccustomed to the yoke.' Spiritual distempers must be most laid to heart. God's children in some degree are inflexible and insensible; there is too great touchiness, and impatiency to be admonished, too much disobedience to the Spirit's sanctifying motions; they are too often benumbed with the delights of the flesh, and cares of the world.

[2.] Hasten your repentance and return to God: Ps. cxix. 60, 'I made haste, and delayed not to keep thy commandments;' Gal. i. 16, Immediately I conferred not with flesh and blood.' To press this, let us consider these things—

(1.) How soon God may take an advantage against us we cannot tell. He hath not told us at what number of calls he will depart, and give us over to our own hearts; but he hath bid us not to delay, and lose the present season: Heb. iii. 7, 8, 'To-day if ye will hear his voice, harden not your hearts.' The command is as express for the time as for the duty; there is no season like the τὸ νῦν, the present season. It is but a flattering presumption to think that God will always stand waiting. Felix had but one call that we hear of, and he fooled it away to a more convenient season.

(2.) Every day spent in an unregenerate condition brings us nearer to destruction, and puts us upon a greater disadvantage: Rom. xiii. 11, 'Now is our salvation nearer than when we believed.' *A pari*, we may say; now is our damnation and final impenitency nearer.

(3.) Every call sets us yet nearer still. Sins are ripened by every call, as iron oft heated and oft quenched is the harder. When men are often sermon-scorched, they prove at length sermon-proof. The holy God will not cast his pearls before swine: Isa. lv. 6, 'Seek ye the Lord while he may be found, call ye upon him while he is near.'

(4.) A presumptuous going on in sin, upon a supposition that we shall repent at last, is the very next door and step to hell. You wittingly continue under the devil's power. Life is uncertain. God may take you away in the act of sin, as he did Zimri and Cosbi, Korah and his accomplices; or he may deny that space to call for mercy that you think of, for death doth not always give warning; or by an apoplexy, or lethargy, or some stupefying distemper, he may deprive you of the use of your reason. Let this rouse and awaken you out of your fond presumptions.

[3.] Beware of tendencies to it, when the heart begins to harden; as—

(1.) When you are not sensible of God's withdrawings, when there are any suspensions of his grace, the comfort and conduct of his Spirit, and the soul is stupid. It is sad not to be sensible of the accesses and recesses of the Spirit: Mat. ix. 25, 'The days shall come when the bridegroom shall be taken from them, and then shall they fast.' Grace stands in a continual watchfulness and observation of all God's dealings. Felt desertions are grievous, but not so dangerous as those that are unfelt. It is some good degree of grace not to be quiet without God.

(2.) When you scorn at reproof, when you are not only actors, but defenders of sin, and bear up yourselves impudently and stubbornly in your transgressions: Jer. vi. 10, 'To whom shall I speak and give warning, that they may hear? Behold, their ear is uncircumcised, and they cannot hearken; behold, the word of the Lord is unto them a reproach.' They are of an unteachable, untractable disposition; they think we rail when we do reprove. The devil hath then two victories—one by the scorn and opposition that is cast on the reprover, and the other by the hardening of the heart of the fretting and reproved sinner; that anger that should be turned upon the sin is turned upon the reproof.

(3.) When ordinances grow powerless. You live under ordinances, and receive no profit by them; you have much means, and can see no fruit: Isa. vi. 9, 10, 'Hear ye indeed, but understand not; and see ye indeed, but perceive not. Make the heart of this people fat, and make their ears heavy, and shut their eyes; lest they see with their eyes, and hear with their ears, and understand with their heart, and convert, and be healed.' The word is powerful; if it softens not, it hardens.

(4.) When our worldly comforts are apt to prove a snare to us: Mal. ii. 2, 'I will curse your blessings, yea, I have cursed them already, because ye do not lay it to heart.' When your table is made your snare, your meat becomes your poison, your estate is but as golden fetters to bind and chain your heart to the world; your honours blow you up. When you do not take comforts as the mercies and blessings of God, to praise him for them, and to devote yourselves in the strength of them to his service.

(5.) When corrections go away without fruit: Jer. v. 3, 'Thou hast stricken them, but they have not grieved; thou hast consumed them, but they have refused to receive correction; they have made their faces harder than a rock, they have refused to return.' God will have an account of every dispensation; afflictions are upon the register as well as mercies. Christians should never advance more in christianity than under the cross.

(6.) When we are lazy and loath to admit Christ into the heart. It being thronged with creature comforts, we keep him at the door knocking, and will not open to him: Rev. iii. 20, 'Behold, I stand at the door and knock;' Cant. v. 3, 'I have put off my coat, how shall I put it on? I have washed my feet, how shall I defile them?' This laziness and spiritual security is a cause and beginning of hardness of heart.

(7.) When trivial and slight temptations prevail against the sense of our duty; when for a piece of bread, and handfuls of barley they will transgress, and sell the righteous for a pair of shoes; when they are as a stone to God's counsels, but as wax to all other things.

(8.) When the heart grows vain and frothy; for a slight heart will be an hard heart; or God gives men over to a reprobate sense and an injudicious mind. These are the forerunners of hardness of heart, which we should beware of, and carefully watch against.

SERMON UPON GENESIS III. 15.*

It (i.e., the seed of the woman) shall bruise thy head, and thou shalt bruise his heel.—GEN. iii. 15.

THESE words are a part of the gospel preached in paradise, or the first promise of grace and life made to mankind, now fallen and dead in sin. As God was cursing the serpent, he draweth out this comfort to our first parents, who were confounded with the sense of sin and their defection from God. Satan's condemnation is our salvation. He did the first mischief, therefore the crushing of his head giveth hope of our deliverance out of that state of misery into which he hath plunged us.

The words are dark in comparison of the larger explications of the grace of God by Jesus Christ which were after delivered to the church. Who would look for a great tree in a little seed? Yet the seminal virtue doth afterward diffuse and dilate itself into all those stately and lofty branches in which the fowls of the air do take up their lodging and shelter. So do these few words contain all the articles and mysteries of the christian faith, which are the fountains of our solid peace and consolation. In the seed of the woman is contained all the doctrine concerning the incarnation of the Son of God; in the bruising of his heel, his death and sufferings; in the crushing of the serpent's head, his glorious victory and conquest. As obscure as the words are, an eagle-eyed and discerning faith could pick a great deal of comfort out of them. The οἱ πρεσβύτεροι, 'the elders,' mentioned Heb. xi. 2, the antediluvian fathers, so famous throughout all ages for their faith and confidence in God, had no other gospel to live upon. Abel, that offered a better sacrifice than Cain, Enoch, that walked with God, Noah, that prepared the ark, did all that they did in the strength and upon the encouragement of this promise.

The words are considerable—

1. For the person who speaketh them, the Lord God himself, who was the first preacher of the gospel in paradise. The draught and plot was in his bosom long before, but now it cometh out of his mouth.

2. For the occasion when they were spoken. When God hath been but newly provoked and offended by sin, and man, from his creature and subject, was become his enemy and rebel, the offended God comes with a promise in his mouth. Adam could look for nothing but that God should repeat to him the whole beadroll of curses wherein he had

* Preached the fifth of November.

involved himself, but God maketh known the great design of his grace. Once more, the Lord God was now cursing the serpent, and in the midst of the curses promiseth the great blessing of the Messiah. Thus doth God 'in wrath remember mercy,' Hab. iii. 2. Yea, man's sentence was not yet pronounced. The Lord God had examined him, ver. 8–10, but before the doom there breaketh out a promise of mercy. Thus mercy gets the start of justice, and triumpheth and rejoiceth over it in our behalf: James ii. 13, 'Mercy rejoiceth against judgment.'

3. They are considerable for their matter, for they intimate a victory over Satan, and that in the nature which was foiled so lately. Man by sin had not only incurred God's wrath, but put himself under the power of the devil, who had a legal power over fallen man, such as the executioner hath from the judge over the condemned person, and a tyrannical power by conquest, man being seduced by him from God. Therefore it is good news to hear of a victory over Satan, and that his power shall be destroyed.

In the former part of the verse you have the combat; in the text the success.

[1.] The conflict and combat: 'And I will put enmity between thee and the woman, and between thy seed and her seed.' It cannot be understood of the hatred and antipathy between men and serpents, though that be alluded unto. To what end should God thunder curses and condemnation upon the serpent, a brute creature, that understood them not? Therefore it is meant of the war between the devil and mankind, Satan and his instruments; for wicked men are called his seed: John viii. 44, 'Ye are of your father the devil;' and Ignatius calleth Menander and Basilides, τὴν τοῦ καηοῦ ὄφιος παραφύοιδα, 'the spawn of the old serpent.' And on the other side, the seed of the woman, by way of eminency, Christ and his confederates. But I shall not consider the conflict now as carried on between the two seeds, but between the two heads, Christ the prince of life, and the devil 'who hath the power of death,' Heb. ii. 14. It was begun between the serpent and the woman; it is carried on between the seed of the woman and the seed of the serpent: but the conflict is ended by the destruction of one of the heads; the prince of death is destroyed by the prince of life.

[2.] The success and issue of the combat. Where observe—(1.) What the seed of the woman doth against the serpent, 'He shall bruise thy head;' (2.) What the serpent doth against the seed of the woman, 'Thou shalt bruise his heel.'

(1.) There is something common to both; for the word *bruised* is used promiscuously both of the serpent and the seed of the woman. In this war, as usually in all others, there are wounds given on both sides; the devil bruiseth Christ, and Christ bruiseth Satan.

(2.) There is a disparity of the event, 'He shall bruise thy head,' and 'Thou shalt bruise his heel;' where there is a plain allusion to treading upon a serpent. Wounds on the head are deadly to serpents, but wounds in the body are not so grievous and dangerous; and a serpent trod upon, seeketh to do all the mischief it can to the foot by which it is crushed. The wound given to the head is mortal, but the wound given to the heel may be healed. The seed of the woman may be cured, but Satan's power cannot be restored. The devil cannot reach to the head, but the heel only, which is far from any vital part.

(1*st.*) For the first clause, 'It shall bruise thy head.' The seed of the woman crushed the serpent's head, whereby is meant the overthrow and destruction of his power and works: John xii. 31, 'Now shall the prince of this world be cast out;' 1 John iii. 8, 'For this purpose the Son of God was manifested, that he might destroy the works of the devil.' The head being bruised, strength and life is perished. His kingdom and strength is his head; that is gone, that $\kappa\rho\acute{a}\tau o\varsigma$ $\theta a\nu\acute{a}\tau o\nu$, 'that power of death,' Heb. ii. 14, the power to deceive and detain captive souls: Col. i. 13, 'Who hath delivered us from the power of darkness.'

(2*d.*) For the other clause, 'Thou shalt bruise his heel.' Where— (1.) Note the intention of the serpent, who would destroy the kingdom of the Redeemer if he could; but he can only reach the heel, not the head. (2.) The greatness of Christ's sufferings; his heel was bruised, as he endured the painful, shameful, accursed death of the cross.

Doct. That Jesus Christ, the seed of the woman, is at enmity with Satan, and hath entered the lists with him; and though bruised in the conflict, yet he finally overcometh him, and subverteth his kingdom.

I. That Jesus Christ is the seed of the woman. That he is one of her seed is past doubt, since he was born of the Virgin, a daughter of Eve. That he is 'The seed,' the most eminent of all the stock, appeareth by the dignity of his person, God made flesh: John i. 14, 'The Word was made flesh, and dwelt among us;' or, God manifested in the flesh,' 1 Tim. iii. 16. As also by his miraculous conception: Luke i. 35, 'The Holy Ghost shall come upon thee, and the power of the highest shall overshadow thee; therefore also that holy thing which shall be born of thee shall be called the Son of God.' So Mat. i. 23, 'A Virgin shall be with child, and shall bring forth a son, and they shall call his name Emanuel, which, being interpreted, is God with us.' He that was God-man in one person, and thus wonderfully conceived, without a male or company of man, might well be looked upon as the seed of the woman here spoken of. Now, if you ask what necessity there was that the conqueror should be the seed of the woman, because the flesh of Christ is the bread of life, and the food of our faith? I shall a little insist upon the conveniency and agreeableness of it.

1. That thereby he might be made under the law, which was given to the whole nature of man: Gal. iv. 4, 'God sent forth his Son, made of a woman, made under the law.' He that came to repair our lost condition needed to subject himself to the precepts of God's law, that by obedience he might recover what by disobedience was lost, and might be to us a fountain and pattern of holiness in our nature; and therefore Christ in our nature truly subjected himself, and conformed himself to the law of God, that general and moral law which all men are obliged unto. He performed the duties of the first table: Luke ii. 49, 'Wist ye not that I must be about my Father's business?' He took all occasions to glorify God. And the duties of the second table, as to his natural and reputed parents: Luke ii. 51, 'He went down with them, and was subject to them.'

2. That he might in the same nature suffer the penalty and curse of

the law, as well as fulfil the duty of it, and so make satisfaction for our sins, which as God he could not do. He was 'made sin for us,' 2 Cor. v. 21, and was 'made a curse for us,' Gal. iii. 13; Phil. ii. 8, 'He became obedient to death, even the death of the cross.' There was a curse denounced against those who yielded not personal obedience; and he came in the sinner's room to undergo it, that the justice of God might be eminently demonstrated, the lawgiver vindicated, and the breach that was made in the frame of government repaired, and God manifested to be holy, and an hater of sin, and yet the sinner saved from destruction.

3. That in the same nature which was foiled he might conquer Satan. As a tempter he conquered him hand to hand in a personal conflict, repelling his temptations, Mat. iv. As a tormentor, and one that had the power of death, so he conquered him by his death on the cross: Heb. ii. 14, 'Forasmuch as the children are partakers of flesh and blood, he also himself took part of the same, that through death he might destroy him that had the power of death, that is, the devil.' Christ would stoop to the greatest indignities to free us from this enemy, and to put mankind again into a condition of safety and happiness, that he having conquered, they might also conquer.

4. That he might take compassion of our infirmities, having experimented them in his own person. Therefore he assumed human nature that he might have assurance of this: Heb. ii. 17, 18, 'Wherefore in all things it behoved him to be like unto his brethren, that he might be a merciful and faithful high priest in things pertaining unto God, to make reconciliation for the sins of the people; for in that he himself hath suffered, being tempted, he is able to succour them that are tempted.' We have now assurance that he will pity us, more than one who is a stranger to our blood. He hath had trial of our nature and our miseries and temptations, and will be more sensible of the heart of a tempted man, and will mind and attend upon our business as his own.

5. That he might take possession of heaven for us in our nature: John xiv. 2, 3, 'I go to prepare a place for you; and if I go and prepare a place for you, I will come again, and receive you to myself, that where I am, there ye may be also.' The devil comes to depress our nature, and Christ came to exalt it; he endeavoured to make us lose paradise, and Christ gave us heaven. Man fallen is strangely haunted with doubts about the other world. Now he that came to save us and heal us did himself in our nature rise from the dead, that he might give us a visible demonstration of the life to come, which he had promised to us, that we might more regard the offer. He himself hath seized upon it, that the rest of the seed may be possessed of it; and hath carried our nature thither, that in time our persons may be translated.

6. That after he had been a sacrifice for sin, and conquered death by his resurrection, he might also triumph over the devil, and lead captivity captive, and give gifts to men in the very act of his ascension into heaven: Eph. iv. 8, 'Wherefore he saith, When he ascended on high, he led captivity captive, and gave gifts unto men.' Having foiled his enemies on the cross, it is fit he should triumph over them, to assure the world of his conquest, and give such a measure of his gifts

and graces to his church as might help them to scatter the ranks of the battle. His victory is shown to be complete as to the head; and as to the rest of the seed of the woman, who are all willing to enter into confederacy with him, he hath left ordinances and an almighty Spirit, that they may get to heaven after him.

II. That Christ is at enmity with Satan, and hath entered into the conflict with him.

1. We must state the enmity between Christ and his confederates, and Satan and his instruments. For it is said in the beginning of the verse, 'I will put enmity between thy seed and her seed;' which is principally to be understood of the Lord Christ, and of his confederates in the second place; against Satan in the first place, and his instruments on the other side. There is a double enmity which Christ hath against Satan, and so he undertakes the war against him as contrary to his nature and office.

[1.] There is a perfect enmity between the nature of Christ and the nature of the devil. The nature of Satan is sinful, murderous, and destructive; for it is said, he was 'a liar and murderer from the beginning,' John viii. 44; and 1 John iii. 8, 'He that committeth sin is of the devil; for the devil sinneth from the beginning: for this purpose the Son of God was manifested, that he might destroy the works of the devil;' again, ver. 12, 'Not as Cain, who was of that wicked one, and slew his brother: and wherefore slew he him? because his own works were evil, and his brother's righteous.' Now the nature of Christ is quite contrary. It is the devil's work to do all the hurt that he can to the bodies and souls of men; and it is Christ's work to do good, and only good: Acts x. 38, 'God anointed Jesus of Nazareth with the Holy Ghost and with power, who went about doing good, and healing all that were oppressed with the devil; for God was with him.' Christ did nothing by way of malice and revenge; he used not the power that he had to make men blind or lame, or to kill any; no, not his worst enemies, when he could easily do it, and justly might have done it. No; he went up and down giving sight to the blind, limbs to the lame, health to the sick, life to the dead. He rebuked his disciples when they tempted him to destroy some for their contempt by calling for fire from heaven, telling them they 'know not what manner of spirit they were of; for the Son of man is not come to destroy men's lives, but to save them,' Luke ix. 55, 56. It was unlike his spirit and design. All his miracles were acts of relief and favour, not pompous, not destructive; bating only two, the blasting the unfruitful fig-tree, which was an emblematical warning to the Jews, and suffering the devil to enter into the herd of swine, which was a necessary demonstration of the devil's malice and destructive cruelty, who, if he could not afflict and destroy men, would enter into the herd of swine, that the poor creatures might perish in the sea. Thus there was a perfect contrariety of nature between Christ and Satan.

[2.] An enmity proper to his office and design. For he came 'to destroy the works of the devil,' 1 John iii. 8; and was set up to dissolve that sin and misery which he had brought upon the world. The devil sought the misery and destruction of mankind, but Christ sought our salvation. Satan is the great destroyer of the creation, and Christ is the repairer of it. Now salvation and destruction are diametrically opposite; so are the kingdom of Christ and the kingdom of Satan, the function and office of Christ as a saviour, and the purpose and design of the devil as Abaddon, the destroyer. And therefore Christ proveth that he had not the least confederacy with Satan; for 'then his kingdom would be divided against itself, and how could it stand?' Mat. xii. 25, 26. It was impossible the Saviour could befriend the destroyer, or the destroyer the Saviour. No; their ends and designs are perfectly opposite.

Now, as there is such an enmity between Christ and Satan, so there is between the rest of the confederates on either side.

(1.) An enmity or contrariety of nature. The seed of the serpent inherits his venomous qualities; for as these are an estate opposite to God, so they are to the people of God, and seek their destruction by all cruel and bloody means. All people of a false religion, whether infidels, idolaters, or heretics, are of bloody and desperate principles, their minds being efferated by their false religion, and the influence of their great guide and leader, who is the devil: Jude 11, 'They have gone in the way of Cain.'

Let me instance in antichrist and his abettors and adherents, who is the devil's eldest son. Witness their bloody practices that have been acted on the stage of Christendom for so many years. What a deal of blood hath been sucked by these leeches in England in Queen Mary's days, in Germany, France, and the Netherlands! Witness of late their horrible slaughters in Ireland, Piedmont, and the hellish powder plot, the deliverance from which we commemorate this day; this was a flash of their malice, by which they would have blown up the whole state at once. On the other side, Christ conveyeth his holy, meek, and lamb-like nature to his sincere worshippers and followers. There is indeed a contrariety of nature to the carnal, so as they do not run with them into the same excess of riot, so as their righteous souls are vexed with the impure conversation of the wicked, so as they are grieved to see people go by droves to hell, and list themselves in the devil's service. But there is no destructive enmity. If they hate the wicked, it is with an hatred opposite to the love of complacency, but not with an hatred opposite to the love of good-will. There is an enmity to Satan, and his works, yet a pity to the persons inveigled and deceived by him. The wicked hate that holy disposition which is in the hearts of God's people, and therefore malign and persecute them. But on the other side there is a contrariety of disposition: Prov. xxix. 27, 'An unjust man is an abomination to the just, and he that is upright in the way is abomination to the wicked.' There is *odium offensionis*, but not *inimicitiæ*; an hatred of offence, but not of enmity. They bear with them with patience, pursue their recovery, strive to rescue poor captives out of the snares of the devil, but aim not at their destruction: 2 Tim. ii. 25, 26, 'In meekness instructing those that oppose themselves, if God peradventure will give them repentance to the acknowledging of the truth, and that they may recover themselves out of the snare of the devil, who are taken captive by him at his will.'

(2.) There is an enmity of design. As Christ actually employeth any as soldiers to fight under his banner, so they participate of the enmity of his design and office. Every private christian is one of Christ's soldiers; for we give up our faculties and powers as weapons: Rom. vi. 13, 'Yield yourselves unto God as those that are alive from the dead, and your members as instruments,' or weapons, ὅπλα, of righteousness unto God.' And the graces of the Spirit are called armour of light: Rom. xiii. 12, 'Let us cast off the works of darkness, and let us put on the armour of light.' And we are bidden 'to put on the whole armour of God, because we wrestle not against flesh and blood, but against principalities, against powers, against the rulers of the darkness of this world, against spiritual wickedness in high places,' Eph. vi. 11, 12. The ministers and those in a public station are leaders under Christ the general, and are by office and employment engaged in this warfare against the kingdom of the devil. And therefore the apostle biddeth Timothy to 'endure hardness as a good soldier of Jesus Christ,' 2 Tim. ii. 3; and the apostle says, 2 Cor. x. 4, 'The weapons of our warfare are not carnal, but mighty through God for the pulling down of strongholds.' They must set themselves against the devil and his kingdom.

2. The enmity being such between the seeds, Christ sets upon his business to destroy Satan's power and works.

[1.] His power. Satan hath a twofold power over fallen man—legal and usurped.

(1.) The legal power is that which the apostle calleth the power of death, and the terrors which follow upon it: Heb. ii. 14, 15, 'That through death he might destroy him that had the power of death, that is, the devil; and deliver them who through fear of death were all their lifetime subject to bondage.' The devil hath no power, as a judge, to condemn sinners: he is not *dominus mortis*, the Lord of death; but *minister mortis*, the minister of death; for, being condemned of God, the poor sinner is put into his hand that he may either terrify or stupefy him, and so more and more involve him in the curse of God's broken law; and also he may hasten his death and everlasting destruction.

(2.) Satan hath a tyrannical usurped power. So the devils are called 'rulers of the darkness of this world,' Eph. vi. 12, the blind, idolatrous, superstitious world; and Satan is called 'The prince of this world,' John xiv. 30, and 'The God of this world,' 2 Cor. iv. 4. God made him an executioner, but we make him a prince, a ruler, and a God. Now Christ, as a priest, disannulleth his legal power by his death and the merit of his sacrifice; and Christ, as a true king, and head both of men and angels, pulls down Satan as an usurper, delivers the poor captive souls out of his power; and as a prophet he discovereth his cheats and delusions.

[2.] His works. There is a twofold work of Satan—the work of the devil without us, or the work of the devil within us.

(1.) The work of the devil without us is a false religion, or those idolatries and superstitions by which Satan's reign and empire is upheld in the world. This is destroyed by the doctrine of the gospel, accompanied with the all-powerful Spirit of God. And therefore, when the gospel was first preached by Christ's messengers, the devil fell from that great and unlimited power which he had before in the world:

Luke x. 18, 'I beheld Satan as lightning fall from heaven.' It is an allusion to his first fall; as lightning flasheth and vanisheth, and never recollecteth itself again, so 'Now shall the prince of this world be cast out,' John xii. 31. When Christ did first set upon the redemption of mankind, the apostles went abroad to beat the devil, and hunt him out of his territories; and they did it with great effect. Therefore this is made one argument by which the Spirit doth convince us of the truth of the gospel: John xvi. 11, 'He shall convince the world of judgment, because the prince of this world is judged.' The silencing of his oracles, the suppressing of his superstitions, the destroying of the kingdom of wickedness and darkness, was an apparent evidence of the truth of the gospel. The old religion, by which the devil's kingdom was supported everywhere, went to wrack, no more the same temples, the same rites, the same gods; all was made to stoop and bow before God as worshipped in Christ.

(2.) There is the work of the devil within us. This concerneth the recovering particular persons out of the snare of the devil, who were taken captive by him at his will and pleasure. Here we must distinguish between the purchase and application. The purchase was made when Christ died: Col. ii. 15, 'Having spoiled principalities and powers, he made a show of them openly, triumphing over them in it;' that is, on his cross. Christ's death was Satan's overthrow; then was the deadly blow given to his power and kingdom. This was the price given for our ransom, and the great means of disannulling all that power Satan had before. The application is begun in our conversion; for then we are said to be turned from Satan unto God: Acts xxvi. 18, 'To open their eyes, and to turn them from darkness to light, and from the power of Satan unto God.' Then we are rescued out of the devil's clutches, and adopted into God's family, that, being made children, we may have a child's portion.

III. That in this conflict his heel was wounded, bitten, or bruised by the serpent.

1. Certain it is that Christ was bruised in the enterprise; which showeth how much we should value our salvation, since it costs so dear as the precious blood of the Son of God incarnate: 1 Peter i. 18, 19, 'Forasmuch as ye know that ye were not redeemed with corruptible things, as silver and gold, &c., but with the precious blood of Christ, as of a lamb without blemish and without spot.' He thought not his whole humiliation, from first to last, too much for the overthrowing of the devil's kingdom, nor any price too dear to redeem poor captive souls.

2. But how was he bruised by the serpent? Certainly on the one hand Christ's sufferings were the effects of man's sin and God's hatred against sin and his governing justice; for it is said, Isa. liii. 10, 'It pleased the Father to bruise him.' Unless it had pleased the Lord to bruise him, Satan could never have bruised him. On the other side, they were also the effects of the malice and rage of the devil and his instruments, who was now with the sword's-point and closing stroke with Christ, and doing the worst he could against him. In his whole life he endured many outward troubles from Satan's instruments; for all his life long he was a man of sorrows, wounded and bruised by Satan

and his instruments: John viii. 44, 'Ye are of your father the devil, and the lusts of your father ye will do ; he was a murderer from the beginning, and abode not in the truth, because there is no truth in him.' But the closing stroke was at last; then did the serpent most eminently bruise his heel. When Judas contrived the plot, it is said, the devil entered into him: Luke xxii. 3, 'Then entered Satan into Judas Iscariot, being one of the twelve.' When the high priest's servants come to take him, he telleth them, Luke xxii. 53, 'This is your hour, and the power of darkness.' The power of darkness at length did prevail so far as to cause his shameful death ; this was their day.

3. It was only his heel that was bruised. It could go no further ; for though his bodily life was taken away, yet his head and mediatory power was not touched: Acts ii. 36, 'This same Jesus whom ye have crucified, God hath made both Lord and Christ.' Again, his bodily life was taken away but for awhile. God would not leave his soul in the grave: Ps. xvi. 10, 'Thou wilt not leave my soul in hell, neither wilt thou suffer thy Holy One to see corruption.' The counsel and purpose of God concerning man's redemption had then been wholly frustrated : 'For if Christ be not risen, your faith is vain ; ye are yet in your sins,' 1 Cor. xv. 17. Once more, though Christ was bruised, yet he was not conquered. When the Jews and Roman soldiers were spoiling him, and parting his garments, then was he spoiling principalities and powers ; and when Satan and his instruments were triumphing over the Son of God, then was he triumphing over all the devils in hell, for by death he destroyed him that had the power of death. This was a necessary means of conquest; and Christ must overcome Satan by suffering himself to be overcome visibly by him. The devil doth not conquer Christ by death, but Christ doth conquer him. And still all the temptations of the devil are but the wounding of the heel ; the loss is not great to Christ or his members: as Dan is compared to 'a serpent by the way, or an adder in the path, that biteth the horse-heels, so that his rider shall fall backward, Gen. lxix. 17. Such is the craft of Satan ; he doth not usually bring temptations before our reason, but they enter in at the backdoor of sensual appetite ; but though he bite the heel, the life of grace is secured. Satan prevailed so far against Christ that his wicked instruments brought him to the cross, pursued him to the death there. But, 2 Cor. xiii. 4, 'Though he was crucified through weakness, yet he liveth by the power of God;' or, as it is in 1 Peter iii. 18, 'Being put to death in the flesh, but quickened by the Spirit.' So for christians, he may divers ways wound and afflict us in our outward interests, but the inner man is safe : 2 Cor. iv. 16, 'Though our outward man perish, yet the inward man is renewed day by day.' Nay, we may be bruised in the heel by divers temptations and slips into sin ; yet the vitals of grace are not hurt, there is no total extinction of our love to God.

I should come now to the fourth branch, that though Christ was bruised in the conflict, yet it endeth in Satan's total overthrow. His heel was bruised, but Satan's head was crushed. But of that anon.

In the meantime, by way of use, let me press you cheerfully to remember and celebrate this victory of Christ. The duty we are engaging in is an eucharist, and we come to rejoice in God our Saviour. Let me bespeak you, in the psalmist's words, Ps. xcviii. 1, 'O sing unto the Lord a new song, for he hath done marvellous things; his right hand and his holy arm have gotten him the victory;' or, Ps. cxviii. 15, 16, 'The voice of rejoicing and salvation is in the tabernacle of the righteous; the right hand of the Lord doth valiantly; the right hand of the Lord is exalted; the right hand of the Lord doth valiantly;' Ps. cvi. 2, 'Who can utter the mighty acts of the Lord? who can show forth all his praise?'

[1.] The conqueror is the seed of the woman, or the Son of God incarnate. Oh! let us bless God for so great a mercy: Luke i. 68–76, 'Blessed be the Lord God of Israel; for he hath visited and redeemed his people, and hath raised up an horn of salvation for us in the house of his servant David; as he spake by the mouth of his holy prophets, which have been since the world began: That we should be saved from our enemies, and from the hand of all that hate us; to perform the mercy promised to our fathers, and to remember his holy covenant, the oath which he sware to our father Abraham, that he would grant unto us, that we, being delivered out of the hands of our enemies, might serve him without fear, in holiness and righteousness before him all the days of our life.' What! shall the Son of God come from heaven to subdue the kingdom of Satan, and to deliver men from this bondage, and we be no more affected with it?

[2.] The manner of overcoming; it is by suffering a shameful, painful, and accursed death: Rev. i. 5, 6, 'Unto him that loved us, and washed us from our sins in his own blood, and made us kings and priests to God and his Father; to him be glory and dominion for ever and ever, Amen.' Again, 'Worthy is the Lamb that was slain to receive power, and riches, and wisdom, and strength, and honour, and glory, and blessing,' Rev. v. 12; and ver. 9, 'For thou wast slain, and hast redeemed us to God by thy blood, out of every kindred, and tongue, and people, and nation;' that by a death which he deserved not he should destroy the death which we deserved.

[3.] Who is overcome? The devil: Rev. xii. 10, 'Now is come salvation, and strength, and the kingdom of our God, and the power of his Christ; for the accuser of our brethren is cast down, who accused them before our God day and night;' ver. 11, 'And they overcame him by the blood of the Lamb, and the word of their testimony; and they loved not their lives unto the death;' ver. 12, 'Therefore rejoice, ye heavens, and ye that dwell in them: woe to the inhabitants of the earth and of the sea; for the devil is come down unto you, having great wrath, because he knoweth that he hath but a short time.' O christians! what will raise your hearts in thanksgiving to God, if not these three arguments which I have plainly mentioned to you? for the matter needeth no descants. The incarnation of the Son of God, who came as the seed of the woman, that he might free mankind from the power the devil had over them by sin. Then the merit and satisfaction of our Saviour, for he was bruised in his heel. And then the dissolution of Satan's power, and the freeing of mankind out of his hands, either as a tempter or a tormentor.

[4.] The effects of the victory when it is applied to us. I shall mention three—

(1.) Our conversion to God, and the destruction of sin in our hearts, or our actual deliverance from Satan: Luke xi. 21, 22, 'When a strong man armed keepeth his palace, his goods are in peace; but when a stronger than he shall come upon him, and overcome him, he taketh from him all his armour wherein he trusted, and divideth his spoils.' This was our case; all was in a sinful quiet and peace. When wind and tide go together, no wonder if their be a calm. Satan's suggestions and our corruptions suited the one with the other. But blessed be God that this carnal security is disturbed, that the kingdom of God is come upon us; that Christ, by a sacred rescue, hath dispossessed Satan, and destroyed sin. Oh! let us 'give thanks unto the Father, who hath made us meet to be partakers of the inheritance of the saints in light; who hath delivered us from the power of darkness, and translated us into the kingdom of his dear Son,' Col. i. 12, 13.

(2.) Remission of sins: Acts xxvi. 18, 'To open their eyes, and to turn them from darkness to light, and from the power of Satan unto God, that they may receive forgiveness of sins, and an inheritance among them that are sanctified, by faith that is in me;' Col. i. 13, 14, 'Who hath delivered us from the power of darkness, and translated us into the kingdom of his dear Son, in whom we have redemption through his blood, even the forgiveness of sins.' Christ's subjects have the privileges of his kingdom. Now 'bless the Lord, O my soul; and all that is within me, bless his holy name: bless the Lord, O my soul, and forget not all his benefits; who pardoneth all thy iniquities, and healeth all thy diseases,' Ps. ciii. 1–3.

(3.) Our own personal victory over Satan's temptations. In part now. We renew that covenant now, wherein we engaged to fight against Satan: 1 John ii. 14, 'I have written unto you young men, because ye are strong, and the word of God abideth in you, and ye have overcome the wicked one.' Fully hereafter: Rom. xvi. 20, 'The God of peace shall bruise Satan under your feet shortly.' The God of peace, as pacified in Christ. Now this is matter of thanksgiving: 1 Cor. xv. 57, 'Thanks be to God, who giveth us the victory through our Lord Jesus Christ;' that Christ will take us along with him in his triumphant chariot, and help our weak faith and faint hope, and that we may conquer the tempter and accuser.

IV. Though Christ's heel was bruised in the conflict, yet it endeth in Satans final overthrow; for his head was crushed, which noteth the subversion of his power and kingdom.

To explain this, we must consider—(1.) What is the power of Satan; (2.) How far Satan was destroyed by Christ.

First, What is the power of Satan? It lieth in sin. And Christ destroyed him, as he 'made an end of sin, and brought in everlasting righteousness, and made reconciliation for iniquities,' Dan. ix. 24; namely, as he reconciled man to God, and restored God's image and life eternal. In short, the power of Satan may be considered either as to single persons, or his interest in the corrupt world, or the sinful race of apostate Adam, who in their degenerate estate make up a confederacy or party, that may be called the kingdom of the devil.

1. As to single and individual persons; all his power over them is by reason of sin, which was introduced by his subtlety and malice.

There are three things in sin—the power, the guilt, the being.

Whilst any of these remain, Satan hath some power; and all these Christ came to dissolve, but by several means and at several times.

[1.] The devil's power lieth in the corruption of our natures; for men continuing in the apostasy from God are of Satan's party: Eph. ii. 1-3, 'And you hath he quickened, who were dead in trespasses and sins; wherein in time past ye walked, according to the course of this world, according to the prince of the power of the air, the spirit that now worketh in the children of disobedience; among whom also we all had our conversation in times past, in the lusts of our flesh, fulfilling the desires of the flesh, and of the mind.' This was the power that Satan had over us, to rule us and govern us by the lusts of the flesh. This was our daily walk and trade, without any remorse for it, or any desire to change our condition. And we are the more confirmed in it by the general and corrupt example of those among whom we live. Now, whilst we follow these sinful motions and suggestions, Satan is our prince and God; the corrupt nature maketh us readily to entertain his motions, and we 'are taken captive by him at his will and pleasure,' 2 Tim. ii. 26.

Now how doth Christ take away this power?

I answer—By converting grace, which is not only a turning from sin to God, but from Satan to God: Acts xxvi. 18, 'To open their eyes, and to turn them from darkness to light, and from the power of Satan to God;' whereby the reign of sin is broken; for as long as sin reigneth, Satan is in peaceable possession: Luke xi. 21, 'When a strong man armed keepeth his palace, his goods are in peace;' and the devil, who hath lost his seat in heaven, hath still a throne in the hearts of men, and lords it over them as his slaves. Now the reign of sin is broken when Christ puts an enmity into your hearts against it: 'I will put enmity between thy seed and her seed;' for sin dieth as your love to it dieth, and is mortified and subdued as your enmity increaseth. Well, then, they that are converted to God are possessed with a spirit of enmity to Satan and his ways, such as they had not before whilst they remained in the degenerate estate. Therefore it is said, Ezek. xxxvi. 26, 'A new heart will I also give to you, and a new spirit will I put within you;' such as none else have till the Redeemer work upon them: 1 Cor. ii. 12, 'We have received not the spirit of the world, but the Spirit which is of God.' The spirit which possesseth the generality of men is the worldly spirit that inclineth to earthly and sensual satisfactions; but this Spirit maketh them look after the great things promised by Christ, and the great things required by Christ; in short, a spirit quite opposite to the satanical spirit. The satanical spirit is contrary to God and man. To God: Col. i. 21, 'And you that were sometimes alienated, and enemies in your mind by wicked works, yet now hath he reconciled.' To man: James iv. 5, 'The spirit that dwelleth in us lusteth to envy.' But this spirit begetteth in us love to God and man, that we may seek his glory and the good of others. Now till this spirit be planted in us, we have not changed parties and masters. The being of sin is found in all, but the reign only in the unconverted; therefore the reign of sin must be broken by the dwelling of this spirit in us. Sin will put strongly for the throne again, but you must pray earnestly: Ps. cxix. 133, 'Order my steps in thy word;

and let not any iniquity have dominion over me.' And watch constantly, as ever mindful of your baptismal vow and covenant: Rom. vi. 11, 'Likewise reckon ye yourselves to be dead indeed unto sin, but alive unto God through Jesus Christ our Lord.' And then you will find Christ overcoming more and more the satanical spirit, and enlarging you into the liberty of God's children.

[2.] The guilt of sin, which is an obligation to punishment, and ariseth from the sentence of condemnation pronounced by the law against sinners. Our misery ariseth first from the violation of the precept of the law, and then from the sanction and penalty threatened. And so also therein lieth Satan's power, as we are obnoxious to the wrath of God; for therein he is the minister and executioner of death, as God maketh use of all his creatures according to their inclination. And so this wrathful revengeful creature is the instrument of his wrath. He hath an advantage against us by the law of God, the precepts whereof we have broken, and so incurred the penalty; and so Satan cometh on as one that hath the power of death. Those obstinate and careless souls who refuse the government of the Lord's grace and spirit are put into his hands; as 'when the Spirit of the Lord departed from Saul, an evil spirit from the Lord troubled him,' 1 Sam. xvi. 14. He doth or may terrify and afright the consciences of men with the dreadful expectation of death and the consequences of it, especially the sick and the dying. He that formerly tempted then beginneth to trouble; and he that formerly showed you the pleasant baits of sin will then show you the hook; he who now representeth pardon easy, will then represent it as impossible. And when death cometh, he hath power to hale away the sinner to torments; for as the good angels carry the souls of the faithful to Christ, Luke xvi. 22, 23, so probably the devil hath a power to carry them to hell. Now, as the devil hath this power of death, he bringeth men into sin that he may bring them into terror. Yea, Satan hath a great hand in the troubles of conscience which befall God's children.

Well, then, how is this power destroyed? By satisfying the law, Christ destroyeth the power of the devil. For first, 'he blotted out the handwriting that was against us,' and then 'spoiled principalities and powers,' Col. ii. 14, 15. And when he doth actually justify, we feel the comfort and benefit of it: Rom. viii. 33, 34, 'Who shall lay anything to the charge of God's elect? It is God that justifieth: who shall condemn? It is Christ that died, yea, rather, that is risen again, who is even at the right hand of God; who also maketh intercession for us.' Our advocate is more gracious in court than our accuser. Having paid our ransom, and interceding for us and pleading it, what accusation from the law can stand against those who have embraced this gospel?

[3.] The being of sin; for while it remaineth there is somewhat of Satan left which he worketh upon. There is a remnant of his seed in the best: the godly are yet in the way, but not at the end of the journey; and therefore he hath leave to assault them while they are here; but Christ will perfect the conquest which he has begun, and so the very being of sin shall at length be taken away: Jude 24, 'To him that is able to keep you from falling, and to present you faultless before the presence of his glory;' and Eph. v. 27, 'That he might present it to himself, a glorious church, without spot or wrinkle, or any such thing; but that it should be holy and without blemish.' At death sin is totally disannulled, the physician of our souls will then perfect the cure. As in the first moment of our birth we were sinners, so in the moment of our expiration all sin dieth. Christ taketh that time to finish his work. No sinner can enter into the state of bliss; but the veil of the flesh being rent, we are immediately admitted into the sight of God, and so made exactly perfect.

2. As to the general case, or his interest in the corrupt world. It is true the kingdom of Satan yet remaineth; but he doth and shall divide the spoil with the strong: Isa. liii. 12, 'Therefore will I divide him a portion with the great, and he shall divide the spoil with the strong.' And though his doctrine and religion meeteth with opposition in the world, yet it doth prevail upon opposition, and against opposition, and by opposition; when in the seasons of it he cometh to set his kingdom on foot: Rev. vi. 2, 'I saw a white horse, and he that sat on him had a bow, and a crown was given unto him; and he went forth conquering and to conquer.' This is an emblematical representation of the rise and progress of Christ's kingdom. Where you may note his furniture, a crown and a bow. The crown noteth his dignity, the bow his armour and strength: Ps. xlv. 3–5, 'Gird on thy sword upon thy thigh, O thou most mighty, with thy glory and majesty; and in thy majesty ride prosperously, because of truth, and meekness, and righteousness; and thy right hand shall teach thee terrible things: thine arrows are sharp in the heart of the king's enemies, whereby the people fall under thee.' Christ having the grant of a kingdom over the nations, is every way furnished with power to obtain it, by means proper to the mediatory dispensation, by his word, Spirit, and providence.

[1.] His word, which is called 'The rod of his strength,' Ps. cx. 2; 'The weapons of our warfare are not carnal, but mighty through God,' 2 Cor. x. 4. When Christ will work, the world cannot resist its convincing power; those that feel it not fear it: John iii. 20, 'Every one that doeth evil hateth the light, neither cometh to the light, lest his deeds should be reproved.'

[2.] His Spirit. Now what can stand before the mighty Spirit of God, convincing men of the truth of his religion? John xvi. 8–11, 'And when he is come, he will reprove the world of sin, and of righteousness, and of judgment: of sin, because they believe not on me: of righteousness, because I go to the Father, and ye see me no more: of judgment, because the prince of this world is judged.' Showing hereby Christ was the Messiah, and therefore they were guilty of great sin who did not believe on him; that he was a righteous and innocent person, and no seducer, because Christ rose from the dead and went to the Father; that he was an exalted prince, above Satan, and whatever things were looked upon as divine powers. Many that were not converted were convinced of this.

[3.] His providence. All judgment was put into Christ's hands, to be improved for the advancement of his mediatory kingdom: John v. 22, 'For the Father judgeth no man, but hath committed all judgment to the Son.' He hath the government of all things, angels, and all events that fall out in the world. None of the creatures are left to their own arbitrament or uncertain contingencies, but under the government of a supreme providence, which is left in Christ's hands. Thus you see, though the devil's interest be held up by the combined interests of the world agreeing together to promote the idolatries and superstitions wherewith he hath inspired them, yet Christ is able to break and dissolve all this force and power.

Secondly, How far was Satan destroyed or his head crushed?
1. Negatively.

[1.] *Non ratione essentiæ*, not to take away his life and being. No; there is a devil still, and shall be, even when the whole work of Christ's redemption is finished; for then it is said, Rev. xx. 10, 'The devil that deceived them was cast into the lake of fire and brimstone, where the beast and the false prophet are, and shall be tormented day and night for ever and ever.' So Mat. xxv. 41, 'Depart from me, ye cursed, into everlasting fire, prepared for the devil and his angels.' Then eternal judgment is executed on the head of the wicked state. Sentence was passed before, and the devil feareth it: Mat. viii. 29, 'Art thou come hither to torment us before the time?' He was condemned before, but then it is executed upon him; he is finally punished, and shall for ever remain with the damned.

[2.] *Non ratione malitiæ*, not in regard of malice; for the enmity ever continueth between the two seeds, and Satan will be doing though it be always to loss: 1 John iii. 8, 'The devil sinneth from the beginning.' Therefore he is not so destroyed as if he did no more desire the ruin and destruction of men. He is as malicious as ever. The devil is always at the old trade of destroying souls, and watcheth all advantages, and observeth our motions and inclinations, to make use of them.

2. Affirmatively, it remaineth that it is *ratione potentiæ*, in regard of his power. But the question returneth, How far is his power destroyed? for he still governeth the wicked, and possesseth a great part of the world. Therefore the devils are called, Eph. vi. 12, 'The rulers of the darkness of this world.' He molesteth the godly, whether considered singly and apart, or in their communities and societies. Singly and apart he may sometimes trouble them and sorely shake them, as wheat is winnowed in a sieve: Luke xxii. 31, 'Simon, Simon, behold, Satan hath desired to have you, that he may sift you as wheat.' And in their communities and societies: Ps. cxxix. 1, 2, 'Many a time have they afflicted me from my youth, may Israel now say: many a time have they afflicted me from my youth.'

Ans. Though he may afflict and molest the people of God, yet he cannot totally prevail over them.

[1.] There is enough done by way of merit to break the power of Satan, or that whole kingdom of darkness which is united under one head called the devil. The price and ransom is fully paid for captive souls: 'The Lamb of God taketh away the sin of the world,' John i. 29. There need no more to be done by way of merit and satisfaction to bruise the serpent's head and to dissolve that woful work which he hath introduced into the world. Now, not only the comfort of particular believers is ascribed to the death of Christ, but the success of the gospel over false religions; as 1 Peter i. 18, 'Forasmuch as ye know that ye were not redeemed with corruptible things, as silver and gold, from your vain conversation, received by tradition from your fathers, but with the precious blood of Christ.' He purchased the power of recovering souls out of their apostasy at a dear rate. Therefore, though the superstitions of the world were entailed on people by a long descent, yet when we go forth to preach the gospel in the virtue and value of the blood of Christ, that will work mighty wonders for the destruction of the kingdom of the devil.

[2.] Christ is upon the throne, and we are under his protection; therefore the devil cannot totally prevail as to those who have interest in him. As to single believers: John x. 28, 'None is able to pluck them out of my hand.' Or as to their communities and societies: Mat. xvi. 18, 'Upon this rock will I build my church, and the gates of hell shall not prevail against it.' The gates of hell signify the power and policy of hell, for there was their armoury and their counsel. Christ expecteth their most subtle and furious assaults, but all should be but as the dashing of waves against a rock, end in foam, and shame to the aggressors and assailants. So that besides his merit on the cross, there is his power in heaven, as now sitting upon the throne.

[3.] The victory is carried on so as that our duty and trials may not be excluded.

(1.) Though Satan's head be crushed, yet still there is room for our duty, that we may use the means for our safety, as good soldiers of Christ, and live as in a continual fight. These are set down, 1 Peter v. 8, 9, 'Be sober and vigilant, because your adversary the devil, as a roaring lion, walketh about, seeking whom he may devour; whom resist steadfast in the faith.'

(1*st.*) Sobriety, or an holy moderation as to the comforts and delights of the present life. The devil, the flesh, and the world are in conspiracy. By the baits of the world he enticeth our flesh to a neglect of God and heavenly things; therefore we must use the world as if we used it not, lest our hearts be burdened and depressed, and disabled from seeking after our great end and happiness.

(2*d.*) Vigilancy and watchfulness is necessary, that we may stand upon our guard, avoiding snares, and forecasting hazards, lest we fall as a ready prey into the mouth of the tempter: 1 Cor. xvi. 13, 'Watch ye, stand fast in the faith, quit yourselves like men, be strong.' The first point of a christian soldier is to watch; conscience must stand porter at the door, examining what cometh in and what goeth out. The devil watcheth all advantages against us, that he may spy where we are weakest; and if the enemy watch and we sleep, we cannot be safe.

(3*d.*) Steadfast resistance in the faith. When we are yielding, Satan gets ground; but when we believingly and steadfastly resist, he is discouraged. This steadfast resistance in the faith is—(1.) Adhering to the privileges of the gospel as our happiness; (2.) Persevering in the duties thereof as our work; resolving not to let go our hold, but by patient continuance in well-doing to wait for the mercy of our Lord Jesus unto eternal life. Now if Christ should so destroy the devil as to exempt from this duty, the whole gospel would be in vain, and the promises and precepts of it to no purpose, and all the furniture of grace which Christ hath purchased for us and promised to us be lost and useless. Surely Christ hath not so crushed the serpent's head but that we need to be sober and watchful and steadfast in the faith ; otherwise we were not his soldiers, but his enemies.

(2.) Not to exempt us from trials of our sincerity. God will have all obedience to be tried and honoured by opposition, and sometimes by sharp and grievous opposition : Rev. ii. 10, ' The devil shall cast some of you into prison, that you may be tried.' Thus Job was remitted to Satan for his trial : chap. i. 12, ' And the Lord said unto Satan, Behold, all that he hath is in thy power.' And Paul had his messenger of Satan for his trial, to see what shift he could make, with sufficient internal grace under outward and vexatious evils, 2 Cor. xii. 7–10. Now better undergo the fiery trial than the fiery torment. Tried we are then, but not destroyed. God may let loose the wolf to drive us into the fold, and exercise us with temptations, but not suffer us to be overwhelmed.

[4.] In the external management of the mediatorial kingdom there are many vicissitudes and interchanges of the outward condition of the church. Sometimes God doth notably defeat Satan and his instruments, and the devil's kingdom visibly goeth to wrack ; as at the first promulgation of the gospel, though the world was captivated under Satan, rooted in former superstitions, yet Christ prevailed and got ground by the rod of his strength and the word of his kingdom, though Satan everywhere had his temples wherin he was worshipped and his oracles were resorted to with great reverence. Till the Hebrew child silenced him, he ate the fat of their sacrifices, and drank the wine of their drink-offerings, yea, often the blood of their sons and daughters, whom they sacrificed to him ; yet all of a sudden his strongholds were demolished, the idols broken, whom they and their fathers had worshipped and prayed unto in their distresses and adversities, and blessed in their prosperities ; the temples broken down, the altars polluted and set at nought, and the world turned from these vanities to the living God. But a little while after the fires were kindled, and the professors of the true religion were butchered and slaughtered ; but then ' they overcame him by the blood of the Lamb, and by the word of their testimony, and not loving their lives unto the death,' Rev. xii. 11. So that when the church seemed weakest and her enemies strongest, then she had more for her than against her. When Satan's instruments were killing christians, then they were pulling down Satan's throne and advancing Christ's ; so that it is better to be a simple soldier on Christ's side than commander of a whole army against him. When the persecutors had done, Satan raised up heretics in the church, as worms that bred in the body, and devoured it ; yet Christ confounded them, and in a little time brake each sect in pieces, and those that were the great scourge and vexation of one age were scarce known to the next but by their names and some obscure reports. The light of the gospel did soon scatter these mists as soon as they did arise. Last of all came the great apostasy of antichristianism, whereby the simplicity of the christian doctrine was turned into school niceties, the worship of the gospel into a theatrical pomp and the pageantry of ridiculous ceremonies, and the discipline of the church into a temporal domination; and all this supported by the blood of the saints and worldly grandeur, and the combined interests of many popish nations. And here are the ebbs and flows between the two shores of Christ and antichrist amongst us. You know by what a bloody design Hagar the bondwoman, that was cast out, sought to weaken and vaunt it over Sarah; but the Lord broke the snare, and our foot is escaped.

[5.] If the promised seed had not bruised the serpent's head the world had been in a worse case than it is. There is some conviction and restraint where conversion taketh not place. Consider how Satan reigneth where Christ hath not pursued him with his gospel, or where Christ hath withdrawn his gospel for the ingratitude of men. Surely there is a difference between the places where people live in the dregs of christianity, and there where the devil is worshipped and idolatry set up.

[6.] Though there be not a total destruction of the kingdom of Satan, yet it is in an absolute subjection to the throne of the mediator. The kingdom of sin and Satan are so far destroyed as not to hinder the demonstration of mercy to the elect, and as to be subservient to the demonstration of his justice to others, who neglect or contemn the remedy offered, which is God's great design that the elect may obtain, though the rest be hardened.

[7.] That in time Christ will destroy all opposite reigns and kingdoms. He doth some sooner, others later; but there will be an universal and absolute subjection to Christ at the day of judgment. Infernal spirits shall then bow the knee to him, Phil. ii. 10, with Rom. xiv. 10, 11, and that with Isa. xlv. 23. Then saints shall judge angels, 1 Cor. vi. 2, and the whole mystery of iniquity will then be finished and come to nothing.

Use 1. Thankfulness and praise to our mediator. The eternal God hath selected a people from the rest of the world to praise him for the mystery of his love here in the assemblies of his people; for 'God inhabiteth the praises of Israel,' Ps. xxii. 3; and hereafter, that he may have the thanks of his glorified saints for ever. Consider to this end how Satan's design is crossed and counterworked in the mystery of our redemption.

1. Satan's design was to dishonour God by a false representation, as if envious of man's happiness: Gen. iii. 5, 'God doth know that in the day that ye eat thereof, then your eyes shall be opened, and ye shall be as gods, knowing good and evil.' And so to weaken the esteem of God's goodness. Now in the work of our redemption God is wonderfully magnified, and represented as amiable to man; not envying our knowledge and delight, but promoting it by all means, even with great care and cost: 1 John iv. 8, 'God is love.'

2. To depress the nature of man, that in innocency stood so near God. Now that the human nature, so depressed and abased by the malicious suggestions of the devil, should be so elevated and advanced, and be set up far above the angelical nature, and admitted to dwell with God in a personal union, oh! let us now cheerfully remember and celebrate this victory of Christ. Our praise now is a pledge of our everlasting triumph. This table is spread for us in the sight of our

enemies, and we come to have intimate communion and fellowship with him at his table.

Use. 2. To exhort us to make use of Christ's help for our recovery out of the defection and apostasy of mankind. Oh! let Satan be crushed in you, and the old carnal nature destroyed. He that so willingly entered into the conflict on the cross, though his heel were bruised, will as willingly employ the power of the Spirit to help you; the one was in order to the other. Christ doth not only enter upon the work by conquest, but hath much to do with every individual person before he can settle his kingdom in their hearts. There is a combat between Christ and Satan for the rescue of every sinner, and we are not easily brought to change masters. Now yield to him, suffer him to save you. You look to the outward interest of Christ in the world, and you do well; but it is easier to bring men to own a true religion than to bring them under the power of it. Christ's greatest victory is the overcoming men's corruptions and carnal inclinations, to purify their polluted souls, and to set up Christ's government in the heart, where once Satan ruled. The kingdom of Christ within us is the most excellent kingdom: Luke xi. 20, 'If I with the finger of God cast out devils, no doubt the kingdom of God is come upon you.' If once we become Christ's, we will more really care for his interest in the world.

Use 3. To show us the nature of Christ's victory, and wherein it consisteth; not in an exemption from troubles, nor in a total exemption from sin for the present.

1. Not in an exemption from troubles. No; you must expect conflicts. Though Satan's deadly power be taken away, our heel may be crushed. Christ hath delivered us from the present evil world: Gal. i. 4, 'Who gave himself for us, that he might redeem us from this present evil world.' Not that the world should trouble us no more, but that the world should not be a snare to us. He came not to exempt us from trouble, but 'to save us from our sins,' Mat. i. 21; 'To deliver us from wrath to come,' 1 Thes. i. 10. We have the victory which he purchased for us, if the devil and the world do not hinder the fruition of eternal glory. Our victory over Satan is mostly gotten by patience even to the death; and so those that are killed all the day long are 'more than conquerers through him that loved them,' Rom. viii. 35–37. Satan's main spite is not at your worldly interests, but your souls. God may give him sometimes a power over your worldly and bodily interests, but he doth not give him a power over your souls. Though he get his will over your bodies, yet, if he get not his will over your souls, it is you that conquer, and not Satan; therefore in the christian sense suffering is conquering. If he do not draw you away from God and Christ, though he and his instruments have great power over you, it is your heel only is bruised, but your head is safe.

2. It is not a total exemption from sin. Necessary vital grace is only absolutely secured; you shall receive no deadly wound to destroy your salvation. The godly sometimes may be foiled. Satan stirred up David to number the people: 2 Cor. xi. 2, 3, 'I am jealous over you with a godly jealousy; for I have espoused you to one husband, that I may present you as a chaste virgin to Christ: for I fear lest by any

means, as the serpent beguiled Eve through his subtlety, so your minds should be corrupted from the simplicity that is in Christ;' 1 Cor. vii. 5, 'That Satan tempt you not for your incontinency.' Yea, God may employ Satan in punishing his people; as when the Israelites murmured, 'he sent evil angels among them,' Ps. lxxviii. 49, and 'they were destroyed of the destroyer,' 1 Cor. x. 10. Because careless souls are apt to fall asleep, God permitteth him to be the executioner of his indignation.

Use 4. To animate and encourage Christ's servants in their war against Satan's kingdom, at home and abroad, within and without: 'Not to give place to the devil,' Eph. iv. 27. Christ whom we serve is more able to save than Satan is to destroy.

1. The devil is a creature, but Christ is the sovereign Lord, who hath power over him and all creatures. The devil's tempting is by leave: Job i. 12, 'And the Lord said unto Satan, Behold, all that he hath is in thy power;' Luke xxii. 31, 'And the Lord said, Simon, Simon, behold, Satan hath desired to have you, that he may sift you as wheat.' He could not enter into the herd of swine without leave from Christ: Mat. viii. 31, 'So the devils besought him, saying, If thou cast us out, suffer us to go away into the herd of swine.' When we are in Satan's hands, Satan is in God's hands.

2. The devil is an usurper, Christ is the heir of all things. Satan is the god of this world by usurpation, but by lawful ordination Jesus is both Lord and Christ: Acts ii. 36, 'Therefore let all the house of Israel know assuredly that God hath made that same Jesus, whom ye have crucified, both Lord and Christ.'

3. The devil hath only a persuasive force, no constraining efficacy. He cannot change the heart, or create any new principles and habits there, which were not before. But God can 'put his law into our inward parts, and write it in our hearts,' Jer. xxxi. 35. He can only propound alluring baits or objects to the outward senses and fancy, but God worketh immediately on the heart.

4. If the devil be vigilant and assiduous in his temptations, he is matched and overmatched. Christ is always mindful of the affairs of his people; he doth ever make intercession for us before God: 'And he that keepeth Israel shall neither slumber nor sleep,' Ps. cxxi. 4. Satan daily bloweth the bellows, inflaming our corruptions, suggesting temptations; but the Spirit is as watchful in our hearts, maintaining his interest there.

5. The devil's malice is restrained, for he is held in chains of darkness: 2 Peter ii. 4, 'If God spared not the angels that fell, but cast them down to hell, and delivered them into chains of darkness to be reserved unto judgment;' meaning thereby not only the powerful restraints of providence, but the horror of their own despairing fears. Chains imply restraint, but chains of darkness, horror. He himself believeth and trembleth: James ii. 19, 'Thou believest that there is one God, thou doest well; the devils also believe and tremble.'

6. The Lord Jesus doth often give out demonstrations of his power and providence. Partly in protecting, strengthening, assisting his people, and prospering their just endeavours for the advancement of his kingdom, so that all the machinations of the wicked against them

come to nought. Partly in making fearful havoc and destruction in Satan's kingdom. In protecting his people, sometimes he destroyeth their enemies: Isa. xxvii. 4, 'Who would set the briers and thorns against me in battle? I would go through them, I would burn them together.' Sometimes infatuateth their counsels: Job v. 12–14, 'He disappointeth the devices of the crafty, so that their hands cannot perform their enterprise: he taketh the wise in their own craftiness, and the counsel of the froward is carried headlong. They meet with darkness in the daytime, and grope in the noonday as in the night.' Sometimes he hideth his people in the secret of his presence: Ps. xxxi. 20, 'Thou shalt hide them in the secret of thy presence from the pride of man; thou shalt keep them secretly in a pavilion from the strifes of tongues.' He smiteth his enemies by an invisible curse: Job xx. 26, 'All darkness shall be hid in his secret places; a fire not blown shall consume him; it shall go ill with him that is left in his tabernacle.' He divideth them: 2 Chron. xx. 23, 'The children of Ammon and Moab rose up against the inhabitants of Mount Seir, utterly to slay and destroy them; and when they had made an end of the inhabitants of Seir every one helped to destroy another.' Christ is the assailant, and makes fearful havoc in the devil's kingdom. The word of truth is come into all the world, and pulleth down idolatrous and false worship: Col. i. 6, 'The word of truth is come unto you, as it is in all the world, and bringeth forth fruit, as it doth also in you, since the day you heard of it, and knew the grace of God in truth.

SERMONS UPON GENESIS XXIV. 63.

SERMON I.

And Isaac went out to meditate in the field at the even-tide.—
GEN. xxiv. 63.

THE context is spent in describing the journey of Rebekah with Abraham's servant, and the text showeth the occasion of the first interview between Isaac and Rebekah; he goeth out into the fields to meditate, and of a sudden he seeth the camels coming.

I cannot pass by this accident without some remark and observation. Isaac goeth to meet with God, and he meeteth with God and Rebekah too Godliness hath the promises of this life and that which is to come; there is nothing lost by duty and acts of piety and worship. Seneca said the Jews were an unhappy people, because they lost the seventh part of their lives, meaning the time spent in the sabbath. This is the sense of nature, to think all lost that is bestowed on God. Flesh and blood snuffeth and crieth, What a weariness is it! and what need all this waste? Oh! let me tell you, by serving God you drive on two cares at once. Worldly interests many times are cast into the way of religion, and, besides the main design, these things are added to us. Wonderful are the providences of God in and about duties of worship. Some have gone aside to pray, and escaped such as lay in wait to destroy them; and Luther tells a story of one that balked a duty and fell into a danger, passed by a sermon, and was presently surprised by thieves. Others there are that thought of nothing but meeting God in his worship, and God hath made their duties an occasion of advancing their outward comforts. Certainly it is good to obey all impulses of the Spirit; there may be somewhat of providence as well as grace in it: 'Isaac went out to meditate in the field at the even-tide; and he lift up his eyes and saw, and behold the camels were coming.'

In the words you have several circumstances: the person, 'Isaac;' his work, 'He went out to meditate;' the place, 'In the field;' the time, 'At even-tide.'

1. For the person, Isaac, I need not say much, because I would not digress. He was Abraham's son, and God said of Abraham, Gen. xviii. 19, 'I know him, that he will command his children, and his household after him, and they shall keep the way of the Lord, to do justice and judgment, that the Lord may bring upon Abraham that

which he hath spoken of him.' Good education leaveth a savour and tincture upon the spirit, at least an awe and a care of duties and exercises of religion; and therefore it is no wonder to hear of Abraham's son that had been trained up in the way of the Lord, to go out to meditate; it is a seal of the blessing of education. again Isaac was now in his youth; certainly he could not be very old. Sarah was ninety years old when the promise was first made to her of a son: Gen. xvii. 17, 'Then Abraham fell upon his face and laughed, and said in his heart, Shall a child be born unto him that is an hundred years old? and shall Sarah, that is ninety years old, bear?' Now Sarah was but one hundred and twenty-seven years old when she died, Gen. xxiii. 1, and this match was immediately after her death; for just as he received Rebekah he left off his mourning for Sarah: Gen. xxiv. 67, 'And Isaac brought her into his mother Sarah's tent, and took Rebekah, and she became his wife; and he loved her: and Isaac was comforted after his mother's death.' Probably Isaac was now a little above thirty. Isaac, a young man, that was now entering into the world, goeth out to meditate. Usually we make religious exercises the work of grey hairs, and after we have spent the heat and flower of our spirits in the vanities of the world, we hope to make amends for all by a severe and devout retirement. Young and green heads look upon meditation as a dull melancholy work, fit only for the phlegm and decay of old age; vigorous and eager spirits are more for action than thoughts, and their work lieth so much with others that they have no time to descend into themselves. But the elder world was more innocent; the exercises of Isaac's youth were pious; he went out into the fields to meditate.

2. To open his work to you, 'to meditate,' or, as it is in the margin, to pray, לָשׂוּחַ, the word used in the original is indifferent to both senses; it properly signifies muttering, or an imperfect and suppressed sound. The Septuagint sometimes renders it by $ἀείδεω$, to sing, but here they render it by $ἀδολεσχῆσαι$, which signifies to exercise himself, and most properly a sportive exercise, as if his going abroad had been only to sport and recreate himself after the toil of the day. But that is not so probable; the Holy Ghost would not put such a mark upon such a circumstance. Therefore I suppose the Septuagint's word must be taken more largely to comprise also a religious exercise. But how is it? To pray or meditate? I would not recede from our own translation without weighty cause; most other translations look that way. Symmachus renders it $λαλῆσαι$, to speak; Aquila, $ὁμιλῆσαι$, to discourse as with others, that is, with God and his own soul; and so it suiteth with the force of the original word, which properly signifies to mutter, or such a speaking as is between thoughts and words. So that the meaning is, he went aside privately to discourse of God, and the promises, and of heavenly things.

3. The place, 'In the field.' Partly for privacy; deep thoughts require a retirement. Many of David's psalms were penned in the wilderness. He that would have the company of God and his own thoughts had need go aside from other company, and be alone that he may not be alone, that the mind, being sequestered from all distractions, may solace itself the more freely in these heavenly thoughts: Exod. iii. 1, 'Moses led the flock to the back-side of the desert and came to

the mountain of God, even to Horeb.' He goeth aside from the other shepherds, that he might converse with the great shepherd and bishop of our souls, and there he seeth the vision of the burning bush. When God would communicate his loves to the church, he inviteth her into the wilderness: Hosea ii. 14, 'Therefore behold I will allure her, and bring her into the wilderness, and speak comfortably unto her.' The most familiar and intimate converses between God and the church are in private. So the spouse inviteth the bridegroom: Cant. vii. 11, 'Come, my beloved, let us go forth into the field, let us lodge in the villages.' In these solitary and heavenly retirements, to which no eyes are conscious and privy, we have most experience of God and of ourselves. Duties done in company are more easy; byends and man's eye and observance may have an influence upon our worship, and therefore meditation is difficult and tedious, because it is a work of retirement, that hath approbation from none but our Father that seeth in secret. Partly because the field is an help to meditation, fancy and invention being elevated and raised by the sweetness, variety, and pleasure of it, there being on every side so many objects and lively memorials of God. However in this sense the circumstance is not binding. Some do better in a closet than in a field or garden, where the senses being locked from all other objects, the mind may fall more directly upon itself, which otherwise in a field or garden would skip from object to object, without pitching upon any seriously.

4. The last circumstance in the text is the time, 'In the even-tide,' which is also a matter of an arbitrary concernment. Time in itself is but an inactive circumstance; all hours are alike to God; he taketh no more pleasure in the sixth or ninth hour than in the first hour; only you should prudently observe when your spirit is most fresh and smart. To some the morning is quickest, the fancy being fittest to offer spiritual and heavenly thoughts, before it hath received any images and representations from carnal objects abroad. Morning thoughts are, as it were, the virgin thoughts of the mind, before they have been prostituted to these inferior and baser objects, and so are more pure, sublime, and defecate; and then the soul, like the hind of the morning, with a swift and nimble readiness climbeth up to the mountains of myrrh and frankincense: Cant. iv. 6, 'Until the day break, and the shadows flee away, I will get me to the mountain of myrrh, and to the hill of frankincense;' and it tendeth much to season the whole day when we can talk with the law in the morning: Prov. vi. 22, 'When thou awakest, it shall talk with thee.' To some the evening seemeth fitter, that, when the gayishness and vanity of the spirit hath been spent in business, their thoughts may be more serious and solemn with God; and after the weights have been running down all day through their employments of the world, they may wind them up again at night in these recesses and exercises of piety and religion; as David says, Ps. xxv. 1, 'Unto thee, O Lord, do I lift up my soul.' To others the silence and stillness of the night seemeth to be an help, and because of the curtain of darkness that is drawn between them and the world, they can the better entertain serious and solemn thoughts of God. David speaks everywhere in the psalms of his nocturnal devotions: Ps. lxiii. 6, 'When I remember thee upon my bed, and meditate on thee in the

night-watches.' The expression is taken from the custom of the Jews, who divided the night into so many watches. <u>Whilst others were reposing their bodies on their beds, David was reposing his soul in the bosom of God, and he gave the less rest to his eyes that he might give the more to his soul.</u> So Ps. cxix. 148, 'Mine eyes prevent the night-watches, that I might meditate in thy word.' Certainly in the night, when we are taken off from other business, we have the greatest command of our thoughts, and the covert of darkness that God hath stretched over the world begetteth a greater awe and reverence. Therefore Mr Greenham, when he pressed any weighty point, and perceived any careless, used to beg of them that, if God by his providence should suffer them to awake in the night, they would but think of his words. Certainly the mind, being by sleep emptied of other cares, like a mill falleth upon itself, and the natural awe and terror which is the effect of darkness helpeth to make the thoughts more solemn and serious. So that you see much may be said for the conveniency of either of these seasons, evening, or morning, or night. It is your duty to be faithful to your own souls, and sometimes to take the advantage either of the night, or of the day, or of the morning, or of the evening, as best suits us. David saith, Ps. cxix. 97, 'Oh! how love I thy law! it is my meditation all the day.' So he describes his blessed man: Ps. i. 2, 'His delight is in the law of the Lord, and in his law doth he meditate day and night;' that is, sometimes in the day, and sometimes in the night; no time can come amiss to a prepared spirit. Isaac's hour was in the even-tide; in the evening he went out to meditate, in which two things are notable—

[1.] That he made duty his refreshment. He had wrought all the day, and in the evening he goeth to recreate himself with God. What a shame is it that what was his solace is our burden! If we had a spiritual discerning, we should soon see that there is no delight to that of duty, and no refreshment like that which we enjoy in the exercises of religion and in communion with God. The world's delights are vain and dreggy; they may provoke laughter, but they cannot yield any pure, solid, and true contentment. It was Christ's meat to do his Father's will: John iv. 34, 'My meat is to do the will of him that sent me, and to finish his work.' It was sweeter to Job than his appointed food to hear God's word: Job xxiii. 12, 'I have esteemed the words of his mouth more than my necessary food.' And David saith, Ps. cxix. 54, 'Thy statutes have been my songs in the house of my pilgrimage.' All the comfort he had to drive away the sad and disconsolate hours of his pilgrimage was to exercise himself in the study and meditation of God's word. And it was Isaac's evening comfort to go out and meditate. <u>Gracious hearts must have spiritual delights, the word, and obedience, and prayer, and meditation.</u> As one said, *Aut hoc non est evangelium, aut nos non sumus christiani*—Either these histories are not true, or our hearts are much unlike theirs. Oh! how sweet would it be if we could make duty a recreation and our work our pleasure; that in the close of the day this might be our solace, after the work of the day to take a turn with God in the mount, and to walk in the garden of love, and, as David saith, Ps. civ. 34, 'My meditation of him shall be sweet; I will be glad in the Lord.' Isaac went out at even-tide.'

[2.] That at the evening his spirit was still fresh and savoury ; this was the time not of necessity, but choice. Many spend their heat and strength in the world, toiling all day, and in the evening come and offer God a drowsy yawning prayer, when all the vigour of their spirits is wasted. You should bring forth the best wine at last ; never so engage in the world as to hinder a duty. It should be the wisdom of christians to guide their affairs with such judgment that duties may not become a burden and a weariness. Now a soul encumbered with business cannot act with such delight and freedom as it ought. Too often do we suffer the lean kine to devour the fat. Mary hath cause to complain of Martha ; so much time is spent in the world that we have no heart or strength for communion with God ; and usually when all are asleep and wearied out with the world, then we call to duty. Oh ! remember in the evening and close of the day your affections should be quick and free for spiritual things. Isaac went out ' at evening-tide.'

I shall sum up the intent of the whole verse in this one point—

Doct. That it is the duty of christians to sequester and set apart some time and place for solemn meditation, or the exercising their souls in heavenly and holy things.

My purpose is to speak of meditation, a duty unaccustomed and unpractised ; both the practice and the knowledge of it are become strangers to us. The times are times of action and tumult, and we all think that we have so much to do with others, that few desire to converse with God and themselves. Our case is somewhat like theirs in Nehemiah's time, Neh. iv. 17, ' With one hand they wrought in the work, and with the other hand held a weapon.' We are forced to fight and quarrel for our religion, that we may rescue the innocent and holy principles of it from violation and scorn. I observe that many christians use the sword, they spend the heat and strength of their spirits in controversies ; but I doubt they do not use the trowel enough, and are not so serious in private retirements as they are earnest in public defences. Therefore I shall make it my work to press the duty of meditation. My method shall be this : I shall show—(1.) What meditation is ; (2.) The necessity and profit of it ; (3.) The rules that serve to guide us in this holy work and business ; (4.) The lets and hindrances of it, with the helps and remedies against them ; (5.) The object or matters upon which you are to meditate, which I shall handle—first, generally ; secondly, particularly.

I shall give you some hints of meditation on those objects which are most usual and most practical.

I. What meditation is. Before I can define it I must distingush it.

1. There is that which we call occasional meditation, which is an act by which the soul spiritualiseth every object about which it is conversant. A gracious heart is like an alembic, it can distil useful meditations out of all things it meeteth with. Look, as it seeth all things in God, so it seeth God in all things. Our Lord at the well discourseth of 'the water of life,' John xxi. 10. At the supper of the pharisee one discourseth of ' eating bread in the kingdom of God,' Luke xiv. 15. There is a chemistry and holy art that a christian hath to turn water into wine, brass into gold, to make earthly occasions and objects to minister spiritual and heavenly thoughts. God trained up the old

church by types and ceremonies, that upon a common object they might ascend to spiritual thoughts; and our Lord in the new testament taught by parables and similitudes taken from ordinary functions and offices among men, that in every trade and calling we might be employed in our worldly business with an heavenly mind, that, whether in the shop, or at the loom, or in the field, we might still think of Christ and heaven. There is a parable of merchant-men, a parable of the sower, a parable of a man calling his servants to an account. In all these similitudes Christ would teach us that we should still think of God and heaven. So small a matter as a grain of mustard-seed may yield many spiritual applications.

2. There is set and solemn meditation. Now this is of several sorts, or rather, they are but several parts of the same exercise.

[1.] There is a reflexive meditation, by which we wholly fall upon ourselves. This is nothing else but a solemn parley between a man and his own heart: Ps. iv. 4, 'Commune with your own hearts upon your bed, and be still.' When in a solemn retirement, reason and inward discourse returneth and falleth back upon itself. Of all the parts of meditation this is the most difficult, for here a man is to exercise dominion over his soul, and to be his own accuser and judge; it is against self-love, and carnal ease. We see all our shifts are to avoid our own company, and to run away from ourselves. Guilty man, like a basilisk dieth, by seeing himself. Hence the worldly man choketh his soul with business, lest his thoughts, for want of work, like a mill should grind upon itself. The voluptuous person melteth away his days in pleasure, and charmeth his soul into a deep sleep with the potion of outward delights, lest it should awake and talk with him. Oh! then, necessary it is that a christian should take some time to discourse with himself, to ask of our own souls, what we are? what we have been? what we have done? Jer. viii. 6; what straits, what temptations we have passed through, and how we have overcome them? You would think it strange of two men that conversed every day for forty or fifty years, and all this while they did not know one another; yet this is the case between us and our souls; we live a long time in the world, and are strangers to ourselves.

[2.] There is a meditation, which is more direct, and that is of two sorts—(1.) Dogmatical, whose object is the word; (2.) Practical, whose objects is our own lives. There is more of search and apprehension in the first, there is more of plot and contrivance in the second; the one is more conversant about doctrines, the other about things; the latter catcheth hold of the heel of the former, for where dogmatical meditation endeth, there practical meditation beginneth.

(1.) Dogmatical meditation is when we exercise ourselves in the doctrines of the word, and consider how truths known may be useful to us. It differeth from study, partly in the object; study is conversant about a thing unknown in whole or in part: Rom. xii. 2, 'That ye may prove what is that good and acceptable and perfect will of God;' but meditation is an act of knowledge reiterated, or a return of the mind to that point to which it arrived before; it is the inculcation or whetting of a known truth, the pause of reason on something already conceived and known, or a calling to remembrance what we know before. Partly in the end; the end of study is information, but the end of meditation is practice, or a work upon the affections: Josh. i. 8, 'This book of the law shall not depart out of thy mouth, but thou shalt meditate therein day and night, that thou mayest observe to do according to all that is written therein.' Study is like a winter's sun, that shineth but warmeth not; but meditation is like the blowing up of the fire, where we do not mind the blaze, but the heat. The fruit of study is to hoard up truth, but the fruit of meditation is to practise it. Curious inquiries have more of the student in them than the christian. In study we are rather like vintners, that take in wines to store themselves for sale; in meditation we are like private men, that buy wine for our use and comfort. A vintner's cellar may be better stored than a nobleman's, but he hath it for others' use. The student may have more of notion and knowledge, his cellar may be fuller, but he hath it not for taste and necessary refreshment, as the christian hath.

(2.) More practical and applicative meditation is when we take ourselves aside from worldly distractions, that we may solemnly debate and study how to carry on the holy life with better success and advantage, when we are wise in our sphere: Luke xvi. 8, 'The children of this world are in their generation wiser than the children of light, εἰς τὴν γενεὰν, in their generation;' it is an Hebrew phrase for the manner, course, and sphere of our lives: Gen. vi. 9, 'These are the generations of Noah; Noah was a just man, and perfect in his generation, and Noah walked with God;' so to be wise in our generation is to be wise in our manner of living and business. So it is said, Ps. cxxii. 5, 'He will guide his affairs with discretion,' which noteth plotting and wise foresight, choosing our way, or devising our way, as Solomon calleth it: Prov. xvi. 9, 'A man's heart deviseth his way.' It is a great part of a christian's employment. The scriptures call for it for a minister: 2 Tim. ii. 15, 'Study to show thyself approved unto God, a workman that needeth not to be ashamed, rightly dividing the word of truth,' to devise how to carry on his ministry with most honour and success. So for private christians: Heb. x. 24, 'Let us consider one another, to provoke unto love and to good works.' We should consider one another, each other's gifts, dispositions, and graces, that so our spiritual converse and commerce might be the more improved. By this kind of meditation piety is made more prudent, reasonable, and orderly. Christians that live at haphazard, and order their lives at adventure, without these rational and wise debates, if they do not stain their profession with foul indiscretions, yet find much inconvenience and toil in the holy life, and are not half so useful as others are. Certainly we should learn this of the children of this world. A wicked man is plotting for his lusts: Rom. xiii. 14, 'Make no provision for the flesh to fulfil the lust thereof,' μὴ ποιεῖσθε πρόνοιαν. They make provision, they are catering how they may feed such a lust and satisfy such a carnal desire. Therefore certainly we should take care for the conveniencies of the holy life, how we may be most useful for God, and pass through our relations with most advantage, and cast our businesses that they may be the least disadvantage to religion, and consider how particular duties may be the most dexterously accomplished: Ps.

cxvi. 12, 'What shall I render unto the Lord for all his benefits towards me?'

These are the kinds of meditation. The definition may be formed thus: Meditation is that duty or exercise of religion whereby the mind is applied to the serious and solemn contemplation of spiritual things, for practical uses and purposes.

I shall open the description by the parts of it.

1. It is a duty and exercise of religion.

[1.] That it is a duty and exercise of religion appeareth by the evidence of scripture, where it is commanded, Josh. i. 8, 'This book of the law shall not depart out of thy mouth, but thou shalt meditate therein day and night.' It is made a character of a godly man: Ps. i. 2, 'His delight is in the law of the Lord, and in his law doth he meditate day and night.' It is commended in the practice and example of the saints that were most famous in scripture; Isaac in the text, Moses and David. And as it is plain by the evidence of scripture; so by the light of nature and reason. God that is a spirit deserveth the most pure and spiritual worship, as well as such as is performed by the body. The thoughts are the eldest and noblest offspring of the soul, and the solemn consecration of them is fit for God. In the gospel meditation is called for. I find in the Old Testament the main thing there called for is meditation in the law; in the gospel we are directed to a new object, the love of Christ: Eph. iii. 17–19, 'That ye, being rooted and grounded in love, may be able to comprehend with all saints what is the breadth, and length, and depth, and height, and to know the love of Christ, which passeth knowledge;' that is the study of saints. I confess it is more called for in the Old Testament; being gross and carnal, they needed greater enforcements to spiritual duties; but now it suiteth every way with the nature of our worship: John iv. 24, 'God is a spirit, and they that worship him must worship him in spirit and in truth.' Now worship in spirit and in truth is more agreeable to our state. Meditation is a pure and rational converse with God; it is the flower and height of consecrated reason.

[2.] It is not a duty of an arbitrary concernment. It is not only a moral help that may be observed or omitted, but a necessary duty, without which all graces would languish and wither. Faith is lean and ready to starve unless it be fed with continual meditation on the promises; as David saith, Ps. cxix. 92, 'Unless thy law had been my delight, I should then have perished in my affliction.' Thoughts are the caterers of the soul, that purvey for faith, and fetch in food and refresh it with the comfort of the promises. Hope is low, and doth not arise to such a fulness of expectation till by meditation we take a deliberate view of our hopes and privileges: Gen. xiii. 17, 'Arise, walk through the land, in the length of it, and in the breadth of it, for I will give it unto thee.' Our hopes arise according to the largeness of our thoughts. It is a great advantage to have our eyes open to view the riches of our inheritance, and to have a distinct view of the hope of our calling. The apostle prays for the Ephesians, chap. i. 18, 'The eyes of your understandings being enlightened, that ye may know what is the hope of his calling, and what the riches of the glory of his inheritance in the saints.' Men of barren thoughts are usually of low hopes, and for want of getting to the top of Pisgah to view the land, our hearts sink within us. Certainly hope thriveth best on the mount of meditation. Then for love, the sparkles of affection will not flow out unless we beat upon the will by constant thoughts. Affection is nourished by apprehension, and the more constant and deliberate the thoughts are, the love is always the deeper. Those christians that are backward to the duty of meditation find none of those impulses and meltings of love that are in others; they do not endeavour to comprehend the height and breadth and length, and depth of the love of Christ, and therefore no wonder that their hearts are so narrow and so much straitened towards God. Affections always follow the rate of our thoughts, if they are ponderous and serious. Then for obedience, or keeping the spirits constantly in a religious frame; to others good motions come like flashes of lightning, and are as soon gone, as their thoughts are slight and vanishing, but deep musing maketh the fire burn, and keepeth a constant heat and flame in the spirits, not by flashes. And as for duty, so for comfort; a man that is a stranger to meditation is a stranger to himself. In acts of review you enjoy yourselves, and you enjoy yourselves with far more comfort in these private recesses; you have most experience of God, and most experience of yourselves. Moses when he went aside to meditate had the vision of the fiery bush. Usually God cometh in, in the time of deep meditation, and an elevated heavenly mind is fittest to entertain the comforts and glory of his presence.

Thus you see it is a necessary duty. Many think it is an excuse to say it doth not suit with their temper; that it is a good help, but for those that can use it. I answer—

(1.) It is true there is a great deal of difference among christians; some are more serious and consistent, and have a greater command over their thoughts, others are of a more slight, weak spirit, and are less apt for duties of retirement and recollection. But our unfitness is usually moral rather than natural, not so much by temper as by disuse; and moral unfitness cannot exempt us from a moral duty. Inky water cannot wash the hand white, or a sin exempt me from a duty. Indisposition, which is a sin in me, doth not disannul my engagements to God; as a servant's drunkenness doth not excuse him from work. That it is a moral unfitness appeareth by two things—

(1*st.*) Disuse and neglect is the cause of it. Those that use it have a greater command over their thoughts. Men count it a great yoke, but custom would make it easy. Every duty is an help to itself, and the more we meditate the more we shall. It is pleasant to them that use it: Ps. i. 2, 'His delight is in the law of the Lord, and in his law doth he meditate day and night.' Fierce creatures are tame to those that use to command them, and if a man did use to govern his thoughts, he would find them more obedient.

(2*d.*) Want of love. Thoughts are at the service of love; we pause and stay upon such objects as we delight in: Ps. i. 2, 'His delight is in the law of the Lord, and in his law doth he meditate day and night.' Love naileth and fasteneth the soul to the object or thing beloved; as we see we can dwell upon carnal pleasures because our heart is there; as Solomon gives this reason why a carnal man cannot dwell upon a sad and solemn object, because 'his heart is in the house of mirth,'

Eccles. vii. 4. We usually complain we want temper and we want matter; but the truth is we want an heart. David saith, Ps. cxix. 97, 'Oh! how love I thy law; it is my meditation all the day.' Delightsome objects will engross the thoughts. Therefore see if it be not a moral distemper.

(2.) Suppose it be a natural unfitness, yet while you have reason it is not total and universal, and therefore cannot excuse. We see in other duties, some have the gift of utterance, and have a great savouriness and readiness of expression for prayer; others are more bound up and restrained; but this can be no plea for them wholly to neglect prayer. Duty must be done as we are able; God will hear the breathing, panting soul as well as the rolling tongue. So it is in meditation; some are more for musing, and can better melt out their souls in devout retirements, others can show their love better in zealous actions and public engagements for the glory of Christ; yet still, though there be a diversity of gifts, we are all bound to the same duties, and though we be fitter for some rather than others, yet none must be neglected in their order and course.

(3.) The rank and place that meditation hath among the duties. Meditation is a middle sort of duty between the word and prayer, and hath respect to both. *The word feedeth meditation, and meditation feedeth prayer; we must hear that we be not erroneous, and meditate that we be not barren.* These duties must always go hand in hand; meditation must follow hearing and precede prayer.

(1st.) To hear and not to meditate is unfruitful. We may hear and hear, but it is like putting a thing into a bag with holes: Hag. i. 6, 'He that earneth wages, earneth wages to put it into a bag with holes;' James i. 23, 24, 'He is like unto a man beholding his natural face in a glass; for he beholdeth himself, and goeth his way, and straightway forgetteth what manner of man he was.' Bare hearing begets but transient thoughts, and they leave but a weak impression, which is rather like the glance of a sunbeam upon a wall; there is a glaring for the present, but a man never discerneth the beauty, the lustre, and the order of the truths delivered till he cometh to meditate upon them; then we come clearly to see into the truth, and how it concerneth us, and how it falleth upon our hearts. David saith, Ps. cxix. 99, 'I have more understanding than all my teachers, for thy testimonies are my meditation.' The preacher can but deliver general theorems, and draw them down to practical inferences; by meditation we come to see more clearly and practically than he that preacheth. We see, in outward learning, they thrive best that meditate most; knowledge floateth, till by deliberate thoughts it be compressed upon the affections.

(2d.) It is dangerous to meditate and not to hear because of errors. Man will soon impose a deceit upon himself by his own thoughts. Fanatic spirits that neglect hearing pretend to dreams and revelations. We have a sophister and an heretic in our own bosoms, 'which soon deceiveth without a stock and treasure of some knowledge;' for men would be vain in their imaginations were not their thoughts corrected by an external light and instruction. Jude calleth those fanatic persons ἐνυπνιαζόμενοι, 'filthy dreamers,' Jude 8. All practical errors are men's natural imaginations gotten up into a valuable opinion.

(3*d*.) It is rashness to pray and not to meditate. What we take in by the word we digest by meditation and let out by prayer. These three duties must be so ordered that one may not jostle out the other. Men are barren, dry, and sapless in their prayers for want of exercising themselves in holy thoughts: Ps. xlv. 1, 'My heart is inditing a good matter;' and then it follows, 'I will speak of the things which I have made touching the King; my tongue is the pen of a ready writer.' The heart yieldeth matter to the tongue; the word signifieth, boileth and frieth; a word from *mincha*, their meat-offering; the oil and the flour was to be kneaded together, and then fried in a pan, and then offered to the Lord; implying we must not come with raw dough-baked offerings, till we have concocted and prepared them by mature deliberation. It is notable that often in scripture prayer is called by the name of meditation, because it is the product and issue of it; as Ps. v. 1, 'Give ear to my words, O Lord: consider my meditation. Implying that his prayer was but the expression of his deliberate and premeditated thoughts. So Ps. xix. 14, 'Let the words of my mouth and the meditation of my heart be acceptable in thy sight, O Lord, my strength and my redeemer.' It is the vent of the thoughts.

2. Whereby the mind is applied to the serious and solemn consideration. I add this to distinguish it from occasional meditation, and those good thoughts that accidentally rush into our minds, and to note the care and intenseness of the soul in such an exercise: Prov. xviii. 1, 'Through desire a man, having separated himself, seeketh and intermeddleth with all wisdom;' then is a man fit for these solemn and holy thoughts, and for intermeddling with all wise and divine matters, when he hath divorced himself from other cares, and is able to keep his understanding under a prudent confinement.

3. Of spiritual things. This noteth the object, and so I call matters that are of an useful consideration; as for instance, God, that we may fear him; sin, that we may abhor it; the works of God for the Creator's glory; any useful subject. So David limiteth it: Ps. xlix. 3, 'My mouth shall speak of wisdom; and the meditation of my heart shall be of understanding.' He meaneth of the state and end of man. Generally the object in the Old Testament is of the law.

4. For practical uses and inferences. This noteth the end. Meditation is not to puzzle the head with notions, but to better the heart. The proper use of this exercise is to set on those great practical heads of religion, to work the heart to a greater care of duty and detestation of sin. To a greater care of duty: Ps. cxix. 15, 'I will meditate in thy precepts, and have respect unto thy ways;' and to a greater detestation and hatred of sin: Ps. cxix. 11, 'Thy word have I hid in mine heart, that I might not sin against thee.'

SERMON II.

And Isaac went out to meditate in the field at the even-tide.—
GEN. xxiv. 63.

II. I AM now come to the necessity and profit of meditation, or motives to press to this duty. I shall urge such as will serve also for marks; for when it is well performed, you will find these effects wrought in you. Meditation is the mother and nurse of knowledge and godliness, the great instrument in all the offices of grace; it helpeth on the work of grace upon the understanding, affections, and life, for the understanding of the doctrine of godliness, for the provoking of godly affections, and for the heavenly life.

1. In point of understanding it is of great advantage to us in the entertainment of the doctrines of religion.

[1.] To give us a clearer and more distinct sight of them. A man seeth the meaning, scope, and order of all points of religion, when he cometh to meditate on them. Knowledge without meditation is but an hearsay knowledge; we talk after one another like parrots, and as the moon that shineth with another lustre without any light rooted in its own body: Rom. ii. 20, 'Which hast the form of knowledge, and of the truth in the law,' $\mu\acute{o}\rho\phi\rho\sigma\iota\nu$ $\tau\hat{\eta}s$ $\gamma\nu\acute{\omega}\sigma\epsilon\omega s$, a map of knowledge; we have nothing but the lean apprehension of others. As the philosopher said, $\tau\grave{a}$ $\mu\grave{\epsilon}\nu$ $\lambda\acute{\epsilon}\gamma o \upsilon \sigma \iota \nu$ $o\grave{\iota}$ $\nu\epsilon\acute{o}\iota$, $\grave{a}\lambda\lambda\grave{a}$ $o\grave{\upsilon}$ $\pi\iota\sigma\tau\epsilon\acute{\upsilon}o\upsilon\sigma\iota\nu$, they repeat them by rote, without affection and belief; so we speak one after another by rote, but do not so distinctly discern the worth and excellency of christianity as when we come to meditate upon it: John iv. 42, 'Now we believe, not because of thy saying, for we have heard him ourselves, and know that this is indeed the Christ, the Saviour of the world.' Most men's knowledge is but traditional; they never made an essay, and tasted the sweetness of Christ, or of their own thoughts. Oh! do but try; bare apprehensions of the report of Christ is but tradition, not religion. When we come to exercise our own thoughts thereon, then we see him ourselves; the sight is more clear when it is steady and fixed. To one that passeth by, to see men dancing and frisking seemeth lightness and madness, but when he cometh nearer, and heareth the music, and observeth that they keep time, and pace, and measure with it, he findeth art in that which he thought frenzy. The beauty and excellency of religion is not discerned by a transient glance; when we come to meditate, and so see what is our beloved above all beloveds, then we admire him. The christian religion is not to be taken up by chance, but by choice; not because we know no other, but because we know no better; then our affections to it are the more rational, the judgment having had a clearer sight and trial.

[2.] That we may the better retain them. When an apple is tossed to and fro in the hand, it smelleth of it when the apple is gone, as when civet hath been long kept in the box the scent remaineth when the civet is taken out. A constant light is a great friend to memory, and sermons meditated on are remembered long after they are delivered. We do not forget those friends whom we have entertained with any solemnity. Solemn and serious thoughts leave a charge upon the memory.

[3.] That they may be always more ready and present with us. All sins do arise out of incogitancy or forgetfulness. As for instance, distrust: Heb. xii. 5, 'Ye have forgotten the exhortation which speaketh unto you as unto children;' Luke xxiv. 6, 'He is not here, but is risen: remember how he spake unto you when he was yet in Galilee.' A temptation gets the start of holy thoughts. It were a mighty advantage to have truths always ready. Now this is the Spirit's office: John xiv. 26, 'But the Comforter, which is the Holy Ghost, whom the Father will send in my name, he shall teach you all things, and bring all things to your remembrance, whatsoever I have said unto you.' But now, for an outward help, there is no such thing as meditation: Prov. vi. 21, 22, 'Bind them continually upon thine heart, and tie them about thy neck: when thou goest, it shall lead thee; when thou sleepest, it shall keep thee; and when thou awakest, it shall talk with thee;' that is, shall be always present with thee. Continual meditation maketh religious thoughts actual and present.

2. It is a great advantage to the work of grace upon the affections. Ponderous thoughts are the bellows that kindle and inflame the affections; they blow up those latent sparkles of grace that are in the soul. Impure thoughts stain the heart, and convey a taint and filth to the soul: 2 Peter ii. 14, 'Having eyes full of adultery.' When the fancy is rolled upon unclean objects, lust is kindled. Lust, revenge, covetousness, they are all fed with thoughts; a wicked spirit distilleth sin into the quintessence of villany, the imaginations of the heart are evil. So suitably good thoughts leave a forcible impression upon the soul. The papists talk of St Francis and St Clara, that had the wounds of Christ impressed on them. It is true, in a spiritual way, deep thoughts leave the wounds and sorrows of Christ upon the heart, and do crucify us; it is true morally, as well as mystically: 'I am crucified with Christ,' Gal. ii. 20. Certainly you find this by experience, that when you know not things, you are not so thoroughly affected with them. Serious meditation hath this advantage, that it doth make the object present, and as it were sensible; therefore faith, which is a deep acting of the thoughts upon the promises, and upon glory to come, is called ὑπόστασις, 'the substance of things hoped for, and the evidence of things not seen,' Heb. xi. 1. It giveth the future blessedness a present subsistence in the soul, and therefore it must needs ravish it. It is a principle in nature, appetition followeth knowledge, and desire is answerable to that certain and clear judgment that we have of the worth, value, and dignity of the object. Now it is not enough that the judgment be once convinced, but that it stay upon the object, for things lose their virtue when we do not keep them in the eye of the soul. When the bird often leaveth her nest and is long absent, the eggs grow cold, and do not come to be quickened; so do our desires grow cold and dull, which otherwise by a constant meditation are hatched into some life. Instance in any affection. Hope and trust are ripened by constant thoughts of the grace, power, truth, goodness, and unchangeableness of God: 2 Tim. i. 12, 'I know whom I have believed, and I am persuaded that he is able to keep that which I have committed to him against that day.'

Presumption is an inconstant careless apprehension, and therefore soon overborne: Ps. ix. 10, 'They that know thy name will put their trust in thee;' that is, that seriously consider it; for the Hebrew word is used for *consider*; they that know what a God thou art, how merciful, true, and powerful thou art, they will trust thee. So for fear, so far as it is sanctified it is fed by a consideration of the dreadfulness of Gods wrath and displeasure: Ps. xc. 11, 'Who knows the power of thine anger? according to thy fear, so is thy wrath;' that is, who doth seriously consider of it? According to those awful apprehensions that they form within themselves doth God's wrath more or less move them. So for desire, either of Christ or of heaven. Of Christ; a serious consideration of the excellency of Christ is that which ravisheth the heart. The spouse formeth a description of Christ, and then she saith he is all desires: Cant. v. 16, 'His mouth is more sweet, yea, he is altogether lovely.' Enough to ravish all our desires. The value of things lieth hid when we do but slightly and superficially look upon them, but when we meditate of them, they are double to that which is seen at the first blush: Job xi. 6, 'And that he would show thee the secrets of wisdom, that they are double to that which is.' In natural things serious thoughts are necessary, much more in spiritual, because the mind, by long use, having been inured to earthly objects and profits, had need to be much raised. We see that we do insensibly receive taint from those objects with which we do converse, and therefore we had need to be often and serious in meditating of the excellences of Christ, that by a spiritual art he may be as usual an object to us as the world. So for heaven, when we do not hold our hearts to the consideration of the glory of it, it doth not work upon us. Moses, Heb. xi. 26, 'Had respect to the recompense of the reward,' $\dot{\epsilon}\pi\acute{\epsilon}\beta\lambda\epsilon\pi\epsilon$; he had an eye to it. The word noteth a serious and intent consideration; we should again and again consider it, and be sending our thoughts as spies into the land of promise, to bring us reports and tidings of it, as love between men is maintained by constant visits and letters. So for sorrow for sin past: Ps. li. 3, 'My sin is ever before me;' and Jer. xxxi. 19, 'Surely after that I was turned I repented; and after that I was instructed I smote upon my thigh; I was ashamed, yea, even confounded, because I did bear the reproach of my youth.' When we come deeply to consider our errors, and the unkindness of them, that begetteth a sad sense. So for hatred and displicency against sin. Evil affections are nourished by thoughts, and kept up in life and strength, for thoughts are *pabulum animæ*, the food of the soul: Rom. vii. 13, 'Sin, that it might appear sin, working death in me by that which is good, that sin by the commandment might become exceeding sinful.' The sinfulness of sin appears by considering the purity of the law, the majesty of God, and the kindness of Christ. So for joy and delight; the soul is feasted by meditation, it turneth the promises into marrow: Ps. lxiii. 5, 6, 'My soul shall be satisfied as with marrow and fatness, and my mouth shall praise thee with joyful lips, when I remember thee upon my bed, and meditate on thee in the night-watches.' Hereby we discern their relish and savour: Ps. xxxiv. 8, 'Oh! taste and see that the Lord is good;' the thoughts, taste, and the relish is left on the affections.

3. It is an advantage to the fruits of grace in the life; it maketh the heavenly life more easy, more sweet, more orderly and prudent.

[1.] More easy, because it calleth in all the rational help that may be. Reason, which otherwise would serve the senses, and be enslaved to appetite and worldly desire, now is employed in the highest and purest use; and therefore when reason is gained, which is the leading faculty, the work cometh on more easily. Meditation putteth reason in authority, and rescueth it from being prostituted to sense: 2 Cor. x. 5, 'Casting down imaginations,' λογισμοὺς, reasonings, 'and every high thing that exalteth itself against the knowledge of God, and bringing into captivity every thought to the obedience of Christ.' And then for sense, it maketh our eyes to furnish us with matter: Job xii. 7, 8, 'But ask now the beasts, and they will teach thee; and the fowls of the air, and they shall tell thee: or speak to the earth, and it shall teach thee; and the fishes of the sea shall declare unto thee.' Every element giveth in an help; he that doth not want an heart cannot want an object; the air, the sea, the earth giveth fuel for wisdom and spiritual advantage. But for want of consideration a man is worse than the beasts: Prov. vi. 6, 'Go to the ant, thou sluggard; consider her ways, and be wise.'

[2.] More sweet. It bringeth the heavenly life into more liking with us. Duty to worldly men is irksome and unsavoury, because they lose the sweetness and blessedness of communion with God: Ps. xxvi. 3, 'For thy loving-kindness is before mine eyes; I have walked in thy truth.' This constraineth and enforceth to holiness, and gives encouragement to it. Others only attempt this work, but do not consider the fruit of it.

[3.] More orderly and prudent. Others do good duties by chance: Phil. iv. 8, 'Finally, brethren, whatsoever things are true, whatsoever things are honest, whatsoever things are just, whatsoever things are pure, whatsoever things are lovely, whatsoever things are of good report; if there be any virtue, and if there be any praise, think of these things.'

III. That which I am now to do is to give you the rules to guide you in this weighty affair of the christian life. There are rules to be observed to fit the soul, but those I shall handle under the term of helps. I handle such now as must guide the soul.

1. Whatever you meditate upon must be drawn down to application: Job v. 27, 'Lo this, we have searched it, so it is; hear it, and know thou it for thy good.' In meditation our aim and design is to promote the good of our souls. The heathen Emperor Antoninus had observations, which he called τὰ εἰς ἐμαυτὸν, 'things for myself;' that is the proper end of this exercise, things for ourselves. In conference we aim at the good of others, but the end of meditation is to fall directly upon our own souls. All the while we stay in generals we do but bend the bow; when we come to application we let fly the arrow, and we hit the mark when we come to return upon our own souls. Now this application must be partly by way of trial, partly by way of charge.

[1.] The first reflection upon ourselves must be by way of trial. This should always be the close of all, How is it with thee, oh! my soul? or, Is not this my state? When the apostle had taken a view of the doctrine of justification, he shutteth up all with a practical return upon his own heart: Rom. viii. 31, 'What shall we then say to these things?' How am I concerned in this truth? So Nazianzen in his 41st Oration saith his custom was ἀποχωρῆσαι Θεῷ τὸ μικρὸν, to go aside to converse with God, but always in the course of the duty he did ἑαυτὸν ἐπισμέψασθαι, search himself.

[2.] By way of charge and command. You should charge yourselves to serve God with greater care. Meditation is as it were the heat of the cause, and after the debate you should give sentence, and issue forth a practical decree, as David; now I see 'It is good for me to draw nigh to God,' Ps. lxxiii. 28. When he had been meditating of the providence of God in punishing the wicked, now, O my soul! thou seest what is best for thee, even to keep close to God. So in two psalms, when he had been meditating of the mercy and power of God, he layeth a charge upon his soul to bless God for his mercy: Ps. ciii. 22, 'Bless the Lord all his works, in all places of his dominion; bless the Lord, O my soul!' Of his power: Ps. civ. 35, 'Let the sinners be consumed out of the earth, and let the wicked be no more; bless thou the Lord, O my soul! praise ye the Lord.'

2. Do not pry further than God hath revealed; your thoughts must be still bounded by the word. There is no duty that a fanatic brain is more apt to abuse than meditation. When men are once able to raise their thoughts, they soar too high, and being puffed up with their fleshly mind, intrude themselves into things that they have not seen, Col. ii. 18. They are dazzled with ungrounded subtleties, and so, like a lark that have flown high, of a sudden fall down again. David saith, Ps. cxxxi. 1, 'Lord, my heart is not haughty, nor mine eyes lofty, neither do I exercise myself in great matters, or in things to high for me.' In spiritual exercises you must stint your thoughts with what is revealed; μὴ ὑπερφρονεῖν παρ᾽ ὃ δεῖ φρονεῖν, ἀλλὰ φρονεῖν εἰς τὸ σωφρονεῖν, Rom. xii. 3, 'Not to think of himself more highly than he ought to think, but to think soberly, according as God hath dealt to every man the measure of faith;' that is, as God hath revealed and dispensed the measure of faith to you. To pry into the mysteries of the divine decrees were to disturb affection, not to raise it; nice disputes feed curiosity, not religion. Again, regard must be had not only to the word, but to your own abilities. Those that soar too high fall low enough ere they have done. Consider what is fit for your pitch and size. Again, do not leave bread and wine and gnaw upon a stone, or leave practical matters for intricacy of dispute.

3. When you meditate of God you must do it with great care and reverence; his perfections are matter rather of admiration than inquiry. Some dispute whether it be best to meditate of God's essence or no. Certainly as it is discovered to us in his attributes it is very comfortable and useful: Ps. civ. 34, 'My meditation of him shall be sweet, I will be glad in the Lord.' And though you should get as large thoughts as possibly you can of his majesty and power, yet you must not pry too curiously into his nature, lest you be oppressed by his glory. The mysteries of the trinity are matters of belief rather than debate, we may well cry out, ὦ βάθος, Oh, the depth! It is enough to know that it is so, we cannot search how. It is said, 1 Tim. vi. 16,

'Who only hath immortality, dwelling in the light which no man can approach unto, whom no man hath seen, nor can see;' and Ps. xviii. 11, 'He hath made darkness his secret place, his pavilion round about him were dark waters, and thick clouds of the skies.' God is said to dwell in light to show his majesty, and to dwell in darkness to show his incomprehensibleness. Do not entangle yourselves while you go about to raise your zeal; the full knowledge of these things is our portion in heaven.

4. In meditating on common things, keep in mind a spiritual purpose. God hath endowed man with a faculty to discourse, and employ his mind on earthly objects to spiritual purposes: Eccles. iii. 11, 'He hath set the world in their heart.' *Mundum tradidit disputationi eorum* ; the meaning is, he hath endowed him with natural light to contemplate on his handiwork. The mind is soon apt to grow common and vain, and therefore here you have need of more care and watchfulness: Ps. viii. 34, 'When I consider the heavens, the work of thy fingers, the moon and the stars, which thou hast ordained, what is man that thou art mindful of him, and the son of man that thou visitest him?' Basil calleth them διδασηαλεῖον καὶ παιδευτέριον ψύχων, a school to teach us not knowledge but religion: Ps. xix. 1, 'The heavens declare the glory of God, and the firmament showeth his handiwork.' Philosophers study the creatures to find out their natural causes, we to find out arguments of worship and religion.

5. Take heed of creating a snare to your souls. Some sins are catching, like fire in straw, and we cannot think of them without infection and temptation; the very thoughts may beget a sudden delight and tickling, which may pass through us like lightning, and set us all on fire: Ezek. xxiii. 19, 'She multiplied her whoredoms in calling to remembrance the days of her youth, wherein she had played the harlot in the land of Egypt.' Though the prophet speaketh of spiritual fornication, yet there is a plain allusion to outward; it is an allusion to an unchaste woman, who feedeth a new fire by remembering her vile lusts. Some temptations cannot be supposed without sin; it is less dangerous to suppose the temptation of Peter than the temptation of Joseph, of Peter that was tempted to deny his master, than of Joseph who was tempted to folly with his mistress. This direction is not unnecessary; you know not how apt a carnal heart and busy devil may be to taint the best duties, and how soon an innocent thought may degenerate into an unclean glance. The apostle would have some sins not named among the saints: Eph. v. 3, 'But fornication and all uncleanness, or covetousness, let it not be once named among you, as becometh saints.'

6. Meditate of those things especially which you have most need of. There is the greatest obligation upon the heart. The matter is not arbitrary; there you will find most help, and there the benefit will be most sensible. Seasonable thoughts have the greatest influence. The servants of God have sometimes meditated on his power, sometimes on his mercy, sometimes on his providence, according as their affairs and temptations call for it: Ps. lvi. 3, 'What time I am afraid, I will trust in thee.' In a time of fear he would think of arguments of trust.

7. Whatever you meditate upon, take heed of slightness. Transient thoughts leave no impression. See that you meditate but of one thing at once. *Hoc age*, mind the work you are about, is a good rule in meditation as well as prayer, the thoughts should be under a restraint and wise confinement. A skipping mind, that wandereth from one meditation to another, seldom profiteth. In meditation be not like the dogs of Nile, that snatch here and there, or like the bee, that passeth from flower to flower. A constant fixed light worketh most. The apostle speaketh of apostates that they have flashy tastes: Heb. vi. 4, 5, 'They were once enlightened, and tasted of the heavenly gift, and were made partakers of the Holy Ghost, and tasted the good word of God, and the powers of the world to come.'. They had vanishing and fleeting motions: James i. 25, 'He that looketh into the law of liberty,' ὁ δὲ παρακύψας, he that boweth down to take a deliberate view; it is a metaphor taken from them that stoop down, and bend their bodies toward a thing that they may narrowly pry into it. The same word is used to imply that narrow search which the angels use to find out the mysteries of salvation by: 1 Peter i. 12, 'Which things the angels desire παρακύψειν, to look into,' an allusion to the cherubim, whose faces bowed down towards the ark, as desirous to see the mysteries therein contained. There must be a deep sight and serious inculcation: Luke ii. 19, 'But Mary kept all these sayings, and pondered them in her heart,' συμβάλλουσα; she examined, compared them, traversed them to and fro in her mind, which is afterwards expressed, ver. 51, 'She kept all these sayings in her heart.' There is a folly in man, when once we apprehend a thing; curiosity being satisfied, we begin to loath it, the first apprehension having as it were deflowered it, but at last they lose their power and virtue. When digestion is precipitated there is no nourishment, and when the meditation is not deep and ponderous we have no comfort, no lively perception and feeling of it in our hearts. A glance doth not discover the worth of anything; he that doth but cast his eye upon a piece of embroidery doth not discover the art of it.

8. Come not off from holy thoughts till you find profit by them, either sweet tastes and relishes of the love of God, or high affections kindled towards God, or strong resolutions begotten in yourselves. Usually God droppeth in sweetness into the hearts of his people, as all those ecstasies of love in the Canticles were occasioned by meditation. But we cannot always expect raptures and high elevations; it is some fruit if it maketh you fall to prayer and holy complaints.

9. Be thankful to God when he blesseth you in meditation, or else you will find difficulty in the next. Christians often forget to return God the glory: Cant. i. 4, 'Draw me, we will run after thee, the king hath brought me into his chambers; we will be glad and rejoice in thee, we will remember thy loves more than wine; the upright love thee.' That which goeth up in vapours cometh down in showers. So the psalmist, Ps. lxvii. 5, 6, 'Let the people praise thee, O God, let all the people praise thee; then shall the earth yield her increase, and God even our own God, shall bless us.' There is a mutual access and recess between the rivers and the sea, so there is between blessings and praises. In this duty God is jealous lest we should give the honour to ourselves, because there is so much work of our own thoughts: Ps. lxiii. 4, 5,

'Because thy loving-kindness is better than life, my lips shall praise thee: thus will I bless thee while I live, I will lift up my hands in thy name.' Not only in my necessity, but for ever, for such sweet experiences.

10. Do not bridle up the free spirit by the rules of method. That which God calleth for is religion, not logic. When christians confine themselves to such rules and prescriptions, they straiten themselves, and thoughts come from them like water out of a still, not like water out of a fountain. Voluntary and free meditations are most smart and pregnant. In all arbitrary directions, that make only for the conveniency of the duty, you must remember we come to you like Paul to the Corinthians: 1 Cor. vii. 12, 'To the rest speak I, not the Lord.' We do not prescribe, but advise.

11. Your success in the duty is not to be measured by the multitude and subtlety of the thoughts, but the sincerity of them. Christians puzzle and disquiet themselves because they look too much at gifts; you should covet the best gifts, but not inordinately: Ps. li. 6, 'Thou desirest truth in the inward parts.' In prayer God looketh more to the impulses of zeal than the flowers of rhetoric; so in meditation, if we are less subtle, it is no matter, so we be more devout.

12. You must begin and end all with prayer. Duties are subservient one to another. In the beginning you must pray for a blessing on the duty, and in the end commend your souls and resolutions to God. There is no hope in your own promises, but God's. They were in an high pang of zeal when they offered so freely to the service of the house of God; but David prays, 2 Chron. xxix. 28, 'O Lord God of Abraham, Isaac, and of Israel, our fathers, keep this for ever in the imaginations of the thoughts of the heart of thy people, and prepare their hearts to seek thee.' Our motions are fleeting and vanishing; God must preserve in us these resolutions of consecrating ourselves and all that is ours to him.

SERMON III.

And Isaac went out to meditate in the field at the even-tide.—
Gen. xxiv. 63.

My work now is to handle the lets or hindrances of meditation, together with the helps and means that may quicken you to the performance of it. The lets may be sooner discovered than remedied, as the nature of many diseases is better known than the cures, and therefore they are called *opprobria medicorum*, the disgrace of the physician's skill; so these remain as marks and memorials of the fall. Entire and uninterrupted visions are the privileges of heaven; we must be contented with our broken and imperfect measures; it is enough that we have 'doves' eyes,' Cant. iv. 1; that we can peck and look upward, and enjoy some temperate glances on the glory of our hopes, though we be not transported with the ravishments of a constant and steady vision. We cannot expect to be absolute; we shall still have cause to be humbled; it is enough if we can be encouraged against despair; for many find themselves so unfit that they have not hopes enough to attempt the duty. To these I shall speak chiefly in this discourse. I had thought to have handled the lets severally, and then the helps; but I think it would be better to suit each discouragement with its proper helps.

The lets and hindrances are of several sorts, some common to this with other duties, and others more peculiar to the duty of meditation.

First, I begin with the first sort, such hindrances as are common to other duties, and they are four—sloth, love of pleasure, a guilty conscience, and an unwieldy mind.

1. There is a spiritual slothfulness. Men lie upon the bed of ease, and are loath in good earnest to apply themselves to what is painful and difficult. If grace would drop to them out of the clouds, or God would be contented with some faint lazy wishes, or some cold and yawning expressions of a drowsy devotion, they would be religious; but where duties must cost labour and self-denial, and put them to pains, men withdraw the shoulder, and hang off. Therefore Solomon saith, Prov. xxi. 25, 'The desire of the slothful killeth him, for his hands refuse to labour.' They would fain have grace, and perform what God requires, but are loath to take pains. Now, as this is a prejudice against all other duties, so especially against the duty of meditation; partly because of all duties it is most difficult and tedious to the flesh; it is a duty lying within the soul; we cannot so easily command our own thoughts. Now inward duties are the most difficult, because we cannot always exercise a dominion over our own spirits. Partly because it is a private duty, to which God alone is conscious. In public duties secular interests and ends have a great constraint, and therefore we excite the heart to be more intent and serious. We see byends make men deny themselves, but where there is not this to prompt them, they either omit the work, or turn it into a slight and idle practice.

How shall we do to shake off this spiritual sloth? I answer—

[1.] You must consider that a lazy spirit is most unfit for christianity. The whole christian life is carried on with much labour and diligence. You were as good never look after Christ and heaven as refuse labour. There is nothing required in the whole compass of religion but what will cost you a great deal of pains. Faith is a work: John vi. 29, 'That is the work of God, that ye believe on him whom he hath sent.' It is not a barren idle speculation, nor a naked apprehension, but a matter of difficulty and diligence to bring Christ and the soul together, and to lodge the soul in the bosom of Christ. Love is labour: Heb. vi. 10, 'God is not unrighteous, to forget your work and labour of love.' It is not a naked profession, but there is labour in it; take it either for love to God or men. For love to God, that is not a fellow-like familiarity, but a laying out ourselves in his service; or for love to men, that doth not consist in a few good words. Debts are not paid with a noise of money; you do not satisfy the commandment by saying, 'Depart in peace, be ye warmed, be ye filled, if you give them not those things which are needful to the body,' James ii. 16. So for obedience : it is expressed by a constant course of work and labour : 1 Cor. xv. 58, 'Be ye steadfast and unmovable, always abounding in the work of the Lord, forasmuch as you know that your labour is not in vain in the Lord.' Religion is a constant exercise ; there are no loiterers in heaven. God's work must not be followed with a faint wish and a slack hand. Men mistake religion if they think it a broad and easy way where men may live at large. No ; the gate is narrow and the path is strait, and few there be that find it; it is a work, not a sport and play ; and men had as good lay all thoughts of God and Christ aside as to resolve upon an easy course, and flatter themselves with an expectation that they shall go to heaven with a lazy wish, and fancy such a short cut and passage to heaven as will cost no pains.

[2.] It is better to take pains than to suffer pains, and to be bound with the cords of duty than with the chains of darkness. The bonds of duty are not gyves, but ornaments, for duty is the greatest freedom : Ps. cxix. 45, 'I will walk at liberty, for I seek thy precepts.' You will never be more free than when you once make experience of God's service. How sad is it to see men prejudiced against such pains as yield freedom and comfort for the present and glory for the future, and take pains for that for which they shall suffer eternal pains ! Isa. v. 18, 'Woe unto them that draw iniquity with cords of vanity, and sin as it were with cart ropes.' They moil and toil in the work of Satan as a horse in a mill, and labour for their own destruction. Consider the devil's work is drudgery and his reward is death ; yet such is the wretchedness of man, that he accounteth nothing toilsome but God's work, and nothing pleasant but the accomplishment of his own lusts, to be lust's vassal and pride's slave, and to be at the command of every covetous and unclean desire. How do men toil in the world, go to bed late, rise early, eat the bread of sorrows, exhaust and waste their strength and spirits, and yet there is sin in the work, and hell in the wages! Oh ! consider, if it seem difficult, which is better, to labour for a season, or suffer for ever ? which is the end of them that live in the constant neglect of a known duty.

[3.] There is nothing so hard in God's service but he hath manifested love enough to sweeten it. We begrudge a few thoughts of God, and God had thoughts of us before all worlds : Ps. xl. 5, 'Many, O Lord my God, are the wonderful works which thou hast done, and thy thoughts which are to us-ward ; they cannot be reckoned up in number unto thee : if I would declare and speak of them, they are more than can be numbered ;' Ps. cix. 13, 'How precious also are thy thoughts unto me O God ! How great is the sum of them ! ' Who can tell what a condescension it was for infiniteness to think of poor worms, and that he should before all worlds plot and design our salvation ? And when the plot came out, there was a great deal of love to sweeten duty. The Lord Jesus Christ thought no danger too great, no suffering or extremity too hard, no work too difficult for our sakes, what a mercy is this! God hath not only required obedience, but discovered a love that may sweeten the difficulties of it.

[4.] There is no difficulty in religion wholly insuperable and too hard for an active and industrious spirit. Those that follow on after God do at length find him to their comfort. A faint pursuit is the cause of discouragement. When a flint doth not strike fire at the first, we strike again: Prov. x. 4, 'He becometh poor that dealeth with a slack hand, but the hand of the diligent maketh rich.' It is a rule in grace as well as nature; let us therefore follow on till we have overcome the difficulty that is before us.

[5.] A lazy backward heart must be urged forward with the greater importunity. When David was shy of God's presence, he lays a command upon himself: Ps. xxxii. 5, 'I said I will confess my transgressions unto the Lord;' he maketh reason to issue out a decree and positive conclusion. So Ps. xxxix. 1, 'I said I will take heed to my ways, that I sin not with my tongue.' So by just analogy we may gather that the soul should in this case determine, I will go and try, and see what may be done; I will keep off from God no longer, but will go to him.

2. Another let and hindrance is love of pleasures. Men that would pass their time in mirth are unwilling to be so solemn and serious. When children's minds are set to play, it is irksome to hear of school or of their books; so when the heart is set for pleasure, it is a hard matter to bring the soul to religious performances.

How shall we do to wean the soul from pleasures?

[1.] Consider to love pleasure is to gratify the beast in us rather than the angel. Man is in part an angel and in part a beast; he hath a nature common to both. Now when men study altogether to gratify their sensual part, it is to turn men into beasts. To serve our lowest faculty, and to enjoy pleasures without remorse, is the happiness of the beasts; to eat, and drink, and sleep, and sport is but to do as the beasts do; a man's delight should be in the pure and free exercises of reason. If men would exercise themselves herein, they would find the greatest delectation would be in the contemplation and view of truth: Ps. xix. 8, 'The statutes of the Lord are right, rejoicing the heart.' That taste which hypocrites have of the good word of God, Heb. vi. 5, is merely such as scholars have in the height of speculation and study, because the gospel is such an excellent contrivance, and a sublime satisfying truth. *Nulla major voluptas quam fastidium voluptatis;* there is no greater pleasure than a disdain of sensual pleasures.

[2.] Consider the sweetness of religious exercises is far better than that of carnal pleasures, as that heat is more manly that is gotten by exercise than by hovering over the fire. It is hard, I confess, to abjure accustomed delights; pleasantness is connatural to us; but we should consider that by communion with God in spiritual exercises delight is not abrogated but preferred, and advanced to a more noble becoming object; it is taken out of Egypt that it may grow in Canaan, transplanted out of a fen into a paradise, that it may thrive in a better soil; it is less dreggy, but more masculine and grave: Ps. civ. 34, 'My meditation of him shall be sweet; I will be glad in the Lord;' Eph. v. 4, 'Neither filthiness nor foolish talking nòr jesting which are not convenient, but rather giving of thanks.' We keep the affection, but change the object. The comforts of christianity are expressed by terms proper to the delights of the senses, to teach us this excellent art, to keep the affection and change the object, and by an holy sleight and wile to cozen the soul into better joys. Here delight is most pure and more free, no excess is vicious. *Castæ deliciæ meæ sunt scripturæ tuæ*; thy scriptures are my chaste delights. The pleasures of the world are but sugared baits; a man may soon lose himself; but here by trial you will find the same sweetness with less hazard and danger.

[3.] We may make choice of matter more pleasant to allure the soul. All the objects of meditation are not dark and gloomy; there are some things pleasing to nature—the variety of providences, the beauty of the creation, the excellent contrivance of the gospel. All objects are not mournful, and in case of such a temptation we may allure the soul; and when we are not so fit for the severe exercises of the closet, we may, as Isaac, go out into the fields to meditate, and heighten fancy and imagination by objects more pleasant.

3. The next general hindrance is a guilty conscience. When the soul is under the burden of guilt, we are loath to be serious and alone, lest the mind should fall on itself; of all things we then desire to flee the company of ourselves, and therefore meditation is an unpleasant duty. We cannot think of God but as of a judge, nor of a world to come but as of our own ruin. A guilty conscience would fain obliterate the thoughts of God; as the guilty heathens, Rom. i. 28, 'They did not like to retain God in their knowledge;' that is actual, sound, distinct thoughts of God. It is said, James ii. 19, 'The devils believe and tremble.' Thoughts of God impressed the more horror on them, therefore they cried out, Mat. viii. 29, 'Art thou come hither to torment us before the time?' So guilty men are under these horrors, 'They are all their lifetime subject to bondage,' Heb. ii. 15; which, though it be not always felt, is soon awakened: Job xxi. 14, 'Therefore they say unto God, Depart from us, for we desire not the knowledge of thy ways.'

What shall we do to remedy this.

[1.] Get your conscience cleansed by the hearty application of the blood of Christ. A galled conscience is much discomposed and unsettled, and unfit for such an exercise; musing requireth a quiet sedate mind.

[2.] There are matters comfortable that may be of excellent relief to the spirit. When the soul is sadly humbled, and bondage is indeed revived, there is an hope set before us to which we may fly for refuge: Heb. vi. 18, 'That by two immutable things, in which it is impossible for God to lie, we may have strong consolation, who have fled for refuge to lay hold upon the hope set before us.' The wounded soul may run up to the mountains of myrrh and frankincense. So David, Ps. xciv. 19, 'In the multitude of my thoughts within me thy comforts delight my soul.'

4. Another let and hindrance is unwieldiness of spirit to spiritual and heavenly duties. The heart is many times burdened and oppressed, and sunk down with its own burden and weight, that it cannot be lifted up to any holy duties, and so is unfit for any exercise of religion. This our Saviour bids his disciples have a care of: Luke xxi. 34, 'Take heed to yourselves, lest at any time your hearts be overcharged with surfeiting and drunkenness and cares of this life.' Pleasures and cares do as it were hang a weight upon the soul that it cannot mount up to God in heavenly exercises. This is expressed by a fat heart: Isa. vi. 10.

'Make the heart of this people fat;' that is, spiritually dull, as it is observed of the ass, which is the simplest of all creatures, it hath the fattest heart. There is a spiritual dulness and listlessness that is apt to seize upon us.

What shall we do to help this?

[1.] Learn a holy moderation and sobriety in outward businesses and pleasures. As the apostle says of prayer, Eph. vi. 18, 'Watching thereunto;' the same rule holds good in meditation. Watch that you may always keep the soul in a fitness for the duty; order your affairs with great wisdom, that you may not jostle out so necessary a duty. When a man is encumbered with business, there is no room left for such an exercise; if he let loose his heart disorderly all the day, he will find this spiritual dulness to seize on him.

[2.] Keep the body in a fit frame, that it may not be a clog to the soul, but a dexterous instrument. There is a sanctification of the body: 1 Thes. v. 23, 'And the very God of peace sanctify you wholly, and I pray God your whole spirit and soul and body be preserved blameless unto the coming of our Lord Jesus Christ.' And the apostle commands, 1 Thes. iv. 4, 'That every one of you should know how to possess his vessel in sanctification and honour.' Men emasculate and weaken their strength and spirits, and so the body loseth its fitness.

Secondly, There are hindrances that are peculiar to the duty of meditation. I shall name but two—barrenness of thoughts and inconstancy.

1. Leanness and barrenness of thoughts. When we go about to meditate, we have no matter whereupon to bestow our time and thoughts, and so christians are much discouraged. This is opposite to that which the scripture calls the abundance of the heart: Mat. xii. 34, 'Out of the abundance of the heart the mouth speaketh;' that is, when there is a holy treasure in the soul.

Now to remedy this—

[1.] You must not give way to it, but try and use constant exercise. When we give way to such indispositions, they prove an utter bondage. Voluntary neglects are punished with penal hardness, and evils grow upon us; as to lie in the dirt will make us more filthy, and by little and little men are hardened through the deceitfulness of sin. The apostle speaks of them that have $αἰσθητήρια\ γεγυμνασμένα$: Heb. v. 14, 'Who by reason of use have their senses exercised to discern both good and evil.' All habits are increased by frequent acts, long disuse makes the duty uncouth. Wells which are at first a puddle are the sweeter for draining. If we are under indisposition, should we not strive to come out of it? The more we work, the more vigorous and free is the soul for the work of God.

[2.] Get a good stock of sanctified knowledge. Let there be a treasure in your hearts: Mat. xiii. 52, 'Every scribe which is instructed in the kingdom of heaven is like unto a man that is an householder, which bringeth forth out of his treasure things new and old.' Those that buy by the penny will be sometimes in want: Prov. vi. 21, 22, 'Bind them continually upon thine heart, and tie them about thy neck. When thou goest it shall lead thee, when thou sleepest it shall keep thee, and when thou awakest it shall talk with thee.' This is the way to make truths present and ready in the thoughts; when we have laid them up, we can the better lay them out.

[3.] When the heart is barren, think of your own sins and corruptions, and the experiences of God to your own souls. If we did not want an heart we could never want matter, did we but consult with our own experiences: Ps. xl. 12, 'Innumerable evils have compassed me about; mine iniquities have taken hold upon me, so that I am not able to look up; they are more than the hairs of mine head, therefore mine heart faileth me.' And if nothing else will come to hand, meditate upon your present unfitness for any holy duty.

[4.] You may season and affect your mind before meditation with some part of God's word. Reading is a good preparative, and when we have taken in food, we may exercise our depastion and digestion upon it.

2. A loose garish spirit, that is apt to skip and wander from thought to thought. There is a madness in man; his thoughts are light and feathery, tossed to and fro, and like the loose wards in a lock, only kept up whilst we are turning the key. This doth much discourage christians, that they cannot keep up their affections and command their thoughts.

How shall we help and remedy this?

[1.] When you go to meditate, you should exercise a command and restraint upon yourselves. This is expressed in scripture by trussing up the loins of your minds: Luke xii. 30, 'Let your loins be girded about;' an allusion to their hanging garments, that they trussed up when they went about any work, that they may be compact and succinct. Lay a command upon yourselves: Zeph. ii. 1, 'Gather yourselves together, yea, gather together, O nation not desired!'

[2.] Pray and call in the help of God's Holy Spirit: Ps. lxxxvi. 11, 'Unite my heart to fear thy name.' Lord, make my heart one. He that could stay the sun can stay the fleeting of your thoughts.

[3.] Dry up these swimming toys and fancies with the flame of heavenly love. Love unites the heart, and where we have a pleasure, there we can stay: Ps. cxix. 97, 'Oh, how love I thy law! it is my meditation all the day.'

[4.] Let the course of your lives be grave and serious. The mind is according to the course of the life. You flatter yourselves when you think you are able to command spiritual thoughts on a sudden, when you have suffered your thoughts to rove and wander: Prov. xvii. 24, 'Wisdom is before him that hath understanding, but the eyes of a fool are in the ends of the earth;' here and there and everywhere.

[5.] Watch against the first diversion; how plausible soever it be, look upon it as an intruding that breaks the rank. The devil injects good thoughts sometimes that he might divert your other thoughts. Charge your thoughts that they may not disturb your meditation: Cant. iii. 5, 'I charge you, O ye daughters of Jerusalem, that you stir not up, nor awake my love till he please.'

[6.] When you come to meditate in God's presence, do not bring the world with you; purge yourselves of all carnal affections: Ezek. xxxiii. 31, 'Their heart goeth after their covetousness.' Always consider this, the prevailing lust will engross the thoughts. To a distracted mind no place is a solitude; the very closet is a market-place. Therefore before meditation we should purge our hearts of worldly affections.

SERMON IV.

And Isaac went out to meditate in the field at the even-tide.—
GEN. xxiv. 63.

I SHALL not wholly divert from the subject in hand, though I shall a little interrupt the method of it. My purpose is now to speak of that meditation that is proper to the sacrament.

The main part of that worship is dispatched in thoughts. Here we come to put reason to the highest and most sublime use, to be an instrument and servant to faith and love.

But now the thoughts proper to the Lord's supper are many. There are an union of mysteries, yea, so many, that they are a burden to some christians, and a snare to those that are most scrupulous. It will be necessary therefore to give you some directions how you may guide yourselves in this duty for your best advantage. It is a matter of great profit to be wise and skilful in duties. Many that know the general nature of them know not how to manage them. David saith, Ps. cxix. 27, 'Make me to understand the way of thy precepts, so shall I talk of thy wondrous works;' intimating that then we perform duties with most success when we go about them with most wisdom and understanding; and when we are skilled in the way of God's precepts, we shall understand those marvellous acts of grace which he vouchsafeth to his people.

Now it is good that every one according to his talent should help one another's joy, and therefore I shall now speak a little to this purpose, and the rather because it will much conduce to the opening of the doctrine of meditation in the general. My method shall be this— (1.) I will show the usual defects of christians in this service, with their necessary remedies; (2.) I shall handle some cases.

First, The usual defects and faults of people in this duty, I mean so far as they concern meditation, and they are four—barrenness, stupidity, roving of thoughts, and a lazy formality.

1. Barrenness. This is a great trouble to christians, when their understandings are unfruitful, and they cannot enlarge themselves in pertinent and necessary thoughts.

Now how shall we do to get our hearts to be fruitful in holy thoughts?

[1.] There must be a solemn preparation for this service. It is good to breathe ourselves in some religious exercises beforehand, that we may run the more freely without fainting. Spiritual dispositions do not come on us of a sudden; christians are deceived that look for rapt and sudden motions; there must be a time to put off the shoes off our feet when we come upon holy ground to converse with God in so sweet a service; we must lay aside the distractions of the world, and not come reeking from the world into God's presence. There must be a time to raise the soul into a zealous height and ardour; there must be a blowing of the fire, for here you come to flame, your thoughts are to flame out in great and raised ascents: Cant. i. 12, 'While the king sitteth at his table, my spikenard sendeth forth the smell thereof.' Wood doth not blaze and flame as soon as it is laid on.

[2.] Those solemn and preparative thoughts are chiefly to be spent in these two things—the nature of the supper, and the love of Christ in the institution of it.

(1.) The nature of the supper. You are to consider the great things that are offered to you, and the great blessings and benefits which God cometh to represent, exhibit, and seal up to your souls: Mat. xi. 7, 'What went ye out into the wilderness for to see?' Christ examineth the grounds of their resort and concourse to him. It is good to consider what we are about, and the dainties of the banquet we are invited to, what assurance the outward signs are to give you, what communion we have with Christ and his graces. We are barren, because we do not consider our work, and the nature and importance of it.

(2.) The love of Christ in the institution of it. (1.) The time when it was instituted: 1 Cor. xi. 23, 'The Lord Jesus Christ the same night in which he was betrayed, took bread.' The Lord Jesus Christ had thoughts of the greatest good to man when man was executing the greatest spite and malice against him. And the rather because it is an act of mercy that Christ frequently useth to surprise sinners in the midst of their wickedness. When Saul was breathing out threatenings against the disciples, God had a design of love to him, and smites him from his horse. Some are smitten with conviction in the height of provocations. We read in ecclesiastical story of a young man that came to stab St John who was converted by him; so many come to jeer and catch at a sermon, and have been converted by it. (2.) The rights which he instituted, appointing bread and wine, symbols of pleasure and delight. As a physician conveys health to us in a golden pill, so doth Christ convey spiritual nourishment to us by those elements which we take pleasure in. The outward observance is comfortable. God doth not require us to lance ourselves, and to exercise the body with whips and cords; the rites are not bloody, as in circumcision, but bread and wine. And yet this is nothing to the inward sweetness, meat and drink which the world knows not off: John iv. 32, 'I have meat to eat which ye know not of.'

(3.) The advantage and relief that faith has from these things of sense. God speaketh to you now, not by words, but things. He doth as it were embody religion, and represent it to the senses: Gal. iii. 1, 'O foolish Galatians! who hath bewitched you, that you should not obey the truth, before whose eyes Jesus Christ hath been evidently set forth crucified among you?' that is, in the word or sacraments; here God doth as it were hold forth Christ dying before your eyes. It is a pleasure to see things by picture, though we know the person; so though we have an image of Christ in the word, and may know his person there, yet it is a great relief to us to see Christ in the supper by these outward symbols, where sense may teach faith what strength of grace and what sweetness of comfort to expect from Christ. These thoughts through the blessing of God will raise the soul into a frame of religion, that when you come to this ordinance you will not be so dry and barren.

2. Wandering when the heart is prepared and set towards God, how shall we do to keep it from roving, and prevent those excursions which are apt to carry away the heart.

[1.] Get an awe and dread of God. Labour to have the deepest apprehensions of the presence of God as possibly may be. Strong affections, especially fear, lock up the mind, and do not suffer it to flit abroad. Now fear is not unseasonable to this duty, but rather proper, because of the excellent mysteries by which God condescendeth and approacheth us. Chrysostom calls it *terribilis mystica mensa*, the dreadful mysterious table, and therefore now our apprehensions should be most aweful. When Jacob had a sight of God, says he, Gen. xxviii. 17, 'How dreadful is this place!' And the psalmist saith, Ps. lxviii. 35, 'O God! thou art terrible out of thy holy places.' Mixed affections do best in the sweetest worship: Ps. ii. 11, 'Serve the Lord with fear, and rejoice with trembling;' Hosea iii. 5, 'They shall fear the Lord and his goodness in the latter days.' Here we are to have distinct thoughts of his holiness and goodness, and therefore we should fear before him, lest we forget ourselves to be poor guilty creatures; and fear confineth the soul, and will not suffer it to run abroad.

[2.] Chide the heart for your vain excursions. Christians might have more command over their hearts if they would but hold the reins a little straiter, and check their souls; they are not so sadly sensible of the idle roving of the brain, which do not so directly carry them after the evil, though they make them to neglect the good. Take up yourselves, as David doth about his lumpishness: Ps. xlii. 5, 'Why art thou cast down, O my soul? and why art thou disquieted in me?' Did I come hither to think of anything but Christ and heaven? Did I come to think of news, vanity, business, and lust? My work is to discern the Lord's body, not to think of worldly toys. Is this to remember and fruitfully to insist upon his death? Look, as Christ did chide his disciples, Mat. xxvi. 40, 'What! could ye not watch with me one hour?' so chide your heart. Cannot I keep my heart free for God a little while? In heaven duty will be my constant work, and if my heart wander now, how shall I be able to hold it for ever? In the supper God ties my soul by outward rites; lest my eyes should carry away my heart, God would exercise my eyes. Certainly if you would chide your souls the heart would not steal so many glances. But usually our hearts do not steal away; we dismiss them, and let them go. God gave reason a command of your thoughts at first, and we might exercise it more than we do.

3. Stupidness. Many times the soul is surprised with deadness and amazement; it neither actually thinks of evil nor of good, but is at a dead pause and stay. For this I shall urge a double help.

[1.] By earnest ejaculations call in the help of the Spirit: Cant. iv. 16, 'Awake, O north-wind, and come, thou south; blow upon my garden, that the spices thereof may flow out.' Desire God to breathe upon the soul with a fresh gale and excitement; that he would take a coal from his own altar, that the perfume might burn bright. Censers must not be kindled with strange fire. Oh! raise and quicken this dead soul! Remember 'the first Adam was made a living soul, the last Adam was made a quickening spirit,' 1 Cor. xv. 45.

[2.] Call upon your own hearts. It is a mistake of christians to think they are only to call upon God; you are also to call upon yourselves, and to deal with your own souls by way of quickening: Ps. lvii. 8, 'Awake up, my glory; awake, psaltery and harp: I myself will awake early.' Charge your souls, awake to the consideration of heavenly mysteries. Speak to your own hearts, as David lays a charge upon himself: Ps. ciii. 1, ' Bless the Lord, O my soul; and all that is within me bless his holy name.' The children of God are brought in speaking to themselves, Oh! my drowsy, blockish heart! how coldly dost thou think of Christ! This dead heart will not become the service of the living God.

4. A lazy formality. Either we cannot get the soul to this worship, or we perform it slightly. We content ourselves with a few careless glances, and lazy barren thoughts. To remedy this, consider, in so sweet a duty God doth not only require affection, but height of affection, an holy ardour, earnestness and raisedness of spirit: Cant. iv. 6, 'Until the day break and the shadows flee away, I will get me to the mountain of myrrh, and to the hill of frankincense;' an allusion to the censers used in the Levitical worship. God requires such thoughts as will comfort, revive, and quicken our souls. Such thoughts as end in affection. Leave not off till you can say as the spouse, Cant. ii. 5, 'Stay me with flagons, comfort me with apples, for I am sick of love.' Do not leave meditating of Christ till you can bring your souls to a holy ravishment, and your hearts are wounded with impatient desires after communion with Christ. No thoughts will work but those that are serious.

Secondly, I will propound some cases, which shall not only concern the duty of the Lord's supper, but some of them the duty of meditation in general.

Case 1. How can we do, because of variety of matter that is to be meditated upon, that plenty makes us barren? And in such straits of time, how can we run through all? I shall answer to this in three propositions.

1. The mind of man is $\dot{\epsilon}\nu\epsilon\rho\gamma\dot{\eta}s$, working, and much may be done by thoughts in a short time. The mind's motion is not so slow as that of the body, which is burdened with a mass and clod of flesh, and therefore must have time for its action, but the soul is quick. There are two sorts of meditations in the supper, as indeed in all other matters—pregnant apprehensions and enforcing reasons. (1.) Pregnant apprehensions, suitable to each circumstance of the duty. Now these are absolutely necessary; as in blessing the elements, and setting them aside for this use, think of the eternal decrees of God, by which Christ was separated to the office of mediator. In breaking the bread, your thoughts must act afresh on the sorrows of Christ's cross, and those bruises wherewith he was broken for our iniquities. Thus it is good to follow every part of the duty with some devout and religious

thoughts. (2.) Enforcing reasons, when we pitch upon one matter, and inculcate it, and whet it upon the soul according to our present distress and exigencies, which is a pleading with our own hearts from the main design and end of the duty.

2. It is not good to skip from matter to matter hastily; partly because a light touch leaves very little impression, and therefore, as long as milk cometh, suck on the breasts of consolation. Hold reason and faith to its work; when things drop thus on their own accord, they are sweetest, as life-honey that drops of itself from the comb, or as marrow, that the bone droppeth of its own accord; as the lamb sucks the dam's dugs till they cease dropping. When thoughts come, freely entertain them. Partly because we cannot think of all at once; one thought would but intrude and thrust out another ere we have received comfort and profit, and in a throng and crowd of thoughts there is little good done. And besides it would draw a tediousness upon the soul if every time we should renew the same thoughts; God appointed this variety for our relief, not our burden.

3. There must be a wise choice in such variety of matter according to your necessities and wants: Job v. 27, 'Hear it, and know thou it for thy good.' Things that nearly concern us do most affect us, and thoughts in season are most affecting; while we are here in the world we are always humbled with some present want. Now these wants are known by search and trial, and therefore is examination appointed as a preparative to receiving, that we may know our wants.

Case 2. Is it good to bind ourselves to such or such a meditation? Will not this hinder much sweetness, which we should otherwise reap by the duty? and will it not exclude other thoughts which God by his spirit might raise up in our minds? and so we shall defraud ourselves of much sweetness and comfort in the duty. To this I answer—

1. In every particular duty a christian should have one main particular aim, either the removing of such a doubt the relieving of such a want, the beating down of such a corruption, or the receiving of such a grace. Upon a trial you will find some special need for the supply of which you wait upon God. And there are several reasons why it is good for a christian to be thus particular; partly because it discovers sincerity, and prevents much guile; partly because one case may be best managed and carried on at one time, either in prayer, by wrestling with God, or in meditation by argument and pleading with ourselves; partly because the comfort and success will be most sensible, as a needle that toucheth but in one point entereth sooner than a blunt thick piece of iron that toucheth many, so particular things are most sensible, and leave a quicker and smarter sense upon the soul; partly because when you are thus particular it will make you come with fresh and renewed affections. It is good to drive on this main care, and the bent and design of your thoughts must run that way: 2 Cor. xii. 8, 'And for this thing I besought the Lord thrice that it might depart from me.'

2. God usually comes in over and above our aims and expectations: Eph. iii. 20, 'He is able to do exceeding abundantly above all that we ask or think.' Solomon asked wisdom, and God gave him riches and honour in great abundance. Jacob desired of God to be kept in the way, and God made him two bands. The prodigal comes with a

modest request, Make me a hired servant, and the father puts on him the best robe, and entertains him with the fatted calf. We seek to subdue such a lust, and the Lord comes in with an overflow of comfort. He would have such a doubt removed, and it may be the Lord comes in with a high tide of sensible appearance to his soul and increase of grace.

3. You should do in the Lord's supper as in prayer. You meditate in prayer, but not to exclude supervenient thoughts and sudden motions; so here, you meditate on your own wants and needs, and leave the Spirit to his free assistance. When we use the most prudent course, it is no straitening to the Spirit of God. In all preparations we leave ourselves at a liberty to receive his free breathings and coming into our souls. We keep matter ready at hand to kindle our thoughts to feed our confessions and petitions, so it is good to keep matter ready at hand to feed our meditations, and to drive on the main care, waiting for supervenient assistances.

Case 3. Whether there be required of a christian a fixing of the soul in a steady view and contemplation of God in quietness and silence, without any variety of discourse? Or whether God doth now raise and heighten the soul to a sole act of vision and intuition without any discourse, or the traverses of reason, in the supper or any other ordinance?

That you may understand the case, you must know that the schoolmen and other writers of devotion usually distinguish between consideration, meditation, and contemplation. Consideration is a thinking of truth, and a rolling of it in the understanding and memory. Meditation is an enforcing of truth upon the soul by discourse or variety of pressing arguments. Contemplation is the fruit and perfection of meditation; and this they make a supernatural elevation of the mind, by which it adhereth to God, and pauseth in the sight of God and glory without any variety of discourse; the soul being dazzled with the majesty of God, or the glory of heaven, and transported into a present joy, the use of reason is for a time suspended, and the soul is cast into a kind of sleep and quietness of intuition, staring and gazing with ravishing sweetness upon the divine excellences and the glory of our hopes. In short, contemplation is a ravishing sight without discourse, the work of reason not discoursing, but raised and ecstasied into the highest way of apprehension.

Now it is inquired whether there be any such thing required of a christian? or whether there be any such dispensation in these latter times of the gospel? As, for instance, Paul had the glory of God and Christ presented to him; he did not barely think of these things by the apprehensions of the mind, or discourse of these things by the enforcement of reason, but he had an intuition, a steady view or sight of these things, such as did, as it were, ravish his soul from his body. Doth God use such a dispensation now? I answer in these propositions—

1. In the primitive times these dispensations and raptures were more usual. We read of John's rapture, Rev. i. 10, 'I was in the Spirit on the Lord's day.' Mark, he doth not say the Spirit was in him, as it is present in the heart of every child of God; but he was 'in the Spirit,'

which intimateth height and plenty of revelations. So we read of Peter's rapture while he was praying: Acts x. 10, 'He fell into a trance,' ἐπέπεσεν ἐπ' αὐτὸν ἔκστασις, a trance fell upon him, noting that those raptures are things of dispensation rather than choice and duty; they fall upon us, we do not work ourselves into them. So we read of Paul's rapture: 2 Cor. xii. 2, 'I knew a man in Christ above fourteen years ago (whether in the body I cannot tell, or whether out of the body I cannot tell, God knoweth), such an one caught up to the third heaven.' Whether these things were framed by way of representation to the soul, or whether the soul were for a time separated from the body and was transported into heaven, Paul himself was at a loss, and could not determine and resolve the case.

2. These dispensations may still be, though not in the same height and manner which the apostles enjoyed. God may do it still, for he is left to the liberty and sovereignty of his own dispensations; and though sight, and the beatifical vision and contemplation be the happiness of the next world, yet in some measure God may begin it here, that his children may enter into their inheritance by degrees, and may be beforehand led into the suburbs of heaven. As a father gives the child not only a part of the estate, but sometimes the liberty of the whole house, so God may give us here in this world not only those more temperate enjoyments of peace and joy in the Holy Ghost, and the first-fruits of the Spirit, but he may lead us into the suburbs of heaven, and put us above the clouds into the glory of the world to come. Though there may be such a dispensation, yet not in the same manner that the apostles enjoyed it, for that was peculiar to them; and therefore when the apostle Paul had reported his rapture, he pleaded that he had the sign of an apostle: 2 Cor. xii. 12, 'Truly the signs of an an apostle were wrought among you in all patience, in signs, and wonders, and mighty deeds. With these raptures there was a concomitant revelation of the will of God. And they were for other ends; these raptures were not so much excesses of religion, but revelations for the great ends of the gospel. John's rapture was to receive the visions of God for the comfort of the churches; Peter's to go to the Gentiles; Paul's that he might have commission for the apostleship, and the mark and sign of an apostle. Therefore though God may use some such dispensation (for we know not what he may do out of sovereignty), yet not in the same way, and for the same end.

3. Those raptures and transportations, which the children of God now feel sometimes, proceed from strong pangs and ecstasies of love, which for a while do suspend and forbid the distinct use of reason, and cast the soul into a quiet silent gaze. Observe that love, where it is moderate, venteth itself in thoughts and words, and it is a great help to make the inward sense more acute and sharp; but where it is vehement and strong, it is contented with itself, and satisfied with its own heat, ardour, and intenseness, therefore there is not such a distinct actual discourse. As when a man huggeth and embraceth a friend, the closer he huggeth him, the less distinctly doth he behold and take a view of him; so in the embraces of love, when the soul falleth into the arms of Christ, and claspeth about Christ with the arms of its own love, it hindereth the distinct exercise of reason, and

those offices of discourse by which the soul would otherwise reflect upon him. A man that desireth a precious jewel, at first he vieweth it with greediness and delight, but afterwards he layeth it up in his bosom, and wholly pleaseth himself in the possession of it; so the soul that thirsts after Christ pleaseth itself in the consideration of his beauty and perfection, and dwells upon it with religious thoughts, but afterwards love growing very strong, and being heightened unto the utmost degree, shutteth the eyes of our souls, and we only please ourselves in a more intimate feeling, and in the sweetness of our embraces. Great and high affections must needs hinder the use of reason, because all our strength and vigour runneth out into one faculty, and then such a poor limited creature as man is cannot attend other offices and employments of the soul. It is very notable in the whole life of Christ that he had no ecstasy, *propter maximam capacitatem supernaturalem animæ*, because of the extraordinary perfection of his person, and the large capacity of his soul; he had a transfiguration, yet all the while in the midst of that he had a temperate use of reason, Mat. xvii. The disciples were indeed surprised by those glimpses and emissions of his glory; they were overwhelmed, so that 'they fell on their faces, and were sore afraid,' ver. 6. Poor man, being of a lesser capacity, cannot suffer such a feeling and high tide of affection without some transportation and ravishment beyond the support of reason, for the strength and vigour of his soul is melted out to Christ in love. Now the soul being of a limited power and capacity, the more strongly it attendeth one office and function, the less can it serve others. Look, as a flame, when it ascendeth, endeth in a point, and groweth narrower and thinner, so such high flames and such glorious ascents of affection usually mind but one thing, and do not permit the soul any variety of discourse, but fix it in one thought, and in one steady and deliberate gaze.

4. Usually such experiences of God's children are given in to them in the most social duties. As in the time of prayer; Peter's trances fell upon him in prayer. Ordinary ecstasies carry some proportion with that which is extraordinary, and usually the soul flames out to God, and breaks forth in religious accents in the time of prayer. And so such strong affection oversets the soul in the time of the Lord's supper: Cant. v. 1, 'Eat, O friends; drink, yea, drink abundantly, O beloved.' Be drunk with loves. That whole song concerneth our communion with Christ in heaven and in the ordinances; above all, in the ordinance of the supper, which is the pledge of heaven. So also in the height of meditation; when the soul hath been spent and much exercised itself in that work, after the labour of meditation God giveth in this silence and rest in the steady contemplation of his love and glory, and the mind being inflamed and heightened with spiritual thoughts and exercises, suffereth a kind of transportation. It is very notable that those ravishments that were between Christ and the spouse were in the palm-tree: Cant. vii. 8, 'I said, I will go up to the palm-tree, I will take hold of the boughs thereof; now also thy breasts shall be as clusters of the vine, and the smell of thy nose like apples.' There Christ would satisfy himself with the church's breasts, and there she should be satisfied with his love. The palm-tree hath a long naked bark, and carrieth all its leaves, branches and fruits upwards;

it noteth the religious ascent of the soul in spiritual exercises, when the thoughts do not run out in underwood and lower branches, in earthly thoughts and carnal distractions. Well, then, in the top of the palm-tree there we taste the sweetness of Christ, and the soul is ravished and spiritually made drunk with the clusters of his grapes.

5. These experiences, where God seeth fit to give them, are given to persons of much holiness and religion : Mat. v. 8, 'Blessed are the pure in heart, for they shall see God.' Those bright and clear souls are more fit to enjoy the sight of God ; when by constant and daily exercise the heart hath been subdued to a religious frame, the Lord may then give in those ravishing sweets, and those gazes upon his beauty and glory. There are degrees in the sense of God's love. Hypocrites have but a taste and a little sip, as the merchant that selleth wine will give a taste to those that do but cheapen it. Christians whose spirits are not defecated or cleared from the clouds of passion or purged from the dregs of carnal interests seldom meet with those sweet and rich experiences; to such an intimate discerning the senses had need be exercised. The lute had need be rightly strung and tuned that maketh a ravishing melody ; easy, lazy, and gross hearts feel none of these rapt motions and strong qualms of affection : God usually gives them to those that are purged and purified.

6. These rich experiences are very fleeting and vanishing, and but now and then bestowed. We have not such high experiences under lock and key, and at the command of our own endeavours. God gives them when he seeth fit, and when he pleaseth they pass away again. If they were constant, and God should continually pour in, the vessel would break, and the soul could not sustain itself under the burden of it. The disciples in the transfiguration were astonished and fell down for fear, they could not bear the glory, though but for a little while : Mat. xvii. 6, 'And when the disciples heard it, they fell on their faces, and were sore afraid.' Our present state is not capable of these transports long ; the soul is not extended and enlarged to such a capacity and fitness, neither is the body qualified. We are in the animal state now, the deliberate contemplation is our portion in heaven, when sin and weakness is done away, and when we have that which the apostle calls a spiritual body, 1 Cor. xv. 44 ; that is, a body fit for those high communications, and for the continual presence of God. This is an extraordinary indulgence, which, if continued, would destroy and abrogate the economy and dispensation of grace. This pause of reason upon the majesty of God and the glory of heaven is somewhat like the sun's standing still in Joshua's time, which, if it were so always, would burn up the frame of nature ; therefore God hath ordained that it should roll hither and thither. Motion and change is fitter for this state to which God hath subjected us.

7. Such ravishing experiences are not to be sought for, but referred to the good pleasure of God. We cannot pray for them in faith, having no promise of them, and we must not be too hasty to eat of the fruits of paradise before our time. It is enough for us to go to heaven in the usual roadway, and not like Elijah, in a fiery chariot. Look, as in outward things we are not to desire riches, but a competency ; if God casteth them in upon our endeavours, we should be thankful ; so

in meditation we must mind those enjoyments which are more temperate, and leave other things to God. It is good to content ourselves with grace, and peace, and joy in the Holy Ghost, though we have not those transports and high ecstasies of love and affection. We must not tempt God with immodest requests and expectations, but sit down humbly and quietly, and if the master of the feast bid us to sit higher, and call us to a more choice dispensation, well and good. These experiences are not to be ranked among duties, but among enjoyments; we shall not be called to an account for the want of them, for we are not obliged to pursue them; they are acts of God's magnificence and indulgence to the soul. Many times christians oppress their souls by their indiscreet aims; it is good to keep an even hand, that we may not vex ourselves with the disappointment of a rash and foolish trust. Some are altogether careless, and content themselves with any frame of spirit in worship; others are not satisfied but with ecstatic and rapt motions. Look, as it is with a lute-string, if it be too slack, it doth not sound at all, if it be too high stretched, it is hoarse and screeching; so it is with our souls in duty; when we are careless, there is no melody made to God, but if we be too high strained, then the soul is oppressed with its own aims, and with a pursuit of things above our reach; the temperate middle way should be our aim.

8. Upon all such experiences we should be careful and watch our hearts, because many times herein we delude ourselves; we call that a rapture which is but the suppositions of a troubled fancy, or some fanatic delusions by which Satan abuseth an over-credulous and superstitious soul. Dotage many times passeth under the pretence of vision, and the extravagances of a wild zeal seemeth rapture. Always observe their end and scope; if they end in pride, and prove a temptation, they are from the devil, and not from God. Experiences from God enlarge our hearts for service, and make us more humble, as the highest flames tremble most. These souls that are called to the highest enjoyments are most humble. It is true we are apt to be puffed up with a revelation from God, as Paul was puffed up with the abundance of revelations, but there was a subsequent dispensation, some cross to humble him: 2 Cor. xii. 7, 'And lest I should be exalted above measure through the abundance of the revelations, there was given to me a thorn in the flesh, the messenger of Satan to buffet me, lest I should be exalted above measure.' This is through the corruption of our nature, which God preventeth in his children by such dispensations. But if it tendeth to make us neglect piety, and to be above duties, it is against the nature of religion, which presseth us to wait upon God with the more encouragement, because we have already discerned his beauty and glory: Ps. lxiii. 2, 'To see thy power and glory so as I have seen thee in the sanctuary.'

Thus I have done with this case, in which I have been in the high mountains. I shall come to the valleys, which, as they are more easy of access, so usually they are more fruitful. What follows will be more plain.

SERMON V.

And Isaac went out to meditate in the field at the even-tide.—
Gen. xxiv. 63.

Case 4. When must we meditate?

1. In the general, something should be done every day; seldom converse begetteth a strangeness to God, and an unfitness for the duty. It is a description of God's servant, Ps. i. 2, 'His delight is in the law of the Lord, and in his law doth he meditate day and night.' At least we should take all convenient occasions. It is an usual way of natural men to make conscience of duties after a long neglect; they perform duties to pacify a natural conscience, and use them as a man would use a sleepy potion or strong waters; they are good at a pinch, not for constant drink. Alas! we lose by such wide gaps and distances between performance and performance; it is as if we had never done it before.

2. For the particular time of the day when you should meditate, that is arbitrary. I told you before you may do it either in the silence of the night, when God hath drawn a curtain of darkness between you and the things of the world; or in the freshness of the morning, or in the evening, when the wildness and vanity of the mind is spent in worldly business.

3. There are some special solemn times, when the duty is most in season; as—

[1.] After a working sermon; after the word hath fallen upon you with a full stroke, it is good to follow the blow; and when God hath cast seed into the heart, let not the fowls peck it away: Mat. xiii. 19, 'When any one heareth the word of the kingdom, and understandeth it not, then cometh the wicked one, and catcheth away that which was sown in his heart.' Ruminate on the word, chew the cud; many a sermon is lost because it is not whet upon the thoughts: James i. 23, 24, 'He is like a man that beholdeth his natural face in a glass; for he beholdeth himself, and goeth his way, and straightway forgetteth what manner of man he was:' Mat. xxii. 22, 'When they heard these things, they marvelled, and left him, and went their way.' You should roll the word in your thoughts, and deeply consider of it.

[2.] Before some solemn duties, as before the Lord's supper, and before special times of deep humiliation, or before the sabbath. Meditation is, as it were, the breathing of the soul; that it may the better hold out in religious exercises, it is a good preparative to raise the spirits into a frame of piety and religion. When the harp is fitted and tuned, it doth the better make music; so when the heart is fixed and settled by a preparative meditation, it is the fitter to make melody to God in worship.

[3.] When God doth specially revive and enable the Spirit. It is good to take advantage of the Spirit's gales; so fresh a wind should make us hoist up our sails. Do not lose the Spirit's seasons; the Spirit's impulses are good significations from God that now is an acceptable time.

Case 5. What time is to be spent in the duty?

I answer—That is left to spiritual discretion. Suck the teat as long as milk cometh. Duties must not be spun out to an unnecessary length. You must neither yield to laziness, nor occasion spiritual weariness; the devil hath advantage upon you both ways. When you rack and torture your spirits after they have been spent, it makes the work of God a bondage; and therefore come not off till you find profit, and do not press too hard upon the soul, nor oppress it with an indiscreet zeal. It is Satan's policy to make you out of love with meditation by spinning it out to a tediousness and an unnecessary length.

Case 6. Whether should the time be set and constant?

I answer—It is good to bind the heart to somewhat, and yet leave it to such a liberty as becomes the gospel. Bind it to somewhat every day, that the heart may not be loose and arbitrary. We see that necessity quickeneth and urgeth, and when the soul is engaged it goes to work the more thoroughly. Therefore the Lord asks, Jer. xx. 21, 'Who is this that engaged his heart to approach unto me?' It is good to lay a tie upon the heart; and yet I advise not to a set stinted hour, lest we create a snare to ourselves. Though a man should resist distractions and distempers, yet some business is unavoidable, and some distempers are invincible. I have observed this, that even religious persons are more sensible of their own vows than of God's commands; when men have bound up themselves in chains of their own making, their consciences fall upon them, and dog them with restless accusations, when they cannot accomplish so much duty as they have set and prescribed to themselves. And besides, when hours are customary and set, the heart groweth formal and superstitious.

Case 7. Are all bound to meditate? are the ignorant? are men of an unquiet nature? are servants? are ministers?

1. Are the ignorant, and men of barren minds, that have not a good stock of knowledge? I answer—Yes, they are bound to this as well as other duties, though they cannot do it well; it is their duty to strive that the word of God may dwell richly in them. It is a mark of a godly man; every man is bound to be skilful in the scriptures: Jer. xxxi. 34, 'They shall all know me, from the least of them to the greatest of them, saith the Lord.' God hath no child so little but he knows his father, therefore all are bound in some measure to be able to discourse of God and of the things of God.

2. But some are of an unquiet nature, fit for public duties, but not for private exercises; are they bound as well as those of softer spirits, and fitter for meditation? I answer—This is not temper, but distemper, the unquiet spirit must not *totaliter cessare*, wholly discontinue this work. They are to mind wherein they may serve God most, but not totally desist from a work so necessary, and of such great importance.

3. Are servants bound to it, whose time is not their own? I answer —They should do what they can; God is more merciful to them, but those that are in bondage to others may find some leisure for God.

4. Are ministers obliged? Their whole work is a study, their employment is a continual meditation. I answer—There is a difference between meditation and study. In study we mind the good of others, in meditation the good of our own souls. Things work with us accord-

ing to our end and the aims that we propose to ourselves. Public teaching is no such trial of our hearts; there is a natural pride in us to urge us to teach others, and that makes so many intrude into the ministry; there is some kind of authority in it, that we exercise over others; but we are to mind the good of our own souls, and to regard private duties. There is a greater engagement upon us than others, because we have the help of art and education, and have greater advantages than others, and therefore we should not lose so sweet a comfort. It is strange that papists confine it altogether to spiritual men, as if it were not a lay duty, and usually we lay it aside, as if study would serve the turn, and it did not belong to us.

V. My work is now to speak of the object of meditation, which I am first to handle in general, and then in special.

First, In the general consideration of the object I am to speak—(1.) Of the choice of the object; (2.) The manner how to work upon it.

1. For the choice of the object, I need not press you to choose that which is seasonable, and what suiteth with your own case. A sermon worketh more forcibly when it is suitable, so do thoughts when they are seasonable, and direct to the present case of the soul: Ps. xciv. 19, 'In the multitude of my thoughts within me thy comforts delight my soul;' he meaneth sad thoughts, then it was his advantage to exercise himself in seasonable comforts, like a shower of rain on new-mown grass; it would be burnt up with the drought, which if rain had come seasonably might have flourished and grown up with a fair herbage; so the soul is parched with a temptation, if it be not watered with suitable thoughts. 'We faint not,' saith the apostle, 'for we look not to the things that are seen, but to the things that are not seen,' 2 Cor. iv. 16-18, viz., by reviving our christian hopes; and therefore the exigencies of the soul must be served. Food in thirst doth enrage rather than please. It is not enough to consider what is good, but what is seasonable. Things mistimed and misplaced lose their force and operation; as the blood when it is in vessels is the continent of life, but when it is out it breedeth diseases, so truths out of their order and place do not nourish the heart, but oppress it; as if you should talk of hell and the severity of God's judgment to those that are dejected, this were to speak to the grief of those whom God hath wounded, and when the back is ready to break to lay on more load.

I shall for the present (having spoken largely in the general directions) give you but two rules—

[1.] Choose that which is profitable. There is a great deal of difference between the objects of meditation; some are more speculative, others altogether practical. There are matters speculative revealed in the word which yet have their use and profit; as the fall of the angels, the order of providence, &c.; yet out of these the heart may distil matter of practical use and profit. All the benefit we receive from these truths lieth in our meditation of them. But then there are others that are altogether practical, and these should chiefly be chosen. The mind of man is the mill of God, not to grind chaff, but wheat. Matters practical are there to be ground for bread to the soul; they that hunt after fancies do but misemploy their thoughts, and beat chaff into dust, and do not grind good corn for nourishment; and that is the reason why many times mean christians excel those of the best gifts, because they spend their time in subtle inventions and inquiries, and whilst we strive to be more subtle they are more sincere. Oh! consider the soul is diseased while it is only fed with quails and fine notions; there is more delicacy but less nourishment. Notions that are airy tickle the fancy, and move the lighter part of the affections, but those considerations that are grave and masculine convince most soundly, and work most deeply: 'Wisdom entereth into the heart,' Prov. ii. 10. Look, as wicked men do not please themselves in abstractions of sin, they devise wickedness to accomplish it, so the christian should not satisfy himself with nice speculations, but employ his thoughts about practical matters to promote holiness in his heart and life.

[2.] Choose matters to meditate upon in an orderly and apt method. But you will say, Do you think this useful to confine the soul to method in meditation, to prescribe a set course to ourselves? Shall we not jostle out seasonable thoughts? I answer—

(1.) It is lawful and necessary to prescribe to ourselves a course and method, partly that we may know our work, and that we may not be to seek both of a subject and how to work upon it; therefore, that you may keep your religious exercises together, and know how to pass from one to another, it is good to keep a set course. Partly because things work with us according to method; it is the way of knowledge and affection; the soul finds it an excellent advantage when things are aptly suited and ranked in their order. God himself hath disposed all his works in order, so should we ours. You will find an advantage when you take your rise low, and go on from matters more plain and obvious to those that are more mysterious. There are shallows for the lambs of God, and there are deeps for those of an higher growth and stature. You must pass from the most obvious matter of christianity to those that are of more sublime speculation. The rise of the sun is first low, and gildeth with its beams the eastern parts, and then riseth higher to the top of the heavens; so in your progress there are the third heavens to which you must ascend, but first you must pass the first and second heavens. Before we search the depths of the Spirit, it is good to search the depths of the belly (I compare Paul's expression with Solomon's), to begin with the knowledge of ourselves before we come to the knowledge of God. *Prius redi ad te quam rimari præsumas quæ supra te*, is a rule of Bernard, who was of much experience in these exercises; first return to ourselves, and by an orderly progress to go on from examination of ourselves, before we soar up to the contemplation of the divine glory. You know what Christ saith, John iii. 12, 'If I have told you earthly things, and ye believe not, how shall ye believe if I tell you of heavenly things?' They were spiritual matters he spake of, regeneration and principles of religion; yet in comparison of deeper mysteries of religion, and because he had set them out by earthly similitudes of generation, water and the wind, he called them 'earthly things.' Christ trained up his own disciples this way; first he begins with plain matters: John xvi. 12, 'I have yet many things to say unto you, but you cannot bear them yet.' There were greater mysteries above the reach and size of their present capacity. So the apostle Paul speaketh of wisdom for them that are perfect : 1 Cor. ii. 6, 'Howbeit we speak wisdom to them that are perfect;' that is, for them that had made some progress in religion ; perfect, not absolutely, but in comparison with babes and novices. Therefore it is good, with Mary, to sit at the feet of Jesus, and not presently with the spouse to beg the kisses of his mouth, but to go on by degrees.

(2.) Though we must contrive a method and course, yet there must be a liberty left for things, for all seasons and occasions. As in the world, though a man hath disposed his business, yet he reserveth a liberty for incidental and unthought of occasions; so in these spiritual matters, and in the course of religious exercises, you must not bind up yourselves from these occasions. I shall name four—

(1st.) Working and forcible sermons. It is not good to lose the heat that we have gotten at the word, but to go home and chew the cud. In the word there is ingestion ; in meditation you turn it into nourishment. There must be a time for concoction, and when the seed is scattered, it must be covered.

(2d.) For present impulses, keep yourselves free, that you may not lose the advantage of such impulses. Many times Christ cometh 'leaping upon the mountains, and skipping upon the hills,' Cant. ii. 8. He impelleth our hearts on a sudden and unlooked for, by causing holy thoughts to shoot into our minds; by representing our unworthiness, coldness, and deadness of life ; or else he inflameth us by representing the beauty and loveliness of grace. Then it is good those thoughts should take the next turn, and our method must give way to God's dispensation. As general nature altereth its course in some great particular exigencies, fire descendeth, and water ascendeth, so in this case the general work must be interrupted. It is a kind of resisting God not to entertain these motions; I do not mean when they come upon you in the necessary work of your callings, but only that they may have the next turn.

(3d.) For remarkable providences, when God casteth us upon such objects as stir up special veneration and reverence, as some marvellous events, or creatures that discover his wisdom and glory, or sudden death of one near us, it is of excellent use while such experiences are warm to go home and consider of them; as Waldo, a rich merchant of Lyons, was conversing with a friend, and he fell down dead, and presently he went home, and thought of the uncertainty of life, and the necessity of providing for a future state, and God blessed these thoughts for his conversion. Or else the sad falls of a person eminent for religion, when we see some glorious star fall like lightning from heaven, these are accidents that must not be passed over without some mark and consideration, and then God doth as it were call you off from your usual thoughts.

(4th.) The present exigence of the Spirit. Choose that which is seasonable, and what suits with your own case ; a sermon works more forcibly when it is seasonable. Thus David: Ps. xciv. 19, 'In the multitude of my thoughts within me thy comforts delight my soul.' He means his sad thoughts; it was an advantage to him then to solace himself with those comforts God had provided. The scripture useth this similitude of rain upon new-mown grass. Rain when it comes seasonably refresheth the grass and causes it to spring up, which otherwise would be burnt up with the drought and heat of the season; so the soul would be parched with a temptation if it be not watered with seasonable thoughts. But I have spoken to this point before.

But you will say, What is the method that we should use?

Ans. Though I cannot exactly prescribe it, yet give me leave to advise—

(1.) For those that are wholly to begin this duty, it is best first to meditate about meditation, the nature, use, and excellency of it, and how they may carry it on with success; it is a good preparative to the whole work. I do direct you to this course, because this is that which the soul standeth in need of; this will lay a charge and necessity upon the soul. As to pray is a good preparative to prayer, so to meditate on meditation is a good preparative to meditation. To quicken you, consider the motives alleged, and when you have done all, say, O soul! do but go and try! O Lord! help me, and keep this up in the thoughts of thy servant!

(2.) For the general method, it is good to keep the method of the Spirit. The method of meditation should follow that of God's dispensation: John xvi. 8, 'When the Spirit is come, he shall reprove the world of sin and of righteousness and of judgment.' First begin with sin, which is more easy and familiar to the understanding; it is good to lay the foundation of all in the mortifying and purgative way; and then go to righteousness, and after the extermination of sin we shall be fitter to entertain the love of God, and then go to judgment. Take another method; first consider the great end of man, that you may come to yourselves; then the evil of sin, that you may bemoan and avoid it; then the miseries of the world, or the vanity of the creature, that you may contemn it; then the horrors of death, the severity of judgment, the torment of hell, that you may prevent it; then the excellences of Christ, the privileges of the godly, the rare contrivance of the gospel; then of providence, of heaven, of God and his attributes, his power, his wisdom, his eternity, &c., with suitable scriptures for each of these.

2. For the manner how you must work upon these objects.

[1.] There must be pregnant thoughts and apprehensions. Deep consideration begins the work; you must set your hearts to consider the subject, for when the heart is once set, these thoughts through the blessing of God will come in freely. It is often spoken in scripture of setting our hearts to seek the Lord; when the heart is set for prayer, God comes in with a great enlargement; so when the heart is set to consider, you will have serious and solemn thoughts. If vain thoughts trouble you and interpose, yet still set the heart and go on; as a man in a journey, though dogs come out and bark upon him, he rideth on; to run after every cur would be a great hindrance and diversion; so if you stand quarrelling with ever vain thought, you lose your purpose, and so the devil will gain that by a reflex act which you seek to reject in a direct act; as criers in a court in calling for silence many times make the greatest noise. Mr Greenham was wont to lift up his heart in a short ejaculation, and so go on.

[2.] There are serious enforcements and rational inculcations. Things barely propounded do not work; it is by lively reasons they are whetted upon the soul. Look, as it is in going to sea, those that only mind passage do not stay upon the ocean, and therefore do not fetch up the treasures of the great deep, but those that go to fish cast out the net again and again, so must you; you must cast in reason upon reason, enforcement upon enforcement, till you bring up treasure, cast on weight upon weight till it weigh down. Now these rational enforcements are four—by arguments, similitudes, comparison, colloquies or soliloquies.

(1.) By arguments that are most effective. Inquire what kind of arguments have most force upon the spirits. The usual arguments you should look after are causes and effects; by the one knowledge is increased, and by the other affections are stirred. Do not emptily declame, but see that your eye may affect your heart. Choose such arguments as are evident and strong; you have them in the word and in sermons, and you should have them in your hearts: Luke vi. 45, 'A good man out of the good treasure of his heart bringeth forth that which is good, and an evil man out of the evil treasure of his heart bringeth forth that which is evil, for out of the abundance of the heart the mouth speaketh.' A good man should be able to bring forth good arguments, that he might bring his heart powerfully to the acknowledgment of the will of God; for what did God give you faculties, and the use of reason and discourse, and such helps in the ministry, but for such a purpose?

(2.) By similitudes. The word will furnish you upon every point. Heaven speaketh to us in a dialect of earth. Heavenly mysteries are clothed with a fleshly notion. In the Book of Canticles communion with Christ is set forth by banquets and marriages, and spiritual things are shadowed out by corporal fairness and sweetness. In other places of scripture Christ's kingdom is set forth by an earthly kingdom, the word of God by a glass, the wrath of God by fire. Now apt similitudes have a great force upon the soul for two reasons—partly because they help apprehension, and partly because they help discourse. There is as it were a picture for the thoughts to gaze upon. By similitudes we come to understand a spiritual thing that we know not, being represented by sensible things with which they are acquainted; the thing is twice represented to the soul—in reality and in picture, as a double medium helpeth the sight, the glass and the air in spectacles; a shilling in a basin of water seemeth bigger, so it is here. Yea, they yield matter for much enlargement, and help discourse, as when they brought God the blind and the lame: Mal. i. 8, 'Offer it now unto thy governor; will he be pleased with thee, or accept thy person? saith the Lord of hosts.' Sin is expressed by death; now the soul may reason thus: I tremble at death, why do I not tremble at sin? So mortification is physic; I can dispense with the trouble of physic for my body, this will make my soul healthy.

(3.) By comparisons, wherein other things are like or unlike the things we meditate upon. I urge this because it is a natural help; it is a rule of nature that contraries being put together do mightily illustrate one another; as when you compare fairness and deformity, black and white, deformity is more odious, and black is more black. So if I would contemplate the beauty of virtue and of the spiritual life, I would compare it with the filthiness of vice, and of the profane life. So when you compare the pleasant path of wisdom with the filthy and dreggy delights that are in the path of sin, you gain upon the soul. Put earthly things into the scales with heavenly, and see which weigheth heaviest, set heaven against hell, and heaven against the world. Our Saviour teacheth us to meditate by way of comparison: Mat. xvi. 26, 'For what is a man profited if he shall gain the whole world and lose his own soul? or what shall a man give in exchange for his soul?' So by comparing yourselves with other creatures, as thus; when you would shame yourselves for your disobedience, you may argue thus: All things obey the law of their creation, the sun delighteth to run his race, the stars keep their course, and do not go beside the path God hath set them, and I only have found out my own path. So for your uncomfortableness in the ways of God; you may say, Wicked men delight to do wickedly, but I do not delight in the service of God; shall it not be a pleasure to me to be exercised in the duties of religion? shall I not rejoice in the Lord?

(4.) By colloquies and soliloquies; colloquies and speeches with God, and soliloquies with ourselves. Thoughts are more express and formal, but when turned into words and speeches, it is a sign the affections are stirred. Strong affections must have vent in words; speech is an help in secret prayer.

(1*st.*) In colloquies with God, either by way of complaint: Lord, I am poor, and needy, and worldly. Lord, my heart is naked, and void of grace. Or else by way of request; as the infant will show the apple or jewel, or whatever it hath received, to the parent or nurse, so the soul representeth to God whatever it hath gotten by meditation, and taketh occasion further to converse with God, and beg grace of him.

(2*d.*) In soliloquies with your own souls, and these are either by way of urging the heart or charging it. (1.) By way of urging the heart. As suppose you have been meditating on the glorious salvation that was purchased by Jesus Christ, let this be the close of all, 'How shall we escape if we neglect so great salvation?' Heb. ii. 3. So if you have been meditating on the sinfulness of sin, fall upon your own hearts: Rom. vi. 21, 'What fruit shall we have in those things whereof ye are now ashamed, for the end of those things is death?' Or if you have been meditating of hell and the wrath of God, speak to your heart: Ezek. xxii. 14, 'Can thy heart endure, or can thine hand be strong in the day that I shall deal with thee?' Art thou stronger than God, that thou canst wrestle with him? Or if you have been meditating on your sinfulness, or the course of your own wicked lives, you may return upon your heart: Micah vi. 8, 'He hath showed, O man, what is good, and what doth the Lord require of thee;' and ver. 6, 'Wherewith shall I come before the Lord, and bow myself before the high God?' How shall I get a ransom to redeem my soul from the guilt of sin? (2.) By way of charge and command. Suppose you have been meditating of the benefit of God's service, and the danger of going a-whoring from him: Hosea ii. 7, 'She shall say, I will go and return to my first husband, for then was it better with me than now.' Or if you have been meditating of the benefits of God to your souls, you may return upon your hearts by way of charge: Ps. cxvi. 7, 'Return unto thy rest, O my soul, for the Lord hath dealt bountifully with me.' God hath opened his good treasure to thee, this hath been thy portion, therefore 'Return unto thy rest.' Well, then, thus do, and then be watchful that you do not lose what you have wrought. Isaac digged wells and the Philistines dammed them up; so when the soul hath digged a well of salvation, Satan will seek to dam it up; therefore be watchful.

SERMON VI.

And Isaac went out to meditate in the field at the even-tide.— GEN. xxiv. 63.

SECONDLY, I come now to the particular objects of meditation—

First, I begin with that which is the chief end of man, a necessary work that you may come to yourselves: Luke xv. 17, εἰς ἑαυτὸν δὲ ἐλθών, 'When he came to himself, he said, How many hired servants of my father's have bread enough and to spare, and I perish with hunger!' That is, when he began to consider of his condition, it put better thoughts into him. Therefore, that we may come to ourselves, it is good to consider the end why we were created, and the errand upon which God sent us into the world, to reason thus with ourselves: Why was I sent into the world? Why do I live here? to get an estate, or to get into Christ? to wallow in pleasures, or to exercise myself in communion with God? to heap up perishing things together, or to make my everlasting state more sure? When the end is rightly stated, men know their work, and so live up to the purposes of their creation. But alas! many know other things, but are ignorant of themselves, and so pass on carelessly to their own ruin; like him that gazed on the stars, and fell into a deep pit, their eyes are upon the ends of the earth, but they do not consider their souls. Others, for want of considering the end of their lives, are so far from living as christians, that they scarce live as men, but either as beasts or as devils. Delight in the pleasures of the world transformeth a man into a beast; it is their happiness to enjoy pleasures without remorse, and to gratify the body; and delight in sin transformeth a man into a devil. Worldly pleasures are not bread, and sinful pleasures are poison. You that are allured by the pleasures of the world, which are lawful in themselves, you lay out your money for that which is not bread; and you to whom it is meat to do evil, you feed upon that which is rank poison; the world cannot satisfy, and sin will surely destroy. Thus men beguile themselves, and do not consider of the end of their lives, till their lives be ended, and then they make their moan. Usually when men lie a-dying, then they cry out on this world how it hath deceived them, and how little they have fulfilled the end of their creation. Partly because then conscience is awake, and puts off all disguises; and partly because present things are apt to work upon us, and when the everlasting estate is at hand, the soul is troubled that it did no more think of it. Oh! consider, it is better to be prepared than to be surprised. Think not only of your last end, but of your chief end; what should be the great aim of your lives, even before death comes? All religion lies in this, in fixing the aim of your life; all the difference between men and men is in their chief good and utmost end.

In the managing of this meditation, I shall pursue it in this method; not that I prescribe to you, but that I may set some bounds to my own discourse. However I shall use such a method as is most facile and obvious, not exceeding the capacity and reach of the meanest. The work of such a meditation may be divided into three parts—(1.) The considering work; (2.) The plotting and contriving work; (3.) The arguing work.

First, In the considering work you may propound these or such like things to your thoughts.

1. Man was made for some end. All God's works are referred to the service and use of his glory: Prov. xvi. 4, 'The Lord hath made all things for himself, yea, even the wicked for the day of wrath.' God, being a wise agent, must have an end; now God could have no other end but himself and his own glory, for the end must be more worthy than the means, something better and above all created things; and if God made all things for himself, then man, who was the visible masterpiece of the creation, the lesser world, the compendium and sum of all God's other works. So the apostle, Rom. xi. 36, 'For of him, and through him, and to him are all things.' All things are of him as a creator, through him as a preserver, and to him, or to his glory; from him as the first cause, to him as the last end. Certainly God did not make such a glorious creature as man for any low use. The whole creation was for man's use, and man was for God's glory: Ps. viii. 3, 4, 'When I consider the heavens, the works of thy fingers, the moon and the stars that thou hast ordained, what is man that thou art mindful of him, and the son of man that thou visitest him?' He was God's deputy and vicegerent, created to enjoy the comfort of other creatures, and to exercise dominion over them; the whole world is his palace, arched with heaven, and floored with earth, but still, that he might be faithful to his Maker, and do his homage to God, and give him the rent and tribute of his glory and praise. And therefore if the heavens do declare the glory of God, and the creeping things, and all beasts in their rank and place, much more should man, who was furnished with higher privileges, and with an higher capacity. We have faculties that are especially suited to this purpose; therefore it is said, 1 John v. 26, 'He hath given us an understanding that we may know him that is true.' Certainly God never made such a glorious creature for wealth or pleasures, but for an higher use and purpose, even for himself. If you do but look upon his mind and understanding, you will find it to be a wrong and debasement to take it off from a spiritual use, and put it to a carnal.

2. This end is the enjoying and glorifying of God. To enjoy God is man's happiness, and to glorify God is man's work; by glorifying God he comes to enjoy him, and he enjoyeth him that he may glorify him. Herein he differeth from other creatures; they were made only to glorify him, not to enjoy him, but man to glorify him, and enjoy him too.

[1.] He was made to enjoy him, for that is his happiness. *Domine, fecisti nos propter te, et irrequietum est cor nostrum, donec perveniat ad te.* The soul is made up of unlimited and restless desires; there are such crannies and chinks in the soul that cannot be filled up but by the enjoyment of God; we were made for him, and we are not quiet till we do enjoy him. Nature will teach us to grope after an eternal good, as the Sodomites did after Lot's door in the dark: Acts xvii. 28, 'That they should seek the Lord, if haply they might feel after him, and find him.' So Ps. iv. 6, 'There be many that say, Who will show us any good?' It should be translated, The many say, &c.; for this is the voice of the multitude; all are for good, for something that is every way satisfying and contentful. There are some remains of entire reason and right nature, as Job's messengers said, Job i. 15, 'And I only am escaped alone to tell thee.' There are some obscure instincts that are alone escaped out off the ruins of the fall, to tell us that God is our chiefest good, and therefore must be our utmost end. But the scriptures go further, and teach us that there is no way of enjoying God but in Christ, and till then man can never be happy. God is the centre of the soul, the place of the soul's rest. All things move to their own place, so should man to God. It is monstrous to see things move contrary to the impulse of nature, to see fire to descend, or a stone to leap upward; so it is as monstrous in grace for our souls to descend, and to cleave to those things which are without us, which were made only to rest in God; our souls are of a heavenly original, and therefore should tend thither. Say then, This is that which will make me happy here and hereafter, and therefore why should I run elsewhere? It is against grace and nature. There is a principle in nature by which all creatures aim at their own satisfaction; there is a weight and propension that poiseth them to their happiness. If I would show myself a christian or a man, all my comfort lieth in enjoying God in Christ: Isa. xlvi. 8, 'Remember this, and show yourselves men.' He is a beast that can satisfy his soul with the world, and he is a devil that can satisfy his soul with sin. Let me show myself a man, and return to my own rest. Things are miserable when they do not attain their end; so shall I be out of my place, tossed to and fro till I return to God; the faculties of the soul are misplaced, and are as a member out of joint.

[2.] He was made to glorify God. The creatures do it necessarily; we must do it voluntarily and by choice. This must be the care of our hearts—(1.) In every business; (2.) In every enjoyment.

(1.) In every business, be it never so trivial and low, even in the ordinary refreshments of nature: 1 Cor. x. 31, 'Whether therefore ye eat or drink, or whatsoever ye do, do all to the glory of God.' These common actions of eating and drinking must be done upon reasons of religion. In a king's house there are many officers, but they are all to please the king; so in my calling, in my duties, all must be done for the glory of the great God. All things must be measured by this rule, and give place to this great end, how I may glorify God, whether in the shop or in the closet, in my outward calling or in my private duties, or in my public relations or engagements, so far am I to mingle with any outward business as I may still enjoy God, and be serviceable to his glory.

This is to make religion your work, and not your play and recreation, when still in every business God is at the utmost end, whatever present ends I have. If nature interpose to make us look after our particular conveniences, yet this is but in subordination to God's glory.

(2.) In every enjoyment, whether it be natural or spiritual. I am to desire outward increase and estate, but I cannot desire it lawfully, but so as I may honour God with it. Agur measureth every estate by ends of religion: Prov. xxx. 8, 9, 'Give me neither poverty nor riches, but feed me with food convenient for me, lest I be full and deny thee, and say, Who is the Lord; or lest I be poor and steal, and take the name of God in vain.' As God should be at the end of every business, so at the end of every enjoyment, though it be spiritual. It is a mistake in christians to think that spiritual blessings are only to be desired for themselves. I must desire the pardon of my sins, not merely for itself, but that God may be glorified in pardon. I must desire grace not only that I might be saved, but that God may be glorified in my salvation: Eph. i. 6, 'To the praise of the glory of his grace, wherein he hath made us accepted in the Beloved.' The creature's aims are never regular but when they suit with God's. In the work of redemption Jesus Christ pleased not himself, but had an aim at the Father's glory: Rom. xv. 3, 'For even Christ pleased not himself.' So should we in the comforts of redemption, not please ourselves merely in the consideration of our own happiness, but rejoice in it as God's ends are promoted in it, that God is glorified in pardoning my sin, or giving me grace and salvation. Though it be a difficult, yet it is a necessary piece of self-denial to desire salvation in a subordination to God's glory.

Secondly, For the contriving plotting work. The end being once fixed, we are to consider generally by what means it may be accomplished, and more particularly how you may observe and carry it on to the glory of God.

1. Generally, by what means we may accomplish it. Every end is obtained by apt and fit means, and God, as he hath ordained the end, so he hath appointed the means. The whole duty of man is to 'fear God and keep his commandments,' Eccles. xii. 13. The whole duty is comprised in obedience and fear; obedience respects the rule, and fear the principle. Or obedience and love; he instanceth in that principle that was most suitable to the present dispensation. In the Old Testament, fear is the beginning of wisdom, fear is represented as the great principle of duty and worship, as in the New Testament, love: 2 Cor. v. 14, 'The love of Christ constraineth us;' 1 John v. 3, 'This is the love of God, that we keep his commandments.' The meaning of that place is, that God hath required entire obedience out of an holy and upright principle. Look, as God hath appointed to the creatures a law of creation by which they are bounded to their stated times and paths, as the psalmist saith of the waters of the sea, Ps. civ. 9. 'Thou hast set a bound, that they may not pass over, that they turn not again to cover the earth,' so God hath given a moral law and rule to the rational creature, which must be observed by love and reverence. So it is said, Eph. ii. 10, 'We are the workmanship of God, created in Christ Jesus to good works, which God hath before ordained that we

should walk therein.' God having by the same decree and wise counsel ordained both end and means, he hath given us a rule by which we are to be guided in serving his glory.

2. More particularly, how you may observe and carry it on in this way according to the will of God. A christian is to be wise in his generation; that is, in the course and sphere of his employments to manage the holy life by a wise foresight. A man that is a child of God hath wisdom if he would improve it: Luke xvi. 8, 'For the children of this world are in their generation wiser than the children of light.' Christ makes it to be the application of the parable of the unjust steward; he was plotting aforehand how he should maintain himself when he was turned out of his service; so Christ would hence commend to us spiritual wisdom, how the children of light should plot and contrive how to manage their course according to the will of God; as the prodigal contrives aforehand how he shall make his address most acceptably to his father: Luke xv. 18, 'I will arise and go to my father, and will say unto him, Father, I have sinned against heaven and before thee.' He is searching out meet words, words of humbleness and submission, by which he might work upon his father's bowels. So if this be my end, to enjoy God and glorify him, how shall I order my life so as to maintain most communion with him, and so as I may most promote his glory? Neh. i. 11, 'Grant me mercy in the sight of this man; for I was the king's cup-bearer.' He showeth the reason why he did undertake the work; he was a courtier, and had the liberty of address to Artaxerxes; Mnemon, he was devising what he might do for God in that station. So you should be contriving: This is my place, and these are my relations; what shall I do for God as I am a minister, a magistrate, a master of a family? how may I serve the great end of my creation, and promote the glory of God? Such foresights make the holy life to be a life of care and choice; not merely of chance and peradventure, but managed and guided with discretion for the glory of God.

Thirdly, For the arguing work. In such a meditation as this is you must dispute and argue with the soul, that you may gain it from base and inferior objects, which would divert you from looking after the great end of your conversation, which is the glorifying and enjoying of God.

Follow the method formerly prescribed by pregnant reasons, apt similitudes, forcible comparisons, and by holy colloquies and soliloquies.

1. By pregnant reasons. Debate thus with yourselves, Why should I look after other things, when my end is to enjoy God? Take these reasons—

[1.] Other things cannot satisfy and yield any solid contentment to the spirit: Isa. lv. 2, 'Wherefore do you spend your money for that which is not bread? and your labour for that which satisfieth not?' Carnal affections are most irrational; why should I lavish away my choice respects upon those things that will do me no good? The things of this world cloy rather than satisfy. A man is soon weary of worldly comforts, therefore he must have shift and change. When we have wealth and honour, we want peace and contentment; nay, sometimes the particular pleasure must be changed because of satiety and loathing which will grow upon us. A man may be weary of life itself, and it may be a burden to him, but never of the love of God; you never heard any one complain of too much communion with God. Heavenly comforts are more lovely when they are attained than when they are desired; one taste ravisheth, and imagination is nothing to feeling. Worldly things cannot satisfy the affections. Man's heart is made up of vast and unlimited desires, because it was made for God, and cannot be quiet till it enjoy God. He that is all-sufficient can only fill up those crannies and chinks that are in man's heart. But alas! if they could satisfy the affections, they cannot satisfy the conscience; they cannot calm and lull conscience asleep. There is no proportion between conscience and worldly things; these are a covering too short for us; there will be trouble, though we have abundance.

[2.] They are not durable and lasting. An immortal soul is for an eternal good. It is the greatest misery that can be to outlive our happiness. We have a soul that will never perish, and why should we labour after things that perish? When the things are gone, our affection will increase our affliction; we shall be the more troubled because we loved them so much. All things under the sun are therefore vexation, because vanity: Eccles. i. 14, 'I have seen all the works that are done under the sun, and behold all is vanity and vexation of spirit.' That which is vain and flashy will vex the soul with disappointment; we can enjoy nothing with contentment but what we enjoy with security: Isa. xl. 6, 'All flesh is grass, and all the goodliness thereof is as the flower of the field.' The flower may be gone, the blustering of the wind and the scorching of the sun may soon deface the beauty and glory of the flower, and then it remains a rotten and neglected stalk: Prov. xxiii. 5, 'Wilt thou set thine eyes upon that which is not?' The men of the world call them substance; they think they are the only things, when of all these Solomon says they are not. How fading are honours! Haman was one day high in honour, and the next day high on the gallows. Therefore these things being so fickle and of such uncertain enjoyment, they cannot give the soul any quiet.

[3.] They are inferior, and below the soul; they do not perfect nature, but abase it; they suit only with the outward and baser part of man, and serve only the conveniences of the body. That which makes a man happy must be something above a man, better than himself; now this is beneath your souls. You would count it absurd to adorn gold with dirt, or lay on brass upon silver; it is a stain and disgrace, not an ornament to it. One soul is more worth than a whole world: Mat. xvi. 26, 'What is a man profited if he shall gain the whole world and lose his own soul? or what shall a man give in exchange for his soul?' God created the world only with a word, but Christ redeemed the soul with his blood and sufferings, and why should you degrade yourselves? Heaven thought your souls worthy of the blood of Christ, and you should think them too worthy to be prostituted to the world. Men do not know the worth of a soul till they come to die, and then what would a man give in exchange for his soul, to redeem his soul from the destruction of fears? Job xxvii. 8, 'For what is the hope of the hypocrite, though he hath gained, when God taketh away his soul?' When God comes by a fatal stroke or a mortal disease to take away your soul, you will see that a soul once lost can be redeemed by no price, and how little doth the hypocrite then think of all his gain that he hath heaped together? Oh! then do not debase your souls. It is dishonourable among men to match beneath their birth and dignity; oh! why will you match your souls, that are of a heavenly original, to these base outward things?

[4.] All these things which we think increase our happiness do but add to our trouble, both to our outward, inward, and eternal trouble.

(1.) Many times to our outward trouble. The greater gates do but open to the greater cares, and the more any are endowed with any excellency in the world, they have proportionable sorrow and encumbrances. Moral wisdom is the best of all outward enjoyments, yet that increaseth our portion of sorrow: Eccles. i. 18, 'For in much wisdom is much grief, and he that increaseth knowledge increaseth sorrow.' Many have observed that never was a man eminent for any outward endowment, but the joy of it was abated with an answerable proportion of sorrow and trouble, and their encumbrances have been every way suitable to their comforts. Those that have been most famous for outward qualities have come to some dismal end, as Sampson for strength, Saul for stature, Absalom for beauty, Achitophel for counsel and parts, Asahel for swiftness, Alexander for warlike prowess, Nabal for riches; and God hath made it good by many experiences in our times; the wheel of providence hath rolled upon them, and they have come to some sad end. So for wit and parts. Wit has been many a man's ruin: Isa. xlvii. 10, 'Thy wisdom and thy knowledge hath perverted thee.' Many are undone by their own wisdom and knowledge, and the greatness of their parts, and come to sad accidents.

(2.) For inward troubles. As children catch at painted butterflies, and when they have taken them, their gaudy wings melt away in their fingers, and there remaineth nothing but an ugly worm, so we catch at those things which perish in the using, but the worm of conscience remaineth. Many times outward blessings are salted with a curse; we never have outward things as a blessing till we have an higher interest in them: Ps. cxxvii. 2, 'So he giveth his beloved sleep.' Those that have an interest in God can rest quietly in the bosom of providence; and outward comforts are given as a blessing when they are additionals and appendices to the covenant of grace: Mat. vi. 33, 'Seek ye first the kingdom of God and his righteousness, and all these things shall be added unto you.' God doth not say, Seek the world, and heaven shall be added to you; but, Seek heaven, and the world shall be added; for by seeking of heavenly things first, you drive on two trades at once—for earth and heaven. But when men cumber themselves with the world, there is a snare upon the conscience, and they cannot enjoy the comfort of their condition. It will add to your inward trouble when God is neglected and the world sought.

(3.) For eternal trouble. These things are temporal, and we hazard the loss of eternal things for them. We never leave God but with disadvantage to ourselves: Jonah ii. 8, 'They that observe lying vanities forsake their own mercy.' Whenever you go off from God for a fleeting shadow, you loose an eternal joy. The comfort of the world is but for a time; but our punishment is for ever. *Ea quæ ad usum diuturna esse non possunt, ad supplicium diuturna sunt.* Why should we look after those things that we cannot use for ever, and so wound and destroy our souls for ever? An immoderate seeking after temporal things will be our eternal ruin. Oh! that men would be wise, not to run so great a hazard for so small a pleasure! Riches are uncertain, but the love of them brings a sure damnation: Phil. ii. 19, 'Whose end is destruction, who mind earthly things.' Oh! say then, Shall I overturn the quietness of my life? shall I wound my conscience? shall I contract guilt and terror for the time to come, for that which will perish in the using and is uncertain in the enjoyment? Let us leave things that perish to men that perish. Shall I adventure my soul upon so vain a pursuit? Shall I lose eternal glory for a little vainglory? Shall I make my children or kindred rich, and be poor to all eternity? Shall I bereave my soul of all my hopes, and of those eternal joys which God hath provided for them that love him, for a possession that is so uncertain and so ensnaring?

2. You should deal with your hearts by apt similitudes. The word will afford you several. Who would dwell in a ditch that may have a goodly house in a city? Who would leave treasures and feed off husks? Who would refuse a pleasant bride for a company of nasty harlots? Or who would sit on the stairs when he is called up to sit on the throne? I may enjoy God in Christ, and shall I think it my happiness to enjoy the world?

3. By comparisons. Compare the world with heaven. Here you have the fuller wealth, and but a foretaste of heaven, but the grapes of heaven are better than the vintage of the world, and these present enjoyments are sweeter and more sure than all honours and riches in the world. These things are gotten with care, kept with fear, and lost with grief. Reason thus with yourselves: What are these pleasures to the joys of the Spirit? These gratify the body, the beast, and are so disproportionable to reason itself, that when we have sucked out the quintessence of all earthly delights, they cannot yield a perfect contentment. Therefore Solomon saith, Prov. xiv. 13, 'Even in laughter the heart is sorrowful, and the end of that mirth is heaviness.' We see that laughter, by too much extension and dilatation of the spirits, causeth an aching in the sides; in the outward expressions of jollity God would show how painful it is; you will find carnal delights always go away, and leave some sad impressions. God's worst is better than the world's best; the groans of the Spirit are better than the joys of the world. The groans of the word never go away, but they leave a contentment and drop some sweetness; but the joys of the world never go away but clouds of sorrow are left behind. God's children rejoice in the midst of their mourning, and a glory hath risen upon their spirits even when they seem to be disconsolate in the eyes of the world.

4. By colloquies with God. Either by way of complaint that thou hast sinned and been ungrateful to God: Ps. lxxiii. 22, 'So foolish was I and ignorant; I was as a beast before thee.' Lord, this hath been my brutishness, to choose outward pleasure before communion with God, and to prefer the contentments of the world before the

delights of thy presence. Go and humble yourselves, and say, Lord, I have traded with vanity, and vexed myself in unprofitable pursuits; I have lived so long in the world, and have scarce minded the end wherefore I was sent into the world; as if I was put into the world only as leviathan in the sea, to take my fill of pleasure, and bathe my soul in carnal delights. Or else by way of thanksgiving, if the Lord hath taught thee better; as David, when he had chosen the Lord for his portion, Ps. xvi. 7, 'I will bless the Lord, who hath given me counsel.' My own reason would never have taught me so much; that is a dim light; there were some obscure instincts to sway me to my happiness in general, but I might have groped about for the door of grace, but not have found it, but God gave me counsel. As Austin saith, *Errare per me potui, redire non potui*—Lord, I could go astray of myself, but I could not return of myself; so we could go astray fast enough out of the inclination of our own nature, but thou hast brought home a poor lost sheep on thine own shoulder; if I had been left to the counsels of my own heart, what would have become of me!

5. By soliloquy with your own souls. Expostulate with yourselves for your former errors and follies: Rom. vi. 21, 'What fruit had ye in those things whereof ye are now ashamed? The end of those things is death.' Why should I melt away my spirit and emasculate my soul by stooping to such low contentments? What have I got by turning away from God, but a wound and disquiet in my conscience? Then charge your souls, issue out a practical decree, determine with yourselves, Well, now I see it is best to cleave to God, I will choose God for my chiefest good and utmost end. Oh! my soul, I see, with David, Ps. lxxiii. 28, 'It is good for me to draw nigh to God.' Therefore, farewell my pleasure, that pleased my childish age. When I was a child, I did as a child; it shall be my care now to enjoy communion with God, to be ruled by his word, to live to his glory. Those things that have intercepted the delight and contentment of my spirit, I will leave them to the men of the world.

SERMON VII.

And Isaac went out to meditate in the field at the even-tide.—
Gen. xxiv. 63.

Secondly, I am now to propose to you another object of meditation, which is the sinfulness of sin, an argument very necessary and practical. It is necessary in several respects. Partly to humble us; we have low thoughts of sin, and therefore we are but slight in the matter of humiliation. Until we understand the evil of sin sufficiently, we do not think it worthy of a tear or one hearty sigh; but when the understanding is once opened, the heart is deeply affected: Ps. vi. 6, 'I am weary with my groaning; all the night make I my bed to swim; I water my couch with my tears.' We see such filthiness in sin as cannot be washed away without a deluge of sorrow. And it is necessary partly to awaken us to a greater care and conscience. Who would adventure upon a sin that doth but know and seriously consider what it is? Gen. xxxix. 9, 'How can I do this great wickedness, and sin against God?' That will be the issue of such a consideration. The child will thrust his fingers into the fire that doth not know the pain of being scalded, or play with a snappish cur that hath not been bitten. Men are the more bold in adventuring upon sin because they do not know the danger. And it is necessary partly to urge us to come to Christ; none look to the brazen serpent but those that are stung, so none regard salvation but those that have been stung with some remorse in their consciences for the great evil of sin; when the poor soul feels the weight and burden of sin, then it will come to Christ. And it is necessary partly that we may more loathe ourselves when we come into the presence of God. Gracious men are most self-abhoring. Elijah covered himself with a mantle; Isaiah said, chap. vi. 5, 'Woe is me, for I am undone, because I am a man of unclean lips.' Peter had such a sense of his sins that he says, Luke v. 8, 'Depart from me, for I am a sinful man, O Lord!' Though there was something of excess and sin in these dispositions, that is, so far as they do exclude the encouragements of the gospel, but yet there is somewhat worthy of imitation, so far as they had a deep sense of their own unworthiness.

It is a necessary argument you see, and of much practical use, but very large, and will yield great plenty of thoughts; it will be harder to to know what we should omit in the consideration of it, than what we should pitch upon. I shall pursue it in this method—

1. I shall give you some general rules and observations concerning meditating on the sinfulness of sin.

2. What arguments you should propound to your souls to work your hearts to a sense of it.

I. For the general observations and rules concerning the sinfulness of sin.

1. None can know the utmost evil of sin perfectly but God. There is a kind of infiniteness in sin, because it is committed against an infinite object, and therefore a finite and limited understanding cannot conceive of the evil of it. The greatness of sin is known by the party offended and the party satisfying; both are infinite: 1 John iii. 20, 'If our heart condemn us, God is greater than our heart, and knoweth all things.' As if he had said, Your heart doth not suggest half the evil that there is in sin, for the infinite God knows there is a great deal more evil in it than you can conceive. What is our light to the eye of God? We are the guilty parties, and so are apt to be partial in our own cause; but God is the party offended, and therefore he can best judge of the measure of the offence. Again, God's whole nature setteth him against it; we have but a drop of indignation against sin, God hath an ocean; he is most good, and therefore most hateth what is evil. The truth is, there is nothing properly an object of divine hatred but sin; it is wholly and only carried out against it, and therefore he seeth more evil in it than any creature possibly can.

2. Man's knowledge of sin is more clear at some times than at others

When conscience is opened there is not a greater load and burden. David could say, Ps. xl. 12, 'Innumerable evils have compassed me about; mine iniquities have taken hold upon me, so that I am not able to look up; they are more than the hairs of my head, therefore my heart faileth me.' It is a rule in philosophy, *Elementa non gravitant in suis locis*—Elements are not heavy in their proper place. A fish in the water feeleth no weight, though it would break the back of a man if that weight of water lay upon him; so wicked men are in their element when they are in the heat of their sinful pursuit; here they sport and play, and feel not the burden of sin. Sometimes when men come to die conscience is touched, and then they cry out of the burden of sin: 1 Cor. xv. 56, 'The sting of death is sin;' then their hearts are filled with a sad despair; this makes death to be dreadful and terrible to the soul, and keeps the soul in bondage: Heb. ii. 15, 'Through fear of death they were all their lifetime subject to bondage.' But certainly it shall be at the day of judgment, then we shall see the folly of it; conscience shall then be extended and enlarged, and the sinner shall remember the wickedness of his past life. You will then find the devil, that is now a tempter, will prove an accuser. Oh! what kind of apprehensions will you have when the devil shall come forth and plead, Lord, adjudge this person to me; I never died for him, I never shed my blood for him, I could promise him no heaven and glory, yet he easily hearkened to my temptations? *Tuus esse noluit per gratiam, sit meus per culpam; ostende tales tuos munerarios, O Christe.* He would not be thine for all the grace and kindness thou didst show him, and all the rewards thou didst propound and promise to him. Then all disguises will be laid aside. A little consideration and search, and prayer for conviction for the present, would help us to the same apprehensions. If conscience should be now extended as it will be then, we should soon be weary of our lives. At least, do not rest in your own valuation and account, for then the secrets of all hearts shall be opened.

3. The less sin appeareth, many times it is the greater sins are not to be measured by the smallness of the matter of them, but by the offence done to God. The first sin to a vulgar and common apprehension was but the eating of an apple; it seemed a small matter if we did not consider the offence against God. It is an aggravation mentioned by the prophet, Amos ii. 6, 'They sold the righteous for silver, and the poor for a pair of shoes;' that is, upon so small an occasion, or for such a contemptible matter they would oppress the poor. The lesser the occasion and temptation is, the greater the impudence, the imprudence and the unkindness; the greater the impudence that they will dare God to his face for a trifle; the greater is the imprudence that we will hazard our souls for a mean thing; the greater is the unkindness that we will stand with God for a little. Sins that are accounted small in the matter of them have been overtaken with the sad revenges of God; he that denied a crumb could not receive a drop of water to cool his tongue. The contempt of God is the greater when we break with God for a small matter, and transgress his commandments upon every light occasion. In short, sin is in no case small, but only in regard of God's mercy and Christ's merits.

4. None are exempted from bewailing the evil of sin. Though the children of God shall never feel it, nor have the dregs of God's displeasure wrung out to them for it, yet they must bewail the evil that there is in sin. The death and merit of Christ doth not change the nature of sin nor put less evil into it. Why should we look upon it with a different eye after conversion than we did before? Sin is still damning in its own merit and nature, and it is still the violation of an holy righteous law, and an affront to the holy God, and an inconvenience to the precious soul. Sin is the same as it was before, though the person be not the same. Nay, the children of God are not altogether exempted from the effects of sin neither; it is a disease, though not a death; and who would not groan under the heat of a burning fever though he be assured of life? God hath still a bridle upon you to keep the soul in awe; and though the godly can never lose their right in the covenant, that doth remain, yet they may lose the fruition of it, and this is enough to make a child of God mourn. Notwithstanding all the privileges of grace, you may be branded, though not executed; and though the Lord hath made them vessels of mercy, yet he doth not use and employ them as vessels of honour, but they are set aside as useless vessels. Sin will still be inconvenient, it will bring disgrace to religion and discomfort to your souls, and furnish the triumphs of hell, and make Satan rejoice, and eclipse the light of God's countenance; and who can brook the loss of God's favour and of intimate communion with him without sadness and bemoaning his case? I may ask you that question, Job xv. 11, 'Are the consolations of God small with thee?' Do you make so little reckoning of those rich comforts of the Holy Ghost? Though you cannot be damned, for 'there is no condemnation to them that are in Christ,' Rom. viii. 1, yet your pilgrimage may be made very uncomfortable; and he that prizeth communion with God would not lose the comfort of it for the least moment. Besides, if there were no inconvenience, yet love is motive enough to a gracious person? Where is your love? Christians, you sin against mercy; the warm beams of mercy should melt the heart: Ezek. xxxvi. 31, 'Then shall ye remember your own evil ways, and your doings that were not good, and shall loathe yourselves in your own sight for your iniquities, and for all your abominations.' As long as there is love in the heart, you can never want an argument to represent the odiousness of sin. Put the matter in a temporal case; it would be ill reasoning for an heir to say, I know my father will not disinherit me, therefore I do not care how I offend him. Where is your love to God if you do not hate sin? Ps. xcvii. 10, 'Ye that love the Lord, hate evil.' Though your right in the covenant be safe, yet you should still have the evil of your own doings in remembrance.

5. Many speak much of the evil of sin in prayers and confessions, yet loathe it never the more, yea, the less. What should be the reason of it? All their thoughts are spent in empty declamations and forms of satire or anger, and these do not subdue affections. Or else it may be we only paint sin in our fancies, and that worketh no more than a picture or image, which doth not allure and draw love so much as a living beauty; it only pleases and tickles a little. Things foul in their nature are pleasant in their picture and description. What more

dreadful than war? and yet what more pleasant than in a strain of poetry or rhetoric, or in a lively picture to describe the fury and heat of battle? What more ugly than a toad? and yet a toad painted to the life pleaseth. So when we merely paint sin by the help of the imagination or fancy, it moves only the lighter part of the soul. It is good to be rational in our considerations, and where there is the less art, it leaveth the deeper stroke upon the heart. Imagination and fancy is a great instrument in the work of meditation, but still it must be wisely ordered and guided by reason. Sound conviction by God's blessing doth the work, or else they rest in generals; they are not serious, particular practical discourses, brought home to their own case against the sin they are struggling with. Lusts take the throne by turns, and that our thoughts may fall with the greatest sense and feeling upon our souls, it is good to bend the strength of our thoughts against our iniquity. It is good to be particular, to fetch the aggravations of sin out of thine own heart, or else men soar high, and in affected strains. To draw an arrow always to the head breaketh the bow. Sin, Christ, heaven, and hell admit of an hyperbole, but yet a man may strain too much, that a soul may be discouraged by it, and much hurt may be done. Men look upon matters of religion as abstracted ideas, and high strains, and matters of fancy. Certainly the more simple and natural your thoughts are, the more working. Forced, high-flown arguments, if they raise the affections, it is but like fire in stubble, that flashes for the present, not like a fire furnished with fit materials, that yields a constant heat. Modest arguments fitted to our present state do better. I will bring it to the matter in hand. Men usually overlash, while they should set out sin as exceeding heinous, and forget those material and natural arguments that should work the soul into a hatred of it That saying of Anselm is justly censured by Mr Fox, *Si hic peccati pudorem, et illic inferni horrorem, &c.* If here were the filthiness of sin, and there were the horrors of hell, I had rather be in hell without sin than in heaven with it. These expressions do not come from a modest virtue, but the over-daring of fancy, and besides they leave a snare and temptation upon weak christians. God doth not put us to that trial to choose hell or sin, and, as Mr Fox urgeth, God in the gospel will bring sinners though sanctified to glory. Or else if they use solid reasons and arguments, they rest in their own discourse and reason, and then it is said, Job vi. 25, 'What doth your arguing reprove?'

II. Having premised these observations, I will give you a few arguments whereby you may come to understand a little of that evil that there is in sin. And they shall be drawn—(1.) From the nature of sin; (2.) From the effects of sin; (3.) From the circumstances and aggravations wherewith sin may be clothed.

1. From the nature of sin, and so it may be considered as to God and as to ourselves.

[1.] Consider the nature of sin as to God.

(1.) It is an aversion from God, a turning from the chiefest good to the chiefest evil. The very nature of sin is punishment enough to itself; it is misery enough to depart from God, the centre of rest, and the fountain of life and blessing. It is a dishonour to God and a disadvantage to ourselves. A dishonour to God to prefer carnal sweets and the satisfaction of sin before the comforts of his presence, and yet this is the root of every sin : 2 Tim. iii. 4, ' Lovers of pleasures more than lovers of God.' Every natural man loves the pleasures of sin more than communion with God. You are angry at Judas for betraying Christ, and at the Jews for preferring Barabbas before Christ, a murderer before a saviour, and yet you do the same almost every day : Job xv. 1, ' Why doth thine heart carry thee away ? and what do thine eyes wink at ? ' You forfeit the best things for the basest, as children part with a pearl for an apple or a nut. Nay, I may go higher ; it is a preferring the devil before God. Sins are called his lusts : John viii. 44, ' Ye are of your father the devil, and the lusts of your father you will do ;' and duty is enforced by God's law, and will you gratify the devil and displease God ? You will find him to be an ill master at length. He that now tempts will hereafter accuse, and that for this very thing, that you were so easy to be entreated to leave God and follow him ; as Austin brings him in pleading against us to God, Though thou didst try him by thy grace, and direct him by thy law, though thy Son did die for him, yet he would not be thine, and therefore let him be mine : I never died, and shed my blood for him, I could not promise him heaven and glory ; I only brought him the bait and temptation, and he easily hearkened unto me. When the tempter shall thus become an accuser, you will know what it is to turn from God and to prefer the devil before a Saviour. Then it is a great disadvantage to yourselves ; you turn your back upon your own happiness. Sin will make you shy of God's presence, and it will make you hated of God, that he will not endure your presence ; he will have no communion with you, nor you with him. It is the comfort of God's children, whatever befalls them in the world, that they can go in secret, and their eyes can pour out tears to God ; but now God will turn away from you, God who is the centre of your rest, the God of your mercies; and then to whom will you unbosom yourselves ? Isa. lix. 2. ' Your iniquities have separated between you and your God, and your sins have hid his face from you, that he will not hear.' They set you at a distance from God, and God at a distance from you. Oh ! reason thus with yourselves : Shall I commit that which will cause me not to endure God, nor God to endure me ? that I shall not care to have to do with him, nor he with me ? Sin has always been attended with a casting out from God. It cast the angels out of heaven, where God is present in a glorious manner ; it cast Adam out of paradise, where God was present by his own image ; and it cast Cain out of the church, where God was present in his ordinances and worship ; and it will make God cast you out as an abominable branch. If you are not sensible of this at present, yet you will be sensible hereafter, when God shall say, ' Depart, ye cursed.'

(2.) It is enmity against God. It is not only a turning from God, but an opposition to and turning against God : Rom. viii. 7, ' The carnal mind is enmity against God, for it is not subject to the law of God, neither indeed can be.' The more the heart is set upon sin, the more it hateth God formally or virtually. The soul hates God as a lawgiver though not as a creator, because he comes in with a restraint between us and our carnal desires: Col. i. 21, 'You were sometime alienated, and enemies in your mind by wicked works.' In the original it is ἐχθροὺς τῇ διανοίᾳ ἐν τοῖς ἔργοις τοῖς πονηροῖς, 'by your mind in wicked works;' because your minds were set upon wicked works, you were vexed God should restrain your desires; for we cannot endure one should restrain the exercise of our carnal affections. Now this enmity is mutual; God hates us, and we hate God. On man's part it is driven on with fury; he doth so hate God that he seeks the destruction of his being; as he that hates another seeketh the destruction of his goods, life, and honour, so he that hates God seeks to un-God him. The sinner wishes there were no such being as a God in the world: Ps. xiv. 1, 'The fool hath said in his heart there is no God.' The heart is the seat of desires; these are the fool's wishes; it is a sweet pleasing thought to him. Though he cannot get rid of these impressions of a Godhead, yet he wishes he could. A man that would live at liberty could wish there was no judge to call him to an account; he could let loose the reins of vile affections if there were no God; were it not for this restraint he could live as he list. Nay, they deny God in their lives: Titus i. 16, 'They profess that they know God, but in works they deny him.' Sin in effect doth lay God aside, and, to put the greater affront upon him, it sets up something base in his stead; it sets up the belly for God: Phil. iii. 19, 'Whose god is their belly;' the choicest respects of the soul run out upon the sensual part. Or it sets up a little wealth for God. Or if sin cannot take away the being of God, yet it strikes at his honour, and would make him to be an unjust or an evil God. Sin deprives God of the honour of all his attributes; of his omnisciency, for though we are ashamed to sin before man, yet, though God seeth all things, we do not blush if we can carry on a wicked design under the veil of darkness, and dig deep to hide our counsels from the Lord. Doth such a sinner think God is all-seeing and all-knowing? Jer. ii. 26, 'A thief is ashamed, when he is found;' when the eye of man hath surprised him, but alas! we are always found of God. It robs him of his omnipotency and power, as if he were impotent and weak, as if we could make our party good with him. The apostle useth a smart question, 1 Cor. x. 22, 'Do we provoke the Lord to jealousy? are we stronger than he?' As if he had said, Man, consider what thou doest; by sinning thou dost enter into the lists with God, and art thou able to deal with him? It is a contest with God, as if we could arm our lusts against his mighty angels. Will you contend with him that can command legions of angels? When you go about to sin, you do as it were wage war with heaven, and enter into combat with God. That is the reason the Lord by the prophet asketh sinners, What do you think? Is there such a thought in thee as if thou wast able to deal with me? Ezek. xxii. 14, 'Can thy heart endure, or can thine hands be strong in the day that I shall deal with thee?' Are you able to grapple with my omnipotent arm, and snatch judgment out of my hands, and oppose my mighty angels? Can thy heart endure when my almighty hand shall seize upon thee, and divine displeasure shall break out against thy soul? The angel when contending with the devil 'durst not bring a railing accusation,' Jude 9. He knew the mighty God would avenge him, therefore he durst not be malicious; yet we dare enter the lists with heaven. Thus is sin an enmity against God; it would either have no God, or an impotent, unjust, unwise God. Nay, there is an enmity in sin against every person in the Holy Trinity. Against God the Son: When Christ came into the world, his great work was to dissolve the works of Satan: 1 John iii. 8, 'For this purpose the Son of God was manifested, that he might destroy the works of the devil;' that he might unravel all those webs which Satan had been weaving, and you strive as much as in you lies to set it up, and make his death of none effect: Heb. x. 29, 'Of how much sorer punishment shall he be thought worthy who hath trodden underfoot the Son of God, and hath counted the blood of the covenant wherewith he was sanctified an unholy thing?' You make a low thing of it, tread it underfoot; it is an allusion to the sprinkling of the lintels of the door, but they sprinkled it on the threshold. And it puts an affront upon the Holy Ghost; it grieveth and vexeth the Spirit of God; it is a setting up lust against lust, and a direct thwarting of his motions and impulses: Gal. v. 17, 'The flesh lusteth against the Spirit, and the Spirit against the flesh.' You do as it were reproach him, and say he shall do no good upon your hearts, this shall not gain upon you. Moses, when he speaks of a presumptuous sinner, saith, Num. xv. 30, 'The soul that doth ought presumptuously, the same reproacheth the Lord;' when you do thus deliberately sin, you do as it were reproach the Spirit of God. Likewise on God's part; he hateth us too, and though he be full of kindness, yet he cannot give sin a good look: Hab. i. 13, 'Thou art of purer eyes than to behold evil, and canst not look on iniquity.' God loveth all his creatures, and loveth to look upon them, but he hateth that which is properly man's creature, and that is sin; there is no antipathy greater than between these two natures. You may sooner reconcile fire and water, light and darkness, cold and heat, than God and sin. The enmity of all creatures is as their beings are, finite and limited; but God's being is infinite; his whole nature sets him against sin; therefore there is no comparison which serves to set out the indignation the Lord hath against sin, there is no antipathy like it.

(3.) Sin is a transgression of the law. Do but consider what a disgrace sin puts upon the law that forbiddeth it; it doth in effect condemn the law, as if it were not good and useful and righteous, as if it were an idle restraint. There is a notable expression, James iv. 11, 'He that speaketh evil of his brother and judgeth his brother, speaketh evil of the law and judgeth the law;' that is, he puts this affront upon the law, as if it were injurious, as if God were not righteous in making such a law against passion and evil-speaking. Therefore Nathan comes to rouse up David's conscience, and tells him his sin: 2 Sam. xii. 9, 'Wherefore hast thou despised the commandment of the Lord, to do evil in his sight?' In every sin there are some implicit thoughts by which the law is disvalued and disapproved; we secretly tax it of envy, folly, and rigour, as if God had dealt harshly with his creatures; they look upon it as a weak and simple law: Ezek. xviii. 26, 'Yet ye say, The way of the Lord is not equal.' The devil, when he inspired the first sin, would suggest to our first parents as if

God had envied the perfection of man by prescribing a law to him: Gen. iii. 5, 'God doth know that in the day ye eat thereof then your eyes shall be opened, and ye shall be as gods, knowing good and evil.'

[2.] Consider the nature of sin with respect to yourselves, and so the evil of it appears in these respects.

(1.) It is a degradation of your natures, and sets you beneath the rank of men, and equals you with beasts: Ps. xlix. 12, 'Nevertheless man being in honour abideth not; he is like the beasts that perish.' In the original it is, he abideth not for a night. Adam sinned the very same day that he was created. So Ps. xxxii. 9, 'Be ye not as the horse or as the mule, that have no understanding;' implying that inconsiderate and rash men, that never consider their ways, are like the horse and mule, which are void of understanding, and are guided only by their own instinct. To what use do men put their reason that do not reflect upon their consciences? It would be an odd sight to see a man with the head of a mule or the feet of a horse, yet there is a greater affinity between the body of a beast and the body of a man than between a beast and a man's soul; the former are in the same degree of being, as material substances.

(2.) It is the defilement of your natures. The scripture, when it speaks of sin, sets it out by 'filthiness and superfluity of naughtiness,' James i. 21; an allusion to the brook Kedron, where the garbages of the sacrifices were wont to be cast. So it is called a blot. These notions are to heighten our souls into a detestation of it. *Omne malum naturam, aut timore, aut pudore perfudit.* There is such a filthiness in sin, that it is ashamed of itself, and therefore it always seeketh for a disguise. There needeth no argument against it, but to be seen in its proper colours; it either seeketh a show of virtue, or a veil of darkness. Pray why doth the adulterer seek for the twilight (Prov. vii. 9, 'In the twilight, in the evening, in the black and dark night') but that he is ashamed of sin? Sin is so monstrous and deformed that it seeks to hide itself from those that love it most, from the conscience of the party that committeth it, or from the sight of others. Nay, there is such a turpitude in it that some sins beget shame in their very name and mention. The apostle speaks of a sin that 'is not so much as named among the gentiles,' 1 Cor. v. 1; and Eph. v. 3, 'But fornication, and all uncleanness, and covetousness, let it not be once named among you, as becometh saints.' Socrates hid his face whenever he spake against wantonness.

(3.) It is the bondage of your natures. Oh! what worser captivity can there be than this, for reason to be put out of its empire, and that you should be under the command of vile affections, a slave to pride, and a drudge to your lusts and carnal pleasures? Sin is a bondage here and hereafter; here it binds you with the cords of vanity, and hereafter with the chains of darkness. This is the preposterous judgment of men, that they look upon the service of God as their greatest bondage: Ps. ii. 3, 'Let us break their bands asunder, and cast away their cords from us;' but then it is otherwise; there is no greater freedom than to be employed in the service of God, and to be free for the actions of a holy life: Ps. cxix. 45, 'I will walk at liberty, for I seek thy precepts.' The bonds of duty are not gyves, but ornaments;

and there is no greater bondage than to be a slave to sin : 2 Peter ii. 19, 'While they promise them liberty, they themselves are the servants of corruption ; for of whom a man is overcome, of the same is he brought into bondage.' What a bondage is this, to be a vassal of hell, to be at the command of our lusts, a slave to pride and uncleanness, and we know not how to help it!

SERMON VIII.

And Isaac went out to meditate in the field at the even-tide.—
GEN. xxiv. 63.

2. ANOTHER argument to prove the evil of sin is taken from the effects of sin. We being in a lower sphere of understanding, know causes by their effects : Jer. ii. 19, 'Know therefore and see, that it is an evil thing and bitter that thou hast forsaken the Lord thy God ;' when they had seen the sad effects of it, their cities wasted and destroyed. And where shall we not find the sad effects of sin? Survey the story of sin since it came into the world.

The first news we hear of sin is in the fall of the angels, and what a dreadful instance is that? The angels, that were the most noble part of the universe, the courtiers of heaven, and as soon as they had sinned, in a moment from angels they were made devils, and cast down into the pit of darkness, for one aspiring thought against God's imperial majesty. If we should see ten thousand princes executed in one day, we would wonder at the cause of it, and yet this is but a short resemblance of this case. Think of those princes of the creation, those morning-stars, those sons of God ; now if one sin cast down these angels, what will become of us who have millions of sins ? If God be so angry with the nobles, how may the scullions tremble ? If God will cast angels out of heaven for one sin of thought, what will become of us poor dwellers in clay, who are but a little enlivened dust, that may be soon crumbled into nothing ? Yet Christ was not made an angel for angels, as he was made a man for me. If you should hear of a drop of gall that should embitter a whole ocean of sweetness, you would wonder at the pestilential influence of it; here one sin of thought embittered the whole ocean of the angelical sweetness.

The next news we hear of sin is in the fall of man. Who would taste of that poison that poisoned all mankind at once ? Adam did but taste of the forbidden fruit, and all his posterity were poisoned ; in the morning he was God's favourite, and in the evening the devil's slave ; he slept not one night in innocency. Nay, this is not all, you shall see the venom of sin went further ; it did not only ruin all mankind, but it gave a crack to the whole creation. All the creatures groan under sin : Rom. viii. 20, 21, 'For the creature is made subject to vanity, not willingly, but by reason of him who hath subjected the same in hope, because the creature itself also shall be delivered from the bondage of corruption into the glorious liberty of the children of God.' When

God looked upon the creatures that he had made, he saw all was good, but when Solomon looketh upon God's works, he seeth nothing but vanity; what is the reason of this? Sin intervened, so that the creatures are not only the monuments of God's power, but of man's rebellion.

The next dreadful instance of sin is in the old world, and there all mankind except eight persons were swept away at once.

The next news of sin is in the instance of Sodom, and there sin was of such an evil influence that it made God to rain hell out of heaven; as one expresses it, *Gehennam misit e cœlo:* Gen. xix. 24, 'Then the Lord rained upon Sodom and upon Gomorrah brimstone and fire from the Lord out of heaven;' *dominus a domino,* the Lord Christ from the Lord Jehovah. Jesus Christ himself will become the executioner upon such a wicked people.

Go from Sodom to Sion, and further trace the story of sin. Who can read the Lamentations without lamentation, or run over the story of Jerusalem's sorrows with dry eyes? There was not such a people under heaven both for mercies and judgments, the dearly beloved of his soul given up to a sad ruin! Lam. iii. 39, 'Wherefore doth a living man complain, a man for the punishment of his sins?' What is the reason of all this but sin?

Will you go further, and see the effects of sin upon the Son of God himself, who was the Son of his love, 'the man God's fellow,' as he is called, Zech. xiii. 7; his associate; they solaced themselves mutually in each other: Prov. viii. 30, 'There was I by him, as one brought up with him; I was daily his delight, rejoicing always before him.' See what sin did to him that was but imputed to him. Look into the garden, see him in his agonies; go to Golgotha, see Christ hanging on the cross, if you would know sin. Gold and silver would not ransom us, nothing would serve but the blood of Christ. Oh! come and wonder. The boundless sea of the Godhead was stopped by the bank of sin. For a candle to be put out is no such matter, but for the sun to be quenched and darkened, this is dreadful. So for a poor creature to be forsaken is nothing, but when the Son of God shall complain that he cannot actually enjoy the comfort of the Godhead, when the Sun of righteousness shall complain of an eclipse, and of a suspension of consolation, this is dreadful. Though the human nature recoiled out of a just abhorrency of the sufferings he was to endure, and he came to his Father, Mat. xxvi. 39, 'O my Father! if it be possible, let this cup pass from me;' and again, ver. 42; and again, ver. 44, saying the same words; yet divine justice would not bate him one farthing. What then would have become of us if Jesus Christ had not catched the blow?

Then survey common experience. If all the charnels in the world were emptied upon one heap, and all the bones of all that ever died were laid together, you might say, All these were slain by sin. Whenever you see sin, you may entertain it as Elisha did Hazael, Thou art the murderer. All diseases, pestilences, wars, famines, tumults, earthquakes, these are but the births of sin; it hath laid houses desolate, wasted kingdoms, destroyed cities. Sin may say, Zeph. iii. 6, 7, 'I have cut off the nations; their towers are desolate: I have made their streets waste, that none passeth by; their cities are destroyed so that there is no man, there is none inhabitant: I said, Surely thou wilt fear me;' that which we feel we may fear.

But we may come nearer home. Do but consider the effects of it within yourselves in the terrors of conscience. What a sorry creature is man when God arms his own thoughts against him, and sets home one sin upon his conscience! He longs for death rather than life. Heman, who was a child of God, complains, Ps. lxxxviii. 16, 17, 'Thy fierce wrath goeth over me, thy terrors have cut me off; they came round about me daily like water, they compassed me about together.' What a sad thing is this, that a man should be *magor missabib*, fear round about, that his own thoughts should be his hell, and wherever he goes, he carries his hell with him! When he lies down in his bed, hell lies down with him; when he walks out into the field or garden, hell walks with him; when he goes about his business, hell goes with him. Sin is its own executioner; however it smiles in the first address, yet afterwards it scourgeth the soul with horror and despair.

Consider the horrors in death. There is a natural abhorrency from death as an evil to our life and being, but that which increaseth horror is sin: 1 Cor. xv. 56, 'The sting of death is sin.' Oh! what agonies will it raise in our souls when we come to die if we die in our sins! Though we were immortal, yet sin is so great an evil that it were not to be committed; but when we are to die, and give an account, how doth it fill the soul with horror and diffidence and shame and anger! Some wicked men indeed die stupid and careless, at least doubtful; and some may be foolhardy; like a man that fetcheth a leap in the dark over a bottomless gulf he doth not know where his feet may light. A wicked man is like a tree that grows on the bank of a river; he is on the borders of hell, and when he dies, he falls into it. When they come to die, sin will be accusing, conscience witnessing, the law condemning, Satan insulting; heaven will be shut up against them, and hell enlarging her mouth. Oh! how will the body curse the soul for an ill guide, and the soul curse the body as a wicked instrument! It is a sad parting when these two loving friends, body and soul, part with curses, and can never expect to meet again but in torment. A godly man, when he dies, takes a fair leave of his body, and says, Farewell, flesh! He goes down to the grave with the covenant of grace in his hand, My flesh shall rest in hope; but a wicked man dreadeth it, that ever his body and soul must be united again; they part with an expectation never to meet but in flames.

But all this is nothing to the everlasting estate that follows after it. Consider either the loss or the pain; both will represent the evil of sin. Consider the loss; by sinning thou losest God and heaven and glory for a trifle; for a little dreggy pleasure thou thrustest away eternal joys. Thou dost as it were say, I care not for heaven, so I may have carnal satisfaction; as of Esau it is said, Gen. xxv. 34, 'Thus Esau despised his birthright;' it is not worth a mess of pottage. With what sad reflections wilt thou declaim against sin when thou shalt see the holy ones of God stand at the right hand of Christ, and thou art haled to thy own place! How will thy heart turn upon thee for thy own folly then! As one dreamed that his heart was boiling for his sins in a kettle of scalding lead, and it cried out to him, 'Ἐγὼ σοὶ τούτου αἰτία, It is I that have been the cause of this. Were it not for sin I might have had a place in Abraham's bosom, but now I am going to everlasting torment; then you will know what sin is. Every sinner is as a mad gamester; he ventures a kingdom, the largest and fairest that ever was, at every throw, and he is sure to lose it too. Then consider the pains of hell; they will set out the greatness of sin; and consider them either in regard of God's ordination or appointment, or in regard of your own feeling. (1.) In regard of God's ordination and appointment. That the good God, who is meekness and sweetness and bowels itself, should adjudge his creature to eternal torments; certainly there is some cause. We pity a dog if he should be cast into a furnace for half an hour; yet those tender bowels of mercy shrink not up at the sight of sinners, though man be the work of his own hands; and though the creature screech and howl under these pains, yet he will not lessen and take them away. Surely there is some great evil in sin that hath tied up the hands of mercy. (2.) Consider it in regard of yourselves and your own feeling. Oh! for a short temporal pleasure thou runnest the hazard of eternal pains. We that cannot endure the scratch of a pin or the aching of a tooth, how shall we endure the torment of so many thousand years, and yet still to look for more? Heb. x. 31, 'It is a fearful thing to fall into the hands of the living God.' Mark the attribute, 'the living God,' who lives for ever to see the vengeance accomplished. As long as God is God, hell will be hell; there can never be any hope that God's being can be destroyed, or that there will be a cessation of those torments and pains. God ever liveth to reward the godly and to punish the wicked.

3. The third sort of arguments are from the aggravations of sin, that may enhance it, and show the greatness of it to your thoughts.

[1.] It is natural to us. It is necessary to reflect upon this circumstance, because it is the hardest matter in our humiliation to be sufficiently affected with our birth-sin. Evils that come by accident are objects of pity, but evils of nature are objects of hatred. We pity a dog that is poisoned, but we hate a toad that is poisonous by nature. Oh! how may the Lord hate us that have evil in our nature! It is not accidental to us. It is the great fondness of men to make that an excuse which is in itself the greatest aggravation. Some will say when they are reproved for sin, I cannot do otherwise; it is my nature. This will be the cause of thy ruin without an interest in Christ. The waters that come out of a pure fountain may be soiled and dirtied, but they will be clear again; but a puddle that runneth out of a dunghill will be always nasty and filthy. Our sins are not by accident, but by nature; they are not like the muddying of a clear fountain, but like the unsavoury liquor that comes out of a dunghill. Original sin (however you think of it) is the sin of sins; we are born with such a sin, and it is worse than any other sin. Actual sins are but as a transient act, whereby there is a violence offered to one of God's commandments, but this is a constant, rooted, abiding contrariety to God's own nature. Actual sins are a blow and away, but this is a remaining enmity. Actual sins are like a fit of anger and displeasure, soon up and soon down, but this is a rooted hatred. This is the cause of all other sins, the bitter root that diffuseth a poison into all the branches. All other sins that a man commits are but original sin acted and exercised. Look, as in the art of numbering, the greatest number that can be numbered is but one multiplied, so the whole fry of actual transgressions is but original sin multiplied, this spawn diffused and spread abroad; all those traitorous actions that we are guilty of in the course of our lives are all summed up in this sinning sin.

[2.] Our sins are many. We sin in praying, in eating, in ploughing, in trading; and any one of these is enough to undo a world. The angels became devils for one sin, for one sin of thought, a proud thought against God's empire and greatness, and for this they were thrown into places of darkness. What ruin then will a great many sins procure to thy soul! If single sins seem light in themselves, yet what are they all together? There is nothing lighter than one sand, and yet nothing heavier than sand in a great quantity. A gnat, a fly, a locust are poor inconsiderable creatures, yet when they come in multitudes they are called God's great army, and destroy whole countries: Joel ii. 11, 'The Lord shall utter his voice before his army, for his camp is very great.' If every pore in the body were but pricked with a pin, the veins would soon be emptied of blood. One sin was deadly, but what are they altogether, when from top to toe there is nothing but sores and putrefaction? Herod was eaten up with lice, a small inconsiderable kind of vermin, yet the abundance of them destroyed him; so though sins seem small in themselves, yet when they come in clusters, how soon will they devour and eat out the life and comfort of the soul! Ps. xl. 12, 'Innumerable evils have encompassed me about; mine iniquities have taken hold upon me, so that I am not able to look up; they are more than the hairs of mine head; therefore my heart faileth me.' And if David may say so, may not we much more? Nothing can be little that is committed against the great God. But suppose them small, yet they are a company. Oh! this will make your hearts fail. The little finger of sin is weighty, but when all the loins of it are laid upon the soul, how great will the burden be! Look upon all the troubles of the servants of God, and you will find they were first occasioned by a small sin, as Mr Peacock's by eating too freely at a meal; but when innumerable evils shall compass you about, that wherever you look there is sin—if you look on duty there is sin, if you look on your calling there is sin, if you look on your recreations there is sin, if you look on the hours of your repast there is sin—oh! this will make your hearts fail indeed.

[3.] If they have been such as have been committed against knowledge. There is more of the nature of sin in such acts, for the nature of sin is $\dot{a}\nu o\mu\acute{\iota}a$, a transgression of the law. Now the more we know the law the greater is the transgression; according to the sense we have of the law so the offence is elevated and raised. He that hath knowledge is *magis particeps legis*, the law is a piece of himself; it is impressed upon his conscience, and he offereth violence to the principles of his own bosom. This is the reason why the children of God use this aggravation; as David: Ps. li. 6, 'In the hidden part thou shalt make me to know wisdom.' God had taught David wisdom and some spiritual skill, and yet he sinned against him. So Christ: John xv. 22, 'If I had not come and spoken to them, they had not had sin;' that is, none in comparison. According to the proportion of light, so the rate of sin riseth; the more you know of the law, the more you sin against the law. It is sad to put the finger in nature's eye, but it is worse to sin against the light of the word, that will make sin rise high indeed. Then there is more of enmity and malice in it. When a man will break through the convictions and restraints of conscience, it is a sign a man does love sin, and sins for its own sake; which is sensibly and clearly discerned in apostates, who are carried on with most wilful malice and rage against the truth which once they professed. *Apostatæ sunt maximi osores sui ordinis.* Hosea v. 2, 'The revolters are profound to make slaughter.' Forward professors, when they revolt, turn violent persecutors. They set themselves against the light. Alexander was once a disciple, yet he 'made shipwreck of the faith,' 1 Tim. i. 19, 20; and he is the man that must set on the multitude against Paul: Acts xix. 33, 'And they drew Alexander out of the multitude, the Jews putting him forward.' The same man is intended, for by the epistles to Timothy we learn that he dwelt at Ephesus, where Timothy was when those epistles were directed to him. Now the Jews set him up as the fittest accuser of Paul;' he knew his doctrine, and he must appear to turn all the blame of the uproar on the christians. Once more we read of this Alexander as a desperate adversary to the truth: 2 Tim. iv. 21, 'Alexander the coppersmith did me much hurt.' Certainly their rage and malice is the greater because of the abundance of light which they have forsaken. No vinegar is so tart as that which is made of the sweetest wine; so when knowledge is once corrupted, it fills the heart with most rage: Prov. xxviii. 4, 'They that forsake the law praise the wicked.' They not only commit sin, but like it in others; they are the most violent and forward men to defend wicked ways and unjust courses. Sins against knowledge have the greatest marks of the divine vengeance and displeasure. When men abuse knowledge, God giveth them up to sottishness, madness, hardness of heart, or despair. To sottishness: Rom. i. 21–23, 'Because that when they knew God, they glorified him not as God, neither were thankful; but became vain in their imaginations, and their foolish heart was darkened: professing themselves wise, they became fools, and changed the glory of the incorruptible God into an image made like to corruptible man, and to birds, and four-footed beasts, and creeping things.' Heathens, that had some common knowledge of the divine nature, when they sinned against their light, God darkened their hearts and made them more foolish. The heathens that were most civil and had most light were given up to the most beastly errors about the nature of God. The Romans worshipped fevers, passions, and paltry gods; the Egyptians, thunder and the sun. Or else the Lord gives them up to madness. The most moral heathens were the sorest persecutors, as Severus, Antoninus; they abused their light, and therefore God gave them up to fury and madness against his ways. Or else they are given up to hardness of heart. Iron oft heated and oft quenched groweth harder. God justly punisheth contempt of light with obduracy; when a man hath had frequent convictions, and still he quencheth them, he grows the harder. Or else the Lord gives them up to a sad despair. God opens their consciences, and makes them to see how they have gone against their own light. Much knowledge not digested is like meat in the stomach, that, being not concocted, breedeth the colic; it breedeth sad gripes in the conscience.

[4.] If they are committed against love. It is sad to sin against God's laws, it is more to sin against God's love. Suppose it be but against common love, against God that giveth us food and raiment, rain from heaven, and fruitful seasons. The apostle calls this a 'despising the goodness of God,' Rom. ii. 4, either by employing it to vile uses, or else by a careless slighting and not taking notice of it. You that slight the kindness of God do as it were say, God shall not gain me to his ways for all this. Every sin is not committed against knowledge, but every sin is against love and bowels. Christ may say to every sinner, as he said to the Jews, John x. 32, 'Many good works have I showed you from my Father; for which of those works do you stone me?' Thus the Lord may plead, I have given you protection and provision, and food and raiment, for which of these do you violate my law and put such an affront upon me? It is I that have been so liberal to you, in giving you the fruits of the earth, the fish of the sea, the fowls of the air; it is I that have caused your sheep to bring forth thousands, and your fields to yield meat; and will you return upon me with my own weapons? Malefactors are punished in the same things in which they offend, and you seek to do me despite by my own blessings, as if I did you wrong when I did you good. But much more if you sin against special love. You that are Christ's favourites, every sin of yours is as a stab at the heart of mercy; as when the multitude forsook him, says Christ to his disciples, John vi. 61, 'Will ye also go away?' That went to his heart. God reckoneth upon you that he shall have much service and obedience from you, and disappointment is the worst kind of vexation: Gen. xviii. 19, 'I know Abraham, that he will command his children, and his household after him, and they shall keep the way of the Lord;' Isa. lxiii. 8, 'Surely they are my people, children that will not lie.' That which in others is but single fornication in you is adultery; others sin against common mercies, but you against the bowels of Christ; they are not thankful for a piece of bread, nor you for the bread of life. As Absalom said to Hushai, 2 Sam. xvi. 17, 'Is this thy kindness to thy friend?' so is this the fruit of all those tender loves and mercies which God hath meted out to you? It is unnatural, as if a hen should bring forth the egg of a crow.

[5.] If it be against vows and covenants, against frequent and reiterated promises and purposes. By such sinning you break double chains—God's and your own. It is not a simple sin, but treachery; Judah hath dealt treacherously: Jer. iii. 7, 'Her treacherous sister Judah saw it.' You commit a sin under the show of friendship. Obedience is due, though it were never promised, but it is a help to our weakness that we vow. It is God's condescension to make a covenant; his laws bind, though we do not seal and subscribe to them; they bind as a law though not as a covenant; but vows and promises make the covenant more explicit. A lawful thing vowed and dedicated to God could not be alienated without sin. Ananias was smitten dead for receding from his purpose: Acts v. 4, 'Whilst it remained, was it not thine own? and after it was sold, was it not in thine own power? why hast thou conceived this thing in thine heart? thou hast not lied unto men, but unto God.' But much more in vows in things necessary that are not in your power. When you have promised obedience, you have promised a thing necessary. God might require duty from you, and punish you for the violation of his law, whether you vowed or no. It was never left to your pleasure to deal falsely in your covenant with men; it is the sin the Lord doth always avenge. Such solemn obligations should be sacred and inviolable; what then is it to break vows with God after we have solemnly renewed our covenant with him?

[6.] If it be against former experiences, and that either of the sweetness of grace or the evil of sin. (1.) Of the sweetness of grace: The Lord takes it ill that you should sin against him after 'you have tasted his good word,' Heb. vi. 5. It is a mighty affront to Jesus Christ to go off from him after we have had experience of the sweetness of his ways. The apostle calls this a 'denying the Lord that bought them,' 2 Peter. ii. 1; that this, *in foro ecclesiæ*, in the court of the church, and with respect to the outward covenant that is between the Lord and every church member. An apostate doth as it were proclaim to the world that Jesus Christ is no good master; that, after he hath made trial of both, the devil is a better master than Christ, for he seemeth to have known both masters. So we find the Lord contests with his people about their provocations: Jer. ii. 5, 'What iniquity have your fathers found in me, that they are gone far from me, and have walked after vanities, and are become vain?' You have gone far from me, and departed from my ways; what is the matter? Did I ever do you hurt? have I ever been a land of darkness to you, or a hard master? So Micah vi. 3, 'O my people, what have I done unto thee, and wherein have I wearied thee? testify against me.' When we go off from God, we do as it were proclaim that we have found just discouragement in the ways of Christ, as a man that goeth off from you showeth his expectation is deceived in you. (2.) If you have done it after experience of the evil of sin. When a man hath found the bitterness of sin, suppose it be of drunkenness or anger, when it hath weakened his body and broken his peace, and yet he runs into it again, it is a sad aggravation; as that king that would adventure another captain and his fifty when one captain and his fifty were consumed with fire from heaven, 2 Kings i. 10, 11. When we will be tampering with the carnal sweets again which have cost us so much trouble, when we have found the hand of God meet us in a carnal way, yet we will venture again, and enter into the lists with him, and set ourselves against him, it is as the breaking of a bone in the same place: James iv. 2, 'Ye lust, and have not, yet kill and desire to have, and cannot obtain; ye fight and war, yet ye have not.' This is a plain contest with God, when, after ye have been broken in pieces, you will again gather and associate yourselves, as it is Isa. viii. 9, 'Associate yourselves, O ye people, and you shall be broken in pieces; and give ear, all ye of far countries; gird yourselves, and ye shall be broken in pieces; gird yourselves, and ye shall be broken in pieces.' Thus the children of Israel argued with the Reubenites and Gadites and the half tribe of Manasseh: Josh. xxii. 17, 18, 'Is the iniquity of Peor too little for us, from which we are not cleansed until this day (though there was a plague in the congregation of the Lord), but that ye must turn away this day from following the Lord?'

[7.] If sin has been committed against a special relation, as suppose that of a magistrate or a minister, this doubles the offence. Your sins are imitated; you should be fountains of religion and justice, and you poison the fountains. You are as the first sheet that is printed off, and all others are stamped after your copy. It was a sad title that was given to Jeroboam, that 'he made Israel to sin;' so when you do not show forth a special strictness of religion according to your place, it is a great aggravation.

SERMON IX.

And Isaac went out to meditate in the field at the even-tide.—
Gen. xxiv. 63.

THIRDLY, The matter I am now to propose to you is the excellent contrivance of the gospel as a subject for your meditation; an argument that challengeth all our reverence and thoughts and wonder, a mystery of mysteries, the fairest draught and picture that ever came out of the workhouse of God: 1 Tim. iii. 16, 'And without controversy great is the mystery of godliness.' This is a depth that cannot easily be fathomed; here are miracles enfolded in miracles, and mysteries within mysteries; God would astonish mankind, and save it at the same time. Christ is called the wisdom of God: 1 Cor. i. 24, 'Christ, the power of God and the wisdom of God;' not only as the treasures of wisdom and knowledge are hid in him, and through him conveyed to the creatures, but because herein is God's wisdom most discovered by disposing and putting our salvation into the hands of Christ; not only as a fountain of wisdom, but as a map of wisdom, as discovering the excellent contrivance of God, and the curious variety that is in his counsels. God showeth wisdom in all things: Ps. civ. 24, 'O Lord, how manifold are thy works! in wisdom hast thou made them all.' Every creature is disposed into apt cells and storehouses, and contributes to the glory of their creator. But here God would discover the curiosity of his wisdom. The world is his work, but the gospel is his plot. And therefore in your solemn and most deliberate thoughts you should take a view of it. It is the great duty of saints: Eph. iii. 18, 19, 'That ye may be able to comprehend with all saints what is the breadth, and length, and depth, and height, and to know the love of Christ, which passeth knowledge.' This should be your continual task and search. There are two great mysteries in the world—Christ and antichrist, the mystery of the gospel and the mystery of iniquity. It is the great advantage of christians to discern the mystery of iniquity, and to meditate upon the mystery of godliness; to observe antichrist's cunning, and to consider the contrivance of the gospel. Oh! then exercise your thoughts herein, and study the excellency of God's design; bring hallowed and reverend thoughts, that by a deliberate gaze you may raise your souls into an holy wonder and admiration.

1. I shall lay down some preparative considerations.
2. I shall come to the work itself.

I. To prepare you to consecrate your thoughts for the entertainment of so great a mystery, consider these things—

1. When you have done your utmost, your thoughts will still fall short: Isa. xl. 28, 'There is no searching of his understanding.' There is an excess in every attribute above all human thought and conceit, and though we follow on after God, yet we cannot find him out to perfection. Now among all his attributes none is more hidden from us than his wisdom, as children that are only busied in puppets and baubles cannot imagine what it is to govern a commonwealth. Power is obvious, but our foolish spirits cannot trace the wisdom of providence, much more his wisdom discovered in the gospel. One of the names of Christ is Wonderful, Isa. ix. 6. It is a point that we should always be studying, and yet we can never come to the bottom of it, and therefore what is wanting in thoughts must be supplied by wonder. When we have done all, we must cry out, Rom. xi. 23, 'O the depth of the riches both of the wisdom and knowledge of God! how unsearchable are his judgments, and his ways past finding out!' As if he had said, I have done as much as I can, I have discovered as much as I am able; but I must leave off disputing, and fall now to wondering. The light of the scripture doth not discover him fully: 1 Cor. xiii. 9, 'We know in part, and we prophesy in part.' Full knowledge is our portion in heaven; these are but partial discoveries we have even in the word of God. However this is no excuse for negligence and barrenness. Not for negligence, for we must 'follow on to know the Lord,' Hosea vi. 3. It is the fault of christians that they keep always to their milk and first childish thoughts and apprehensions; we should rise higher in our considerations and admirations of the love and wisdom of God. It is notable that Moses his first request to God was, 'What is thy name?' Exod. iii, 13. and then, 'I beseech thee show me thy glory,' Exod. xxxiii. 18. We must follow on from considering God's name to clearer sights of his glory. Not for barrenness; empty thoughts void of argument and discourse beget a confused stupor, not a wonder; the thoughts are only stayed, not raised.

2. Not only men, but angels themselves are at a loss in this great mystery; they study it as well as we, and cannot come to the bottom of it: 1 Peter i. 12, 'Which things the angels desire to look into.' The word παρακύψαι signifies to bow down and bend the body; it is an allusion to the cherubim, that were pictured over the ark stooping, and as it were bending their bodies, as prying into the mysteries of the ark. The mysteries of the gospel are so sublime that the angels which do continually behold the face of God cannot perfectly comprehend them; they are learning and improving their knowledge by learning and improving the dispensations of God to the church: Eph. iii. 10, 'To the intent that now unto the principalities and powers in heavenly places might be known by the church the manifold wisdom of God;' that they may know the curious contrivances of God's wisdom by observing the revelations that are made, and the dispensations God hath used towards his church. And possibly this may be the meaning of the apostle in that expression, 1 Tim. iii. 16, 'Seen of angels;' that

is, with reverence, admiration, and wonder, to see Christ stoop so low, to be clothed with flesh, to condescend to a nature so much beneath their own. This is the work of angels, either they desire to know more of Christ, or they delight themselves in beholding of that they know. Oh! we should never be weary of searching into these holy mysteries, and acting our thoughts upon them.

3. They wonder most at the contrivance of the gospel that have most interest in it; to others it is but a cold story or naked plot. Concernment sharpeneth invention and affection, a man doth then more seriously consider of it; their eyes are open, and they have more of sense and feeling. And that is the reason why the enjoyments of the saints have notes of wonder annexed to the expressions of them; as Phil. iv. 7, 'The peace of God, which passeth all understanding,' &c. 1 Peter i. 8, 'Joy unspeakable and full of glory;' they that have a taste of it know what it is to enjoy a calm and serene conscience through the application of the promises of the gospel. They can best wonder at the contrivance of the gospel, who are 'called out of darkness into his marvellous light,' 1 Peter ii. 9. They wonder in their thoughts that God and Christ should design their heaven, be plotting and contriving their salvation before all worlds, how they may be vessels filled up with glory. O marvellous light! wonderful, unutterable joy! These are the apprehensions of God's children; others may look upon the gospel as a probable truth, but they have found it a comfortable truth, therefore their hearts are raised in wonder.

II. I come to the work itself. You may manage it three ways—(1.) By observations; (2.) By arguments; (3.) By comparisons.

1. By observations. Observe what is beautiful and excellent in the gospel.

[1.] God did not contrive to save the fallen angels: Heb. ii. 16, 'For verily he took not on him the nature of angels, but he took on him the seed of Abraham.' He was not made an angel for angels, as he was made a man for men. O Lord! thou sawest angels sinning, but not returning; in them thou didst discover the severity of thy justice, but in us the riches of thy mercy. God would not so much as treat with fallen angels, but plotted a way to recover man. In the election of angels mercy is not so much glorified as in the election and calling of men; there was grace showed in the election of angels, but not mercy; none of the fallen angels were saved, but fallen man is called to grace in Christ. Certainly whatever the causes were, there was much of wisdom and mercy in it. Whether it be for this cause, that when Adam sinned the whole human nature fell, but the whole angelical nature did not fall, but only a part of it; the kind itself needed not to be repaired, but all the mass of mankind was poisoned; or whether this be the cause, merely the will of God, certainly there is much of mercy in it. Love after a breach is more glorious; it is more to be reconciled than to be confirmed. *Pœnitens*, the penitent, have more cause to glorify God than *innocens*, the innocent; those that are received to mercy than those that are confirmed by grace. Or else was this the cause? Because the angels sinned out of their own motion. Angels had no other temptation but their own ambition and aspiring thought, but man sinned by the devil's suggestion. Certainly it is more to be a tempter than a sinner, and he that sinneth himself doth not offend God himself so much as he that made Israel to sin. However it be, we have cause to bless God that he hath revealed his justice against them and his mercy to us.

[2.] Observe God's wisdom fetched a large compass and circuit; and those things which we count the ruin of man were through the wisdom of providence his preservation. The fall of angels, the fall of man, those crooked things which seemed to be the destruction of the creature, through the overruling of God made for the manifestation of his glory. Gregory called the sin of Adam *fœlix scelus*, because it occasioned the coming of Christ. Providence hath many creeks and turnings, but all concur to the beauty of the whole frame. The apostle calls it πολυπόικιλος σοφία, 'the manifold wisdom of God,' Eph. iii. 10. Therefore we are not to judge by present sense. God's mending is better than his making; he would have all fall to pieces to discover more of his mercy. Man must commit a shameful act, and Christ must suffer a shameful death, and all this to advance his own glory. As a vessel that is cracked and soldered is the stronger there, or a leg that has been broken, and set again by a skilful hand, is the stronger; so the Lord would first have man to fall and ruin himself, that he might be the better established by his own grace.

[3.] Observe again, that God should pitch upon this way of sending his Son. God was not limited or bound up; he could have done it by an angel, or of his own will have released the creature of his offence; but 'it pleased the Father that in him should all fulness dwell,' Col. i. 19; it was God's will that salvation should be brought about this way. In the whole business of salvation God would proceed by choice, not necessity. I confess, supposing the determination of the divine decrees, no creature was qualified to do us good; the angels do but their work, they could not so fitly supererogate for us; but if God would send his own Son, he might have come as a king in glory and triumph, and wrestled with Satan, and rescued all the elect out of his hands. But the Lord would not now discover power, but love; he had discovered power in creation: Rom. i. 20, 'For the invisible things of him from the creation of the world are clearly seen, being understood by the things that are made, even his eternal power and godhead;' but in redemption he discovered his wisdom; every attribute of God was to be discovered in its season. Again, the Lord would meet with the sin of men and angels. The angels had lost their holiness out of a desire of greatness, they would be over all, and under none; and man was sick of the same disease, and did desire to be rather great than good. Adam would be as God; Adam fell by pride, and to counterwork this, Christ was to restore mankind by humility. When he cometh to save mankind, he lays aside his majesty, and puts on a humble garb; he would not save mankind by power, but by suffering; the Lord's design was by the quality of the remedy to show the nature of the disease.

[4.] Observe, man or angel could not have found out such an excellent plot or design as this is. It could not have come into our heads or hearts, and therefore it came merely from the breast of God; it was devised by Father, Son, and Holy Ghost: Rom. xi. 34, 'Who hath known the mind of the Lord? or who hath been his counsellor?' What creature did prescribe to God, or direct him to such a way? The apostle showeth it could not enter into the creature's thoughts: 1 Cor. ii. 9, 'Eye hath not seen, nor ear heard, neither have entered into the heart of man the things which God hath prepared for them that love him.' You will find by the context he speaks of the doctrine and contrivance of Christ crucified; neither sense, nor fancy, nor reason could suggest such a thing to the creature. There are some seeds of the law in nature, but not the least seeds of the gospel. We see in other nations they cannot so much as think of a way of a recovery': Isa. lvi. 19, 'He saw that there was no man, and wondered that there was no intercessor, therefore his arm brought salvation unto him;' it is chiefly understood of the everlasting salvation by Christ. If the Lord had tarried till man had devised a way for his own comfort, we had been miserable to all eternity.

[5.] Observe, God discovered this design before it was accomplished in the fulness of time: Isa. xlii. 9, 'Before they spring forth I tell you of them.' This love was too big to be contained in his heart, but he must open his mind. The prophecies and promises of the Old Testament were the eruptions and overflows of God's love; his heart was so full of love, that it could not be contained within the bounds of secrecy. He openeth his heart, and gives vent to his love in the midst of anger. As soon as man had displeased him, God drops out the promise that the seed of the woman should break the serpent's head.

[6.] Observe again, God discovered this by degrees, first in types, then in truths; first in promises, then in performances. God spake to his people formerly not so much by words as by things. We teach children to fight with puppets, and in the oriental nations it is their genius to be taken with allegories and figures. God would prepare the world by degrees, as the day groweth till it cometh to high noon; to us he hath opened all his good treasure. And further, it was for our instruction, that wickedness should be perfectly discovered. And besides the former ages needed restraints more than comforts. Every age had sufficient revelation for what God required of them.

2. Follow this meditation by arguments. There could not have been a better way to save the creature, whether we respect God's glory or the creature's comfort and profit.

[1.] If we consider God's glory.

(1.) It was the best way to commend his love: Rom. v. 8, 'But God commended his love towards us, in that, while we were yet sinners, Christ died for us.' Herein was the commendation of the divine love, that God would give up the Son of his own love and bosom to die for us that were sinners. As the apostle saith, Heb. vi. 13, 'When God made promise to Abraham, because he could swear by no greater, he sware by himself.' So when the Lord could give us no greater gifts, he gave us his Son. David seems to be amazed with wonder when he considers the power of God in making such creatures as the moon and stars, much more when he considers the love of God in framing of man: Ps. viii. 3, 4, 'When I consider the heavens, the work of thy fingers, the moon and the stars which thou hast ordained; what is man, that thou art mindful of him? and the son of man that thou visitest him?' But here the Son of God himself is become man for us. Oh! that Jesus Christ should stoop so low! that he that fills all things should be shut up in the narrow straits of the virgin's womb! that Christ should disrobe himself of all his glory, and submit to the greatest abasement! John iii. 16, 'For God so loved the world that he gave his only-begotten Son, that whosoever believeth in him should not perish, but have everlasting life.'

(2.) Hereby his justice is discovered. One attribute is not to be exercised to the wrong and prejudice of another. Now in this excellent contrivance God did glorify his mercy so as his justice was no loser, that being sufficiently satisfied in the Lord Jesus Christ. Therefore justice, which in itself is our dread, is in Christ the ground of our comfort and support, and that attribute which would discourage sinners doth now invite and draw unto Christ: 1 John i. 9, 'If we confess our sins, he is faithful and just to forgive us our sins, and to cleanse us from all unrighteousness.' So Rom. iii. 25, 26, 'Whom God hath set forth to be a propitiation through faith in his blood, to declare his righteousness for the remission of sins that are past, through the forbearance of God; to declare at this time, I say, his righteousness, that he might be just, and the justifier of him that believeth in Jesus.' God would dispense acts of grace with the greatest advantage to his justice. This is the beauty of his design, he would be just in justification, and those acts which to us are acts of mere grace, are now made acts of righteousness.

(3.) Hereby the authority of the law is still preserved. God in innocency had written a law in man's heart, and he was to preserve the honour of it. Man transgressed this law. Now by appointing Jesus Christ to die for us, the dignity of the law is kept up. Impunity maketh sin to be lightly esteemed; when laws are relaxed there must be some commutation or recompense, or else their authority is not preserved: Mat. v. 18, 'Till heaven and earth pass, one jot or one tittle shall in no wise pass from the law till all be fulfilled.' The omission of punishment would detract from it, therefore Christ must be made under the law: Gal. iv. 4, 5, 'But when the fulness of time was come, God sent forth his Son, made of a woman, made under the law, to redeem them that were under the law, that we might receive the adoption of sons.' Christ endured the severity of it.

(4.) Hereby God's essence is discovered, even the whole Trinity, Father, Son, and Holy Ghost. The doctrine of the Trinity was but darkly revealed in the Old Testament till Christ came in the flesh. One of the main designs of our redemption was to discover God the Father, God the Son, and God the Holy Ghost. There is a God that must be satisfied, there is a God that must satisfy, and there is a God that must seal up all this to the soul. At Christ's baptism, when he was solemnly inaugurated into the mediatorship, there was a discovery of the Trinity, the Father in a voice, the Son in person, and the Holy Ghost in the shape of a dove.

[2.] If we consider the creature's comfort, it was the best way to establish that.

(1.) Here is excellent provision made against the infiniteness that is in sin by the infiniteness of Christ's sufferings; for though sin be but a temporary act, yet it is infinite because of the object, being committed against an infinite majesty; so Christ's sufferings were but a temporary act, yet they were infinite, he being a person that was both God and man. Therefore as sins receive a value from the person against whom they are committed, so Christ's sufferings receive a value from the person by whom they are performed. The apostle puts a 'how much more' upon the blood of Christ: Heb. ix. 14, 'How much more shall the blood of Christ, who through the eternal Spirit offered himself without spot to God, purge your consciences from dead works to serve the living God?' His Godhead did put a value and merit upon his blood to expiate the guilt of sin, and therefore the blood of Christ is called the blood of God: Acts xx. 28, 'Feed the church of God, which he hath purchased with his own blood.' So that if sin did abound, grace had superabounded; if sin be put into one scale, put the blood of Christ into the other. The great purpose and design of God was to give us triumph over the clamours of our own conscience. Sin is expiated and done away by the blood of the Son of God.

(2.) There is an excellent provision made for all that the creature stands in need of. There are three things which trouble the creature, and they are only accomplished and made good in this great contrivance of God—the bringing of God and man together, the bringing of justice and mercy together, and the bringing of comfort and duty together. How God and man are brought together, who were separate by sin: 1 Peter iii. 18, 'Christ also hath once suffered for sin, the just for the unjust, that he might bring us to God.' To unite man fallen to God, there is mortal and immortal, greatness and baseness, finiteness and infiniteness brought together. There is God and man in one person, that there might be a commerce between us and God; our nature, as it were, grafted and planted into the person of Christ, that our persons might have social communion with God. Then justice and mercy are brought together. The great inquiry of nature is, how to have a satisfaction for justice, that mercy might have a free course? What shall we do to recompense justice? Creatures would sacrifice themselves, and all they have: Micah vi. 6, 7, 'Wherewith shall I come before the Lord, and bow myself before the high God? Shall I come before his face with burnt-offerings, with calves of a year old? Will the Lord be pleased with thousand of rams, or with ten thousand of rivers of oil? Shall I give my first-born for my transgression, the fruit of my body for the sin of my soul?' But it is not our first-born, but God's first-born. So also comfort and duty are sweetly united together, the Lord having provided a merit against our defects, and a spirit against our weaknesses; the Lord is at peace with us, and we are enabled comfortably to serve God.

[3.] If we consider the profit of the creature.

(1.) This way serves to represent sin. You have nowhere such a sight of sin as upon Mount Calvary, when you see the Son of God stretched out upon the cross, and crying out, 'My God, my God, why hast thou forsaken me?' When the punishment of our sins was laid upon Christ, God showeth how displeasing sin was to him.

(2.) To wean us from vanity. We make great matters of trifles, and are apt to idolise every petty and vain thing in the world; therefore in Christ the Lord would show us the highest self-denial when he took the human nature on him, and endured the wrath of the Father. The whole world wondered after the beast, and the disciples wondered at the goodly stones of the temple, Mat. xxiv. 1. Oh! what will you do at the Son of God, in whom the fulness of the Godhead dwelt bodily? This should beget a special veneration and reverence towards God.

(3.) To overcome us by love. There is a great engagement laid upon a sinner hereby. When the king of Moab was pressed hard by Israel, 'he took his eldest son, that should have reigned in his stead, and offered him for a burnt-sacrifice upon the wall,' 2 Kings iii. 27, according to their superstition, who were wont in extreme dangers and desperate cases to sacrifice their children, whereupon they raised the siege, and went home. God hath taken his own Son, and sacrificed him, that we might leave off fighting against heaven. God would overcome sin by the highest act of goodness and kindness imaginable, hereby he would shame and overcome the heart of a poor sinner.

(4.) That we might have a high and glorious pattern of obedience. We are referred to angels, and to Christ himself, who would leave us a more glorious example.

3. Magnify this great contrivance of your salvation by comparisons. Compare it with creation, with other deliverances, and with the works of nature.

[1.] Compare it with creation. The Lord discovered much of his glory in making the world out of nothing, but he discovered more of his glory when Jesus Christ was born of his own creature, a vine out of the berry or grape. This was his masterpiece and grand design, in which he purposed to gain to himself most honour and glory. The world was made with a word, but redeemed with a serious plot and contrivance. The world was made for man and woman, but Christ was made out of a woman. In the creation God made us like himself, but here the Lord made himself like us. In the creation all things were made out of nothing, here order came out of confusion. In the creation man was made out of the earth, but here God was made man. In the creation God went the high way to do us good, in redemption he came the lower way; Jesus Christ abased himself for our sakes.

[2.] Compare it with other deliverances. It was a great thing to be delivered out of Egypt and Babylon, but it is far greater to be delivered out of hell, and from damnation and wrath to come. Read the story of the children of Israel's deliverances, Ps. cvii. They were delivered from the oppression of Pharaoh, but we from Satan. God gave them food, and satisfied the longing soul, and filled the hungry; but Jesus Christ incarnate is made bread and food to the soul. They had deliverance from diseases, but we from sin, the sickness and disease of the soul, and from the vanity of our own spirits. Then he goes on to the wonders in the deep, but we may see the depth of mercy swallowing up the depth of sin, and the glorious love of God breaking out in such a wonderful deliverance by Jesus Christ, that we may well cry out with them, ver. 31, 'Oh! that men would praise the Lord for his goodness, and for his wonderful works to the children of men.'

[3.] Compare it with the miracles of nature. There are strange things among the creatures, yet there may be some footsteps of reason seen; but it cannot enter into the heart of man to conceive of this glorious salvation brought about by the Son of God. Therefore bless God for the revelation, and complain of thyself for not thinking of these things with serious admiration, scarce vouchsafing to look into these things, but are more pleased with every bauble and vain contrivance than the great and serious plot of the gospel.

SERMON X.

And Isaac went out to meditate in the field at the even-tide.—
GEN. xxiv. 63.

FOURTHLY, The object which I shall now propose is providence, a large field, and full of useful matter. It is a draught which God hath been plotting from all eternity, and accomplishing these thousands of years. Take it altogether, and it is a continued contexture or concatenation of decrees, actions, and events, from the creation to the day of judgment. It is our duty to understand it for the present, and it will be our happiness to understand it perfectly hereafter: Ps. cvii. 43, 'Whoso is wise, and will observe those things, even they shall understand the loving-kindness of the Lord.' It is an excellent piece of wisdom to be able to link events together that we may see the wisdom and love of God in the usual occurrences that happen out. We being of short narrow thoughts, fail most herein. Power is such an attribute as is visible and obvious to a common and careless eye; the heathens knew it: Rom. i. 20, 'For the invisible things of him from the creation of the world are clearly seen, being understood by the things that are made, even his eternal power and Godhead.' But to find out the beauty and wisdom of God's work, there needs the light of faith and some acquaintance with God himself; therefore it is said, Job xi. 5, 6, 'O that God would speak, &c., and show me the secrets of wisdom, that they are double to that which is.' Power is obvious to sense and reason, but wisdom is scarce discernible to faith. There is an outside and an inside in all divine dispensations; the outside is full of beauty, but that is but dark to the inside, to the secrets of wisdom. God's works are full of mysteries as well as his word, and we cannot understand them unless God himself be our teacher; we are blind and see not, and then we murmur. But the full knowledge of the mysteries of providence is reserved for our portion in heaven, when we shall know as we are known: 1 Cor. xiii. 12, 'Now we see through a glass darkly, but then face to face; now I know in part, but then I shall know even as also I am known.' We shall view all the passages of providence by which we have been brought to glory, and see the beautiful order and links of them. Now 'we have known God, or rather are known of God,' Gal. iv. 9. God knoweth what is the meaning of such a providence, what is in the womb of such a dispensation. Here there is a handwriting upon the wall, but we, as Belshazzar, cannot read it. As when we see a woman with child, we cannot tell what it will prove; but when we are on the top of the mount, we shall look back, and see how many are the crooked lanes we have passed, the uphill and downhill we have trod, and God knew us all along, and did not only lead us in, but lead us out; then we shall know the multitude of his thoughts, and what the great number of them is. I confess by narrow observation we may discern a little for the present; as David: Ps. cxxxix. 17, 'How precious also are thy thoughts unto me, O God! how great is the sum of them!' When he looked back, how God had carried him through many difficulties, and brought him to rule his people, and watched over him with a careful eye of providence, and ordered every event for his comfort. Some general view and knowledge we may have for the present.

Now, to direct your meditations upon the providence of God—(1.) I will show what it is; (2.) That it is; (3.) I will give you some observations; (4.) I will press you to treat with your own hearts about the use and comfort of it.

I. To open the nature of it, what it is. Consider—(1.) The grounds of providence; (2.) The acts of providence.

1. The grounds of providence; it is founded in God's nature and attributes, three especially—omniscience, wisdom, and power.

[1.] God's omniscience, or knowledge of all affairs in the world. God, like the sun, is all light and all eye: Prov. xv. 3, 'The eyes of the Lord are in every place, beholding the evil and the good;' in the congregation, in the closet, in the shop, the eyes of the Lord are everywhere, and do not only behold the evil and the good person, but the evil and the good action. But chiefly God's eyes are upon his children; they fall under his special care: 2 Chron. xvi. 9, 'The eyes of the Lord run to and fro throughout the whole earth, to show himself strong in the behalf of them whose heart is perfect towards him.' God minds their whole condition, takes notice of their wants and dangers and troubles, and will show himself strong in their supply and deliverance. He doth not only know their persons, but their way: Ps. i. 6, 'The Lord knoweth the way of the righteous.' God takes notice of every particular step he takes and every case he is in; by one intuition all things are present to God. Therefore when Christ would comfort his disciples, and fence them against worldly care, he saith, Mat. vi. 32, 'Your heavenly Father knoweth that you have need of all these things.' God takes an exact and particular account of all your wants and necessities. So the psalmist: Ps. lvi. 8, 'Thou tellest my wanderings; put thou my tears into thy bottle; are they not in thy book?' There is not a tear you shed but it is treasured up in God's bottle; not a weary step you take for his name's sake but it is recorded in God's book. He speaks of those weary steps he took through the two forests of Ziph and Hateph. But if this be not full enough to commend the particularity of God's care, he goes higher: Isa. xlix. 16, 'Behold, I have graven thee on the palms of my hands; thy walls are continually before me.' When we are apt to forget, we fix a memorial on our hands; and if we forget a thing recorded in our book, we shall not forget what is imprinted on our hands.

[2.] God's wisdom. He knoweth their wants and ordereth their deliverance. There is something of counsel in all that the Lord doeth: Eph. i. 11, 'Who worketh all things after the counsel of his own will.'

Therefore his will is called his counsel: Acts iv. 28, 'For to do whatsoever thy hand and thy counsel determined before to be done.' There is not only a mighty hand seen in all the dispensations of God, but a wise counsel. So these two attributes are coupled: Job ix. 21, 'He is wise in heart and mighty in strength.' We are rash and precipitate, carried on with more resolution than reason; our desires beget an heat that oversetteth us; but whatever God doth it is with exact judgment. If we have eyes to see it, we should see that all the circumstances of providence are disposed with much art.

[3.] God's power to execute and administer that which his wisdom hath devised. God's counsels and purposes are always followed with a shall be, or shall not be; he hath infinite power to accomplish them. His power is as it were the midwife to his blessed decrees; he conceiveth all things in the womb of his will, and then he educeth and bringeth them forth by his mighty power: Ps. xxxiii. 9, 'He spake and it was done, he commanded and it stood fast.' 'Let it be' was sufficient to make the world, and 'I will' is enough to preserve it. God pleadeth this as the privilege of the Godhead: Isa. xliv. 7, 'Who, as I, shall call, and shall declare it, and set it in order for me?' that is, that can by calling ordain or create. Therefore Christ, when he would discover the power of his godhead, cured by a word of omnipotency: Mat. viii. 3, 'I will; be thou clean.' Now this power of God is discovered in providence three ways—by his ability and sufficiency to work without means, by unlikely means, or by contrary means.

(1.) By working without means. God is not bound to the road of nature, or tied to the course of second causes; he can create where he doth not find; therefore when God is represented as an object of trust to his people this expression is used: 1 Peter iv. 19, 'Wherefore let them that suffer according to the will of God commit the keeping of their souls to him in well-doing, as unto a faithful Creator;' as one that is able to create where nothing is found. So God promiseth, Hosea i. 7, 'I will have mercy on the house of Judah, and will save them by the Lord their God, and will not save them by bow, nor by sword, nor by battle, by horses, nor by horsemen.' These were the only means they could pitch upon to re-establish themselves, but, saith the Lord, I have a purpose to save them, but it shall not be by these. God would do it by an invisible sway and turn of things, that they should enjoy the mercy but not see the means. So Isa. xlviii. 7, 'They are created now, and not from the beginning; even before the day when thou heardest them not, lest thou shouldst say, Behold, I know them.' Sometimes God by an immediate sovereignty will help us: Mat. iv. 4, 'Man shall not live by bread alone, but by every word that proceedeth out of the mouth of God.' Sometimes God will not reach out a supply by the ordinary means, but by the powerful word of his providence or commanded blessing.

(2.) By working with unlikely means. There is nothing so evil or so inconsiderable but God can work by it. In the story of Joseph (which is one of the fairest draughts of providence), a lie cast him into prison, and a dream fetched him out; so evil a thing as a lie, and so inconsiderable a thing as a dream. So the Lord makes use of the neglect and errors of men. Possidonius hath two remarkable stories in the life of Austin; one was that in travel he lost his way and found his life, for he escaped an ambush of the Donatists. At another time, being to preach, he forgot both his text and matter, and fell upon that which through the blessing of God converted Firmius. Omnipotency needeth no outward advantage. So in public deliverances. God's instruments are usually despicable. A straw is as good as a spear in the hands of omnipotence. Most of the judges that rescued Israel were taken from the plough and sheepfold. So for judgments; God by weak means punishes sinners. Egypt was plagued with flies and lice; they were strong to execute God's word.

(3.) By working with contrary means. Christ used clay and spittle, that one would think should put out the eyes, to restore sight to the blind man. Joseph was first made a slave and then a favourite; his brethren first sell him and then worship him; he is cast into the dungeon to be preferred to court. There are strange contrivances and contrarieties in providence; the way seemeth contrary to the aim, and the means disproportionable to the end. When we see great confusions in the world, we wonder how this should tend to God's glory and the church's good, and are apt to say, as Joshua, chap. vii. 9, 'What wilt thou do unto thy great name?' and as the prophet, Amos. vii. 2, 'By whom shall Jacob arise, for he is small?' We wonder how God means to save when Babylon destroyeth, and how confusion and mischief can end in order and beauty. But God knows the sufficiency of his own power, and is able to bring about these things, to bring light out of darkness, and one contrary out of another.

2. The acts of providence; they are three—conservation, gubernation, and ordination.

[1.] Conservation, conserving and keeping all creatures in their being. Therefore the apostle saith, Heb. i. 3, 'He upholdeth all things by the word of his power;' Isa. xxii. 23, 24, 'I will fasten him as a nail in a sure place, and he shall be for a glorious throne to his father's house, and they shall hang upon him all the glory of his father's house.' If God should take away the shoulder of his providence, all things would return to their first nothing, and vanish and disappear; as a seal upon the waters, the impression is defaced as soon as the seal is gone. Providence is a continual creation; everything that is kept in working and being is, as it were, newly born, newly brought forth, newly produced. Nay, Chrysostom saith it is $\mu\epsilon\iota\zeta\acute{o}\nu$ $\tau\iota$, something greater than creation. As it is more to support a burden long in the air than to raise it up from the earth, so it is more to keep all things from returning to nothing than to educe and bring them out of nothing. That is the reason why the Holy Ghost speaks in the present tense: Ps. civ. 2, 'Who stretcheth out the heavens like a curtain;' and Isa. xl. 22, 'It is he that stretcheth out the heavens as a curtain, and spreadeth them out as a tent to dwell in.' It is not in the future tense, because God is always a stretching them out. So our Saviour: John v. 17, 'My Father worketh hitherto, and I work.' Though there be a cessation of work in regard of new kinds, yet there is a continuation of work in regard of their preservation and God's providential influence. The power which raised from nothing must still preserve from nothing: Rom. xi. 36, 'For of him, and through him, and to him, are all things.' This Solomon intends when he saith, Prov. xx. 12, 'The hearing ear and the seeing eye, the Lord hath made even both of them.' He doth not mean spiritually, but naturally; he doth not only give the faculty, but the exercise; as he gives the eye, so the seeing, and as he gives the ear, so the hearing: this could not be done without new acts of providence, assistance, and supportation from God. Therefore we read Hagar did not see the well of water till the Lord opened her eyes: Gen. xxi. 19, 'And God opened her eyes, and she saw a well of water.' So the disciples: Luke xxiv. 31, 'And their eyes were opened, and they saw him.' When the Lord suspended his influence, the fire could not burn the three children. God did not destroy the property of the fire, but only suspended the efficacy of it. No creature can put forth itself in a way of operation without a new providential assistance from God.

[2.] Gubernation, or governing all things according to his will and pleasure. All things keep their course, for God sitteth at the helm and steereth all: Dan. iv. 35, 'He doth according to his will in the army of heaven, and among the inhabitants of the earth; and none can stay his hand, or say unto him, What doest thou?' God doth all according to his pleasure; he is not confined by any external law, nor straitened by the course of nature, but acts with a great deal of sovereignty and freedom, and sometimes inverts the order of second causes. God's will is sometimes called $\theta\acute{\eta}\lambda\mu a$, sometimes $\epsilon\nu\delta o\kappa\acute{\iota}a$; his pleasure is all. There are indeed some standing ordinances of nature, as the ordinances of sun and moon and the covenant of day and night: Jer. xxxi. 35, 'Thus saith the Lord, which giveth the sun for a light by day, and the ordinances of moon and stars for a light by night;' and Gen. viii. 22, 'While the earth remaineth, seed-time and harvest, and cold and heat, and summer and winter, and day and night shall not cease.' God can alter the course of these, as in Joshua's time and at Christ's death; there were three days' darkness in Egypt: Mat. v. 45, 'He maketh his sun to rise on the evil and on the good, and sendeth rain on the just and on the unjust.' There is nothing so casual but it is governed by God, and falls under the ordination of his wise counsel. It is said, 1 Kings xxii. 34, 'And a certain man drew a bow at a venture, and smote the king of Israel between the joints of the harness.' It was a mere chance as to him, but God directed it into the sides of the king. So Exod. xxi. 13, 'If a man lie not in wait, but God deliver him into his hand;' compared with Deut. xix. 5, 'As when a man goeth into the wood with his neighbour to hew wood, and his hand fetcheth a stroke with the axe to cut down the tree, and the head slippeth from the helve, and lighteth upon his neighbour that he die.' God slew him. There is nothing so casual but it is directed by the wise ordination of God: Prov. xvi. 33, 'The lot is cast into the lap, but the whole disposal thereof is of the Lord.' There seems to be nothing so trivial and casual as the casting the lot into the lap, yet it is overruled by him; he doth not only permit, but govern. God governs all his creatures; in such a throng of stars there is no interfering. We wonder at strange events when the great sway is discovered. The sea is higher than the earth, yet it doth not transgress its bounds and limits. We live and breathe as the Israelites did in the midst of the Red Sea; this is a daily miracle.

[3.] Ordination. All things are overruled by God's great sway; it is not as the creature will, but as God will; and many times the creatures are serviceable to the designs of God contrary to their intentions: Isa. x. 6, 7, 'I will send him against an hypocritical nation, and against the people of my wrath will I give him a charge to take the spoil, and to take the prey, and to tread them down like the mire of the streets. Howbeit he meaneth not so, neither doth his heart think so, but it is in his heart to destroy and cut off nations not a few.' The king of Assyria was moved with a principle of ambition, rage, and cruelty, but the Lord sent him on his work. So Augustus his covetousness in taxing the whole world God orders it for the occasioning Christ's birth at Bethlehem, Luke ii. The actings of the creature are disposed and carried on besides the purpose of the creature to another end. He discovers his wisdom by man's folly, and his righteousness by man's sin. Look, as in a ship some sleep, and some walk contrary to the ship's motion, so in the world some men are negligent, others keep bustling and stirring and seek to resist the designs of God, but the ship goes on: Acts iv. 28, 'For to do whatsoever thy hand and thy counsel determined before to be done.' The devil thought to ruin all mankind by seducing of Adam, yet that made way for Christ. Herein is the great beauty and order of providence seen, that God can make hindrances to be helps, and while men seek to cross his will most, they do but accomplish and fulfil it.

II. That there is such a thing as providence. Heathens granted it, though they had but a dim sight of it; and therefore Tully saith, *Dii magna curant, parva negligunt*—The gods take care of great things, but neglect little things. We count them atheists that deny a providence, as well as they that denied a God.

That there is a providence may be proved from the being of God: there is a God, therefore there is a providence. His wisdom and his goodness enforceth it; he is so wisely good: Ps. cxix. 68, 'Thou art good, and thou doest good.' The divine wisdom ordereth all things for an end, and the divine power governs all things in order to that end. We read it in the order of the world and the sense of our own conscience; if there were no providence, the devils would soon overturn all things, honesty would be folly, a title without substance, labour without reward: 1 Cor. xv. 19, 'If in this life only we have hope in Christ, we are of all men most miserable.' The godly would have no relief; they would not call God to witness, nor acquaint him with their sorrows, which is their great solace: Job xvi. 20, 'My friends scorn me, but mine eye poureth out tears unto God.' God's works discover it. Who feedeth the beasts? Job xii. 7-9, 'But ask now the beasts, and they shall teach thee; and the fowls of the air, and they shall tell thee: or speak to the earth, and it shall teach thee; and the fishes of the sea shall declare unto thee. Who knoweth not in all these that the hand of the Lord hath wrought this?' His judgments show it: Ps. lviii. 10, 11, 'The righteous shall rejoice when he seeth the vengeance; he shall wash his feet in the blood of the wicked: so that a man shall say, Verily there is a reward for the righteous, verily he is a God that judgeth in the earth.' Some men's sins are open beforehand, and God keeps a petty sessions before the general assize cometh.

The great objection that is against providence is because all things come alike to all; but that which seemeth the blemish of providence is the beauty of it. The prosperity of wicked men complieth with God's ends; that there is such a checker-work of providence is for the exercise of the godly, as the stones that are for a temple are hewed and squared; and hereby wicked men are left without excuse; they have prudence, but not grace; and they cannot complain, having common mercies.

III. I will give you some observations.

1. Providence reacheth to the least and most inconsiderable things, as the flight of a sparrow, the falling of a hair: Mat. x. 29, 30, 'Are not two sparrows sold for a farthing? and one of them shall not fall on the ground without your Father; but the very hairs of your head are all numbered.' God takes particular account of every concernment and circumstance of your lives: Ps. cxlvii. 4, 'He telleth the number of the stars.' It is much that God should be at leisure to tell the stars; much more that he should take particular notice of the hairs of your head.

2. Though providence extends to all things, yet it is chiefly exercised about the most noble creatures, men and angels. The psalmist saith, Ps. xxxvi. 6, 'Lord, thou preservest man and beast;' but chiefly man. For mark it, these are not only governed by God, but by themselves. Other things, that are void of understanding, are only guided by an external principle without the knowledge of an end, as arrows shot out of a bow; but rational creatures have a principle of their own, viz., prudence, which is a shadow of divine providence. In these providence is most discovered. Man's will is rebellious; it is harder to rule a skittish horse than it is to roll a stone. God challengeth this as his own prerogative: Jer. x. 23, 'O Lord, I know that the way of man is not in himself; it is not in man that walketh to direct his steps.' He can bridle, rule and restrain the hearts of men, and turn them as he pleaseth: Prov. xxi. 1, 'The king's heart is in the hand of the Lord; as the rivers of water, he turneth it whithersoever he will.' The hearts of kings, those that seem to be most led by will and passion, God can turn them, and rule them at his pleasure.

3. Though the providence of God chiefly concerns man, yet the chiefest care of providence is about the good of the elect: Mat. vi. 26, 'Behold the fowls of the air, for they sow not, neither do they reap, nor gather into barns; yet your heavenly Father feedeth them: are ye not much better than they?' 1 Tim. iv. 10, 'We trust in the living God, who is the saviour of all men, especially of those that believe.' He is a saviour in this sense in regard of providential administration, but all dispensations towards his people are more exact, and have more of care; God particularly looks after them: Amos ix. 9, 'For lo, I will command, and I will sift the house of Israel among all nations like as corn is sifted in a sieve, yet shall not the least grain fall upon the earth.' Mark, above all nations God would have a care of Israel; whatever becomes of the chaff, God watcheth over the corn. The elect are the darlings of providence; the world is continued for their sakes, that all the elect may be gathered in: Isa. xliii. 3, 4, 'I gave Egypt for thy ransom, Ethiopia and Seba for thee. Since thou

wast precious in my sight, thou hast been honourable, and I have loved thee; therefore I will give men for thee, and people for thy life.' All the rest of the world are but as dust and refuse, which God will give up to his justice. If justice must have an object whereon to exercise itself, I will give up Seba and Ethiopia and Egypt to justice; a thousand of them shall perish rather than my people. So ver. 14, 'For your sake I have sent to Babylon, and have brought down all their nobles.' God will stain the glory of all the world for the elect's sake. If God throw them into the furnace, he sitteth by the furnace, prying and looking after his metal: Mal. iii. 3, 'And he shall sit as a refiner and purifier of silver, and he shall purify the sons of Levi, and purge them as gold and silver, that they may offer unto the Lord an offering of righteousness.' The fire shall not be too hot, that nothing be lost.

4. Providence must not be considered by pieces, but all together. You must consider the way of God with the aim of God, and the means with the end. You must not measure things by present feeling: Rom. viii. 28, 'All things shall work together for good to those that love God, to those that are the called according to his purpose.' A single part of providence taken out of the frame is odd and unseemly. Providence is a draught of many pieces; there is the manifold wisdom of God in it. All the links of the chain of providence are not of one size. If you would think aright of providence, you must take in your own case and God's aim. (1.) Consider your own case; not what is absolutely good, but what is respectively good for you. Gold absolutely is better than a draught of water, but not to Sampson, who was ready to die for thirst. Cutting a vein is in itself ill, but good in a fever; so such or such a providence, though not good in itself, may be better for you. (2.) You must take in God's aim with your own case; the single links of providence are not all of a sort; like Nebuchadnezzar's image, partly gold, partly iron, partly brass, and partly clay. To an observant eye there is a wonderful beauty in the providences of God. There is no beauty in the parts of a building till they be set together; no more is there in the several pieces of providence till you consider them together and compare one with the other. The first dashes of a picture are uncomely, therefore do not look on God's work by halves, but all together.

5. God doth manage and govern all things without labour and difficulty. It is much for us to spread a small net; the care of a family and the care of a congregation is too great for our shoulders, but the Lord governs all the world without difficulty and pain; he is not burdened with the multitude of cares; it costs him no more to govern angels than to govern ants, to govern palaces than cottages. Look, as the sun doth as easily shine upon a thousand places at one time as upon one field, so the Lord doth as easily manage the affairs of the whole world as of any one place in the world; his care is without trouble, his work is without pains. Lucian scoffs at God's running here and there. No; all things are represented to him in one view.

6. God's providence is conversant about sin, yet without sin. God doth συνεργεῖν, work with us, but he doth not συναμαρτάνειν, come into the fellowship of our sin or guilt. As the sunbeams may shine upon a dunghill, and in a filthy place the warm sun draweth forth

stinking vapours, but the sun is not stained hereby. The apostle saith, Acts xvii 28, 'For in him we live and move.' We are moved by him; but as the lameness of the horse is no blemish to the rider, so neither is the defect of the creature to be imputed to the providence that doth support it.

7. Providence doth not take away either the industry or the liberty of the creature: Acts xxvii. 22, compared with ver. 31; it is said, ver. 22, 'There shall be no loss of any man's life among you, but of the ship;' and yet, ver. 31, 'Except these abide in the ship ye cannot be saved.' We must plough though the clouds drop fatness; still there is a place for human industry, and human counsel and deliberation: Ezek. xxi. 21, 'For the king of Babylon stood at the parting of the way, at the head of the two ways to use divination,' &c. There were two ways; one way led to his country, the other way led directly to Jerusalem. God had determined which way he should go, yet freely out of his own spirit he is moved to take the way he went; still there was place for human counsel and human deliberation.

8. Observe the providences of God to yourselves, in the womb and from the womb: Ps. cxxxix. 12, 'How precious also are thy thoughts unto me, O God! how great is the sum of them!' Gen. xxxii. 10, 'With my staff I passed over this Jordan, and now I am become two bands.' Broad rivers come from a small fountain: Job viii. 7, 'Though thy beginnings were small, yet thy latter end should greatly increase.'

9. The great aim of providence is God's glory and the salvation of the elect. God's glory: Rom. xi. 36, 'For of him, and through him, and to him are all things, to whom be glory for ever, Amen;' Ps. cxix. 91, 'They continue this day according to thine ordinance, for all are thy servants.' The salvation of the elect: Rom. viii. 28, 'All things shall work together for good to them that love God, to them that are called according to his purpose.' The world would soon shatter to pieces, but that God had some elect to gather out of it.

IV. When you have meditated, and taken some view of providence, treat with your own hearts about the use and comfort of it; either about the providences of God in general, or to yourselves in particular.

1. About the providences of God in general. Consider of the care which God hath over all creatures. Urge the providences of God against your fears. Is it fear of man's policy? Oh! consider divine providence is above human prudence: Job v. 13, 'He taketh the wise in their own craftiness, and the counsel of the froward is carried headlong.' Suppose they be able to contrive mischief, yet God can hinder the execution of it, that they cannot find their hands for their enterprise. Or do you fear the cunning of Satan? Consider providence is chiefly exercised for this end, to defeat the power of Satan. There is a providence over the swine, much more over the flock of Christ; and as Tertullian saith, He that has told the bristles of swine hath much more numbered the hairs of the saints. Urge your hearts with the providence of God to encourage your trust in God for outward provision. When you are humbled with straits, and pinched for maintenance of your families, consider there is a providence. The world is God's great common, and he doth not overstock his own common. All things wait upon God; how do the beasts live but upon providence? Ps. civ. 27,

'These all wait upon thee, that thou mayest give them their meat in due season.' Who is it that feeds the ravens? Ps. cxlvii. 9, 'He giveth to the beast his food, and to the young ravens which cry;' and Ps. cxlv. 16, 'Thou openest thine hand, and satisfiest the desire of every living thing.' Compare it with ver. 19, 'He shall fulfil the desire of them that fear him; he also will hear their cry, and will save them.' Urge your hearts herewith to patience under miseries. Not a sparrow falls to the ground without a providence, therefore certainly your crosses fall under the wise dispensation of God: Ps. xxxix. 6, 'Surely every man walketh in a vain show; surely they are disquieted in vain.' Again, urge your hearts to thankfulness for mercies; look upon the first cause, and acknowledge the providence of God in all that you enjoy.

2. Consider the providences of God to yourselves in particular, for thou art a little world. Consider how the providence of God watched over thee in the womb; when he took thee out from thence, how he provided two bottles to sustain thee; how he hath borne thee up from the womb hitherto; especially how he took care of thee when thou hast been in distress. Oh! it is sweet when we can say, as David, Ps. xxxiv. 6, 'This poor man cried, and the Lord heard him, and saved him out of all his troubles.' I have been in these and these distresses, yet the Lord hath heard and delivered me. Especially if he hath blessed thee from small beginnings, and increased thy substance, urge thy heart to trust in him for the future: 1 Peter v. 7, 'Casting all thy care upon him, for he careth for thee.'

Fifthly, The next object of meditation is the excellency and happiness of our estate in heaven. (See this subject treated on in a sermon on Titus ii. 13, 'Looking for that blessed hope.')

SERMONS

ON

SEVERAL TEXTS OF SCRIPTURE.

PART II.

THE EPISTLE DEDICATORY.

To the Lady Bawdon.

Madam,—It needs no apology that I have prefixed your ladyship's name to this part of the late Reverend Dr Thomas Manton's works, since the memory of the author is so precious with you, by whom you and your children were baptized into the christian faith, under whose ministry you were brought up in the knowledge of the mysteries of the gospel, and whose works published both before and since his death, have been so highly valued by you. But your ladyship has a more especial title to these sermons, because a great part of them being committed to my care to publish, the preparing them for the press was performed in a great measure under your ladyship's roof, when the providence of God called me there in my attendance on your honoured mother, the Lady Wharton, in the last scene of her life.

The duty I owe to the memory of that great person obliges me to testify to the world what I, as well as others who had the honour of knowing her, observed in her. She was one whom God had endowed with more than common gifts and graces; one of a piercing judgment, quick apprehension, great presence of mind, useful in all her relations. But that which adorned all was her eminent godliness, which was visible in the whole course of her conversation. She had a great understanding of the mysteries of the gospel; and though she abounded in good works, yet she knew how to account all things loss and dung for the excellency of the knowledge of Christ Jesus her Lord. She was often in the admiration of the riches and freeness of God's grace in Jesus Christ; and all her hopes, trust, and confidence were in his merits and righteousness. She had a very high valuation and esteem of the ordinances of God; and when her long sickness had for some time hindered her from a public attendance on the worship of God, she would often complain of it, that she was as a leper shut out from the sanctuary of God. She was of a noble, generous, and charitable frame of spirit; and her charity was dispensed with great prudence. I cannot but mention one branch of it, viz., the relieving of sick persons, especially providing and giving medicines to the poor who had no money to buy them; and God did wonderfully own her with great success herein.

In her latter days God was pleased to exercise her with great trials, her sickness was long and tedious, her pains great and sharp; but under all, her steady adherence to God showed the strength of her faith and the truth of her patience. I have often heard her say—this one thing silenced all complaints—It is God who hath done it. All the breaches God made upon her made no breach between God and her soul. In her languishing hours, when her strength failed her, she expressed the inward tranquillity and repose of her mind; it being almost the last words she said, 'All is well, all is well.'

Thus she lived and thus she died, and is now joined to that great assembly of glorified saints who are always praising, blessing and adoring God, where she is always beholding the face of her God in glory, and fully understands the meaning of all the dark providences of God towards her in the latter part of her life.

I mention not these things to renew your ladyship's grief for so great a loss, and to make your wounds bleed afresh, but to provoke you to a holy imitation of so great a pattern, and to be a follower of her, as she was of Christ. Good examples have a powerful influence upon us, for we are led more by pattern than by precept, especially the examples of those we love, for such we are prone to imitate; but more especially of those who are in nearest relation to us, for there nature sides with grace. And what an advantage your ladyship has had in having such a precedent before your eyes appears by the fair transcript you have been of so fair a copy.

Madam, God hath been pleased to exercise your ladyship also with great trials, but you have had your comforts and supports. God hath taken away some of your nearest relations, but he hath continued others to you. What a blessing hath God bestowed upon you in those excellent daughters that have sprung from you! But, alas! we are too apt to pore on our losses and overlook our enjoyments, to make our afflictions the grave of our mercies. God hath given your ladyship a better frame of spirit, and taught you how to see his love in the losses you have sustained and the blessings you enjoy. But were it worse with you as to outward comforts, yet ' the foundation of God standeth sure,' having this seal, the Lord knoweth them that are his.' And certainly there is more in God, and a covenant relation to him, to support your joy, than there can be in any outward affliction to cause grief and sorrow of heart; and a due sense of God's afflicting hand is not inconsistent with a holy rejoicing in him. Now that God would fill you more and more with the joys and comforts of his Holy Spirit, and multiply his blessings upon yourself, and those that have descended from you, is the prayer of, honoured madam, your ladyship's most obliged, and most humble servant,

WILLIAM TAYLOR.

February 9, 169$\frac{2}{3}$.

SERMONS UPON LUKE XVI. 30, 31.

SERMON I.

And he said, Nay, father Abraham : but if one went unto them from the dead, they will repent. And he said unto him, If they hear not Moses and the prophets, neither will they be persuaded though one rose from the dead.—LUKE xvi. 30, 31.

It hath been a question whether this is a parable or a history. A parable, surely, for otherwise many incongruities would be asserted; for it supposeth body and soul already in hell: ver. 23, 'And in hell he lift up his eyes, being in torment.' And it would suppose charity, and care of conversion of others in hell, therefore it is not a history. The scope of this parable is to teach us three lessons—

1. To show that the godly poor are blessed, and the unmerciful rich are in everlasting torments. *Desideravit guttam, qui non dedit micam*—He desired a drop of water that would not give a bit of bread.

2. The irreversible estate of the damned: ver. 26, 'Between us and you there is a great gulf fixed, so that they which would pass from hence to you cannot; neither can they pass to us that would come from thence.'

3. That the direction of the holy scriptures is the only means to escape these torments.

This latter is represented in a dialogue between Dives and Abraham. Dives would have one sent from the dead to his father's house, supposing that would work on them to repent. Christ's parables do impersonate our thoughts; we always dislike the present dispensation which God useth to reclaim us, and would have extraordinary means, and then we presume we should believe and repent; these are our thoughts. But Abraham thinketh otherwise, or rather Christ, who is the author of the parable: 'If they hear not Moses and the prophets, neither will they be persuaded though one rose from the dead.'

By 'Moses and the prophets' are meant the whole scriptures of the Old Testament and the New. These are mentioned because these only were then written and received by the Jews; and these include the rest, the same truth being carried on in all the books, though more explicit in the latter.

Doct. That the word of God is a more conducible means to persuade us to repentance than if one should come from the dead.

There are two ways of proof of this doctrine, and therefore let us see what may be said for and against one coming from the dead.

First, If one coming from the dead be presumed to be a more effectual means to bring men to repentance and conversion to God, it must be either because he can bring a more necessary doctrine, or could urge better arguments, and more persuasively, or propound these truths with more certainty, or could by his own strength convey a power with his words, or rationally expect a greater concomitancy and co-operation of grace than is ordinarily dispensed by the word. One or other of these things it must be, or else the conceit is vain and frivolous. But now, proceeding from one consideration to another, I shall show you that the word of God hath clearly the pre-eminence, and is a far more accommodate instrument to work upon the hearts of men than any extraordinary dispensation whatsoever.

1. One coming from the dead, angel or man, cannot bring a doctrine more necessary, there being in the scriptures sufficient direction about the way to true happiness, for which we have not only express testimony, but apparent reason and sensible experience.

[1.] Express testimony, which should sway with christians: 2 Tim. iii. 16, 17, 'All scripture is given by inspiration of God, and is profitable for doctrine, for reproof, for correction, for instruction in righteousness; that the man of God may be perfect, thoroughly furnished unto all good works.' A man of God, or minister of the gospel, thoroughly furnished, hath from the scriptures full out enough to guide man to the enjoyment of God; nothing is wanting for information as to doctrine, conviction, arguments of quickening or exhortation, for instruction or directions concerning the whole duty of man. And—

[2.] Apparent reason. If God be a sufficient teacher of divine things, and if we suppose him willing to inform the creatures (neither of which can be denied without blasphemy), then surely, supposing the scriptures to be the word of God, as all christians do, and in this debate it is fit we should suppose, then certainly we have enough in the scriptures, and need not that the rest of the dead should be discomposed that there may be a fit messenger found out to invite us to return to God. If it need proof, who can teach us the way to blessedness more than the blessed God? Ps. cxix. 12, 'Blessed art thou, O Lord; teach me thy statutes.' Who more willing to show man what is good than the good God? Ps. cxix. 6, 8, 'Thou art good, and doest good; teach me thy statutes.' The blessed God needeth not to envy us the perfection of knowledge, as the devil insinuated: Gen. iii. 5, 'God doth know that in the day ye eat thereof, then your eyes shall be opened, and ye shall be as gods, knowing good and evil.' Wherein is his happiness lessened by our perfection? And the good God, who is so full of goodness and love to mankind, would give us a sufficient direction, especially since his Son appeared in human nature, and became his messenger. Would God reveal himself to any one from the dead, yea, to an angel, more than to his own Son? Or could he see, feel, or hear more than God hath made known to Christ? or be presumed to have a greater charity to mankind than the Lord hath, whose creatures they are? No, no; it cannot be: 'He hath showed thee, O man, what is good,' Micah vi. 8. Abide by that, and thou hast enough.

But let us confirm it. Compare the provisions of the word with your own necessities. What! would you have a rule? Then see if you have it not in the holy scriptures: Titus ii. 11, 12, 'For the grace of God that bringeth salvation hath appeared to all men, teaching us that, denying ungodliness and worldly lusts, we should live soberly, righteously, and godly in this present world.' By 'the grace of God' is meant the gospel; and what doth the gospel teach us? To 'live soberly, righteously, and godly;' to enjoy God, to live with man, and the government of ourselves. We have enough if we have all this. But we have all this in as ample manner as heart can wish for, and therefore he that cometh from the dead must either preach the same doctrine, and then it is needless and superfluous, or contrary things, and then how shall we believe him, who are forewarned? Gal. i. 8, 'But though we or an angel from heaven preach any other gospel unto you than that which we have preached unto you, let him be accursed.' Christ enters a caution against them.

2. Better arguments cannot be urged, nor more persuasively. The gospel is 'the wisdom of God,' 1 Cor. i. 24; and surely God knoweth all the wards of the lock, and what kind of keys will fit the heart of man. He hath laid forth the riches of wisdom and grace upon this blessed design, and hence it is that we have such mysterious doctrines, such dreadful threatenings, such sweet promises, such strong obligations from the death and incarnation of the Son of God, from the example of Christ, which doth secure our direction and encourage our practice. Out of what rock was man hewn if all this will not work upon him? What must God do? provide a better heaven, a hotter hell, another Son to die for us? or a more forcible and encouraging example than that of Jesus Christ? What is the matter that the wicked sinner will not be allured and made tame, charm the charmer never so wisely? What do we need more to move us? Shall God pipe to you in a sweeter strain than that of gospel grace or gospel promises? Is the giving himself and his Christ a price too cheap to purchase your hearts? or must he thunder to you in a more dreadful accent than the horrors of everlasting darkness? Are these but poor and mean scarecrows to tell you of a pit without a bottom, of a worm that never dieth, of a fire that shall never be quenched? Or what is the matter that the sinner stirreth not? Is the scripture a dead letter? and needeth it to be actuated and enforced by a living voice? God hath provided us apostles and prophets to write scriptures, so pastors and teachers to explain and apply scriptures: Eph. iv. 11, 'He gave some apostles, and some prophets, and some evangelists, and some pastors and teachers;' men who are concerned as well as ourselves, the value of whose credit we know by their faithfulness in other things, that have the same temptations, affections, and necessities as we have; men with whom we may more familiarly converse, and with less fright, than with one from the dead. Oh! but one that cometh from the dead is supposed to testify his own sight and knowledge, and so to speak more feelingly. And have not God's messengers some experience? Cannot they say, We declare to you the things which we have seen and heard and felt? Have they not been scorched by the spirit of conviction, tasted comfort, felt a change in their own hearts? What can any messenger from the dead say that hath not been told you over again and again a thousand times? Would he say that all

shall die?—that you see with your eyes. That presently after death cometh judgment?—that you pretend to believe already. That the torments of hell are terrible and insupportable?—this God hath told you over and over; and 'if we receive the witness of men, the witness of God is greater,' 1 John v. 9. That you must repent and be converted?—this is that that is sounded in your ears every day. Therefore we are better provided already than to need the horror of an apparition or a warning from one among the dead.

3. It is not because he could propound these truths with more certainty, for these things are already propounded to our understandings, and we have sensible confirmation.

[1.] They are propounded to our understandings with a fair and full credibility. The holy scriptures have in themselves a self-evidencing light, by which they make it out to the consciences of men that they are of God. Everything that hath passed the hand of God discovereth its author; all God's works have his signature and impression upon them, which is legible and visible to every attentive beholder: Rom. i. 20, 'For the invisible things of him from the creation of the world are clearly seen, being understood by the things that are made, even his eternal power and godhead; so that they are without excuse;' Ps. xix. 1, 'The heavens declare the glory of God, and the firmament showeth his handiwork.' Not a pile of grass but showeth its maker— *Præsentem refert quælibet herba Deum;* and surely his word, which he 'hath magnified above all his name,' Ps. cxxxviii. 2, is not altogether without such an impress and stamp of God upon it, therein being revealed things most worthy of the truth, wisdom, goodness, and holiness of God, and suitable to that wisdom and truth that is in us, so far as there is any in us. What shall I speak of the most satisfactory way of reconciliation with God, the fairest draught of moral perfection, far beyond all that which is of mere human recommendation? Here is no dead fly in this box of ointment, but all pure and holy, without mixture; nothing so accommodate to the necessities of man, and fit to bring us to the enjoyment of that which the reasonable nature aimeth at. What shall I speak of the majesty of the style, the genuine simplicity of the narrations, the harmony of the parts, the sublimity of the doctrines, the impartiality and purity of the precepts, the overflow of God's love in the promises, the glorious rewards, the certainty of the prophecies?— all which are so many innate characters and evidences of the divine authority of these writings, by which they clearly insinuate themselves with wonderful force and power into the consciences of men: 2 Cor. iv. 2, 'But have renounced the hidden things of dishonesty, not walking in craftiness, not handling the word of God deceitfully; but by manifestation of the truth commending ourselves to every man's conscience in the sight of God.' There was an evidence in the truth itself preached by the apostles, so there is in the word written by the apostle, for the voice could add nothing to it, and the writing take nothing from it. A man of art and judgment discovereth himself in every book he writeth. Aristotle's writings show him a person of great knowledge. Can a book have God for its author, and have nothing to discover its author? It is unreasonable. Masters in writing or painting show their hand; the scripture doth not stand or fall to the courtesies of man. Well, then, if these things be so (as certainly they are so), we have more certainty by the word itself than possibly we can have by a messenger from the dead, yea, or a voice from heaven, for it hath such a signature of God upon it that we need go no further: 2 Peter i. 18, 19, 'And this voice which came from heaven we heard when we were with him in the holy mount, who have also βεβαιότερον λόγον, a more sure word of prophecy, whereunto ye do well that ye take heed, as unto a light that shineth in a dark place, until the day dawn, and the day-star arise in your hearts.' What greater confirmation could the apostles expect than that voice from heaven, 'This is my beloved Son, in whom I am well pleased?' Mat. xvii. 5. Yet Peter who heard that voice telleth us that comparatively we have greater security from and by the written word; not in itself, but as it is given in evidence to us, so that there is no compare between it and one from the dead.

[2.] We have sensible confirmations. We are wrought upon by sense. Now is not ordinarily the word as sensibly confirmed to us as it would be by a vision or apparition from the dead?

(1.) There is the holiness of professors: 1 Cor. xiv. 25, 'And thus are the secrets of his heart made manifest, and so, falling down on his face, he will worship God, and report that God is in you of a truth;' 1 Peter iv. 4, 'Wherein they think it strange that ye run not with them to the same excess of riot, speaking evil of you.' Is it not more wonder to see a living man that hath not divested himself of the interests and concernments of flesh and blood to deny himself for things to come, than to hear a tale from a dead man?

(2.) There is the constancy of the martyrs, that have ratified this truth with the loss of their dearest concernments: Rev. xii. 11, 'And they overcame by the blood of the Lamb, and by the word of their testimony; and they loved not their lives unto the death.' It is possible a man may suffer for a false religion, and sacrifice a stout body to a stubborn mind. But is there no true gold because there hath been some counterfeit coin? The devil's martyrs have not been so many for number, nor for temper and quality, so holy, so wise, so meek, as the champions of the truth. The christian religion can show you persons of all ages, young and old; of all sexes, men and women; of all conditions of life, noble and of low degree; of all qualities, learned and unlearned. (See Sermons on John xvii.)

(3.) Then there is the inward feeling of God's children; they find a power in the word, convincing, changing, comforting, fortifying their hearts. These can speak of what they hear, feel, and taste, as well as one that cometh from the dead. They have answerable impressions on their hearts: Heb. viii. 10, 'I will put my laws into their mind, and write them in their hearts;' 2 Cor. iii. 3, 'Ye are manifestly declared to be the epistle of Christ ministered by us, written not with ink, but with the Spirit of the living God, not in tables of stone, but in fleshly tables of the heart.' All this stamped upon the heart in legible characters. A true christian is the lively transcript of his religion; the scriptures are the original, and every believer is the copy; it is gone over again in his heart.

(4.) Those that have no experience of this have a secret fear of the power of the word: John iii. 20, 'For every one that doeth evil hateth the light, neither cometh to the light, lest his deeds should be reproved.' He will not come to the light because he is afraid of the majesty of God shining forth in the scriptures. Men dare not muse upon and seriously consider the doctrine therein contained. Atheism lieth in the heart, the seat of desires: Ps. xiv. 1, 'The fool hath said in his heart, There is no God.' Men question the word, because they would not have it true; they are willing to indulge their lusts, and therefore they are afraid of the word that forbiddeth them; as Ahab was loath to hear Michaiah, because he prophesied evil. Strong lust maketh us incredulous. A malefactor desireth to destroy the records and evidences that are against him.

(5.) There are also outward effects of the power of the word; its propagation throughout all the world within thirty years or thereabout; The doctrine itself, contrary to nature; it doth not court the senses nor woo the flesh; it doth not make offers of splendour of life or pleasures and profits, but biddeth us deny these things and expect troubles. The drift of it is to teach men to row against the stream of flesh and blood, to renounce our lusts, deny our interests. And this was done by a few fishermen, who had no long sword, no public interest or authority to back them, and that in the face of the learned world, when all civil disciplines were in their $ἀκμή$ and height. The word prevailed against ancient customs; the ark was to be set up in the temple that was already occupied and possessed by Dagon.

(6.) Then consider the many sensible effects of the word, as the accomplishment of prophecies, promises, threatenings, and answer of prayers. God's providence is a comment upon scripture. It is an authentic register, and infallible prognostication and calendar. We need not have one come from the dead to tell the truth of it; it is fulfilled before our eyes every day.

4. Or else they can convey a power, or expect that God will co-operate more with their report than with the holy scriptures. Surely they are finite creatures though passed out of this life. Nothing can convert and turn the heart of man but the infinite power of God; all the angels in heaven cannot pluck one sinner out of the state of nature. We read one angel could destroy one hundred and eighty-five thousand in Sennacherib's host, 1 Kings xix. 35; but all the angels cannot convert one soul.

But will God co-operate? Alas! when all prejudices are removed, men are nothing the better till the Lord puts in his grace. The Jews suppose Moses and the prophets to be of God; they were confirmed by notable miracles, the fame of which continue among them. But the matter is about God's efficacy. But now God concurreth with his instituted course; common means of God's appointing have a singular efficacy annexed; as reading, Acts viii. 32, hearing, Mark iv. 24, meditation, Acts xvii. 11. Christ died to sanctify ordinances, Eph. v. 26; and there if ever shall we meet with the power and grace of God.

Secondly, Against it. There are more rational prejudices that lie against any other way than this way that God hath taken. As to instance in the matter in hand.

1. It is no mean scruple about the lawfulness of hearkening to one that should come from the dead, since they are out of the sphere of our commerce, and it is a disparagement to the great doctor of the church. Against consulting with the dead, see Deut. xviii. 10–12, with 14, 15, 'There shall not be found among you any one that maketh his son or his daughter to pass through the fire, or that useth divination, or an observer of times, or an enchanter, or a witch, or a charmer, or a consulter with familiar spirits, or a wizard, or a necromancer; for all that do these things are an abomination unto the Lord, and because of these abominations the Lord thy God doth drive them out from before thee. For these nations which thou shalt possess hearkened unto observers of times, and unto diviners; but as for thee, the Lord thy God hath not suffered thee so to do. The Lord thy God will raise up unto thee a prophet from the midst of thee, of thy brethren, like unto me; unto him ye shall hearken.' It would make religion ridiculous, like a story of hobgoblins and bugbears, wherewith we fright children, or like the fond superstitions of the heathens, that held the world under the servility and bondage of scrupulous fears.

2. It is not so sure a way. How could we trust or believe any one that should bring a message from the dead, since impostors are so rife? Satan can turn himself into an angel of light. What security can we have against delusions? how miserably we may be deceived by stories from the dead is to be seen in popery. Therefore it is a favour that we have such a sure rule: Gal. i. 8, 'But though we or an angel from heaven preach any other gospel unto you than that we have preached unto you, let him be accursed.' We shall never be free from evil designs.

3. It is not so effectual a course as some think. The great doctor of the church arose from the dead, which was confirmed by five hundred witnesses; nothing so credible, and yet they would not believe and repent for all that. The Jews would not believe Lazarus, when, after he had been four days dead, he was raised up again.

4. It is not so familiar a way, and therefore not so fit to instil faith, and reduce men to God's purpose by degrees, as the written word, to which we may have recourse without affrightment, and that at all times. This spirit must be supposed to appear but rarely; for if it were frequent, and settled into a constant converse, the way would be contemned. But here we may view and review the counsel of God in our most deliberate and serious thoughts, and by searching come to know the mind of God. Faith groweth in a rational way: Acts xvii. 11, 'These were more noble than those in Thessalonica, in that they received the word with all readiness of mind, and searched the scriptures daily, whether these things were so.'

Use 1. Information.

1. That man is apt to indent with God about believing and repenting upon terms of his own making: Mat. xxvii. 42, 'If he be the king of Israel, let him now come down from the cross, and we will believe him;' Ps. lxxviii. 19, 'Can God furnish a table in the wilderness?' Mat. iv. 3, 'If thou be the Son of God, command that these stones be made bread.' Many require miracles or new apostles, that maketh them turn seekers; or a testimony from the dead, a spirit or a vision,

and that maketh them turn atheists; or an infallible interpreter, that should solve all questions, or excuse them from the pains of study and prayer, and that maketh them turn papists. Thus foolishly would we give laws to heaven, and prescribe to God how he shall reveal his mind to men. God will not always give sensible confirmation.

2. There lie more prejudices by far against any way of our devising than against the course which God hath instituted for the furthering of our repentance. Man is an ill caterer for himself. The people slighted Moses, and would hear God himself speak; but when he thundered upon the Mount, then they say, let us no more hear the voice of God, for then we shall die: Exod. xx. 19, 'And they said unto Moses, Speak thou with us, and we will hear; but let not God speak with us, lest we die.' All God's institutions are full of reason, and if we had eyes to see it, we could not be better provided for.

3. God in giving the scriptures hath done more for us than we could imagine, yea, better than we could wish to ourselves. He hath certainly done enough to leave us without excuse. You think if one came from the dead this would be better, but you have more; and therefore, if you be damned, it will not be for want of power, but want of will; you have more than if one came from the dead. Try what you can do with Moses and the prophets. It is a great mercy to have a rule by which all doctrines are to be tried, to have a standard and measure of faith, and that put into writing to preserve it against the weakness of memory and the treachery of evil designs, and that translated into all languages. That we have such a rule, and so thoroughly finished, is a great mercy.

4. That we are apt to betray present advantages by wishes of another dispensation, as that we may have oracles and miracles. It is but a shift to think of other means than God hath provided. They that believe not the word will not believe one that should come from the dead. Extraordinary means will not work upon them upon whom ordinary do not prevail. Whatever dispensation God uses, man is man still: Ps. lxxviii. 22–24, 'They believed not in God, and trusted not in his salvation, though he had commanded the clouds from above, and had opened the doors of heaven, and had rained down manna upon them to eat, and had given them the corn of heaven.' There were unbelievers and carnal wretches when there were miracles, and so there would be still. Though there were never so sufficient proof yet such is our perverseness, that we shall slight God's counsel. Man is ever at odds with the present dispensation. It is a sign the heart is out of order, or else any doctrine that is of God would set it a-work.

5. Those that like not the message will ever quarrel at the messenger; and when the heart is wanting, something is wanting. We have means enough to believe; it is our own carelessness and obstinacy that we do not: Mat. xi. 18, 19, 'John came neither eating nor drinking, and they say, He hath a devil. The Son of man came eating and drinking, and they say, Behold a man gluttonous, and a wine-bibber, a friend of publicans and sinners.' There is always one exception or another.

6. How credulous we are to fables, and how incredulous as to undoubted truths; spirits and apparitions, these things are regarded by

us, but the testimony of the Spirit of God speaking in the scriptures is little regarded.

Use 2. To exhort us to improve the scriptures to repentance. This is the great work.

Here I shall show you—(1.) What repentance is; (2.) What the holy scriptures offer to work us to repentance; (3.) How we may improve these.

I. What repentance is. It is a turning of the whole heart from sin and Satan to serve God in newness of life; or a turning from sin because God hath forbidden it, to that which is good because God hath commanded it. There are in it, as in every action, two terms—*a quo* and *ad quem*.

1. The *terminus a quo*, that from which we are to turn. We turn from something; from sin: Acts viii. 22, 'Repent of this thy wickedness;' $\dot{a}\pi\dot{o}\ \tau\hat{\eta}s\ \kappa\alpha\kappa\iota\alpha s$, from thy wickedness. From dead works: Heb. vi. 1, 'Repentance from dead works.' And Satan is sometimes made the term from which, because the sinner falleth to his share: Acts xxvi. 18, 'To turn them from darkness to light, and from the power of Satan to God.'

2. The *terminus ad quem*, the term to which we are to turn, that is, to God: Acts xx. 21, 'Repentance towards God;' to the truth: 2 Tim. ii. 25, 'If God peradventure will give them repentance $\epsilon\dot{\iota}s\ \dot{\epsilon}\pi\iota\gamma\nu\omega\sigma\iota\nu\ \dot{a}\lambda\eta\theta\epsilon\iota as$, to the acknowledgment of the truth.' To holiness and newness of life: Rom. vi. 4, 'Even so we also should walk in newness of life.' To life: Acts xi. 18, 'Then hath God also to the gentiles granted repentance unto life.' According to which terms there is a double action required of us—humiliation and reformation; humiliation or compunction, and a due remorse for sin; reformation, or a change of course. Which answereth to the double work of God upon the soul—mortification, or the subduing of sin; vivification, or the infusion of life. So suitably there are aversion from sin and a conversion to God and the things of God; which is expressed by two duties—confession of sin, and entering into covenant with God. Serious confession of sin is mortification acted; entering into covenant with God is vivification acted, or the desire of grace expressed. Confession of sin is required, that a man, laying aside all extenuations, evasions, and excuses, may take shame to himself, giving glory to God. Entering into covenant with God is required that a man may be under a firm obligation of obedience, and be cautious over his own heart and ways; the one respects sin past, the other sin to come.

First, Let us speak of the first act, the *terminus a quo*, turning from sin. Supposing the judgment enlightened and the heart made tender by grace, the work doth mainly discover itself in the affections of fear, shame, grief, and indignation. True humiliation is begun in fear, continued in shame, carried on by sorrow, and endeth in indignation. And so sin is renounced, and the power of it broken. And indeed, whenever we renew our repentance upon special occasions, these are the affections that are to be exercised. They all have a proper ground and consideration to set them at work. (1.) Fear leadeth the rank. That trembleth at the wrath of God and judgment to come; an accusing conscience telling us that we are in a state of damnation. (2.) Shame looketh upon sin not only as hurtful but filthy and brutish. It is φόβος δικαίο ψύγου, a fear of just reproach for the filthiness and folly of sin. (3.) Sorrow looks upon God's goodness and sin's unkindness, lamenting that ever we should lose the favour of such a God as this is, who hath made us, and kept us, and gave his Son to die for mankind; now that we should forfeit his favour! (4.) Indignation is stirred up by the unseemliness and disproportion of sin to the nature of man, much more to grace infused, or that interest we have or would have by Christ. In short, fear looketh upon sin as damning, shame as defiling, sorrow as offensive to God; indignation is misbecoming our present resolutions, hopes, and interests. The guilt of sin causeth fear; the stain, shame; the unkindness, sorrow; the unsuitableness, indignation. By this means did we come to be divorced from sin, and by these means it is daily weakened.

1. The first awakening of the soul is by the sense of the wrath of God, and everlasting woe denounced on impenitent sinners. You have done that which in its own nature deserveth you should suffer eternal torments, and be separated from the Lord, and be cast forth with the devil and his angels. And then the sinner, being under a fear of being condemned, crieth out, Oh! what shall I do to flee from the wrath to come! I am undone and lost unless God help me. I say here the work beginneth; punishment is soonest felt, and the first notion that we have of sin is the guilt of it, which causeth fears and terrors with respect to the wrath that is to ensue. So it is said of those converts, Acts ii. 37, 'That they were pricked at their hearts;' they were troubled about their condition. It requireth a quicker and more tender sense to be sensible of the folly and filthiness of sin. A man that is covered with noisome boils and sores, the first thing that affecteth him is the pain, though he also abhorreth the sight and smell of them. First we tremble at the thought of God's judgments, before we are ashamed of sin or grieve for it. In renewing our repentance this is an ingredient. It is not against the liberty of the gospel to make use of threatenings; we are sluggish, and need all kind of helps.

2. There is shame and self-loathing, which ariseth from an apprehension of the odiousness of sin: Ezek. vi. 9, 'They shall loathe themselves for the evils which they have committed in all their abominations;' Job xlii. 6, 'I abhor myself, and repent in dust and ashes.' So Ezra ix. 6, 'O my God! I am ashamed, and blush to lift up my face to thee, my God.' They are ashamed to look God in the face, they have dealt so unworthily with him. This is to hate sin as sin, when a man is not only afraid of it, but ashamed of it, as it is against the revealed will of God; not only as it bringeth misery, but as it crosses God's will; not only for the evil after sin, but the evil in sin; that you have polluted your souls, defiled your natures, defaced the image of God, become as a beast before him: Ps. lxxiii. 22, 'So foolish was I, and ignorant; I was as a beast before thee.' Oh! what a fool I was to turn my back upon God; to imagine that any good could come of sin, which God hateth, and to practise a thing so unbefitting the reasonable nature!

3. Sorrow and lamentation to the Lord, which ariseth from a thought of the Lord's goodness and sin's unkindness: Zech. xii. 10, 'They shall look upon me whom they have pierced, and they shall mourn for him;'

Luke vii. 47, she wept much because 'she loved much.' Sin will affect the heart most when the wrong done to God is considered, who never showed any backwardness to our good, but who gave his Son to die for us. He made us at first, and how soon can he take from us that which he hath given us. He hath obliged us with a multitude of benefits: Isa. i. 3, 'I have nourished and brought up children, and they have rebelled against me;' Rom. ii. 4, 'Or despisest thou the riches of his goodness and forbearance and long-suffering, not knowing that the goodness of God leadeth thee to repentance?' And shall we use all these as weapons of unrighteousness! food, raiment, peace, plenty? Ah! but his Christ above all! Oh! never any sinned as I have done. The devil sinned, but Christ never died for him, as he did for me. Judas sinned, but he was never pardoned, as I have been. Achan sinned, but he had not that light and knowledge of the gospel that I have had; he did not live under such means as I have enjoyed. We content ourselves with a hasty sigh. Oh! but it is a deep sorrow that is required, and an active pungent grief, 'rending the heart,' Joel ii. 13; 'Afflicting the soul,' Lev. xvi. 29; Mat. xxvi. 75, 'Peter wept bitterly.' When we are touched with a sense of our unkindness to God, we shall mourn.

4. Indignation, which is an act of our hatred against sin, hatred quickened into a zeal against it. Indignation is the soul's expulsive faculty, when we heartily renounce it, as unsuitable to our present resolutions, professions, and hopes: Isa. xxx. 22, 'Thou shalt cast them away as a menstruous cloth; thou shalt say unto them, Get ye hence.' So Hosea xiv. 8, 'Ephraim shall say, What have I any more to do with idols?' The soul saith first when it is convinced, Oh! what have I done? and then, What shall I do? and then, What have I any more to do? If a christian did remember what he is and what he hopeth for, these questions would be more rife with him. Repentance is not a bare purpose to leave sin, but to leave it with a hatred and deep displeasure against it.

SERMON II.

And he said, Nay, father Abraham: but if one went unto them from the dead, they will repent. And he said unto him, If they hear not Moses and the prophets, neither will they be persuaded though one rose from the dead.—LUKE xvi. 30, 31.

SECONDLY, I now proceed to the next term, which is the *terminus ad quem*, turning to God, which is done in two things—

1. A settled purpose and solemn dedication of ourselves to his use and service, which is a resolution taken up upon debates of conscience: Luke xv. 17, 18, 'And when he came to himself, he said, How many hired servants of my father's have bread enough and to spare, and I perish with hunger; I will arise and go to my father.' First he came to himself, then I will go to my father. This ariseth out of a sense of

God's mercy in Christ: Rom. xii. 1, 'I beseech you, brethren by the mercies of God, that you present your bodies a living sacrifice, holy, acceptable to God, which is your reasonable service.' Lord, accept me for thine; and is the fruit of supernatural grace: James i. 18, 'Of his own will begat he us with the word of truth;' and is accompanied with shame that God so long hath been kept out of his right: 1 Peter iv. 3, 'For the time past of our life may suffice us to have wrought the will of the gentiles, when we walked in lasciviousness, lusts, excess of wine, revellings, banquetings, and abominable idolatries;' and a purpose to serve him with all our might.

2. It is seconded by a real performance: Mat. iii. 8, 'Bring forth therefore fruits meet for repentance;' Acts xxvi. 20, 'That they should repent, and turn to God, and do works meet for repentance.' Without these he is a liar, and deceiveth his own soul, if the heart be not more watchful over itself, afraid to offend God, and grieve his Spirit, more tender of the least sin, more careful to please God in all things, more close at work in the business of eternal life. These are fruits worthy of repentance; this is that περισσόν τι, that which we do more than carnal hypocrites, fruits suitable to the power of grace working in us, and to our professions of respect to God. This is the sum of the doctrine of repentance.

II. What doth the scripture offer to persuade us to this work?

1. It clearly layeth down the absolute and indispensable necessity of it in grown persons, or such as are come to years of discretion: Acts iii. 19, 'Repent ye, therefore, and be converted, that your sins may be blotted out, when the times of refreshing shall come from the presence of the Lord;' Luke xiii. 5, 'Except ye repent, ye shall all likewise perish;' Ezek. xxxiii. 11, 'Say unto them, As I live, saith the Lord God, I have no pleasure in the death of the wicked, but that the wicked turn from his way, and live: turn ye, turn ye, from your evil ways, for why will ye die, O house of Israel?' One way or the other, turn or die: it is no mootpoint or matter of controversy. There are many controversies about other things, but in this all is clear. Many will say, There is such a doubtfulness, that every one bringeth scripture, and maketh a nose of wax of it, ductile and pliable to his own fancy. But in points of absolute duty it is fully clear, and in the marks of one that shall go to heaven or to hell, especially in the doctrine of repentance. Make use of the scriptures, and practise conscientiously according to your light, and God will clear up his mind to you. By study and prayer and practice you will come to an increase of knowledge: John vii. 17, 'If any man will do his will, he shall know of the doctrine whether it be of God, or whether I speak of myself.'

2. It doth not only call for repentance, but a speedy repentance: Heb. iii. 7, 8, 'Wherefore, as the Holy Ghost saith, To-day, if ye will hear his voice, harden not your hearts;' Joel ii. 12, 'Therefore also now saith the Lord, Turn ye even to me with all your heart.' God standeth upon *now*. If the season were not determined, yet the nature of the thing would bear it. A necessary work, that is to be once done, should not be left to uncertainties. But because men are loose and arbitrary, and think they may make use of repentance at their leisure, therefore the scripture is as peremptory for the time as for the thing:

'Now, and to-day, if you will hear his voice, harden not your hearts.' As soon as you are convinced of your sinful estate. Why not now? Sin is such an evil that you cannot be rid of it too soon. Sin is as a poison in the bowels, a fire in a building. Now who will say, We will get an antidote next week? or quench the fire hereafter? Sin is a wound, and shall we let it alone till it fester and rankle? No wound so dangerous as that which destroyeth body and soul; no fire so dreadful as the wrath of God; no poison so hurtful as that of sin; it robbeth us of eternal life. God hath not given us leave for a day, nor for a moment. If a man were banished by proclamation, and it were death whoever should entertain and harbour him after ten days, till the time were out there were no danger; but God saith *now*. When we are in any trouble, we cannot brook any delay: Ps. cii. 2, 'In the day when I call, answer me speedily.' We must have a present answer; and shall God stand waiting when there is danger of his dishonour? Therefore now while it is to-day turn unto God. To-morrow is a very uncertain thing. Besides if you were certain of to-morrow, it is folly to lie under the wrath of God any longer. If really you are convinced of a sinful state, why do you not repent and return to God now? In every sinful action thou art laying thy soul at pawn, and one sin more may fill up the measure of your iniquity. Besides, every day will make you more unfit to turn to God; and it is base self-love to think of indulging the flesh longer, provided at length you can be saved.

3. The scripture showeth the profit of it.

[1.] What a remedy it is against sin: Ezek. xviii. 30, 'Repent, and turn yourselves from your transgressions; so iniquity shall not be your ruin.' Every man is a sinner, but every man shall not die by sin. There is in sin *reatus, culpa, pœna, macula*. (1.) *Reatus*, the guilt that is blotted out: Acts iii. 19, 'Repent, and be converted, that your sins may be blotted out, when the times of refreshing shall come from the presence of the Lord.' Sin is written in two books, one in God's keeping, the other in our own. He doth not say that we may blot out our sins out of God's book; that is not the debtor's, but the creditor's work to cross the book: Isa. xliii. 25, 'I, even I, am he that blotteth out thy transgressions for mine own sake, and will not remember thy sins. There is a handwriting against us, but it is blotted out when we repent. Our own book is the book of conscience: Heb. x. 22, 'Having our hearts sprinkled from an evil conscience.' The worm of conscience gnaws us till we repent, then the Spirit blotteth it out of our hearts. (2.) *Macula*, the stain; the more a man sinneth, the more he is inclined to sin, as a brand that hath been once in the fire is apt to take fire again. We lose tenderness by every act of sin, and the smart of repentance is a means to kill the sin, as breaking up the fallow ground doth destroy the weeds: Jer. iv. 3, 'Break up your fallow ground, and sow not among thorns.' (3.) *Culpa*, the blame. God will not upbraid us with former sins: Mark xvi. 7, 'Go tell my disciples and Peter.' It is judged in one court already; not a word of Peter's miscarriage: Tell him, I am risen. (4.) *Pœna*, the punishment; that is done away by repentance; we may look for days of refreshment.

[2.] The comfort it will bring. God hath comforts for his mourners:

Mat. v. 4, 'Blessed are they that mourn, for they shall be comforted.' Never such sweet revivings as after godly sorrow: 2 Cor. vii. 10, 'For godly sorrow worketh repentance to salvation never to be repented of.' Many have repented of their carnal mirth, but never any of their godly sorrow; you will never curse the day of your new birth.

4. The scripture offereth grace and help of God to work this in us: Ezek. xi. 19, 20, 'I will give them one heart, and I will put a new spirit within you; and I will take the stony heart out of their flesh, and will give them an heart of flesh; that they may walk in my statutes, and keep mine ordinances, and do them; and they shall be my people, and I will be their God.' Men will say they cannot repent; come and wait upon God, and he will give you to repent: Acts xi. 18, 'Then hath God also to the gentiles granted repentance unto life.' God doth not only give occasions of repentance, time of repentance, means of repentance, but power to repent, yea, repentance itself: Acts v. 31, 'Him hath God exalted with his right hand, to be a prince and a saviour, to give repentance to Israel, and forgiveness of sins.' So that if we would turn wrangling into prayer, and bemoan ourselves, and say, Jer. xxxi. 18, 'Turn us, O Lord! and we shall be turned.' If we would follow him close, we need not be discouraged.

5. The scripture layeth down powerful arguments to quicken us to repentance, which have a marvellous tendency and influence that way. I shall single out three—The death of Christ, the day of judgment, and the torments of hell.

First, The death of Christ. A serious consideration of the death of Christ will further humiliation and reformation.

[1.] Humiliation.

(1.) Here is the highest instance of the love of God, and the purest fountain of tears is God's love. Mary wept much, because much was forgiven her. Nothing thaweth the heart more than the warm beams of mercy. Wrath causeth sorrow to flow like water out of a still by the force of fire; but love gently melteth the heart, and causeth it to run out at the eyes in a flood and stream of tears. Here is the highest instance of God's love. Christ is the greatest gift that ever he gave the world. When he gave us life, and breath, and all things, though he gave them to us, yet he gave us nothing from himself; but now out of his bosom he gave us Christ, that is love: John iii. 16, 'God so loved the world that he gave his only-begotten Son.' It cannot be told, it can only be wondered at: Rom. v. 8, 'But God commended his love towards us, in that, while we were yet sinners, Christ died for us.' So great a person for such vile creatures! How can an ingenuous heart think of this! I have sinned against God that gave his Christ: I have grieved his Spirit, that loved me, and died for me. Saul had a hard heart, and yet he wept when David told him how he had spared him when it was in his power to kill him, 1 Sam. xxiv. 16. Had God done no more for us but spared us, that should melt us; but he commended his love that Christ died for us.

(2.) Here is the truest spectacle of sin; for all that was done to Christ, sin did it. What could men or devils do? Men could do nothing: John xviii. 6, 'As soon as he said unto them, I am he, they went backward, and fell to the ground.' Poor dust and ashes swooned at the breath of his mouth. Not devils; he could cast them out with a word. Not God's justice; that hath no place against innocency. No; it was we, not Judas, nor Pilate, nor the Romans, nor the Jews, but we that have pierced him: Zech. xii. 10, 'They shall look upon me whom they have pierced.' This will give us the truest spectacle of sin. The old world was a sad spectacle, but that is no wonder; a filthy world to be washed with a deluge. Sodom was another sad spectacle; hell was rained out of heaven; but it is no wonder to see combustible matter burn. But Christ was a green tree, the Son of God, holy and undefiled, who was made sin only by a voluntary susception; but when he was made sin, God spared him not. Now the heinousness of sin appeareth—(1.) In the value of the sacrifice; (2.) The extremity of his sufferings.

(1st.) In the value of the sacrifice. Nothing could expiate sin but the blood, and shame, and agonies of the Son of God. A man would have thought that a word of Christ's mouth would have pacified God; but so great was the offence, that though he cried with strong cries, God would not hear him till he had endured his wrath. Christ prayed, Mat. xxvi. 39, 'O my Father! if it be possible, let this cup pass from me.' But God would not bate him a farthing. If you would know sin, go to Golgotha.

(2d.) The extremity of his sufferings. His outward sufferings were much. If you consider the majesty of his person, he was the great God, that filled heaven and earth with his glory, and yet was sold for thirty pence, the price of a slave. His back was mangled with whips, his body nailed to the cross, he was scorned in all his offices, a variety of sorrow was poured in by the conduit of every sense—seeing, smelling, tasting, hearing, and feeling. If you consider the excellency of his constitution, his body, being framed by the Holy Ghost, was of a more exact temper, his senses more lively; they that enjoy life in a higher measure than others, the more delicate the sense, the higher the pain; the back of a slave is not so sensible of strokes as of one that is nicely and tenderly bred. His senses were kept lively and in their full vigour; he refused the stupefying cup that was given to him. He kept his strength to the last; this appeared by his strong cry when he gave up the ghost; Luke xxiii. 46, 'And when Jesus had cried with a loud voice, he said, Father, into thy hands I commend my spirit; and having said thus, he gave up the ghost.' But what is this to what is inward, the agonies of his soul under the curse and wrath of God due for sin, his desertion of the Father. It is more to see the sun eclipsed than to see a candle put out. He complained that 'his soul was exceeding sorrowful, even unto death,' Mat. xxvi. 38. His soul dwelt with God in a personal union. Christ knew how to value his Father's wrath; he had an excellent judgment and tender affections. When he sweat drops of curdled blood, he needed support from an angel. Now put all these circumstances together, and see if sin be a light thing.

Object. But many think this lesseneth sorrow. Christ hath endured so much, what need they be troubled?

Ans. (1.) These know not what faith and love meaneth. Can a man love Christ, and not mourn for that which was the cause of his sufferings? Thou art the man that laid all this upon Christ. (2.)

Slight thoughts of sin are a disparagement of Christ's sufferings: you make nothing of that which cost him so dear. (3.) Christ's death doth not nullify our duty in this kind, but ratify it. He died not only to expiate the guilt of sin, but also to show the heinousness of it. God might have taken another course. This for humiliation.

[2.] As to reformation. The death of Christ furthereth this—

(1.) By way of obligation: Gal. ii. 20, 'I am crucified with Christ: nevertheless I live, yet not I, but Christ liveth in me, and the life which I now live in the flesh, I live by the faith of the Son of God, who loved me, and gave himself for me.' The great argument that quickeneth us to the spiritual life is that it is a thing pleasing and acceptable to him. If we knew anything pleasing and acceptable to a man that had redeemed us out of a miserable thraldom, we would do it. They are unthankful wretches that dare to deny Christ anything.

(2.) By way of purchase. Our liberty from sin was bought at a dear rate; not with silver and gold. You disparage your redeemer and seek to put him to shame, if you live in sin, for you go about to make void the purchase, and to overturn the whole business which Christ hath been establishing with so great a cost. He paid dear for that grace which you slight; you tie the bonds which he came to loosen.

(3.) By way of conformity to the purity of our sacrifice. He was without spot and blemish. A carnal christian dishonoureth his head, and puts him to an open shame, as if the church were but a sanctuary for naughty men, and christianity a design to make us less careful and holy. What a spotted Christ do we hold forth to the world! We are to look upon Christ crucified so as to be crucified with him.

Secondly, The day of judgment. The serious consideration of that day is an help to repentance: Acts xvii. 30, 31, 'He hath commanded all men everywhere to repent; because he hath appointed a day in which he will judge the world in righteousness.' As hell worketh on fear, so this on shame. It helpeth humiliation and reformation.

[1.] Humiliation. It is a means to prevent the shame of that day; if we do not call sin to mind, God will call it to mind: Ps. l. 21, 'I will set thy sins in order before thee.' The book of conscience shall be opened, and not only ours, but God's book too. Now it will cost us grief to look upon our sins, then grief with desperation; terms of grace are ended, and we can have no hope. A sinner now blots the book that is in his own keeping, but then he cannot. We will not own the convictions of the word when it showeth our face, but then, Jude 15, 'He will convince all that are ungodly of all their ungodly deeds that they have ungodly committed, and of all their hard speeches which ungodly sinners have spoken against him.' Confession now is neglected, but then all shall be brought to light out of our own reins: 1 Cor. iv. 5, 'Judge nothing before the time until the Lord come, who both will bring to light the hidden things of darkness, and will make manifest the counsels of the hearts; and then shall every man have praise of God.' Let us take shame before it be imposed on us. Sins repented of will not be mentioned to our confusion, but only to the glorifying of the riches of the Lord's grace. They that repent, their sins shall be then blotted out: Acts iii. 19, 'Repent and be converted, that your sins may be blotted out when the days of refreshing shall come from the presence of the Lord.'

[2.] Reformation. It includeth faith and obedience. (1.) Faith. Let us get our discharge before that day cometh; then we shall have boldness: 1 John ii. 28, 'And now, little children, abide in him, that when he shall appear we may have confidence and not be ashamed before him at his coming.' The members of Christ's mystical body need not be afraid of Christ's judgment; their advocate shall be their judge; their hearts are sprinkled with his blood, as the door-posts against the destroying angel. They that are not careful to be found in Christ, surely they do not believe that God will make inquisition for sinners. Is the day of judgment a fable? Scripture and conscience saith the contrary. Or are we innocent? Or hath God provided another way than Christ? (2.) Obedience. Everything is written, and must be reviewed. If things were forgotten as soon as we forget them, we need not revise our acts or be so careful of our conversation. Oh! but we must come to an account: James ii. 12, 'So speak ye, and so do, as they that shall be judged by the law of liberty;' Ps. i. 5, 'Therefore the ungodly shall not stand in the judgment, nor sinners in the congregation of the righteous.' What a shameful story will there be produced against careless sinners! All the business of our lives is to stand in the great congregation, and to appear with confidence. Would a man give way to vain thoughts if he knew he were to give an account? or to vain discourse if he thought every idle word would be brought to judgment? or to carnal actions, though never so secret, if he thought that all these would come to a review? or neglect the duties of his calling if he knew he were to give an account of his stewardship? or be unmerciful to the poor if he did think of, Have you fed? have you clothed? or that he should be examined upon these questions?

Thirdly, The consideration of hell, or the dreadful punishment of sin; for this is the matter in this text. This is useful to think of hell that we may shun it. Presumption is a coward: Mat. iii. 7, 8, 'O generation of vipers! who hath warned you to flee from the wrath to come? Bring forth therefore fruits meet for repentance.' There is a forced repentance; they that do not weep for their sins for a while here, shall there mourn for ever with a fruitless repentance. It is peace upon earth. What is hell? (1.) There is *poena damni*, the punishment of loss; a separation from the presence of God, and everlasting exile: 'Depart from me, ye cursed,' Mat. xxv. 41; Luke xiii. 25, 26, 'When once the master of the house is risen, and hath shut the door, and ye begin to stand without, and to knock at the door, saying, Lord, Lord, open to us; and he shall answer and say unto you, I know ye not whence ye are;' and ver. 28, 'When ye shall see Abraham, and Isaac, and Jacob, and all the prophets in the kingdom of God, and you yourselves thrust out.' When God turned Adam out of paradise, it was sad, but then he clothed him, made him coats of skins. Adam was a rebellious child, and was turned out of doors, but God had a care of him, would not turn him out of doors without his garments, gave him the promise of the seed of the woman, hopes of a better paradise. This is the worst part of hell, to have a glimpse of God, the remembrance of which shall remain with them for ever, and then to be shut out.

Thou shalt see it with thine eyes, but not taste it; as a prodigal reduced to rags goeth by the lands and houses he hath sold with a sad heart. (2.) The *pœna sensus*, the punishment of sense, the worm of conscience and the fire of God's wrath. The worm of conscience; the sting of conscience when we think of our folly and imprudence. A man may run away from his conscience now by sleeping, reading, working, drinking, sporting, as Cain built cities and Saul called for music; but in hell there are no such diversions, not a thought free day nor night, but *memoria præteritorum*, the remembrance of what is past, slighted means, abused comforts, wasted time, and *sensus præsentium*, a sense of what is present; the understanding maketh heaven or hell; and *metus futurorum*, a fear of what is to come for ever and ever. O blind fools! that we did not think of these things aforehand. The pleasures of the world for a thousand years will not countervail one minute's torment. And then the fire shall never be quenched: Heb. x. 31, 'It is a fearful thing to fall into the hands of the living God.' Do but make trial, and put your finger in the candle, and see how you can bear it: Isa. xxxiii. 14, 'Who among us can dwell with the devouring fire? who among us shall dwell with everlasting burnings?'

III. How to improve the scriptures to repentance.

1. Believe them as you would an oracle or one from the dead. Consider the authority and veracity of God. The authority of God: God commandeth men to repent; charge the heart in the name of God, as it will answer to him another day. If God had bidden thee do some greater thing, wouldst not thou have done it? Will you contradict your maker? The veracity of God; these things are true. If you had heard a voice from heaven, as Abraham, or had a vision, or a messenger sent out of the other world, you would believe. You would think him to have a very hard heart that is not warned by an oracle or frighted by an apparition. God himself hath spoken in his word, and is not he of credit? You would fly in the face of him that should give you the lie, and will you give the lie to the God of truth? We should be ashamed that the word, which is a greater and surer revelation than oracles or apparitions, should prevail no more with us, and that all those arts of grace which are used in the scriptures do not persuade us to obedience and amendment of life. There is more reason to persuade a rational man that the scriptures are true and worth the heeding, than to persuade him of the truth of any voice from heaven or message by one from the dead. There you are warned that if you are unbelieving, unholy, or uncharitable, you shall go to hell, and as Lot seemed to his sons-in-law 'as one that mocked,' Gen. xix. 14, so we are looked on as if we were in jest, and it were a matter of course to make one another sad by repeating of matters mournful and lamentable. If thou hadst seen a ghost this last night, or a devil had appeared to thee in man's shape, thou wouldst have been terrified; and shall not the threatenings of the word startle thee? So when you are spoken to concerning the joys of heaven, it should not seem ὡσεὶ λῆρος, as an idle tale; as it is said, Luke xxiv. 11, 'And their words seemed unto them as idle tales, and they believed them not.' The report of Christ's resurrection was an idle tale. If an angel had told you that within such a compass of years you should be in another world, he would have

been credited; but you have a more sure word of prophecy; we tell you the same from God's word, and yet we are not regarded, as the Israelites did not believe the spies.

2. Urge thy heart with it; recollect yourselves: Rom. viii. 31, 'What shall we then say to these things?' Come to yourselves: Luke xv. 17, 'And when he came to himself.' The prodigal came to himself before he thought of returning to his father: Ps. xxii. 27, 'All the ends of the earth shall remember, and return unto the Lord.' Think with yourselves, Whence am I? whither am I going? what have I done in the work of repentance? what will become of me to all eternity? Here in the scriptures God himself hath told me what I must look for, and will God deceive me? Oh! let me take God's directions for the saving of my soul.

I might take occasion hence to press you to bless God for transmitting such a doctrine to us, and to give you caution not to look after other revelations; there are none, or, if there were, none can be so certain and so sufficient as this. And whatever is pretended as a message from God, bring it to the scriptures: Isa. viii. 20, 'To the law and to the testimonies; if they speak not according to this word, it is because there is no light in them.' Some cry up the church; some the Spirit, in contradiction to the scriptures. Do you take the middle course; go to the word opened and dispensed in the church, and wait for the Spirit's teaching; and whatever is pretended, if it be not according to this, there is no light in it; and if there be no light of knowledge, there will be no light of comfort, and no light of happiness.

SERMON UPON HEBREWS XIII. 20, 21.

*Now the God of peace, that brought again from the dead our Lord Jesus, that great shepherd of the sheep, through the blood of the everlasting covenant, make you perfect in every good work to do his will, working in you that which is well-pleasing in his sight, through Jesus Christ ; to whom be glory for ever. Amen.—*HEB. xiii. 20, 21.

THE words carry the form of an apostolical blessing or prayer for those christian Hebrews to whom he wrote. Consider in them—(1.) The person to whom he prayeth; in which the grounds of audience are implied, ver. 20 ; (2.) The matter which he prayeth for, ver. 21.

I. The person to whom the prayer is directed ; who is described—

1. By a proper title, 'The God of peace.'

2. By his great work, 'He brought again from the dead our Lord Jesus Christ;' who is set forth—

[1.] By his office, 'The great shepherd of the sheep.'

[2.] By his merit and satisfaction, 'Through the blood of the everlasting covenant;' which may relate—

(1.) To God's title ; he is become 'the God of peace through the blood of the everlasting covenant.'

(2.) To God's work, 'Through the blood of the everlasting covenant,' 'he brought him again from the dead.'

(3.) To Christ's office, 'Through his blood shed for sinners' he is become the 'great shepherd of the sheep.'

II. The matter which he prayeth for ; the continued sanctification of man once regenerate; set forth by both its parts—the will, and the deed, Phil. ii. 13. First, the will or remote power, 'Make you perfect,' or fit you 'for every good work to do his will;' secondly, the deed, or actual assistance, 'Working in you that which is well-pleasing in his sight.' We have both by Jesus Christ, for it is added with a doxology, 'Through Jesus Christ, to whom be glory for ever and ever, Amen.'

The text is long; I must give you but short strictures upon it, and I will begin with the second branch, the matter prayed for ; and therefore let me observe—

Doct. 1. That the beginning, progress, and accomplishment of every good work is from God through Jesus Christ. This appeareth plainly from the 21st verse, which may be reduced to two heads—

1. The expressions which concern man's duty, which is to be 'perfect in every good work,' that we may do God's will, and that which is pleasing in his sight.

2. The expressions which concern God's power to enable us for this duty; there are two words, *perfecting* and *working*. The first relateth to his habitual grace, the second to his assisting grace.

I. The first expressions which import man's duty are four—(1.) Perfecting; (2.) Every good work; (3.) Doing his will; (4.) So as may be pleasing in his sight.

1. We must be made perfect, or the begun work of grace must be carried on to perfection. We all come short of that perfection which is attainable in this life, therefore those that have attained some good measure of grace should not rest satisfied with it. We need to be more able for duties, more fortified for trials. A man groweth till he be fit for all manly actions; and a christian groweth and must be made more perfect till he be fit for every good work. An artisan must be so long learning his trade till he be fit for all those functions which belong to his trade. A sick or wounded man is under the hand of the physician or chirurgeon till he be perfectly cured. So is a christian under the care of his spiritual physician till he be fitted for all the parts and duties of a christian. Here upon earth, 'Christ by one offering hath perfected for ever them that are sanctified,' or dedicated to God, Heb. x. 14; but now he is in heaven, he perfecteth us by degrees. The sacrifice needeth not to be repeated, but his intercession is continual, because we still need new influences of grace. Absolute perfection is not attainable in this life; but the perfection of sincerity is here required, that we should mortify all our lusts, and serve God in every good work, and please him by an universal and impartial obedience: Phil. iii. 12, 'Not as though I had already attained, either were already perfect; but I follow after, if that I may apprehend that for which also I am apprehended of Christ Jesus;' that is, I aim at that which Christ aimed at, that I may be thoroughly and exactly perfect.

2. 'In every good work.' Not in one, but all. Many will do some good, but are defective in other things, and usually in those which are most necessary. They cull out the easiest and cheapest parts of religion, such as do not contradict their lusts and interests. We can never have sound peace till we regard all: Ps. cxix. 6, 'Then shall I not be ashamed, when I have respect to all thy commandments.' Shame is φόβος δικαίου ψόγου, fear of a just reproof. This reproof is either from the supreme or the deputy judge. The supreme judge of all our actions is God. This should be our principal care, that we may not be ashamed before him at his coming, nor disapproved in the judgment. But there is a deputy judge which every man hath in his own bosom. Our consciences do acquit or condemn us as we are partial or sincere in our duty to God; and much dependeth on that: 1 John iii. 20, 21, 'But if our hearts condemn us, God is greater than our hearts, and knoweth all things. Beloved, if our hearts condemn us not, then have we confidence towards God.' Well, then, that our hearts may not reprove or reproach us, we should be complete in all the will of God. Alas! otherwise you will never have evidence of your sincerity.

3. The next expression is, 'That you may do his will.' The rule of man's duty is the will of God. The will of God signifieth two things— either his decree concerning them, or else that law which he hath given concerning our duty. This last is intended. The works of man are

the actions and operations of a reasonable creature subject to the laws of God. If his actions be conformable to his law, they are good ; if not, they are evil. Therefore a man cannot be a good christian without doing God's will. If it be the will of God he should forbear such a practice, custom, or evil action, he dareth not go forward : Jer. xxxv. 6, 'We will drink no wine, for Jonadab the son of Rechab, our father, commanded us, saying, Ye shall drink no wine, neither ye nor your sons for ever.' If it be the will of God he should do such a thing, he will do it ; he dareth not omit it, how cross soever to his inclinations and interests : James iv. 17, 'Therefore to him that knoweth to do good, and doeth it not, to him it is sin.' This is the reason of all reasons : 1 Thes. iv. 3, 'For this is the will of God, even your sanctification ;' 1 Thes. v. 18, 'In everything give thanks, for this is the will of God in Christ Jesus concerning you ;' 1 Peter ii. 15, 'For so is the will of God, that with well-doing ye may put to silence the ignorance of foolish men.' Well, then, it is not enough that we should well and thoroughly understand the will of God, but we should do it. And I will add this one consideration : the more we do it, the more we will understand it : John vii. 17, 'If any man will do his will, he shall know of the doctrine whether it be of God.' It is doing that God looks at and we must most regard ; not who can acutely plead or eloquently declaim about it, but readily frame his heart to do the will of God ; for the precepts of God are given, not to try our wit or memory, but practice.

4. We must do it so as may be 'well-pleasing in his sight ;' where note—

[1.] That all that we do is done in the sight of God. He observeth who break and who keep his law, and nothing can escape his view and knowledge : Luke i. 75, 'In holiness and righteousness before him.' We are ever in his eye, and he is our witness, approver, and judge : 'Will he force the queen,' saith Ahasuerus, 'before my face ?' Esther vii. 8. Will ye, God looking on, be vain, foolish, and carnal ?

[2.] This must be our great aim and scope, 'to please God.' It is a well-tempered religion that beginneth and endeth in God. Man-pleasing is the hypocrite's religion, but God-pleasing is sincere and true religion : Col. i. 10, 'That ye may walk worthy of the Lord unto all pleasing.' And the apostle often inculcateth this as the right end of all our duties : 'Not as pleasing men, but God.'

[3.] Our work must be so ordered as it may be 'pleasing and acceptable to God ;' for every slight thing will not please him, but when it is agreeable to his will. Therefore it is not enough to do what is for the matter good, but what is for the manner pleasing to him ; that is to say—(1.) It must come from a right principle, love to God : 2 Cor. v. 14, 'The love of Christ constraineth us ;' and faith in Christ : Heb. xi. 6, 'Without faith it is impossible to please God.' Not as forced, nor as a mere natural act, but as depending on the Redeemer for our acceptance. We are sinners ; we are not exact. (2.) Then for the manner, it must be with seriousness : Heb. xii. 28, 'Wherefore we receiving a kingdom which cannot be moved, let us have grace, whereby we may serve God acceptably, with reverence, and godly fear ;' so as will become so great a majesty with that diligence which our aim at perfection calleth for : 1 Thes. iv. 1, 'Furthermore then we beseech you, brethren, and exhort you by the Lord Jesus Christ, that as you have received of us how ye ought to walk and to please God, so ye would abound more and more.'

II. The words which express the necessary concurrence of the divine power; they are two—

1. The first is, 'Make you perfect.' He prayeth not now for framing the new creature, but for perfecting it. God, that maketh man, new maketh him, and then he perfecteth him. God is wonderful in the first creation, in raising such a beautiful piece out of the dust of the ground as the first man was; and in ordinary generation David telleth us, Ps. cxxxix. 14, 'I am fearfully and wonderfully made.' So God is wonderful in re-making or regenerating us: Eph. ii. 10, 'For we are his workmanship, created in Christ Jesus unto good works;' Eph. iv. 24, 'And that ye put on the new man, which after God is created in righteousness and true holiness.' There is much of the wisdom, goodness, and power of God seen in the new creature, to enable a man to captivate those lusts which the generality of the world are mastered by, and to live a divine life in the flesh. He is also wonderful in perfecting us till we grow up to our full stature in spiritual things. As it is not in man's power to make himself or regenerate himself, so it is not in man's power to perfect himself. No; but the Spirit of regeneration abiding in us doth renew us more and more. Well, then, it is not meant of regeneration when we are created to good works, but of the increase of his sanctifying grace, which is to regeneration as preservation and providence is to creation. God, that begun the work, must continue it and strengthen it, otherwise we shall be unfit for every good work, or as a member that is out of joint, as the word importeth which is there used.

2. 'Working.' God doth continually co-operate and work in us and with us, without which we cannot fulfil his will, or do anything that will please him. So will and deed are joined together: Phil. ii. 13, 'For it is God which worketh in you both to will and to do.' God worketh in us a power to will, and maketh us actually to will; and a power and strength, or ability to do it. The new creature dependeth absolutely on his influences from first to last: 2 Peter i. 3, 'According as his divine power hath given unto us all things that pertain unto life and godliness.' He giveth us spiritual life, and he giveth us godliness. He first giveth supernatural faculties, and then the use and exercise of them in our walk or conversation; the first motions, and then the flowing forth of these motions into acts suitable.

Use 1. To establish our dependence. In doing any good we must depend on God, both for the power given at first and continued unto us. Will and deed come from him, and they come from him through Christ, who purchased and conveyeth this power to us by his constant intercession and the influence of his Spirit. Of unwilling he maketh us willing, and causeth us to do what he would have us to do. He doth not only give us the will, that is, the desire, and purpose, but the grace that we may do that good which we will and purpose. These are distinct; many may have assistance in one kind, not in another. Paul showeth us that willing and doing are different: Rom. vii. 18,

'For to will is present with me, but how to perform that which is good, I find not.' To will is more than to think, and to exert our will into action is more than both. In all we need God's help, both to think a good thought or conceive a good purpose, much more to perform a good action. Man is mutable, and here is much opposition.

Use 2.' Exhortation to several duties.

1. Let us shake off carnal security and laziness. Here is not only God's grace represented, but man's duty. God's doing all doth not warrant us to lie upon the bed of ease, but stir us up to diligence: Phil. ii. 12, 13, 'Work out your salvation with fear and trembling, for it is God which worketh in you both to will and to do of his good pleasure.'

2. We are not to neglect the motions of the Spirit lest we grieve him: Eph. iv. 30, 'And grieve not the Holy Spirit, whereby we are sealed to the day of redemption.'

3. We are to use the means, and God will bless our endeavours: 1 Peter ii. 2, 'As new-born babes desire the sincere milk of the word, that you may grow thereby.' We are to attend upon the word and frequent the sacrament.

4. We must pray earnestly, for a twofold reason—(1.) That we may humbly own our wants: James i. 5, 'If any man lack wisdom, let him ask it of God.' (2.) That we may express our desires and longing for grace: Mat. v. 6, 'Blessed are they that hunger and thirst after righteousness, for they shall be filled.'

5. We must improve our talents, lest we be accounted evil and slothful servants, that receive grace in vain: 2 Cor. vi. 1, 'We beseech you that you receive not the grace of God in vain.'

Doct. 2. That the continued sanctification and perfecting of man once regenerate cometh from God as the God of peace.

This is the blessing prayed for, and when the apostle prayeth for it, he calleth God 'the God of peace.' So elsewhere: 1 Thes. v. 23, 'The very God of peace sanctify you wholly; and I pray God your whole spirit, and soul, and body be preserved blameless unto the coming of our Lord Jesus Christ.' He prayeth there for the whole progress of sanctifying grace, till it hath attained its end and final perfection, and giveth God the same title.

Here I shall open to you these five things—(1.) In what sense God is said to be the God of peace; (2.) The ground and foundation of this peace; (3.) The evidences how it appears that God is pacified; (4.) The conveyance of it to us, or how we come to be interested in this peace; (5.) The reasons why all increase of grace cometh from him as such.

I. What is the meaning of this title? God is called 'the God of peace' in two respects—

1. With respect to union and peace with men, especially our fellow-christians. God is the God of peace as he is the author and approver of this peace: 1 Cor. xiv. 33, 'For God is not the author of confusion, but of peace, as in all the churches of the saints;' 2 Thes. iii. 16, 'Now the Lord of peace himself give you peace always, by all means.'

2. With respect to our reconciliation with himself after the breach that was between us. Heaven and earth are at an accord, and the great

quarrel between us and God is compromised and taken up. In one place the angels come to proclaim 'peace on earth,' Luke ii. 14. At another time, when Christ solemnly entereth as the Messiah into Jerusalem, they cried out, Luke xix. 38, 'Peace in heaven, and glory in the highest.' One of the parties at variance is in the earth, the other in heaven. The angels, the inhabitants of the other world, proclaim peace on earth; and men, that dwell here below, echo to them again peace in heaven, and that when they gave Christ the honour of the Messias, showing that his great business was to make reconciliation. It is not a primitive original peace, but a reconciliation after a breach, a restoring of peace when it was lost. We had all broken with God, and God was angry with men for sin; now while God was angry and offended there was no hope to receive any gift of grace from him; therefore with respect to this is God called 'the God of peace.'

II. The grounds and foundation of this peace; and that is 'by the blood of the everlasting covenant,' which is the only propitiatory sacrifice which could appease God, and give his justice full satisfaction and recompense for our offences. Before this peace could be made and this woful breach repaired, there were two things to be removed which stood in the way—God's wrath, and our rebellious nature. The righteous wrath of God is appeased by the blood of Christ; our rebellion is cured and healed by his Spirit. The latter is but a consequent of the former. The first foundation for this peace was laid in the blood of Christ: Col. i. 20, 'And having made peace through the blood of his cross, by him to reconcile all things unto himself;' Isa. liii. 5, 'The chastisement of our peace was upon him, and with his stripes we are healed.' The enmity had been irreconcilable and impossible to be removed, unless God had taken this way, unless the Son of God had died for a sinful world, that by the merit of his obedience he might give satisfaction to a provoked God for the wrong we had done him.

III. The evidences that God is pacified. Here are three mentioned—

1. The bringing back of Christ from the dead. This showeth that God was propitiated, that he hath accepted the ransom that was given for souls. Christ's resurrection is called by the prophet a being 'taken from prison and from judgment,' Isa. liii. 8. While Christ was in the state of the dead, he was in effect a prisoner, under the arrest of divine vengeance; but when he rose again, then was our surety let out of prison. The expression is notable in the text, 'Brought again the Lord Jesus from the dead.' The force of the word may be explained with allusion to that carriage of the apostles when they were cast into prison: Acts xvi. 35, 37, 39, 'And the magistrates sent to let them go. Nay, verily,' say they, 'but let them come themselves and fetch us out, and they came and brought them out of prison.' So was Christ brought again. Though Christ had power to rise, yet was he rather raised. The Lord sent an angel to remove the stone, not to supply any lack of power in Christ, but as a judge when he is satisfied sendeth an officer to open the prison doors. Though Christ had power to rise, yet not authority, till the angel rolled away the stone. He did not break prison, but was brought again from the dead. Neither did he perish in prison; then we could have no assurance of our discharge; but as 'he died for our offences, so he rose again for our justification,'

Rom. iv. 25, as having perfectly done his work. As the Father delivered him to death, so he brought him back again from the dead. The apostle lays a great weight upon this: Rom. viii. 34, 'Yea, rather, that is risen from the dead.' There is some special thing in Christ's resurrection comparatively above his death, which hath influence on our justification. Was not Christ's death enough to free us from sin? Yes; but the visible evidence was by his resurrection. It is as it were an acquittance from those debts of ours which he undertook to pay; as Simeon was dismissed when the conditions were performed, and Joseph satisfied with the sight of his brother: Gen. xliii. 23, 'He brought Simeon out unto them.'

2. Christ's office is allowed, so that he is 'the great shepherd of the sheep;' that is, the blessed Saviour into whose hands God hath put his flock, to be justified, sanctified, and saved, and from whom we may expect all that comfort which a flock hath from a good and faithful pastor. We are put into his hands as he is Mediator, not by way of alienation, for they are in the Father's hands still: John x. 29, 'My Father which gave them me is greater than all, and no man is able to pluck them out of my Father's hand;' but an oppignoration laid at pledge in his hands. A shepherd is not lord of the flock, but as a servant to take care of them. They are not his as Mediator by way of original interest and dominion, but in point of trust and charge. He hath an office about them, and giveth an account of them at the last day. He is sometimes called simply, without any addition, 'The shepherd,' 1 Peter ii. 25, 'Ye are returned unto the shepherd and bishop of our souls.' Sometimes ποιμὴν ὁ καλός, The 'good shepherd,' as John x. 11; and here, 'The great shepherd;' and 'The chief shepherd,' 1 Peter v. 4, because of the dignity of his person and office. And surely if we put ourselves into the hands of this shepherd we can lack nothing: Ps. xxiii. 1, 'The Lord is my shepherd, I shall not want.' We may look for all manner of supplies from Christ.

3. God is so far appeased that there is a new covenant procured and constituted, called here 'the everlasting covenant;' partly because it shall never be repealed, and continueth unalterable, and the called obtain by it the title and possession of an eternal inheritance: Heb. ix. 15, 'They which are called may receive the promise of eternal inheritance.' And partly because Christ's blood is the foundation of this covenant, and the virtue of it never ceaseth; therefore this covenant is everlasting also, and made effectual and able to obtain its ends, which is the eternal salvation of sinful man once converted and reconciled to God. This covenant also is called the covenant of God's peace, because it is a public demonstration that God is pacified: Isa. liv. 10, 'But my kindness shall not depart from thee, neither shall the covenant of my peace be removed;' Ezek. xxxvii. 26, 'I will make a covenant of peace with them.' Partly because in this covenant this peace and reconciliation is published, and offered to us, that man may not stand aloof from God as a condemning God. So it is said, Eph. ii. 17, 'Christ came to preach peace to those that are near, and to those that are afar off;' Acts x. 36, 'The word which God sent unto the children of Israel, preaching peace by Christ; he is Lord of all.' Partly because in this covenant the terms of this peace between us and God are stated.

God bindeth himself to sinful man to give him remission of sins, and eternal life begun by the Spirit, and perfected in heaven upon the conditions of faith. Rom. v. 1, 'Being justified by faith, we have peace with God;' and repentance: Acts iii. 19, 'Repent and be converted, that your sins may be blotted out;' at our entrance and new obedience as to continuance: Heb. v. 9, 'He became the author of eternal salvation to all that obey him.'

IV. How we come to be interested in this peace and reconciliation, or the conveyance of it to us; for this peace may be considered as to the impetration and application of it.

1. As to the impetration and laying down of the price; that was done by Christ on the cross. Therefore it is said, 2 Cor. v. 19, 'God was in Christ reconciling the world to himself.' Then was God propitiated, and the merit and ransom interposed, by virtue of which we are pardoned and reconciled.

2. As to application, when God is actually reconciled with us, and we enter into his peace, and are restored unto his favour. This may be considered either as to the first gift. God is never actually reconciled to us, nor we to him, till he give us the regenerating Spirit; that is our 'receiving the atonement,' Rom. v. 11. It was made on the cross, but received at our conversion and regeneration. Or else it may be considered as to the further measure of his sanctifying grace, called here, 'Perfecting us for every good work, and working in us that which is pleasing in his sight.' This is given with respect to our reconciled estate, as we are actually at peace and in covenant with God: 2 Cor. v. 17, 18, 'Therefore if any man be in Christ, he is a new creature: old things are passed away, behold all things are become new: and all things are of God, who hath reconciled us to himself by Jesus Christ.' The sum is this: at the death of Christ there was such a foundation laid that we need no other ransom nor propitiation. He hath so far satisfied divine justice that he hath obtained the new covenant. The first grace is given us merely with respect to the merit of his sacrifice; for Christ purchased the mercies promised, and power to perform the conditions. Further grace is given us because we are already reconciled unto God, which is a ground of the greater joy and confidence; for our actual reconciliation giveth us a title to all consequent acts of friendship which can be expected or received, for in God's way we shall have further sanctification, and after that salvation.

V. The reasons why all increase of grace comes from God as the God of peace.

1. From the giver. God will not set us up with a new stock of grace till satisfaction be made for the breach of his law. We must not look upon him as *pars offensa*, the offended party, but as *rector mundi*, the governor of the world. Private persons may forgive offences as they please, but the governor and judge of the world would not pass by the offence of man till the ends of government be secured, or that the law fall not to the ground, which it doth not whilst God standeth upon the satisfaction of Christ and the submission of the sinner. The right of passing by a wrong, and the right of releasing a punishment, are different things; because punishment is a common interest, and is referred to the common good, to preserve order, and for an example to

others. Certainly punishment doth not belong to the wronged party as such; then every one would have a right to punish, and so invade the power of the magistrate. A private person hath a right of seeking restitution or compensation for the wrong done to him, unless higher reasons of charity forbid him, but not a power to compel them to punishment unless satisfaction be given. But the case is different; here God punisheth *non qua læsus, sed qua rector*, not as the offended party, but as a governor. Now the government of the world requires God's holiness should be demonstrated, and his laws vindicated, and a brand put upon sin.

2. From the gift, which is the sanctifying Spirit, which, being the gift of his love, must needs be the fruit of his peace and reconciliation with us: Rom. v. 5, 'Because the love of God is shed abroad in our hearts by the Holy Ghost.' Other things may be given us during his anger, for God showeth himself placable in the whole course of his providence. Yea, they may be given in anger, but the regenerating Spirit is never given us during his anger or in anger. Sanctifying grace doth evidence his special favour. Look, as the payment of the ransom was testified by the visible pouring out the Spirit, Acts ii., so is our particular reconciliation by the gift of the Spirit to us.

Use 1. Is of instruction.

1. How we are to look upon God in our prayers, as the God of peace, reconciled to us by Jesus Christ. When we pray to him, we look upon him as a God of grace: 1 Peter v. 10, 'But the God of all grace, who hath called us,' &c. This showeth his propension and inclination to communicate his grace freely to unworthy sinners. We also pray to him as the God of power: Rom. xvi. 15, 'Now to him that is of power to establish you according to my gospel.' But here we are directed to look upon him as the God of peace, as pacified in Christ, which is a greater ground of confidence. If a socinian were to pray to him, he could only use the plea of Benhadad to Ahab, 'We have heard the kings of Israel are merciful kings;' so we have heard the God of Israel is a merciful God. If the papist would pray with confidence, he thinketh he must appease God by himself, by his penal satisfactions and costly offerings; as Jacob would appease Esau by sending gifts to him, Gen. xxxii. 20; but the penitent believer is reconciled to God by Christ: Rom. v. 1, 2, 'Therefore, being justified by faith, we have peace with God through our Lord Jesus Christ, by whom also we have access by faith,' &c. He cometh to God in his name, and no other: John xvi. 23, 24, 'In that day ye shall ask me nothing: verily, verily, I say unto you, Whatsoever ye shall ask the Father in my name, he will give it you. Hitherto you have asked nothing in my name; ask and you shall receive, that your joy may be full.' He runneth to the horns of the altar, accepteth of the peace published in the gospel, devoteth himself to God, and rests upon Christ's mediatorial sacrifice as sufficient. Here is his hope and confidence.

2. How careful we should be that no breach fall out between us and God, lest we stop grace at the fountain-head. Continued sanctification cometh from the God of peace, as well as the first renovation of the heart. The giving the Spirit is a sign of God's love, and the withholding of the Spirit is a sign of his anger and displeasure; the one is

the greatest mercy, the other the greatest misery. In his internal government, the one is the highest reward, the other the greatest punishment. As a reward it is spoken of Prov. i. 23, 'Turn you at my reproof: behold I will pour my Spirit upon you; I will make known my words unto you.' As a punishment: Ps. li. 10-12, 'Create in me a clean heart, O God, and renew a right spirit within me; cast me not away from thy presence, and take not thy Holy Spirit from me: restore unto me the joy of thy salvation, and uphold me with thy free Spirit.' The one is to be sought: Luke xi. 13, 'How much more will your heavenly Father give the Holy Spirit to them that ask him?' the other to be deprecated: 'Take not thy Holy Spirit from me;' Ps. li. 11. Therefore take heed the Spirit be not grieved, but obeyed.

3. What ground of thankfulness to Christ—

[1.] That he hath made our peace with God at so dear a rate. All your repentings, if you had wept out your eyes for sin, would not have made your peace with God, nor have satisfied his justice, nor procured pardon and life for you. Now God is appeased, Christ having 'slain the enmity by his cross,' Eph. ii. 16.

[2.] That the new covenant is procured, wherein pardon and salvation is offered to you, as sealed by the blood of Christ, who hath paid our debts: Luke xxii. 20, 'This cup is the new testament in my blood, which is shed for you.' There had been else no place for your repentance, faith, prayer, or hopes.

[3.] That such free and easy conditions of mercy, with power to perform them, are propounded in the gospel: 'Lord, thou wilt ordain peace for us, for thou also hast wrought all our works in us,' Isa. xxvi. 12.

[4.] That he should call us, and have such favourable thoughts to us, who for a long time were dead in sin, and in hostility against him: Rom. v. 10, 'For if, when we were enemies, we were reconciled to God by the death of his Son, much more, being reconciled, we shall be saved by his life.'

SERMON PREACHED ON A DAY OF PUBLIC THANKSGIVING.

But Hezekiah rendered not according to the benefit done unto him; for his heart was lifted up: therefore wrath was upon him, and upon Judah and Jerusalem.—2 CHRON. xxxii. 25.

THAT I may not detain you in a preface, let me tell you the words hold forth—

1. A sin, 'But Hezekiah rendered not according to the benefit done unto him.'
2. The proof and argument of it, 'For his heart was lifted up.'
3. The sad effects and punishment of it, both as to his own person and the people under his government.

Let me explain these branches, and then come to observe something in order to the work of the day. I know, christians, you look not for things luscious, but savoury.

1. In the sin there was a benefit done unto him, and Hezekiah's fault is that he 'rendered not accordingly.' The benefit done him implieth a complication of mercies; not only his miraculous recovery out of sickness, and fifteen years added more to his life, but also the destruction of his enemies the Assyrians; mercies which fell out near about the same time; though I dare not say, with the Jewish writers, that three days before the slaughter of the Assyrians this sickness and recovery fell out; yet certainly they were near together, as appeareth from 2 Kings xx. 6, 'And I will add unto thy days fifteen years, and I will deliver thee and this city out of the hand of the king of Assyria.' The report of which flying abroad, all the princes round about him stood in awe of him; his neighbours sent him presents; his treasures were increased; yea, nations remote, and those of no small power, as the king of Babylon, reckoned to be seven hundred miles distant from Jerusalem, sent congratulatory embassies to his court. Well, then, Hezekiah was looked upon as one highly in favour with God, honoured of men, courted on every side with costly and precious presents, and so grew full of treasure and wealth. When such strong winds fill the sails, it is hard to steer right. This was the benefit done to him; all things fell out according to his heart's desire, and concurred to the lift-

ing up his heart: 'Hezekiah rendered not according.' How can that be? He was a holy man and a thankful man. He penneth a psalm of thanksgiving, and sung it yearly as a memorial of God's mercies to him: Isa. xxxviii. 9, 'The writing of Hezekiah, king of Judah, when he had been sick, and was recovered of his sickness.' God will not be complimented with. It is not words and ceremonies, formal acknowledgments and days of thanksgiving, that God standeth upon, but holy and humble carriage under mercies; and therefore Hezekiah, though he rendered somewhat to God, he 'rendered not according.' There was a defect which is here charged as his sin. He should have carried it more humbly, as holding his life and kingdom and everything of the grace of God.

2. The proof and argument. How doth it appear that he rendered not according? 'His heart was lifted up.' There is a twofold lifting up of the heart—in a way of zeal and encouragement in the Lord's ways. So it is said of Jehoshaphat, 2 Chron. xvii. 5, 6, that he had 'presents, and riches, and honours in abundance; and his heart was lifted up in the way of the Lord: moreover he took away the high places and groves out of Judah.' This is a good lifting up, when a man groweth cheerful and undaunted in the Lord's work, and therefore falleth a-reforming, whatever it cost him. He knoweth the God of his mercies will bear him out. But there is a carnal lifting up of the heart, in a way of pride and vainglory, or daring violence and oppression. Thus it is said of Amaziah, after he had smitten the Edomites, 2 Chron. xxv. 19, 'That his heart was lifted up to boast;' and this was in part Hezekiah's sin. Indeed it is not easy to state the kind of his pride.

[1.] Whether the pride of arrogancy or self-ascription, or taking God's part to himself, as if the blessings were merited by him; a disease incident to the creature when exalted: Deut. ix. 4, 'Speak not thou in thine heart after that the Lord thy God hath cast them out from before thee, saying, For my righteousness the Lord hath brought me in to possess this land;' and therefore God puts in a caution against it.

[2.] Or else conceit, musing upon and admiring his own greatness; as the king of Babylon strutteth and vaunteth, 'Is not this great Babylon, which I have built for the house of the kingdom, by the might of my power, and for the honour of my majesty?' Dan. iv. 30. Pride, of all sins, puts men upon vain musings: Luke i. 51, 'He hath scattered the proud in the imaginations of their hearts.' Proud men, of all others, are subject to imaginations, or self-admiring thoughts. His heart was too much tickled. In the story it is said, when Merodach Baladan sent letters and a present to Hezekiah, Isa. xxxix. 2, 'He was glad of them;' wherein the secret intimation of his spirit was discovered. Or else—

[3.] The pride of security or self-dependence. When we are well, God is forgotten; good men are apt to sleep upon a carnal pillow or bolster, and dream many a pleasant dream, till God taketh it away from under their heads: Ps. xxx. 6, 'And in my prosperity I said, I shall never be moved.' Carnal confidence is very natural. Or—

[4.] The pride of vainglory or ostentation. He seemeth to be tainted with a spice of that vanity by showing his treasure to the ambassadors of the king of Babylon: 'He showed them the house of his precious things, the silver, and the gold, and the spices, and the precious ointment, and all the house of his armour, and all that was in his treasures; there was nothing in his house, nor in all his dominion, that Hezekiah showed them not,' Isa. xxxix. 2. Whether one or more, or all, I will not determine; they are all branches of the same root. Certainly, vain men are apt to be puffed up in all these kinds, that have had deliverances far less strange than was this of Hezekiah.

3. Come we now to explain the punishment and sad effects of this great failing: 'Wrath was upon him, and upon Judah and Jerusalem.'

[1.] Upon his particular person, 'Wrath was upon him.' There is a near link between pride and wrath. His 'heart was lifted up,' and presently 'wrath was upon him:' Prov. xviii. 12, 'Before destruction the heart of man is haughty.' It is a sure sign of the loss of our comforts, parts, estate, children, authority, when we grow proud of them. It is a sin that God deeply detesteth, and will severely chasten it, even in his own dearest children: 'Wrath was upon him;' sentence was passed, but execution respited. All was well for the present. Wrath is said to be upon us as soon as sentence is passed. Men think not so, but God judgeth so: 'Wrath was upon him.' Doth it stay there? No.

[2.] Upon his people. It followeth, 'And upon all Judah and Jerusalem.' The whole land smarts for the sins of magistrates. *Delirant reges*, kings offend. 'Hezekiah's heart was lifted up.' *Plectuntur Achivi*, the people are punished. Judah and Jerusalem are obnoxious to the stroke of God's vengeance. But how can this stand with the Lord's justice? 'What have these sheep done?' as David said in a like case, 2 Sam. xxiv. 17. I answer—They had done enough to ruin them long since. Hezekiah's sin was not the main cause, but one great occasion of hastening the judgment. Sometimes God takes occasion to punish magistrates for the people's sin: Prov. xxviii. 2, 'For the transgression of a land many are the princes thereof.' The government is often altered, and they are tossed from hand to hand as a just punishment. At other times the people are punished for the magistrates' sins: Zech. x. 3, 'Mine anger was kindled against the shepherds, and I punished the goats.' A great oak cannot fall but all the little shrubs about it suffer loss. On the other side, when the burning beginneth at a cottage, it may increase till it come to the palace. If the dispensation seem harsh, remember that God would involve us in one another's judgments, to make us more careful of one another's duties; that when magistrates transgress, the people may mourn, and, with that modesty which will suit with the duty of their place, give warning of the danger. And magistrates may not give liberty to the wickedness of the people, lest they bring a judgment on their own heads.

I have given you some view of the words, let me come to the points.

1. That those that have received mercies must be careful to give in answerable returns, or to render according to what they have received.

2. That it is a sign we are unthankful for mercies when our hearts are lifted up under the enjoyment of mercies.

3. Pride and unthankfulness is a sad intimation of approaching wrath and destruction.

4. When a ruler's heart is lifted up, and doth not thankfully improve the mercies received from God, the whole land may smart for it.

I shall speak but to the two first of these points—

Doct. 1. That those that have received mercies must be careful to give in answerable returns, or to render according to what they have received. It was Hezekiah's sin that he did not render according.

Here I shall inquire what it is to render according to what we have received. Observe—(1.) There must be a rendering; (2.) A rendering according to the rate and kind of our receipts.

I. A rendering. There is a reflection upon God from all his works. Hell-fire casts back the reflection of the lustre of his justice and the power of his wrath. The world is round, and the motion of all things circular; they begin in God, and end in God; their being is from him, and the tendency of their motion is to him: Rom. xi. 36, 'For of him, and through him, and to him are all things.' All things do thus reflect upon God: 'The wrath of man shall praise thee,' Ps. lxxvi. 10. We should want many occasions of rejoicing in God if it were not for the wrath of man; thus God is glorified passively. All events turn to a good account; thus all creatures praise him: Ps. cxlv. 10, 'All thy works shall praise thee, O Lord;' the creatures offer matter of praise to God.

But we speak of the active rendering and returning praise to God. There are many words used in this matter. Those three which are most solemn are, praise, blessing, and thanksgiving; which last is the solemn word of the new testament, as being proper to the dispensation of it, God's benefits being now fully manifested and accomplished. There is a difference between these three terms. Praise respects God's excellency, as I may praise a man that never did me good. Blessing, God's benefits; it is an echo to him: Eph. i. 3, 'Blessed be the God and Father of our Lord Jesus Christ, who hath blessed us with all spiritual blessings in heavenly places in Christ Jesus.' And thankfulness is not only declared in word, but in deed. These three should always go together. We should gather up God's excellences out of his providences, and acknowledge the mercy, and live the life of love and praise. Or, if you will, in rendering praise to God these things concur—(1.) We must be affected with the mercies; (2.) Solemnly praise God for them; (3.) Renew the remembrance of them; (4.) Improve them to some good use.

1. We must be affected with the mercy. Formal speeches are but an empty prattle, which God regardeth not. David first calleth upon his heart: Ps. ciii. 1, 'Bless the Lord, O my soul, and all that is within me bless his holy name.' The noblest faculties must be exercised in the noblest work. Is the soul raised into an admiration of God? church adversaries took up the customary form: Isa. lxvi. 5, 'Your brethren that hate you, that cast you out for my name's sake, said, Let the Lord be glorified.' In an instrument of music, the more the sound cometh out of the belly of it the sweeter; if we expect flame, we presuppose fire. When the heart is full of gracious affections, the tongue will be loosed to praise God: Ps. xlv. 1, 'My heart is inditing a good matter, my tongue is the pen of a ready writer.'

2. Solemn praising God for them. It is an honourable work; love

is the grace of heaven, praise the duty of heaven. There is no room for faith nor use of prayer. It is angels' work, as sin is the devil's work. It is good to be preparing for our everlasting estate. It is comely for the saints: Ps. cxlvii. 1, 'Praise the Lord, for it is good to sing praises unto our God; for it is pleasant, and praise is comely.' Usually we thrust gratulation into a narrow room: it is a stranger in our public worship. Self-love will put us upon supplication, and our wants will beget a natural fervency in prayer. We are eager to have blessings, but we forget to return to give God the glory: Hosea v. 15, 'In their affliction they will seek me early.' This is self-love, not religion. All the ten lepers could say, 'Jesus, Master, have mercy upon us,' Luke xvii. 13, but only 'one of them, when he was healed, turned back, and with a loud voice glorified God,' ver. 15. Pharaoh could pray when God's hand was upon him. Oh! it is the more honourable thing to give thanks, and it is profitable: Ps. lxvii. 5, 6, 'Let the people praise thee, O God, let all the people praise thee; then shall the earth yield her increase.' There is a $\kappa v \kappa \lambda o \gamma \acute{\epsilon} v v \epsilon \sigma \iota \varsigma$, a circular generation, between vapours and showers. Vapours cause showers, and showers cause vapours. The course of mercy is stopped when God is not praised. Where do husbandmen bestow their seed most plentifully, but where the ground yieldeth most increase? When the land faileth year after year, men withhold their seed. God will not bury mercies in the grave of unthankfulness. It is a due to God; it is his bargain with us: Ps. l. 15, 'Call upon me in the day of trouble, I will deliver thee, and thou shalt glorify me.' He expects it as the return of all his mercies. Glory and praise are the revenues of the crown of heaven, the rent reserved to God. We have the comfort and use, God will have the glory and praise. We promised it to him: Ps. li. 15, 'O Lord, open thou my lips, and my mouth shall show forth thy praise.' Want of mercies maketh us prize them. If we would look upon the vows of our affliction, we should find cause to value our enjoyments. It is our privilege, as men, that we have a tongue to bless God: James iii. 9, 'Therewith bless we God, even the Father.' Therefore our tongue is called our glory: Ps. cviii. 1, 'I will sing and give praise, even with my glory.' Beasts have no reason, angels no tongue. Praise is necessary to give vent to our affections, yea, to increase them. Fire warmeth the hearth, and then the warmth of the hearth doth preserve the fire. Praise is necessary to convey our affections to others, as one bird may set the whole flight on chirping.

3. Renewing the remembrance of them: Ps. cxi. 4, 'He hath made his wonderful works to be remembered; the Lord is gracious and full of compassion.' Great deliverances are things not to be once mentioned, and no more, whilst the experience is warm upon our hearts; when the act is over, we should be remembering again and again.

4. The mercies must be improved to a greater trust in God, and love and fear of God, and obedience to him.

[1.] Trust. The more we know of his name, the more should we trust him: Ps. lxiv. 10, 'The righteous shall be glad in the Lord, and shall trust in him.' That is true praise and thanksgiving that endeth in trust. It is the purest respect of the creature, and that which keepeth up a respect between God and us; faith is the best thanks.

I doubt we are not spiritual enough in our returns to God. We content ourselves with verbal praises, and do not look after the growth of faith and trust: 2 Cor. i. 10, 'Who delivered us from so great a danger, and doth deliver; in whom we trust that he will yet deliver us.' He findeth it growing upon him whilst he was mentioning of it. Every experience we have is a condescension in God towards the strengthening of our faith.

[2.] Love; it is a special part of this rendering. God will be loved again where he loveth first. *Radius reflexus languet.* The cold wall will reverberate and beat back the sunbeams; a little water put into a pump fetches up more: Ps. cxvi. 1, 2, 'I love the Lord, because he hath heard my voice and my supplication; because he hath inclined his ear to me, therefore I will call upon him as long as I live.' God is more endeared to us. Love him as thy Father in Christ. Every mercy cometh wrapped in his bowels to the saints, and swimming in his blood. When Moses had received mercies, Deut. x. 12, 'Now,' saith he, 'what doth the Lord require of thee, but to fear the Lord thy God, and to walk in his ways, and to love him, and to serve the Lord thy God with all thy heart and with all thy soul?' We have a good master, and love is one chief part of our work. We were bound to love him if he had never done us good, much more when he is so gracious. It is the end of all common mercies: Deut. xxx. 20, 'That thou mayest love the Lord thy God, and that thou mayest obey his voice, and that thou mayest cleave unto him, for he is thy life, and the length of thy days.'

[3.] Fear, that we dare not offend so good a God. That is a true improvement: Hosea iii. 5, 'Afterwards shall the children of Israel return and seek the Lord their God, and David their king, and shall fear the Lord and his goodness in the latter days.' When we grow more presumptuous because we are well at ease, that is naught; but when it increaseth our reverence of God, and holy fear and trembling, then it works kindly. You that have been conscious to the terrible things of righteousness which God hath executed in the high places of the field, you should fear, love, and trust him more than others. You see what a great God he is, that he will find out those that hate him. How suddenly can he blast worldly confidence, however supported! and how able is he to protect those that trust in him! Will you offend such a God? These changes do not only speak duty to the enemies, but to you. Habakkuk trembled at the thought of God's judgments on Babylon: Hab. iii. 16, 'When I heard, my belly trembled, my lips quivered at the voice;' and David: Ps. cxix. 120, 'My flesh trembleth for fear of thee, and I am afraid of thy judgments.' It is an appearance of God, and tender hearts melt at it, as a lion trembleth to see a dog beaten. Tender hearts are affected with the wrath that lighteth upon others, especially when they are the instruments.

[4.] Obedience. You should walk the more humbly and strictly with God. David was at a loss: 'What shall I render?' This was one of his resolutions: Ps. cxvi. 9, 'I will walk before the Lord in the land of the living.' This is your duty, to bind yourselves to a more humble and holy walking with God. This is a good use of experiences. The army that have seen so much of God should be a school of piety to the nation. There is a notable place: Judges ii. 7, 'And the people served the Lord all the days of Joshua, and all the days of the elders that outlived Joshua, who had seen all the great works of the Lord that he did for Israel.' Whilst there were any to keep alive the memorial of such experiences, what an awe was it upon their hearts! Oh! that you could get your hearts in such a frame. Methinks you should have such arguings as this: Shall I, that have seen the wonders of the Lord, be proud, vain, carnal, contemptuous of holy things? Such holy reasonings argue a good frame: Ezra ix. 13, 'Seeing that thou our God hast given us such deliverance as this, should we again break thy commandments?' Certainly none sin so dearly, and with so much expense, as a people saved by the Lord's mercies.

II. To render accordingly, What is that? It implieth two things—

1. Real mercies require real acknowledgments. When your lives were in jeopardy in the high places of the field, did God compliment with you, or save in jest? And now, in the day of your thanksgivings, will you compliment with God, and put him off with a little bodily presence? What is a little cold thanks if you be proud and injurious, and despisers of the ministry, regardless of God's institutions, cavilling at his ordinances, neglectful of church-communion, a thing grown into fashion with many; they content themselves with a loose profession of Christ, living out of the communion of any particular church; a sad thing! God would have coals lie together. Wine is best preserved in the hogshead, and saints in communion. Did God take their thanks well that would own a mercy but oppress the people? Zech. xi. 5, 'Whose possessors slay them, and hold themselves not guilty, and they that sell them say, Blessed be God, I am rich.' They were grown great and high, and God must have the glory by all means; but they used the people severely at their own pleasure. There was a thanksgiving, but withal there was disobedience and abuse of authority; and in that case keeping a day will be to no purpose. The devil's leading Christ to the top of the pinnacle was but to persuade him to cast himself down again.

2. The acknowledgment must answer the proportion of the mercy, be it in word or deed. It is true we cannot vie with God for degree and measure, but we must do what we can.

[1.] If the acknowledgment be in word: Ps. cxlv. 3, 'Great is the Lord, and greatly to be praised;' it must be taken notice of in a more than ordinary manner. The more of God is manifest, the more it should be taken notice of: Ps. cl. 2, 'Praise him according to his excellent greatness.' According to the great appearances and manifestations of God so must our praises be: 'Let the high praises of God be in their mouth,' Ps. cxlix. 6. There are higher and lower praises, more and less solemn according to the proportion and size of our mercies. The spouse's eyes were as 'dove's eyes,' Cant. iv. 1, to peck and look upward.

[2.] If in deed, some notable thing must be done for God. When Ahasuerus had heard of a good deed done by Mordecai, he saith, What honour and dignity hath been done to Mordecai for this? Esther vi. 3. So, what honour hath been done to the Lord? What have we done for him? Saith David, 2 Sam. vii. 2, 'I dwell in a house of cedar, but the ark of God dwelleth within curtains.' The Lord hath advanced me from a sheep-hook to a sceptre; what love have I showed to God? what excellent thing have I done for God? wherein am I carried out with zeal for God?

Use. To reprove—

1. Those that, instead of rendering according, render the quite contrary, who, the more God hath blessed them, grow unthankful, proud, sensual, dead, formal in prayer, less in communion with God, more licentious in their actions. They are like tops, never well but when they are scourged; abuse their mercies to the contempt of God, as the Israelites took the earrings of gold and silver, which were the spoils of the Egyptians, and made a golden calf of them. As the sea turneth all the sweet dews and influences of heaven into salt water, so they turn all their mercies into occasions of sin.

2. Those that do not render aught at all. They are crying for mercy, but think not of returning thanks to God, but, when they have what they would have, turn the back upon God, not the face: Jer. ii. 27, 'In the time of their trouble they will say, Arise and save us;' then their face is to God. There was a law in Ezekiel xlvi. 9, 'He that entereth in by the way of the north gate to worship shall go out by way of the south gate,' &c. He that went in at one gate was not to go out at the same gate, but an opposite; some say, lest he should turn his back upon the mercy-seat.

3. Those that render something, but not suitable. If you would render according, you must be in a capacity. Under the law, the peace-offering was brought at the top of a burnt-offering, Lev. iii. 3. We must be first reconciled to God before we can do anything acceptable. Awaken the heart to the work. David awakens his soul: Ps. ciii. 1, Bless the Lord, O my soul; and all that is within me, bless his holy name.' Search out the works of God: Ps. cxi. 2, 'The works of the Lord are great, sought out of all them that have pleasure in them.' Consider what the world gaineth by every discovery of God, what attributes of God are manifested, what promises are accomplished, how church hopes thrive. Desire God to give you the heart to render, that he that gave the occasion would give the disposition: Ps. li. 15, 'Lord, open thou my lips, and my mouth shall show forth thy praise.' We are spiritually dumb and tongue-tied. Reason and argue from your experiences to your duty: Ezra ix. 13, 'Seeing thou hast given us such a deliverance as this, shall we again break thy commandments?' When you have done all, you will be at a loss: Ps. cxvi. 12, 'What shall I render to the Lord for all his benefits towards me?' He that hath a right sense of God's mercies will be forced to say so; and therefore be striving more and more.

Doct. 2. That it is a sign we are unthankful under mercies when the heart is lifted up upon the enjoyment of them. The Spirit of God bringeth this as the evidence against Hezekiah.

Reasons of the point.

1. Because God can never be rightly praised and exalted while the heart is proud: Isa. ii. 17, 'And the loftiness of men shall be made low, and the Lord alone shall be exalted in that day.' God is exalted in

the creatures' self-abasement; as two buckets in a well, when one goeth down, the other cometh up. The ark and dagon cannot stand together, 1 Sam. v. 3. Set up the ark, and dagon must come upon his face. If you would have God exalted in the riches of his grace, you must lie in the dust.

2. A proud, lifted-up heart cannot be rightly conversant about blessings. It doth not give them their due rise, nor their due value, nor their due end.

[1.] Not their due rise. Many will say God did it. 'God, I thank thee,' was in the pharisee's mouth, Luke xviii. 11; but they do not stand wondering why God should do it; as David: 2 Sam. vii. 18, 'Who am I, O Lord God? and what is my father's house, that thou hast brought me hitherto?' that God should look upon a worm, whence is it? what did God see in me? They actually disclaim all respect, and worth, and merit in themselves, that praise God aright.

[2.] A proud heart doth not give blessings their due value. He looketh for more still, he entertaineth crosses with murmuring, and blessings with disdain. It is but thus and thus, and still set God a new task to do: Ps. lxxviii. 20, 'Behold he smote the rock, and the waters gushed out, and the streams overflowed; can he give bread also? can he provide flesh for his people?' They slight what is past if they have not what they look for: 'All this availeth me nothing, as long as I see Mordecai the Jew sitting at the king's gate,' Esther v. 13; Mal. i. 2, 'I have loved you, saith the Lord; yet they say, Wherein hast thou loved us?' Where are all those mercies and glorious experiences? It is all forgotten and undervalued. If the mercies fit not our mould, all is nothing.

[3.] It doth not give blessings their due ends. God giveth us mercies that we might be more holy and humble, and pride maketh us more carnal and insolent and secure; and so we feed our lusts of the Lord's provision. He gives mercies that 'we may be lifted up in his ways,' 2 Chron. xvii. 6, that we might promote his interest the more cheerfully, without baseness, fear, or carnal respects. But pride abuseth it to carelessness, contempt of holy things, insultation over those that are fallen under God's hand: Deut. xxxii. 15, 'Jeshurun waxed wanton and kicked.' They despise the ordinances of God, and dispute away duties, and cavil at religion. Is this the fruit of our deliverances?

How shall we know when the heart is lifted up? Pride is a capacious sin, therefore called 'pride of life,' 1 John ii. 16, because it is a sin that diffuseth itself throughout all affairs and conditions of life, children, estate, beauty, strength, parts, honours, graces. A worm may breed in manna. Paul was puffed up: 2 Cor. xii. 7, 'Lest I should be exalted above measure through the abundance of the revelations, there was given to me a thorn in the flesh, the messenger of Satan to buffet me, lest I should be exalted above measure.' But the text speaketh of a pride after deliverances, which is a self-blessing and self-depending confidence; which is mainly shown—(1.) In security; (2.) In insolency.

(1.) In security. Men live as if they were above changes. God is neglected, or but coldly owned, as if now we had no more need of him: Lam. i. 9, 'She remembered not her last end, therefore she came down wonderfully;' that is, she was not mindful of the changes and mutations to which all things are obnoxious. Men usually lose their sense of duty with their fears. The heart groweth flat and dead in prayer, not carried out with such zeal and earnestness as when we were in distress. Or it takes us off from what we proposed in our affliction, and all our vows and promises are forgotten.

(2.) In insolency. This is manifested—

(1*st*) By contention. When we are delivered, then we revive the old quarrels; as timber warpeth in the sunshine. When God giveth us success, then follow divisions. The greatest strife is in dividing the spoil: 'Only by pride cometh contention,' saith Solomon, Prov. xiii. 10. Plenty and ease begetteth pride. Dioclesian's persecution was brought on by the factious carriage of the christians themselves, contending for the honours of the church. In king Edward's days, when there was a little breathing, then was there a contention for ceremonies.

(2*d*) By insultation over enemies. True they are under, but it is unmanly to speak to the grief of those whom God hath wounded. If our mercies cannot be advanced but by the fall of our brethren, let us not insult, but pity them. David grieved when Saul fell, and fasted for his enemies. Those whom the hand of the Lord hath touched have a kind of reverence due to them; as places blasted with thunder and lightning were accounted sacred Judges xxi. 6, 'And the children of Israel repented them for Benjamin their brother.'

(3*d*) By oppression and violence: 'Because it is in the power of their hands,' Micah ii. 1. Power doth mightily draw forth corruption. Tenderness of conscience should be a restraint where public force is not. This I can do, but I dare not. But when men employ their power for hurt, not for good, and think to be borne out in a sinful course by their strength and power, it is pride and carnal confidence.

Use. O christians! beware of being lifted up in any kind.

1. Take heed of secret thoughts of merit: Deut. ix. 4, 'Speak not thou in thine heart after that the Lord thy God hath cast them out from before thee, saying, For my righteousness the Lord hath brought me in to possess this land.' Though there be not such formal thoughts or downright expressions, yet this is the implied thought. There are explicit thoughts and implicit thoughts; the one is actually and sensibly conceived in the mind, the other lurk and lie hid there, and our actions being interpreted, are necessarily resolved into such thoughts. As when you are scornful and pitiless, vaunting yourselves above others, and do not actually admire the riches of the Lord's goodness, surely there is some latent thought of merit in the heart. You may take notice of God's justice, but still you must admire free grace.

2. Take heed of ascribing to your wisdom, power, and conduct. Man would fain be *faber fortunæ suæ*, the author of his own happiness, jostling God out of his thoughts: Hab. i. 16, 'They sacrifice to their net, and burn incense to their drag, because by them their portion is fat and their meat plenteous;' insulting and glorying in their wisdom and strength. Though a man doth not fall down as a gross idolater, and perform rites of devotion, yet his thoughts run this way, and so God is laid aside. God giveth his people warning of this: Deut. viii. 14, 'Let not thine heart be lifted up, and thou forget the Lord thy

God which brought thee out of the land of Egypt;' and ver. 17, 'And thou say in thine heart, My power and the might of my hand hath gotten this wealth.' Why should the Lord give so many warnings if we were not exceeding prone to this? We should throw our crowns at God's feet. It is enough for us to be poor instruments in God's hand. I hope you came here before the Lord with such a design this day, to strip yourselves, and give all the glory to God.

3. Take heed of the pride of self-dependence. Hereby the heart is taken off from God, and then the devil hath us upon the hip. He that swimmeth in a full stream is apt to be carried away with the stream. It is a hard matter to see the nothingness of the creature when we enjoy the fulness of the creature. Man's thoughts are always swallowed up with his present condition. In misery we think we shall never come out of it; in prosperity, that it will never be otherwise. Paul could say, 'As having nothing, yet possessing all things,' 2 Cor. vi. 10. Few can say, As possessing all things and having nothing, so as to sit loose from our worldly dependences: 'I have learned to abound;' it is an harder lesson than 'I have learned to be abased;' Phil. iv. 12, as there is more of choice in it, and less of necessity. We are beaten to the other. We use to say, Such a one would do well to be a lord or a lady. It is an harder matter than you are aware of. Many have done well in a low condition that could not manage an higher. 'Ephraim is a cake not turned,' Hosea vii. 8; not baked of both sides, so as to walk with an holy equality and evenness of spirit in all conditions. You think it is hard to bear miseries; it is as hard to master comforts, to carry a full cup without spilling, and to keep from surfeiting at a rich and luscious banquet. Few know how to abound.

To prick these windy bladders in solemn remembrances of mercy, such things as these are necessary.

[1.] A special recognition and recalling of sins is not unseasonable. Let the warm sun melt you: Ezek. xxxvi. 30, 31, 'I will multiply the fruit of the tree, and the increase of the field, that ye shall receive no more reproach of famine among the heathen; then shall ye remember your ways and doings that have not been good, and shall loathe yourselves in your own sight for all your iniquities.' When mercies humble us and set us a-mourning, it is a kindly work. Moses bowed himself when the Lord proclaimed the name of his mercy. Oh! bow yourselves; poor worthless creatures, that God should look upon us!

[2.] Meditate upon the changes of providence. Things are at a great uncertainty in the world. Hezekiah is delivered and then falls sick; he is delivered again, and then groweth proud; and then came wrath upon him, and upon all Judah and Jerusalem: Ps. xxxix. 5, 'Verily every man at his best estate is altogether vanity;' not only in his worst, but at his best estate; when he is in his zenith, then he is at the vertical point. Verily this is a truth should be stamped deeply upon all our hearts. Belisarius, a famous general to-day, and within a little while forced to beg for a halfpenny. Things and persons are as the spokes of a wheel, sometimes in the dirt, and sometimes out. The church complaineth, Ps. cii. 10, 'Thou hast lifted me up and cast me down;' a sad dejection after some comfortable elevation. All outward glory is like a glass, transparent, but brittle. Paul was rapt in the third heaven, and was full of unspeakable ravishments and revelations, yet presently he talketh of a thorn in the flesh. Now, at your best think of this, that you may inure your thoughts to changes, and settle your solid happiness in God. David, when he had a glorious victory, speaketh of losing, and God's blasting their armies, Ps. lx. 10, compared with the title; he acknowledgeth past judgments as the fruit of God's displeasure. In the Roman triumphs there was one to remember them of their mortality in the midst of their pomp. Yea, under the law leavened cakes were allowed in peace-offerings and sacrifices of thanksgiving, which were forbidden in other sacrifices: Lev. vii. 13, 'He shall offer for his offering leavened bread with the sacrifice of thanksgiving of his peace-offerings,' to teach us to temper our joys with the thought of sorrow and affliction.

SERMON UPON LUKE XXII. 31, 32.

And the Lord said, Simon, Simon, behold, Satan hath desired to have you, that he may sift you as wheat: but I have prayed for thee, that thy faith fail not; and when thou art converted, strengthen thy brethren.—LUKE xxii. 31, 32.

IN the words observe two things—(1.) A warning of danger approaching, ver. 31; (2.) A comfort propounded, ver 32.

First, In the first branch observe—

1. The person to whom Christ directeth his words; to Peter, though they concerned all the rest, for it was not him only whom Satan desired to sift, but all of them; but Christ speaks to him in particular, because it most concerned him. The devil would vex all of them, but our Lord foresaw that he would more grievously fall than his fellow-disciples, and, being more fervent and confident than the rest, was more exposed to temptations; and when he addresseth his speech to him, he calleth him not Peter, but Simon. It was, Mat. xvi. 18, 'Thou art Peter, and upon this rock will I build my church;' *q. d.*, the name by which thou art known to me signifieth a rock and stone. But this was when he uttered his good confession; but now he was to be an instance of human frailty, he calleth him not Peter, but Simon. And mark the ingemination of his name, 'Simon, Simon.' This doubling of his name doth partly intimate affection, and is as much as to say, My dear Simon; partly to stir up a serious attention, that he might mark what is said.

2. The danger itself, 'Behold Satan hath desired to have you, that he may sift you as wheat.' Where observe—

[1.] The author and procurer of this trouble, the devil, called here Satan, that is an adversary. Our danger is mainly from the devil; he hath a great hand in the troubles of God's people. He assaulteth them himself by his wiles, and fiery darts, Eph. vi. 11 and 16, and stirreth up his instruments to persecute them: Luke xxii. 53, 'This is your hour, and the power of darkness.' That was the time when the devil and his instruments were permitted to work their wills on Christ; when the shepherd was smitten, and the flock scattered abroad.

[2.] The way how he bringeth it about, 'He hath desired to have you.' It intimateth two things—

(1.) He asketh leave; for Satan and his instruments cannot touch any of God's children without God's permission; therefore he asketh leave to have the disciples of Christ in his power to vex them. So for Job; he has leave to touch his substance, but must not meddle with his person: Job i. 11, 12, 'But put forth thine hand now, and touch all that he hath; and he will curse thee to thy face. And the Lord said unto Satan, Behold, all that he hath is in thy power, only upon himself put not forth thy hand.' Then to afflict his body with boils, and sores, but he must spare his life: Job ii. 5, 6, 'But put forth thine hand now, and touch his bone and his flesh, and he will curse thee to thy face. And the Lord said unto Satan, Behold, he is in thine hand, but save his life.' Nay, he was fain to ask leave to enter into the herd of swine: Mat. viii. 31, 'So the devil besought him, saying, if thou cast us out, suffer us to go away into the herd of swine.' Surely then the flock of Christ's sheep need not be troubled. If the bristles of the swine be numbered, much more are the hairs of your heads.

(2.) It is a kind of suing out of his right. The word signifieth the putting in of a plea and suit, not a bare asking leave; $\dot{\epsilon}\xi\eta\tau\acute{\eta}\sigma\alpha\tau o\ \dot{\upsilon}\mu\hat{\alpha}s$, *poposcit vos ad pœnam.* Sin giveth Satan some right of claim, and when we have committed some sins, we provoke God to give us over to Satan to be disciplined. Therefore this 'desiring to have you' is his accusing you to God, and requiring that he may have the shaking of you. For the devil is an adversary: 1 Peter v. 8, 'Because your adversary the devil as a roaring lion walketh about, seeking whom he may devour.' The word is $\dot{\alpha}\nu\tau\acute{\iota}\delta\iota\kappa os$, an adversary. Satan is an enemy at law; he is always indicting and accusing you before God, that he may get you into his power and reach. Oh! how watchful should the children of God be, when they have an adversary that pleadeth law and equity on his side, and pursueth his right against them to bring them to the trial! But how could he do so in the case of the apostles, and of Peter in particular? Possibly it might be something criminously done by them in that contention of the disciples about primacy and superiority, who should be chiefest, mentioned ver. 24, 'And there was a strife among them, which of them should be accounted greatest;' and the indignation of the ten against the two brethren, James and John; and in that contest Peter might be most faulty, he being with them too. Those of the disciples whom Jesus most loved, Peter, James, and John, were often admitted to his privacies when others were excluded. Oh! it is a sad thing when we give occasion to Satan to demand us to the judgment.

[3.] His aim and purpose, 'To sift you as wheat,' that is, to toss and shake you as grain in a sieve. The meaning is, the devil would have permission from God wholly to subvert you, and cast you away. A great judgment is expressed by this phrase: Amos ix. 9, 'I will sift the house of Israel among all nations like as corn is sifted in a sieve.' This is the devil's aim, utterly to destroy God's people. But he can obtain no more than to shake and molest them for trial. In sifting, two things are considerable—(1.) The agitation of tossing to the corn, now this way, now that way, from one side to another; (2.) The separation of the wheat from the chaff. The devil only intends the former, but God the latter. He would have Peter and the rest of the apostles given to him that he might trouble and vex them, and not suffer them to have any rest; but God would turn it to an holy use, to purge you from your dross, your worldly and carnal affections. Satan desireth to trouble us, but thereby God doth cleanse and refine us. He would have liberty to do his worst to drive you from the faith of Christ; but though somewhat of that is granted to him, yet the power of the devil is limited, both as to tempting and hurting. *Cribratione Satanæ non perditur, sed purgatur frumentum.* The corn is not spoiled but cleansed by Satan's sifting.

Secondly, Here is comfort propounded to sustain them under this great danger; where observe two things—

1. The means of disappointing Satan, 'I have prayed for thee, that thy faith fail not.'

2. The event, delivered in the form of a direction. Peter should recover out of this lapse, and be a means to strengthen others: 'And when thou art converted, strengthen thy brethren.'

1. The means of disappointing Satan, 'I have prayed for thee,' &c. Mark, to Satan's desires there are opposed Christ's prayers. There is more force in Christ's prayers than in Satan's temptations. More particularly consider—(1.) Who prayeth; (2.) For whom he prayeth; (3.) For what.

[1.] Who prayeth; Jesus Christ, the Mediator and advocate of his people. The devil is the accuser, but Christ the advocate, to whose mediation and intercession it must alone be ascribed that we do not finally miscarry. Christ is ready to pray, for he knoweth the heart of a tempted man: Heb. ii. 17, 18, 'Wherefore it behoved him in all things to be made like unto his brethren, that he might be a merciful and faithful high priest in things pertaining to God, to make reconciliation for the sins of the people; for in that he himself hath suffered, being tempted, he is able to succour them that are tempted.' And his prayer is effectual: John xi. 42, 'And I know that thou hearest me always.' Christ doth not only perfume our prayers, or stay till we pray for ourselves, but prevents them by his own intercession when he foresees the danger.

[2.] For whom he prayeth: 'I have prayed for thee;' that is, for Peter. What! for him only? No; but the rest of the disciples also. The remedy was prepared for them before the trials came, and the plaster fitted before the wound was made. But was it for the apostles only? No, but for all believers: John xvii. 20, 'Neither pray I for these alone, but for them also which shall believe on me through their word.' Christ here upon earth did pray first for the college of the apostles, and then for all believers; so in heaven he hath a watchful care over us, that we may not faint under the temptations of Satan.

[3.] For what he prayeth: 'That thy faith fail not;' that is, may not utterly miscarry. Here observe—

(1.) The grace prayed for, faith, the grace most necessary, and upon which other things depend. All matters that concern Christ and his kingdom depend upon faith: 2 Peter i. 5, 6, 'Add to your faith virtue, and to virtue knowledge, and to knowledge temperance, and to temperance patience, and to patience godliness.' If faith fail not, other graces will not fail: 1 Peter v. 9, 'Whom resist, steadfast in the faith.' And faith is the grace most assaulted in the present trial; for Peter was put to it whether he would own and acknowledge Christ to be his Lord and Master. To faith there belong two acts—Believing with the heart, and confession with the mouth : Rom. x. 9, 10, 'If thou shalt confess with thy mouth the Lord Jesus Christ, and believe in thy heart that God hath raised him from the dead, thou shalt be saved; for with the heart man believeth to righteousness, and with the mouth confession is made unto salvation.' This last was put to the trial.

(2.) How far it was prayed for, in the word, 'Fail not.' Christ prayeth not that our faith should never be tried and assaulted, nor that we should be exempted from trouble, but kept from the evil: John xvii. 15, 'I pray not that thou shouldst take them out of the world, but that thou shouldst keep them from the evil.' Not that we should be never oppugned, but not expugned; neither that it should be not in any degree weakened, but not extinguished. Faith doth not fail totally as to the habit and root of it in their heart, though the habit may be much weakened and diminished, and its proper and natural action obstructed and interrupted, such as is confession with the mouth. Christ foresaw his approaching denial of him, and foretold it; but Peter did not utterly forsake the faith, as appeareth by his speedy repentance. As a candle smoking and newly blown out easily sucketh light and flame again, so did he recover himself out of that surprise.

2. The event, delivered in the form of a direction; wherein—

[1.] Is intimated his recovery and being converted. Peter had denied Christ with oaths and execrations, a foul fault; but Christ recovered him by his look, that no man might despair; and after his resurrection bringeth him to a threefold confession: John xxi. 15, 16, 'Lovest thou me more than these? and lovest thou me? and lovest thou me?' Now the core of his distemper was gotten out: 'Lovest thou me more than these?' Is thy love to me so great as thou didst seem to affirm it when thou saidst, 'Though all men forsake thee, yet will not I'? Is thy love surpassing the love of all other my disciples? What was Peter's answer? 'Lord, thou knowest that I love thee;' that is, sincerely. Being taught by his smart experience, he dareth not make comparison with all others; no more comparisons now. Peter had been under a severe discipline, which taught him humility, and before all the disciples he testifieth his repentance, which was first acted in secret. Now he was grown more jealous of himself, he would not boast of such a singular love.

But observe the term, converted. Recovery out of a sore temptation is a kind of second conversion. Grace is battered and bruised, and so many things are necessary to put us in joint again. Denial of Christ, even out of weakness, is a loss not easily recovered. First, Peter had Christ's look: Luke xxii. 61, 'And the Lord turned, and looked upon Peter;' which pierced his very heart, upon which 'he went out, and wept bitterly,' ver. 62. And then Christ's message: Mark xvi. 7, 'Tell his disciples and Peter that he goeth before you into Galilee; there ye shall see him.' Be sure to tell Peter, a little to revive and comfort him. He was now full of tears, and grieved at heart for his former offence; then Christ appeared to him alone, as Luke xxiv. 34, 'The Lord is risen indeed, and hath appeared to Simon.' Therefore the apostle saith, 1 Cor. xv. 5, 'That he was seen of Cephas, then of the twelve.' Then afterwards he is brought publicly upon the stage to acknowledge his love to Christ, John xxi. 15–17. So hard a matter is it to set a member in joint again that is once out. So David: Ps. li. 10, 'Create in me a clean heart, O God, and renew a right spirit within me.' He speaketh of it as a second creation and renovation; not that there was a total expulsion of faith or charity, but to show that the loss is not soon repaired.

[2.] There is counsel given him, 'Strengthen thy brethren.' When by repentance thou art recovered out of thy sin, be more careful to confirm and strengthen others.

(1.) To prevent falling, pray for them, warn them, be an example of constancy to them, that they may not fall or fail in like manner; which he did by his threefold profession of love to Christ, and in glorifying God in his whole life and death: John xxi. 19, 'This spake he, signifying by what death he should glorify God.' Christ warneth him of his future sufferings, showing that he should be more stout than in his former trial. Such a difference there was between Peter trusting in his own strength and Peter supported by God. He that before was blown down by the weak blast of a damsel's question, could then confidently look a cruel death in the face.

(2.) Recover them if lapsed with meekness, that they may not despair: Gal. vi. 1, 'If a man be overtaken in a fault, ye which are spiritual restore such a one in the spirit of meekness, considering thyself, lest thou also be tempted.' If the possibility of falling be an argument, the actual experience is much more. Christians should not exercise too great severity on them that are fallen, considering we have or we might fall into like sin in the time of temptation. Thus would Christ season and prepare his servants for their office, and by their own experience teach them meekness and tenderness to others. In general it is said, 2 Cor. i. 4, 'Who comforteth us in all our tribulations, that we may be able to comfort them which are in any trouble with the comforts wherewith we ourselves are comforted of God.' Such comforts are not only for our good, but for the benefit and advantage of others. 'Confirm thy brethren,' saith Christ here to Peter. They are brethren, and they need to be strengthened; for all these afflictions are incident to all our brethren which are in the flesh, and our example and consolation from experience are a great relief to them.

Thus you have a full view and prospect of the words. I shall observe this point from the whole.

Doct. That though Satan by God's permission may sorely trouble and vex his people, yet we are not wholly exposed to his fury to be dealt with as he pleaseth. Let me show you how many ways Satan may vex and trouble God's people; either by inward suggestion, or by outward persecution and affliction.

1. By inward suggestions; as when he tempted David to number the people: 1 Chron. xxi. 1, 'Satan stood up against Israel, and provoked David to number Israel.' Namely, as he moved him to pride and glory in the arm of flesh, or in his grandeur or multitude of subjects. God had an hand in it: 2 Sam. xxiv. 1, 'And the anger of the Lord was kindled against Israel, and he moved David against

them to say, Go, number Israel and Judah;' to punish David and his people for their sins, God as a just judge using Satan as his minister therein. God by permission and a wise ordination of it for good, and Satan by suggestion and malicious intention for evil. God as a judge in a just punishment for sin, and Satan as an enemy and an actor of sin. It is no excuse to Satan or David that God moved, nor any blot in God that Satan moved, they acting from diverse principles and diverse ends. Well, but to our present purpose, Satan moved David, a man after God's own heart. Alas! the best have their infirmities, and Satan hath many hidden secret arts to mischief souls which we think not of.

2. By persecutions or afflictions. Many of Satan's temptations are conveyed by afflictions, that he may make the people of God weary of their profession, and either quit the truth or cast off their duty to him. Thus when the apostle telleth us of the devil's unwearied malice and enmity to souls, he biddeth us 'resist him steadfast in the faith, knowing that the same afflictions are accomplished in our brethren which are in the world,' 1 Peter v. 9. And again, Rev. ii. 10, 'The devil shall cast some of you into prison.' Surely they were put in prison by men, but these men were Satan's instruments. They have their hour sometimes and seasons when they work great trouble to the people of God. God doth not so altogether bind up Satan but that he suffereth him to act many strange parts in the world, either by himself immediately or by his instruments.

Again, our trials are the more sore because Satan hath an hand in them.

1. Not only because that is cumulative to the malice of men, or superadded to it. And so the apostle: Eph. vi. 12, 'We wrestle not against flesh and blood, but against principalities, against powers, against the rulers of the darkness of this world, against spiritual wickednesses in high places.' Our business lieth not with men, with flesh and blood only, but with Satan. Men are but the devil's instruments. Human and bodily powers are Satan's auxiliaries, whom he stirreth up and employeth; so that there is a double party—the visible agents, and the invisible powers by which they are assisted and acted. But—

2. There are special reasons why the devil is a more terrible and dangerous party than any human power: as partly—

[1.] Because of his great enmity to mankind, especially the redeemed by Christ; because he looketh upon them as likely to possess the vacant places from which he and his angels are fallen. He is always called the enemy with respect to war; adversary, or opposite litigant party, with respect to law

[2.] Partly because of his unwearied activity. He is always going about 1 Peter v. 8, 'Your adversary the devil as a roaring lion walketh about, seeking whom he may devour;' and in the book of Job, chap. i. 7, 'From going to and fro in the earth, and from walking up and down in it.' And—

[3.] Partly for his insatiable cruelty. His malice is bitter and extreme, 'Seeking whom he may devour.' His aim is utter ruin and damnation, to prejudice us in our eternal estate or our spiritual and heavenly concernments. It is not your temporal and bodily interests that he would mainly bereave you of. He can let you enjoy the pleasures of the world that he may deprive you of your delight in God. He can be content that you shall have dignities and honours, ease and safety, so they prove a snare to you; all is to ruin your souls. If he cannot prevail so far, yet he would thereby draw you to scandalous sins, that you may dishonour God: 2 Sam. xii. 14, 'By this deed thou hast given great occasion to the enemies of the Lord to blaspheme;' and destroy your own peace: Ps. xxxii. 3, 'My bones waxed old through my roaring all the day long.'

[4.] Partly for his subtlety. He is of a spiritual nature, and so the devil is invisible both in his nature and approaches, and doth often reach us a deadly blow before we know it is he; and he seeketh by all means to conceal himself: 2 Cor. xi. 3, 'I fear lest by any means, as the serpent beguiled Eve by his subtlety, so your minds should be corrupted from the simplicity which is in Christ.' The devil maketh as if he meant all kindness, when he cometh to ruin and destroy souls. He playeth of all hands; tempteth Peter to dissuade, and Judas to betray, and the high priests to persecute. He endeavoureth to keep out of sight, that he may not be seen himself in the temptation, as the fowler and hunter hide themselves till the bird or beast is gotten into the snare or toil. Alas! little do we think the devil is so near, and hath so great an hand in the business which we are about to perform, as we afterwards find him to be. It is not he that seemeth to do it, but such a neighbour, such a minister, or wise man.

3. Why God permitteth this. For many holy and wise reasons.

[1.] To glorify the power of his grace in preserving us: 2 Cor. xii. 9, 'My grace is sufficient for thee, for my strength is made perfect in weakness,' 'Made perfect,' that is, found or discovered to be perfect; for God's strength cannot be more perfect than it is. There are no degrees in infiniteness, much less can our weakness add anything to it. The meaning is, it is manifested to be perfect. The greater the pressures are, the more visible and conspicuous is the perfection of the divine assistance. More goeth to the keeping of a saint here in the world than to the preserving of an angel; for the angels are ἔξω βέλους, out of gunshot and harm's way, but we are making our way to heaven almost every step by conflict and conquest.

[2.] To abate our carnal confidence. For till we have experience of the strength of sin, danger of temptations, and our own weakness, we are too confident of our own resolutions, which, because they are sincere and undissembled, we think they may be easily maintained; therefore God, to show us ourselves, suffereth Satan to tempt us and his instruments to vex us, that by experience we may see how weak that faith is in the temptation which we thought to be strong out of the temptation. This is the meaning of that counsel our Lord giveth his disciples: Mat. xxvi. 41, 'Watch and pray that ye enter not into temptation: the spirit indeed is willing, but the flesh is weak.' To enter into temptation hath a peculiar sense and signification in that place, and the meaning is, to be overcome by temptations, to enter so as to abide under the power of them, to be encompassed so as we cannot get out. Therefore watch and pray that it be not so with you; for however your mind and resolution be good, and your professions for the time zealous, yet you may fall from your stoutest resolutions if you be not careful. Or thus, though the spirit or the renewed part be willing to resist and oppose temptations, yet the natural and unrenewed part is weak and ready to be overcome by them. They were confident, secure, and unconcerned when that danger was approaching which would make them either to forsake Christ or to deny and forswear him, as Peter did; therefore it were better for them to be watchful and importunate with God, that they might not be overcome with this temptation. In many cases we find that those that thought their faith strong find it very weak when the temptation cometh: John xvi. 31, 32, 'Do ye now believe? Behold the hour cometh, yea, is now come, that ye shall be scattered every man to his own, and shall leave me alone.' There is a great deal of difference between trials in imagination and trials in actual experience. Trials in imagination do not affect us so much, because we only know them at a distance, or by guess and supposition; but evils in sense and feeling are another thing than we could imagine. It is a lamentable thing to see what a cowardly spirit there is in most christians, how soon they are discouraged with every petty assault or slender temptation, and their resolutions shaken with the appearance of any difficulty, how confident soever they were before.

[3.] God sendeth temptations to abate our pride, and so to humble us as well as prove us, that we may not be proud of what we have, or conceit that we have more than we have. Paul giveth this reason: 2 Cor. xii. 7, 'Lest I should be exalted above measure through the abundance of revelations, there was given me a thorn in the flesh, a messenger of Satan to buffet me, lest I should be exalted above measure.' There is a difference about the interpretation what this $\sigma\kappa\acute{o}\lambda o\psi$ $\tau\hat{\eta}$ $\sigma\alpha\rho\kappa\grave{\iota}$, thorn in the flesh, was; either a racking disease or some other sharp affliction. Surely it was not stirrings of sin or some boiling lusts, for Paul was aged, and he would then speak of it in other words. Some think it was some racking disease, like the stake thrust into the fundament of a slave that ran from his master, and came out at his back. Whatever it was, it was a messenger of Satan. Now, whether God would permit Satan to have such power over Paul's body, I leave it to you to consider. Therefore some think it was some sore affliction. In the general, I remember the pricking brier and grieving thorn is put for the despisers and persecutors of Israel: Ezek. xxviii. 24, 'And there shall be no more a pricking brier unto the house of Israel, nor any grieving thorn of all that are round about them that despised them.' This may be called a thorn in the flesh. A sad and sharp affliction questionless it was, inflicted on Paul by the power of the devil. But whatever the event was, God's end was clear, that he might not be elevated with his transcendent revelations: he twice repeateth it, 'Lest I should be exalted above measure.' When the instruments of Satan deal roughly with him, this was designed by God to keep him humble.

[4.] God sendeth these temptations in justice to correct us for other sins: 2 Sam. xxiv. 1, 'The anger of the Lord was kindled against Israel, and he moved David to say, Go, number Israel and Judah.' The Lord permitted Satan to move David, as I explained it before; but mark, it was because God was angry with Israel, when they had abused their plenty and prosperity to licentiousness and forgetfulness of God. Satan is permitted to tempt David, that God might take that occasion to punish them. And it is observed in the censures of the church; a scandalous sinner is 'delivered over to Satan for the destruction of the flesh, that the spirit may be saved in the day of the Lord Jesus,' 1 Cor. v. 5; that is, permitted for a while to the devil's power, that he might be recovered to God. And in the text, Satan hath desired, ἐξητήσατο, hath required him of God, demands to have him delivered up to him as to an executioner; and if God thinks fit to answer this request, then he delivereth them up to Satan. Now this should be regarded by us. It is a sad thing when the devil hath a just plea in law against us. The apostle warneth christians 'not to give place to the devil,' Eph. iv. 27. This may be done *effectivè* or *meritoriè*. Effectually, when you comply with his insinuations, and give way to your inordinate passions and carnal affections; then you set open the door to Satan, for he watcheth for any opportunity to recover his old possession and exercise his former tyranny again. Pharaoh was not so hasty to pursue after the Israelites as this malicious spirit is to recover the prey taken out of his hands. When you give way to any known sin, and continue and lie asleep in it, Satan is encouraged and God provoked. And so *meritoriè;* meritoriously you give place to Satan as you make God to withdraw his assistance or to give Satan leave to tempt you: 2 Chron. xxxii. 31, 'God left him to try him, that he might know all that was in his heart.' And so fearful havoc is made in the soul, not only of comfort, but grace as to many degrees of it. One sin prepareth for another, as a spark doth for a flame; and the longer and oftener we sin, so much the worse it is for us. Repentance is the sharper, because of the wrong done to God; and the harder, because it is not easy to settle and restore such a soul, that the influences of God's grace and favour may have their wonted course.

4. That God doth not expose us to the fury of Satan, to be dealt with as he pleaseth, but doth bridle and restrain his rage.

[1.] God is the sovereign orderer of this business of temptations. As the shaking and tossing of the saints is by his leave, so is the protection of their faith from his grace. The devil is a creature under government, as all other creatures are; and it is a great comfort to the saints that, when they are in Satan's hands, Satan is in God's hands. Neither the devil nor the world can help or hurt us without his leave. The devils are represented to be 'under chains,' and 'chains of darkness,' Jude 6, 2 Peter ii. 4. These chains are God's irresistible power and terrible justice; either the restraints of his powerful providence, called therefore 'chains,' or the horror of their own despairing fears, called therefore 'chains of darkness.' They can do nothing but as far as God's justice and holy wisdom permitteth them.

[2.] As our protection cometh from God, so it cometh to us by the intercession of Christ, who prayeth for his people; a copy whereof we have, John xvii., and a pledge of which is this. He hath intendered his own heart by experience, and so is more likely to pity us: Heb. ii. 18, 'For that he himself hath suffered, being tempted, he is able to succour them that are tempted.' There is ability of power, ability of idoneity and fitness, as it is proper and agreeable that he should become compassionate, and willing to relieve those that fall into the like or same evils, namely, sharp persecutions in this world for his name's sake: Heb. iv. 15, 'He was in all points tempted as we are.' He hath felt the weight and trouble of temptations himself, and will be sensible of our condition; as a man that has had the stone or gout knows better how to sympathise with others in the like case, and as Israel was commanded to be merciful and pitiful to strangers, because they knew the heart of a stranger. *Non ignara mali, miseris succurrere disco.*

[3.] Christ's love is never more at work for us than when under temptations. He hath a tender sense of our danger by Satan. When he followeth them out of malice and spite, then God puts forth the strength and efficacy of his mediation: Zech. iii. 1, 2, 'And he showed me Joshua the high priest standing before the angel of the Lord, and Satan standing at his right hand to resist him: and the Lord said unto Satan, The Lord rebuke thee, O Satan.' When his people are assaulted by Satan he hath most love for them, and taketh care aforehand: John xiii. 1, 'Having loved his own that were in the world, he loved them to the end.' Saith Christ of them, Poor creatures! they are left to storms and tempests, and they are undone if I help them not.

[4.] Though he permit the temptation, yet he alloweth not a total victory, as he prayed that Peter might not utterly forsake the faith. *Non pugna sublata est, sed victoria.* He doth not hinder the fight, but the victory. He overcame the devil and the world, therefore fear not. God promiseth help for human frailty, not for rashness and sloth. We are sure of victory whilst we resist and keep up the fight: James iv. 7, 'Resist the devil, and he will flee from you.'

[5.] Being kept from the evil is better than to be exempted from the trouble of vexatious temptations. Our Lord prayeth so: John xvii. 15, 'I pray not that thou shouldest take them out of the world, but that thou shouldest keep them from the evil.' He teacheth us to pray so: Mat. vi. 13, 'Lead us not into temptation, but deliver us from evil.' There is a direct prayer, and a prayer by way of reserve. First, if it be the will of God, 'lead us not into temptation;' but if that be, then 'keep us from the evil.' It is a more wonderful providence to be kept from the evil than to be kept from temptation. A garrison never assaulted is easily kept. And partly because the evil of sin is greater than the evil of trouble. Sin separateth from God, affliction driveth us to him; and to be preserved from the reign of sin is better than not to be permitted to fall into a signal act of sin; for the act may be consistent with grace, but not the reign.

Use 1. Let us not be secure. Christ was tempted, so was Job, so was Paul. We have a fierce and subtle adversary to encounter with, many trials we must look for. None are so tempted as the best christians; the pirate doth not set upon an empty vessel. Wicked men are not troubled; they are already in the snares, slaves and vassals to Satan, of whom he is sure already: Luke xi. 21, 'Where a strong man keeps his palace, his goods are in peace.' A middle sort of men God permitteth not to be tempted: 1 Cor. x. 13, 'God will not suffer you to be tempted above what you are able.' They are not seasoned enough, nor furnished with life and light. Satan's malice aimeth at the best, but he prevaileth with the presumptuously confident and fool-hardy. They know not their own weaknesses. If we slight these things, and thrust ourselves into temptations, we fall as a ready prey into the mouth of the roaring lion. You know how many a good purpose hath come to nothing; and will not you watch? This is the cause why we are so often surprised; we live and walk as if we were not among our enemies, as if the devil did not haunt us, and we gave him no occasion to solicit God against us.

2. Being forewarned, let us be forearmed or prepared against Satan's devices; otherwise, when we think, as Samson, to go forth and shake ourselves as at other times, we shall find that our strength is gone, and we have permitted ourselves too much to the power of the enemy. Our preparation mainly lieth in two things—

[1.] That we be dead to the flesh and the world. Be sober and watchful. Sobriety is a moderation in all earthly things. The devil usually gets the world on his side. Therefore, till we be dead to applause, commodity, honour, and profit, and resolve to be holy and obedient to God though it cost us dear, we shall do nothing in christianity. Satan will tempt the flesh, and that will soon say, Spare thyself: Mat. xvi. 22, 'This shall not be unto thee.' Therefore as long as there is a bias of worldly inclination upon us, and we are set on the pleasures, profits, or honours of the world, or be taken too much with its ease, peace, and prosperity, we are not prepared; and what work will Satan make when he comes to toss us!

[2.] Keep faith upright. Christ prays that Peter's faith may not fail, and 1 Peter v. 9, 'Whom resist, steadfast in the faith.' Faith has many things to pitch on, the whole gospel, but chiefly the promises and threatenings of the gospel; they will inform you what will be the end of godliness and sin, and a man that hath his eyes opened, and seeth the end of godliness and sin, hath a mighty advantage. As to the promises of Christ, surely Christ is no deceiver. Will you credit the devil, whom you have found to be false, and suspect the promises of Christ? Luke xii. 32, 'Fear not, little flock; for it is your father's good pleasure to give you the kingdom.' Christ promiseth more than the devil. As to the threatenings, let not the threatenings of men affright you; if they threaten a prison, God threateneth hell; if they threaten to molest the body, God can cast body and soul into hell. God can preserve you from what men threaten, and he threatens what is worse than man threatens; and therefore, to have our eyes in our head, and see the end of godliness and sin, is a mighty help in this case, that our faith may not fail.

SERMON UPON HEBREWS I. 9.

Thou hast loved righteousness, and hated iniquity; therefore God, even thy God, hath anointed thee with the oil of gladness above thy fellows.—HEB. i. 9.

IN the context the apostle is proving that Christ hath obtained a more excellent name than the angels. They are servants, he a son; they are creatures, he is God; they are to worship, he is to be worshipped, in which divine honours they can have no communion; they are spectators of the mystery of redemption, he is the head of the redeemed world, as being solemnly appointed thereunto by God. This is the argument of the text, which is a quotation out of the 45th Psalm, 'Thou hast loved righteousness,' &c.

In these words we have—(1.) A description of Christ; (2.) The exaltation of Christ; (3.) The respect of the one to the other, 'therefore.' The one is the foundation of the other.

1. In the description of Christ his holiness is taken notice of; and—

[1.] Both branches are mentioned, 'loved righteousness,' 'hated iniquity.'

[2.] The habitual inclination of his heart is asserted in all that he did or now doth do; all proceeded from his love to righteousness, and his hatred to sin.

[3.] This commendation or description doth not only concern his personal practice, but his design. His heart was set upon it, not only to practise holiness himself, but to promote it in the world; for the holiness of God incarnate is essentially necessary both to his person and employment. By it he was fitly qualified. Nothing puts us on to do a thing thoroughly more than love; this was Christ's principle; and therefore he would express the most effectual means.

2. His exaltation: 'God, even thy God, hath anointed thee with the oil of gladness above thy fellows;' that is, exalted thee above men and all angels. Anointing is often applied to Christ: Ps. ii. 2, 'Against the Lord and his anointed;' Acts iv. 27, 'Thine holy child Jesus, whom thou hast anointed;' Isa. lxi. 1, 'The Lord hath anointed me to preach good tidings to the meek.' Therefore he is called in the Hebrew Messiah, and in the Greek Χριστός. This anointing usually signifieth three things—

[1.] The giving of power and authority, as Saul by being anointed was made king of Israel, 1 Sam. x. 1, and Aaron and his sons made priests, Exod. xxx. 30. So Christ was anointed to authorise his dispensation, or to invest him in the authority and power of the mediatory office.

[2.] To fit and enable the person so authorised for the discharge of the office unto which he was called; for the oil was typical, and signified the gifts and graces of the Spirit. So Jesus Christ was 'anointed with the Holy Ghost, and with power,' Acts x. 38, to fit his human nature for so high a function.

[3.] His welcome and entertainment at his return to heaven; and so the glorious exaltation of our Lord Jesus Christ, when he solemnly sat down at the right hand of majesty, and entered upon his kingdom, was his anointing; for then was he solemnly 'made both Lord and Christ,' Acts ii. 36, and evidenced to be the Lord's anointed one, as I shall show more fully by and by.

3. The respect or relation of his exaltation to his description, 'therefore.' At least it is a consequent of what he had done in the world in love to righteousness and hatred of sin, but moreover it is to him a recompense: Phil. ii. 9, 'Wherefore God hath highly exalted him, and given him a name which is above every name;' Rom. xiv. 9, 'For to this end Christ both died, and rose, and revived, that he might be Lord both of the dead and living.' Which is no lessening of his merit; for therein he considered not himself, but us, that he might be a merciful high priest to us, or a powerful king to defend his people. The Son of God had before his incarnation a glory to which nothing can be added, and a full right which cannot be increased; and whatever glory he received as mediator, it concerneth us more than him.

Doct. That Jesus Christ as mediator, because of his love to righteousness and hatred of sin, is dignified and advanced by God, not only above all men, but also above all angels.

In handling of this point—(1.) I shall speak of the holiness of Christ; (2.) His unction, which is the consequent and fruit of it.

First, Of the holiness of Christ, both as to his person and office.

1. As to his person. There we must consider the original holiness of his natures, divine and human. Divine; he is called, Isa. xlv. 21, 'A just God, and a saviour.' Human; he was wholly free from that original contagion wherewith others that come of Adam are defiled: Luke i. 35, 'That holy thing that shall be born of thee shall be called the Son of God.' Now add to this his perfect actual obedience to God both in heart and life, and this either to the common law of duty that lieth upon all mankind, for it 'became him to fulfil all righteousness,' Mat. iii. 15, or that particular law of mediation which was proper to himself: Heb. v. 8, 'Though he were a son, yet he learned obedience by the things he suffered;' by which he answered the end of the law which we have broken, and was also the meritorious cause of the covenant of grace, by which all blessings are conveyed to us: 2 Cor. v. 21, 'For he hath made him to be sin for us who knew no sin, that we might be made the righteousness of God in him.' Well, then, his personal holiness did make him acceptable to God, and should make him amiable to us. He loved righteousness, and hated iniquity. Adam in the state of innocency did perfectly love righteousness and hate sin

but not constantly, for he soon fell. Believers in the state of regeneration love righteousness and hate iniquity sincerely and constantly, but not perfectly; but Christ, when he assumed our nature, did love righteousness and hate iniquity both perfectly and constantly, in heart and practice, and this even to the death. This qualified him for his office of prophet, priest, and king. As a prophet, who is so fit to teach the world holiness as one that hath a perfect love to holiness and hatred of sin, and this manifested in our nature? Angels are holy and righteous, but not so as Christ, who, besides the essential purity and holiness of the Godhead, hath also assumed our nature, and preserved it in purity and innocency. And therefore his nature and practice agreeth with his design: 1 John iii. 5, 'He was manifested to take away our sins, and in him is no sin.' So as a priest; his holiness gave a value both to the merit of his sacrifice and intercession: Heb. vii. 25, 26, 'Wherefore he is able to save them to the uttermost that come to God by him, seeing he ever liveth to make intercession for them: for such an high priest became us, who is holy, harmless, undefiled, separate from sinners.' Here was a pure, unspotted sacrifice, offered up to God here upon earth, and pleaded and represented in heaven. He that was to satisfy in the behalf of others needed to be free from the defilement of sin himself, that he might be not only our ransom but our pattern. Then as a king, this purity and holiness is necessary, not only that he might powerfully affect, but also favour and patronise all that is good, holy, and just in the world; for, Prov. xv. 9, 'The way of the wicked is an abomination to the Lord, but he loveth him that followeth after righteousness.' The one are the objects of his abomination, the other of his love. The wicked are for a while prosperous and successful, therefore they think God loveth them, but they are an abomination to him into whose hands all judgment is put. They cannot collect or conclude his approbation from his forbearance. No; nor any neglect of human affairs, as if they were left to their own chance and arbitrament. No; all that can be gathered from thence is his great forbearance and mercy to the worst, while he is inviting them to repentance. On the other side you have the disposition of the regenerate set forth, who do not perfunctorily and by-the-by do that which is holy and righteous, but set their whole heart and desire to it. They follow after righteousness; their business is to be eminently holy; and surely they are loved by Christ: for he that hateth iniquity and loveth righteousness will love those that follow after it, than which nothing more sweet, honourable, and blessed can be thought of by us than to be loved by our Redeemer. To have a prince love us, or a wise or learned man love us, we highly value it; what is it then to have Christ love us? This will not be a barren or an empty love. Well, then, he is fit to be the king of the world.

2. All this while we have spoken of his personal holiness, which maketh him acceptable to God and amiable to us, and qualifieth him for his office. Now let us see how he showeth this love to holiness and hatred to iniquity in his office as well as in his person. The general term whereby this office is expressed is *mediator*. The three particular functions are those of prophet, priest, and king.

[1.] As to the general term mediator, whose work it is to bring heaven and earth to kiss each other, or to make peace between God and man, God offended, and man guilty, all that he did therein was out of his love to righteousness and hatred of iniquity, which was the great makebate between God and us; therefore surely his chief design was to destroy sin and to promote holiness. So much we are told, Dan. ix. 24, that the Messiah shall come 'to finish transgressions, and to make an end of sins, and to make reconciliation for iniquity, and to bring in everlasting righteousness, and to seal up the vision and prophecy, and to anoint the Most Holy.' The great business for which the Mediator came into the world was to destroy the reign and power of sin, and to advance the practice of all goodness and holiness, and to recover the lost world to God. Now, because his heart was so much set upon this, God 'anointed him with the oil of gladness above his fellows.'

[2.] Come we to those three particular functions wherein this office is exercised, those of prophet, priest, and king.

(1.) As a prophet, by his doctrine he showeth that he loveth righteousness and hateth iniquity, for the whole frame of it discovereth and breatheth out nothing else but an hatred against sin and a love to holiness: John xvii. 17, 'Sanctify them through the truth; thy word is truth;' Ps. cxix. 140, 'Thy word is very pure.' All the histories, mysteries, precepts, promises, threatenings, aim at this one business, that sin may be subdued in us, and brought into disrepute and disesteem in the world. The histories are certain patterns and examples of holiness, and those taken from men and women that had not divested themselves of the interests and concernments of flesh and blood no more than we have, and yet pleased and served God in their several generations, to excite us to like diligence and self-denial: Heb. vi. 12, 'Be followers of them who through faith and patience inherit the promises.' The mysteries are not only to raise our wonder, but breed a true spirit of godliness: 1 Tim. iii. 16, 'And without controversy great is the mystery of godliness.' The whole gospel is called, Titus i. 1, 'The truth which is after godliness;' and 1 Tim. vi. 3, 'A doctrine which is according to godliness;' because it delivereth the exact and most perfect way of serving God. The Lord Jesus was desirous that this doctrine should take place in the world, therefore he himself was pleased to assume our nature to preach it to us. So for his precepts, they all prescribe an universal adherence to God, and dependence on him, that we may not be carried away by the false offers and delights of sin, but may live in perfect obedience to God, and justice and charity to men. Besides, the word discovereth all the cheats and fallacies we put upon ourselves, to keep us from all impure mixtures of worldly and carnal aims: it discovereth the crafty pretences, and the most insinuating and cunning contrivances to disguise and hide sin: Heb. iv. 12, 'For the word of God is quick and powerful, and sharper than any two-edged sword, piercing even to the dividing asunder of soul and spirit, and of the joints and marrow, and is a discerner of the thoughts and the intents of the heart.' In short, the whole aim of it is that we may please God and be beloved by him: John xiv. 21, 'He that hath my commandments and keepeth them, he it is that loveth me; and he that loveth me, shall be loved of my Father, and I will love him, and will manifest myself to him.' The promises call for the greatest purity and cleanness of heart and life: 2 Cor. vii. 1, 'Having therefore these promises, let us cleanse ourselves from all filthiness both of flesh and spirit, perfecting holiness in the fear of God.' So the threatenings; why doth Christ tell us of torments without end and ease, of a pit without a bottom, of a fire that shall never be quenched, but to make sin more odious and hateful to us? Surely not to terrify us, but to sanctify us; for his government is rather by love than by fear. Now, whosoever wisely considereth the christian religion, he will soon discern that it was framed and set afoot by one that loved righteousness and hated iniquity.

(2.) His priestly office consists in his oblation and intercession, as the high priest under the law did both offer sacrifice and intercede for the people. Now what was the intent of Christ's sacrifice but to put away sin? Heb. ix. 26, 'Now once in the end of the world hath he appeared, to put away sin by the sacrifice of himself;' that is, not only to destroy the guilt, but the power of it. There are three things in the death and sufferings of Christ to make us hate iniquity, and so by consequence to love righteousness—(1.) By way of representation; (2.) By way of impetration; (3.) By way of obligation.

(1*st*.) By way of representation. His bitter sufferings are an instance of God's great wrath against sin and sinners: for if Christ must thus be handled rather than sin shall go unpunished, it warneth us to be very cautious how we meddle with the forbidden fruit. When we remember his bitter agonies, his accursed, shameful death, we should cry out Oh, odious sin! This is the meaning of that expression, Rom. viii. 3, 'And for sin he condemned sin in the flesh;' that is, by a sin-offering, or the sacrifice of Christ, he hath condemned sin, he hath left a brand or mark of his displeasure against sin, which should induce us to be very cautious and watchful against it; for if these things be done in the green tree, what shall be done in the dry?

(2*d*.) By way of impetration and purchase. Christ came not only to expiate the guilt of it, but to get it out of our hearts. As he pacified the wrath of God, so he purchased the Spirit; in which sense our old man is said to be crucified with him, Rom. vi. 6, namely, as grace was obtained whereby it might be crucified. Now we are sluggish and cowardly if we tamely yield to our lusts, and pretend want of power, when it is want of will to cast them off.

(3*d*.) By way of obligation, by this great instance of his love to induce us to kill our love to sin: 1 Peter ii. 24, 'Who his own self bare our sins in his own body on the tree, that we, being dead to sin, should live unto righteousness, by whose stripes we are healed.' Since he hath borne the weight of our sins, and endured the wrath due to them in his own person, if we have any esteem of Christ's love, certainly we would not spare our most beloved lusts, nor be still alive to sin and dead to righteousness, nor wittingly and allowedly do the least thing that is offensive to him: Ezra ix. 14, 'Should we again break thy commandments, and join in affinity with the people of these abominations, wouldst thou not be angry with us till thou hadst consumed us, so that there should be no remnant nor escaping?'

(3.) The next is a king. He is one whose heart was so set upon the love of righteousness, and the hatred of all iniquity, that he would come as a prophet himself to teach the sinful lost world how to become holy again. And as a priest to die for the guilty world to reconcile them to God. Surely he was fit also to rule and govern the world. There are two parts of government—laws and actual administration. His laws are all good and equal, the same with his doctrine. As he giveth notice of these things as a prophet, so he giveth charge about them as a king. Of his laws we need not further speak, but the administration is under our consideration. Now in the righteous ordering the affairs of his kingdom he showeth himself to be one that loveth righteousness and hateth iniquity. As the laws are good and equal, so the administration is right and just. The administration of this kingdom is twofold —internal and external.

(1*st.*) Internal. Christ is set over the church of God as a glorious head and chief, who is to recover a lost people unto God. His internal administration is either effective or remunerative.

(1st.) Effective by his preventing grace, as he changeth our hearts, bringeth us into his kingdom, worketh faith in us, and maketh us willing subjects to him. Conversion is one of his kingly acts, wrought in us by the efficacy of his preventing grace; otherwise we cannot enter into his kingdom: Mat. xviii. 3, 'Except ye be converted, and become as little children, ye shall not enter into the kingdom of heaven;' Col. i. 13, 'Who hath delivered us from the power of darkness, and hath translated us into the kingdom of his dear Son.' Till he subdue the power of sin and Satan in our hearts, we shall still groan under that tyranny: Acts xxvi. 18, 'To open their eyes, and to turn them from darkness to light, and from the power of Satan unto God.'

(2d.) Remunerative, by the rewards of godliness here and hereafter. Here: Rom. xiv. 17, 'For the kingdom of God is not meat and drink, but righteousness, and peace, and joy in the Holy Ghost.' Peace of conscience, increase of grace, joy in the Holy Ghost. They shall not want encouragement who seriously set themselves to love righteousness and hate iniquity: 2 Peter i. 11, 'For so an entrance shall be ministered unto you abundantly into the everlasting kingdom of our Lord and Saviour Jesus Christ.' Hereafter, heaven is the portion of the sanctified: Acts xx. 32, 'And now, brethren, I commend you to God and the word of his grace, which is able to build you up, and to give you an inheritance among all them which are sanctified.' He doth sanctify all that believe on him, and then gives them eternal life.

(2*d.*) External, in the course of his providence. Christ hath set up a government wherein he will favour and protect those that walk uprightly: Ps. xi. 7, 'For the righteous Lord loveth righteousness; his countenance doth behold the upright.' But with the disobedient 'God is angry every day,' Ps. vii. 11. Only it is the day of God's patience. God is preparing himself. Well, then, we must neither rebel against his government nor distrust his defence; for Christ administereth justice in his kingdom, defending the good, and destroying the wicked, and he will in time earnestly espouse the cause of all holiness and righteousness.

Secondly, I come now to the unction of Christ, which is the consequent fruit of the former: 'God, even thy God, hath anointed thee with the oil of gladness above thy fellows.' There you may observe—(1.) The author of this unction, 'God, even thy God;' (2.) The privilege itself, to be 'anointed with the oil of gladness;' (3.) The partakers of this privilege, or the persons to whom it is applied. One principal and singular, who hath the pre-eminence, and that is the Mediator; others inferior, and in a lower degree of participation, called here 'his fellows.' Let us a little explain these things.

1. The author of this unction, 'God, even thy God.' Is this spoken to him as God or man? It may be true in both senses. As to his divine nature he is God of God, or, as it is in John i. 1, 'The Word was with God, and the Word was God.' As to his human nature, he is a creature made of a woman, and so God is his God, as he is the God of all flesh. But especially is this spoken of him as Mediator, so Christ is one of God's confederates. There is a covenant between God and him: John xx. 17, 'I go to my Father and your Father, to my God and your God.' The sum of the covenant was, that after he had suffered here upon earth, and satisfied God's justice by being made a curse for us, he was at length to be raised out of the grave, and exalted to his regal power in heaven. All that belongeth to a covenant is found in this transaction between God and Christ.

[1.] God propoundeth the terms, or demandeth of his Son that he lay down his life; and for his labour he promiseth that he shall see his seed, that God shall give him many children: Isa. liii. 10, 'He shall see his seed, he shall prolong his days, and the pleasure of the Lord shall prosper in his hands.'

[2.] The Son consenteth, and saith, 'A body hast thou prepared for me; Lo, I come to do thy will,' Ps. xl. 6, 7; 'Sacrifice and offering thou didst not desire; mine ears hast thou opened: burnt-offering and sin-offering thou hast not required. Then said I, Lo, I come; in the volume of the book it is written of me.' Here the eternal Son of God doth agree and contract with his Father to perform that perfect obedience to his laws, and to offer up himself such a divine and spotless sacrifice for the sins of the whole world as was necessary for the expiation of sin.

[3.] Christ hath not only consented, but doth with all joy and delight set about this whole will and counsel of God, and go through with the work and office assigned unto him very cheerfully and heartily, till he had brought it to a good end and issue: Ps. xl. 8, 'I delight to do thy will, O my God; yea, thy law is in my heart.'

[4.] After this ready and willing obedience he is to plead the covenant: Ps. lxxxix. 26, 'He shall cry unto me, Thou art my Father, my God, and the rock of my salvation;' Ps. ii. 8, 'Ask of me, and I will give thee the heathen for thine inheritance, and the uttermost parts of the earth for thy possession.' Upon this there is—

[5.] God's answer, 'God, even thy God, hath anointed thee with the oil of gladness above thy fellows;' and Ps. cx. 1, 'The Lord said unto my Lord, Sit thou at my right hand until I make thine enemies thy footstool.' Thus doth the scripture lisp to us in our own dialect, or in such language as we can best understand, concerning that bill of contract or transacted bargain between God and Christ from all eternity, wherein Christ, undertaking perfectly to fulfil the will of God, and to perform all active and passive obedience even unto death, had the promise from God that he should become the author of eternal salvation to all that obey him. The redemption of sinners is not a work of yesterday, nor a business of chance, but well advised, and in infinite wisdom contrived. There was a preparatory agreement to that great work before it was gone about, and therefore it should not be slighted by us, nor lightly passed over.

2. The privilege itself; to be anointed with the oil of gladness. It noteth his solemn exaltation and admission to the exercise of his office. By oil all agree is meant the Spirit, by which Christ was anointed: Luke iv. 18, 'The Spirit of the Lord is upon me, because he hath anointed me.'

[1.] Christ was anointed at his conception in his mother's womb, when he was sanctified by the Holy Spirit; for the work of the Spirit was not only to form his body out of the substance of the virgin, which nature could not do of itself; but chiefly to preserve it from sin, and endow it with the gift of holiness; from which time he grew in wisdom and grace, as well as in stature: Luke ii. 52, 'And Jesus increased in wisdom and stature, and in favour with God and man.'

[2.] Again, Christ may be said to be anointed at his baptism, which was the visible consecration to his office, when the Holy Ghost descended upon him 'in the form of a dove,' Mat. iii. 16, 17, and John i. 33. Once more—

[3.] He may be said to be anointed at his ascension, when he received of the Father the promise of the Spirit to pour him forth upon his disciples: Acts ii. 33, 'Therefore being by the right hand of God exalted and having received of the Father the promise of the Holy Ghost, he hath shed forth this, which ye now see and hear.' This I take to be the sense here, his glorious exaltation at the right hand of God, where, being possessed of all power, he joyfully expecteth and accomplisheth the fruits of his redemption. I am the more confirmed in this—

(1.) Because the exaltation of Christ is as it were his welcome to heaven; God doth as it were take him by the hand, and set him upon the throne after all the sorrows of his humiliation. As we welcome a stranger or a guest whose coming is pleasing to us by taking him by the hand and bringing him into our houses, so is Christ exalted by the right hand of God, and welcomed into heaven, as having done his work, and made full provision for the glory of God and the obedience of the creature; as we are also received into glory after we are guided by his counsel: Ps. lxxiii. 24, 'Thou shalt guide me by thy counsel, and afterward receive me to glory;' and then all tears shall be wiped from our eyes.

(2.) The term, 'the oil of gladness,' implieth it; for that was the entertainment of honourable guests invited to a feast. We see it practised to Christ by one woman: Luke vii. 37, 'And behold, a woman in the city, which was a sinner, when she knew that Jesus sat at meat in the pharisee's house, brought an alabaster box of ointment.' And by another: Mat. xxvi. 7, 'There came unto him a woman having an alabaster box of very precious ointment, and poured it on his head as he sat at meat.' And the psalmist, speaking of God's festival entertainment: Ps. xxiii. 5, 'Thou preparest a table before me in the presence of mine enemies; thou anointest my head with oil.' Another mention of this practice is, Ps. civ. 15, 'Wine to make glad the heart of man, and oil to make his face to shine.' All these places, and many more in the scripture, allude to the custom of pouring some fragrant precious ointments on the heads of guests of special eminency, called 'the oil of gladness,' because the use of it was to exhilarate and cheer the spirits. Now, because this was an extraordinary respect paid them, this phrase came at length to signify the preferring one above another; and so it is fitly applied to Christ, whom God hath dignified above all men and angels, in that he hath received power spiritual and divine above what was communicated to any other.

3. The persons anointed.

[1.] One singular in this unction, the Lord Jesus Christ. There are two sorts of privileges—(1.) Some things only given to Christ, not to us; as the name above all names to be adored, Phil. ii. 9; to be the head of the renewed state, Eph. i. 21, the saviour of the body, Eph. v. 23; to have power to dispense the Spirit, to administer providences, &c. All this is proper to Christ; neither men nor angels share with him in these honours. (2.) There are other things given to Christ and his people; as the sanctifying and comforting Spirit, the heavenly inheritance, victory over our spiritual enemies, the devil, the world, and the flesh; these are given to us and him; only God doth grace his Son above his fellows: Rom. viii. 29, 'That he might be the first-born among many brethren.' He must have the honour due to the first-born. Anciently the first-born was lord of the rest of the family: Gen. xxvii. 37, 'And Isaac answered and said unto Esau, Behold, I have made him thy lord, and all his brethren have I given to him for servants.' And also the first-born gave the rest of the brethren a share of the father's goods, reserving to himself a double portion: Deut. xxi. 17, 'He shall acknowledge the son of the hated for the first-born by giving him a double portion of all that he hath, for he is the beginning of his strength, the right of the first-born is his.' Christ being the first-born, he must in all things have the pre-eminence. In our conflicts and trials he is 'the captain of our salvation,' Heb. ii. 10. In holiness he is our pattern, or the copy which we must transcribe: 2 Cor. iii. 18, 'Are changed into the same image from glory to glory.' *Primum in unoquoque genere est mensura et regula cæterorum*—The first in every kind is the standard for all the rest. In our glory and blessedness he is our forerunner, Heb. vi. 20, having actually taken possession of that felicity and glory which he will bestow upon his followers; so that Christ's honour is reserved, and believers are comforted whilst they follow their head in every state and condition.

[2.] Others are admitted to be partakers of this grace in a lower degree, called 'his fellows.' They are also dignified and graced by God above the rest of the world, but not as Christ was. Two things I will observe here—

(1.) They must be his consorts and fellows. Sometimes they are called 'his brethren,' Heb. ii. 11; sometimes members of his mystical body, Eph. i. 22, 23; sometimes 'joint-heirs with Christ,' Rom. viii. 17; meaning thereby all believers, who are companions with him both in grace and glory. Thus we must be before we partake of this anointing. *Actus activorum sunt in passivo unito et disposito*—They that receive influence from another must be fitted for what they receive, and united to him from whom they receive it. Therefore none but Christ's members and fellows do partake of his unction. But who are they? All such as are like-minded with himself, that love righteousness, and hate iniquity, that set themselves seriously to promote the glory of God, and to destroy the reign of sin in the world, both in themselves and others; in short, those that are regenerated and planted into his mystical body by the Spirit.

(2.) The next thing which I observe is, that all these may have somewhat of this unction according to their measure and part which they sustain in the body: 1 John ii. 20, 'But we have an unction from the Holy One;' compare Ps. cxxxiii. 2, 'It is like the precious ointment upon the head, that ran down upon the beard, even Aaron's beard, that went down to the skirts of his garments.' The ointment poured upon our head in such plenty that it diffuseth itself to all his members, God is the author thereof: 2 Cor. i. 21, 'Now he that establisheth us with you in Christ, and hath anointed us, is God.' It is a divine work but the pipe or means of conveying it to us is Christ, who is the great receptacle from whence the whole family is supplied: John i. 16, 'Of his fulness have all we received, and grace for grace.' And it mainly consisteth in the gift of the Spirit, sanctifying and preparing us for our present work and final reward, and comforting us with our present interest in the love of God and hopes of glory: 2 Cor. v. 5, 'Now he that hath wrought us for this self-same thing is God, who also hath given unto us the earnest of the Spirit.'

Use. I shall exhort you to two things—(1.) To holiness; (2.) To get more of the oil of gladness.

1. To holiness. If there were no more than that it is pleasing to Christ, and visibly exemplified in his own person, this should induce us. It was love to holiness and hatred of sin that brought him out of heaven, and put him on the work of our redemption. Nothing doth more urge us to do a thing than love, or to forbear it than hatred. These were Christ's motives to undertake the redemption of sinners. Now we should love what he loveth, and hate what he hateth: Rev. ii. 6, 'Thou hatest the deeds of the Nicolaitans, which I also hate;' Prov. viii. 13, 'The fear of the Lord is to hate evil, pride, and arrogancy; and the evil way and the froward mouth do I hate.' But there is more in the argument than so. This was the design of our Redeemer: 1 John iii. 8, 'For this purpose the Son of God was manifested, that he might destroy the works of the devil.' Now it doth not become christians to contradict the designed end of their Redeemer. But this is not all; it is to slight the price of our redemption, as if there were no such great mystery in it, that the Son of God should die; for if we slight the benefits we slight the ransom, 1 Peter i. 18. Yea, there is this further in it, we neglect the grace that may be had upon such easy terms. Surely the coming of our Lord Jesus Christ did somewhat shorten the power of sin, or else he came in vain. He obtained the grace he purchased: John xii. 31, 'Now is the judgment of this world; now shall the prince of this world be cast out.' These are the glorious fruits and effects of his death, that it shall tend to the glory of God and the bringing down

the kingdom of sin and Satan in the world. They to whom this purchase is revealed, and yet reject the offer, are guilty of sluggish cowardice, and if they be not delivered from the power of the devil, and restored to a life of holiness, their condemnation is just. In our natural estate by the fall of Adam we were all corrupted and out of frame, but the second Adam came to restore things that were in confusion and out of frame to their right and primitive order. Man hath fallen from holiness and happiness; sin and Satan have reigned and raged in this world; the children of this world have blessed themselves in their bad condition, and delighted in their slavery and bondage. Now if Christ come to make an end of sin and bring in everlasting righteousness, shall it be so still as it was before? shall the disordered world go on in its ancient wont? Surely there should be more visible fruits of his coming seen among us. If men should lie in wickedness still, and turn their backs upon God, after whose image they were created, and sin and Satan rule them at their pleasure, how are things put in frame that were out of course? What hath the Son of God done by all his holy life and bloody sufferings? Surely either the purchase is not so great and glorious, or we make but little use of it, and so are quite strangers in God's Israel.

I have not done with the argument yet. We have no communion with Christ, yea, we renounce it, if we continue to be so unlike him: 1 John i. 6–8, 'If we say we have fellowship with him, and walk in darkness, we lie, and do not the truth; but if we walk in the light, as he is in the light, then have we fellowship one with another, and the blood of Jesus Christ his Son cleanseth us from all sin. If we say we have no sin, we deceive ourselves, and the truth is not in us.' Such a solemn preface introduceth that truth, to show that if we live in our sins, we shall die in our sins, and then farewell all happiness.

2. To look after more of this unction. He is Christ the anointed of God; we must be christians: Acts xi. 26, 'The disciples were called christians first in Antioch;' anointed with the Holy Ghost and with power, that we may understand the mind of God, consecrate ourselves to him, work his work, and engage in his warfare, fighting against the devil, the world, and the flesh, till we triumph with Christ in heaven. All must be anointed.

[1.] This is the fruit of Christ's exaltation, to send and shed abroad the Spirit. There are effects of Christ's humiliation and effects of Christ's exaltation. The effects of Christ's humiliation are taking away the curse of the law, pacifying God's wrath, satisfying his justice, the annihilation of the right which the devil had over sinners, a right to return to God and enjoy eternal life. The exaltation of Christ also hath its effects; the application of this grace and the execution of this right, by quickening us who were dead in trespasses and sins, and pardoning our transgressions, and putting us into the way everlasting. Now we should seek in Christ not only the force of satisfaction but the force of regeneration, and his efficacious grace to apply what he hath purchased for us, that he may be 'made sanctification to us' as well as 'righteousness,' 1 Cor. i. 30. Since Christ is so able and willing to dispense this grace freely and abundantly into men's hearts, surely it should not be neglected.

[2.] Consider the necessity of this grace. Our love to righteousness and hatred of iniquity is the fruit of this unction, for affections follow the nature. When we live in the Spirit we shall walk in the Spirit: Ps. xcvii. 10, 'Ye that love the Lord, hate evil.' All that pretend to return to God must show the reality of it this way. Therefore, as you would be pleasing to Christ, do not neglect this grace.

[3.] Consider the utility and profit. It is for our comfort. The Spirit is called 'the oil of gladness,' because the benefits whereof we are partakers are matters of great joy: Acts xiii. 52, 'The disciples were filled with joy and with the Holy Ghost;' Acts viii. 39, 'He went on his way rejoicing;' Acts xvi. 34, 'He rejoiced, believing in God with all his house.' It is for our honour we are dignified above others, the more we are made partakers of the Spirit: 1 Peter ii. 9, 'Ye are a chosen generation, a royal priesthood, a holy nation, a peculiar people.'

SERMONS UPON ACTS XXIV. 14-16.

SERMON I.

Believing all things which are written in the law and the prophets: and have hope towards God, which they themselves also allow, that there shall be a resurrection of the dead, both of the just and unjust. And herein do I exercise myself, to have always a conscience void of offence towards God, and towards man.—ACTS xxiv. 14–16.

THESE words are part of Paul's apology against the accusation of Tertullus. Among other things, he chargeth him to be an heretic, or an apostate from the Jewish religion. When the Romans had conquered the Jews, they submitted upon this condition, that they should innovate and change nothing in their religion, but defend it against the disturbers of it. Now the christians being accused of innovation and disturbance of such a religion as was under the caution of the Roman laws before a Roman tribunal, it concerned them to show the harmony and agreement of both religions as to the substance. This is Paul's business, and therefore he giveth an account of his faith, worship, and conversation. He did indeed observe the way of the christian worship, which they called sectarism or heresy, and Paul was accused 'to be a ringleader of the sect of the Nazarenes,' ver. 5; but yet this was agreeable enough to the religion of the Jews for the substance, which he proveth by his faith, hope, carriage, and conversation.

Here is in effect all christianity delivered to us in one prospect and view.

1. An account of his faith at the bottom of all, 'Believing all things which are written in the law and the prophets.'

2. His hope, as the immediate fruit of it, 'And have hope towards God;' and the principal object is, 'The resurrection of the dead, both of the just and the unjust,' when we shall enjoy the full of what we wait for.

3. An account of his manners, where you have a brief description of a christian conversation, 'Herein do I exercise myself, to have always a conscience void of offence both towards God and towards men.' My business is not to discuss all these branches of christianity apart, and in their full latitude, but to give you the sum and delineation of all religion in one view. Therefore observe—

Doct. That true christianity is such a believing the truths contained in the scriptures as produceth an hope of eternal life, and is expressed in an impartial, uniform, and constant obedience.

Here is Paul's apology; faith at the bottom, hope as the immediate effect and product of it, and an holy conversation as the fruit and consequent. The same method is observed in other scriptures; as 1 Tim. i. 5, 'The end of the commandment is charity, out of a pure heart, and of a good conscience, and of faith unfeigned.' The commandment is the gospel institution, and this received with a pure heart and faith unfeigned produceth a good conscience, which shows itself in love to God and men, by a true and lively faith in Christ. The Holy Ghost purifieth the heart and conscience, and so produceth love: 2 Peter i. 5, 6, 'Add to your faith virtue, and to virtue knowledge, and to knowledge temperance, and to temperance patience, and to patience godliness.' In the chain of graces faith is the root of all. I shall—
(1.) Examine the expressions here used; (2.) Give some reasons why this is true christianity.

I. Examine the expressions here used.

First, Concerning faith, 'Believing all things that are written in the law and the prophets.'

1. Here is the object, or things believed, 'Things written in the law and the prophets.'
2. The extent, 'All.'
3. The act, 'Believing.'

1. The object, 'Things written in the law and the prophets.' Law and prophets is an expression commonly used for all the scriptures then extant: Mat. xi. 13, 'For all the prophets and the law prophesied until John;' and Luke xvi. 29, 'They have Moses and the prophets; let them hear them.' The books of the Old Testament are thus called. We christians, who have received the canon and rule of faith more enlarged, are said 'To be built on the foundation of the prophets and apostles,' Eph. ii. 20; so that now the object of our faith is prophets and apostles. The object of faith may be considered formally or materially. Materially, such things as God hath revealed; formally, because God hath revealed them. If God hath revealed what is in the writings of the apostles, then we are to believe them. God's veracity is the ground and support of our faith, into which it is ultimately resolved. His instruments in revealing are the prophets and apostles. We know God hath revealed the things written by them, partly because these writings are delivered to us by the universal tradition of the church, and the testimony of christians through all successions of ages, in whose experience God hath blessed these writings for conviction, conversion, and consolation; and partly because of the consent between the prophets and the apostles, the one foretelling whatever the other declared as accomplished: Acts xxvi. 22, 'Having therefore obtained help of God, I continue unto this day, witnessing both to small and great, saying none other things than those which the prophets and Moses did say should come.' Partly because the doctrines have an impress of God upon them, as everything that hath passed his hand hath. How do I know a fly, gnat, or any other creature to be made by God? God hath set his signature upon them: Ps. xix. 1, 'The heavens

declare the glory of God, and the firmament showeth his handiwork.' So the scriptures agree with the nature and properties of God. As God is wise, powerful, and good, these doctrines become his wisdom; they have the stamp of his moral goodness, which is his holiness; and as for his power, they that feel it not fear it: John iii. 20, 'For every one that doeth evil hateth the light, neither cometh to the light, lest his deeds should be reproved.' There is something that alarmeth the conscience. And partly because it agreeth with the nature of man, so far as a man hath any good left in him. It agreeth with the necessities of man, his guilty fears and his desires of happiness. For his guilty fears, men, that by reason of sin are afraid of God's justice, cannot be quieted by any other means, but are by this: Jer. vi. 16, 'Stand ye in the ways, and see, and ask for the old paths, where is the good way, and walk therein, and you shall find rest for your souls;' Mat. xi. 28, 'Come unto me, all ye that labour and are heavy laden, and I will give you rest.' In life and death the conscience is quieted. So for desires of happiness. Men rove and grope about for some satisfying good: Acts xvii. 27, 'That they should seek the Lord, if haply they might feel after him, and find him;' And Ps. iv. 6, 'There be many that say, Who will show us any good?' Life and immortality are brought to light in the scriptures, and the way to obtain it clearly revealed: Ps. xvi. 11, 'Thou wilt show me the path of life; in thy presence is fulness of joy, and at thy right hand are pleasures for evermore.' Partly because God hath witnessed and attested it by his Spirit: Acts v. 32, 'We are witnesses of these things, and so is also the Holy Ghost.' Without, by miracles and other wonderful effects; within, by enlightening the heart and mind, inclining and exciting us to believe it upon these motives and arguments: 2 Cor. iv. 6, 'God, who commanded the light to shine out of darkness, hath shined in our hearts, to give the light of the knowledge of the glory of God in the face of Jesus Christ;' so as to discern God's impress. Upon these accounts we receive what is written in the prophets and apostles as revealed by God.

2. The extent, 'All things.' A believer receiveth all truths which are of divine revelation, whether precepts, promises, threatenings, doctrines, or histories. But then we must distinguish of an implicit or explicit faith. With the latter we can only believe those things which we know; what we know not we cannot believe with an explicit faith. Some christians know not all things which are contained in the prophets and apostles, and yet in a sense they do believe by an implicit faith; as Agrippa believed the prophets: Acts xxvi. 27, 'King Agrippa, believest thou the prophets? I know that thou believest.' Yet he was ignorant of some things revealed by them. So all christians own the writings of the apostles and prophets as the rule and warrant of faith, yet they do not discern every truth therein contained; they do believe that whatever the prophets and apostles say and have written is true, and so are ready to believe all things which shall be demonstrated to them to be written or said by them. But by an explicit faith they believe all fundamental truths, such as are absolutely necessary to salvation, and usually most other truths which are next to fundamentals. The fundamentals are set down, John xvii. 3, 'This is life eternal, to

know thee the only true God, and Jesus Christ, whom thou hast sent.' That God is to be known, loved, obeyed, worshipped, and enjoyed, and that the Lord Jesus is our Redeemer and Saviour, to bring us home to God, with his gifts of pardon and life, to be begun by the Spirit here, and perfected in heaven.

3. The act, 'Believing.' It is not enough not to deny or not to contradict, but we must actually and positively believe. The reason why the generality of people living in the christian world feel so little force of their faith is from their inadvertency; they leap into the christian faith by the advantage of their birth, but do not consider what they believe, nor why they should believe it, and how they are concerned in it; and so may be rather said not to contradict than to believe. But true faith is a positive, firm assent, excited in us by the Spirit of God. As the apostle saith of some that were zealous for the law, 'Understanding neither what they say, nor whereof they affirm,' 1 Tim. i. 7, so the rabble of common christians may be zealous for the gospel, yet are not instructed in the nature and grounds of it, what and why they should believe. A sound belief requireth a thorough understanding of what we believe, and a deep consideration of the grounds and reasons why we are to believe it. And then it is such a fixed assent as is not perplexed and haunted with doubts about the truth of it, and such a close adherence as is not discouraged with difficulties and oppositions. It would be much better with the christian world if every one that carrieth the name of a christian could say, 'I believe all that is written in the prophets and the apostles.' In short—

To a sound belief there is necessary—

[1.] A knowledge or full instruction in the things which we believe; for it is said, 1 John iv. 16, 'We have known and believed the love that God hath to us;' first known and then believed.

[2.] A due conviction of the certainty of them: Luke i. 4, 'That thou mayest know the certainty of those things wherein thou hast been instructed;' and John vi. 69, 'We believe and are sure, that thou art that Christ, the Son of the living God;' and John xvii. 8, 'They have known surely that I came out from thee, and they have believed that thou didst send me.'

[3.] This faith doth not only imply a bare intellectual assent, but a practical trust and affiance; for the nature of the object requireth so much. Christianity doth not only propound bare truths to be assented unto, but joyful, comfortable truths suitable to our necessity and desires; and therefore we must depend upon them, seek our happiness in them in the way appointed by God, which is nothing but practical trust and affiance. Therefore it is not a bare opinion, but a reliance upon God, that he will make good his word to us, whilst we continue with patience in well-doing. Therefore we are said to belong to Christ, 'If we hold fast the confidence and the rejoicing of the hope firm unto the end,' Heb. iii. 6.

[4.] Those truths which are contained in the word are to be considered with application, that we may know them for our good: Job v. 27, 'Hear it, and know thou it for thy good.' Every doctrine, which upon search we find to be sound and good, we must make application of it to ourselves, that it may affect our own hearts; if threatenings, that we may escape the curse; if comforts or promises, Rom. viii. 32, 'What shall we say to these things?' The promise of pardon to all believers is so universal, that it includeth you as well as others. Christ is offered to every creature, that he may be yours as well as another's; and the offer of heaven and eternal life is so propounded that you should engage your hearts to seek after it, and closely to adhere to it till you obtain it. But to apply it so as to be persuaded that your own sins are already pardoned, that you are an heir of glory, that you are Christ's as to actual interest, you must have good evidence for that from a spiritual sense of your own qualifications: but it belongeth not to faith simply taken. Thus we have set forth a christian in his first part, as a believer.

Secondly, The apostle asserts his hope, 'And have hope towards God, which they themselves allow, that there shall be a resurrection of the dead, both of the just and unjust.'

1. Mark that he propoundeth his hope as the immediate effect and product of faith; for when I believe, then I must look and long, and prepare for the blessedness offered, otherwise my faith is but a cold opinion, not such a faith as will subdue the inclinations and interests of the flesh, nor make the labours and sufferings of the spiritual life tolerable: and that is true faith which breatheth and longeth after the end of all religion, and looketh for it. What good will it do me to believe the doctrines of the prophets and apostles, if I expect no good from thence? Faith would be vain, and religion vain. Only note here that hope is twofold—

[1.] One the fruit of regeneration, or the immediate effect of conversion to God: 1 Peter i. 3, 'Blessed be the God and Father of our Lord Jesus Christ, which according to his abundant mercy hath begotten us again unto a lively hope.' And this is nothing else but a seeking and looking for a happiness in another and an unseen world, with a longing desire and diligent care to obtain it. It is faith to place my happiness so high and so far from sense; now when my desires and delights are there, and my daily care is to get thither, and to live in a continual preparation for it, and desirous expectation of it, and to deny myself, and suffer any loss and pain to get thither, this is the work of hope.

[2.] There is an hope built upon experience: Rom. v. 4, 5, 'And experience hope, and hope maketh not ashamed, because the love of God is shed abroad in our hearts by the Holy Ghost.' This dependeth upon the sense of my qualification and interest, and is confirmed by experience of God's love to my soul, for grace hath the force of an evidence and pledge.

2. Observe that he pitcheth upon the resurrection as the great thing hoped for, because then is our full and final happiness. We do not believe in Christ unless we believe in him for eternal life: 1 Tim. i. 16, 'That in me first Jesus Christ might show forth all long-suffering, for a pattern to them that should hereafter believe on him to life everlasting;' John xx. 31, 'But these things are written that ye might believe that Jesus is the Christ, the Son of God, and that, believing, ye might have life through his name.' This is the great thing which we hope, wait, and labour for. Nobody would trouble themselves about religion, which abridgeth us of present delights, and exposeth us to

great troubles and sufferings, but for these things. Who would deny himself, and devote himself entirely to God, but for these things? 1 Cor. xv. 19, 'If in this life only we have hope in Christ, we are of all men most miserable;' but at the resurrection all shall be recompensed to us, all the effects of sin cease.

3. Observe that he proposeth the double resurrection, of good and bad; all that ever lived shall be judged and rewarded, whether good or evil; though with a hope to be found among the good and among the sheep, not the goats. This is the true way of christian reflection upon the great day; however we are assured of our own interest, that whilst we strengthen faith and hope, we weaken the security of the flesh. Some may miscarry, though I have hopes to be accepted: 1 Cor. ix. 26, 27, 'I therefore so run, not as uncertainly; so fight I, not as one that beateth the air; but I keep under my body, and bring it into subjection, lest that by any means, when I have preached to others, I myself should be a castaway.' We have a covenant wherein to trust, as long as we continue faithful with God, and deny the flesh its satisfactions.

Thirdly, See what account he giveth of his manners and conversation: ver. 16, 'And herein do I exercise myself, to have always a conscience void of offence both towards God and towards men.'

Observe here three things—(1.) The encouragement; (2.) The integrity of his obedience; (3.) The laborious diligence wherewith he carried it on.

First, His encouragement, $\grave{\epsilon}\nu$ $\tau o \acute{u} \tau \varphi$. Interpreters diversely expound this $\grave{\epsilon}\nu$ $\tau o \acute{u} \tau \varphi$ ($\chi \rho \acute{o} \nu \varphi$), *interea temporis*, in the meantime, till faith be turned into vision, hope into fruition. There is a time between believing and possessing, hoping and having; and during that time there is much exercise for our faith and patience: Heb. vi. 12, 'That ye be not slothful, but followers of them who through faith and patience inherit the promises.' Again, $\grave{\epsilon}\nu$ $\tau o \acute{u} \tau \varphi$, by virtue of this faith and hope, upon this hope and encouragement. Faith and a good conscience are often coupled: 1 Tim. i. 5, 'Now the end of the commandment is charity, out of a pure heart, and of a good conscience, and of faith unfeigned.' We cannot keep the one without the other; not a good conscience without faith, nor faith without a good conscience. Not the first, for no man will make conscience of his duty unless he believeth in God and hopeth for salvation; for unless we believe in God and hope for his promises, we shall not be so careful to keep a good conscience, by eschewing evil and doing good. Sometimes faith is said to work by love, and sometimes by hope. By love: Gal. v. 6, 'For in Jesus Christ neither circumcision availeth anything, nor uncircumcision, but faith that worketh by love.' The soul is never fit for duty till it be possessed with the love of God and man. Sometimes by hope: 1 John iii. 3, 'He that hath this hope in him purifieth himself as God is pure.' And the second is evident, for it is said, 1 Tim. i. 19, 'Holding faith and a good conscience, which some having put away, concerning faith have made shipwreck.' Any great lust cherished will destroy our faith and hopes, as a man cannot long subsist in a leaky vessel. So 1 Tim. iii. 9, 'Holding the mystery of faith in a pure conscience.' Precious liquors are best kept in a clean vessel.

Secondly, The integrity of his obedience, set forth in all the necessary requisites.

1. There is sincerity asserted. For his conscience was in it, and a good conscience. Now conscience is that faculty which is apt to take God's part, and is the judgment a man maketh upon his actions, morally considered, in order to praise and dispraise, reward and punishment; and the goodness of conscience consisteth in its ability to do its office, in its clearness, purity, tenderness, quietness, or peaceableness. For its clearness: a blind conscience is an evil conscience; for 'without knowledge the heart is not good,' Prov. ix. 2. As a judge that understandeth not the laws of the country is unfit to give judgment in any matter that cometh before him, or as a dim eye cannot do the office of an eye, so a blind conscience is no competent judge of our duty to God. So for the purity of conscience: 1 Peter iii. 21, 'Not the putting away of the filthiness of the flesh, but the answer of a good conscience towards God;' and Heb. xiii. 18, 'We trust we have a good conscience, willing in all things to live honestly.' A good conscience is an heart set to please God in all things, an heart hating sin and loving holiness. Again, tenderness is another property of a good conscience when it is wakeful, and smiteth for sin upon all occasions offered. This property may be understood by what the apostle saith of heathens for gross sins: Rom. ii. 15, 'Which show the work of the law written on their hearts, their consciences also bearing witness, and their thoughts in the meantime accusing or else excusing one another.' In David: 1 Sam. xxiv. 5, 'David's heart smote him because he had cut off Saul's skirt;' and by what Job saith, chap. xxvii. 6, 'My heart shall not reproach me as long as I live.' The opposite is a seared conscience that hath no feeling: 1 Tim. iv. 2, 'Having their consciences seared with a hot iron.' This we contract by frequent heinous sinning, or by a customary practice of that which is evil, by which the heart groweth as hard as the highway which is trod upon. Quietness of conscience is another property, whereby the goodness of it is discerned; only this quietness must arise from the former properties, else it is a dead, sleepy, seared conscience. For in this we must consider not who hath most quiet, but who hath most cause; as in buildings, not the fairness of the structure, but the foundation of it is to be regarded. There is a quiet evil conscience: Luke xi. 21, 'When a strong man armed keepeth his palace, his goods are in peace.' When wind and tide go together there is a calm, but the quiet good conscience is from faith in Christ: Rom. v. 1, 'Being justified by faith, we have peace with God;' from a sense of our sincere dealing with God: 2 Cor. i. 12, 'For our rejoicing is this, the testimony of our conscience, that in simplicity and godly sincerity, not with fleshly wisdom, but by the grace of God, we have had our conversation in the world.' A serenity resulting from our peace with God and close walking with him.

2. The strictness and exactness of the apostle's course. He would keep this good conscience 'void of offence.' It may be understood passively or actively. Passively, that conscience be not offended and suffer wrong; actively, that we offend not, or offer wrong to others.

[1.] That conscience be not offended, or receive wrong by any miscarriage of ours, for it is a tender thing. The least dust in the eye hindereth its use, so doth sin offend and trouble the conscience. Take those four notions before mentioned. Clearness: Mat. v. 8, 'Blessed are the pure in heart, for they shall see God.' A dusty glass hindereth the sight of the image, so lust cloudeth the mind. In regard of purity; so far as we give way to sin, conscience is defiled. The apostle speaketh of some 'whose minds and consciences were defiled,' Titus i. 15. It is defiled by sin. In regard of tenderness, nothing bringeth a brawn upon conscience so much as frequent and allowed sinning in small things. First it is wounded, and then hardened, and so groweth dead and sleepy; though it may write, it refuseth to speak; it is a register when it is not a witness. So it is offended in regard of quietness. An offended conscience will offend us, and 'a wounded spirit who can bear?' Prov. xviii. 14. You may as well expect to touch the flesh with a burning coal without pain as to sin without trouble of conscience. Sin will bring shame and horror ever since Adam's experience, who was afraid and ashamed, Gen. iii. 7.

[2.] The second sense, that we offend not, nor offer wrong to others, will fall in with the next head.

3. The impartiality of his obedience, 'Both towards God and towards men.' There are two tables, and we are to take care we do not give offence to God or men, by neglecting our duty to either.

[1.] Our chief care should be that we do not make a breach upon our love to God. Conscience standeth always in dread of God's eye and presence, to whom it is most accountable: Acts xxiii. 1, 'I have lived in all good conscience before God until this day;' O 'grieve not the Spirit!' Eph. iv. 30. Offend not the pure eyes of his glory.

[2.] That we do not offend men: Rom. xii. 17, $\pi\rho o\nu o o \dot{\upsilon} \mu \varepsilon \nu o \iota\ \tau \grave{\alpha}\ \kappa \alpha \lambda \grave{\alpha}$, 'Provide things honest in the sight of all men.' We must be careful of our conscience before God and frame with men, that we neither seduce them by our example nor grieve them by any unjust or uncharitable carriage of ours, but be blameless to men.

4. The constancy, $\delta \iota \alpha \pi \alpha \nu \tau \grave{o} \varsigma$, 'always,' in all cases, by all means, at all times. A conscience brought forth at times, and for certain turns, is not a good conscience: Job xiii. 18, 'Behold now I have ordered my cause; I know that I shall be justified.' A man is tried by his course, not by a step or two: 1 Peter i. 15, 'As he that hath called you is holy, so be ye holy in all manner of conversation,' $\dot{\varepsilon}\nu\ \pi \acute{\alpha} \sigma \eta\ \dot{\alpha} \nu \alpha \sigma \tau \rho o \phi \hat{\eta}$; in every creek and corner of your lives, not in an humour and in good moods. A christian is everywhere like himself, and never dareth to do anything knowingly against conscience.

Thirdly, The laborious diligence wherewith he carried it on: 'I exercise myself.' We must make it our constant labour and endeavour, by a diligent search into the mind of God: Rom. xii. 2, 'That we may prove what is the good and acceptable will of God;' Eph. v. 17, 'Be not unwise, but understanding what the will of the Lord is;' Eph. v. 10, 'Proving what is acceptable unto the Lord,' that we may not offend him in worship or daily conversation. By a serious inquiry into the state of our own hearts and ways: Ps. iv. 4, 'Stand in awe, and sin not; commune with your hearts upon your bed, and be still.' If we would have conscience speak to us, we must often speak to conscience: Jer. viii. 6, 'I hearkened and heard, but they spake not aright; no man repented him of his wickedness, saying, What have I done?' Ask questions of your hearts. And also by a constant watchfulness and taking heed to our feet: Ps. xxxix. 1, 'I said, I will take heed to my ways, that I offend not with my tongue.' Many live as if they had no conscience, and by a broken-hearted making use of Christ's death: Rom. v. 1, 'Being justified by faith, we have peace with God, through our Lord Jesus Christ;' and 1 John ii. 1, 'If any man sin, we have an advocate with the Father, Jesus Christ the righteous;' and Heb. ix. 14, 'How much more shall the blood of Christ, who through the eternal Spirit offered himself to God without spot, purge your conscience from dead works to serve the living God.' By a serious resistance and mortification of sin, cutting off the right hand, and pulling out the right eye, Mat. v. 29, 30; and Gal. v. 24, 'They that are Christ's have crucified the flesh with the affections and lusts;' and by the use of all holy means which God hath appointed.

II. The reasons why this is true christianity.

1. The necessity of it. It is a great question how far obedience belongeth to faith, whether as a part, or as an end, fruit, and consequent? I answer—Both ways. Consent of subjection is a part of faith, actual obedience a fruit of it. In the covenant there is a consent first before practice. Faith believeth the precepts as well as the promises: Ps. cxix. 66, 'Teach me good judgment and knowledge, for I have believed thy commandments;' Heb. x. 22, 'Let us draw near with a true heart, in full assurance of faith, having our hearts sprinkled from an evil conscience, and our bodies washed with pure water.' It believeth the promises to sweeten obedience to us; it hath a persuasive oratory, as it worketh by love or hope. It worketh us to an observance of the precepts by the hopes of the resurrection, lest we be enticed from them either by things grateful or troublesome to present sense: 1 Cor. xv. 58, 'Be steadfast and unmoveable, always abounding in the work of the Lord, forasmuch as you know that your work is not in vain in the Lord.' If you believe things written in the law and the prophets, you will see your labour is not in vain in the Lord.

2. The comfort of obedience to us. We cannot make out our evidence and plea but by a uniform, constant, and impartial obedience. Principles are latent till they discover themselves by their fruit. Our faith and hope is but a fancy unless it prevail over sensitive inclinations to present things, that we may live in the patient and delightful service of God, and an entire obedience to his holy will. The sap is not seen, but the apples and fruit appear: Acts xxvi. 20, 'That they should repent and turn to God, and do works meet for repentance;' Mat. iii. 8, 'Bring forth therefore fruits meet for repentance;' we can else have no comfortable evidence of it.

3. It is for the honour of Christ, as well as our own comfort and safety. Obedience maketh faith visible and sensible: 2 Thes. i. 11, 12, 'And fulfil all the good pleasure of his goodness, and the work of faith with power, that the name of our Lord Jesus Christ may be glorified in you, and ye in him.' An holy conversation bringeth doctrines near to our senses, and thereby it is more clear and powerful to gain upon others: Christ hath the honour, we the reward: John xv. 8, 'Herein is my father glorified, that ye bring forth much fruit, so

shall ye be my disciples;' and Phil. i. 11, 'Being filled with the fruits of righteousness, which are by Jesus Christ unto the glory and praise of God.' Uniform practice is such a fruit of grace as representeth the doctrine of life with advantage to the consciences of others; otherwise we shall never do any great things for Christ in the world.

SERMON II.

Believing all things which are written in the law and the prophets: and have hope towards God, which they themselves also allow, that there shall be a resurrection of the dead, both of the just and unjust. And herein do I exercise myself, to have always a conscience void of offence towards God and towards man.—
ACTS xxiv. 14–16.

USE 1. Is disproof of the nullifidians, and solifidians; those that cry up good life without faith, and, on the other side, that cry up empty faith without obedience and holiness.

1. Nullifidians, who are very rife among us, who do as wisely as those that would plant a tree by the top, and not by the root; so they cry up a morality without the faith and hope of the gospel, and that love to God which is engendered by it; and so, out of a fondness of pagan strictness and philosophic institution, defy the religion they were bred up in. There can be no true love to God or man without the faith of the gospel. The apostle telleth us, Rom. vii. 4, 'That we are married to him who was raised from the dead, that we may bring forth fruit to God.' As the children who are born before marriage are illegitimate, so all that justice, and temperance, and charity which is not cherished in us by the love of God, and faith in Christ, and the hopes of the other world, is but mock grace and bastard holiness, and is not acceptable to God.

I shall prove two things—

[1.] That morality is not kindly unless it be founded on the gospel, and never so thoroughly promoted as by the principles laid down there: Titus ii. 11, 12, 'The grace of God, that bringeth salvation, hath appeared to all men, teaching us, that, denying ungodliness and worldly lusts, we should live soberly, righteously, and godly in this present world.' The more we believe all things contained in the writings of the prophets and apostles, the more we are taught how to live soberly, righteously, and godly in the present world. There we have the true principle of obedience, viz., love to God fed and bred in us by his love to us in Christ; the true encouragement and motive of obedience, the hopes of the other world; the true rule of obedience, God's mind revealed in his word, and perfecting the light of nature so far as it discovereth anything of our duty to God, neighbour, and self. Here is better furniture than we can have elsewhere, a forcible principle and a glorious hope, and an exact rule. Now they that would cry up right reason in defiance of these are not Christ's disciples, but would make him theirs, and teach him and his apostles how to speak and teach the way to true happiness; and so are guilty of great unthankfulness for this blessed revelation which we have in the gospel.

[2.] That true morality and good conscience cannot be had without the faith of the gospel; so that we are not only better provided, but indeed cannot perform such obedience as is acceptable to God without faith in Christ. And therefore I shall show you the defects that are in men's obedience till they believe in Christ.

(1.) There is a defect in their state. They are not reconciled to God till they be in Christ; and therefore he will not accept an offering at their hands who neglect his grace, and will not sue out their atonement with him in that penitent and broken-hearted way which he hath appointed in the new covenant. Let them first sue out their pardon in the name of Christ, and then begin with a new course of obedience. God is first *placandus*, then *placendus*. First his wrath is to be appeased, and then he will accept of our duties and actions; first our persons are accepted, and then our duties and offerings: Gen. iv. 4, 'The Lord had respect to Abel and to his offering;' Abel being a believer, and under grace, as the apostle explaineth it, Heb. xi. 4, 'By faith Abel offered unto God a more acceptable sacrifice than Cain, by which he obtained witness that he was righteous, God testifying of his gifts, and by it he, being dead, yet speaketh;' that is, he was justified and accepted with God. This is such a principle of reason, that Lilius Gyraldus saith it was the custom of the heathens, *Ut prius iratos deos placarent, et postea invocarent propitios*—First to appease their gods, and then to pray unto them. Man cometh as a sinner to God, and therefore first he must deprecate his wrath, and use all means how God may be pacified and appeased.

(2.) There is a defect in the actions themselves.

(1*st*.) In the root; there is not a clear fountain or principle of grace in their hearts; and then, 'Who can bring a clean thing out of an unclean?' Job xiv. 4; a clear stream out of a dirty puddle? How can he perform a good action which is naturally corrupt? Without the Spirit of Christ all our good actions have a blemish: 'The fruit of the Spirit is in all goodness, and righteousness, and truth,' Eph. v. 9. It is but wild fruit unless it be the fruit of the Spirit, and floweth from the grace of regeneration, and that new state of heart into which we are put by Jesus Christ: John xv. 5, 'I am the vine, ye are the branches: he that abideth in me, and I in him, the same bringeth forth much fruit; for without me ye can do nothing.' One that is in Christ will be fruitful to God, but without him, $\chi\omega\rho\iota\varsigma$ $\dot{\epsilon}\mu o\upsilon$, *seorsim a me*, or apart from him, there is no bringing forth fruit to God. It is not *nihil magnum*, some great thing, ye cannot work miracles without me, but *nihil*, nothing, nothing saving and acceptable to God.

(2*d*.) In the manner. They do not obey God with that purity, that life and affection, that he hath required. Their actions are superficial, shadows of good things; they draw nigh to him with their lips when their hearts are far from him: Mat. xv. 8, 'This people draweth nigh to me with their mouth, and honoureth me with their lips, but their heart is far from me.' Their duties to men are but shadows of good actions, not flowing from a hearty love and a good conscience, but from interest or natural temper.

(3*d.*) There is a defect in the end; they do not regard God's glory: Col. iii. 17, 'Whatsoever you do in word or deed, do all in the name of the Lord Jesus, giving thanks to God and the Father by him;' 1 Cor. x. 31, 'Whether ye eat or drink, or whatsoever ye do, do all to the glory of God.' The most commendable actions of carnal men have either a natural aim, as self-preservation; so in their worship: Hosea vii. 14, 'They have not cried unto me with their heart when they howled upon their beds;' they howl upon their bed for corn and wine. Or self-quiet and ease; so in their duties to men, more 'for wrath than conscience' sake,' Rom. xii. 5. Or for vain-glory, 'To be seen of men,' Mat. vi. 1. Or a legal aim; when most devout, to quiet conscience, or to satisfy God for their sins by their duties: Micah vi. 6, 7, 'Wherewith shall I come before the Lord, and bow myself before the high God? Shall I come before him with burnt-offerings, with calves of a year old? will the Lord be pleased with thousand of rams, or with ten thousands of rivers of oil? shall I give my first-born for my transgression, the fruit of my body for the sin of my soul?' Usually the sacrifice of the wicked is 'brought with an evil mind,' Prov. xxi. 27; to buy our indulgence in some sins by avoiding others, or by performing some duties to pay for their neglect of others which are more weighty. Duties are performed as a sin-offering, not as a thank-offering; to pacify God, not to glorify him. There is no delight in God or obedience. In short, all is as flowers strewed upon a dunghill.

2. The solifidians, that cry up an empty faith without obedience and holiness, these are to be dealt with as well as the other.

[1.] The end of all religion is practice. Christianity was not brought into the world that we might talk of great things, but do great things for God. All the mysteries of our most holy faith are mysteries of godliness; and if it be not so, the word of God is come to us in word only, and not in power, and we are christians of the letter, not of the spirit. The law of grace was never intended to try the acuteness of men's wits, who could reason most profoundly of these glorious things, nor the firmness of their memories, who could best carry in mind these holy truths, nor the readiness of their invention, who could most plausibly discourse about them, but the willingness of their obedience, who would most entirely practise them: John xiv. 21, 'He that hath my commandments and keepeth them, he it is that loveth me.' The practical christian hath the truest sense of his religion.

[2.] The end of our redemption is obedience. Christ hath ends of his own, as well as those which more immediately concern our benefit: Rev. v. 9, 'Thou wast slain, and hast redeemed us to God by thy blood.' Sin had made us unserviceable to God, and the end of Christ's death was to put us in joint again, and to bring us into a course of service and obedience unto our Creator: Rom. xiv. 9, 'For to this end Christ both died, and rose, and revived, that he might be Lord both of dead and living.' He came to redeem us not only from wrath, but from sin; not only to abolish guilt, but to establish holiness: Titus ii. 14, 'Who gave himself for us, that he might redeem us from all iniquity, and purify unto himself a peculiar people, zealous of good works.'

[3.] It is the end of his renewing grace. He hath altered the constitution of our hearts, that we may live unto God: 2 Cor. v. 17, 'Therefore if any man be in Christ, he is a new creature: old things are passed away; behold, all things are become new.' We are renewed in heart, that we might walk in all newness of conversation.

[4.] It is the end of our faith and hope. Faith and hope are but means subservient to love, which is the grace by which we are inclined to perform our duty to God and man; and therefore the strength of our faith is to be judged by the readiness of our obedience: Gal. v. 6, 'For in Christ Jesus neither circumcision availeth anything, nor uncircumcision, but faith which worketh by love.' That carrieth away the prize of justification. It is the love of God, stirred up in us by faith which maketh us watchful against sin, and careful to please him in all things.

Use 2. To press us all, if we would be complete christians, to take all the three parts. (1.) Let us be sound in the faith; (2.) Let us keep up hope; (3.) Let us be thorough and exact in obedience.

1. Let us be sound in the faith, believing all things that are contained in the word of God, not contenting ourselves with a light credulity or common tradition, but have a faith of the Spirit's working. Your love to God dependeth upon the principles laid down in the gospel, which discover to you his love in the Redeemer, and the provision made for your souls; therefore you are 'to build up yourselves in your most holy faith, that you may keep yourselves in the love of God,' Jude 20, 21.

2. Let not hope be left out as an unnecessary grace. This is not a cursory and slight, but a desirous expectation, so as not to be weakened by the lusts of the flesh: 1 Peter i. 13, 'Wherefore gird up the loins of your minds; be ye sober, and hope to the end for the grace that is to be brought unto you at the revelation of Jesus Christ.' When Christ cometh all your labours and self-denial shall be recompensed: Rom. viii. 24, 25, 'For we are saved by hope; but hope that is seen is not hope, for what a man seeth, why doth he yet hope for? but if we hope for that we see not, then do we with patience wait for it.'

3. Be sound and thorough, and exact in obedience. Many hold sound doctrine, and have some lazy expectation of eternal life, but they are defective in the third branch; they are not careful to keep a good conscience, and do their duty in all things to God and man. Here I shall press you to two things—

[1.] Let conscience be your guide.

[2.] Exercise yourselves in this, that conscience may be a good guide to you.

First, Let conscience be your guide. I shall press you hereunto by two considerations—

1. From the nature of conscience. It is not only a monitor, but a judge. As a monitor it warns us of our duty; as a judge it censures our neglects of it. Science is one thing, conscience is another. Science is a man's knowledge of other things; conscience is a man's knowledge of himself, his state, and ways, to know what he is to do, and to know what he hath done; that is conscience. It is the judgment of a man concerning himself and his actions with respect to reward and punish-

ment. God, that is our Lord, is also our proper judge; but it pleaseth God to put a faculty into man, this spirit within him, that he should have something in his own bosom to be a rule and judge, but yet a subordinate rule, and a deputy-judge, accountable to God; but a judge it is. However it much conduceth to the glory of God and to the safety of man.

[1.] To the glory of God.

(1.) As it is an evidence of his being, whose law is the ground of conscience, and before whom conscience doth accuse, and whose sentence it doth dread and stand in fear of. Why doth conscience scruple this or that, if there be not a God by whose will good and evil are distinguished? To whom doth it accuse us but to God? Why is conscience sometimes afraid, sometimes comforted, if there were no God to mind things here below? We find conscience appalleth the stoutest sinners after the commitment of some offence, though it be secret, and beyond the cognisance and vengeance of man: Ps. liii. 5, 'There were they in great fear where no fear was;' that is, no outward cause of fear, where none sought to hurt them; accusing themselves when none else could accuse them, as Joseph's brethren: Gen. xlii. 21, 'We are verily guilty concerning our brother's blood;' or where none had power to reach them, as princes and worldly potentates feel the stings of conscience as well as others. Felix trembled, who was the judge, at Paul's words, who was the prisoner: Acts xxiv. 25, 'And as he reasoned of righteousness, temperance, and judgment to come, Felix trembled.' What is the reason of this, but that they know there is a supreme judge and avenger?

(2.) It is for the glory of his judicial proceedings. Self-accusers and self-condemners have no reason to quarrel with God and impeach his justice. Man hath principles and sentiments graven upon his heart, which justify all God's dealings with him: Luke xix. 22, 'Out of thine own mouth will I judge thee, thou wicked servant!' and Ps. li. 4, 'That thou mayest be justified when thou speakest, and be clear when thou judgest.' Hereby he is left without excuse: Rom. i. 20, 'So that they are without excuse,' ἀναπολογήτους; Titus iii. 11, 'Knowing that he that is such is subverted, and sinneth, being condemned of himself,' αὐτοκατάκριτος. Hence the frequent appeals to conscience: Isa. v. 3, 4, 'Judge, I pray you, betwixt me and my vineyard: what could I have done more to my vineyard that I have not done in it?' I have produced these scriptures to show that by conscience man is better induced to give a testimony to God concerning all his dealings with him.

[2.] To the safety and benefit of man, that he may have an oracle in his own bosom to direct him to his duty, and to warn him of his danger if he doth amiss. Conscience is spoken of in scripture both ways; as instructing us in our duty: Ps. xvi. 7, 'My reins also instruct me in the night season;' that is, conscience showed him his duty, and how he was concerned in the law of God, or the rule which God had given to his creatures. And as it showeth us what to do, so it reflecteth upon what we have done. If evil, it smiteth us for it: 2 Sam. xxiv. 10, 'And David's heart smote him after that he had numbered the people.' If good, it cheereth us with it: 2 Cor. i. 12, 'For our rejoicing is this, the testimony of our conscience, that in simplicity and godly sincerity, not with fleshly wisdom, but by the grace of God, we have had our conversation in the world.' It smiteth as it exciteth fear of punishment; it cheereth as it stirreth up hope of reward, and we do very much understand hereby how God standeth affected towards us: 1 John iii. 19-21, 'And hereby we know that we are of the truth, and shall assure our hearts before him; for if our heart condemn us, God is greater than our heart, and knoweth all things. Beloved, if our heart condemn us not, then have we confidence towards God.'

2. Conscience is God's vicegerent and deputy. You may know much of his mind by the voice and report of conscience; therefore, next to the judgment and sentence of God, a man should regard the judgment and sentence of conscience: 1 John iii. 20, 21, 'If our heart condemn us, God is greater than our heart, and knoweth all things. Beloved, if our heart condemn us not, then have we confidence towards God.' Observe what conscience speaketh; doth it condemn thee or acquit thee? and upon what terms doth it either? The voice of conscience is often the voice of God, and men would sooner come to know themselves, and might make a right judgment upon their estates, if they would look inward, and regard the voice of conscience, doth it condemn or acquit? Indeed there lieth an appeal from court to court, and from judge to judge.

[1.] From court to court. In what court doth conscience condemn you? In the law court? You ought to own the desert of sin, clearing God, if he should inflict it upon you: 1 Cor. xi. 31, 'For if we would judge ourselves, we should not be judged.' But yet you may take sanctuary at his grace, and humbly claim the benefit of the new covenant: Ps. cxxx. 3, 4, 'If thou, Lord, shouldst mark iniquity, O Lord, who shall stand? But there is forgiveness with thee, that thou mayest be feared.' If it condemn you in the gospel court for no sound believer, the case must not be lightly passed over, but examined, whether there be a sincere bent of heart towards God: Heb. xiii. 18, 'We trust we have a good conscience, in all things willing to live honestly.'

[2.] There is an appeal to an higher judge. Doth conscience write bitter things against thee? Yet if God justifieth, Rom. viii. 33, 'Who shall lay anything to the charge of God's elect? it is God that justifieth.' God's act is authoritative and powerful: Isa. lvii. 19, 'I create the fruit of the lips, peace, peace to him that is afar off, and to him that is near, saith the Lord, and I will heal him;' Ps. lxxxv. 8, 'I will hear what God the Lord will speak, for he will speak peace unto his people and to his saints.' But sometimes he speaketh in the sentence of his word when not in the conscience; his authority may comfort when we feel not his power. So for acquitting; conscience is not the highest judge: 1 Cor. iv. 4, 'For if I know nothing by myself, yet am I not hereby justified; but he that judgeth me is the Lord;' Prov. xvi. 2, 'All the ways of a man are clear in his own eyes, but the Lord weigheth the spirits.' We must consult his word, and thereby clear our case, so as to assure our hearts before him.

3. Conscience is easily offended, but not easily appeased; as the eye is easily offended with the least dust or mote, which soon gets in, but

is not easily gotten out.' 'But then to appease it costs a great deal of trouble.' Therefore, if we would, as Paul, keep a conscience void of offence, there needeth much tenderness and watchfulness, for by the commission of deliberate and wilful sins you may raise a tempest that is not easily laid again; as David felt broken bones after his foul fall: Ps. li. 8, 'Make me to hear joy and gladness, that the bones which thou hast broken may rejoice.' Before the action conscience showeth what is to be done; in the action it guideth us in doing; after the action it censureth it as well or ill done; and so either comforteth us with hopes of a reward, or terrifieth us with fear of punishment. As a man acteth, so conscience is a party; as the action is censured, so conscience is a judge. After the action the force of conscience is usually seen more than before the fact or in the fact, because before and in the action the judgment of reason is not so clear and strong, the affections raising mists and clouds to darken the mind and trouble it, and draw it on their side by their pleasing violence. By the treachery of the senses and revolt of the passions the mind is betrayed; but as the violence of the affections ceaseth, and is by little and little allayed, guilt flasheth in the face of conscience, and reason hath the greatest force to affect the mind with grief or fear. The act being over, and the affection satisfied, the soul giveth place to reason, which was before contemned; and when it recovereth the throne, it striketh through the heart with a sharp sentence and reproof for obeying appetite before itself, and brings in terror and trouble, which causeth the soul to sit uneasy: Mat. xxvii. 4, 'I have sinned in that I have betrayed the innocent blood;' Rom. i. 32, 'Knowing the judgment of God, that they which commit such things are worthy of death.' Therefore do not go like an ox to the slaughter, nor a fool to the correction of the stocks.

4. Conscience is the best friend and the worst enemy. It is the best friend, partly for its comfort: Prov. xv. 15, 'He that is of a merry heart hath a continual feast;' 2 Cor. i. 12, 'For our rejoicing is this, the testimony of our conscience;' no bird sings so sweetly as the bird in the bosom. Partly for its nearness; it is always with us, in health and sickness, in life and in death. Husbands and wives, who are most together, yet because they live a distinct life, they are often apart; death looseth the bond and knot, but this remaineth with us. So it is the worst enemy. Partly for its universal nearness. It is sad for a man to be at odds with himself, and fall out with his own heart. It is a domestical tribunal, which always remaineth with us; and therefore Job could bear the reproaches of others, but his own heart should not reproach him as long as he lived, Job xxvii. 6. Partly because of the grievousness of the wound and stroke: Prov. xviii. 14, 'A wounded spirit who can bear?' It is no less than the fear of the wrath of the eternal God. A man cannot run away from his conscience, no more than he can run away from himself; and therefore for a man to please others and offend his conscience, what folly is that! or to please a lust, to wound his conscience. A lust or vain appetite is an unjustifiable thing, and will soon appear so, but the fears of conscience are justified by the highest reason, the law of God. The satisfaction of a lust is a poor vanishing pleasure, but the observing and keeping a good con-

science breedeth a solid joy, which will stick by thee to the very last; and when thou comest to die, will be a support to thee: Isa. xxxviii. 3, 'Remember now, O Lord, I beseech thee, how I have walked before thee in truth, and with a perfect heart, and have done that which is good in thy sight.' When thou must leave riches, honours, and pleasures, which are the baits of thy lust, this will stick by thee: 1 John ii. 17, 'The world passeth away, and the lust thereof; but he that doeth the will of God abideth for ever.' Therefore now thou shouldst mortify thy lust and gratify thy conscience.

5. Thy conscience is the beginning of heaven and hell. A good conscience is the beginning of heaven, and peace and joy in believing is a foretaste of that fulness of joy and pleasure which we shall have when we come into God's immediate presence. The glorified spirits carry a good conscience with them to heaven; 'their works follow them,' Rev. xiv. 13; and the damned carry their stings and convictions with them to hell: Mark ix. 44, 'Their worm dieth not, and the fire is not quenched.' Oh, think of this! The joys of the Spirit are an antepast of glory, called often an earnest in scripture: 2 Cor. i. 22, 'Who hath also sealed us, and given the earnest of the Spirit in our hearts.' And the horrors of conscience are the suburbs of hell. Oh! therefore be sure to keep all quiet within, and whatever be your temptations, do not offend conscience, but unfeignedly discharge your duties to God and men.

6. If there be a crack and a flaw in your conscience, all your trading with heaven is at a stand; there cannot be any serious dealing with God, nor holy boldness in prayer: 1 John iii. 31, 'If our hearts condemn us not, then have we confidence towards God.' When you have sinned away your peace, a strangeness and distance groweth between God and you: Ps. xxxii. 3, 'When I kept silence, my bones waxed old through my roaring all the day long;' Gen. iii. 8, 'And Adam and his wife hid themselves from the presence of the Lord God among the trees of the garden.' Adam ran to the bushes. Your hearts will grow shy of God, and you cannot so comfortably look him in the face, and so the sweetness of holy privacy and communion with God will be lost. Time was when you could go boldly, and open your hearts to God, but now you are afraid of him, and every act of commerce is a reviving of your bondage; the remembrance of God is a trouble to you.

7. If conscience speaketh not, it writeth, for it is not only a witness, but a register and book of record: Jer. xvii. 1, 'The sin of Judah is written with a pen of iron, and with the point of a diamond.' We know not what conscience writeth, being occupied and taken up with carnal vanities, and carried away with foolish and hurtful lusts, but we shall know afterwards, when the book of conscience shall be opened: Rev. xx. 12, 'And I saw the dead, small and great, stand before God; and the books were opened; and another book was opened, which is the book of life; and the dead were judged out of those things which were written in the books, according to their works.' These books are the book of conscience and the book of God's remembrance. The remembrance of our actions shall be forced upon us. Conscience is God's register, and keepeth a diary, and sets down everything. This book, though it be in the sinner's keeping, cannot be razed: what con-

science writeth is written to eternity, unless it be blotted out by repentance and a serious application of the blood of Christ. Well, then, consider a sleepy conscience will not always sleep: if we suffer it not to awaken here, it will awaken in hell, where there is no remedy; for the present it sleepeth in many, in regard of motion, check, or smiting, but not in regard of notice and observation. This secret spy is privy to more than it speaketh of; it is laid up as matter for the worm that never dieth to feed upon.

8. If the stings of an evil conscience be not always felt, yet they are soon awakened by serious thoughts of death and judgment to come, and then forced upon us. There is a fire smothering in our bosoms, and it is soon blown up into a flame. Sometimes by the word: Acts xxiv. 25, 'And as he reasoned of righteousness, temperance, and judgment to come, Felix trembled.' Belshazzar's edge was taken off in the midst of his carousing: Dan. v. 6, 'Then the king's countenance was changed, and his thoughts troubled him, so that the joints of his loins were loosed, and his knees smote one against another.' Sometimes by some great troubles: Isa. lix. 12, 'For our transgressions are multiplied before thee, and our sins testify against us: for our transgressions are with us, and as for our iniquities, we know them.' Therefore 'we roar like beasts, and mourn like doves,' ver. 11. In a tempest, that which is at the bottom cometh a-top. Or by death; whatever silence there be in conscience before, yet death usually reviveth these fears: 1 Cor. xv. 56, 'The sting of death is sin.' Men are wise and more serious as they are entering on the confines of eternity; near things affect us; the baits of the flesh have then lost their allurement. The devil, that was before a tempter, will then be a tormentor. Things overlooked before are then seriously considered; then the stings of sin work more sensibly, and in a lively manner, and the deluded sinner begins to see what he would not take notice of before.

9. If conscience do not speak to you, you must speak to it, and call upon it to do its office. Call yourselves to an account for the expense of your time and employment: Ps. iv. 4, 'Commune with your own heart upon your bed, and be still;' Ps. lxxvii. 6, 'I commune with mine own heart, and my spirit made diligent search.' Take a time to parley with yourselves, and consider how matters stand between you and God. When the clock striketh not, it is a sign the plummets are down, and we must wind them up again. Every day we must do something, as Job sacrificed for his sons day by day: Job i. 5, 'It may be that my sons have sinned, and cursed God in their hearts.' And God himself reviewed every day's work, and 'saw that it was good,' Gen. i. 4, 10, 12, &c. So should we review every day's work, and cast up the account at the foot of every page. Short reckonings prevent mistakes. Pythagoras taught his scholars that they should never give way to sleep till they had posed themselves with these questions, *Quid feci*, &c.—What have I done? what good have I omitted? wherein have I transgressed? Conscience, what hast thou to say to me? And Seneca telleth of his friend Sextius, that before he would betake himself to rest he would ask his soul, *Quid hodie malum tuum sanasti? cui vitio obstitisti? qua parte melior es?*—What evil hast thou got rid of to-day? what sin hast thou resisted? wherein art thou

better than thou wert before ? And he saith of himself, *Quotidie apud me causam dico, totum diem mecum scrutor, dicta et facta mea remetior* ; that he scanned all his actions and speeches in the day. Shall heathens be more serious, and shall christians, who are acquainted with eternity, never take time to set conscience a-work ? Oh ! let us be ashamed of our slightness and negligence !

10. We can never have a sound conscience till we be sincere with God in a constant uniform course of self-denying obedience : 1 John iii. 19, 'Hereby we know that we are of the truth, and shall assure our hearts before him;' and this is described in the text by 'keeping a conscience void of offence both towards God and towards men.' So 2 Kings xx. 3, 'I beseech thee, O Lord, remember now how I have walked before thee in truth and with a perfect heart, and have done that which is good in thy sight,' and this not in an act or two, but in a man's whole course : Ps. cvi. 3, 'Blessed are they that keep judgment and he that doeth righteousness at all times.' Not by starts and good moods only, but constantly and at all times. And our obedience must be self-denying as well as constant and uniform. That religion is worth nothing that costs nothing : 2 Sam. xxiv. 24, ' I will not offer burnt-offerings unto the Lord my God of that which doth cost me nothing.' When we value God's interest above our own, and we can deny ourselves upon the hopes of glory, then is our sincerity most evidenced. But if we embrace only the safe, cheap, and easy part of religion, and cannot deny our ease, profit, and honour, we do not set up Christ's religion, but a christianity of our own making : Mat. xvi. 24, 'Then said Jesus unto his disciples, If any one will come after me, let him deny himself, and take up his cross, and follow me.'

11. If we would have conscience to do its office, there must be great heed and watchfulness, for it is corrupt as well as other faculties, and from a judge it may become an advocate, excusing the partialities of our obedience. To evidence this more fully with respect to conscience, men may be considered three ways—as acting without conscience, or according to conscience, or against conscience.

[1.] A man may act without all conscience, so a man may do either good or evil.

(1.) Good, as those that act rashly, inconsiderately, or customarily. As when men pray, give alms, go to church ; conscience did not send them thither, but custom, inducement of friends, persuasions of parents, or the like. These do that which is good, but they do it not well ; Luke viii. 18, 'Take heed how you hear.' Conscience doth not put them upon it. To this first sort may be reckoned those that intended to do evil, but by accident do that which is good ; as Joseph's brethren : Gen. l. 20, ' But as for you, ye thought evil against me, but God meant it unto good.' And those that perform the duties of christianity so far as the interest of the flesh will give them leave, for the flesh itself will command you to do well, and sin itself forbid sin, that it may not disgrace them in the world, and bring some hurt and inconvenience on them. Conscience doth not guide them herein, but hypocrisy or sin sets them a-work.

(2.) Evil, as Lot's incest with his daughters : Gen. xix. 33, 34, 'He perceived not when they lay down, or when they arose.' Conscience was laid asleep; it did not stir and chasten or rebuke him. So when the people of Ephesus came together, Acts xix. 32, 'The most part knew not wherefore they were come together;' they were in a hurry, tumult, and sudden passion. These consult not with conscience in their actions, and the evil they do is not against conscience; yet evil it is, and doth not exempt from punishment, for a man is bound not to act rashly, but according to the dictate of conscience.

[2.] A man may act out of conscience, or according to conscience, and so he may act either good or evil.

(1.) Good, either lawful, because it is permitted, or necessary, because it is commanded; in the one, conscience is sensible that he may, in the other that he ought to do so. This he doth not out of terror, but the sweet force of love and willing obedience unto God; for fear and conscience are opposed: Rom. xiii. 5, 'Wherefore ye must be faithful, not only for wrath, but also for conscience' sake;' but he doth it in obedience to God: Ps. xxvii. 8, 'When thou saidst, Seek ye my face, my heart said unto thee, Thy face, Lord, will I seek.' I acknowledge thy power over me.

(2.) Evil. So Paul out of conscience persecuted Christ, for his erring conscience told him that the precepts and ceremonies of the law of Moses were all of eternal obligation, and necessary to a man's justification towards God, and therefore that Christ, abolishing the ceremonies, was an enemy to Moses: Acts xxvi. 9, 'I verily thought with myself that I ought to do many things contrary to the name of Jesus of Nazareth.' Error of conscience dictated it to him. But did Paul do well or ill herein? As to the manner of the action, it was well, for he did it with a good mind, and according to his conscience; thus far Paul sinned not. But as to the matter of the action, he did wickedly, that he followed the dictates of a misguided conscience, and did not subject his conscience to that higher revelation of God which is in scripture, but to the tradition of the elders. So many persecutors do evil, and do not think they do evil, but do God good service: John xvi. 2, 'They shall put you out of the synagogues; yea, the time cometh that whosoever killeth you will think that he doeth God service;' and this through ignorance and blind zeal. This erring conscience is their bane; it may urge them to do evil, but it cannot oblige them to do evil, for they are bound to know better; and according to the means of their conviction, so is the greatness of their sin.

[3.] A man may act against conscience.

(1.) So he may do good. As a papist communicating with the reformed churches in the word, and prayer, and sacraments, he doth that which is good, but he doth it against his conscience, because he thinks it is not lawful to have communion with heretics. To this head belongeth those things that we do with scruple of conscience, fearing the things which we do are not right. So many times we do things which are lawful, yet fearing they are unlawful; we do them not without some scruple, and terror of conscience; as, for instance, a self-condemning sinner coming to the Lord's supper, yet because he hath not a clear sense of the love of God, his conscience troubleth him, and he is afraid he eateth and drinketh unworthily. The apostle saith, Rom. xiv. 22, 23, 'Happy is he that condemneth not himself in that thing which he alloweth; and he that doubteth is damned if he eat, because he eateth not of faith; for whatsoever is not of faith is sin; that is, to the party that doeth it, though it be good in itself. Therefore we must endeavour that, whatever we do, we may be assured out of the word of God that it is lawful: Rom. xiv. 5, 'Let every one be fully persuaded in his own mind.'

(2.) So he may do evil. When a man doeth good against his conscience, it is evil; but when he doeth evil against his conscience, it is a double evil, because he doth not only transgress the rule that should guide him, but affronts the judge which God hath set over him in his own bosom, and kicketh against the pricks, the urgings of his own conscience: James iv. 17, 'Therefore to him that knoweth to do good, and doeth it not, to him it is sin.' But especially it is a greater sin, when not only by light natural, but by the checks and motions of the Spirit, he understandeth the evil which he doth, or the necessary good which he omitteth, for this is to resist the Holy Ghost: Acts vii. 51, 'Ye stiff-necked and uncircumcised in heart and ears, ye do always resist the Holy Ghost.' Especially when he wilfully and blasphemously rejects that sufficient evidence that is given him of the ways of God, 'and hath done despite unto the Spirit of grace,' Heb. x. 29; for that is 'the sin unto death,' 1 John v. 19. In short, we should be careful we sin not against conscience, for it is our best friend or our worst enemy. It is God's deputy, and to resist the officer is to resist the prince or magistrate. Therefore do nothing without conscience, do nothing against conscience, but do all things with conscience, rightly informed by the word of God.

Secondly, Exercise yourselves in this, that conscience may perform its office, and be a good guide unto you. There are two offices of conscience—to direct and to censure; to judge rightly *de jure*, what you ought to do; and to judge rightly *de facto*, what you have done or what you are, that you may neither have a blind and erring nor a sleepy conscience.

1. That you may not have an erring conscience, or a blind one, you must consult with your rule: Rom. xii. 2, 'That ye may prove what is that good and acceptable and perfect will of God;' Eph. v. 17, 'Wherefore be not unwise, but understanding what the will of the Lord is;' with a mind fully resolved to do his will: John vii. 17, 'If any man do his will, he shall know of the doctrine whether it be of God, or whether I speak of myself.' This rule is the word of God: Ps. cxix. 105, 'Thy word is a lamp unto my feet, and a light unto my path.' Beg the light of the Spirit: ver. 133, 'Order my steps in thy word, and let not any iniquity have dominion over me.' And be not rebellious against this light, for our sins and lusts blind the mind, and a naughty heart defileth the conscience, so that it groweth loose and indulgent, and from a judge it becometh an advocate, excusing the partialities of our obedience to God and our injuries to men. Therefore there must be a resolute endeavour to overcome every sin you are convinced of: Heb. xiii. 18, 'Pray for us, for we trust we have a good conscience, in all things willing to live honestly.'

2. That you may not have a dead, sleepy, stupid conscience, you

must often excite it. For your actions, bring them to the rule: Hag. i. 5, 'Now therefore thus saith the Lord God, Consider your ways;' Ps. iv. 4, 'Commune with your own heart upon your bed, and be still.' For your state, try it often: 1 Cor. xi. 28, 'But let a man examine himself, and so let him eat of that bread and drink of that cup;' 2 Cor. xiii. 5, 'Examine yourselves whether you be in the faith; prove your own selves: know ye not your own selves, how that Jesus Christ is in you, except ye be reprobates?' The acts of conscience are three—to be an accuser, witness, and judge.

[1.] As an accuser, hearken to its voice; what doth it say to you, good or evil? Job xxvii. 6, 'My heart shall not reproach me so long as I live.' If it speak not to you, you must speak to it. God complaineth, Jer. viii. 6, 'I hearkened and heard, but they spake not aright; no man repented him of his wickedness, saying, What have I done?'

[2.] As a witness, consider the evidence it bringeth, that it may be matter of joy or sorrow to you, of confession or thanksgiving. If it reproach you, do not smother the check: Acts xxiv. 25, 'And as he reasoned of righteousness, temperance, and judgment to come, Felix trembled, and answered, Go thy way for this time; when I have a more convenient season I will call for thee.' If it cheer you, see upon what grounds: Rom. ix. 1, 'I speak the truth in Christ, I lie not, my conscience also bearing me witness in the Holy Ghost.' It is no matter what others think, but what conscience thinketh. Nothing is nearer to us than ourselves; it is a domestical tribunal, that we always carry about with us.

[3.] As a judge it passeth sentence; if it be wrong, there is an appeal from court to court: Ps. cxxx. 3, 4, 'If thou, Lord, shouldst mark iniquities, O Lord, who can stand? but there is forgiveness with thee, that thou mayest be feared.' Conscience is a judge, but it is an inferior judge; there lieth an appeal to a higher: 1 Cor. iv. 4, 'He that judgeth me is the Lord;' Heb. xii. 23, 'And to God the judge of all.' But it should be done with great admiration of grace. But if the judgment be right, it is ratified; its judgment we must yield to: 1 Cor. xi. 32, 'But when we are judged, we are chastened of the Lord.' Thus should we keep up the force of conscience.

SERMON UPON ZECHARIAH XIV. 20, 21.

In that day there shall be upon the bells of the horses, Holiness unto the Lord; and the pots in the Lord's house shall be like the bowls before the altar. Yea, every pot in Jerusalem and in Judah shall be holiness unto the Lord of hosts.—ZECH. xiv. 20, 21.

THESE words describe the purity and holiness of the gospel church in such terms and notions as are proper to the old testament dispensation. In them observe—(1.) The inscription or impress; (2.) The things on which it is engraven; (3.) The time when it is done.

1. The inscription or impress, 'Holiness to the Lord.' This was of old written on the priest's mitre: Exod. xxviii. 36, 'And thou shalt make a plate of pure gold, and grave upon it like the engravings of a signet, Holiness to the Lord;' to show that he was a person sacred, and designed for special holy uses: therein he was a type of Christ. Now what was upon the high priest's frontlet was inscribed on everything, to show they should consecrate their all to God.

2. The things inscribed, particularly enumerated, first, the horse-bells, or the ornaments of their horses; secondly, their bowls or basons; thirdly, their pots.

[1.] What was used in the kitchens of the temple.

[2.] The utensils of every ordinary house and family. There were kitchens belonged to the temple, wherein the thank-offerings were dressed for their sacred feasts. The bowls of the altar were for an higher use, namely, to receive the blood of the sacrifices to make the sprinklings, as 'Solomon made an hundred basons of gold' for that use, 2 Chron. iv. 8.

3. The time, 'In that day.' He speaketh not of any peculiar time, but the whole state of things under the gospel, which is as it were but one day. And it is called 'that day' by way of excellency. Thus the time of the gospel are days indeed full of light and grace, and 'that day' by way of limitation. It should be reserved for this day, and not found in such a degree and measure at any other time; even then when there should be no sacrifices, no altars, then the bells, pots, and basons should be sanctified or separated from a common, and dedicated to an holy use, that is, there shall be such special universal holiness, as if it were so done upon all these things.

But you will say, When and where is it? Alas! considering the degenerate state of the christian world, where is this universal holiness to be found? How shall we make it good?

Ans. 1. Prophecies of things belonging to our obedience are to be understood many times *quoad officium*, of our duty, rather than *quoad eventum*, of the event; it is their duty to be thus holy in all their employments and affairs; that dispensation requireth it as our duty.

2. As to the event, it is to be understood comparatively, not absolutely, to show that there shall be a far greater holiness under the gospel than under the law; both *intensivè* as to the degree of the holiness itself, and *extensivè* as to the persons sanctified. Intensively the holiness itself is greater, because the ordinances of the gospel are rational, and not typical, and the duties of it moral more than ceremonial. God taught them by ceremonies to hate sin by the types of legal uncleanness, to devote themselves to God by offering their beasts in sacrifice. Theirs was like a training, ours a real war, as much as the difference is between shooting at a puppet or painted castle and fighting with an enemy. And because more of the Spirit is poured out; now grace is not given upon trust, but the price is actually paid. Extensively, more persons are sanctified, as the pale is enlarged, and the gospel prevaileth on them: Rev. v. 9, 'Thou wast slain, and hast redeemed us to God by thy blood, out of every kindred, and tongue, and people, and nation;' Mark xvi. 15, 'Go into all the world, and preach the gospel to every creature.'

3. The gospel state hath its ebbs and flows in several ages. Sometimes there is a notable vigour and power of godliness, at other times a great increase of wickedness, and men do so far corrupt their way, that we are forced to put another sense upon words, or expect a better time when the prophecy shall be more amply fulfilled. We can hardly reconcile the words with the state of the times.

Doct. God in and by the gospel will effect an eminent and notable sanctification both of things and persons. (1.) Let us consider how gospel holiness is set forth in this prophecy; (2.) I shall speak of holiness in the general; (3.) Give you the reasons.

I. That degree of holiness which is here prophesied of.

1. All such things as were before employed against God should be then employed and converted to his service, for the horse-bells shall be inscribed. He speaketh before of horses employed against the church, which God would overthrow, ver. 15. It was the fashion of those oriental countries to adorn their war-horses and camels with golden chains and bells, Judges viii. 26. This prophecy intimateth that now these bells should be converted to another use, to make golden pots and bowls for the temple, and be inscribed by God's motto and impress. In our natural estate we employed our time, and wit, and parts, and strength against God; but if converted, then for him. As one of the fathers glosseth upon Eve's seducing Adam, she was a rib, but she proved a dart. We fight against God by his own weapons, but conversion maketh a change: Rom. vi. 13, 'Neither yield ye your members as instruments of unrighteousness unto sin; but yield yourselves unto God, as those that are alive from the dead, and your members as instruments of righteousness unto God.' The ὅπλα ἀδικίας, the weapons or 'instruments of unrighteousness,' are become ὅπλα ικαιοσύνης, 'instru-

ments of righteousness.' So ver. 22, 'For now, being made free from sin, and become servants to God, ye have your fruit unto holiness.' There is a manifest change in the use of all things.

2. Upon all the utensils of the temple there shall be 'Holiness to the Lord,' whether pots or bowls. The great and immediate duties of the worship of God should have special holiness in them, for God will be sanctified in all that draw nigh unto him: Lev. x. 3, 'I will be sanctified in them that come nigh me, and before all the people I will be glorified.' There should be a special awe and reverence upon our hearts in our conversing with God, when the blood of the sacrifice is presented to him, as it was in the bowls, or the flesh of the sacrifice eaten by ourselves, as it was by the priests when it was sodden in the pots of the Lord's house. We read of 'discerning the Lord's body,' 1 Cor. xi. 29. We receive it not in an holy manner if our eating be not in a different manner from eating our ordinary meal. The impression of our great end should be upon our ordinary and common actions, but in worship the nature of the work is holy, and the manner of our deportment should be very reverent and serious.

3. The expressions imply a proficiency and growth in holiness; for the pots of the kitchen of the temple shall become as the bowls of the altar for purity and holiness. There were degrees of holiness in the several vessels belonging to the temple; the meanest things in sacred use shall be advanced to an higher degree of esteem and holy employment than before, which some understand thus: that the meanest things in the christian church shall be as precious as the most glorious things in the Jewish church; rather that holiness should be upon the growing hand, and increasing from degree to degree, till all be perfected in the everlasting estate. The bells or neck-ornaments of their horses shall be turned into pots of the Lord's house, and the pots in the kitchen become as the bowls on the altar. O christians! the holiness of the gospel is a growing holiness; we should go on 'from strength to strength,' Ps. lxxxiv. 7, 'from glory to glory,' 2 Cor. iii. 28. The inner man must be 'renewed day by day,' 2 Cor. iv. 16. There should be a continuance in gospel holiness. Carnal men seek to grow greater and greater, and higher and higher, and attain further degrees of their worldly happiness, and shall not we seek to grow better and better? One drachm of holiness is worth a whole world of greatness. Holiness is the glory of saints, the beauty of angels, the delight of God; you cannot be too holy. But alas! many lose ground in religion; holiness is in the wane, not in the increase; sin is not so hateful as it was before. What will this come to at length? How can he be rich who groweth every day poorer? or reach the goal who goeth every day a step back? who lose their zeal, and, the older they grow, live in more indulgence to the flesh?

4. As it is a progressive holiness, so it is also a diffusive holiness, that spreadeth itself throughout all actions, civil and sacred; in things which belong to peace and war. (1.) In things civil and sacred, all the pots of the Lord's house, and all the pots in Jerusalem. (2.) In things of war and peace, for here are horse-bells and pots; all things should now become holy, and holily used. In every point and ordinary action of the christian life, a christian should devote himself to God. True holiness will extend itself, and shine forth in a man's most com-

mon things and employments, and the sincere man referreth all to God, even in his ordinary conversation, as if he were about immediate worship: 1 Peter i. 15, 'For as he which hath called you is holy, so be ye holy,' ἐν πάσῃ ἀναστροφῇ, 'in all manner of conversation.' In every creek and turning of your lives, or in every particular passage of your christian course. Oh! what a blessed thing is it when godliness runneth through a man's whole life as the woof through the web! when our whole conversation savoureth of godliness and true holiness, and our common and civil actions are done in the Lord and for his glory, and upon all occasions you show yourselves haters of sin and lovers of what is good! Everything that passeth God's hand discovereth the author; there is not a gnat or a pile of grass but you may see God in it as well as in the more stupendous works of the creation. So should a christian in every condition, prosperous and adverse, in an high or low condition, whether he be abased or do abound, carry himself like a christian: Phil. iv. 12, 'I know both how to be abased, and I know how to abound; everywhere and in all things I am instructed both to be full and to be hungry, both to abound and suffer need;' Hosea vii. 8, 'Ephraim is a cake not turned,' baked but on one side, and dough on the other. So in every action, civil or sacred, there must not only be a spirit of holiness breathing in our duties, but shining forth in our ordinary employments and recreations. Every action, morally considered, is in itself a step forward to hell or to heaven; in every relation, in love to our maker, in duty to our fellow creatures: Acts xxiv. 16, 'And herein do I exercise myself, to have always a conscience void of offence towards God and towards men.' To all men, and to our fellow-saints: 2 Peter i. 7, 'And to godliness brotherly kindness, to brotherly kindness charity;' in justice and charity. When the web is one thing, and the woof another, the Lord abhorreth it.

II. Of holiness in the general. What it is? It may be considered relatively or positively.

1. Relatively; so that thing or person is holy which is set apart from a common to a holy use.

2. Positively; so it implieth the renovation of our natures and the rectitude of our actions; for holiness may be applied to persons or actions. An action is holy by its conformity to the rule; a person by the prevalency of his principle. Holiness with respect to our actions is an universal endeavour of conformity to the will of God. A person is holy by the prevalency of his principle, when his heart by those divine qualities which we call graces is constantly bent and powerfully inclined to please God in all things.

1. For holiness relatively considered, or with respect to our relation to God. These four things are in it—

[1.] An inclination towards God. There is a new bias upon the heart, which bends it to God, which before bended and tended towards carnal vanities. Conversion is a turning to God, and the holy life is a living to God: Gal. ii. 19, 'For I through the law am dead to the law, that I might live unto God.' The great work of grace is to set and fix the heart towards him from whom we departed by our folly and sin, that we may serve, please, and glorify him in all things, and finally come to enjoy him as our chief happiness: 1 Chron. xxii. 19, 'Now set your heart and your soul to seek the Lord your God.'

[2.] From this tendency towards God ariseth a dedication of ourselves and all that we have to the Lord's use and service: 2 Cor. viii. 5, 'But first gave their own selves to the Lord, and unto us by the will of God;' Rom. vi. 13, 'But yield yourselves unto God, as those that are alive from the dead, and your members as instruments of righteousness unto God;' Rom. xii. 1, 'I beseech you therefore, brethren, by the mercies of God, that ye present your bodies a living sacrifice, holy, acceptable unto God, which is your reasonable service.' They are ashamed they have so long kept God out of his right, therefore now they resign themselves to be what he will have them to be, and to do what he will have them to do.

[3.] From this dedication there results a relation of the persons so dedicated to God, so that from that time forth they are not their own, but the Lord's: Ezek. xvi. 8, 'Now when I passed by thee, and looked upon thee, behold, thy time was the time of love, and I spread my skirt over thee, and covered thy nakedness, yea, I sware unto thee, and entered into a covenant with thee, saith the Lord God, and thou becamest mine;' Rom. xiv. 7, 8, 'For none of us liveth to himself, and no man dieth to himself; for whether we live, we live unto the Lord, and whether we die, we die unto the Lord; whether we live, therefore, or die, we are the Lord's.'

[4.] There is another thing, and that is the actual using of ourselves for God. We are vessels set apart for the master's use: 2 Tim. ii. 21, 'If a man therefore purge himself from these, he shall be a vessel unto honour, sanctified, and meet for the master's use, and prepared unto every good work.' And accordingly we must live, not to ourselves, but unto God; it resulteth from all the former: 2 Cor. v. 15, 'And that he died for all, that they which live should not henceforth live unto themselves, but unto him which died for them.' If we love God, and have a thankful sense of his love and kindness to us, we will do so; there needeth no other law to bind this upon us but our love. Love is the poise which inclineth the soul to God. If we are dedicated to God, the sincerity of our dedication is known by our use. Many give up themselves to God, but in the use of themselves there appeareth no such matter; they use their tongues as their own, their hearts as their own, their bodies as their own, their wealth, strength, and time as their own; but a sincere christian maketh conscience of his dedication: 1 Cor. vi. 15, 'Know you not that your bodies are the members of Christ; shall I then take the members of Christ, and make them the members of an harlot? God forbid!' Our members are members of Christ, as we are in covenant with him; in point of fidelity, we must not do so. And his interest in us obligeth us: Mat. xxii. 21, 'Render therefore to Cæsar the things which are Cæsar's, and to God the things which are God's.' We are not our own, but God's: 1 Cor. vi. 19, 20, 'Ye are not your own, for ye are bought with a price; therefore glorify God in your body and in your spirit, which are God's.' Do not rob God of his own; you should make conscience of alienating that which is the Lord's.

Once more, this is bound upon us by another argument, the certainty of our future account: Luke xix. 23, 'Wherefore then gavest not thou my money into the bank, that at my coming I might have received my own with usury?' He will require his own with usury. We should keep a constant and faithful reckoning how we lay out ourselves for God; we must not spare God something only, but the main drift and business of our lives must be to honour God; he must have a share in all things we have and do.

I might add, as another binding consideration, the constancy of divine inspection. We are always in the eye and presence of the great God, who still looketh upon us, and considereth whose business we are about, his or our own: Luke i. 75, 'In holiness and righteousness before him all the days of our life.' We are always before him, and observed by him.

2. Positive holiness may be considered either with respect to our persons or actions.

[1.] Our persons, when we are renewed by the Spirit, or there is an inward principle of sanctification wrought in our hearts. Other things, when dedicated to God, are changed only in their use, as gold, silver, and goat's-hair; but when man is dedicated to God, he is changed in his nature; there is not only a difference between him and others, but a difference between him and himself. There is a difference between him and others, not only as he is set apart for God and dedicated to an holy use; the godly are set apart for God: Ps. iv. 3, 'But know that the Lord hath set apart him that is godly for himself;' but as he is cleansed, purified, and renewed by the Holy Ghost, and so there is a difference between him and himself: 1 Cor. vi. 11, 'And such were some of you; but ye are washed, but ye are sanctified, but ye are justified, in the name of the Lord Jesus, and by the spirit of our God.' Now this is necessary, that a man should be holy before his actions shall be holy; for till a man be regenerated, and act from a principle of grace in his heart, all that he doth is but the shadow and imperfect imitation of a good action, as an ape would imitate a man, or as a violent motion doth resemble that which is natural. We are bidden to be holy as God is holy: 1 Peter i. 15, 'But as he that hath called you is holy, so be ye holy in all manner of conversation.' God as to his essence and being is holy, and all his acts carry a condecency with his nature: 'He is righteous in all his ways, and holy in all his works,' Ps. cxlv. 17. So we are 'made partakers of a divine nature,' 2 Peter i. 4, and so live and walk in a godlike manner: 2 Peter i. 3, 'According as his divine power hath given unto us all things that pertain to life and godliness.' Grace is given to beget life, and then we are visibly to express it in a course of godly walking. Grace is planted in the heart, and then the influence of it is diffused throughout all the parts of his life. First there is internal holiness, in the hatred of sin and the love of that which is good, and then external holiness is expressed in avoiding the one and pursuing after the other. In short, actions without life are the motions of puppets, not living creatures. On the other side, if there be a change of heart, there must be fruits becoming it. Habits are known by their acts, and resolution by our practice, and the new nature by newness of conversation. A principle of grace there must be, and a prevalent principle, such as gets the mastery of sin, before a man can be denominated holy. There are mixed principles and mixed operations in a christian, but one is in predominancy though there be a mixture of principles and of operations, yet there is not a mixture of interests; there is but one chief good; their great design is to please God in all things.

[2.] As a person is holy by his principle, so an action is holy by the rule, when it agreeth with it as to manner and matter and end. The substance of the matter must be such as is warranted by the law of God, which meteth and sets out the bounds of sin and duty: 'For by the law is the knowledge of sin,' Rom. iii. 20; Rom. xii. 2, 'That ye may prove what is that good, and acceptable, and perfect will of God;' Gal. vi. 16, 'As many as walk according to this rule, peace be on them, and mercy, and upon the Israel of God.' So for the manner; it must be done in such a way as will suit with the nature of the action we are about. A man may sin in doing good when he doth not do it well: Luke viii. 18, 'Take heed how you hear;' Eccles. v. 1, 'Keep thy foot when thou goest into the house of God, and be more ready to hear than to give the sacrifice of fools; for they consider not that they do evil.' And in our ordinary conversation: Eph. v. 15, 'See then that ye walk circumspectly, not as fools, but as wise;' Prov. iv. 26, 'Ponder the path of thy feet, and let all thy ways be established.' The end must be to glorify God: 1 Cor. x. 31, 'Whether therefore ye eat or drink, or whatsoever ye do, do all to the glory of God;' Col. iii. 17, 'Whatsoever ye do in word or deed, do all in the name of the Lord Jesus, giving thanks to God and the Father by him.' A common rule for all our actions, that they be undertaken in Christ's name, and thanks be given unto God for the event and success of them. In short, to be ruled by Christ's command, depending on his help, aiming at his glory; the heart must be habitually inclined to all things in him and for him, so as in the issue and close of their actions to yield them matter of thanksgiving to God; this is that universal holiness which is required of all christians.

III. Reasons why this eminent holiness, both of persons and actions, should take place in the gospel, above the times of the law.

1. Because of our principle, the new nature wrought in us by the Spirit of God, which is suited to the whole will of God: Eph. iv. 24, 'And that ye put on the new man, which after God is created in righteousness and true holiness.' As thou art a creature, thou art bound to do the whole will of God, for no creature can be exempted from subjection to his creator; but now as new creatures, so are we fitted and prepared or put into a capacity to serve and please God in all things: Eph. ii. 10, 'For we are his workmanship, created in Christ Jesus unto good works, which God hath before ordained that we should walk in them.' Every creature is fitted for the operations which belong to that life which it hath; so the new creature, if created anew, is fitted anew, and therefore the new nature must show itself in all our actions towards God and men. The new nature must still show itself in all our actions with God, our neighbour, and ourselves: Titus ii. 12, 'Teaching us that, denying ungodliness and worldly lusts, we should live soberly, righteously, and godly, in the present world.' In our worship, taking all occasions of conversing with God; as Cornelius, 'a devout man, and one that feared God with all his house, which gave much alms to the people, and prayed to God alway,' Acts x. 2. In

our dealings with men: Rom. xii. 17, 'Provide things honest in the sight of all men.' In charity: Acts ix. 36, Dorcas, a devout woman, 'full of good works and alms-deeds which she did.' Nay, in our recreations and delights of the present life, use them still in order to God: 1 Tim. iv. 4, 5, 'For every creature of God is good, and nothing to be refused, if it be received with thanksgiving; for it is sanctified by the word of God and prayer.' God's permission, and prayer calling for a blessing on it. The word showeth what is commanded as necessary, what is lawful or indifferent. Prayer on all things showeth the seriousness of a christian; in lesser matters, he would go about nothing but what is recommended to God.

2. Because of the exactness of our rule, which teacheth us how to walk in our several businesses and employments. A christian in his walk, either as to faith or manners, is not left indifferent to choose what rule pleaseth him best; but there is a fixed determinate measure of all our actions, how we shall enter into a state of grace, how we should behave ourselves in it: Micah vi. 8, 'He hath showed thee, O man, what is good; and what doth the Lord God require of thee, but to do justly, and to love mercy, and to walk humbly with thy God?' and Ps. cxix. 105, 'Thy word is a lamp unto my feet, and a light unto my path.' Carnality is a walking κατὰ τὸν αἰῶνα τοῦ κόσμου τούτου, 'according to the course of this world,' Eph. ii. 2. Holiness is walking κατὰ κανόνα, 'according to the rule,' Gal. vi. 16. The one according to the fashions of men, and the guise of fleshly-minded creatures, the other according to the holy will of God: Rom. xii. 2, 'Proving what is that good and acceptable and perfect will of God;' or, 'as becometh the gospel,' Phil. i. 27; a conversation strict, spiritual, and heavenly.

3. Because of our pattern and example, Jesus Christ, who was exact in all his actions. He declared himself to be the Son of God, useful in all his converses, still aiming at the honour of his father: John viii. 50, 'I seek not mine own glory; there is one that seeketh and judgeth.' He was careful to please him in all things. Christ came from heaven not only to expiate our offences, but to give us an example; and 'he that saith he abideth in him, ought himself also so to walk, even as he walked,' 1 John ii. 6. Wherein lieth this example? He telleth us he came 'not to do his own will, but the will of him that sent him,' John v. 30. In temptations, sufferings, reproaches, in the midst of the ingratitude of men, and poverty and meanness of condition, in all his fastings, labours, and death, he sought still to please his father and promote his will: John viii. 29, 'For I do always those things that please him.' This is your pattern, christians; and it is true religion to imitate him whom we worship: likeness to him is the true note of our communion with him; if your life be such a life, then there is 'Holiness to the Lord' written upon it from first to last.

4. Our obligations to Christ; partly because of his dominion, as the Lord-redeemer, by right of purchase: Rom. xiv. 9, 'For to this end Christ both died, and rose, and revived, that he might be Lord both of dead and living.' In all conditions and states of life he hath a right in us, therefore in every state of life we should glorify him. Partly from our gratitude to Christ as a Saviour as well as a Lord. What doth he expect from thee, when he hath done so much for thee already,

and will do much more, but that thou shouldst love him, and live to him ? 2 Cor. v. 14, 15, 'For the love of Christ constraineth us, because we thus judge, that if one died for all, then were all dead; and that he died for all, that they which live should not henceforth live unto themselves, but unto him who died for them, and rose again.' What hadst thou been were it not for his love? What wouldst thou have answered to an accusing conscience in the midst of thy griefs and fears? How wouldst thou have looked God, the judge of all the world, in the face? Who could free thee from the curse of the law, and the flames of hell, but the Son of God, who parted with all his glory that he might redeem thee to God? And if thou wilt not part with thy sins, thou justly deservest to suffer for them. Thou lookest for more from him than ever yet thou hast received, to live with God for ever; what then is thy business, but to glorify him upon earth, that thou mayest be glorified with him for evermore? Partly by thine own covenant vow; thou art baptized in his name, and hast often ratified the bond of the oath into which thou art entered; and what is baptism but a dedication unto God, not to be thine own, but his? Acts xxvii. 23, 'Whose I am, and whom I serve.' If thou art this, thy whole life should be Christ's. 'We are debtors not to the flesh, to live after the flesh,' Rom. viii. 12; with Gal. v. 3, 'I testify to every man that is circumcised, that he is a debtor to do the whole law.'

Use. Is to persuade you to this universal obedience. None enter upon God's service but with a consecration, and none entirely give up themselves to God unless they give up all things with themselves, not one thing reserved; and if nothing be reserved, nothing must be used but for his glory, otherwise the dedication is a mockery. The considerations are plain. Now I shall give you sundry directions, and they will mostly come to the same purpose, but altogether will bind this holiness upon you.

1. Undertake nothing but what will bear this inscription upon it, 'Holiness to the Lord.' This question should be put to ourselves, Can I dedicate this to God? In worship, Am I now acting for God or for myself? In your callings, Is this for God? Is it inconsistent with my great end, or impertinent to it? If it be inconsistent, it is plain treachery to my covenant vow; if impertinent, it is a diversion not voluntarily to be allowed: 2 Cor. v. 9, 'Wherefore we labour that, whether present or absent, we may be accepted of him.' In your sports and delights, Eccles. ii. 2, 'What doeth it?' When you are carding away your precious time or your substance, which might be better employed, is this 'Holiness to the Lord?' That should be legible in all you are and do. In the choice of your relations, disposal of your condition of life, here is your measure still.

2. Be sure to exercise your general calling in your particular; your general calling is to be a christian, your particular calling is that way of life to which God hath designed you by your abilities and education for the common good. Now the one falleth into the other. I am to guide myself in my calling by the general duty of a christian, as a minister, magistrate, gentleman, or tradesman, as one fearing and loving God: John xvii. 4, 'I have glorified thee upon earth, I have finished the work thou gavest me to do;' Acts xiii. 36, 'David served

his generation by the will of God.' As an instrument of providence, I must consider how my particular calling will serve my great end : 1 Cor. vii. 21, 22, 'Art thou called, being a servant? care not for it; but if thou mayest be made free, use it rather. For he that is called in the Lord, being a servant, is the Lord's freeman; likewise also he that is called, being free, is Christ's servant;' Neh. i. 12, 'The Lord show me favour in the sight of this man; for I was the king's cup-bearer.' He had improved his place for God.

3. Turn all second-table duties into first-table duties: Heb. xiii. 16, 'But to do good, and to communicate, forget not; for with such sacrifices God is well pleased.' Sacrifice is a first-table duty, yet relieving the poor is called a well-pleasing sacrifice: James i. 27, 'Pure religion ($\theta\rho\eta\sigma\kappa\epsilon\iota\alpha$, worship) and undefiled before God and the Father is this, to visit the fatherless and widows in their affliction.' Whatever we do must be a sacrifice; then in serving men you serve the Lord Christ. This is to turn common pots into temple pots, and pots into bowls of the altar: Eph. v. 21, 'Submitting yourselves one to another in the fear of God.' Be conscientiously careful and tender of your duty to man: Col. iii. 22, 'Servants, obey in all things your masters according to the flesh, not with eye-service, as men-pleasers, but in singleness of heart, fearing God;' 'Wives, submit yourselves to your own husbands, as unto the Lord,' Eph. v. 22; out of love to Christ: Eph. vi. 1, 'Children, obey your parents in the Lord.'

4. Go about your earthly business with a heavenly mind: Phil. iii. 20, 'But our conversation is in heaven.' All is a journey thither; look to the unseen world.

5. Content not yourselves with the natural use of the creature, as brute beasts do, but see God in all. The creature is as a glass and image wherein to read your Creator's goodness, and as helps and means to enable you to his service; therefore still they must be received with thanksgiving: 1 Tim. iv. 3, 'For every creature of God is good, and nothing to be refused, if it be received with thanksgiving.' Man is to use the inferior creatures for God, not as the lord of them, but as the steward of the Creator, to whom he is accountable for that use; not to sacrifice them to his own pleasure and will, and to gratify his fleshly mind; they are neither his, nor for him, but for God; for he hath not the right of a lord, but a servant.

6. In all your ways acknowledge God, depending upon him for direction and success, and consulting with him, and approving thy heart and life unto him: Prov. iii. 6, 'In all thy ways acknowledge him, and he shall direct thy paths.' Especially duties must be done by virtue of influence from Christ: Phil. ii. 13, 'For it is God which worketh in you both to will and to do of his good pleasure;' Gal. ii. 20, 'I live by the faith of the Son of God.' In our ordinary actions, we must still ask his leave, counsel, and blessing, acknowledging his dominion over us and all that we do; there we must call in his help, and aim at his glory: 1 Cor. x. 31, 'Whether you eat or drink, or whatsoever you do, do all to the glory of God;' that, doing things by him, we may do them for him.

7. God should be worshipped by every faithful person in his own

house in as God-like a manner as he was worshipped by the Jews in the temple. A christian must be alike everywhere, at home and abroad: Phil. ii. 12, 'Wherefore, my beloved, as ye always have obeyed, not as in my presence only, but now much more in my absence, work out your own salvation with fear and trembling.' So David: Ps. ci. 2, 'I will walk within my house with a perfect heart.' There where we familiarly converse, we should show most of holiness, ordering all our affairs and actions as may best demonstrate the sincerity of our hearts.

SERMON UPON JOHN III. 14, 15.

And as Moses lifted up the serpent in the wilderness, even so must the Son of man be lifted up, that whosoever believeth in him should not perish, but have eternal life.—JOHN iii. 14, 15.

The former part of this chapter is spent in a discourse with Nicodemus. (1.) About regeneration. That great pharisee needed to be catechised and taught the plainest principles of christianity. (2.) About salvation by Christ, the great secret which our Lord brought out of his Father's bosom. He instructed him in two things mainly—(1.) The manner of purchasing; (2.) The manner of applying, this salvation. As the whole context may be comprised under these two heads, so also the words read to you. The manner of purchasing is by Christ's coming into the world and dying for sinners; the way of applying is by faith in the Son of God. He instructeth him in the manner of purchasing; partly that he might not think light of sins, seeing he must die for them; partly that he might not be scandalised at his sufferings, as afterwards he buried Christ, and provided a mixture of myrrh and aloes for his funeral, John xix. 39. He instructeth him in the way of applying and obtaining the purchased benefits, partly that he might not be ashamed of professing himself one of Christ's followers and disciples; partly to engage his heart to own him as the Saviour of lost sinners, having sufficient virtue to cure the sinfulness and misery of such as fly to him by faith. These things are represented to him by a type, and that a notable one, the type of the brazen serpent. In the words take notice—

1. Of the πρότασις, or proposition, 'As Moses lifted up the serpent in the wilderness.'

2. The ἀπόδοσις, or the reddition or explication of it, 'Even so must the Son of man be lifted up, that whosoever believeth in him should not perish, but have eternal life.' In which—

[1.] The way of saving mankind, 'The Son of man must be lifted up.'

[2.] The means of applying it, 'That whosoever believeth in him.'

[3.] The benefit propounded, negatively, he 'Should not perish;' positively, 'But have eternal life.'

I shall open the words by a short illustration, and then come to the point.

1. For the protasis. 'As Moses,' by God's appointment, though the minister be only mentioned: Num. xxi. 8, 'The Lord said unto

Moses, Make thee a fiery serpent;' it was not his device, but God's ordinance; no invention and institution of his; he had God's express command and warrant for it. 'Lifted up;' that is, set upon a perch or pole, as an object to be looked upon by the stung Israelites. 'The serpent;' that is, the brazen image and figure of a serpent. Signs are often called by the name of the thing represented and signified. 'In the wilderness;' a figure of this world, through which we have our passage to the heavenly Canaan. You may add, that the πρότασις, or proposition of the type, may be more full, 'That the people might not perish, but be healed and live,' for then the reddition or explication of the type will run more smoothly.

2. The apodosis. 'Even so must the Son of man;' that is, Christ, spoken of in the former verse; the Son of man that ascended and descended, that was in heaven, and knew the depths of God's counsel, and came down to make them known to us. This Son of man must 'be lifted up,' believed on, or looked unto by faith, and then the guilty sinner is healed, and shall not perish, but have eternal life. The lifting up of the Son of man in the sound and first hearing seemeth to note his exaltation; but it doth not carry that notion here, but such a lifting up as is correspondent to the erection of the brazen serpent on a tree or pole. It signifieth the crucifixion of the Son of God, not his exaltation, but the lowest act of his humiliation. So in many other places: John viii. 28, 'When ye have lifted up the Son of man, then shall ye know that I am he.' He speaketh it to the wicked Jews; and how did the Jews lift him up but by crucifying him? Surely they intended no honour to him, yet there it is made their act. So John xii. 32, 33, 'I, if I be lifted up from the earth, will draw all men after me. This he said, signifying what death he should die,' as the evangelist there explaineth his meaning; so that there needeth no further scruple about the sense of the words. It followeth, 'that whosoever;' all persons are invited, without exclusion of any; that universal particle comprehendeth sinners of all sorts and sizes, of all ranks and conditions in the world. 'Believeth in him;' this answereth to looking upon the brazen serpent. Believing is a looking to Christ, a looking upon him by the eye of faith. 'Shall not perish, but have eternal life.' He shall escape the present danger which he feareth. Souls shall be healed, and delivered from hell, and life eternal is restored to them.

Doct. That we ought to consider salvation by Christ as prefigured and represented by the history of the brazen serpent.

'As Moses lifted up the serpent in the wilderness, even so must the Son of man be lifted up.' And Christ here propoundeth it to Nicodemus.

1. It is useful to consider the types, partly to confirm our faith, when we see the harmony between the testaments. There are historical types and prophetical types. Historical types are only patterns and examples: 1 Cor. x. 11, 'All these things happened to them for τύποι,' ensamples or types; so the providences of God to his ancient people: 1 Cor. x. 9, 'Neither let us tempt Christ, as some of them also tempted, and were destroyed of serpents.' Prophetical types were instituted to prefigure a thing to come, as the ceremonies of the law were figures of better things to come. Now we see the gospel is not a novel inven-

tion, only hatched in that age when it was first set afoot. No; it was long since foretold, not only by words, but things; there was a preparation made for it. And partly to help our meditation; we reflect upon these things with more delight and sweetness, whilst we view the agreement between the truth and the type. When we know the person, yet we delight to see the picture; and so we may take a view of things with a grateful variety. We see them double when we consider both the shadow and the mystery. Partly to increase our thankfulness; we have not such dark and long prospects, through which they only could look to Christ; we may see him more clearly in the doctrines of the gospel, where he is evidently set forth unto us, and, as it were, 'crucified before our eyes,' Gal. iii. 1. Surely then we are more obliged to mind these things. The more clearly and convincingly Christ is represented to us, the more will our negligence be aggravated, and our contempt the greater, if we make light of these things.

2. Among other types, the brazen serpent must not be forgotten; partly because it doth in a most lively and full manner represent Christ. Here a word is a sermon; and we cannot think of the brazen serpent but the necessity, the remedy, the means of application, do presently offer themselves to our thoughts. And partly because this took off the great scandal and Jewish exception against Christ, which was the ignominy of the cross. Therefore to a doctor of the law he doth not produce the paschal lamb or other figures, but the brazen serpent, as clearly representing the cause, quality, and fruit of his sufferings.

3. To help you in this consideration, I shall—(1.) Give the history; (2.) The typical use of it.

First, The history, in Num. xxi. 6-9, 'And the Lord sent fiery serpents among the people, and they bit the people; and much people of Israel died. Therefore the people came unto Moses, and said, We have sinned; for we have spoken against the Lord, and against thee: pray unto the Lord, that he take away the serpents from us: and Moses prayed for the people. And the Lord said unto Moses, Make thee a fiery serpent, and set it upon a pole; and it shall come to pass, that every one that is bitten, when he looketh upon it, he shall live. And Moses made a serpent of brass, and put it upon a pole; and it came to pass, that if a serpent had bitten any man, when he beheld the serpent of brass, he lived.' The sin occasioning the judgment was their murmuring at Moses and Aaron, and their loathing of manna; for this God sendeth fiery serpents. Observe how God suiteth the judgment to the sin; venomous tongues are plagued with venomous serpents. It is said, Eccles. x. 11, 'Surely the serpent shall bite without enchantment, and a babbler is no better.' And again, Ps. cxl. 3, 'They have sharpened their tongues like a serpent; adders' poison is under their lips.' They have a bag of water under their tongues, which is most poisonous and inflaming, which in biting is broken. But this was not the asp, but the *chersydrus*, a sort of serpent which abideth on land as well as in water; whilst it liveth in the water, it is not altogether so venomous as when it cometh to live on the dry land, and in this part of the thirsty howling wilderness these kind of serpents were most fiery and burning, and at that time of the year when the Israelites were there, which was about the end of August; for 'Aaron died in the first day of the fifth month,' Num xxxiii. 38, which was about the 10th of July, and the children of Israel mourned thirty days before they journeyed, Num. xx. 29. And when they journeyed from Mount Hor, then we read of their murmuring and God's plaguing them with fiery serpents. Observe, again, that God, that bringeth manna from heaven, can also send serpents. God is not all honey; abused mercy is turned into fury, and when his favours are despised, he hath judgments to sting us; and if men will loathe their food, God will chastise them with poison.

But again to the history. These serpents which God sent are called 'fiery serpents,' partly for their colour, being of a shining glistering skin; the word in the original is *seraphim-burners,* a name given to the angels: Isa. vi. 2, 'Above it stood the seraphims,' which angels are called elsewhere 'flames of fire,' Ps. civ. 4; partly because their venomous stinging and biting did cause a raging heat and grievous burning in the bodies of the Israelites. And it seemeth they were a kind of serpents with wings, not of feathers, but of a cartilaginous substance, like the wings of a bat, and did here and there seize upon them and bite them; or at least they are said to fly because of their swift motion, where by suddenly jerking they shoot themselves forward, or dart themselves out of trees on men or beasts as they pass by them. There is a plain allusion to those flying serpents, Isa. xiv. 29, 'Out of the serpent's hole shall come forth a cockatrice, and his fruit shall be a fiery flying serpent.' And indeed that wilderness through which the Israelites passed did abound with many sorts of these serpents; therefore it is said, Deut. viii. 15, 'Who led thee through that great and terrible wilderness, wherein were fiery serpents and scorpions.' Well, then, they go to Moses, and said, 'We have sinned; for we have spoken against God, and against thee: pray to God for us, that he take away the fiery serpents.' In adversity men will own the faithful servants of God, against whom they have murmured when all is well. Moses forgetteth the injury, and prayeth to God for them; and God, though he doth not take away the serpents, yet he provideth a remedy unlikely in appearance, a brazen serpent to cure the bites of living serpents; but divine institution conveyeth a blessing. The word of command is that they should 'look upon the brazen serpent;' and the word of promise is 'that they should be healed:' Num. xxi. 8, 'Make thee a fiery serpent, and set it upon a pole, and it shall come to pass, that every one when he is bitten, that looketh upon it, shall live.' This is, in short, the history.

Secondly, The mystery, or typical use of the brazen serpent. The chief things represented in it are sin, Christ, and faith; the deadliness of sin, the manner of our deliverance by Christ, and the nature of faith.

1. The Israelites' deadly sin and misery occasioned the setting up of the brazen serpent; so the occasion of Christ's sending into the world was man's sin and misery, we being all bitten by the old serpent, and so liable to the curse. The devil is called 'the old serpent,' Rev. xii. 9; and in the appearance of a serpent he deceived our first parents; therefore we read that 'the serpent beguiled Eve,' 2 Cor. xi. 3. Human

nature was then stung to death by Satan, and the venom dispersed itself throughout the whole race of mankind. Among the Israelites there were but a few stung, here all; there their bodies, here the soul; there temporal death followed, here eternal. In the sting of these fiery serpents two things representeth our misery by sin—(1.) It is painful; (2.) Deadly.

[1.] This sting is painful. The bitings did presently cause pains, and an intolerable thirst and burning, which was very grievous to them; so the sting of sin is painful; not always felt, but soon awakened. In spiritual things we are more stupid, and are not so sensible of the maladies of the soul as they were of the pains of the body. We are 'subject to bondage,' Heb. ii. 14. Though we do not always feel actual horror, there is a fire smothering in our bosoms, though it be not blown up into a flame. One of our spiritual diseases is a lethargy, and it is a great part of our misery not to know our misery. If conscience were not lulled asleep we would be more sensible. Surely Satan's bites are more painful than those of these serpents. His darts are called 'fiery darts,' Eph. vi. 16. His darts are dipped in the gall of asps and vipers. Boiling lusts will in time awaken raging fears and despair. Oh! what horror and torment will sin procure to us if it be not speedily cured! Sin is an evil and a mischief, whether we feel it, yea or no; but we shall soon feel it an evil, as the stung Israelites felt the biting of the serpents. Sin in the life will make hell in the conscience; it seemeth a sweet draught while we are taking it down, but there is rank poison at the bottom. A wounded spirit findeth it now: Prov. xviii. 14, 'A wounded spirit who can bear?' Horror and anguish of conscience is insupportable. Ask any man whose heart is well awakened, and he will tell you that the sense of the guilt of sin is more bitter to the soul than the gall of asps; no terror comparable to the terror and sting of an accusing conscience. God's terrors are compared to a fire that drinketh up the blood and spirits: Job vi. 4, 'The arrows of the Almighty are within me, the poison whereof drinketh up my spirit; the terrors of God do set themselves in array against me.' No poison more burning than sin in an awakened conscience. It may lie asleep till you come to die in sin, stupid and benumbed creatures; but then 'the sting of death is sin,' 1 Cor. xv. 56. Death is made terrible by those sad horrors and apprehensions which sin raiseth in us.

[2.] This sting is deadly. As the biting of the fiery serpents could not be cured, but was present death till God found out a remedy, so this sting of sin is deadly: Rom. v. 12, 'By one man sin entered into the world, and death by sin, and so death passed upon all men, for that all have sinned;' Gen. ii. 17, 'In the day thou eatest thereof thou shalt surely die;' dying thou shalt die: Rom. vi. 23, 'The wages of sin is death;' death temporal, eternal. Thou art a dead man, lost for ever, if thou art not cured. Those who were not solicitous about their cure are a figure of the impenitent, who obstinately continue in their sins though they bring destruction upon them. Not only death temporal, which consists in the separation of the soul from the body; but death spiritual, which consists in an estrangement from God as author of the life of grace; yea, death eternal, which consists in a separation both of body and soul from the presence of God for evermore, and is a perpetual living to deadly pain and torment. This second death is set forth by two solemn notions, 'The worm that never dieth, and the fire that shall never be quenched,' Mark ix. 44; by which is meant the sting of conscience and the wrath of God: Prov. viii. 36, 'All they that hate me love death.'

2. Christ is set forth by the brazen serpent. Here I shall show you—(1.) The resemblances; (2.) The superexcellency of Christ above this, and all the shadows and types of him.

[1.] The resemblance between Christ and the brazen serpent.

(1.) The brazen serpent was a remedy of God's own prescribing out of his great mercy; so is this remedy for lost sinners the mere fruit of God's love: John iii. 16, 'God so loved the world that he gave his only-begotten Son.' The *causa προκαταρκτικὴ*, the occasion or outward moving cause, was our misery; the *causa προηγουμένη*, the inward impulsive cause, was his own love and pity to lapsed mankind. God found out the remedy; we neither plotted it nor asked it; he saw the world of mankind was perishing, and involved in eternal ruin, and because there was no intercessor, therefore his own arm wrought out salvation. Herein the antitype differeth from the type. The stung Israelites, having death in their bosoms, go to Moses; Moses goeth to God, for he saw there could be no help elsewhere; then God said, 'Make thee a brazen serpent.' The motion came from them first, but here it is quite otherwise; God is the offended party, yet he maketh the first motion: 1 John iv. 19, 'We love him because he loved us first.' There God found out the remedy, but here his mere love began the whole business, and did set at work all the causes that did concur to our salvation; we neither minded our danger nor asked our remedy.

(2.) The conveniency of this type to set out the low estate and humiliation of Christ. The form of a serpent was chosen to show that he came in such mean estate as if he were a worm and no man: Ps. xxii. 6, 'I am a worm and no man, a reproach of men, and despised of the people.' So also Isa. liii. 3, 'He was despised and rejected of men; a man of sorrows, and acquainted with grief; and we hid as it were our faces from him; he was despised, and we esteemed him not;' as a vile and abominable creature, both 'despised and rejected,' scarce deemed worthy the name of a man, or to have any converse or communion with them. It is the leavings off of men, as we would say, the very list and fag-end of mankind; so low and mean, that the nature of man can hardly descend lower: Mark ix. 12, 'The Son of man must suffer many things, and be set at nought;' it is *ἐξουδενωθῇ*, made nought worth, or nothing. Once more, the serpent, of all the beasts of the field, was the creature which was cursed by God: Gen. iii. 14, 'Because thou hast done this, thou art cursed above all cattle, and above every beast of the field; upon thy belly shalt thou go, and dust shalt thou eat all the days of thy life.' Yet by this form would he represent Christ to the ancient church. God chose this to be a type of Christ, which we would have thought a dishonour and disparagement to him. Yea, this serpent that was now set up was made of brass, not of gold, to show that Christ would not appear in glorious estate and majesty, but in the meanest and most abject form of any creature. All together will help us to meditate upon the great abasement of the Son of God. *Quanto vilior, tanto clarior nobis esse debet.* The more he humbled himself, the higher estimation should we have of our crucified Lord. Never was any child of God before Christ under so much misery as Christ himself was. His own heaven, his own Father, his own Godhead, hid their face and consolation from him. God's wrath pressed the weight of punishment with the full power of justice both upon his soul and body; those for whom he died despised him, he himself being emptied of all things that make men respected in the world, and depressed lower than ever any man was, as a worm to be trod upon. He was made the matter of common talk and reproach in all men's mouths; condemned by the ruling part of the world, and set at nought by the basest of the people; derided and scorned in his most holy behaviour, his bitter sufferings made a matter of sport and laughter, malice feeding itself with pleasure upon his pain and misery, and expressing itself with the basest signs of mockage which disdain could devise, flouting at his saving doctrine, and insulting over him as if he had been neither the Son of God nor an honest man. And all this was counted little enough for satisfaction of justice, exacting of him the due punishment of our sins. We tenderly resent contempt, and cannot endure to be despised and thrust down, when the Sun of righteousness went back so many degrees in the dial of honour.

(3.) The brazen serpent had the shape and figure of the serpent, but not the sting and the poison. *Figuram habuit, non naturam ;* it had the figure, not the nature of a serpent. Let us pause upon this a little. God would cure the bite of a serpent by a serpent; a serpent stung, and a serpent healed : 'God sending his own Son in the likeness of sinful flesh, and for sin condemned sin in the flesh,' Rom. viii. 3 ; that is, by Jesus Christ in our nature, who was made a sin-offering, and therefore called sin there. The parties to be cured were men, therefore 'the Son of man must be lifted up;' that title is given him here in the text. Christ was debased by this title, by being called 'the Son of man,' but yet the sons of men are dignified by it; 'he came in the likeness of sinful flesh.' As the brazen serpent was in all things like the true serpent, but without any hurtful quality, so Christ in all points was like us, 'but without sin ;' Heb. iv. 15. He came in the likeness of sinful flesh, yet was 'holy, harmless, and separate from sinners.'

(4.) The precise place where the brazen serpent was lifted up. Moses doth not tell us in the story where this matter is recorded; but it may be collected from other places. Moses telleth us that the Israelites going from thence pitched their tents in Oboth, Num. xxi. 10 ; from whence it follows that the place was Punon, for from Punon they came to Oboth, Num. xxxiii. 42, 43. Now this Punon was a place belonging to Idumæa, very famous for mines of brass or copper, as is commonly known in ancient writings, the brass being called from thence 'the metal of Punon.' Eusebius in the eighth book of his Ecclesiastical History tells us that Sylvanus and thirty-nine more were beheaded for the faith's sake, κατὰ τὰ ἐν Φύνῳ χάλκου μέταλλα, near the mines of brass in Punon ; and Eutychius speaketh of divers christians condemned to work in these mines. So also doth Epiphanius and Theodoret. So that the brass out of which the serpent was made was taken out of the very place in which they were bitten; it was the brass of Punon, not without a mystery. That body which Christ assumed was not brought from elsewhere, but born there and formed there where he was manifested in the flesh for the salvation of the world; and where the mischief was, there was the remedy at hand.

(5.) The similitude chiefly holdeth in this, that as the brazen serpent was lifted up upon the perch or pole, so was Christ lifted up on the cross: 1 Peter ii. 24, 'Who his own self bare our sins in his own body upon the tree.' The serpent first stung us by the fruit of a tree, and Christ saved us by suffering upon a tree. David had foretold that his hands and his feet should be pierced: Ps. xxii. 16, 'They pierced my hands and my feet.' And the curse of the law was to be borne: 'Christ hath redeemed us from the curse of the law, being made a curse for us; for it is written, Cursed is every one that hangeth on a tree,' Gal. iii. 13. The apostle obviates an objection; if the law do curse all men, how are any freed from the curse of the law? Even by Jesus Christ, who took upon him the curse due to us, while he was obedient to death, even the death of the cross; for that kind of death was pronounced to be accursed: Deut. xxi. 23, 'He that is hanged is accursed of God.' He came as a surety in the sinner's name, and would take our burden upon himself, and therefore chose a death of all others most cruel and painful and contemptible, ordained for the wickedest and vilest wretches, thereby to assure us of a full ransom and satisfaction to divine justice for our wrongs, and to imprint upon our minds the horrors of our sins. Well, then, here is the spectacle offered to our faith, Jesus Christ hanging upon a tree. We should look upon Christ crucified as if the thing were now a-doing before our eyes: Gal. iii. 1, 'Before whose eyes Jesus Christ hath been evidently set forth crucified before you.' Though it be past long ago it is present to faith; for he is lifted up, that by the eye of faith we should look to him, and see not only the thing, but the end, use, and virtue of this mystery. The brazen serpent was a sufficient remedy for the stung Israelites; none that looked towards it perished, the cure never failed; and Jesus Christ lifted up, and being eyed, is sufficient to cure the guilt of sin, and pain of conscience through sin, and to heal our diseased souls, and free them from the power of corruption. For being made a curse for us, the blessing cometh freely upon the believing gentiles, even the gift of the Spirit: Isa. liii. 5, 'He was wounded for our transgressions, he was bruised for our iniquities; the chastisement of our peace was upon him, and with his stripes we are healed.'

[2.] The superexcellency of Christ above this and all the shadows and types of him. The type doth express the thing signified, but yet the truth doth much exceed the shadow. The brazen serpent was but 'a sign of salvation;' so called in the Book of Wisdom, chap. xvi. 6. But Christ 'is the author of salvation,' Heb. v. 9. The serpent benefited only the Israelites, but Christ all nations, both Jew and gentile: Isa. xi. 10, 'In that day there shall be a root of Jesse, which shall stand for an ensign of the people; to it shall the gentiles seek, and his rest shall be glorious.' It freed them from present death, but yet so that they might die by other means; but Christ hath freed us not only from the death of the body, but of the soul, and this for ever, as in the text, 'That they should not perish, but have everlasting life.' So John xi. 26, 'Whosoever liveth and believeth in me, shall never die.' There natural life is preferred[1] but for a while, here eternal life obtained. This benefit might last for a day or two, but 'Jesus Christ is the same yesterday, and to-day, and for ever,' Heb. xiii. 8. Christ ever retaineth his healing virtue. This was but a piece of brass while they lodged it in the temple, but Christ is a mediator to all eternity. It was a great wickedness to worship the brazen serpent, therefore Hezekiah broke it in pieces, when once he understood the people to be guilty of that idolatry: 2 Kings xviii. 4, 'He brake in pieces the brazen serpent that Moses had made, for unto those days the children of Israel did burn incense to it; and he called it Nehushtan,' or a piece of brass; but it is our duty to worship Christ: 'All men must honour the Son as they honour the Father,' John v. 23; and Heb. i. 6, 'Let all the angels of God worship him;' Phil. ii. 9, 10, 'Wherefore God hath highly exalted him, and given him a name which is above every name, that at the name of Jesus every knee should bow.' When the Israelites worshipped the brazen serpent, it was broken in pieces; but they shall be broken in pieces themselves that deny Christ his due worship: Ps. ii. 9, 'Thou shalt break them with a rod of iron, thou shalt dash them in pieces like a potter's vessel;' Dan. ii. 44, 'And in the days of these kings shall the God of heaven set up a kingdom which shall never be destroyed; and the kingdom shall not be left to other people, but shall break in pieces and consume all these kingdoms, and shall stand for ever.' The kingdom that will not submit to him shall be broken in pieces: Luke xix. 27, 'Those mine enemies that would not that I should reign over them, bring them hither, and slay them before me.' Thus it sets forth Christ.

3. Faith is set forth, or the way and means how we come to have benefit by Christ. It is not enough to look to what Christ hath done, but what we must do that we may be partakers of him. The way of cure was by a look; so it is believing in him that bringeth home the blessing to our souls.

From this type we learn—

[1.] The necessity of faith. None had benefit by the brazen serpent but those that looked on it. The promise was made to those that observed the command: Num. xxi. 8, 'Every one that is bitten, when he looketh upon it, shall live.' If a man turned away his eyes and refused God's remedy, the biting was mortal to him. As there is a necessity Christ should die, so there is a necessity you should believe; for besides impetration there must be application; and the work of the Spirit is as necessary to apply grace as the work of the Mediator to obtain grace for us. A deep well will do you no good without a bucket, nor the purchase of salvation unless you apply it.

[2.] An encouragement of faith.

(1.) To broken-hearted sinners; if you are stung with sin, you may look to Christ. It was ground enough for any bitten Israelite to look to this brazen serpent, because he had need; he found himself bitten, and thirsted for cure by this appointed means. A felt sense of sin is warrant enough to look to Christ as the offered remedy. Look not

[1] Qu. preserved'?—ED.

altogether to your sore, to your sins, but to Christ as the means of healing. Indeed there must be a feeling and a sense of sin, or else there is no work for Christ to do; what should a hale Israelite do with the brazen serpent? Their looking began in a sense of pain; none troubled their thoughts about it till they were stung. Compunction goeth before faith. The Israelites cried out, Oh! what shall we do for these fiery serpents? So Acts ii. 37, 'When they heard this, they were pricked in their heart, and said unto Peter and the rest of the apostles, Men and brethren, what shall we do?' An empoisoned dagger was flung into their souls, and then, 'What shall we do?' The jailer 'came trembling, and fell down before Paul and Silas, and said, Sirs, what must I do to be saved?' Acts xvi. 29, 30; 'And they said,' ver. 31, 'Believe on the Lord Jesus Christ, and thou shalt be saved.' Only look upon the serpent. A sinner must first feel himself a sinner before he will or can come to Christ, but then come: 'The Son of man is lifted up, that whosoever believeth in him should not perish but have eternal life.' Some that know not themselves believers have been welcome to Christ; but never any that know not themselves sinners.

(2.) To lapsed believers. The serpents were left to sting the Israelites while they were in that place, only the brazen serpent was lifted up. God did not presently take away the serpents, only he gave a remedy for such as were bitten. Sin is not abolished, but whilst we are in this station the remedy is still offered; we are never so cured but we may be bitten again. The disobedient Israelites needed this motive and chastisement to keep them in awe; we cannot imagine that any would provoke these serpents to sting him that he might be healed. So say I, as the apostle, 1 John ii. 1, 'These things I write unto you, that ye sin not; and if any man sin, we have an advocate with the Father, Jesus Christ the righteous.' For the present, stings of conscience is one of God's rods over us, but when we fall, there is forgiveness by Jesus Christ; as Peter of Alexandria destroyed the idols, but only left one for a monument.

[3.] The nature of faith, which is a looking to Christ. It is usually said that faith is ὀφθαλμος της ψυχῆς, 'the eye of the soul.' Certain it is that the act of faith is often expressed by seeing or looking, and faith itself by an eye; as Zech. xii. 10, 'They shall look upon me whom they have pierced.' So Isa. xvii. 7, 'At that day a man shall look to his Maker, and his eyes shall have respect to the Holy One of Israel.' So John vi. 40, 'This is the will of him that sent me, that every one which seeth the Son, and believeth on him, may have everlasting life,' ὁ θεωρῶν καὶ πιστεύων. And faith is described to be 'the substance of things hoped for, and the evidence of things not seen,' Heb. xi. 1. By faith 'Moses saw him that was invisible,' Heb. xi. 27.; Heb. xii. 2, 'Looking to Jesus.' So faith itself is said to be the eye of the soul: Eph. i. 18, 'That the eyes of your understandings being opened,' Gal. iii. 1; 'Before whose eyes Jesus Christ hath been evidently set forth crucified among you.' The mystery of Christ crucified was so evidently set forth as if he had been crucified before their eyes. So where the work of faith is impeded and hindered, it is said 'the god of this world hath blinded the minds of them which believe not,' 2 Cor. iv. 4; that is, hindered their faith. Therefore I shall here inquire—(1.) What sights are proper to faith; (2.) What kind of looking faith is.

(1.) The objects proper to faith are matters that lie out of the view of sense, τα μὴ βλεπόμενα, things that cannot be seen by any other faculty or discerning power. Some things are invisible in regard of their nature, and some things because of their distance from us, because either they are past or to come. Things invisible, because of their nature, are all spiritual things, which are not obvious to the eye of sense. Sense is only conversant about bodily things, which may be seen, heard, tasted, or felt; reason can only see things in their causes. Things invisible, by reason of their distance, are either things past, as the creation of the world, or the sufferings of Christ; or things to come, as the glory and happiness of the other world. Let us explain this by applying it to the matter in hand, the Son of man lifted up on the cross. This was sometimes a matter of sense, namely, at the time when Christ suffered; and therefore then if a man had seen him, or looked upon him, it had done him no good, as it did not to those that wagged their heads at him and mocked him, though it did to the centurion, who cried out, Mat. xxvii. 54, 'Truly this was the Son of God.' But in another regard this is always matter of faith, namely, if we consider his deity, and offices; as the Son of God dying and healing wounded consciences, this is a thing invisible in its nature. Therefore the soldiers that turned subjects to him, and confessors of his name, even then when he is hanging dead on the cross, they that could see his Godhead, and confess it in its deepest humiliation, were believers; they saw Christ not with the eye of sense, but of faith. Now go to the other things invisible, viz., by reason of their distance, because they are either to come or past. Christ crucified was sometimes a thing to come. The fathers had need of clear eyes, who could see salvation at such a distance, and represented under such dark figures and shadows; yet some had such an eagle-eye of faith: 'Your father Abraham rejoiced to see my day; and he saw it, and was glad,' John viii. 56; and Heb. xi. 13, 'All these died in faith, not having received the promises, but having seen them afar off, and were persuaded of them, and embraced them.' To us now it is a thing past; there needeth faith both to believe the history and the mystery too. When we believe the history so clearly as if we saw it, Gal. iii. 1, that is faith; and the mystery: 1 Cor. ii. 2, 'For I determined to know nothing among you but Jesus Christ and him crucified;' and ver. 4, 'My speech and my preaching was not with enticing words of man's wisdom, but in demonstration of the Spirit, and of power.' This ἀπόδειξις πνεύματος, this 'demonstration of the Spirit,' is the ground of faith, when the object is so represented that it maketh a powerful impression, and so affected as if we had seen him with our eyes. Well, then, it is some faith to believe the history, to see it as a thing now done. So John xx. 29, 'Blessed are they that have not seen, and yet have believed.' But to believe the end and the use, that was always matter of faith, whether past, present, or to come. And herein all believers stand upon the same level. Christ is not now lifted up upon the cross, but it is our duty to lift him up, that poor sinners and wounded consciences may look on him with an eye of faith: Isa. xi. 10,

'There shall be a root of Jesse which shall stand for an ensign of the people; to it shall the gentiles seek;' Isa. xlix. 22, 'Behold, I will lift up my hand to the gentiles, and set up my standard to the people; and they shall bring thy sons in their arms, and thy daughters shall be carried upon their shoulders.' Christ is lifted up in the ministry of the word as a sign of salvation to draw people to him, so to see him as to follow him, and as to submit to him. If David prayed God to 'open his eyes to see the wonders of his law,' Ps. cxix. 18, we may much more pray to God to open our eyes to see Christ, and own him in the gospel, and to see him crucified in the symbols of bread and wine for our comfort.

(2.) We have showed you what is to be seen by faith, now what kind of sight faith is. Not a bare speculation, but such as was the look of the Israelites on the brazen serpent, serious, applicative, affectionate, engaging to thankfulness and obedience, when they went away and were healed.

(1st.) Serious; not a glance, but a fixed eye. A stung Israelite would not cast a careless glance on the sign of salvation and health, neither should we upon Christ. Ponderous thoughts take hold of the heart; musing maketh the fire to burn, and a steady sight hath the greatest influence upon us.

(2d.) Applicative. So Job v. 27, 'Hear it, and know thou it for thy good.' The Israelite came for the cure of his own wounds; so must we look upon Christ as our own Saviour, with application to ourselves: John xx. 28, 'My Lord and my God.'

(3d.) Affectionate, with desire and trust. With desire longing for cure; there must be hearty groans and desires: 'Our eyes are upon thee,' 2 Chron. xx. 12. The having our eyes to anything noteth our desire: Ps. cxxi. 1, 'I will lift up mine eyes unto the hills, from whence cometh my help.' Earnestly desire to be partaker of these benefits by Christ: 1 Peter i. 7, 'To them that believe he is precious;' and with trust: Isa. xvii. 7, 'At that day shall a man look to his Maker, and his eyes shall have respect to the Holy One of Israel;' that is, he shall seek to him, trust in him, depend upon him, because what men trust to they are wont frequently and wistly to look after, and to have their eyes fixed upon: Ps. cxxiii. 2, 'Behold, as the eyes of servants look unto the hand of their masters, and as the eyes of a maiden to the hand of her mistress; so our eyes wait upon the Lord our God, till he have mercy on us;' Ps. xxxiv. 5, 'They looked to him, and were lightened;' that is, comforted in the midst of their darkness and trouble; Ps. cxli. 8, 'Mine eyes are unto thee, O God the Lord; in thee I trust.'

(4th.) Engaging; we need to get open eyes to see him and contemplate him, till we see beauty in him that may allure us to love him, and esteem him as the fairest of ten thousand, to renounce ourselves and the vanities of the world, and betake ourselves to his discipline, to see all is nothing in comparison of his excellency: Phil. iii. 8, 'Yea, doubtless, and I count all things but loss for the excellency of the knowledge of Christ Jesus my Lord.' A true knowledge of Christ is called $\dot{\epsilon}\pi\dot{\iota}\gamma\nu\omega\sigma\iota\varsigma$, Eph. i. 17, which is elsewhere rendered 'acknowledging,' so as to give due honour, respect, and reverence to him. We may know strangers, and those whom we contemn and despise, but we do not acknowledge them.

Use. Let us look upon the Lord Jesus for cure. He calleth upon us in his word, 'Look unto me, and be ye saved, all the ends of the earth,' Isa. xlv. 12. It is little that we can afford Christ if we cannot afford him a serious look. It may be you will think that this is so slight a work that it will not produce any great effects in the soul; that a look should heal is strange. Surely, you will say, this is not a full notion of faith, nor an act that will do us any good. I answer— Indeed it will not if it be done slightly. Therefore let me tell you that there are several notions of faith, which all have their use. Some notions are fitted for soul-examination, as faith that worketh by love, that conquereth the world, that purifieth the heart; these do best for a deliberate search, and the stating of our interest. Some for anxious thoughts at the first awaking of the soul out of the sleep of sin, as coming, running, flying, and seeking. When the soul is under trouble, and hangeth off from the grace offered, we press them to come; as our necessities are great, we press them to run. A soul deeply pressed with a sense of its necessity and danger is always in haste, so we press them to fly for refuge. When comfort appeareth not presently, we press to seek, and to a diligent attendance on the appointed means. Some for agonies of conscience after some former manifestations of God's love; these we exhort to staying and resting: Isa. l. 10, 'Who is among you that feareth the Lord, that obeyeth the voice of his servant, that walketh in darkness, and hath no light? Let him trust in the name of the Lord, and stay upon his God.' We press recumbency and adherence: Isa. xxvi. 3, 'Thou wilt keep him in perfect peace whose mind is stayed on thee, because he trusteth in thee.' Some for agonies of death; and great and imminent dangers, when long debates are not so seasonable, these we press to committing: 2 Tim. i. 12, 'I know whom I have believed, and am persuaded that he is able to keep that which I have committed unto him against that day;' 1 Peter iv. 19, 'Let them that suffer according to the will of God commit the keeping of their souls to him in well-doing, as unto a faithful Creator.' Jesus Christ himself did so: Luke xxiii. 46, 'Father, into thy hands I commend my spirit;' and David: Ps. xxxi. 5, 'Into thine hand I commit my spirit.' Some for holy duties, as word, prayer, Lord's supper; we press to acceptance of Christ in the word, to coming to Christ, or to God by Christ in prayer; we accept him from God in the word of promise, we present him to God in prayer as the ground of our confidence and hope for the mercies prayed for. In the Lord's supper, as religion is made visible, and we are to make use of the help of sense, eye, taste, and hand, so we press you to take, eat, and look; this is a notion for this use when Christ is crucified as it were before our eyes. Well, then, this is one great work, to look to Jesus, the author and dedicator of our faith, to spy out Christ under his memorials; here he is set forth dying and hanging on a tree. Pilate, when he had scourged him, brought him forth and showed him to the Jews; he said, 'Behold the man!' John xix. 5. We say, to you in God's name, Behold your dearest Redeemer bleeding and dying.

Now he is evidently set forth to you, your business is to behold him. And that this look may be serious, remember—

1. This is supposed, that you come hither as stung with sin, and that your hearts are deeply affected with your malady. Alas! otherwise here is no work to do. If men are not sensible of their malady, why should they look after a remedy: Mat. ix. 12, 13, 'They that be whole need not a physician, but they that are sick; for I am not come to call the righteous, but sinners to repentance.' None but the burdened will look out for ease, or the self-condemned for pardon. If sin be not sin indeed, grace will not be grace indeed. Christ was anointed 'to heal the broken-hearted,' Luke iv. 18.

2. Your sight of Christ must not merely be historical and literal, the work of the understanding and memory, but of faith. A few cold thoughts raised upon this occasion do not warm and comfort the heart. You are to look to him so as that the heart be affected with mourning, desire, and trust.

[1.] Mourning for sin. If you are sensible of your case you will do so. A slight glance of the thoughts leaveth no impression. Look, as the three Marys, Mary the mother of Jesus, Mary the wife of Cleophas, and Mary Magdalen, they were affected when they saw Christ dying, John xix. 25, 26; of one of them it is said, Luke ii. 35, 'Yea, a sword shall pierce through thine own soul also;' so do you: Acts ii. 37, 'When they heard this, they were pricked in their heart.'

[2.] Desire. Would not the stung Israelite desire a cure? So must you: Mat. v. 6, 'Blessed are they that hunger and thirst after righteousness, for they shall be filled.' Saith the church, Lam. iii. 51, 'Mine eye affecteth my heart.'

[3.] Trust. You see nothing by the eye of sense but his memorials, which God hath instituted as helps of faith, yet to appearance as despicable and as unlikely to produce any great effect as a figure of brass to cure a raging wound. But things under an institution are under a blessing: 1 Cor. i. 21, 'It pleased God by the foolishness of preaching to save them that believe.' You may think a crucifix a more lively representation. No; that is not under the blessing of an institution, as bread broken and wine poured forth is; that is too much a matter of sense, and begetteth bare thoughts, which stirreth up fond pity and gross and wrong thoughts. This conveyeth a blessing: You are to behold not only a dying man put to a cruel death, but the Son of God in his deep exinanition; not carnally to pity him, but to see his love and the wrath of God and the desert of sin, that you may abhor it; to see the great price paid for our ransom, the necessity of having the virtue of his cross, and finally our thankful subjection to God. Behold him that you may bless and praise God for your redeemer. The type had its effect, and shall not Christ? Oh! labour to feel the comfortable effects of his death.

3. Beg of God the Spirit to open your eyes. Christ crucified is only seen in the light and evidence of the Spirit: 1 Cor. ii. 4, 'My speech and my preaching was not with the enticing words of man's wisdom, but in demonstration of the Spirit and of power.' The eyes of our minds are opened by the Spirit of wisdom and revelation, for our light is but darkness.

4. See him so as to expect not only comfort, but healing: Isa. liii. 5, 'With his stripes we are healed.' That heart is to be suspected that looks to comfort more than duty. Look to him that you may live by him: Gal. ii. 20, 'I live, yet not I, but Christ liveth in me; and the life which I now live in the flesh, I live by the faith of the Son of God, who loved me, and gave himself for me.' Look to him that you may be like him: 2 Cor. iii. 18, 'For we all with open face, beholding as in a glass the glory of the Lord, are changed into the same image from glory to glory, even as by the Spirit of the Lord.' Look to him that you may loathe sin: Ezek. xxxvi. 31, 'Then shall you remember your own evil ways, and your doings that were not good, and shall loathe yourselves in your own sight, for your iniquities, and for your abominations.'

SERMONS UPON 1 THESSALONIANS V. 16.

SERMON I.

Rejoice evermore.—1 THES. v. 16.

THE words are brief and short, and therefore they may be easily carried away. They are independent on the context, and therefore will need no long deduction. They press you not to a painful, but pleasant duty; therefore you should be readily induced to practise it. But yet, when we look more intrinsically into the nature of it, it is not so easy as we first imagined. Every one cannot receive this saying; it is hard to keep the heart in such an exact frame as to 'rejoice evermore, pray without ceasing, and in everything to give thanks;' as Christ saith in another case, 'He that is able to receive it, let him receive it,' Mat. xix. 12. But what if we prove it to be a duty incumbent on all christians, and that at all times? The text seemeth to enforce it, 'Rejoice evermore.'

In which words take notice of two things—

1. The duty to which we are exhorted, 'Rejoice.'
2. The constancy and perpetuity of it, in the word, 'Evermore.' Delight and pleasure are greedily sought after; in christianity it is not only part of our wages, but much of our very work.

Doct. That God's children should make conscience of rejoicing in God at all times and under all conditions.

Here is a precept for it; not only a liberty given, but a command. If you look upon the words as a licence or liberty given, you may conceive of them according to the apostle's speech of marriage: 1 Cor. vii. 39, 'She is at liberty to be married to whom she will,' μόνον ἐν κυρίῳ, but only 'in the Lord.' But it is not only a liberty given, but a command; for he addeth, ver. 18, 'This is the will of God in Christ Jesus concerning you.' The will of God is the supreme reason of all duties, and the will of God in Christ Jesus falleth upon the conscience with a double force; the law of the mediator binding us to delight in God, as well as the primitive duty which we owe to God as the Creator. And that this clause respects all the three duties is evident to any considering mind. In the opening of this duty I shall shew you—(1.) What rejoicing the apostle intendeth; (2.) How this must be constant and perpetual; (3.) The many reasons which do enforce this duty upon us.

I. What rejoicing the apostle speaketh of. There is a double rejoicing—a carnal rejoicing, and a spiritual rejoicing.

1. The carnal rejoicing is in the world, and the good things of this

world apart from God : Luke xii. 19, 'Soul, thou hast much goods laid up for many years; take thine ease ; eat, drink, and be merry.'

2. The spiritual rejoicing is in God: Phil. iii. 1, 'Finally, my brethren : rejoice in the Lord ;' Phil. iv. 4, 'Rejoice in the Lord always, and again I say, rejoice.' These two sorts of rejoicing must be carefully distinguished, for they differ in their causes. To the one we are prompted by carnal nature, which taketh up with present things, and the other is excited in us by the Spirit of God, therefore often called 'joy in the Holy Ghost.' The one is called the joy of sense, the other the joy of faith. The joy of faith is in God, the joy of sense in the creature ; the joy of faith is most in future things, the joy of sense in present things ; the joy of faith is in the good of the soul, the joy of sense in the good of the body or the provisions of the flesh ; the joy of faith is built on the covenant and the promises of God: Ps. cxix. 111, 'Thy testimonies have I taken as an heritage for ever; they are the rejoicing of my heart.' The joy of sense on the blessings that flow in the channel of common and general providence. Now the first sort of rejoicing the apostle would not press us unto. Nature there needeth a bridle rather than a spur ; but to the latter, delight in God, and in all things that come from God and lead to him.

This delighting ourselves in God must be the thing, which must be further explained.

[1.] God himself, as God, is a lovely nature, and the object of our delight; for he is good, even before and without the apprehension of his doing good : Ps. cxix. 68, 'Thou art good, and doest good ;' and 'of him, and to him, and through him, are all things,' Rom. xi. 36. God's essential goodness is not, I confess, the first inviting motive to draw our hearts to him, but his beneficial goodness ; yet the infinite perfection of his nature is also an object of our love and delight; for the creature was made for him, and our good and benefit is not the last end. As the angels admire and adore God not only for his benefits, but also for his holiness and sovereign majesty and dominion : Isa. vi. 3, 'Holy, holy, holy, is the Lord of hosts ; the whole earth is full of his glory ;' so should we, who are to laud God and serve God on earth as he is served in heaven, Mat. vi. 10. Admire him, and delight in him for his holiness and the infinite perfection of his nature. Surely we are not only to bless him, but praise him : Ps. cxlv. 2, 'Every day will I bless thee, and I will praise thy name for ever and ever ;' and ver. 10, 'All thy works shall praise thee, O Lord, and thy saints shall bless thee.' These two words have their distinct reference ; blessing to his benefits, and praise to his excellences; and when we praise God for his glorious being, we should do it in a delightful manner : Ps. cxxxv. 3, 'Praise ye the Lord, for the Lord is good ; sing praises unto his name, for it is pleasant.' It is pleasant and delightful to think of, or speak of, or show forth the excellences of his heavenly majesty. Again, his holiness is an amiable thing, and therefore the object of our delectation. If we must delight in the saints because of their holiness, though they have never done us good : Ps. xvi. 3, 'But to the saints that are in the earth, and to the excellent, in whom is all my delight ;' if we are to account them the excellent ones of the earth because of the image and beauty of God that is upon them, then surely we are much more to love God, not only because of his benefits, but because of his holiness. Yea, if we are to love the law of God, and to delight in it, as it is pure: Ps. cxix. 140, 'Thy word is very pure, therefore thy servant loveth it;' then surely we are to love God also because of the immaculate purity of his nature, and to delight in him. At least this is one, though not the only nor the first reason of our love to him and delight in him.

[2.] We are to delight and rejoice in God as he hath discovered himself to us in Christ. That was the foundation of his beneficial goodness, and the greatest discovery of the amiable nature of God that ever was made to the creature: John iii. 16, 'God so loved the world, that he gave his only-begotten Son;'. Rom. v. 8, 'But God commendeth his love towards us, in that, while we were yet sinners, Christ died for us.' That we might not conceive God to be all wrath and inexorable, unless upon hard terms, therefore Christ came as the express image of his person, full of grace and truth. Well, then, God reconciled in Christ is the life and spirit of all our joy and gladness. In Christ we see him accessible, near to us, and within the reach of our commerce, as dwelling in our nature. In Christ we see him gracious and propitious to us, ready to do us good: Luke i. 46, 47, 'My soul doth magnify the Lord, and my spirit hath rejoiced in God my Saviour.' We have a great and a good God in Christ; he is God and our Saviour.

[3.] We rejoice in God as we rejoice in the fruits of our redemption, or in all those spiritual blessings which are offered or given to us by Christ; such as reconciliation, or God's admitting of us into the privileges of his holy covenant: Rom. v. 11, 'We joy in God through our Lord Jesus Christ, by whom we have now received the atonement.' Clear that once, and the cause of all our sadness and drooping discouragements is taken out of the way. The bottom cause of our bondage and fears is the quarrel God hath against us by reason of sin; we can never be soundly merry and comfortable till that be taken up; for as long as we apprehend him an enemy and an avenger, how can we rejoice in him? So Ps. xxxii. 11, 'Be glad in the Lord, and rejoice, ye righteous: and shout for joy, all ye that are upright in heart.' The Psalmist speaketh of the pardon of sins; it is David's Maschil, an instruction from his own experience; he begins the psalm, 'Blessed is he whose iniquity is forgiven, whose sin is covered: blessed is the man unto whom the Lord imputeth not sin.' Then he concludeth, 'Rejoice, ye upright.' A man that is condemned for some criminal offence, and ready to be executed, oh! what joy hath he when he hath received his pardon! So we should rejoice in God, who are as it were brought back again from the gibbet, and have received our atonement. So also in the gift of the Holy Spirit to sanctify and heal our natures; if the angels, who are but the spectators and lookers-on, rejoice in the conversion of a sinner, should not the parties interested: Luke xv. 10, 'There is joy in the presence of the angels of God over one sinner that repenteth.' So in the hopes of glory: Luke x. 20, 'Rejoice, because your names are written in heaven;' Rom. v. 2, 'We rejoice in hope of the glory of God.'

[4.] We rejoice in God when we delight to do his will, and are fitted for his use and service. To be set and kept in the way to heaven is a greater comfort to us than if we had all the world bestowed upon us: Ps. cxix. 14, 'I have rejoiced in the way of thy testimonies as much as in all riches.' David had experience of both as a puissant king, and as God's servant. So 2 Cor. i. 12, 'For our rejoicing is this, the testimony of our conscience, that, in simplicity and godly sincerity, not with fleshly wisdom, but by the grace of God, we have had our conversation in the world.' In carnal rejoicing men seek to conceal and hide the grounds of their joy, as being ashamed of them; the worldling in his bags, the voluptuous in the instruments of his pleasure. The glutton will not point to his dishes, nor the drunkard to his pots, and say, This is my rejoicing; but a christian dareth own his joy, This is my rejoicing, that God hath taught me his ways, and enabled me to walk in them.

[5.] We also rejoice in God when we rejoice in the blessings of his providence, as they come from God and lead to God: Joel ii. 23, 'Be glad then, ye children of Zion, and rejoice in the Lord your God; for he hath given you the former rain moderately, and he will cause to come down for you the rain, the former rain, and the latter rain in the first month.' So God's care in protecting us: Ps. v. 11, 'But let all those that put their trust in thee rejoice; let them ever shout for joy, because thou defendest them: let them also that love thy name be joyful in thee.' These common favours and benefits manifest God's respect to us, and should be as a step to the Lord's people to lead them up to rejoice in God. This was God's quarrel with his people: Deut. xxviii. 47, 48, 'Because thou servest not the Lord thy God with joyfulness and with gladness of heart for the abundance of all things, therefore shalt thou serve thine enemies, which the Lord shall send against thee, in hunger and thirst and nakedness, and in want of all things; and he shall put a yoke of iron upon thy neck, until he hath destroyed thee.' Whatever we have, we should look upon it as a token of God's love to us, and so rejoice in them; not as satisfied with these worldly things, but as they direct us to God. Carnal men rejoice in the creature, but in a carnal and sensual manner; their joy neither ariseth from God, nor endeth in God; they neither look to God as their author, nor make him their end; and it is a naughty heart that can rejoice in anything without God and apart from God.

II. How this must be constant and perpetual, 'Rejoice evermore.'

1. In all estates and conditions; this joy must not be infringed. God's children have or may have cause of rejoicing in God, whatever their outward condition be; and therefore they should make conscience of it, whether their affairs be adverse or prosperous.

[1.] A state of worldly sorrow and affliction is reconcilable and agreeable enough, or consistent with our rejoicing in the Lord. The scriptures abound in the proof of this: 2 Cor. vi. 10, 'As sorrowful, yet always rejoicing;' 1 Peter i. 6, 'Wherein ye greatly rejoice, though now for a season, if need be, ye are in heaviness through manifold temptations;' 2 Cor. vii. 4, 'I am filled with comfort, and am exceeding joyful in all our tribulations. So David: Ps. xciv. 19, 'In the multitude of my thoughts within me thy comforts delight my soul.' Paul and Silas sung in the dungeon at midnight: Acts xvi. 25, 'At midnight Paul and Silas prayed and sang praises unto God.' Tribulation disturbeth not the harmony of a well-composed mind. The reason is, because there is more matter of delight in God than can be taken from him in the creature: John xvi. 22, ' Your heart shall rejoice, and your joy no man taketh from you.' Whatever falleth out, God's all-sufficiency and heaven's happiness are everlasting grounds of rejoicing. (1.) God's all-sufficiency: Hab. iii. 18, 'Yet I will rejoice in the Lord; I will joy in the God of my salvation.' Your right and interest in God is not made void by the blasting of the creature. So (2.) Hopes of glory remain unshaken: Mat. v. 12, ' Rejoice and be exceeding glad, for great is your reward in heaven.' Though the world be bent against us with all manner of spite and hatred, yet there is more cause of joy than sorrow. There cannot be more evil in our sufferings than there is good in God and happiness in heaven.

[2.] A state of sorrow and affliction is not only consistent with this holy rejoicing, but doth much promote it; partly as afflictions conduce to refine, and purge the soul from the dregs of sense, and make it capable of the comforts of the Spirit: Jude 19, 'Sensual, having not the Spirit.' Till our taste be clarified from the feculency and dregs of sense, we cannot relish spiritual comforts, nor know their worth and value. Whilst we flow in worldly comforts, the carnal gust and taste is too strong upon us, and so we have mean thoughts of God's consolations. They do best relish with the afflicted, as cordials are for the fainting, not for those whose stomachs are full of phlegm and filth. Partly as they occasion greater experiences of God: 2 Cor. xii. 10, 'Therefore I take pleasure in infirmities, in reproaches, in necessities, in persecutions, in distresses for Christ's sake; for when I am weak, then I am strong.' So Rom. v. 3–5, 'And not only so, but we glory in tribulations also; knowing that tribulation worketh patience, and patience experience, and experience hope: and hope maketh not ashamed, because the love of God is shed abroad in our hearts by the Holy Ghost, which is given unto us.' Partly as they are sanctified, and increase grace; and an increase of grace will bring with it an increase of comfort: Heb. xii. 11, 'Now no chastening for the present seemeth to be joyous, but grievous; nevertheless afterward it yieldeth the peaceable fruit of righteousness unto them which are exercised thereby.' Now from all these considerations, though afflictions may a little damp it, yet they do not extinguish it.

2. We must rejoice evermore, because it is not a duty to be done now and then, or which doth only belong to some eminent christians, that are assured of God's love; but from our first acquaintance with Christ till the last period of our lives it is of use to us.

[1.] Some act of joy our first entrance into christianity is begun with, before our interest is well settled and cleared. There are general grounds of rejoicing which oblige all; as that there is a good God, and poor drooping spirits should apply themselves to him who hath comforts for his mourners: Isa. lvii. 15, ' For thus saith the high and lofty One that inhabiteth eternity, whose name is Holy; I dwell in the high and holy place, with him also that is of a contrite and humble spirit, to revive the spirit of the humble, and to revive the heart of the contrite ones.' That there is a merciful and able Saviour a gospel, or new covenant, that bringeth glad tidings to sinners: Luke ii. 10, 11, 'Fear not, for behold, I bring you glad tidings of great joy, which shall be to all people. For unto you is born this day in the city of David a Saviour, which is Christ the Lord.' The world being fallen under God's wrath and deserved condemnation, it is matter of joy that God hath found a ransom, and that he offereth pardon and life to those who will seek it and accept it upon his blessed terms. It is matter of joy before we have interest in these things; a possible conditional reconciliation with God, that dreadful controversy taken up, heaven and earth kissing each other, that life and immortality is brought to light, and such a blessedness discovered as satiateth the mind of man, without which man would have been but as leviathan in a little pool. In short, the gospel showing a sure way of reconciliation with God, and the everlasting fruition of him in glory; the very offers of it stir up a joy in us. And wherever the gospel cometh, it hath at its first coming upon these accounts been entertained with joy. As when Philip preached the gospel in Samaria, Acts viii. 8, 'There was great joy in that city;' not only joy, but great joy. So it is said of the jailer, that new convert, Acts xvi. 34, that 'he rejoiced, believing in God, with all his house;' he was but even recovered out of the suburbs of hell, ready to kill himself just before, ver. 27, so that a man would think he should easier fetch water out of a flint, or a spark of fire out of the bottom of the sea, than to find joy so soon in such an heart, yet he rejoiced, though he was still in danger of his life, for treating those as guests whom he should have kept as prisoners. So 2 Cor. viii. 2, we read of 'the abundance of their joy,' and 'deep poverty,' because they were acquainted with the gospel. So Zaccheus received Christ joyfully, because salvation was come to his house: Luke xix. 6, 'He made haste and came down, and received him joyfully.' And the man that found the true treasure, 'for joy thereof goeth and selleth all that he hath,' Mat. xiii. 44; he parted with all his satisfactions, comforts, and contentments. This is so sure a truth, that wherever the gospel of Christ is received in any degree and proportion, though not to a converting degree, there is some joy. In converts I have showed you, and you may cast in that text by way of overplus: Acts ii. 41, 'Then they that gladly received the word were baptized; and the same day there were added to the church about three thousand souls.' It is a degree not amounting to conversion. Luke viii. 13, the stony ground 'received the word with joy.' Herod had some kind of joy in hearing John the Baptist: Mark vi. 20, 'He did many things, and heard him gladly;' and his other hearers 'rejoiced in his light for a season,' John v. 35. These had a joy, but not in such a predominant degree as to be able to control their affections to other things, and so this joy could not maintain itself or keep itself alive. Therefore it is said, that 'we are his house, if we hold fast the confidence, and the rejoicing of the hope firm unto the end,' Heb. iii. 6. The first offers of pardon and life by Christ do stir up this joy in us, as the gospel showeth us a way how to come out of the greatest miseries, and get an interest in the greatest happiness. The possible hope of relief and deliverance cannot but affect us if we be serious.

[2.] As to our progress in the duties and hopes of the gospel, it is still carried on with joy. Therefore believers are described by it as their vital act: Phil. iii. 3, 'We are the circumcision, which worship God in the spirit, and rejoice in Christ Jesus, and have no confidence in the flesh.' What is the constant work of a christian but a rejoicing in Christ Jesus, or a thankful sense of our Redeemer's mercy? And therefore the whole life of a christian is represented by keeping a feast: 1 Cor. v. 7, 8, 'Christ our passover is sacrificed for us; therefore let us keep the feast.' Seven days the Jews kept their feast of unleavened bread, which figureth the whole time of our pilgrimage till we enter into the everlasting sabbath. Every day is a holyday and a feast-day with a christian, now Christ his passover is sacrificed for him; partly through a sense of God's love, partly through the testimony of a good conscience, and partly through the hopes of glory. He is always rejoicing in God, if he be in a right frame and liveth up to his gospel-privileges. Let me chiefly instance in two duties—of prayer, and praise or thanksgiving, which take up a great part of our commerce with God; and especially because they are connected with the duty we are upon, for we must 'Rejoice evermore, praying without ceasing, and in everything give thanks.' The duties that follow serve to act and cherish this joy.

(1.) Rejoice evermore so as 'to pray without ceasing.' They that delight in God will be often with him, and can come cheerfully, and unbosom themselves to him, as a man would to his friend. They are not dragged into his presence as into the presence of a judge, but they come freely to him as children to their father. They that love God as their portion and happiness will much converse with him; they are out of their element but when they are praying to God, or speaking of God, or thinking of God; therefore they are still with him. But this is denied of the hypocrite: Job xxvii. 10, 'Will he delight himself in the Almighty? will he always call upon God?' They may sometimes cry to him, not because they love him and his service, but because they love their own ease, and to be free from trouble; their straits may force a little service from them. Well, then, without delight we cannot keep a continual course of communion with God in prayer.

(2.) For praise or giving of thanks: 'In everything give thanks;' that is both the fruit of our delight in God and a means to quicken it. One that delights in God will have cause enough to give thanks, whether the creature come or goes. Whatever is taken from him, his joy is not taken from him. He can bless God for his mercies in Christ when retrenched and cut short in the world; though he hath lost some comforts, yet others are yet remaining. Shall one cross embitter all our comforts, as one string broken puts the whole instrument out of tune? They can bless God for taking as well as giving: Job i. 21, 'The Lord gave, and the Lord hath taken away; blessed be the name of the Lord.' If the Lord gave all, why may he not take away a part? A thankful heart can praise God for God himself, for choicer mercies yet continued, for some outward mercies remaining. If God gave all, and take but a part, have we any cause to complain?

[3.] Still I prove this joy must be continued throughout the whole course of the spiritual life, because the beginning, progress, and ending is carried on by it; the joy of God is our support in our declining time, the staff of our age ; for then christians grow more dead to the world and worldly things, and are less moved by them, whether they keep or lose, have or want them ; and then they are nearer to eternity, and have more of that 'Rejoicing in hope,' spoken of Rom. xii. 12. This joy is a beginning of the joys in heaven; here we have a sip, there a full draught. Our delight in God now is of the same nature with that which the saints and angels have in heaven. There is indeed a vast difference in the degrees ; here a little joy entereth into us, but there we 'enter into our master's joy,' Mat. xxv. 23. But though they differ in degree, yet the object and affection is the same. It is the same God and the same glory which delighteth us; only now they are seen by faith, then they shall be objects of direct sight and fruition; we shall see him face to face. In short, rejoicing in God is a beginning of the employment we shall then have in heaven. Therefore, when we expect in a few days to be swallowed up of this joy, shall we be no more affected with it now? We that shall so shortly be so full of joy, shall we be empty now? Shall not we rejoice, who have now a title to heaven, and shall in a little time be in the full and perpetual possession of it?

III. The many reasons which show we should have a greater inclination to this blessed work than usually we have, and be oftener in it.

1. Because God hath done so much to raise it in us. All the persons of the Godhead concur and contribute their influence, in that way of operation which is proper to each, to give us grounds of joy.

[1.] The Father giveth himself to us, and his favour as our felicity and portion. God's love is the bosom and bottom cause of all our happiness, which sets all other causes at work; and when we have the sure effects of it, can anything so bitter befall us that will not be sweetened by the love of God? or so evil that this shall not be ground of comfort to us : Ps. iv. 6, 7, 'There are many that say, Who will show us any good? Lord, lift thou up the light of thy countenance upon us. Thou hast put gladness in my heart, more than in the time that their corn and their wine increased.' Carnal men must have something good to sense, but godly men take their full delight in God. This doth them good to the heart; it is not like a little dew that wets the surface, but like a soaking shower that goeth to the root. And 'more;' enough to draw us off from the world, enough to swallow up all our infelicities; yea, to encounter the thoughts of death, hell, and judgment to come.

[2.] The Son is also matter of rejoicing to us, as our Redeemer and Saviour. You are to consider what the Lord Jesus hath done to deliver you from sin, and the bitter curse of the law, and the fears of death, and the flames of hell. The eternal Son of God came to heal our wounds: Isa. liii. 5, 'By his stripes we are healed;' to make our peace with the Father by the blood of his cross, Col. i. 20 ; to vanquish our spiritual enemies, and triumph over them, Col. ii. 14, 15 ; to be the ransom of our souls, 1 Tim. ii. 6 ; the captain of our salvation, Heb. ii. 10 ; the head of his church, Eph. i. 22 ; the treasury and storehouse of all our comforts, John i. 16 ; and, in short, he hath recovered us to God, and hath given us an interest in the comforts of his gospel and the promises thereof, which are in him Yea, and in him Amen; and is not this matter of joy and rich comfort? The whole covenant breeds 'strong consolation' in the hearts of God's people, Heb. vi. 18; and David saith, Ps. cxix. 111, 'Thy testimonies have I taken as an heritage for ever, for they are the rejoicing of my heart.' It doth our hearts good when we take these things for our happiness. Abraham rejoiced in the forethought or foresight of Christ's day: John viii. 56, 'Your father Abraham rejoiced to see my day, and he saw it, and was glad.' And should not we rejoice, that live under the clearest dispensation of it? The benefits of our redemption by Christ should be so esteemed that no affliction should be grievous. The kingdom of Christ is everywhere represented as a kingdom of joy and comfort: Rom. xiv. 17, 'The kingdom of heaven is not meat and drink, but righteousness and peace, and joy in the Holy Ghost.' And if we be real members of it, we should see more cause of rejoicing in Christ Jesus.

[3.] The Holy Ghost concurreth in his way of operation, as a sanctifier, guide, and comforter. As a sanctifier he layeth the foundation for comfort; for it is the spirit of delusion that comforts us in our sins, that by imaginary comforts he may keep you from those that are real, solid, and everlasting; but the true Spirit is a sanctifier, and therefore a comforter; he first poureth in the oil of grace, and then the oil of gladness. Comfort and joy follow holiness, as heat doth the fire. And then as a guide, either in his restraining motions, as he mortifieth sin, or in his inviting motions, as he exciteth and quickeneth to holiness; these are helps to our comfort. Cannot a man live merrily without sin? And do you think a life of holiness irreconcilable with a life of rejoicing? No such matter; it is the ready way to joy, especially to joy spiritual. But chiefly as a comforter; he is purposely given us to keep in this holy fire, and maintain a constant delight in God in our souls. And therefore it is called 'Joy in the Holy Ghost.' Where God himself taketh upon him the office of a comforter surely there will be comfort. Life will quicken, light will illuminate, and the comforting Spirit will comfort in that season and degree God seeth fit and we are capable to receive. Now he comforteth partly as sealing, partly as giving earnest: 2 Cor. i. 22, 'Who hath also sealed us, and given us the earnest of the Spirit in our hearts.' As sealing us, by stamping the impress and image of God upon us, which is the mark of his children, the sure evidence of his love, and the pledge of our happiness; and as giving us the earnest of a blessed estate to come; that life is begun, which there shall be perfected. Now consider all this. When God himself will be our portion, our saviour, our comforter, should not all this cause us to rejoice in God, whatever our condition be in the world?

2. All the graces tend to this—faith, hope, and love.

[1.] Faith, that is a dependence upon God for something future that lieth out of sight. Now these invisible and future objects are so great and glorious that they support and comfort the heart, how afflicted soever our present condition be: 1 Peter i. 8, 'In whom believing, ye rejoice with joy unspeakable and full of glory;' Rom. xv. 13, 'Now the God of hope fill you with all joy and peace in believing, that ye may abound in hope through the power of the Holy Ghost.' In both these places faith implieth a firm belief of and dependence upon Christ as an all-sufficient Saviour, by whom alone God will give us eternal life. This faith will breed a perpetual rejoicing in the soul, if it be firm, strong, and operative.

[2.] Hope breedeth this joy also: Rom. xii. 12, 'Rejoicing in hope;' and Rom. v. 2, 'We rejoice in hope of the glory of God.' Though we be pressed with miseries for the present, yet there is a better estate to come, the excellency and certainty of which causeth us to rejoice, and giveth us a foretaste of it. Joy is chiefly for enjoyment, but there is a partial enjoyment by hope, which is not only a desirous expectation, but delightful foretaste or preoccupation of the thing hoped for.

[3.] Love to God also causeth us to rejoice in him, for it showeth itself in a complacency and well-pleasedness of mind in God as our chief good: Ps. xvi. 5, 6, 'The Lord is the portion of mine inheritance and of my cup; thou maintainest my lot: the lines are fallen to me in pleasant places.' Certainly they do not love God that do not value and esteem him as better than all worldly things. Other things without him cannot give any solid contentment to the soul, but he without other things is enough; he is all in all to the heart that loveth him. Therefore if we be rooted and grounded in love to God, he will be the delight of our souls and our exceeding joy, whatever we lose in the world. Thus you see faith, hope, and love have a great influence upon this joy.

3. All the ordinances and duties of religion were appointed to breed, and feed, and act, and increase this joy in us. Reading, hearing, praying, meditating, the Lord's supper; all these duties were appointed to quicken the soul to delight in God, and they must all be used to this end. Reading; wherefore were the scriptures written but to beget in us a comfortable sense of the love of God in Christ? 1 John i. 4, 'These things write we unto you, that your joy may be full.' The word doth beget and keep up our delight in God by those discoveries which it maketh of his goodness to us, in doctrines, counsels, and promises, that every time we look into God's blessed book we might have a fresh delight acted and stirred in us. So for hearing; its main end is to increase our joy, therefore was the ministry appointed: 'not for that we have dominion over your faith, but as helpers of your joy,' 2 Cor. i. 24. That is the main end of our ministry, because the gospel dispensation is a dispensation of grace. We must press repentance, but it is to cure you of your vain rejoicings in order to more solid comfort; to put you out of your fool's paradise, that you may prize and esteem your Saviour, and set more by him than by all the pleasures, honours, and riches of the world. Holy mourning is in order to comfort, the vain delight and carnal rejoicing is checked and deadened, that we may raise in you the true joy. We are helpers of your joy in God's way, and truly that is the only way. We need not over-gospel the gospel, as honey needs not to be sweetened with other things. So prayer; we put promises in suit that we may have new experiences of the love and bounty of God: John xvi. 24, 'Ask and ye shall receive, that your joy may be full.' In prayer you come to solace yourselves with God and to

unbosom yourselves to him as your best friend. Meditation on God's excellences and benefits, it is still to maintain this delight in God: Ps. cxl. 34, 'My meditation of him shall be sweet, I will delight in the Lord.' The Lord's supper was appointed for the elevation of our joy to the height; it is our spiritual feast and refection, that we may go on our way with joy; as the eunuch, when baptized, 'He went on his way rejoicing,' Acts viii. 39. Here the whole gospel is applied and sealed to us; and bread and wine doth not so much cheer the body as the body and blood of Christ doth the soul. You come not only to remember your privileges by Christ, but it is your solemn investiture; here you take possession of Christ and all his benefits.

SERMON II.

Rejoice evermore.—1 Thes. v. 16.

Use. To press you to this spiritual rejoicing. God never hath our hearts till he hath our delight. To enforce this exhortation, I must— (1.) Take off prejudices; (2.) Persuade by arguments; (3.) Direct you in the exercise of this great duty.

First, To take off prejudices and objections which may lie in the hearts of men against this duty.

1. Prejudice. How can this rejoicing evermore stand with that sense which we should have of afflictions coming from God? Is it not a stupid thing to be merry when God is angry? Must we rejoice in troubles notwithstanding the breaches God hath made upon us? I answer—

[1.] Carnal rejoicing is a very provoking thing, because it is an affront to God's providence. It is a defiance of the dispensation we are under when we are not affected with our own or our brethren's misery, or our father's anger: Isa. xxii. 12–14, 'In that day did the Lord God of hosts call to weeping, and to mourning, and to baldness, and to girding with sackcloth: and behold joy and gladness, slaying oxen, and killing sheep, eating flesh, and drinking wine: let us eat and drink, for to-morrow we shall die. It was revealed in mine ears by the Lord of hosts, Surely, this iniquity shall not be purged from you till you die.' So James iv. 9, 'Be afflicted, and mourn and weep; let your laughter be turned into mourning, and your joy into heaviness;' and chap. v. 1, 'Go to now, ye rich men; weep and howl for your miseries that shall come upon you;' and ver. 5, 'Ye have lived in pleasure upon earth, and been wanton; ye have nourished your hearts as in a day of slaughter.' Now compare this with chap. i. 2, 'My brethren, count it all joy when ye fall into divers temptations.' Never any were reproved for rejoicing in God in calamities, but for carnality and for rejoicing in sensual satisfactions. If you say, the answer cometh not home; you may rejoice in unjust dealings and persecutions of men, or in trials; but in corrective dispensations from the immediate hand of God how shall we rejoice? I reply—We are directed to this rejoicing in God in those calamities which come from God's immediate hand: Hab. iii. 17, 18, 'Although the fig-tree shall not blossom, neither shall fruit be in the vines, the labour of the olive shall fail, and the fields shall yield no meat, the flocks shall be cut off from the fold, and there shall be no herd in the stalls; yet I will rejoice in the Lord, I will joy in the God of my salvation.' Surely famine and desolation come from God, and come as a punishment; 'Yet I will rejoice in the Lord.' This spiritual rejoicing is not irreverence, but an honour to God when we are satisfied in him though all creature comforts and means of subsistence are blasted; and we show that we have comfort enough in God, that is out of the reach of trouble, and this can support us when all things beneath God fail: Job v. 22, 'At destruction and famine shalt thou laugh.' Stupidity and carnal mirth are very unseasonable, but to live above the creature and without the creature is an high point of faith and love to God; and to rejoice in him when all outward causes of rejoicing cease, is so far from being a sin, that it is an eminent duty. Our better part and happiness is out of the reach of trouble, though it be never so grievous.

[2.] We must distinguish between the sense of affliction and support under it; for we must neither slight it nor faint under it: Heb. xii. 5, 'My son, despise not thou the chastening of the Lord, nor faint when thou art rebuked of him.' These are the two extremes. The sense of our condition is necessary, that we may not slight the affliction; and the support, that we may not faint under it. Both may and must stand together; for in all worldly cases 'we must weep as if we wept not,' 1 Cor. vii. 30; and again, 'Sorrow not as those without hope,' 1 Thes. iv. 13, and so be without all comfort. In short, the sense is necessary for improvement, the support to make trouble easy.

(1.) If we have not a sense, we cannot make a right use of our sufferings and afflictions, but our hearts will be more hardened in sin. God is their author, repentance is their end, and their cause is sin: Lam. iii. 39, 'Wherefore doth a living man complain, a man for the punishment of his sins?' And therefore, though we be not to droop and languish under our afflictions, yet we must consider the righteous providence of God; and the smart of his displeasure must awaken us to repentance, otherwise the affliction is frustrated, and you leave the thorn in your foot, which caused your first pain and soreness. If you do not repent of your sins, and no cure is wrought, if you still let out your hearts freely to the world, and the prosperities and delights thereof, this is the highway to security and carelessness of soul concernments.

(2.) You must not faint and despair, as if all joy and comfort in God were lost. For—

(1*st*.) We are not utterly undone as long as we have God for our portion: Lam. iii. 24, 'The Lord is my portion, saith my soul, therefore will I hope in him.' Though the creature be blasted, he is alive still, and should be the joy and delight of our souls; for then we are tried, whether he be so or no.

(2*d*.) God is a loving Father when he corrects. Our chastisements are effects not only of his justice, but mercy; it is a rod in the hand of our Father wherewith we are scourged: John xviii. 11, 'The cup which my Father hath given me, shall I not drink it?' and so it is an act of love and kindness to us.

(3*d*.) Our Father hath mercy enough to turn it to our benefit: Heb. xii. 10, 'They verily for a few days chastened us after their own pleasure, but he for our profit, that we may be partakers of his holiness.' And shall we mourn for that which is for our benefit? If we rejoice in God and holiness it will not be so. If God will stir us up to more humility, contempt of the world, confidence in himself, and to place our delight in him alone, shall we be dejected and displeased, as if some great wrong had been done us?

(4*th*.) If this affliction fits us for everlasting happiness, there is cause of joy still left: 2 Cor. iv. 17, 'For our light affliction, which is but for a moment, worketh for us a far more exceeding and eternal weight of glory.' One that must have eternal glory, and eternal glory promoted by such a means, should not grudge at a little suffering and affliction, which is the common burden of the sons of Adam.

2. Prejudice. Christ hath pronounced those blessed that mourn for sin: Mat. v. 4, 'Blessed are they that mourn, for they shall be comforted;' how then can we rejoice evermore?

Ans. 1. Mourning for sin is necessary to cure our vain rejoicing, or delight in carnal vanities; and at our entrance into christianity this is a duty highly incumbent upon us, because of sin and the curse which we naturally lie under. Certainly while we are out of Christ we have nothing to comfort us, nothing to answer to the terrors of the law, or to reply against the accusations of conscience, and the fears of approaching misery and judgment; and what should we do, if we be sensible of it, but bemoan ourselves, and seek after God with weeping and supplications? God's first work in conversion is to put men out of their fool's paradise, who are satisfied with the creature without himself. Therefore humiliation and a broken-hearted sense of misery is required to deaden the relish and taste of sin, and that men may more prize and esteem the healing grace of Christ, and set more by it than all the pleasures, and riches, and honours of the world. Can a man see himself lost, and in danger of condemnation, and not be grieved? But all this while joy is in the making, and we are providing everlasting comfort for ourselves; for God is ready to ease us as soon as our need requireth and our care will permit: Isa. lvii. 15–17, 'For thus saith the high and lofty One that inhabiteth eternity, whose name is Holy; I dwell in the high and holy place, with him also that is of a contrite and humble spirit, to revive the spirit of the humble, and to revive the heart of the contrite ones. For I will not contend for ever, neither will I be always wroth; for the spirit shall fail before me, and the souls which I have made. For the iniquity of his covetousness I was wroth, and smote him; I hid me, and was wroth, and he went on frowardly in the way of his heart.' And he saith afterwards, ver. 18, 'I have seen his ways, and will heal him: I will lead him also, and restore comfort to him, and to his mourners.' The Lord is ready to come in with sweet and heavenly cordials when the physic worketh but a little kindly: Jer. xxxi. 18–20, 'I have surely heard Ephraim bemoaning himself thus; Thou hast chastised me, and I was chastised as a bullock unaccustomed to the yoke; turn thou me, and I shall be turned, for thou art the Lord my God. Surely after that I was turned, I repented, and after that I was instructed, I smote upon the thigh, I was ashamed, yea, even confounded, because I did bear the reproach of my youth. Is Ephraim my dear son? is he a pleasant child? for since I spake against him, I do earnestly remember him still; therefore my bowels are troubled for him, I will surely have mercy on him, saith the Lord.' Well, then, this sorrow may be well allowed, because it prevents greater sorrow, namely, the pains of hell. It is better to mourn for a while than for ever; better to have healing grief than tormenting grief; to mourn now, while mourning will do us good, than to howl at last, when all sorrow will be fruitless, and only a part of our punishment, not of our cure. And besides, this sorrow maketh for comfort: Mat. v. 4, 'Blessed are they that mourn, for they shall be comforted.' When the shower is fallen, the sun cleareth up, and shineth in his full strength and beauty. The vain rejoicing being deadened, we have grounds of everlasting joy, by considering the means God hath appointed for our deliverance from sin, and death, and the flames of hell.

Ans. 2. Mourning for sin and joy in the Lord may stand well together; for grace and grace are not contrary, but grace and sin. Those who most mourn for sin do most rejoice in the Lord, and those who most rejoice in the Lord do most mourn for sin; as that christian Niobe wept much because she loved much; and 'she loved much, because much was forgiven her,' Luke vii. 47. As many times the sun shineth when the rain falleth, so there is a mixture of spiritual rejoicing and holy mourning; a deep sense of God's love, and yet a mourning because of the relics of corruption. Well, then, carnal rejoicing is opposite to holy mourning, but not joy in the Lord, therefore these two must be mixed. Sorrow is a servant to faith, and love, and joy in the Holy Ghost; and joy and thankfulness for the mercy of God in Christ is an help to godly sorrow: the one serves to mortify sin, the other to strengthen grace. None are so displeased with themselves for offending so good a God as those that have tasted how good and gracious the Lord is. But more thoroughly to reconcile this holy mixture to your thoughts, take these considerations—

[1.] Godly sorrow is better than all the pleasures of sin: 2 Cor. vii. 10, 'For godly sorrow worketh repentance to salvation, not to be repented of.' Many have repented of their vain pleasures or of their carnal mirth, but never any repented of their godly sorrow. Many have cursed the day of their birth, but never any cursed the day of their new birth. Whoever had any loathsome remembrance of those hours which they spent in reconciling themselves to God, though it were done with grief and bitterness of spirit? Oh! the remembrance of that happy time is ever sweet and grateful to them!

[2.] That mourning for sin containeth in itself the matter of joy is evident, because a poor christian is glad when his heart can melt for sin. A day of serious and sound humiliation is more to him than all carnal pleasures whatsoever; he would not exchange the comfort that he findeth in his penitent tears for all the mirth in the world. He findeth this helpeth to mortify sin, which would mar his rejoicing in God; it helpeth him to value Christ and taste the sweetness of his love; they are more glad of that measure of grace received than if they were masters and rulers of the world. To be affected with the dishonour done to God is included in their love and esteem of him, and floweth from their delight in him.

[3.] Though they groan under the relics of sin, yet they are glad they are but relics; that they are in any measure gotten out of their former estate is a comfort, though that they are gotten no further be a grief to them. The mourning christian would not change estates with the best and greatest of ungodly men, which showeth there is some solid complacency and delight in their present condition, though not that full joy which they shall have in heaven, when sin shall be no more. Joy is not perfect till holiness be perfect, yet there is joy still, though it be not perfect joy. Here there is *gaudium ineffabile cum suspiriis inenarrabilibus,* a joy mixed with sorrow; groans unutterable, and joys unspeakable and glorious.

Secondly, Having removed the prejudices, let me now persuade you to rejoice evermore by the two arguments of necessity and utility.

1. The necessity of it.

[1.] That you may own God as your God; delighting in God is a duty of the first commandment: 'Thou shalt have no other gods before me;' that is, rejoice in no other, but in me only, as thy full and all-sufficient portion and happiness; and therefore it is a part, not of instituted, but of natural worship, such worship which we are to give God, though he had never given direction about it, which immediately resulteth from the owning and choosing of God for our God; for if God be not loved and delighted in more than anything, or all things else, he is not our God. Now, then, is there not a necessity, if you would worship God as God, that you should rejoice evermore, and delight in him as sufficient to your happiness, whether the world cometh or goeth, whether your creature comforts and relations continue with you or be taken from you? God still must be the heart's delight and your exceeding joy: Ps. xxxvii. 4, 'Delight thyself also in the Lord, and he shall give thee the desires of thine heart.'

[2.] The necessity appeareth by this, how can you be thankful, and prize and value those blessings which you have from God by Christ, unless you rejoice evermore, whatever your condition be in the world? Surely Christ when received must be received with all love and thankfulness, else you do not know the worth and value of his grace; and this esteem is never so much shown in words as in deeds, when you can delight in him more than all things else: Ps. iv. 7, 'Thou hast put gladness in my heart more than in the time that their corn and their wine increased.' Delight in him so as to lose all for him: Phil. iii. 8, 'For whom I have suffered the loss of all things, and do count them but dung that I may win Christ;' Heb. x. 34, 'And took joyfully the spoiling of your goods, knowing in yourselves that ye have in heaven a better and an enduring substance.' And you can esteem a naked Christ ground enough of comfort, though you be stripped of all things. The heart is not sound with Christ, till we be so taken up with the love and praise of our Redeemer that we have scarce leisure to observe whether we be rich or poor, or to regard the honours and dishonours of the world.

[3.] How can you profess to follow the conduct of that Holy Spirit who hath undertaken to be your comforter, unless your solid delight and comfort be in God and heaven? I know the Spirit is not so necessarily a comforter as he is a sanctifier; but I speak of that disposition of soul which belongeth both to his sanctifying as well as his comforting operation, and is necessary to grace; and that is to place your happiness not in this world, but in God and heaven, and so to place it there as that this may be a support to you in poverty and disgrace and pain, that nothing may be able to overcome your joy: John xvi. 22, 'Your heart shall rejoice, and your joy no man taketh from you.' Surely this is a necessary work of the sanctifying Spirit, to teach you to fix your comforts there, where they may be out of the reach of the world, that you may have everlasting grounds of delight, whatever man can do unto you.

2. The utility of it, both with respect to our spiritual benefit and profit, and our acceptance with God.

[1.] With respect to the temper and frame of our own hearts, or our spiritual benefit. There are two parts of regeneration, mortification and vivification; and this rejoicing evermore promoteth both of them.

(1.) As to mortification. It is most profitable to wean us from carnal vanities. The love of sensitive delights is the root of sin; some carnal lure there is, which enticeth and draweth us away from God: James i. 14, 'But every man is tempted when he is drawn away of his own lust and enticed.' This carnal favour is our undoing; pleasure being born and bred with us, and deeply ingrained in our natures, is hardly removed; yet if it should be cherished, it would wholly fasten our souls to earthly things, to riches, pleasures, and honours. Now that we may not be deceived and inveigled with the delights of the flesh, we should think of another joy, which may be continual and perpetual, that so this higher joy may drive out the carnal joy, as a greater nail driveth out the lesser. Man cannot be without some joy, nor can delight lie idle in the soul; it must be occupied and taken up either with the delights of the flesh, and the toys and trifles of the world, or acted upon God and heavenly things. The brutish part of mankind employ their oblectation about trifles, and love pleasures more than God; but the renewed part make God their exceeding joy, and favour the things of the Spirit: Rom. viii. 5, 'They that are after the flesh do mind the things of the flesh, but they that are after the Spirit, the things of the Spirit.' These latter employ their oblectation aright, and being acquainted with better things, the carnal gust dieth away in them by degrees; as men left off the use of acorns when they found out the use of wheat or bread-corn, or as dainty fare maketh us despise coarser viands. When our delight findeth a better object, it is a great check to those dreggy contentments and petty satisfactions which obtrude themselves upon our senses at every turn; the taste of them is marred, they become sapless to a christian who hath higher and chaster delights. Every life hath its taste, and every man's joy is in worldly vanities, or in God, and other things as they have respect to God. He that is acquainted with God and hidden manna cannot relish the garlic and onions and flesh-pots of Egypt: 'We will be glad, and rejoice in thee; we will remember thy love more than wine,' Cant. i. 4. So that you see it is a great help to mortification to rejoice evermore in God. Delight puts out delight, as the sun doth the fire.

(2.) As to vivification. It quickeneth us to the life of holiness; 'The joy of the Lord is your strength,' Neh. viii. 10. There is a natural dulness and deadness in holy duties which we find in ourselves, which is only cured by delight in God, which is as oil to the wheels. Everything goeth on easily and smoothly which is carried on with joy and delight; that maketh us yield to duties which otherwise would be tedious and irksome to us. Shechem yielded to be circumcised for the delight which he had in Dinah, Gen. xxxiv. 19; so the apostle saith, 'But none of these things move me, neither count I my life dear unto myself, so that I may finish my course with joy,' Acts xx. 24. Whatever is done without delight is ingrate and harsh: the mortifying of a lust is like the cutting off an arm with a rusty saw; the performing of a duty like the bringing of a bear to the stake. Delight sweetens things, and puts a life into them. Obedience is done readily, when it is done out of a thankful and delightful sense of our Redeemer's love: Ps. xl. 8, 'I delight to do thy will, O my God; yea, thy law is in my heart.' So 1 John v. 3, 'For this is the love of God, that we keep his commandments, and his commandments are not grievous.' Well, then, this joy is very profitable, both as to mortification and vivification; it is a joy that maketh us better. Carnal joy maketh us worse; it filleth the minds with vanity and folly, and bringeth a slavery upon the heart: Titus ii. 3, ' Serving divers lusts and pleasures;' but this delight doth not corrupt you, but perfect you.

[2.] With respect to God's acceptance. This rejoicing evermore is more honourable to God, and more pleasing to God.

(1.) It is more honourable to God to rejoice in him evermore, as a cheerful servant is a credit to his master. We show forth the goodness of God by the joy of our faith and continual delight in God, however it be with us in the world. God standeth upon his credit that he doth not weary his people: Micah vi. 3, ' O my people! what have I done unto thee? and wherein have I wearied thee? testify against me.' He is not a rigorous and an hard master, but every way good and kind. The Thessalonians that received the word in much affliction, with joy of the Holy Ghost, were ensamples of all that believed in Macedonia and Achaia, and from them sounded out the word of God to others, 1 Thes. i. 6–8. These propagate their profession, and recommend it to others. Surely God is a good master; he hath made joy both our work and our wages, our way and our end. What is our great end and hope but ' to enter into our Master's joy?' And what is our constant business and work but to 'rejoice evermore?' Why then should we dishonour God by our uncheerfulness, and justify the prejudices of the world, who draw an ill picture of religion in their minds, as if it always looked sour, and with a tormenting and discontented look?

(2.) It is most pleasing to God, the life that he is best pleased withal God, that loveth a cheerful giver, loveth a cheerful sufferer, a cheerful practiser of godliness. Men love a thing done cheerfully, because it betokeneth love in the party that doeth it. Surely this rejoicing evermore is very pleasing to God, because he doth so often call for it: Ps. xxxvii. 4, 'Delight thyself in the Lord, and he shall give thee the desire of thy heart;' Phil. iv. 4, 'Rejoice in the Lord always, and again I say, Rejoice;' Ps. lxviii. 3, 'Let the righteous be glad, let them rejoice before God; yea, let them exceedingly rejoice;' and in many other places. Surely that which God calleth for so often and so earnestly should be more cared for by a christian. Be sure of this, that a cheerful spirit is more pleasing to God than a troubled, discontented spirit. When Isaac longed for savoury meat, such as his soul delighted in, a profane Esau taketh his bow to get it for him. When God hath told us how much this is pleasing to him, should we not make more conscience of it?

Thirdly, I must direct you how to perform this great and necessary duty.

1. Be prepared for it. The precept belongeth to the renewed and reconciled: Ps. xxxi. 1, 'Rejoice in the Lord, ye righteous; for praise is comely for the upright.' Delight is not forced by arguments, but drawn forth by inclination; therefore till we have a nature and heart suited to it, we shall never perform it. *Canticum novum, et vetus homo male concordant*—The new song and the old man do not well agree. Well, then, be prepared. It is easy to rejoice after a natural and worldly manner, but not easy to rejoice in the Lord. We are never prepared till our state be altered, heart altered, and life altered.

[1.] Our state must be altered. For naturally we are children of wrath, condemned by the sentence of the law, and under the curse; and doth it become condemned men to rejoice, and go to their execution dancing? No; you must take hold of another covenant, the hope that is set before you, and then you provide matter of joy, yea, of 'strong consolation,' Heb. vi. 18. By taking sanctuary at the Lord's grace, the heirs of promise have strong consolation. When the eunuch was solemnly admitted into God's covenant by baptism, 'He went on his way rejoicing,' Acts viii. 39. By repentance towards God, and faith in our Lord Jesus Christ, we enter into the new covenant, and that is a state of peace, life, and joy. In the new covenant God offers himself to be your reconciled Father, Christ your Saviour, and the Holy Ghost your sanctifier; are you willing to consent to this? And then, why should not you rejoice in the Lord? for you have enough in God.

[2.] Our hearts must be altered; for every man's relish and complacency is according to the temper and constitution of his soul: Rom. viii. 5, 'They that are after the flesh do mind the things of the flesh, but they that are after the Spirit the things of the Spirit.' Know his complacency, what it is that a man is pleased with most, and you know the man. An old corrupted heart and mind cannot delight itself in God: 1 Cor. ii. 14, 'But the natural man receiveth not the things of the Spirit of God, for they are foolishness unto him, neither can he know them, because they are spiritually discerned.' But those that have a divine nature put into them cannot satisfy themselves in the world: 2 Peter i. 4, 'Ye may be partakers of the divine nature, having escaped the corruption that is in the world through lust.' They can easily spare the pleasures of the flesh, and leave these husks for swine to feed on. A change of heart inferreth a change of delights and pleasures; for the new heart is nothing else but new desires and delights; when you have a new understanding and a new heart, then you will discern and relish spiritual things.

[3.] The life must be altered. For holy walking and fruitfulness in obedience raiseth the greatest joy: John xv. 10, 11, 'If ye keep my commandments, ye shall abide in my love, even as I have kept my Father's commandments, and abide in his love. These things have I spoken unto you that my joy might remain in you, and that your joy might be full;' Acts ix. 31, 'Walking in the fear of the Lord, and in the comfort of the Holy Ghost.' The godly life is the only sweet life: 2 Cor. i. 12, 'For our rejoicing is this, the testimony of our conscience, that in simplicity and godly sincerity, not with fleshly wisdom, but by the grace of God, we had our conversation in the world.' If you will but learn what it is to live in the love of God, and the belief and hope of life eternal, and in universal obedience to the laws of Christ, you will soon see what it is to live in a state of joy and comfort. If you fall into great and wounding sins, no wonder if your rejoicing in God be disturbed. Surely a tender heart cannot make light of sin, but it will cost them broken bones and broken hearts.

2. Act it continually. Partly for that the grounds of rejoicing are everlasting, an eternal God, an unchangeable covenant, Jesus Christ, the same yesterday and to-day and for ever; a kingdom that cannot be shaken, an infinite and eternal weight of glory. Now these things should ever be thought of by us, that we may keep up our delight in the Lord. Partly because we need it continually to enliven our duties, to sweeten our crosses, and to wean us from our carnal vanities; for otherwise our duties will go off heavily, our crosses will swallow us up with too much sorrow, or our hearts will be apt to be ensnared by sensual delights, unless we remember that we are continually to rejoice in God and heavenly things. Partly because this delight cannot be maintained in the soul unless it be continually exercised; by constant acting it we keep it, and increase it, till at length it cometh to be predominant in the soul, and able to control our affection to other things. It is said of John the Baptist's hearers that 'they were willing to rejoice in his light for a season,' John v. 35; and of the stony ground, Luke viii. 13, 'That they received the word with joy, and believed for a while, but in time of temptation fall away.' Herod heard John the Baptist gladly for a while, Mark vi. 20. God's offering eternal happiness in Christ may affect us for the present, but this rejoicing faileth, being over-mastered by the appetites and desires of the flesh. Therefore to root it and increase it, that it may be firm to the end, it must be continually acted and exercised.

3. Take heed you do not forfeit it, or damp it by any great and wounding sin. As David speaketh, Ps. li. 8, 'Make me to hear joy and gladness, that the bones which thou hast broken may rejoice.' Sin cloudeth the face of God, wasteth our comfort and joy: Ps. xxxii. 3, 4, 'When I kept silence, my bones waxed old through my roaring all the day long. For day and night thy hand was heavy upon me; my moisture is turned into the drought of summer;' Eph. iv. 30, 'And

grieve not the Holy Spirit, whereby ye are sealed to the day of redemption.' When the Comforter is offended, he showeth his dislike, and withdraweth when we grossly omit any known duty or commit any foul sin; he will show himself displeased with it, and withdraw his gracious and comfortable presence: Isa. lvii. 17, 'For the iniquity of his covetousness was I wroth, and smote him; I hid me, and was wroth.' On such occasions he is wroth and smiteth; he is wroth, and hideth himself, and then our comfort and delight in God ceaseth. Therefore we should deal more dutifully with the Spirit, neither grieving him by the omission or intermission of necessary duties, nor by the commission of any hardening sin, by some error of the concupiscible or pursuing faculty, or the irascible or eschewing faculty; by sins of the tongue, which most easily bewray corruption, for words discover the temper of the heart. I observe that 'grieving the Spirit,' Eph. iv. 30, is put in the middle between a dissuasive from corrupt communication, ver. 29, 'Let no corrupt communication proceed out of your mouth, but that which is good to the use of edifying.' When men endeavour to make themselves glad by carnal discourse, which argueth an heart set for carnal delights, and is contrary to rejoicing in the Lord: Eph. v. 4, 'Neither filthiness, nor foolish talking, nor jesting, which are not convenient, but rather giving of thanks;' and on the other side, ver. 31, 'Let all bitterness, and wrath, and anger, and clamour, and evil-speaking be put away from you.' By discontent, impetuous rage, passionate commotions, contumelious speeches, envy, revenge, we hinder our joy in the Lord. Now all this must be carefully avoided, lest we contract deadness and numbness of conscience.

4. If by sin you have wounded your conscience, and brought smart and mourning upon yourselves, abide not in that estate, but humble yourselves; renewing your repentance and faith in our Lord Jesus Christ, suing out your pardon, and getting your wounds healed. Beg of God to restore the joy of his salvation, that your broken hearts may be revived, and your broken bones restored and set in joint again: Ps. li. 8, 'Make me to hear joy and gladness, that the bones which thou hast broken may rejoice;' and ver. 12, 'Restore unto me the joy of thy salvation.' Never rest till you come again to delight in God, with an hearty resolution not to break with God any more: Ps. li. 6, 'Behold, thou desirest truth in the inward parts, and in the hidden part thou shalt make me to know wisdom;' Ps. lxxxv. 8, 'I will hear what God the Lord will speak, for he will speak peace unto his people, and to his saints; but let them not turn again to folly.' God is ready to receive lapsed penitents, that are sensible of their errors, and are willing to return to their duty: Ps. xxxii. 5, 'I acknowledged my sin unto thee, and mine iniquity have I not hid; I said, I will confess my transgressions unto the Lord, and thou forgavest the iniquity of my sin;' Isa. lvii. 17, 18, 'For the iniquity of his covetousness was I wroth, and smote him; I hid me, and was wroth; and he went on frowardly in the way of his heart. I have seen his ways, and will heal him, I will lead him also, and restore comfort to him, and to his mourners.' Your case is sad and grievous, but not desperate and

hopeless; you may have comfort upon God's terms, mourning for sin, that sin may be made bitter to you, and you may not hazard your peace for trifles another time; and putting your business into the hands of your Redeemer, the advocate must make your peace for you: 1 John ii. 1, 'If any man sin, we have an advocate with the Father, Jesus Christ the righteous.'

SERMON UPON 1 THESSALONIANS V. 17.

Pray without ceasing.—1 Thes. v. 17.

In the words we have—(1.) A duty, pray; (2.) The continuance of the duty, always, ἀδιαλείπτως; from both observe—

Doct. That constant and frequent prayer to God is a duty required of christians.

In handling this doctrine I shall show—

(1.) What prayer is; (2.) How it is to be carried on without ceasing; (3.) The reasons of the doctrine.

I. What prayer is; and here I shall speak—(1.) Of the nature of prayer; (2.) Of the several kinds of it.

First, For the nature of prayer. 'Prayer is the offering up of our desires to God, in the name of Christ, for such things as are agreeable to his will.'

1. It is an offering up of our desires. Desires are the soul and life of prayer, words are but the body. Now as the body without the soul is dead, so are prayers unless they are animated with our desires: Ps. x. 17, 'Lord, thou hast heard the desire of the humble.' God heareth not words, but desires.

2. These desires are offered unto God, or brought before the Lord in this solemn way: Zeph. iii. 10, 'My suppliants, even the daughters of my dispersed, shall bring mine offering;' that is, shall reverently express their desires to God. An offering was either a sacrifice, and prayer is a spiritual sacrifice: 1 Peter ii. 5, 'Ye are an holy priesthood, to offer up spiritual sacrifices, acceptable to God by Jesus Christ.' As a man did then present himself and his offering before the Lord, so do we present ourselves and our desires, and pour out our hearts before him. Or an offering might be the mincah, or meat-offering, which was baked or fried in a pan, and then presented to the Lord: Ps. xlv. 1, 'My heart inditeth a good matter;' not raw indigested services must be performed to God, such as are the eructations of the flesh; or incense was offered to the Lord: 'Let my prayer be set before thee as incense,' Ps. cxli. 2. And we read of 'Vials full of odours, which are the prayers of the saints,' Rev. v. 8. Incense was a mixture of sweet spices, which, being set on fire, the fumes thereof ascended into heaven; so do our holy and ardent desires ascend unto God.

3. They are desires presented in the name of Christ, in whom alone we are acceptable to God: John xvi. 23, 'Whatsoever ye shall ask the Father in my name, he will give it you.'

4. They are desires of things agreeable to the will of God: 1 John v. 14, 'And this is the confidence that we have in him, that if we ask anything according to his will, he heareth us.' All our desires must be regulated by his revealed will, and subordinated to his secret will, so far as God seeth it fit for his glory and our good; for upon other terms he is not bound to us.

Secondly, The kinds of prayer, so there are sundry distinctions.

1. There is mental prayer: Exod. xiv. 15, 'Wherefore criest thou unto me?' Moses cried unto the Lord, and yet no words are mentioned. And vocal prayer: Ps. v. 3, 'My voice shalt thou hear in the morning, O Lord; in the morning will I direct my prayer unto thee, and will look up.' When prayers are put into language, or formalised into some outward expression. Again—

2. There is sudden and ejaculatory prayer; as Neh. ii. 4, 'The king said unto me, For what dost thou make request? so I prayed unto the God of heaven.' That is, some sudden dart of prayer, such as, 'Prosper, I pray, thy servant;' lifting up his heart in a sudden desire to God, to direct or give success to his petition. And solemn prayer, and of greater length: Rom. xv. 30, 'That ye strive together with me in your prayers to God for me;' which words imply a prayer full of earnest pleadings.

3. There are public or church prayers: 1 Tim. ii. 1, 2, 'I exhort therefore that, first of all, supplications, prayers, intercessions, and giving of thanks be made for all men, for kings, and for all that are in authority;' where he giveth directions how the prayers of their public assemblies should be ordered. And private or family prayer: Acts x. 2, Cornelius is said to be 'a devout man, and one that feared God with all his house, and gave much alms to the people, and prayed to God always;' that is, a man that worshipped God with his family, as good men use to do. And it is said, 1 Chron. xvi. 43, that David, after public services, 'returned to bless his house;' that is, to pray for his family, as he had done for the people before. And secret and closet prayer, concerning which Christ giveth direction: 'When thou prayest, enter into thy closet,' Mat. vi. 6. Again—

4. There is ordinary and extraordinary prayer. Ordinary prayer is performed upon ordinary causes, such as daily necessities: Ps. lv. 17, 'Evening, and morning, and noon, will I pray, and cry aloud, and he shall hear my voice.' Extraordinary prayer is upon special weighty occasions, which requireth more than ordinary continuance of time and affection: Joel i. 14, 'Sanctify ye a fast, call a solemn assembly, gather the elders and all the inhabitants of the land into the house of the Lord your God, and cry unto the Lord.' Now all these kinds of prayer are to be made conscience of, and none to be neglected; and in none of these cases must we cease to pray when God requireth it at our hands.

II. What it is to pray without ceasing. This needeth to be explained, because some strain it too far, others straiten it too much; and we must state the matter so as to avoid the extremes on both sides.

First, One extreme is that of the ancient Euchites, and because they seem to be befriended by the letter of the text, we must clear the matter a little. Their senseless error was, as if the act of prayer were never to be discontinued, and therefore they omitted all other duties, and would only pray.

Secondly, The other extreme is of those who keep not up a constant, frequent return of this duty. We must obviate both.

1. For those that would never intermit this exercise.

[1.] We must show them their error by explaining the word. A thing is said to be done continually and without ceasing, which is done at the constant times and seasons as often as they return. As David told Amasa, 2 Sam. xix. 13, 'Thou shalt be captain of the host before me continually;' that is, as often as the army was led forth; so 2 Sam. ix. 12, 'Mephibosheth did eat bread at the king's table continually;' that is, at the constant stated times of eating. So Rom. ix. 2, 'I have great heaviness and continual sorrow in my heart;' that is, as often as he thought of them. So also is the word 'without ceasing' used, 1 Thes. ii. 13, 'For this cause we thank God without ceasing;' that is, as often as he was with God. So 2 Tim. i. 3, 'Without ceasing I have remembrance of thee in my prayers, night and day;' that is, evening and morning, as often as he went to God.

[2.] The matter may bear a good sense if you interpret the apostle's direction either—

(1.) Of the habit of prayer, or the praying temper; that frame of spirit or affection which is fit for prayer must never be lost: Ps. civ. 9, 'But I give myself unto prayer.' In the original there is no more 'but I prayer,' as if he were wholly made up of prayer and supplication; this was the work he was given to, or most intent upon.

(2.) It may be interpreted of a vital prayer. All duties may be resolved into prayer and praise. Now as the life of a christian is a life of love and praise, a kind of confession or hymn to God, so in other respects it is a prayer. *Semper orat, qui semper bene agit;* he that liveth in a constant obedience to God and dependence upon him, doth in effect always pray to him. Now thus doth a christian, both as to life natural and spiritual: Ps. xxv. 5, 'On thee do I wait all the day.', Every minute we depend upon him for the direction and support of his Holy Spirit. So Prov. xxiii. 27, 'Be thou in the fear of the Lord all the day long.' He liveth in an awful regard, loath to displease God because all cometh from him. Now this is virtually a prayer, because he still elevateth his thoughts and desires towards him, and looketh for all from God.

(3.) This praying without ceasing may be interpreted of our continuance in the duty, till we obtain the ends of prayer; and that some competent time is to be spent in it. Prayer is the lifting up of the heart, or the offering of our desires to God in some affectionate manner. In extraordinary occasions the time may be longer; as Christ spent whole nights in prayer: Luke vi. 12, 'He went out into a mountain to pray, and continued all night in prayer to God.' On ordinary occasions the time may be shorter, but the general direction is, continue in prayer: Rom. xii. 12, 'Continue instant in prayer.' A short good-morrow is too slight a compliment for the great God; such interparlance with him is necessary as may warm the heart and serve the ends of prayer.

(4.) Praying without ceasing may express our perseverance in prayer without fainting: Luke xviii. 1, 'He spake a parable unto them to this end, that men ought always to pray, and not to faint;' when we will not let God alone until he bless us. We must not yield to despondency, though we be not heard presently, but let us pray the more earnestly, though the prayer seemeth to be checked and contradicted by God's providence, as the woman of Canaan gets ground by discouragements, Mat. xv. 22–28. We must reiterate our petitions for one and the same thing till it be granted; as Paul prayed thrice: 2 Cor. xii. 8, 'For this thing I besought the Lord thrice, that it might depart from me.' A seeming repulse and denial maketh us the more vehement; for the language of God's rebukes is, not to pray no more, but pray on still; it is yielding to a temptation to desist.

(5.) This praying without ceasing is to be interpreted of the universality and the frequency of the return of the occasions and opportunities of prayer; and we may be said to do that without ceasing which we do very often. So that though the act of prayer be intermitted, the course of prayer should not be interrupted; for we are to pray at all times, in all conditions, and in all businesses and affairs.

(1st.) At all times, never omitting the seasons of prayer, stated or occasional. There are stated times of prayer; something must be done every day. Thus our Lord directeth us to pray: Mat. vi. 11, 'Give us $σήμερον$, this day our daily bread.' Though it be mentioned but in one petition, yet it referreth to all the rest. We need daily bread, daily pardon, daily strength against temptations. Yea, there seemeth to be a double standing occasion; every day in the morning for direction, in the evening for protection; as God appointed a morning and evening sacrifice: Num. xxviii. 4, 'The one lamb shalt thou offer in the morning, and the other lamb shalt thou offer at even.' If any be contentious, let me tell you, it is an ill spirit that doth dispute away duties rather than practise them. So there are occasional times when God by his providence inviteth us to it, as by some special affliction: Ps. l. 15, 'Call upon me in the day of trouble,' or some business in hand, wherein we are to ask his leave, counsel, and blessing: Ezra. viii. 21, 'Then I proclaimed a fast there at the river Ahava, that we might afflict ourselves before our God, to seek of him a right way for us and our little ones.'

(2d.) In all estates and conditions, afflicted and prosperous. In an adverse or afflicted estate: James v. 13, 'Is any among you afflicted? let him pray.' That gives vent to our sorrow, and turneth it into a spiritual channel. In a prosperous estate we are to pray that we may not forget God. Carnal men never come to him but when they have extreme need of him: Jer. ii. 27, 'But in the time of their trouble they will say, Arise, and save us.' That our hearts may not be corrupted, but our portion sanctified to us, for everything is 'sanctified by the word of God and prayer,' 1 Tim. iv. 5. Thus God must hear from us, sick and sound, in pain and well at ease, whether we are abased or abound.

(3d.) In every business, civil or sacred: 'In all thy ways acknowledge him, and he shall direct thy paths,' Prov. iii. 6. In business secular. Abraham's servant beggeth success in his errand: Gen. xxiv.

12, 'O Lord God of my master Abraham! I pray thee send me goodspeed this day.' In matters sacred: 2 Thes. iii. 5, 'The Lord direct your heart into the love of God.' So that a serious sensible christian seldom wanteth an errand to the throne of grace, and if we be not strangers to ourselves, we cannot be strangers to God.

2. To the other extreme we now come, when men are rare and unfrequent with God, upon the pretence that they are not bound to pray always, and the time of duty is not exactly stated in the New Testament. To these we oppose other considerations.

[1.] Though there be not an express rule particularly set down how often we should be with God, yet duties are required in the strictest and most comprehensive terms, and God's expressions about them are very large. For here God saith, 'Pray without ceasing;' and Eph. vi. 18, 'Praying always, with all prayer and supplication in the Spirit, and watching thereunto with all perseverance.' So Col. iv. 2, 'Continue in prayer, and watch in the same with thanksgiving.' So Ps. lxii. 8, 'Trust in the Lord at all times, ye people; pour out your hearts before him.' So Luke xxi. 36, 'Watch ye, therefore, and pray always.' So that here is no gap opened to loose and vain spirits to countenance them in their neglect of God. The scriptures rather speak over than under. Nature is apt to encroach upon grace, as the sea upon the banks, and sloth and strangeness to God will soon creep upon us; therefore the crooked stick is bent the other way. Rather pray always than be always in the world, and always in pleasures; at least take the due occasions. Though these expressions be not to be understood as if we should do nothing else but pray, yet they imply frequency in this duty, at all times when opportunity calleth for it.

[2.] The examples of the saints should move us. David prayed three times a day, at morning, noon, and night: Ps. lv. 17, 'Evening and morning and noon will I pray, and cry aloud.' So did Daniel, and would not omit it in times of persecution: Dan. vi. 10, 'Now when Daniel knew that the writing was signed, he went into his house, and his windows being open in his chamber towards Jerusalem, he kneeled upon his knees three times a day, and prayed, and gave thanks before his God, as he did afore time.' Now, though every one's necessities, abilities, or condition of life will not permit him to do so much, yet in the general we must conclude from thence that we must be constant in our daily worship and attendance upon God.

[3.] The ceasing of the daily sacrifice was accounted to be a great part of the misery occasioned by the abomination of desolation: Dan. ix. 27, 'And in the midst of the week he shall cause the sacrifice and the oblation to cease, and for the over-spreading of abominations he shall make it desolate, even until the consummation, and that determined, shall be poured upon the desolate.'

[4.] Now God trusts love, and would not particularly define the times of our duty and immediate converse with him, surely we should be more open-hearted and liberal to him. God expecteth much from a willing people: Ps. cx. 3, 'Thy people shall be willing in the day of thy power.' Our attendance upon God should be rather more than less, since it is left to our choice.

[5.] God himself was angry with his people, and complaineth of their neglect of him: Jer. ii. 32, 'My people have forgotten me days without number.' Time out of mind, as we say in an English phrase, have I not heard from them. Now these considerations show this expression should not be too much straitened.

III. The reasons why constant and frequent prayer is our duty.

1. With respect to God, that we may acknowledge his being and sovereignty over us and all events that concern us and ours.

[1.] We acknowledge his being in prayer, for, 'He that cometh to God must believe that he is,' Heb. xi. 6. Men of all religions call upon that which they think to be God; as in the storm, the pagan mariners 'cried every man unto his god,' Jonah i. 5. Men take their god to be their sure refuge in all their troubles, distractions, and fears. Now the people of God know him by experience to be the only true God that heareth prayer, therefore they own him as such: Ps. lxv. 2, 'O thou that hearest prayer! unto thee shall all flesh come.' Now this owning of God must not be done in a few rare and disused prayers, but in a constancy of prayer, that we may often call to mind his being and attributes. It is a sin not only to deny God, but to forget him: Ps. ix. 17, 'The wicked shall be turned into hell, and all the nations that forget God.' We are apt to forget God, who is an invisible being, though we have all things from him, and he be necessary to us continually; therefore we must often remember him, and present ourselves before him, and inure ourselves to a reverence of his majesty. God complaineth, Jer. ii. 32, 'My people have forgotten me days without number.'

[2.] We acknowledge his supreme providence by taking all out of his hands, and so are kept more humble and in a constant dependence. We do not enjoy our mercies by chance or by good fortune, but by the gift of his providence. That we may not be forgetful of this, God will have us pray often, yea, thus solemnly take our daily bread out of his hands: Mat. vi. 11, 'Give us this day our daily bread.' The bread you eat is not your own, but God's; you intrench upon his prerogative when you use it without asking his leave.

2. With respect to the nature of prayer. It is the converse of a loving soul with God, the nearest familiarity which a soul dwelling in flesh can have with him. Now acts of friendship and communion must not be rare and unfrequent, but constant and often, therefore called an acquainting ourselves with God: Job xxii. 21, 'Acquaint now thyself with him, and be at peace.' Acquaintance implieth frequent commerce and intercourse. Men that often visit one another, and meet together are acquainted. Prayer is a giving God a visit: Isa. xxvi. 16, 'Lord, in trouble have they visited thee.' The keeping up of this acquaintance is necessary both to our present comfort and future acceptance.

[1.] For our present comfort, it giveth you boldness to come to God in all your necessities and straits, if you daily wait upon him. Frequency of converse begets familiarity, and familiarity begets confidence. When God and you grow strange, you cannot come with that freedom to ask his help as those that familiarly converse with him do: Eph. iii. 12, 'In whom we have boldness, and access with confidence, by the faith of him.' A child is not afraid to go to his father, nor a man unto his friend, to pour out his complaint into his bosom; nor a servant of daily attendance to open his suit to his master; they 'know his name,' Ps. ix. 10, and are acquainted with him.

[2.] For our future acceptance: Luke xxi. 36, 'Watch ye, therefore, and pray always, that ye may be accounted worthy to escape all these things that shall come to pass, and to stand before the Son of man,' viz., at his coming. They that are constant in prayer make up their accounts with God daily, and so may with the better confidence attend his coming. When you have been frequently with him, frequently entertained by him and accepted with him, had your prayers heard and desires granted, it is a great encouragement in the hour of death, when you are to leave the world, and come immediately before him. On the other side, for men to appear before a God whom they never knew nor heartily loved, and with whom they were never acquainted as to any intimate communion and converse, this is a sad case. Alas! at the best it is to an unknown friend, but indeed it is to a certain enemy. They never had experience of his kindness which they would own, nor interest in his love, and now are forced into his presence against their will. Alas! how soon will the time come when men would fain set about prayer, but it is too late. They have then neither leisure nor skill to pray; and the prayers they then make are not the fruits of faith and love, but of despair and horror. They cry, Lord, Lord; but Christ saith, 'I know ye not; ye are workers of iniquity.' But on the other side, they are fitted for everlasting communion with God who are acquainted with him already; and when they come to be translated, they do but change place, not company. Heaven is an access to God, and the throne of grace is the porch of heaven. We begin the heavenly life here by these frequent converses with God, and our access to him now.

3. With respect to the new nature, or the temper and disposition of the saints. Prayer is the cry of the new creature, a work natural and kindly to the saints: Zech. xii. 10, 'I will pour upon the house of David, and the inhabitants of Jerusalem, the spirit of grace and of supplication.' A spirit of grace will soon break out into supplications, and vent itself that way: Acts ix. 11, 'Behold, he prayeth;' Zeph. iii. 9, 'I will turn to the people a pure language, that they may all call upon the name of the Lord, and serve him with one consent.' In the margin it is a 'pure lip.' God's true children are carried to him by a kind of natural motion, as light bodies move upward; they are a sort of men that are seeking after God: Ps. xxiv. 6, 'This is the generation of them that seek him, that seek thy face, O Jacob! Selah!' Therefore we should quite check and cross the bent and inclination of the new nature, unless we be much in prayer and often with God.

4. With respect to the necessities of the saints. Our wants are continual, as well in spiritual as in temporal things. That we need daily bread is evident to sense, and that we need daily pardon and daily strength against temptations should be as evident to faith. The soul hath its necessities as well as the body; yea, they are greater, and of a more dangerous nature. Sometimes we lack wisdom, and who shall give it us but God? James i. 5, 'If any of you lack wisdom, let him ask of God, that giveth to all men liberally, and upbraideth

not, and it shall be given him.' Sometimes we lack strength, and that is to be sought in prayer: Eph. iii. 10, 'That he would grant you, according to the riches of his glory, to be strengthened with all might by his Spirit in the inner man.' Sometimes we lack life and quickening, and to whom should we go but to the life-making Spirit, to him who quickeneth all things? In short, the throne of grace was set up for a time of need, and therefore, when our necessities drive us to it, we should not hang off: Heb. iv. 16, 'Let us therefore come boldly unto the throne of grace, that we may obtain mercy, and find grace to help in time of need.' We always need to be delivered from evil; we always need to be established in good. Sometimes we need a blessing on what we have, that our comforts may be sanctified to us; sometimes a blessing on what we do, that we may begin it and end it in God. All our relations increase our necessities, so do all our enjoyments; new mercies occasion new necessities; and in the variety of our afflictions we have still somewhat to do with God. The receipt of one mercy discovereth the need of another.

5. With respect to the utility and profit of it. It is endless to instance in all things, I shall confine the discourse to spiritual profit, and there—

[1.] The three radical graces, faith, hope, and love, are acted and increased in prayer: Jude 20, 21, 'But ye, beloved, building up yourselves in your most holy faith, praying in the Holy Ghost, keep yourselves in the love of God, looking for the mercies of our Lord Jesus Christ unto eternal life!' Mark there, praying in the Holy Ghost is to be referred in common to them all, to building up yourselves in your most holy faith, to keeping yourselves in the love of God, to looking for the mercy of our Lord Jesus Christ unto eternal life. Surely frequent prayer keepeth every grace active, and more ready than if it were seldom used.

(1.) For faith in this duty: the mysteries of our most holy faith are reduced to practice; even that great mystery of the trinity, and their distinct personal operations; we find the benefit of it in prayer: Eph. ii. 18, 'For through him we both have an access, by one Spirit unto the Father.' To the Father as an all-sufficient fountain of grace: Gen. xvii. 1, 'I am the Almighty God.' By Christ, who hath purchased leave, welcome, and audience: Heb. x. 19; 'By a new and living way, which he hath consecrated for us through the veil, that is to say, his flesh.' And by the Spirit, who hath given us an heart to come, inspiring us with holy motions, enlivening our affections: Rom. viii. 26, 'Likewise the Spirit also helpeth our infirmities;' that we may open our hearts to God. If prayer be prayer indeed, not a few cold heartless words, then is faith solemnly acted.

(2.) Love is acted and increased in this duty, while we desire of God all things in order to God, and show forth our hearty groans after everything that will bring us nearer to himself; praying first for God's love, then the grace of the Redeemer, and all other subordinate blessings and helps as they relate thereunto. Yea, this very opening our hearts to God is a solace to us, and the fruit and act of our delight in him. The groans of the Spirit are the immediate issues of love, and come from a heart strongly bent to God and heavenly things. As faith directeth us to God as the first cause, so love to the chief end, the glory of God, and regulateth all our choices and desires by it. The fruit of prayer increaseth love: Ps. cxvi. 1, 2, 'I love the Lord because he hath heard my voice and my supplications; because he hath inclined his ear unto me, therefore will I call upon him as long as I live.'

(3.) Hope is acted and increased by it, because in prayer this grace is predominant, the certain and earnest expectation of the promised glory. Our thoughts of heaven at other times are cold and heartless; here we enter into the holiest; we beg heaven, and all things in order to heaven, because we expect it from the mercy of God in Jesus Christ. There is desirous expectation in hopes, and prayer is but the expression of our desires, and a certain expectation in hope; so in prayer we plead promises, and show the grounds of our trust, why we look and wait for it, that God will preserve us, and bear our expenses to heaven.

[2.] The three duties pressed in this place are much promoted by frequent prayer: 'Rejoice evermore, pray without ceasing, in everything give thanks.'

(1.) 'Rejoice evermore.' We cherish our rejoicing, or peace and tranquillity of mind in all conditions, by frequent praying. This vent and utterance easeth us of our burden. If anything troubleth us, we go to God, who is able and willing to help us: Job xvi. 20, 'My friends scorn me, but mine eye poureth out tears unto God.' It is our comfort that there is a throne of grace before which to bring our complaint. So Phil. iv. 6, 7, 'Be careful for nothing, but in everything by prayer and supplication with thanksgiving let your requests be made known unto God, and the peace of God, which passeth all understanding, shall keep your hearts and minds through Jesus Christ.' 'Be careful for nothing' is parallel to 'rejoice evermore.' What help have we to pray? 'Let your requests be made known unto God;' and the effect of prayer is 'the peace of God.' When the air is imprisoned in the bowels and caverns of the earth, there are shakings and terrible convulsions till it gets a vent; so is the soul tossed and turmoiled with many tormenting thoughts till we open our hearts to God. Hannah, when she had prayed, 'went her way, and did eat, and her countenance was no more sad,' 1 Sam. i. 18. Now should we not be frequent in this duty, which will keep up our delight in God, and our tranquillity of mind in all conditions on the confidence of his all-sufficiency?

(2.) 'Pray without ceasing.' The duty is promoted by the duty; pray without ceasing and you will pray without ceasing. The way to be fervent is to be frequent. A key that is seldom turned rusts in the lock; wells are the sweeter for the draining. We lose the habit of prayer and fitness for prayer when we are seldom with God, and there is such an intermission between duties. The more we walk, the fitter we shall be to walk; and the more we pray, the fitter we shall be to pray. They find so much sweetness in it that experiment it by practice, that they cannot be without it. It is the strangers to prayer that need to be persuaded. When we intermit this necessary work, we lose our fitness. He that hath often prayed will pray: Ps. cxvi. 2, 'Because he hath inclined his ear unto me, therefore will I call upon him as long as I live.'

(3.) For the last duty, 'In everything give thanks.' They that pray often see all things come from God, and they return all to God again; they take it out of his hands, and use it for his glory. Usually what we win by prayer we wear with thanksgiving. Others do not and cannot observe providence as much as they do that pray often and upon all occasions look to God. Besides, prayer sweeteneth the mercy: 'For this child I prayed, and the Lord hath given me my petition, which I asked of him: therefore have I lent him to the Lord as long as he liveth; he shall be lent to the Lord,' 1 Sam. i. 27, 28.

[3.] It is useful to preserve in us a sense of our duty to God, as it obligeth us to be more cautious and watchful. Who should be so careful of their conversations as they that come often into God's presence? They had need to be careful on a double account—

(1.) That they may be in a readiness always to pray: Eph. vi. 18, 'Praying always, with all prayer and supplication in the Spirit, and watching thereunto with all perseverance;' 1 Peter iv. 7, 'Be sober, and watch unto prayer.' If we would be often with God in prayer, we must watch against anything that would hinder our communion and intercourse with God, that we may look God in the face with comfort; as those that are always to appear in the presence of earthly princes must be more decently clad than other men. How shall we pray at night when we have been offending God all the day.

(2.) The very praying often inferreth an obligation of greater strictness, that we may be such out of duty as we profess to be in duty: 1 Peter i. 17, 'And if ye call on the Father, who without respect of persons judgeth according to every man's work, pass the time of your sojourning here in fear;' 2 Tim. ii. 19, 'Let every one that nameth the name of Christ depart from iniquity.' What! confess sin, and yet commit it? What! pray so zealously, and live so vainly! confute and contradict your prayers by your lives! ask grace so earnestly of God, and cast it away so carelessly in your conversations! Leave off one or the other, for hypocrisy is a double provoking thing, more than open profaneness.

Use 1. Is to reprove those that never call upon God, or very rarely, either in their families, or closets, or both. This cometh to pass—

1. Sometimes through a defect of their faith; they do not believe God's being and providence, and the promises of his holy covenant as made with us. They do not believe his being: Ps. xiv. 1, 'The fool hath said in his heart, There is no God;' and ver. 4, 'They call not upon the Lord.' The practical atheist doth not pray: Job xv. 4, 'Thou castest off fear, and restrainest prayer before God.' As the awe and reverence of God abateth in them, they cast off prayer, especially in secret. God's children may be straitened in prayer, but they do not restrain prayer. Conscience is clamorous; prayer would fain break out, but they smother these checks and sentiments of religion till they wholly quit a course of praying. Sometimes they deny providence: Ps. lxxiii. 11, 'They say, How doth God know?' and is there any knowledge in the Most High?' and ver. 13, 'I have cleansed my heart in vain, and washed my hands in innocency;' Mal. iii. 14, 'Ye have said, It is in vain to serve God, and what profit is it that we have kept his ordinance, and that we have walked mournfully before the Lord of hosts?' Or else they do not soundly believe the covenant of God as made with them in Christ: Rom. x. 14, 'How shall they

call upon him in whom they have not believed?' We cannot address ourselves to God in Christ, if we are not rooted in the faith of the gospel.

2. Sometimes through a defect of their love to God. They have no delight in him, and therefore call not upon his name: Job xxvii. 10, 'Will he delight himself in the Almighty? will he always call upon God?' They may sometimes cry to him to be free from trouble, but they do not always call upon him, nor keep up a constant use of prayer. They are weary of God: Isa. xliii. 22, 'Thou hast not called upon me, O Jacob; thou hast been weary of me, O Israel.' They that left their first love left their first works, Rev. ii. 3, 4. Or else they are glutted with worldly happiness, and so God is neglected: Jer. ii. 31, 'We are lords, we will come no more unto thee.' They are well and at ease, or else they are besotted with carnal pleasures, that they have no heart to come to God: Luke xxi. 34, 'Take heed to yourselves, lest at any time your hearts be overcharged with surfeiting and drunkenness and cares of this life.' The heart is withdrawn from God, and stolen away by carnal vanities.

3. From a defect in their hope; they despair either of assistance or acceptance.

[1.] Of assistance. Having such a wandering, lean, and barren understanding, and dead affections, they think they shall be never able to pray. And though God hath promised a Spirit of grace and supplication, and is ready to give it to those that do not give way to these evils, but strive against them, and the Holy Ghost is appointed to teach them to pray, yet they give way to this dulness and deadness, out of an indulgence to the ease of the flesh, and slothfulness and despair of God's help: Isa. lxiv. 7, 'And there is none that calleth upon thy name, that stirreth up himself to take hold of thee.' There is the lazy despair, as well as the raging despair, when men will not stir up themselves, and overcome the seeming difficulties which at first a course of prayer meeteth with.

[2.] Of acceptance. They have lost their peace by some grievous, wounding sin, and then have not the heart to go to God; as David kept silence, and hung off till he recovered his peace, Ps. xxxii. 3. So others have offended God, and represent him to themselves as an angry judge rather than a gracious father, and so run away from him as guilty Adam did to the bushes, Gen. iii. 8, rather than come to him. In part this may be in God's children when they have grieved the Spirit; but mostly it is in the wicked, who go on impenitently in some grievous and heinous sin, and so can have no heart to go on in a course of lively prayer. The presence of God is terrible to a sinner because of the conscience of their own sinful courses; they expect nothing but wrath and vengeance from God, and they will not take God's way to reconcile themselves, and make their peace with him, but only put off the thoughts of that they cannot put away, and neglect God rather than seek to appease him.

Use 2. It informeth us of a necessary truth; if we must pray evermore, then there must be an endeavour to keep up our hearts still in a praying temper, or in a disposition to go to God upon all occasions, that when God offereth these occasions, there may not want a suitable frame of heart. The disposition and temper of heart fit for prayer must never be lost. Satan is a great enemy to this commerce with God, and our hearts soon grow unfit for it. It is a difficult thing to keep up this praying frame, yet this must be a christian's constant work and care. The whole spiritual life is but a watching unto prayer. Now this praying frame lieth in three things—

1. A broken-hearted sense of our spiritual wants. We have a quick and tender feeling of bodily wants, for these are evident to natural sense, and we love the body more than the soul, and are tender of our bodily interests; but we should be alike affected with soul-necessities, or else there will be no life in our prayers. God 'filleth the hungry with good things, and the rich he hath sent empty away,' Luke i. 53. The poor in spirit do most mourn before the Lord, and hunger and thirst after righteousness: Mat. v. 3–6, 'Blessed are the poor in spirit, for theirs is the kingdom of heaven. Blessed are they that mourn, for they shall be comforted. Blessed are the meek, for they shall inherit the earth. Blessed are they that hunger and thirst after righteousness, for they shall be filled.' Now, that which hindereth this brokenness of heart is carnal pleasures, which bring on a brawn and senseless deadness upon the soul. Therefore the apostle saith, 1 Peter iv. 7, 'Be sober, and watch unto prayer.' Now sobriety is a sparing use of sensual and worldly delights, or a moderation in all earthly things. This you must labour after, if you would keep up your correspondency with God by prayer in a lively manner.

2. A strong and earnest bent of heart towards God and heaven, and so towards spiritual and heavenly things: Isa. xxvi. 9, 'With my soul have I desired thee in the night; yea, with my spirit within me will I seek thee early.' The soul that is set to seek the Lord is most fit for this duty. But unless the heart be thus set towards God and heavenly things, prayer will be as a customary task; we shall ask for fashion's sake, pray from our memories rather than our conscience, and from our conscience rather than heart and affections; or from affections actually excited and stirred, rather than from an heart renewed, or that habitual bent and tendency towards God which is at the bottom of prayer. The heart sensibly stirred in one duty may do well for the time, but it is soon lost, and controlled and mastered by contrary affections. That which doth habitually dispose and incline you to pray always is the fixed bent of heart towards God and heaven. There are three agents in prayer, as in every holy duty—the human spirit, the new nature, and the Spirit of God. The human spirit, or my natural faculties, that by my understanding I may work upon my will and affections, and rouse up myself; for the Holy Ghost doth not work upon a man as upon a block. Then the new nature, which inclineth us to God as our chief good and last end; for the Holy Ghost doth not blow as to a dead coal. Then the divine Spirit, which exciteth those graces in us which incline us to God; as faith or a belief of his being, providence and covenant, love and desire of the full fruition of him in the heavenly glory, and hope of the means and end; of the means by which we attain the end, and the end that we shall thus enjoy by the means. These are the three agents in prayer and every holy work. I must do something as a reasonable creature, something as a new creature, and the Spirit influenceth all. The second we are now speak-

ing of, the new nature or inclination to God; which inclination is not barely natural as the inclination of creatures without life, as in fire or light bodies to ascend, or in a stone or heavy bodies to descend; but voluntary, as in a rational agent, and therefore it is not so indeclinably set but it needeth to be strengthened, excited, and increased in us; and this I now press you to if you would keep up your praying frame.

3. There is a liberty or confidence which ariseth from our peace and friendship with God: 1 John iii. 21, 'If our heart condemn us not, then have we confidence, παρρησίαν, towards God.' When we walk unevenly, we grow shy of God; our mouths are shut, our prayers choked in the utterance. Therefore we should take heed we do not interrupt our peace: 1 Peter iii. 7, 'Dwelling as heirs together of the grace of life, that your prayers be not hindered.' Our access to God in prayer cannot be carried on so cheerfully unless we walk orderly and peaceably in our relations. A christian is very careful that he may not interrupt his communion with God, but must avoid heinous wounding sins. And because, do what we can do, daily infirmities will break out, he often renews his covenant with God, that his heart may be settled.

Use 3. To exhort us to pray without ceasing, Consider—

1. The throne of grace, which God hath erected in the midst of his people, standeth always upon. God doth not keep terms and days of audience. The high priest was not to be too familiar with God to come to him, but once in a year; but we may come every day: Heb. iv. 16, 'Let us therefore come boldly to the throne of grace, that we may obtain mercy, and find grace to help in time of need.' Let us then be often with God.

2. God's compassions and mercies never fail. There is an inexhausted treasure and stock of grace: James i. 5, 'If any of you lack wisdom, let him ask of God, that giveth to all men liberally, and upbraideth not, and it shall be given him.' Compare this with Prov. xxv. 17, 'Withdraw thy foot from thy neighbour's house, lest he be weary of thee, and so hate thee.' You may come too seldom, but you can never come too often to God.

3. We owe this respect to God, that we must not go about his service by fits, but constantly. As the Queen of Sheba pronounced of Solomon's servants, 1 Kings x. 8, 'Happy are thy men, happy are these thy servants, that stand continually before thee, and that hear thy wisdom;' much more may it be said of the servants of God, Prov. viii. 34, 'Blessed is the man that heareth me, watching daily at my gates, waiting at the posts of my doors.' It is a blessed thing to be much with God.

4. We never want occasions of praying, either for ourselves or for the church of God. Therefore we ought always to live in the sense of our own emptiness, and in the faith of God's fulness and willingness to supply our wants; always sensible of our need to pray, and always confident of God's readiness to answer and pray accordingly.

5. Love will not suffer us to keep long out of God's company. They that delight in one another must have their frequent meetings and frequent interviews. An instance of this we have in Jonathan and David: 1 Sam. xviii. 1, 'The soul of Jonathan was knit with the

soul of David, and Jonathan loved him as his own soul, and therefore he could not be long without his friend David. If we have a love to God, we cannot keep long out of God's company, but will be with him pouring out our hearts to him. Consider these things, that you may quicken yourselves to this duty of 'praying without ceasing.'

END OF VOLUME XVII.

PRINTED BY BALLANTYNE AND COMPANY
EDINBURGH AND LONDON

ImTheStory.com

Personalized Classic Books in many genre's

Unique gift for kids, partners, friends, colleagues

Customize:

- Character Names
- Upload your own front/back cover images (optional)
- Inscribe a personal message/dedication on the inside page (optional)

Customize many titles Including
- Alice in Wonderland
- Romeo and Juliet
- The Wizard of Oz
- A Christmas Carol
- Dracula
- Dr. Jekyll & Mr. Hyde
- And more...

CPSIA information can be obtained
at www.ICGtesting.com
Printed in the USA
BVOW06s1815250517
485217BV00017B/161/P